Democratic Socialism in J

Also by the authors

Evelyne Huber Stephens, *The Politics of Workers' Participation: The Peruvian Approach in Comparative Perspective*

John D. Stephens, *The Transition from Capitalism to Socialism*

Democratic Socialism in Jamaica

The Political Movement and Social Transformation in Dependent Capitalism

Evelyne Huber Stephens
University of California, Irvine

and

John D. Stephens
Northwestern University

Princeton University Press
Princeton, New Jersey

First published 1986

Published by
Princeton University Press
41 William Street
Princeton, New Jersey 08540

Printed in Hong Kong

Library of Congress Cataloging-in-Publication Data
Stephens, Evelyne Huber.
Democratic socialism in Jamaica.
Bibliography: p.
Includes index.
1. Jamaica—Politics and government—1962–
2. Jamaica—Social conditions.   3. Jamaica—Economic
conditions.   4. Socialism—Jamaica.   I. Stephens,
John D., Ph. D.   II. Title.
JL639.A15S74   1986   320.97292   85–16963
ISBN 0–691–07697–9
ISBN 0–691–10172–8 (pbk.)

To our Parents

Contents

Tables

Preface and Acknowledgements

Our interest in democratic socialism as a development path has two sources. On the one hand, it stems from the intersection of our previous academic work on social democracy in Western Europe and the reformist military government in Peru; on the other from our intellectual and political discontent with the pessimistic conclusions that have been drawn from many empirical analyses of the Chilean experience and from the theoretical perspective of dependency analysis in its orthodox versions. These conclusions suggest that no serious reform oriented toward greater equity and popular participation is possible in Latin America and the Caribbean without a revolutionary break with the capitalist world system and a revolutionary overthrow and demolition of the existing state apparatus. Given the low potential for a revolutionary upheaval in most countries at intermediate and advanced stages of dependent capitalist development, these conclusions lead to an intellectual dead end and to political paralysis.

The search for an empirical counter-example of a country making serious efforts to transform the social and economic structures of dependent capitalism within a democratic constitutional framework drew our attention to Jamaica. At first sight, the Jamaican experience under the government led by Michael Manley seemed to confirm the pessimistic conclusions, but upon closer examination, the successes that were achieved and the highly unfavorable conditions in which the process started suggested some openings and potential for transformation which might have been realized in Jamaica and might be realized elsewhere in the future.

Two recent historical developments have brought the question of the viability of a democratic socialist development path to greater prominence, namely the interest taken in the Third World by the Socialist International (SI) under the leadership of Willy Brandt, and the democratic openings in South America. The SI and the *North–South Report* of the Brandt Commission have provided the forums for a discussion of changes in the internal and international economic order which could open a development path meeting the criteria of growth, equity, and popular participation. The viability of such a path has become particularly relevant in Latin America with the democratic opening in several countries, most prominently Peru, Argentina and possibly Uruguay, Brazil and Chile. In these

xiv

countries, on the one hand the revolutionary option basically does not exist as the security forces are too strong, and on the other the socialist movements are too weak to carry out a rapid socialization of the economy within a constitutional framework. Thus, the only progressive option open seems to be the democratic socialist path, that is, a gradual process of social and economic transformation which involves reduction of dependence, expansion of the state and cooperative sectors of the economy, redistribution, egalitarian social policies, popular mobilization and deepening of democracy. Given that there is as yet no successful case which could serve as a model for the democratic socialist path, it is important to analyze and learn from the attempts that have been made to chart this path. It is with this purpose and in this spirit that we offer the following analysis of the Jamaican experience.

The relatively small size of Jamaican society (by any but Caribbean standards) made it possible for us to take a total system approach in our research design. That is, we did not single out one aspect of the social transformation process (for example, bauxite policy or sugar cooperatives) as the focus of our primary research and then attempt to put it in the context of the whole process, relying on secondary material. Nor did we settle for outlining the whole process relying on secondary material. Rather, we attempted to study the total system and dynamics based on primary materials. Thus, we employed a variety of methodologies (see Appendices 2–4): reading newspaper accounts; coding reports in the papers; interviewing key political actors, business people and other elites, as well as US policy-makers and aluminum company executives; and investigating a limited number of key topics through collecting documents and interviewing experts in the area.

This is not to say that we did not also rely on secondary material. In fact, we owe a deep debt to West Indian social scientists. Given our resources, we were obviously not able ourselves to do some things essential to our project. One key area was the investigation of mass political behavior and public opinion. Here we were fortunate in that Jamaica in the 1970s was a well-documented case. We also relied on other research on the period, primarily by our colleagues at UWI, in a number of areas; the media, the public bureaucracy and bureaucratic management, and the economy spring to mind as being the most important. These works are cited throughout the text.

It is worth mentioning a few of the remaining gaps in the collective knowledge about the PNP government. We would have liked to cover the reactions of the professional and managerial class in the same kind of detail that we covered the reactions of the capitalist class, given the crucial, but ambiguous, role this class played in the developments of the period and would play in any project of the type the PNP pursued. In our view, this would have demanded at least a medium-size survey of 200–300 people and ideally would have included migrants as well as non-migrants. Such a survey was beyond our capacity given the other tasks we wanted to carry out.

The second gap is the general area of covert activity. In the case of the USA, we went to considerable lengths to investigate covert action in Jamaica, and though we are relatively confident of our findings, we cannot present conclusive evidence. Even after cross-checking our results among our sources and with other investigators, it must be admitted that certain gray areas in our knowledge remain. The gap in the collective knowledge is even larger in the case of the politics of ghetto gun warfare. Every knowledgeable observer in Jamaica is privy to rumors about which politicians are most closely connected to criminal gunmen. Moreover, there is widespread consistency on the identity of these men. For obvious reasons we have not put this in black and white, but any reader who can read between the lines can guess who the main candidates are. Hard evidence on 'who told whom to do what' is not even available to many insiders, nor has the judicial system ever been able to uncover such evidence. Those who know simply are not telling.

In the course of our work on this book we have received invaluable support from many people and institutions. Our field research in 1981–2 was supported by a grant from the Joint Committee on Latin American Studies of the American Council of Learned Societies and the Social Science Research Council, and by a Fulbright Research Award for the American Republics. The Institute for Social and Economic Research at the University of the West Indies at Mona, Jamaica, provided an intellectually stimulating environment during the field research phase and on the occasion of later visits. A fellowship from the Woodrow Wilson International Center for Scholars from July to December 1983 enabled us to do research in Washington, DC, on US policy towards Jamaica and to complete a first draft of the book, and the Department of Sociology at Brown University and its Chair Alden Speare gave critical support for the write-up and processing of the data collected by providing us with funds from its limited research reserve and granting time-off to one of us. We greatly appreciate all this support and hasten to emphasize that the views expressed in this book are not those of any of these institutions.

Of course, we are deeply indebted to all the people whom we interviewed, who were generous with their time and in sharing with us their views and much important information. We wish to thank them all collectively and express our hope that those who disagree with our analysis and conclusions will at least find that we took their views seriously and that our analysis is thorough enough to merit consideration.

For help in the conceptual stages of the project, in obtaining the institutional support already mentioned, and in making initial contacts in Jamaica, we thank Wendell Bell, Peter Evans, J. Edward Greene, Michael

Harrington, Vaughn Lewis, Juan Linz, Michael Mann, John A. Maxwell, Dietrich Rueschemeyer, Alfred Stepan and Charles Tilly. Our research in Jamaica was aided inestimably by George Beckford, Richard Bernal, Carlton Davis, J. Edward Greene, Edwin Jones, Michael Manley, O. K. Melhado, G. E. Mills, Rex Nettleford, Paul Robertson and Michael Witter. Many of them talked to us for long hours and gave us insights which we as outsiders could never have gained on our own. Others made important materials available to us, and still others opened doors which enabled us to pursue further certain research questions.

At the Wilson Center, we found a very congenial atmosphere among our colleagues in the Latin American program, and our work benefitted specifically from feedback offered by Tom Farer, Louis Goodman, and Crawford Young. Kathy Meyer provided much careful, reliable and cheerful research assistance.

We would also like to thank Sandy Thatcher of Princeton University Press for his interest, encouragement and guidance throughout the project, and we are grateful to Jean Evanowski, Pat Sheridan and Carol Walker for typing various parts of the manuscript. Finally, we want to thank all our colleagues who have commented on parts of earlier drafts of the manuscript: Wendell Bell, Richard Bernal, Peter Evans, Richard Feinberg, Carl Feuer, Norman Girvan, Harry Goulborne, J. Edward Greene, Edwin Jones, John A. Maxwell, O. K. Melhado, Orlando Patterson, Peter Phillips, Dietrich Rueschemeyer, Michael Witter and Crawford Young. On the one hand, their comments managed to save us from certain errors of fact and judgement, and on the other hand they forced us to rethink and develop further many of our ideas. Many of the people mentioned above may disagree with some of the opinions we express, which is inevitable given the variety of views they themselves represent. We nevertheless acknowledge our debt to them while taking full responsibility for the views expressed in the following pages.

Abbreviations

ACP	African, Caribbean and Pacific Countries
AIFLD	American Institute for Free Labor Development
AMC	Agricultural Marketing Corporation
API	Agency for Public Information
BITU	Bustamante Industrial Trade Union
CBI	Caribbean Basin Initiative
CDF	Capital Development Fund
CEO	Community Enterprise Organization
CEOPDC	Community Economic Organization Project Development Company
CIA	Central Intelligence Agency (USA)
CLC	Caribbean Labour Congress
CMEA	Council for Mutual Economic Assistance
C. of C.	Chamber of Commerce
CWP	Committee of Women for Progress
DN	*Daily News*
EFF	Extended Fund Facility
EPP	Emergency Production Plan
FIU	Financial Intelligence Unit
G	*Daily Gleaner; Sunday Gleaner*
GROW	Growing and Reaping Our Wealth
HEART	Human Employment and Resources Training
IBA	International Bauxite Association
IBRD	International Bank for Reconstruction and Development
ICSID	International Center for Settlement of Investment Disputes
IDB	Inter-American Development Bank
IDT	Industrial Disputes Tribunal
IMF	International Monetary Fund
ITAC	Independent Trade Union Action Council
JALGO	Jamaica Association of Local Government Officers
JAMAL	Jamaica Adult Literacy
JAS	Jamaica Agricultural Society
JBC	Jamaica Broadcasting Corporation
JBI	Jamaica Bauxite Institute
JCC	Jamaica Council of Churches
JCF	Jamaica Constabulary Force

JDF	Jamaica Defense Force
JDP	Jamaica Democratic Party
JEA	Jamaica Exporters' Association
JEF	Jamaica Employers' Federation
JFL	Jamaica Freedom League
JIS	Jamaica Information Service
JLP	Jamaica Labour Party
JMA	Jamaica Manufacturers' Association
JNH	Jamaica Nutrition Holdings
JNIP	Jamaica National Industrial Promotions Ltd
JOS	Jamaica Omnibus Service
JPL	Jamaica Progressive League
JPS	Jamaica Public Service Company
JTC	Jamaica Telephone Company
JWG	*Jamaica Weekly Gleaner*
JWTU	Jamaica Workers and Tradesmen's Union
JYCBL	Jamaica Youth Construction Brigade League
KSAC	Kingston and St Andrew Corporation
LARRC	Latin America Regional Report Caribbean
LO	Landsorganisasjonen (Norwegian Federation of Trade Unions)
LRIDA	Labor Relations and Industrial Disputes Act
MPLA	Popular Movement for the Liberation of Angola
NEC	National Executive Council
NHT	National Housing Trust
NIEO	New International Economic Order
NIS	National Insurance Scheme
NNICC	National Narcotics Intelligence Consumers' Committee
NPA	National Planning Agency
NPM	National Patriotic Movement
NRA	National Reform Association
NSC	National Security Council (US)
NWU	National Workers' Union
OPEC	Organization of Petroleum Exporting Countries
OPIC	Overseas Private Investment Corporation
PNP	People's National Party
PNPYO	PNP Youth Organization
PSOJ	Private Sector Organization of Jamaica
RJR	Radio Jamaica Rediffusion
SAC	Social Action Centre
SEC	Special Employment Program
STC	State Trading Corporation
TUC	Trade Union Council
TUEI	Trade Union Education Institute

UAWU	University and Allied Workers' Union
UNDP	United Nations Development Program
UP	Unidad Popular/Popular Unity
USDEA	United States Drug Enforcement Administration
UTASP	Union of Technical, Administrative and Supervisory Personnel
UWI	University of the West Indies
WFM	Women's Freedom Movement
WFTU	World Federation of Trade Unions
WLL	Workers' Liberation League
WPJ	Workers' Party of Jamaica
YJ	Young Jamaica
YO	see PNPYO
YSL	Young Socialist League

1

Democratic Socialism: An Alternative Path of Development?

Physically, Jamaica, a tropical island paradise, seems to be an unlikely stage for a political drama that increasingly attracted worldwide attention, but socially, the country was a powder keg by 1972. After ten years of political independence and two decades of rapid economic growth, Jamaican society clearly demonstrated the costs of dependent development. Despite vigorous growth rates of 5 per cent per annum, unemployment increased from 13 per cent in 1960 to 24 per cent in 1972. Affluence and poverty grew in visible sight of one another as the rich built mansions in the hills around Kingston and the unemployed filled the ghetto below. Crime rates doubled in the first decade of independence. Two spontaneous riots directed at privileged groups in society broke out. Political violence assumed ominous tones as political gangs from the two main parties exchanged their rocks and bottles for guns, and a mid-decade clash, the' West Kingston War' escalated to such a level that the government was forced to declare a state of emergency in the ghetto area.

This was the situation which set the scene for the landslide victory of the People's National Party (PNP) under the leadership of the charismatic Michael Manley in the 1972 election. The Manley government proceeded to initiate a broad process of social change, increasing state ownership, introducing employment programs, beginning a national literacy campaign, opening up the educational system and more. Then , in 1974, a showdown with the North American aluminum companies that mined Jamaica's bauxite, in which Jamaica increased its revenue from the mineral sevenfold through unilateral action, and Manley's[1] articulate and vigorous promotion of Third World issues in international forums suddenly catapulted this small island-nation into a role of international importance. Later that year, reviving ideological roots from its early years, the PNP declared its new path of development to be 'democratic socialist'. The next two years saw increasing social polarization, economic decline and rising violence. Despite this, the PNP scored a massive election victory in 1976, but this victory was accompanied by a balance-of-payments crisis which

1

forced the government to turn to the International Monetary Fund. The IMF-imposed austerity program, which reduced the living standard of the Jamaican population by one quarter in a single year, destroyed the PNP government politically. After an election campaign which witnessed unprecedented levels of violence, the PNP was crushed in the 1980 election.

The demise of the Manley government has not reduced controversy about how the experience should be interpreted, particularly in the light of the PNP's comeback in the opinion polls beginning in the fall of 1982. The current (1985) US President and Jamaican Prime Minister have depicted the government as being 'almost communist' and a tool of Cuban expansionism. At the other end of the political spectrum, left socialists argue that what Manley wanted was 'full-fledged capitalist development under control of local capitalists' (Lewin, 1982:57). Even supporters of the PNP disagree on the characterization of the government, with its centrist supporters drawing analogies to European social democracy while the left likened it to African socialism or the 'non-capitalist path' of development.

What lessons can be learned from the Manley government for the viability of the development path it attempted? Not surprisingly, both its left and right critics contend that the Jamaican economic performance and the political demise of the government show that the model itself was not viable, though obviously they point to very different reasons for this. PNP sympathizers, on the other hand, point to the permanent successes of the government, such as increased political mobilization, the bauxite policy and parts of its land reform program. Moreover, they contend that its failures were not due to inherent features of the model, but rather to internal and external opposition pressure, as well as to missed opportunities, mistakes and an inappropriate pace of change (too rapid or too slow, depending on the observer's point of view).

We will argue that, although there are parallels to both African socialism and European social democracy, the Manley government represented an attempt to initiate a distinctive, though not unique, path of development which we will term 'democratic socialist development', adopting the terminology the government itself used. The main task tackled in this book is to analyze thoroughly the experience of the Manley years in order to draw out the lessons of that experience for the viability of this development path, in Jamaica itself, as well as elsewhere in the Caribbean and Latin America.

In arguing that the PNP government attempted to initiate a new development path, we do not mean to imply that the leaders of the party had a clear conception of this path at the outset. Indeed, this lack was one of the key problems, if not *the* key problem, and a source of many of the failures of the government, but, in retrospect, one can piece together the policies and strategies of the government into a more or less coherent whole. In this chapter, we will sketch the basic contours of this democratic socialist development path. In the following chapter, Jamaica's experience with dependent development will be analyzed, focusing on the failures which led the PNP to turn away from this model. Then, we will turn to a detailed study of the Manley period in historical sequence, followed by a brief discussion of the failure of the Seaga government to reinitiate dependent development. Finally, we will present an evaluation of the successes and failures of the PNP government and we will place it in a comparative context and attempt to draw out the lessons that can be learned from the Jamaican case for other countries in the region.

Characteristics of the path

The rationale for the PNP's search for an alternative development path to the dependent capitalist path on the one hand and the revolutionary socialist path on the other hand, and for our efforts to understand the dynamics of this path lies in the realization that neither one of the traditional paths has led to an achievement of the three development goals of growth, equity and democracy, despite a virtually universal espousal of these goals.[2] The dependency literature[3] and studies of the new authoritarianism in Latin America (O'Donnell, 1973; Collier, 1979) have explained the central reasons for the lack of achievement of these goals through the traditional path of dependent capitalist development. Our discussion in the next chapter will show how and why this type of development in Jamaica in the 1950s and 1960s produced growth without equity and began to endanger democracy.

If the dependent capitalist path has not led to the achievement of the three goals, being particularly weak in equity, neither has the revolutionary socialist path, being particularly weak in democracy. Furthermore, the pursuit of a revolutionary socialist path is only possible under special historical circumstances. Certainly, for a government in a country at an intermediate stage of dependent capitalist development and with relatively consolidated democratic institutions this is not a viable option.[4] Nor is it an option for such countries without consolidated democratic institutions but with an entrenched capitalist class and a large professional military establishment (O'Donnell and Schmitter, forthcoming). Thus, there is a need to identify new alternative paths of development for such countries and to understand the particular obstacles likely to be encountered on these paths. An analysis of the experience of the Jamaican government led by Michael Manley with its democratic socialist path can contribute substantially to such an understanding. As a first step, we will briefly outline the key characteristics of this path.

The active pursuit of equity requires a state-sector-led development model. In order to gear the types of goods produced as well as the way in which they are produced towards the satisfaction of basic needs in nutrition, housing, and health and towards the provision of employment, the state needs to gain control over the commanding heights of the economy. Only through planning and state control over the allocation of a substantial share of resources can new patterns of production and distribution be established.[5] Within the parameters of such state control over investment, however, there is a continued important role to be played by the private sector. The technical and managerial expertise of the private sector could hardly be dispensed with, as the state does not have sufficient personnel with such expertise to run the economy, at least in the short run. Even more important, a takeover or freezing-out of the private sector would be potent cause for political dissent and for the potential emergence of a disloyal opposition, which would endanger the maintenance of an open political system. In addition to the state and the private sector, a cooperative or socially-owned and collectively-managed sector has an important function in that it can contribute to a wider distribution of economic power and benefits.

A state-sector-led development model implies a reduction of foreign ownership, in particular its elimination from the commanding heights of the economy, where it tends to be high. Beyond reduction of foreign ownership, it requires a general decrease in economic dependence in order to enlarge the state's capacity to direct the allocation of resources and to ensure accumulation in accordance with an overall economic plan. Product and partner concentration in exports render economies highly vulnerable to market fluctuations, and thus to bottlenecks caused by rapid declines in foreign exchange earnings. Foreign exchange shortages force either cutbacks in imports and thus in domestic consumption as well as in production, as manufacturing tends to be heavily based on imported inputs, or foreign borrowing which tends to become a heavy burden in the long run. Thus, diversification of trading partners and of export products is a key element in efforts to reduce dependence. Where the economy is small and its technological and financial capacity to diversify production on its own highly limited, joint ventures between the state and foreign partners can provide the solution. Partnerships with other states rather than with private corporations may be generally more desirable because of a greater affinity in the definition of goals and strategies by the two partners. Also, reduction of vulnerability to fluctuations in foreign-exchange earnings requires a reorientation of the domestic manufacturing sector from reliance on imported inputs toward domestic backward integration and use of local raw materials. Finally, the effects of disruptions in foreign exchange earnings are particularly detrimental where a high proportion of the food consumed is imported. Accordingly, greater self-sufficiency in food production is an essential element of a less dependent, or more self-reliant development path.[6]

The pursuit of greater social equality as a developmental goal in its own right as well as a pre-condition for genuine political democracy rests on initiatives in the economic, cultural, and political domains. Economically, distribution can be affected by employment creation, land reform, wage and price policies, fiscal policies, and legislation protecting labor organization and workers' rights. Legislation on workers' participation in decision-making in public and private enterprises can modify the distribution of economic power, as can the creation of cooperatives and enterprises under social ownership. Such initiatives not only shift control over production from the private sector and the state bureaucracy to the workers, but also contribute to a redistribution of benefits from production.

Egalitarian initiatives in the field of culture involve a revaluation of indigenous compared with metropolitan culture. Emphasis on the value of popular music and art, both in their traditional folk form and in more contemporary manifestations, greatly reduces the elitist character of cultural production and consumption. This, in combination with an emphasis on the symbolic importance of historical figures defending popular causes, weakens feelings of inferiority and engenders an identification as citizens with equal rights among the lower classes. Such attitudinal changes in turn lead to a decrease in differential political participation and influence between lower and upper classes. Further measures to reduce political inequality are the strengthening of popular organizations, such as unions, neighborhood associations, women's and youth groups, and the creation of a mass-based political party. Organization increases the social and economic power of the lower classes both directly in their dealings with employers, landlords, and providers of services, and indirectly through mobilization for political participation.[7]

Creation and preservation of democracy as a system of rule rests on the protection of civil liberties and political rights, and on periodic free elections of decision-makers at all levels. A deepening of democracy in the sense of a movement towards the ideal of a form of government by the people, the people acting as political equals, requires an expansion of participation both in numbers of people participating and in the range of decisions in which they or their representatives are participating. As just mentioned, the establishment of popular organizations and mass-based political parties expands the number of political participants. Administrative decentralization, inclusion of popular organizations in national planning processes, and introduction of workers' participation in enterprise decision-making expand the range of decisions subject to democratic participation.

A further essential component of the democratic socialist path is a strong productive effort, to be brought about through the introduction of community self-help programs and mobilization for national production at the community and national level. Mobilization for the national productive effort is greatly facilitated by efforts to build a national cultural identity among all citizens, which in turn are related to the revaluation of indigenous culture already mentioned. This is obviously a long-term process, but if a country is to deal with the problems that lack of a strong national cultural identity creates, such as low barriers to exit, limited collective work motivation and the continuation of inappropriate consumption patterns formed in the process of dependent development, this problem must be tackled.

The final characteristic of an alternative development path is the pursuit of an independent foreign policy: Non-alignment is a necessary concomitant of trade diversification and economic cooperation with a variety of partner states.[8] And the promotion of Third World solidarity is a prerequisite for obtaining greater room for maneuver in and greater benefits from the international economic order. Also, active support for an acceptance, at the international level, of the principle of non-intervention is crucial for the security and independence of Third World states, particularly the smaller ones.

Strategic requirements of the path

Constructing a class alliance
Pursuit of a democratic socialist development path within the parameters of a formally democratic political system defines the content of the political strategy that must be followed. On the one hand, the movement must put together a sociological majority to support its program not only at election time but also between elections. Given the class structure of most Caribbean and Latin American countries, this support base must be an alliance of classes, namely, the working class, the peasantry, the lower middle class, and urban marginals, each of whom benefit in objective terms from the development path, if not always in the short run, at least in the long run.

On the other hand, in an open society, a democratic socialist government must secure the voluntary compliance of, and preferably even cooperation from segments of, the professional and managerial class and the capitalist class, who do not materially benefit from the development path, but whose resources (skills and capital) are necessary for national development. Developing a working compromise with these classes is as essential to the successful implementation of the development path as constructing an alliance among the supportive classes. Indeed, the two are linked. Failure to develop a working compromise with the privileged can lead to economic deterioration and thus loss of support among the underprivileged. Conversely a strong class alliance among the lower classes can result in a more favorable compromise with the upper classes.

Building the political movement
The class structure determines the interests of various classes but it does not make members of these classes realize their interests, nor do even

those who realize their interests automatically mobilize themselves actively to support programs and governments promoting them, and, obviously, one cannot count on purely spontaneous transcendence of class interests on the part of even a small minority of the privileged. These are the tasks of the political movement: to articulate an ideology and program, and to organize the people to support the program and promote the movement.

When we speak of ideology here we do not mean dogmatic formulations distilled from cursory readings of leading socialist thinkers. Rather, following Himmelstrand's (1970) definition, an ideology is a set of inter-related statements woven into a coherent whole containing, among other things, an analysis of the defects of the current social order, an image of the desired order, and a program and strategy to initiate the process of social transformation. Creating a consensus on ideology and an ideological understanding among leaders and members of the movement is an essential element of any movement toward social transformation.

In medium-developed dependent capitalist countries like Jamaica, the organizational side of movement-building must be led by the political party because the unions, though also important, cannot effectively penetrate the unemployed (the marginals) and the self-employed (the peasants). The party aims at a large mass membership and at participation in decision-making of the mass membership. This type of ideological, mass-based, participatory party has the greatest potential for carrying out the functions of articulation of the ideology and program and building support for the program, government and movement.

In less-developed countries, attempts to build such a political movement must often seek to transform the clientelistic nature of political life where patronage is the main basis of political support. Clientelistic, patronage-based politics tend to undermine democratic socialist development, since work performance is generally low in patronage-distributed jobs, obviously a critical problem if the state sector is to be expanded, and because reliance on patronage for political support creates an additional pressure towards distributionist expenditure rather than investment and makes it virtually impossible to ask for even short-term sacrifices to further national-development ends.

Theoretical assumptions
The contention that such a development path might be possible rests on some crucial assumptions about the nature of the state, society and the world system, assumptions which we hope to show are borne out in our analysis of the Jamaican case. The first assumption is that the early orthodox statements of dependency or world systems theory overstate their case. These statements argue that Third World countries' partici-pation in the world capitalist system makes it impossible for them to develop economically. The implication of this argument is that there is no

solution to Third World development problems short of a complete break with the world capitalist system, opting for some form of socialist autarky.[9] The failure of cross-national studies consistently to confirm this argument (Bornschier *et al.*, 1978; Stump *et al.*, 1978; Jackman 1980; Nolan 1983) as well as individual cases of dependent development (Evans, 1979; Barrett and Whyte, 1982) have already cast considerable doubt on this contention.

On a strategic level, it seems to us that the problem with this point of view is that it assumes that if a country is exploited in a relationship (trade or investment) this implies that it should terminate the relationship. This is as logical as contending that a worker in a capitalist enterprise should terminate his relationship with his employer because he is exploited. If he is without an alternative, he should continue it and attempt to change the terms of relationship through organizing collective action, and in the long run use the same means to change the relationship itself.

Likewise, a Third World country which is not receiving the full value of its products in a trade relationship or a foreign investment relationship may not find it in its interest to terminate the relationship if it does not have an alternative market for its products. In the meantime, it might attempt to renegotiate the terms of relationship through individual and collective action (that is, cartelization, etc.) and at the same time seek alternative markets. Indeed, this book will document the successful pursuit of such a strategy in the case of Jamaican bauxite. Thus, we would argue, 'renegotiated dependence' or 'partial disengagement' might be a better policy in many cases than the pursuit of autarky.

The second assumption implicit in our sketch of the democratic socialist development path concerns the nature of the state. The path is predicated on the assumption that the Leninist view that the state, even the democratic state, is inevitably a tool of the capitalist class(es) and thus must be 'smashed' to achieve social transformation is not correct. Moreover, the importance attributed to movement-building in democratic socialist strategy implies that class organization can affect state outcomes. This contention is the basis of the 'political class struggle' school of thought on the state in advanced capitalist societies (Esping-Andersen, 1985; Esping-Andersen and Friedland, 1982; Korpi, 1978; J. Stephens, 1979b; Stephens and Stephens, 1982, 1983b).[10] Adherents of this school have marshalled considerable evidence, both statistical and historical, showing that the organized power of the working class has an important effect on the distributive impact of state policy (using nations, states of the USA or cities as units) on social control of the economy, on the level of employment and on the level of strike activity (J. Stephens, 1979b; Cameron, 1978; Hicks *et al.*, 1978; Friedland, 1983; Esping-Andersen and Friedland, 1982, Esping-Andersen, 1985; Stephens and Stephens, 1982; Hibbs, 1977; Korpi and Shalev, 1979). With some important modifications in order to take account of dependency in the world economy, the relative weakness of civil society, and greater autonomy of the state, we hope to convince the reader, in the course of this book, of the utility of this view of the state in analyzing political and economic development in less-developed capitalist societies.

2

State, Party and Society in a Post-Colonial Plantation–Mineral Enclave Economy

The title of the chapter characterizes the Jamaican economy and society well. If we add to the legacy of British colonial rule and of the slave plantation the recently developed bauxite mineral enclave and a few other elements, namely, the independent peasant economy, tourism, and two multi-class party-union complexes, we have a skeletal picture of the Jamaican economy and society in the late 1960s, shortly before the PNP government took power. In this chapter, as a background for the events of the Manley years, we will flesh out this skeleton and outline the impending crisis of the dependent capitalist development path pursued during the 1950s and 1960s.

To 1938: colonial plantation society

A distinctive feature of the Caribbean dependency school, the New World Group and its successors, has been its emphasis on the structure and the legacy of the plantation economy.[1] The plantation economy was created by the union of Caribbean soil, African slave labor and European capital. Insofar as it was possible, all economic activity was geared toward producing sugar for the colonial center while importing everything conceivable from the same. So, from the beginning, Jamaica and many of the other Caribbean economies were characterized by the greatest conceivable degree of economic dependence. In Jamaica, where the indigenous Amerindian population was destroyed by European disease, the plantation was the *raison d'être* of human society on the island. Thus, the economy in the pre-emancipation (1838) period is properly characterized by Best (1967) as a 'pure plantation economy'. Since the social structure of the plantation defined the social structure of the society at large, it seems appropriate to term the society a pure plantation society.[2] The only deviation from this societal pattern were the Maroons, slaves who escaped to the mountains, and who fought the British to a standstill to preserve their freedom.

10

In their 150 years of rule in Jamaica the Spanish did little other than eliminate the indigenous population, so the population, social and economic structuring, and governing of Jamaica was entirely a British affair. In practice, the governing of the colony was left to the local elite, especially after the American Revolution, with the Crown and its ministers stepping in only occasionally to ensure that British interests were protected. The colonial government consisted of a governor, appointed by the Crown, an appointed council and an elective assembly. In practice, most of the power was wielded by the latter, though formally the governor did have veto power. Suffrage was limited to free white males with certain property and income qualifications, and thus to an exceedingly small proportion of the population. To stand for election, a man was required to own property and pay a certain amount of taxes. Invariably, members of the assembly were wealthy planters and, naturally, governed in the interest of their class.

In 1838, soon after the slave rebellion led by the Baptist Deacon Sam Sharpe, slavery was ended in Jamaica. The planters tried to coerce the freed slaves to continue to work on the plantations, but many of them refused, retreating to the hills or to former estate lands to settle on small plots. Many of these plots were too small to sustain a living and people combined independent farming with wage labor. Thus, the black slave mass of the Jamaican society was transformed into three new social classes: a rural proletariat, a peasantry and a third group which had a foot in both classes. The decline of sugar, which had begun well before the end of slavery because of the comparatively low productivity of Jamaican estates, and the rise of the banana industry, which accounted for fully half of exports by 1930, aided this social diversification since bananas are amenable to cultivation on small plots as well as on large estates.

The social structure was further complicated by urban expansion. Filling the urban middle strata were the mulattoes, or brown descendants of master and slave, complementing the brown rural middle class of farmers. The inability of agriculture to absorb the growing population led to significant migration to other Caribbean islands and Panama and to Kingston, where the rural migrants began to form an urban proletariat and lumpenproletariat in the first third of the twentieth century, and, finally, the race–class hierarchy of modern Jamaica was filled out by the immigration of a number of ethnic minorities. In the post-slavery period, planters imported East Indians as indentured servants to work on the plantations, albeit in far fewer numbers than in Trinidad and Guyana. The East Indians populated the rural and urban lower classes, while the Jews, Syrians, Chinese and Portuguese filled the urban upper-to-middle classes.[3]

Though the abolition of slavery was obviously a step forward for the black lower classes, their economic situation continued to be desperate, they had no political rights, and they were abused in the judicial system of the time. It was these conditions that touched off the Morant Bay

Rebellion in 1865, led by Paul Bogle – like Sharpe, a Baptist Deacon, in the parish of St Thomas. Though fewer than two dozen people were killed, the rebellion generated a hysterical reaction from the white oligarchy. The participants as well as potential leaders and sympathizers in other parishes, including brown legislator George Wiliam Gordon, were given summary military trials and were hanged. In all, 439 were killed, 600 flogged and 1000 houses of blacks burned.

The fear among the upper classes was so great that the legislative assembly took the extreme step of turning its powers over to the Crown and Jamaica thus passed over to Crown Colony rule. Initially, all power was lodged in the governor and a legislative council appointed by him. Elected members were later added, but most of the power was still concentrated in the governor's hands. Moreover, there continued to be property qualifications to stand for elections and tax qualifications to vote. With less than 6 per cent of the population eligible to vote, elected members represented elite interests anyhow and there was little if any tension between the governor and the elected members until after the First World War. Even then, the elected members, with a few exceptions such as J. A. G. Smith, opposed democratic change.

From the labor rebellion to the first years of independence

Political change
The impetus to political change in the 1940s, setting in motion a process which resulted ultimately in political independence for Jamaica, came from the labor rebellion of 1938. The 1938 rebellion in Jamaica was part of a Caribbean-wide phenomenon, sparked by the hardships of the depression. It gave rise to organized domestic political life in Jamaica in that it led to the formation of the PNP, to an expansion of unionization, and indirectly to the later formation of the Jamaica Labour Party (JLP), and under pressure from these organized political forces, led by the PNP, British governments gradually consented to institutional changes which enlarged the authority of elected politicians in Jamaica. The formation of the Federation of the West Indies in 1958 further strengthened local autonomy, and the negative result of the referendum on continued Jamaican membership in the Federation precipitated the achievement of full independence in 1962.

The system of modified crown colony rule described in the last section on the one hand created considerable frustration among elected and aspiring local politicians because the number and powers of the members of the Legislative Council were very limited, and on the other hand did not provide for any representation of popular interests because the franchise was highly restricted. The growing brown middle class, with many well-educated members, remained largely marginal to the exercise of political

influence and began to demand constitutional changes toward more effective self-government. These demands were originally articulated primarily
through professional associations, such as the Jamaica Union of Teachers,
founded in 1894, the Jamaica Agricultural Society, founded in 1895, and
various groups of clergymen (Munroe, 1972:16).

The first political party on the island, the People's Political Party, was
founded by Marcus Garvey after his forced return to Jamaica in 1927.[4] This
party had an explicit racial appeal, and, handicapped by the limited
suffrage, Garvey failed to win a seat; disappointed, he left Jamaica for
England in 1935 and the party atrophied. Organizational developments
with a more lasting significance were the formation of the first unions after
the passage of legislation in 1919 which legalized trade unions.[5] In 1922,
the Longshoremen's Union and the Jamaica Federation of Labour were
formed, and in 1935 the Jamaica Workers and Tradesmen Union (JWTU),
which became the base for Alexander Bustamante's rise to fame. In 1936,
the Jamaica Progressive League was formed in New York by Jamaican
residents committed to the advancement of self-government and of social
and economic change in Jamaica. However, these organizations did not
have any major impact on developments in Jamaica until the labor rebellions of 1935 and 1938 shocked the British and local elites into an
awareness of the need for change and prompted the foundation of the PNP
as the driving force in the nationalist movement.

The labor rebellions which occurred all over the Caribbean between
1934 and 1938 were largely a response to the deteriorating conditions
caused by the depression. Between 1929 and 1934, real incomes per capita
declined in the British colonies in the Caribbean because export earnings
declined and domestic production did not expand to the degree required to
compensate for this decline. In Jamaica, sugar prices fell drastically (Post,
1978:88–9), and unemployment was greatly aggravated by the return to
Jamaica of large numbers of workers who had lost their jobs in other
countries also hit by the depression, particularly from Panama and Cuba.
Estimates indicate that between 25 and 33 per cent of urban workers, that
is, wage-earners in the non-agricultural sector, were unemployed in the
late 1930s (Post, 1978:134). Wages had always been low, and the economic
decline and the rising unemployment exerted a further downward pressure
on them.

The first disturbances which had occurred in 1935 in Jamaica had been
more or less confined to banana workers in Oracabessa and dock workers
in Falmouth and in Kingston (Post, 1978:240–1), but renewed outbreaks of
violent protest among construction and factory workers at the Frome sugar
estate in April 1938 escalated into general disturbances which came to
engulf the whole island. A strike of dock workers in late May led to a
march through Kingston which closed many factories, shops, and public
services. Troops were sent in to restore order and violent clashes occurred,

but demonstrations continued for some five days (Post, 1978:276–80). By early June, violent protests had erupted in every parish except Westmoreland, and troops were rushed in by the British to reinforce the local police forces (Post, 1978:281–4).

Though many of the strike actions and riots were of spontaneous origin, the role of the JWTU and its leaders was of importance. The founders and leaders of the JWTU, H. C. Buchanan and A. G. Coombs, had brought in Alexander Bustamante in 1937, a man with exceptional oratory talents, the looks of an elegant Spanish adventurer, and the experience of a widely traveled cosmopolitan.[6] Bustamante had been born in Jamaica in 1884 as Alexander Clarke; he left the island with an elementary education and had a varied career in Cuba and the USA. He changed his name to Bustamante while in Cuba, and when he returned to Jamaica in 1932, he had earned enough to set himself up as a moneylender in Kingston. After being recruited into the JWTU and becoming its treasurer in May 1937, he traveled around the island urging the workers to organize and to demand better wages and working conditions. His oratorical skills and charismatic qualities rapidly catapulted him into prominence; for the workers and the lower classes in general he became a hero, the 'Chief', and for the upper classes he became a most dangerous agitator and villain. Certainly, his speeches and leadership were essential ingredients in the explosive growth of unionization and militant action in the late 1930s. In the longer run, however, the consequences of his political actions had a seriously debilitating impact on the Jamaican labor movement.

In the wake of the rebellion, the British appointed a Royal Commission headed by Lord Moyne to investigate social and economic conditions in the Caribbean colonies. This commission recommended changes not only in social and economic policies but also in the system of government, though its terms of reference had not included the question of constitutional change. The investigation confronted the commission with insistent demands from political forces in formation in Jamaica for a greater role to be assigned to elected politicians, and the commission became convinced that concessions on this point were necessary to enlist the co-operation of the local political leadership (Munroe, 1972:32).

The idea of forming a nationalist political party started to gain currency in 1937 with the launching of *Public Opinion*, a weekly paper devoted to the discussion and promotion of issues of social, economic and political reform.[7] It gave expression to the concerns of the socially, culturally and politically active parts of the Jamaican middle class (Post, 1978:214–15). Almost simultaneously with *Public Opinion*, a new political organization was formed, the National Reform Association (NRA),[8] and shortly thereafter, an abortive attempt was made to form a political party, the Labour Party. In both cases, the founders approached N. W. Manley, a Rhodes scholar and Jamaica's foremost lawyer, to become involved but he refused, as all through 1937 he saw his role primarily in the promotion of social and economic development projects, not in politics (Post, 1978:220).[9] However, the labor rebellion and the government's response to it revealed the serious weaknesses in the political system, and prompted Manley to declare at the end of May 1938 that a political party dedicated to the cause of working-class people was needed in Jamaica (N. W. Manley, 1971:3). Fairclough and others were urging action, and at a private meeting in August a steering committee chaired by Manley was set up to organize the founding conference of the new party (Post, 1978:365). Finally, on 18 September 1938, the PNP was inaugurated at a public ceremony in the Ward Theatre. Its priorities as outlined by N. W. Manley at the inauguration were political education, raising the standard of living and security of the masses of the people and the development of a national spirit and of a movement which would help Jamaica become ripe for self-government (N. W. Manley, 1971:11–22). In 1940, then, the PNP adopted a Fabian-type socialist position, including the advocacy of public ownership or control of the means of production, social justice and equality, and self-government.

Bustamante became a member of the party and was present on the platform at the inauguration of the PNP, symbolizing the intention to weld the working class organized in the unions and the middle class involved in the party into one progressive movement. However, tensions between the flamboyant labor leader and the party leadership soon emerged.[10] Bustamante had been expelled from the JWTU after having pressured the union's president to resign and hand the presidency over to him in late 1937 (Eaton, 1975:35). He then started promoting the formation of a new island-wide trade union, which counted some 8000 members in November 1938 (Eaton, 1975:69) and was formally registered as the Bustamante Industrial Trade Union (BITU) in January 1939. After putting down some initial challenges, Bustamante assumed full personal control over this union and had himself installed as President General of the Union for life in its constitution (Eaton, 1975:72). Bustamante rode high on a wave of popularity among the masses, having been imprisoned for his role in the disturbances, and his union kept growing rapidly in 1938 and 1939. N. W. Manley had been deeply involved during the 1938 disturbances in representing striking workers in negotiations and in court; he had effected Bustamante's release from prison after four days, on 28 May, with an affidavit that no breach of the peace would result (Post, 1978:288–91). However, Bustamante jealously guarded his own leadership position and repeatedly denigrated N. W. Manley's role in speeches to his worker-following (Post, 1978:293). When Bustamante was imprisoned again under the Defence Regulations of 1940, N. W. Manley and other PNP leaders took care of the affairs of the BITU and worked vigorously for Bustamante's release. However, upon his release after seventeen months, in February 1942, Bustamante broke with the PNP and the following year he formed his own party, the Jamaica Labour Party to contest the 1944 general elections.[11]

When Bustamante broke with the PNP, his union had a total membership of 20 612 of whom 13 741 were dues-paying members (Eaton, 1975:79). This split left the PNP without much grass-roots support and necessitated intensive organizational work at the level of the party as well as of the labor movement. Party organization was promoted vigorously by Vernon Arnett who had been appointed general secretary in March 1939. The basic unit of the party was the group, and throughout the 1940s such groups were set up in all parishes, reaching the total number of 190 by 1951 (Munroe, 1972:81). In the trade union field, the PNP strengthened organizational efforts through the Trade Union Council (TUC). The TUC had been set up in February 1939 as an advisory council with twelve members, five of whom were union representatives, namely, Bustamante and two others from the BITU, Nethersole as president of several small independent craft-oriented unions, and N. W. Manley himself as legal adviser to the unions (Eaton, 1975:75). Most of the existing trade unions except for the BITU were affiliated to the TUC by the time of Bustamante's break with the PNP, and thus trade union leaders loyal to the PNP could use the TUC as a base for building a new PNP union wing, drawing members from the unorganized and attempting to induce BITU members to switch to the TUC. However, these organizational tasks required great efforts as Bustamante enjoyed almost legendary respect among the Jamaican lower classes. The JLP far outdistanced the PNP in the 1944 elections (see Table A.1),[12] the first ones with universal suffrage, but by the early 1950s the TUC had managed to break the hold of the BITU over the urban workers in the Kingston area, and these gains in grass-roots support enabled the PNP to win the 1952 elections.

The Moyne Commission's report was so damaging to the image of British colonial administration, particularly in its section on housing conditions that publication of its full version was postponed until after the Second World War.[13] However, in February 1940 the British government published the summarized recommendations concerning the need for labor legislation protecting unions and regulating wages and working conditions, an increase in the sugar quota, fostering of local industries, establishment of new land settlements and of unemployment insurance schemes, and creation of a West Indian Welfare Fund (Post, 1981:90). In order to create the framework for pursuing these policies, a new Colonial Development and Welfare Act was passed. The Commission's recommendations on constitutional changes were very tentative and limited, pertaining to universal adult suffrage, a system of broader representation on the Executive Council and of advisory committees to the Governor (Post, 1981:90–1), but they constituted a step on the path toward strengthening of self-government.

The inclusion of constitutional changes among the commission's recommendations was primarily a response to the demands of the Jamaican nationalist movement, but other forces and circumstances were also favorable to a beginning of the process of constitutional decolonization. The USA, on whose support Britain's war effort depended critically, was clearly bent on expanding its influence in the Caribbean. Also, the Second World War was weakening Britain's colonial hold in other areas of the world and forced the British government seriously to contemplate changes.[14]

A long process of negotiation between the Colonial Office, the Elected Members Association, and the PNP about the extent of political rights to be granted to the Jamaican people and their representatives resulted in the following provisions of the new constitution which was promulgated in November 1944. A bicameral legislature was to be established, with a lower house elected on the basis of universal adult suffrage, the Executive Council was to be the principal instrument of policy, and the Governor's power of certification was to be qualified though the system of Cabinet government was rejected and ultimate power was left in the hands of the Governor. In anticipation of the December 1944 elections, new voters' lists based on the 1943 census were drawn up, to include all adult Jamaicans.

In the 1944 elections, about half the candidates were independent; the remainder were candidates of three parties clearly distinct in their racial and class character. In composition and appeal, the PNP represented primarily the brown urban middle class, the JLP the black lower classes, and the Jamaica Democratic Party (JDP) the white upper class. The results of the election showed how weak was the hegemonic position of the upper class, as none of the JDP's nine candidates managed to win a seat. It also showed how low political mobilization of the lower classes was still, as only 58.7 per cent of the 663 069 electors on the lists cast a vote. Still, the JLP easily carried the day, with 41.4 per cent of the vote and twenty-two seats, followed by the PNP with 23.5 per cent of the vote and five seats, and the independent candidates, all of whom together obtained 30 per cent of the vote but only five of whom won a seat.

The programmatic differences between the JLP and the PNP in the election campaign were most pronounced on the issue of self-government. Bustamante pushed the slogan 'self-government means slavery', whereas the PNP put primary emphasis on nation-building and self-determination. The PNP dropped explicit socialist references contained in a 1943 policy statement from its 1944 election manifesto which emphasized the goals of maximum production and full employment. The JLP did not really present a program but rather based its appeal on loyalty to the leader who would take care of the interests of the working people (Munroe, 1972:37–42).

As already mentioned, the PNP made great efforts throughout the 1940s to gain a foothold among the lower classes through party groups and the

TUC, which were successful to the extent of giving the PNP a slim majority of the vote in the 1949 election, with 43.5 per cent of the vote compared with 42.7 per cent for the JLP and the remainder for independent candidates and other parties. However, the JLP managed to hold on to its seat majority, winning seventeen seats compared with thirteen for the PNP and two for independents. The significance of this election was twofold; on the one hand, it firmly established the dominance of the two major parties, and on the other hand it made the PNP's socialism an issue and generated the strange coalition between the black lower class and sectors of the white upper class which regarded Bustamante's populist and personalist appeal and politics as a lesser evil than the PNP's socialist and organizational appeal and politics. This election campaign also established a pattern of red-baiting of the PNP, which aggravated internal party conflicts between right and left. Important sectors in the leadership became increasingly concerned about the electoral impact of the radical proposals pushed by the party's trade union wing and managed to effect the purge of the party left in 1952.[15] This purge, in turn, signified the beginning of increasing convergence of the two major parties, in ideological as well as in sociological terms.

The PNP had not only grown in importance as an organizational and electoral force, but also as a highly articulate parliamentary force. In contrast to the JLP majority, the PNP minority consistently put forward policy statements and plans for various economic and social programs. Up to 1952, the PNP primarily emphasized state initiatives to promote economic development, including the nationalization of utilities, transport, and communications, and the establishment of public corporations for agricultural and industrial development. In 1952, the PNP changed its position toward advocating the encouragement of foreign investment as an engine for industrial development, and it dropped the issue of nationalization from its platform.[16] Under strong PNP pressure, Bustamante agreed to the establishment of an Agricultural Development Corporation in 1951 and of an Industrial Development Corporation in 1952, thus bringing JLP practice closer to PNP programs. Similarly, Bustamante abandoned his opposition to self-government. Though the PNP clearly remained the driving force behind the demands for self-government, the lack of controversy over this issue also contributed to party convergence. The parties agreed as well on the desirability of the formation of a federation of West Indian territories, which was to become a highly divisive issue in 1960–2. The PNP had been closely involved in the federation efforts through its association with the Caribbean Labour Congress (CLC)[17] and Bustamante publicly accepted the federation plans in 1953.

The lessening of sociological differences between the two parties occurred at all levels – mass, leadership and elite. At the mass level, the

PNP managed to make inroads in the labor movement, and at the leadership level the JLP experienced an influx of brown middle-class professionals interested in political careers and unwilling to wait their turn and earn it through party work in the PNP, where there was a much larger pool of qualified aspirants than in the JLP.[18] The purge of the left wing weakened the PNP's working-class base again, as the left-wingers controlled the TUC and took the union with them. But the PNP immediately embarked on the task of forming a new union wing, the National Workers Union (NWU). The task was formidable, as the NWU had to compete not only with the still thriving BITU, but also with the TUC which had grown very strong in Kingston, particularly since one of its leaders, Ken Hill, had become Mayor of the Kingston and St Andrew Corporation (KSAC). Michael Manley, the younger son of N. W. Manley was recruited as organizer for the NWU, and his first significant success was to gain a foothold among the sugar workers.[19] Other successes, such as the displacement of the TUC from the bauxite industry, added to the rapid growth of the NWU. Thus, by 1955 the NWU had taken most major unions from the TUC and had already recruited 24 361 members, 8961 of whom paid dues. Though the BITU retained a clear numerical majority, with a total of 64 164 of whom 45 876 were dues-paying members (Eaton, 1975:152), the NWU was an important political asset for the PNP in the 1955 elections.

At the level of the economic elite, some sectors of the capitalist class clearly aligned themselves with and supported one or the other party, and some sectors supported both parties, depending on their momentary political strength. The trends of convergence at these different levels, however, did not wipe out the original differences in the social support bases and in the image of the two parties. The JLP continued to be stronger in rural areas, particularly among the small peasantry and agricultural workers, and among the more reactionary sectors of the capitalist class, whereas the PNP predominated among the urban lower and middle classes and the liberal capitalists. The JLP's image as the party of the black man, the uneducated, the 'backwoods', persisted into the 1970s, as did the PNP's image as the party of the better-educated, lighter-skinned urban groups.

A limited degree of convergence also extended into the organizational structure of the parties. In response to the PNP's growing organizational and electoral strength, the JLP in 1951 adopted a formal constitution which established a branch structure analogous to the PNP's group structure. Organizing efforts were apparently taken seriously; by the 1956 party conference, according to the report of the organizing secretary, there were over 100 newly registered branches and a total of over 20 000 JLP members (Munroe, 1972:78). However, neither the new constitution, which stipulated rules for the election of party officers, nor these organizing efforts changed anything in Bustamante's personal control over the party. The

PNP on its part also continued its organizing efforts, increasing the number of party groups from 190 in 1951, to 420 in 1955, and a high of 990 in 1959 (Munroe, 1972:81).

In the 1955 election, the PNP's organizational strength helped the party to a clear victory, with 50.5 per cent of the popular vote, compared with 39 per cent for the JLP, which gave the PNP eighteen seats and the JLP fourteen. Despite the pronounced retreat of the PNP from its socialist position, the JLP's main campaign card was again the danger of socialism, communism, and atheism, conjured up by a PNP victory. Obviously, this tactic failed to have the desired result, and in the 1959 election the JLP's campaign focused primarily on the PNP's unfulfilled promises and the danger that the PNP might sell out Jamaica's interests to the Federation. The PNP countered with emphasis on its achievements in office, particularly the achievement of internal self-government. These achievements, together with the usual patronage to which the PNP as governing party had gained access, gave the party another victory in 1959, with 55 per cent of the vote over the JLP's 44 per cent. The JLP, with its branches languishing because of the lack of access to patronage benefits, was clearly in need of an issue around which to stir emotions and rally support. Thus, Bustamante decided to use Jamaica's withdrawal from the Federation of the West Indies as such an issue.

The idea of a federation to improve administration of the West Indian territories had been harbored by the British Colonial Office for quite some time.[20] The Federation came formally into being in January 1958, with the capital in Port of Spain and Grantley Adams, the Premier of Barbados, as Prime Minister.[21] By that time, Jamaica had achieved virtually full internal self-government, through the introduction of Cabinet government in 1957. Looking for an issue around which to rally opposition to the PNP government, Bustamante declared his irreconcilable opposition to the federation in May 1960, in response to which N. W. Manley decided to hold a referendum on Jamaica's continued membership. The issue thus became totally absorbed in electioneering politics. The referendum in September 1961, with a turnout of 60 per cent, resulted in a majority for withdrawal, with 54 to 46 per cent of the vote. And the elections in the following year gave the JLP a narrow victory, with 50 per cent over the PNP's 49 per cent.

As soon as the referendum was decided, pressures for rapid progress toward full independence generated intensive work on a new constitution. Jamaica achieved full dominion status and the Independence Constitution took effect in August 1962. As Munroe (1972:147ff.) shows, the drafting of the constitution was largely the domain of a small committee and input from organized popular forces was minimal. The constitution followed the British model extremely closely and introduced very few innovations into the framework set by the 1957 constitution. It conferred great powers on the Prime Minister, particularly concerning the dissolution of parliament. It also confirmed the formal role and position of the Leader of the Opposition, which had become political practice in Jamaica because of N. W. Manley's insistence on it during the JLP's first period in office, when Bustamante systematically slighted the PNP representatives in the House.

A highly controversial question, which was to have long-lasting effects, was the inclusion in the constitution of a bill of rights and particularly a clause concerning the right to private property. In the end, Leslie Ashenheim, a representative of the Law Society and a member of one of the wealthiest and most influential sectors of the capitalist class, managed to have a compromise clause entrenched in the constitution.[22] The clause recognized the rights of the state to expropriate property if the public interest so demanded, but it required compensation and assigned to the courts the role of determining the adequacy of compensation. In practice, this meant that expropriation would be prohibitively expensive in that the courts would decide that no less than current market value would constitute adequate compensation.

Economic development

During Crown colony rule, the imperial masters had not encouraged but rather actually discouraged industrialization, as they feared it would damage the interests of British exporters. The war had created a situation in which, because of the disruption of trade, Jamaica was forced to resort to import-substitution, thus beginning local manufacturing in many areas where it was absent earlier. As the country gained some measure of local self-government, its new political leaders turned their attention to the country's economic problems, which though not as serious as during the depression, were still rather desperate: per capita income was less than $125 and over a fifth of the labor force was unemployed.

The thinking, and the policies, of the political leadership were heavily influenced by the writings of the West Indian economist W. Arthur Lewis on the subject of economic development.[23] Lewis argued that, given the threat of overpopulation, the West Indies had to industrialize because agriculture was not capable of absorbing the projected population growth. In contrast to the conventional *laissez-faire* thinking of the day, Lewis contended that protection as well as various government incentives (tax holidays, subsidies, etc.) would be necessary to stimulate industrial development. However, his model was not simply an import substitution model like that of his Latin-American colleagues such as Prebisch. Influenced by the limitations of the small size of the West Indian economies, as well as by the experience of Puerto Rico's 'Operation Bootstrap', Lewis argued that (i) because of the small size of the domestic market the industries must be prepared to export (preferably within the context of a West Indian

Customs Union) and (ii) because of the (alleged) shortage of domestic capital, industrialization must be based on attracting foreign capital. Thus, his model was appropriately termed 'Industrialization by Invitation'.

Successive Jamaican governments in the 1950s and 1960s followed policies which, on the whole, were consistent with Lewis' prescriptions. The state's role was limited to providing infrastructure and protection and incentives to local and foreign capital, which were to be the engines of economic growth. Incentive legislation was passed covering textiles, new industries, industries in general, exporters, bauxite and tourism, variously providing for tax concessions, accelerated depreciation, tax holidays, elimination or reduction of duties and loan guarantees (Jefferson, 1972: 126, 131–2, 151, 172–3). Directly following one of Lewis' (1950:44) suggestions, the government set up the Industrial Development Corporation, whose role it was to give technical and financial assistance and to provide factory space at moderate rental to new industries, labor-intensive industries, import-substituting industries and export industries.

Though the contribution of these incentive laws to growth can be debated, particularly if one considers that the main engine of growth was the bauxite industry (Girvan, 1971), there is little doubt that the country did experience rapid economic growth in the 1950s and 1960s (see Tables 2.1 and 2.2).[24] Not only did gross domestic product increase at an impressive average annual rate of 7 per cent in this period, the economy also underwent a structural transformation. Manufacture increased to 13 per cent of GDP and 9 per cent of merchandise exports; mining to 14 per cent of GDP and 50 per cent of merchandise exports, while agriculture declined to 7 per cent of GDP and 35 per cent of merchandise exports. In the same period, tourist arrivals increased fivefold and by the late 1960s tourism accounted for approximately 10 per cent of GNP and over 25 per cent of gross foreign exchange earnings.

As in the case of a number of other Third World countries in this period, at first glance Jamaican growth must seem to be spectacular by the standards of the historical growth patterns of the advanced capitalist world. However, we must modify this picture immediately, first taking into account population growth, giving us a real per capita GDP growth rate of somewhat less than 5 per cent. Moreover, as Jefferson (1972:51–2) points out, the growth of foreign investment resulted in an increasing gap between GDP and GNP and a corresponding increase from 1 to 7 per cent of GDP that accrued to foreigners. Increasing capital stocks also resulted in increasing depreciation; thus, in 1969, national income was 87 per cent of total product compared with 94 per cent in 1950, and there was some tendency for growth rates to decline through time. Still, real per capita income grew by 4.4 per cent for the whole period, dropping from 5.4 per cent for the 1950s to just over 3 per cent for the 1960s, yielding a satisfactory performance in the later period.

TABLE 2.1   *GDP at factor costs by economic sector, 1950, 1960, 1970*

Sector	1950 J$m	1950 %	1960 J$m	1960 %	1970 J$m	1970 %
Agriculture	43.2	31.5	51.9	12.0	78.9	7.4
Mining	*	*	41.6	9.6	146.7	13.7
Manufacturing	15.8	11.5	58.7	13.6	139.8	13.0
Construction and installation	10.6	7.7	51.1	11.8	155.7	14.5
Electricity, gas and water	1.5	1.1	4.5	1.0	11.8	1.1
Transportation, storage and communication	10.0	7.3	33.4	7.7	62.9	5.9
Distribution	21.2	15.5	77.8	18.0	179.5	16.7
Financial institutions	2.8	2.0	16.2	3.8	43.6	4.1
Ownership of dwellings	8.3	6.1	13.5	3.1	104.7	9.8
public administration	7.0	5.1	26.6	6.2	91.6	8.5
Miscellaneous services	16.6	12.1	56.3	13.0	57.1	5.3
Total	137.0	100.0	431.6	100.0	1072.3	100.0

*The mining sector was virtually non-existent in 1950.

Numbers may not add to 100.0%, because of rounding.

SOURCE   For 1950 and 1960, Jefferson (1972: 42–3). For 1970, Department of Statistics (1973: 44–5).

However, when we turn to employment, the picture is not quite so rosy (see Table 2.3). Though unemployment did decline between 1943 and 1960, this appears to be a product of the economic dislocation caused by the war and unusually high emigration from 1957 to 1960 which caused the domestic labor force actually to shrink in absolute terms.[25] Without this decline, unemployment would have remained at approximately the same level as in 1953 and 1957, about 17 per cent, *despite a real growth rate of 8 per cent per annum* in 1953–60 (or 5 per cent per capita per annum). Moreover, in the 1960 to 1972 period, unemployment actually increased very substantially *despite real growth rates of 5 per cent per annum* (or 3 per cent per capita per annum).

The effects of this kind of development on the structure of inequality are obvious. Income distribution in Jamaica was already very unequal (see Table 2.4); in fact, it was one of the most unequal in the world. The combination of the growth of unemployment and the increase in per capita

TABLE 2.2   *Annual rate of growth of GDP by industrial origin at constant prices, 1950–70*

Industry	1950–5	1955–60	1960–5	1965–70
Agriculture	4.9	–	2.4	1.6
Mining	*	21.8	5.6	11.9
Manufacturing	9.9	7.3	7.1	6.0
Construction and installation	16.0	10.0	2.6	1.6
Public utilities	9.5	10.3	12.2	10.4
Transportation, communication and storage	5.2	9.4	9.3	3.4
Distribution	11.6	8.4	–	6.9
Financial institutions	10.3	–	6.6	9.2
Ownership of dwellings	4.1	−2.2	2.5	0.6
Public administration	8.0	10.2	6.5	9.5
Miscellaneous services	11.5	6.2	7.0	5.6
Total	10.1	7.1	4.6	5.9

*Mining sector was virtually non-existent in 1950.
SOURCE   Jefferson (1972:46); Department of Statistics (1973).

TABLE 2.3   *Growth of population and the labor force, 1943–72 (thousands and %)*

	1943	1960	1972
Total population	1237	1609	1942
Population aged 14 and over	808	975	1077
as % of total population	65.3	60.6	55.5
Labor force	555	654	796
as % of total population	44.9	40.6	41.0
as % of population aged 14 +	68.7	67.1	73.9
Employment	416	566	611
as % of labor force	75.0	86.5	76.8
Unemployment	139	88	185
as % of labor force	25.0	13.5	23.2

SOURCE   Owen Jefferson (1972:27), NPA (various years).

income can only have exaggerated the situation. As the rich built palatial mansions in Beverly Hills and the middle class settled comfortably into the new housing estates in Mona Heights, the impoverished mass growing in absolute and relative terms poured into the West Kingston ghetto (see Table 2.5 for urban growth).

TABLE 2.4   *Percentage of income of quintiles of households, 1958*

Quintile		% of Income
1st	20%	2.2
2nd	20%	6.0
3rd	20%	10.8
4th	20%	19.5
5th	20%	61.5
Top 5%		30.2

SOURCE   Ahiram (1964:337).

TABLE 2.5   *Urbanization, 1943, 1960, 1970* (thousands and %)

	1943	1960	1970
Total population	1237.1	1609.8	1797.4
Urban population*	236.8	519.5	751.2
Urban population as % of total	19	32	42
Corporate area**	201.8	376.5	475.6
Corporate area as % of total	16	23	26

*Excludes places with populations of less than 5000.
**Urban population of Kingston and St Andrew parishes.

SOURCE   Hewitt (1974).

The development of an increasing trade deficit showed another weakness in the economic development model of the 1950s and 1960s. Imports of goods and services grew from 33 to 52 per cent of GNP while exports grew from 26 to 40 per cent. The resulting deficit was financed primarily by investment inflows into bauxite, tourism and manufacture, in that order, and secondarily by loans. Until the late 1960s, no significant section of the political leadership seems to have questioned what would be done if (or rather when) the investment inflow slowed and/or profit repatriation began to accelerate, despite warnings from academic circles (Girvan, 1971).

Jamaican society by the late 1960s

The dependent economy
The rise of unemployment despite vigorous economic growth was the most striking visible feature of Jamaica's pattern of dependent capitalist development. It was not only a great failing in itself but also a symptom of a

dependent capitalist economy suffering from severe structural weaknesses of which unemployment was just one, if the most important, result.

By the 1960s, Jamaica was the world's largest producer of bauxite, the base mineral in the manufacture of aluminum, a metal which played a very important role in post-war development of the world capitalist economy. In 1965, the country supplied 28 per cent of the bauxite used in the market economies of the world. Furthermore, as we saw, bauxite along with tourism fueled post-war Jamaican development and the two provided the country with most of her gross foreign exchange earnings. However, if one goes beyond these surface figures, the contribution of bauxite to Jamaica's development was far less than might be assumed.

The industry was entirely foreign-owned. This meant not only the loss of repatriated profits but, more important, the lack of control over its development.[26] The lack of control resulted in no diversification of outlets (making the country excessively vulnerable to economic cycles in North America) and in very little forward integration. Because of the cost of shipping, Alcan did convert bauxite into alumina in Jamaica, but the other companies did not and, of course, none of them actually smelted aluminum in Jamaica. Because research indicated that a ton of bauxite processed into alumina in Jamaica yielded three times more national income and foreign exchange and one-and-a-half times the taxes than a ton of bauxite exported abroad, the government put pressure on the companies to process more locally, succeeding in 1967 in getting a joint venture agreement between Reynolds, Kaiser, and Anaconda (Alpart) to build a refinery in Jamaica, which was completed two years later. Still, in 1972, 57 per cent of all bauxite mined in Jamaica was exported without further processing (NPA, 1976:127).

In their bid to gain control of Jamaica's reserves of bauxite, the aluminum companies acquired vast tracts of agricultural land, some 142 000 acres. Thus, in a country where land-hunger was widespread, a major chunk of agricultural land was owned by foreign corporations for whom farming was hardly their major concern (though it does not appear that the companies needlessly withdrew major amounts of land from production).

Given the amounts of the mineral being mined, Jamaica's revenues were not great. Since the aluminum industry is a worldwide vertically-integrated oligopoly, there is no world market price for bauxite, so its assumed price and thus profit were the subject of negotiation between the government and the companies. In the initial agreement, the assumed profit was set at a very low level as was the royalty, thus the total revenue from corporate profits, tax and royalties was ridiculously low. This agreement was renegotiated by Norman Manley's PNP government in 1957, resulting in a sixfold increase in revenue. Still, the total returned value from the industry to the Jamaican economy including local purchases, salaries and wages, tax and royalty payments for 1956–67 was only "between 36 per cent and 43 per cent" of the value of bauxite and alumina exports (Girvan, 1976:117). And, astonishingly, the development of Alpart led to a short-run decline in revenues because of financial manipulations which led to massive tax write-offs (Stephens and Stephens, 1985).

The bauxite industry has had very little direct effect on Jamaica's employment problem. Since it is so capital-intensive, it provides direct employment for less than 1 per cent of the employed labor force, though it accounts for 14 per cent of GDP (see Table 2.1). It does, however, provide very high wages, thus putting much more money into the hands of Jamaican workers than do other concerns with similar size workforces. However, some have argued that this was a mixed blessing for the Jamaican economy as a whole, since it is believed that the high wages paid to bauxite workers have had a demonstration effect making it difficult to find workers for work in low-wage sectors such as agriculture.

Finally, as Jefferson (1972:168) points out, net contribution of the industry to national income and foreign exchange, though substantial, is overestimated by bauxite/alumina's share of GDP and exports. If allowances are made for heavy depreciation and other leakages from the domestic income stream, the share of net national income accounted for by the industry was only about 4 per cent in the 1965–8 period. Given the high import content, the net foreign exchange earnings were only about 17 per cent of retained (or net) foreign exchange earnings in the period 1959–68 (compared with 28 per cent of exports of goods and services and 47 per cent of merchandise exports). Jefferson (1972:168) concludes:

> in 1968 the industry provided less than 1 per cent of employment, 4 per cent of national income, 14 per cent of government tax revenue and 17 per cent of retained foreign exchange earnings. Its contribution, while not inconsequential, is far less than would appear from the value of its output. The gap between its actual and potential contribution to the economy is very wide.

Tourism presents a similar picture, albeit on a somewhat smaller scale. Foreign ownership was the dominant pattern, with 56 per cent of hotel capacity (as measured by the number of beds) wholly foreign-owned in 1968. The tourist trade was heavily concentrated: in 1969 77 per cent of tourists came from the USA and another 8 per cent from Canada (Jefferson, 1972:178,181). Jefferson (1972:18) estimates that tourism provided direct employment for about 7000 people and indirectly created an equal number of jobs, thus accounting for about 2 per cent of the employed labor force. As for bauxite, the import content of tourism was high, about 40 per cent. Thus its contribution to net national income and net foreign exchange earnings must be adjusted, with the former figure being 7 per cent and the latter 17 per cent.

Agriculture, which still provided employment for a third of all employed Jamaicans when Michael Manley took office, was, by all accounts, the sick man of the Jamaican economy. Agriculture also bore the mark of dependence, both current and historical. Large estates covered the best land and the bulk of farmers populated the hilly regions of the country. The marketing of all export agriculture was dominated by multinationals who also owned the large sugar estates. Exports were concentrated on a few products, with sugar and its by-products and bananas accounting for three quarters of exports and citrus, pimento, cocoa, coffee and ginger for the rest. Some nine-tenths of these exports went to two countries, the USA and the UK.

Export agriculture grew at a rate of 5 per cent per annum in the 1950s, but then stagnated completely in the 1960s. Were it not for protected markets in the UK, the performance of both sugar and bananas would have been worse. Bananas suffered from quality problems caused by a variety of factors, including transport difficulties, inefficiencies in fertilizing and spraying because of the lack of crop zoning and the windswept character of many places where they are grown. Sugar was also inefficiently produced. The multinationals reaped their profits on the processing, transport, and marketing of sugar and neglected the management of the actual growing and reaping of the cane. Largely because of inefficiency, sugar from estate cane was already being produced at costs above market prices in 1965, the year which marked the peak of Jamaican sugar production. By 1969, the country could no longer meet its quota in protected markets.

Demand for food grew at an annual rate of 4 per cent in the 1950s and 1960s but domestic agriculture grew at only 2 per cent per annum. In the last analysis, it was, of course, the liberal food import policy which allowed this to happen, but the imports were the favored free-market alternative because of the failure of all efforts to increase the production and productivity of small farmers. The small farmer was plagued by lack of funds for basic inputs and poor transportation, storage and marketing. The government programs that were introduced to help these people were hampered by the patronage and the inefficiency of the Ministry of Agriculture. Underlying these difficulties was an extremely unequal distribution of land (see Table 2.6) which resulted in widespread land-hunger. Despite the desire for land, as much as a quarter of the area suitable for continuous cultivation was lying idle in 1961 (Jefferson, 1972:79). Thus, a program for increasing domestic agricultural production would have had to include extensive land reform along with tariff protection, extensive state planning (crop-zoning, new marketing systems, etc.), administrative reform (reduction of patronage, improving extension services, etc.) and financial outlays on infrastructure and inputs.

The pattern of economic dependence could be seen in other sectors also. For instance, the public utilities, with the exception of water, were owned

TABLE 2.6 *Land distribution, 1968*

Size Group (Acres)	Farms		Land in Farms	
	Number	%	Acres	%
Landless	4 768	2.5	–	–
Less than 1	52 969	27.4	22 736	1.5
1–4.9	93 961	48.6	206 480	13.9
5–9.9	25 237	13.0	165 905	11.1
10–24.9	12 370	6.4	174 852	11.8
25–49.9	2 280	1.2	74 718	5.0
50–99.9	775	0.4	52 490	3.5
100 or more	992	0.5	792 007	53.2
Total	193 352	100.0	1 489 188	100.0

SOURCE   Jamaica Department of Statistics Agricultural Census Unit: Census of Agriculture 1968–9, cited in IBRD (1982a:229).

by foreign, mainly British, interests. The banking system was entirely foreign-owned until the late 1960s, when the JLP government initiated its 'Jamaicanization' program, forcing the banks to incorporate locally and offer shares for sale to Jamaicans with the goal of achieving 51 per cent local ownership. Still when Manley took office in 1972, the banks were largely owned and in all cases controlled by foreign interests, mainly Canadian and British.

Sole foreign ownership was much less important in the manufacturing and distribution sectors, though joint ventures between local and foreign capital were relatively frequent in manufacturing. However, these sectors also showed the effects of dependent capitalist development. Domestic commercial capital focused largely on importing goods from the USA and UK and distributing these along with domestically–produced goods on the domestic market. The development of the manufacturing industry was, according to Jefferson (1972:139) 'based to an overwhelming degree on production for the home market behind the protection afforded mainly by quantitative restrictions on imports'. Typically, all capital goods were imported and so, in most cases, were a large proportion of raw materials and other inputs. In some cases, the 'manufacture' was little more than final assembly of knocked–down parts produced in developed countries. Thus the import content in manufacturing was relatively high and the local value added relatively low. This type of development of the commercial and manufacturing sectors was only possible because the inflow of foreign investment, primarily into the bauxite–alumina industry and secondarily into tourism, provided the foreign exchange needed to cover the high import bill. The structure of the capitalist class in Jamaica was thus profoundly shaped by the particular type of dependent development experienced by the country.

The manufacturing sector was also comparatively capital–intensive and becoming increasingly so, a perverse development given the abundance of labor and scarcity of capital in the country. This was in large part a direct effect of government policy. The incentive legislation, such as accelerated depreciation and tax holidays for new investment, tended to make capital cheaper relative to labor and despite the IDC goal of encouraging labor intensive investments little was actually done in this regard.

The final economic activity which made a significant contribution to foreign exchange earnings and employment is difficult to describe and analyze accurately because little reliable data exist on it. This is the illegal marijuana trade. To our knowledge, no estimates exist for the late 1960s, but the US Drug Enforcement Administration estimated that in the period 1979–81 an average of 740–1400 metric tons of marijuana were supplied to the US market by Jamaica, making Jamaica a very distant second to Colombia (NNICC, 1983:52). Exactly how much money was coming into the Jamaican economy depends on one's estimates of how much money per kilogram is received by Jamaican farmers and transporters. The extremely high estimates of up to several hundred million dollars – more than bauxite in the period after the levy – are generally based on excessively high estimates of the return per kilogram, though one source estimates production as being in excess of 4000 metric tons (LARRC, 11 March 1984, also see LARRC, 20 August 1982). An educated guess would put the return between $20 and $30. Thus, allowing also for the export to Canada, the average annual return on the crop would be between $15m and $45m in this period based on the USDEA figures. That is, marijuana's importance to the economy was probably more comparable with that of bananas or sugar rather than that of bauxite or tourism. Moreover, given the great increase in US consumption between the mid-1960s and mid-1970s, it is likely that the figures for Jamaican production for the earlier period were also lower.

In sum, by the late 1960s, the Jamaican economy bore all the marks of dependent development. Foreign ownership dominated the pillars of the economy: bauxite, sugar, tourism, the financial institutions and the public utilities; and it was an important factor in manufacture. The economy was extremely dependent on trade; its exports were heavily concentrated on a few partners and products; its imports on a few partners. Given the labor surplus in the country, the growing sectors were excessively capital-intensive and the one labor-intensive sector, agriculture, was stagnant. The leading growth sectors were marked by a singular lack of forward and backward linkages, and each sector tended to be an enclave in and of itself. Because of this and secondarily profit repatriation, multiplier effects of increases in exports, investment or aggregate demand were extremely small. Finally the country was experiencing ever-increasing trade deficits which were covered by the inflow of foreign investment.

With this overview of the economy as a background, it is now easy to see why the Jamaican post-war patterns of development resulted in such a high degree of inequality. First, because of the legacy of plantation slavery, land distribution was extremely skewed at the outset, which not only had an inegalitarian consequence in and of itself, but also contributed to the development difficulties experienced by this labor-intensive sector (see Table 2.6). Second, the lack of backward and forward linkages from the growth sectors meant that they did little to stimulate growth in other sectors. Third, the capital-intensive nature of the growth sectors resulted in great differences in income between wage-earners in different sectors (see Table 2.7).

Finally and perhaps most important, the capital intensity of growth

TABLE 2.7   *Average weekly earnings per worker in selected industries, 1965 (J$)*

	All workers	Skilled workers	Unskilled workers
Agriculture (excl. sugar)	6.6	19.2	5.8
Agriculture (sugar cane)	9.0	24.2	7.8
Mining	42.4	49.4	27.0
Sugar (factory)	16.2	21.8	11.0
Other manufacturing	14.8	18.0	10.0
Construction (private)	20.8	28.8	13.8
Construction (government)	7.6	19.4	6.8
Public utilities (electricity)	35.2	37.4	10.6
Public utilities (water and sanitation)	8.2	17.6	7.0
Commerce	24.0	28.6	11.4
Transportation, communication and storage	19.6	27.8	14.0
Miscellaneous services	13.8	20.8	11.2
Weighted average	14.4	24.6	9.2

SOURCE   Department of Statistics (1966).

meant that few jobs were created in the process and thus unemployment grew despite vigorous growth. Some crude calculations should demonstrate just how few. A comparison of the growth in the employed labor force and in GDP in the period 1953–72, shows that a 1 per cent increase in GDP created an annual average of about 700–50 new jobs.[27] Unemployment remained at 17.5 per cent from 1953 to 1957 despite a growth rate of 11.5 per cent per annum and a labor-force growth rate of only 0.9 per cent. In the next three years, unemployment did decline to 13.5 per cent, but only because the labor force actually declined in this period, apparently because of migration (Jefferson, 1972:29).[28] However, the average annual growth in the labor force in the period 1960–72 was 1.5 per cent, or about 10 900. It is important to emphasize that this is not unusually high. Indeed, this is only 0.2 per cent above the rate for 1943–53 in Jamaica; only slightly above the average for developed countries (1.2 per cent); and below the average for less developed countries (1.9 per cent) and the USA (1.8 per cent). Given this rate of labor-force growth and the rate of job-creation typical for the capital-intensive nature of Jamaican development in this period, the average rate of economic growth would have to have been about 14 per cent just to maintain the rate of employment that prevailed in 1960!

As Wilber and Weaver (1979:117) point out, this type of high income inequality/low employment creation, capital-intensive growth tends to regenerate itself. By concentrating income in the hands of upper-income earners it creates demand for new, modern, consumer goods, which typically are produced by capital-intensive techniques.

In this regard it is ironic that the incentive legislation actually encouraged the type of capital-intensive development carried out under the leadership of foreign and domestic capital. It is yet a further irony that incentives were either not necessary and/or not justifiable in view of the tax revenues lost. For bauxite and tourism this is clearly the case, and Chen-Young (1966) has demonstrated that even for manufacturing incentives were not economically justifiable.

The dependent society
Bustamante, soon after Jamaica's independence, once boldly stated in a parliamentary debate 'I am for the West and I am for the United States of America . . . I am against communism' (Eaton, 1975:202). Though in practice the JLP's foreign policy was isolationist and it hardly entered the international arena at all, there is no question about where Bustamante and the party stood. Most of the rest of politically influential Jamaicans agreed with the JLP stance. In the 1962 elite study (see Appendix 2), 72 per cent of the elite respondents expressed pro-West attitudes when questioned about the desirable foreign-policy alignment for Jamaica.

There were certainly ideological and historical roots to this posture, as the nature of British rule and the constitutional decolonization process left residues of pro-West attitudes in the middle and upper classes. But there were practical aspects also. The whole economic development model, predicated as it was on Western capitalist investment and trade with the USA, UK and Canada, was a very strong pressure working in the direction of a Western-aligned foreign policy. Moreover, the USA considered the Caribbean its sphere of influence and did not look kindly on independent ventures in foreign policy or otherwise, a fact which could not have been overlooked by the Jamaican leaders in the context of the Cuban missile crisis and the Dominican intervention. Either with enthusiasm or acquiescence, US political and military hegemony was accepted by Jamaica.

This political dependence, the recent colonial heritage, the fact that, unlike India or British African colonies, Jamaica had no indigenous culture, and the peaceful decolonization also contributed to cultural dependence – the penetration of Anglo-American cultural values into the island's own cultural life. Mass media, particularly television but also radio, have also aided this process. The negative consequences of cultural dependence include the adoption of Western consumer tastes, both in terms of level of aspired consumption and type of consumption (in foreign goods instead of locally produceable goods), obviously a barrier to both the development of a more self-reliant economy and the generation of more local investment.

However, the effects of this cultural ideological influence go much further than the development of inappropriate consumer tastes; it is an obstacle to nation-building, the development of a strong national identification, national loyalty and willingness to work for national development among the population. A key negative effect of this, in turn, is the ease with which the decision to migrate is taken. When things get tough in Jamaica, the wealthy and the skilled find it comparatively easy to leave the island for greener pastures elsewhere. This yearly exit of some 1 per cent of the population has resulted in the development of rather large Jamaican communities abroad, especially in New York, London, Miami and Toronto. Indeed, there are half as many Jamaican citizens living abroad as there are living on the island (Kaplan *et al.*, 1976:23).[30] This, in turn, makes it all the easier to make the decision to migrate, since the huge majority of Jamaicans have close relatives living abroad.

The whole cultural complex as well as kinship links gives the USA a positive image in the wider Jamaican society, which it does not have in Latin American countries. This is further reinforced by the perception that the relatives and friends who did succeed in emigrating have 'made it' in material terms. Thus, as novelist George Lamming (*DN* 14 December 1981)[31] observed, 'It is very difficult to get the local population of the Caribbean to think critically of the United States'.

The dependent economy and society also have a negative effect on work motivation. It has become commonplace to link low work-motivation to the legacy of slavery. There is, as we shall argue, some truth to this, but the fallacy lies in positing this low work-motivation as a general cultural characteristic. Indeed, this is very difficult to square with the reputation of US West Indian immigrants as hard-working and entrepreneurial (Lowenthai, 1982:132), with the proven record of Jamaican emigrant farmworkers in the USA as particularly productive and frugal (Foner and Napoli, 1978), and with a similar reputation for Jamaican workers in the Canal Zone. Manley (1975b:46–9) points this out and adds that even in Jamaica one finds a large difference in work-motivation between the self-employed and employees, and goes on to argue that the legacy of slavery and colonialism led to a cultural definition by which hard work in employment (as opposed to self-employment), particularly manual employment, was seen as undesirable, that is, submission to exploitation. Under slavery it was, of course, rational to work as little as allowed by the coercive power, but even in the post-slavery, pre-1938 colonial period, it was irrational for an employee to work hard because he could not reap much of any of the return for his effort because of the absence of trade unions, and he could not advance because of the racist character of colonial society. Thus it was only very recently that effort on the part of a worker was not completely irrational.

However, even this point of view puts too much emphasis on the cultural heritage rather than on the structure of remuneration in world capitalism. Capitalist societies attempt to legitimate their systems of remuneration with the claim that they are meritocratic, arguing that those with more skills, those who are more productive, should and do get paid more. Setting aside the question of what allows one to acquire those skills, education and credentials (that is, social background or innate abilities), there is enough evidence that can be pointed to (doctors earn more than nurses, carpenters more than ditchdiggers, etc.) that this claim backed by the considerable hegemonic power of capital, appears believable.

In a dependent capitalist society so closely linked socially and economically to core capitalist countries the situation appears quite different. From the point of view of the average worker the system of remuneration must appear completely irrational. An unskilled worker in agriculture earns one half of what a similar worker would earn in manufacturing and only one fifth of one in bauxite. Moreover, even the bauxite worker earns only half of what an unskilled worker in the USA would earn. It is hardly a matter of merit but rather connections or just chance that one ends up in one of these jobs rather than another, or even has a job at all!

In the special case of patronage jobs, the patronage system itself was a barrier to motivation as is usually the case in most countries. Workers in patronage jobs take the attitude that the job is a *quid pro quo* for previous party work, thus no additional work effort is necessary to justify holding the job.

This whole problem can be exaggerated and it is important to note that Jamaican employers who manage to transcend the usual elitist and authoritarian attitudes typical of their class, have been remarkably successful in overcoming worker resistance.[32] Nevertheless, the attitude is there; as Manley (1975b:46–7) observes 'Anyone who has ever opened his ears to the language of the Jamaican people is struck by the persistent tendency to describe as 'slave driving' an injunction, or even an appeal, to work harder, provided the call comes from those in authority'. This, along with the infrequency of deep nationalism, stood as an important barrier to any efforts at national mobilization for production.

The race–class structure

The occupational and ownership structure of Jamaica is typical for dependent capitalist countries at medium levels of development, like most countries in Latin America and the Caribbean. It is this structure that underpins the social class structure of a country, with the mediating factor being the degree of intergenerational reproducibility of occupation/ownership groupings as well as the degree of intraclass intermarriage and the degree of closure of social interaction between classes.[33] Unfortunately, no national survey based on studies of mobility patterns and social networks of Jamaica exists. Nonetheless, on the basis of a number of anthropological and sociological studies and labor-force statistics, we can piece together a rough picture of the Jamaican class structure that is a sufficiently close approximation to the Jamaican reality to serve as a basis for our subsequent analysis.[34] Based on a reworking of labor-force data for 1973, Table 2.8 presents this picture.

The percentage estimates in the table are approximate, as are the boundaries between classes. For instance, as we pointed out earlier in this chapter, many very small farmers are also farm workers, thus in reality there is no real 'boundary' between these two classes. Harrison (1982) argues that the marginal population or the lumpenproletariat is actually made up of a number of classes, but that the boundaries between them are fluid both in that movement across them is frequent and in that the exact placing of boundaries is somewhat arbitrary. The categories in the table are not sufficiently sensitive to accommodate some occupations such as higglers (street vendors), who stretch from marginal existence to solid petty bourgeois, with most falling in between. Moreover, as noted earlier, the internal stratification in the working class is relatively great, even when one excludes bauxite workers, a small and very exceptional group. However, on the basic points of relevance to this work, our picture of the class structure is unambiguous: (i) more than three quarters of the population are in the social classes that form the core of the class alliance to be targeted by the democratic socialist movement,[35] and (ii) the three main elements of this core group are very roughly of equal size such that, by size

TABLE 2.8   *Jamaican class structure, 1973*

	Approximate % of population
Capitalist class	less than 0.5
Upper middle class (professionals and managers)	4–5
Urban middle strata Salariat (clerical and sales) Petty bourgeoisie	8–9 4–6
Middle and large farmers	3–4
Urban working class	22–24
Small farmers	17–20
Agricultural working class	4–7
Marginals Marginally employed Unemployed	12–15 22

alone, none of them could be posited as the leading (or vanguard) element. Stone (1980:20–1) using a quite different approach, comes up with a class configuration which would lead to similar conclusions.

In the absence of survey data on the question, the relationship between the class categories presented here and race cannot be accurately mapped. However, data on occupation and race, including a category for Afro-Europeans (browns) not later used, was collected in 1960 and is presented in Table 2.9. The relationship is clear, with the lower classes being predominantly black and whites being almost absent in these groups. On the other hand, it should also be noted that, by 1960, blacks were represented in the professional and supervisory strata (very close to the upper middle-class in Table 2.8) in significant numbers.

By contrast, the capitalist class is predominantly white with some Chinese and brown presence. This fact, which is obvious to any intelligent observer of Jamaican society, is documented by Bell (1964), Holzberg (1977a), Phillips (1977), Reid (1977) and the elite studies by Moskos, Bell and his associates, and ourselves. There are significant ethnic fragments of the white capitalist class: Lebanese and Syrians, Jews and European whites. Although, historically, the European whites were the plantocracy and the other ethnic groups, who immigrated later, moved into commerce

TABLE 2.9 *Occupational and racial composition of the labor force[1] in Kingston and St Andrew parishes, 1960*

Occupational sector Race	Professional and supervisory	Professional services[2]	Clerical and sales	Craftspeople and technical	Manual and services	Not specified or ill-defined	All sectors
African	43	59	59	80	83	77	75
European	14	7	2	–	1	–	2
East Indian and Afro-East Indian	3	3	4	3	2	4	3
Chinese and Afro-Chinese	8	2	9	1	1	1	3
Afro-European	22	20	20	12	10	14	13
Other	9	8	7	4	3	4	5
Total (%)	100	100	100	100	100	100	100
Sectoral share	6	20	28	2	42	2	100
Number of people in each sector	11 802	36 940	51 717	3694	77 575	3694	184 702

[1]14 years and older.
[2]Professional services is a heterogeneous heading comprised of manual and non-manual occupations.

–Less than 0.5 of 1 per cent.

Columns may not all add up to 100% because of rounding.

SOURCE Clarke (1975:153), calculated from Table 31, which was based on the 1960 census.

and later manufacturing, by the late 1960s, all ethnic segments had interests in all sectors of the economy.

Reid (1977) and Holzberg (1977a) have investigated intermarriage, social club membership, and corporate interlocks in the capitalist elite, based on data on directors of public corporations, kinship records, social club membership and, in Holzberg's case, anthropological field-work. The picture that emerges is one of remarkable social and economic cohesion. Twenty-one families account for over half of all corporate directorships and 70 per cent of corporate chairmen. Six families alone account for one-third of all directors (Reid, 1977:24). Intermarriage within the ethnic groups is very frequent and between the groups not infrequent. This elite section of the capitalist class also attended the same schools and are members of the same social clubs. While there are still ethnic differences, and, as we shall see later in this chapter, differences in partisan attachment and in ideology (Chapter 4), these cannot be systematically related to fissures in the structure of capital. That is, there are no socially distinct comprador and manufacturing segments.[36] All of the large empires stretch across these segments and these, along with the smaller concerns, are interlinked by interlocking directorships, intermarriage and social intercourse.

The state

As mentioned above, the independence constitution bequeathed upon Jamaica a political system modelled in all essential respects after the British one.[37] Jamaica became a member of the Commonwealth as a constitutional monarchy, with the Governor-General as head of state representing the Queen. The Governor-General is appointed by the Queen, on the advice of the prime minister. His functions and powers are largely ceremonial, exercised on the advice of the prime minister and, depending on the matter in question, also of the leader of the opposition.

Parliament is sovereign, as in Britain, and it is bicameral, with the Senate as upper and the House of Representatives as lower house. The House of Representatives is elected in direct popular elections at maximum intervals of five years, under single-member district electoral rules. In 1962 the Lower House had forty-five seats, in 1967 and 1972 it was expanded to fifty-three seats and in 1976 to sixty seats. The Senate has twenty-one members appointed by the governor, thirteen on the advice of the prime minister and eight on the advice of the leader of the opposition. The Senate may delay bills, but it can be overridden by the lower house in three successive votes on such bills. Besides being an advisory body and a reservoir of political talent for ministerial appointments of people who are not willing to stand for election, the Senate's key function is the blocking of constitutional changes. Amendments to clauses in the constitution require a two-thirds majority in both houses, that is, at least one Senate member of the opposition has to go along with the party in power. If the Senate refuses to approve proposed constitutional changes, it can be overridden by a special majority of the electorate in a referendum.

The cabinet under the leadership of a powerful prime minister is the principal executive body. In addition to the prime minister it has a minimum of eleven members two or three of whom have to come from the senate. The prime minister is the leader of the majority party; he selects the members of the cabinet and he has the power to call for a dissolution of parliament and new elections. He is subject to the vote of no confidence in the lower house.

The central government exercises all essential legislative powers, as the political system is a unitary one. Local government, in the form of fourteen parish councils, is highly dependent on financial assistance from the central government. This assistance is partly tied to specific areas and only partly available for autonomous disposal by the parish councils. Thus, whereas the parishes are small enough to facilitate some popular participation in political decision-making, the decisions within their discretion are extremely limited. Rather than becoming a school and channel for popular political participation, local government has become a machine for dispensing patronage, strengthening partisan political competition and maintaining popular dependence on the political leadership (for example, see Robertson, 1972:36–8 and Duncan, 1970).

The Jamaican state apparatus in the late 1950s had a distinctively post-colonial character in terms of size, structure, and personnel. Despite constant expansion in the 1950s and 1960s the state had remained comparatively small in size and highly centralized, and the bureaucracy was uninnovative and inefficient. Thus, the state apparatus constituted a poor instrument for directing and regulating economic and social development, though the state was necessarily thrust into this role.

The new tasks faced by the state in the period after the Second World War, particularly the promotion of industrial and agricultural production, caused an expansion of the functions performed by ministries and the creation of new state agencies in the form of public corporations and regulatory boards (Mills, 1970). Actual ownership of industrial and service enterprises, however, as well as direct involvement in the organization of productive activities remained extremely limited. The state's role was mainly the provision of social services, juridical and administrative functions, and of some infrastructure (Phillips, 1982). Only in transport (Air Jamaica and the Jamaica Railway Company) and in communications (Jamaica International Telecommunications, Jamintel and the Jamaica Broadcasting Corporation, JBC) was the state a major owner. However, there were private enterprises in both sectors as well; most importantly, the Jamaica Omnibus Services (JOS) was under private foreign ownership, as was the Jamaica Telephone Company, the Jamaica Public Service Company (JPS) which provided electricity, and the radio station Radio

Jamaica Rediffusion (RJR). The operations of the privately-owned public utility companies were regulated by the state, which caused frequent confrontations over rate increases, expansion plans (or lack thereof) etc.[38] The JLP government also acquired shares in the JPS, thus becoming the largest single shareholder and being able to appoint the chairman of the board, and it required a dispersion of shareholding in the Telephone Company,[39] but the state was not in a position to ensure provision of adequate services, as it did not control sufficient resources and as profit considerations of the private owners remained the decisive criterion for decision-making.

Under the colonial administration, the structure of the state was highly centralized, such as to facilitate effective control by the governor in whose hands power was concentrated (Jones, 1970:116). After the introduction of self-government, elected Jamaican politicians continued in the tradition of exercising control from above and centralizing power in the hands of ministers and, ultimately, the prime minister.[40] The desire to remain in control stood in contradiction to the need for the creation of new, flexible, and at least partly autonomous state agencies in charge of promoting economic and social development. Where ministers managed to bring such agencies under their control, they effectively nullified the rationale for their creation outside the normal civil service structure, as well as the trend to decentralization of decision-making structures accompanying their creation. This contradiction had negative consequences in that it caused frequent duplications of functions and fragmentation of authority and responsibility, which in turn slowed down decision-making and frustrated innovation (Jones and Mills, 1976:331). Finally, the tradition of centralization had not fostered a strong institutionalization of data collection, analysis, and dissemination, but rather a widespread privatization of information by the top levels of the bureaucracy.

The legacy of colonialism was also responsible for a large part of the behavioral obstacles to efficient administration. Under colonialism, civil servants were socialized into faithfully executing decisions, not taking them. Thus the civil service was infinitely better at shuffling papers and abdicating responsibility than at planning and managing the implementation of policies and programs.[41] The negative effects of colonial socialization on the quality of the civil service were aggravated by the scarcity of skills in the society and the decline of the status of the civil service from the 1950s onward.[42] Because of the growth of the economy, the private sector increasingly competed with the civil service for qualified personnel, and successfully so because of the substantially higher monetary rewards offered. Thus, many of the most ambitious and qualified civil servants resigned, and younger people started their careers in the private sector. The strongest attraction of a civil service career came to be job security and virtually guaranteed promotions on the basis of seniority. Rather than inducing civil servants to try to earn promotions through initiative and performance, this situation was conducive to a 'don't rock the boat' attitude and a reluctance to assume responsibility.

The Whitehall model, with its emphasis on administrative neutrality, clashed with Jamaican reality in several major respects. In the context of intense party competition, elected politicians attempted to exert full control over the functioning of the various ministries and wanted to have reliable civil servants, that is, civil servants favorable to the party of the incumbents. Such desires were particularly important because in a small society with closely-knit social circles and family partisan traditions like Jamaica, partisan leanings of top level civil servants were generally well known (Mills, 1979). Since possibilities for politicians to select top level civil servants were limited by the career structure of the civil service, they often attempted to bypass civil servants with the delegation of functions to semi-autonomous state agencies or the appointment of special advisors. Appointments to the boards of such agencies came to be made primarily on the basis of partisan criteria, and thus they became a prime source of patronage for the rich (Jones, 1970). The only alternative solution to satisfy politicians' desires for civil servants committed to the party in power and its policies would have required a constitutional change, that is, the introduction of more layers of appointive positions at the top levels in ministries.

The state's capacity to promote and direct economic and social development in the interest of the mass of the people was severely hampered by the close link of both parties to members of the private sector, one manifestation of which was the domination of boards of state agencies by private sector representatives. Furthermore, since both parties were dependent on private financial contributions and included important capitalist families among their members, many businessmen were appointed as ministers or advisors. As a result of these close links, decision-making in public corporations and agencies increasingly came under the influence of private capital and thus the public sector came to function heavily in the service of private interests.[43]

Jamaica's legal system and court practice were also formed in the British mold. The courts use British law and precedent, and the ultimate instance of appeal has remained the British Privy Council. Locally, the Court of Appeal is the highest legal authority. The status of judicial review of legislation is complex; on the one hand, parliament is sovereign, but on the other hand the constitution is supreme and laws inconsistent with the constitution invalid. The final jurisdiction in the area of judicial review and interpretation of the constitution again rests with the British Privy Council. Independence of the courts from the government is protected by the appointment of judges for life, and appointments being made by the governor in consultation with the prime minister, the leader of the opposition, and a judicial service commission. Not surprisingly, the courts in the late 1960s had a predominantly traditional or even conservative composition and outlook.

The Jamaican security forces are made up of the police, called Jamaica Constabulary Force (JCF), the military, called Jamaica Defense Force (JDF) and of auxiliary police and military forces.[44] In 1968, the JCF had some 3100 regular members. In addition, a variety of auxiliary forces, such as the Island Special Constabulary Force, the Parish Special Constables, the District Constables and the Special District Constables could be armed and brought under the police command. Lacey (1977:104) estimates that mobilization of all these auxiliary forces brought the police force close to 10 000 members in the late 1960s; without mobilization of the Parish Special Constables, which were a genuine emergency organization, the police could count on some 6000–7000 men.

The JDF was set up after Jamaica's withdrawal from the West Indies Federation. It was made up of two battalions, and an air and a coastal patrol unit, which together had between 1500 and 2000 men. The JDF was trained and originally assisted by British forces; accordingly, its original role perception was one of defense against external attack. However, in practice its role became entirely focused on the protection of internal security. Joint operations between the JDF and the JCF assumed increasing importance. The surveillance of the 1966 state of emergency in West Kingston was the first full-scale joint operation (Lacey, 1977:113). As such joint operations became more frequent, they were put under the control of a joint command center. Notable among these joint operations were those during the 1967 election campaign and during the 1968 Rodney riots.[45]

The parties
By the late 1960s, the two parties had come to look alike in many aspects of structure, composition, support base, and political orientation and practice, though some of the traditional differences remained clearly visible. The structural similarities were a formal organization of the mass party type, with groups or branches at the grass-roots level and constitutionally defined procedures for representation of these grass-roots units in higher-level decision-making bodies of the party. Despite this formally democratic set-up, however, decision-making power in both parties was concentrated at the top, in the hands of a small elite among whom the party leader played a predominant role. Robertson (1972:33) found that there was virtually no grass-roots party member input into the selection of candidates for MP or Parish Councillor, and that these members had very little knowledge about the rules and procedures for participation in decision-making organs of the parties. Rather than serving as agents for political education and mobilization and as channels for political participation, the parties served as electoral machines sustained through the dispensation of

patronage. The mechanics of dispensing patronage involved the allocation of government-financed jobs, such as in the Christmas work program, of public housing, of farm-workers' tickets to North America, or of government contracts for construction, etc., either through MPs or the local Councillors. Robertson's findings (1972:37) also confirmed the importance of the instrumental link of rank-and-file members to the parties, mediated through the local-level leadership. The Parish Councillors were the main contact for party members seeking some kind of personal benefits, particularly jobs. This contact, however, was a personalistic rather than an institutionalized one, as Councillors rarely participated in grass-roots party meetings.

Within these essentially similar party structures, there were still certain differences between the PNP and the JLP. Most importantly, the elite circle in the PNP was somewhat wider and more involved in collegial decision-making than in the JLP. In the JLP, Bustamante, the 'Chief', continued to run the party and the union more or less unchallenged, even after his retirement in 1964. All major decisions were cleared with him by Donald Sangster, his successor as Prime Minister, and conflicts between ministers or senior officials were also resolved by him (Eaton, 1975:203). Also, the PNP group structure was better entrenched than the JLP branches.

In terms of party composition at the level of leaders and activists, the two parties had become very similar. The party leadership had largely middle-class backgrounds, being either in elite professions (for example, lawyers, doctors, technical and managerial positions) or in white-collar jobs (such as teachers, ministers of religion, trade unionists).[46] Party activists of both parties came primarily from lower-class backgrounds, that is, the unemployed, the working class and the small farmers.[47] The motivation of these activists was predominantly not of an ideological nature but rather of an instrumental, patronage-seeking nature.

The social support base of the two parties was similar insofar as it had a cross-class character. Both parties had a union wing, as well as some important capitalist supporters. Electorally, the parties attracted some support from all social classes. However, there were still some clearly visible differences. Stone's survey carried out in 1971 in the Kingston–St Andrew area found that the PNP was distinctively stronger than the JLP in the middle classes, that is, among white-collar workers and self-employed artisans, somewhat stronger among blue-collar workers, and distinctively weaker among businessmen and in the lower classes; among professionals and small businessmen, the parties were of roughly equal strength (Stone, 1973:43). A further difference resulting from the traditional image of the PNP as the party of the brown middle-class was visible in the support for the two parties in different color segments within the same social classes. Among white-collar workers, 65 per cent of brown as opposed to 58.5 per cent of black people expressed a PNP preference, and in the working class

56.1 per cent of brown as opposed to 44.5 per cent of black people did (Stone, 1973:46). Finally, there was an urban–rural difference in party strength; the PNP dominated in the Kingston–St Andrew area and in the parishes of St Ann, Manchester, Westmoreland, and St James, all of which have important secondary urban or tourism centers, whereas the JLP clearly dominated in the heavily rural parishes of St Thomas and Clarendon.[48] Accordingly, the JLP had remained the clearly dominant party among small farmers. Among medium farmers, in contrast, the PNP had a strong base, as their organization, the Jamaica Agricultural Society (JAS), had remained close to the PNP.

The main similarities in the political orientation and practice of the two parties were the negligible importance of ideology, and the explicit promotion of industrialization by invitation. Beneath this surface of shared pragmatism and pro-capitalist practice, however, there were different currents in the two parties. In the PNP, there were still some remnants of its earlier ideological orientation and conflicts. N. W. Manley never ceased calling himself a socialist at heart, arguing that the essence of socialism was a commitment to social equality and that the strategy to transform society towards this goal necessarily had to be adapted in practice to concrete historical circumstances. Besides N. W. Manley, there were some members in the PNP leadership with a moderately left-wing orientation, and some younger activists with a neo-Marxist orientation, something virtually entirely absent in the JLP leadership. The only exception in the JLP appeared to be, interestingly enough, given his later role, Edward Seaga, who acquired a reputation as a left-winger through a speech in 1961 about the 'have and have-nots', as well as through his hard line on tax evasion and taxation of corporate profits as Minister of Finance in the late 1960s and early 1970s.

By the early 1960s, N. W. Manley had started to question the social effects of the development model which his government had promoted in the 1950s. The problems of unemployment and poverty contrasting with growing affluence of the top 5–10 per cent of the population caused him to listen to and support the point of view of a group of younger party leaders and members who advocated a return to the PNP's original explicit socialist stand. These younger people, prominent among whom was Hugh Small, had participated in the formation of the Young Socialist League (YSL) in 1962 and attempted to work for their political program by campaigning within the PNP and having themselves elected to leadership positions in the PNP. This revived the old left–right struggle within the PNP, and the PNP Conference in November 1964 saw intense fights about policy statements.[49] By early 1965, N. W. Manley clearly sided with the left and the PNP formally supported a radical platform. The platform advocated nationalization of the utilities, land reform, improvement of social services, eradication of illiteracy, and improvements in the educational system. However, the party contested the 1967 election not on the basis of an explicitly socialist platform but rather mainly on the basis of calls for 'freedom' (Miller, 1981), referring to freedom from repressive actions on the part of the government (see below), and for land for the poor, jobs, free education, youth training, medical care, protection of workers' rights, a social security plan, and equal rights for women (Parris, 1976:167).

The JLP won the 1967 election again with a narrow margin of victory, 50.6 per cent of the popular vote compared with the PNP's 49.1 per cent. However, despite the fact that its electoral majority increased by 0.2 per cent only, the JLP managed to gain seven additional seats, whereas the PNP gained only one additional seat in the newly-expanded House of Representatives. The PNP members of the parliamentary committee in charge of drawing constituency boundaries for the 1967 election had alleged gerrymandering and protested against the committee (JLP) majority report already in 1966 (Lacey, 1977:54–5). Nevertheless, the JLP went ahead with its new boundaries and obtained thirty-three of the fifty-three seats in the lower house.

Though the PNP retreated further from any radical stands between 1967 and 1972, the JLP government's heavy hand towards political dissent, such as the banning of the scholar Walter Rodney and other radical figures, censorship of radio programs, withdrawal of passports of persons who had visited Cuba, bans on books, etc., gave the party the opportunity to continue to differentiate itself from the JLP by emphasizing its role as defender of political rights, including the rights to free speech. Finally, the two parties continued to differ somewhat in their orientation toward the outside world, the PNP's internationalist and cosmopolitan outlook contrasting with the JLP's more parochial one, though both parties professed a clearly pro-Western attitude.

A final important area of similarity in political practice between the two parties was their growing involvement in political violence. Some forms of intimidation and violence, such as verbal threats or stone-throwing and physical attacks on rival party supporters, had been part of Jamaican election campaigns from the beginning. However, in 1966 a new phenomenon entered the scene, namely, the use of guns and the involvement of youth gangs in politically motivated gun violence. Gun violence broke out at the end of 1965 in the Western Kingston constituency where Edward Seaga was attempting to establish his political control to win the 1967 election against the PNP's Dudley Thompson. The government cleared some areas in Western Kingston by simply bulldozing the makeshift housing of squatters, which naturally created great resentment against the government among these urban poor. Seaga, then Minister of Development and Welfare, attempted to strengthen his political base in the area by expanding public housing, notably the Tivoli Gardens project, which like most of such developments, was used as patronage and thus allocated to supporters of the party in power. That this had the desired result can be seen in the 1972 election returns. In one of the polling stations in Tivoli Gardens, for instance, 83 people voted for Seaga, though there were only 82 electors on the voter list, and nobody voted for his PNP opponent, in an adjoining polling station, with 74 electors on the list, 75 votes were cast for Seaga. Other polling places in the area showed similarly lopsided results, with Seaga's PNP opponent polling only a few votes (Chief Electoral Officer, 1972:40). The rising violence led to what was called the 'West Kingston War' and to the declaration of a state of emergency in the area in October 1966.[50] It also earned Seaga the title of 'Minister of Devilment and Warfare' (Lacey, 1977:49). The state of emergency ended in early November, and despite appeals of candidates and party leaders, political violence rapidly assumed alarming proportions. Political violence remained high until after the 1967 elections, and acts of criminal violence, many of them committed with the 'political' guns, increased in number (Lacey, 1977:50). This pattern of inter-party gang violence, carried out with guns distributed with the knowledge of highly placed people in both parties, was to repeat itself and to assume more alarming proportions in subsequent elections. Clearly, the importance of patronage in the political system created the climate supportive of intense and violent inter-party rivalry, which could then be exploited by power-hungry politicians who were willing to build and consolidate a power base by relying on armed strongmen.

The unions

By 1970, the labor movement had grown to a membership of some 146 000 dues-paying members and to a coverage by contract of some 200 000 workers. With a total labor force of 783 000 people, this meant that 19 per cent of the labor force were regular union members and 25 per cent were covered by collective bargaining agreements.[51] If we consider employees with jobs only, that is, excluding the self-employed and unemployed, the figure for dues-paying members comes to 38 per cent of this section of the labor force. By far the largest proportion of union members belonged to the BITU and the NWU, which were of roughly equal strength. By 1959, the NWU had managed to increase its membership to 82 723, of whom 22 140 were dues-paying; the BITU had 74 343 members, 54 943 paying dues (Harrod, 1972:185).[52] However, since the NWU predominated among the better-paid sectors of the working class, particularly the bauxite workers, its income from dues in the same year was £57 564 compared with the BITU's dues income of £48 267, despite the smaller number of dues-paying members (Harrod, 1972:185).

This situation of parity in strength between the two major unions persisted into the 1970s. The NWU had a virtual monopoly in the bauxite/alumina industry and was stronger than the BITU in tourism, communications, and the newer manufacturing enterprises, whereas the BITU remained stronger in the sugar industry. In construction, commerce, and the public sector, both unions had strong bases. Many participants and observers have claimed that the fortunes of the BITU were somewhat in decline by the early 1970s, in accordance with a typical trend for the union identified with the party in power to lose some support to its competitor.[53]

The TUC's importance had greatly and rapidly diminished with the ascendancy of the NWU; in 1966 its membership was down to roughly 2000, or 1 per cent of the combined BITU and NWU membership (Stone, 1973:144). Besides the TUC, there were several smaller unions, some of which belonged to the Independent Trade Union Action Council (ITAC), which was formed in 1969 in an explicit protest action against the two big unions and their alleged politically motivated accommodationist line (Parris, 1976:196–7). The most visible of the nonaffiliated unions were the University and Allied Workers Union (UAWU), headed by Trevor Munroe and linked to the Workers' Liberation League, the Union of Technical, Administrative and Supervisory Personnel (UTASP) and the Jamaica Association of Local Government Officers (JALGO).

Structurally, the NWU and the BITU were (and still are) blanket unions, that is, they covered all industries, trades, services, crafts and occupations. In terms of their constitution regulating internal life, the two unions differed markedly. The NWU had a constitution with a democratic character, stipulating that the annual conference was the highest authority and responsible for the election of the executive council and the President; the Island Supervisor as official with responsibility for industrial relations on an island-wide basis, and the General Secretary as chief administrative officer, were appointed by the executive council (Harrod, 1972:186). Also, shop stewards, delegates, and executive officers of local branches were to be democratically elected by the local membership. According to Manley's own account of his sixteen years as leading NWU figure, reality in the local branches did not always live up to these democratic prescriptions, but the union maintained active local participation in the handling of workers' grievances and contract negotiations (Manley, 1975a:72–3). The BITU's constitution, in contrast, was distinctively undemocratic. Bustamante was President for life, and as President was empowered to appoint the executive committee as well as the General Secretary and the Island Supervisor whose functions were similar to their counterparts in the NWU. The executive committee nominated the Vice President, who was then confirmed in an election, and it also appointed the chairmen of local councils.

In both unions, however, the top-level leadership as well as the paid organizers were from middle-class backgrounds; rank-and-file workers could rarely rise above the level of shop steward or delegate. This, together with the increasing tendency to negotiate contracts at the industry level, caused certain problems of communication between the unions and the rank-and-file members. Breakdowns in communication, which were particularly likely with unions outside the Kingston–St Andrew area, and a certain lack of trust in the union leadership among the members aggravated the propensity to wildcat strikes, which had its roots in the nature of the relationship between workers and employers (to be discussed later). Stone (1973:144) concluded on the basis of his 1971 survey that 'as much as 40 per cent of unionized labor is convinced that the BITU and NWU leaderships do not adequately represent the interests of the working class', a proportion roughly similar to the one in the manual classes as a whole. The most important reasons given for this lack of trust and the antagonism towards the two major unions by working- and lower-class respondents were ineffectiveness, corruption and the alliance to the political parties (Stone, 1973:90).

Union dues were collected through a voluntary check-off system, that is, workers had to authorize these deductions explicitly. There were no closed shops in Jamaica, but the danger of unemployment and social pressure from fellow-workers helped to induce members to pay their dues. The large difference between dues-paying and non-dues-paying members was partly caused by the problem of unstable employment and the resulting difficulty in collecting dues, and partly by the fact that unions did not usually take members who had lost their jobs or had not paid-up off their lists.

The link between the two unions and their respective parties was official and close in both cases, but the BITU–JLP link was the closer of the two. The BITU's representation in the executive organs of the JLP was stronger than the NWU's representation in the PNP. Even more importantly, BITU leaders could retain their union positions while assuming positions as government ministers, whereas NWU leaders were required to resign in such cases (Harrod, 1972:188–9). The precedent, of course, was set by Bustamante himself, but when Hugh Shearer became Prime Minister in 1967, he also retained his BITU position as Island Supervisor. Thus, political control over the union was stronger in the BITU's case. However, in both cases, the party's ability to exercise control over its union and use it for political purposes, such as for strikes to embarrass the government when in opposition or for restraint in wage demands to ease tensions when in government, was severely limited by the highly competitive situation and the low trust of the membership in their unions. The rival union stood always ready to try to convince workers that they were being misled by their leaders who were pursuing their own interests, and where a union failed to deliver the goods, its rival's promises to do better were likely to find open ears.

The main contribution that unions made then and continued to make to the parties was in the electoral area. The unions delivered the votes of a large part of their members and they contributed manpower and some money to election campaigns. Given the income levels of most Jamaican

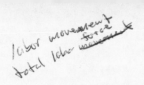

workers, revenues from dues were insufficient to cover operating expenses of the union *and* substantial financial contributions to the parties. Instead, as we have already pointed out, both parties had to rely heavily on contributions from the capitalist class, although in manpower and materials, such as leaflets, loudspeakers, etc., the unions' contribution to mobilizing the vote for their party was important.

The contribution that the parties made to the unions was less tangible. It mainly consisted in a sympathetic attitude when in government *vis-à-vis* labor–capital conflicts and in support for legislation protecting workers and their organizations, though, for instance, a law stipulating compulsory recognition of trade unions was only passed by the PNP government in the 1970s. A further contribution from the parties was the awarding of work to union members on a patronage basis, sometimes directly in the case of government-sponsored projects, and sometimes indirectly in the case of private enterprises undertaken by party leaders or members. Labor recruitment in such cases was frequently done in collaboration between the local MP or Councillor, the employer and union representatives. This practice was particularly strong in the construction industry, with the result that violence with political overtones on construction sites became a rather frequent phenomenon (see, for example, Lacey,1977:51–2).

The most detrimental effects of the party ties on the union movement were obviously the waste of resources and time in inter-union rivalry and the continued inability to cooperate in organizing the unorganized and in forming a strong united working class front to press for job-creation and training policies. In 1967, the NWU attempted to take a first step towards collaboration by proposing the establishment of a single national trade union center for research, educational, and organizational activities. However, the attempt failed as the BITU refused even to enter into negotiations about such a center (Harrod, 1972:272–3). Another earlier example for the BITU's obstruction of moves towards greater trade union collaboration was its refusal to let any delegates attend an annual training course started by the Ministry of Labor in 1955 (Harrod, 1972:317). Only when the American Institute for Free Labor Development (AIFLD) sponsored and financed the formation of the Trade Union Education Institute (TUEI) at the University of the West Indies in 1964 did the BITU agree to participate in a joint activity with other unions (Harrod, 1972:289).

In contrast to developing countries in general and Latin-American countries in particular, the state played a relatively minor role in Jamaican labor relations in the late 1960s.[54] The system of industrial relations was largely built after the British model of voluntary collective bargaining or 'self-government in industry' (Harrod, 1972:190). The Ministry of Labor normally did not interfere in relations between unions and employers at the enterprise level, with the exception of the holding of representational rights polls. As bargaining at the industry level became more widespread,

TABLE 2.10　*Strikes, 1962–82*

Year	Number of strikes*	Number of workers involved	Person-days lost
1962	83	16 081	123 829
1963	75 (30)	10 728	204 056
1964	90 (37)	8 560	67 846
1965	48 (11)	25 316	290 162
1966	73 (4)	23 425	180 628
1967	95	17 849	173 587
1968	104 (20)	22 550	224 781
1969	61 (15)	8 724	91 489
1970	68 (1)	18 097	317 970
1971	77 (27)	18 623	76 069
1972	55 (50)	30 286	266 369
1973	111	18 726	236 805
1974	135	21 309	766 549
1975	205	10 993	112 584
1976	142	8 167	138 655
1977	163	12 557	81 688
1978	N/A	N/A	N/A
1979	182	19 824	82 093
1980	144	N/A	N/A
1981	145	N/A	N/A
1982	142	36 145	316 712

*Number of workers involved refers to the number of strikes indicated. Those numbers in parentheses indicate additional strikes for which the number of workers involved and person-days lost are not accounted.

SOURCE　For 1962, Henry (1972:122–3) for 1963–70, Department of Statistics (1979:315–16); for 1973–82, NPA (various years).

the Ministry of Labor became involved in tripartite Joint Industrial Councils, such as for the Port of Kingston, building and construction, the banana industry, the printing industry and others (Harrod, 1972:191). But the only area where the ministry played a decisive role was in essential services (water, electricity, gas, health, public transport, and communications), where strikes and lock-outs were illegal and deadlocked negotiations were solved by compulsory arbitration.

In general, labor relations in Jamaica were rather conflictful and the militancy of the labor force comparatively high. The available strike statistics (see Table 2.10), which unfortunately cannot be regarded as very accurate and reliable,[55] indicate that between 1965 and 1970 on the average roughly 10–15 per cent of unionized workers participated in strikes every year. This is a high figure in comparative perspective, and becomes even more so if one considers that the data underestimate the actual extent of work stoppages. Certainly, a major reason for this high militancy was the competitive nature of the labor movement.[56] Not only did many work-stoppages result from attempts at raiding, but even more importantly, the imperative of retaining their membership put pressure on union leaders to appear tough and to be constantly ready to fight by threatening and actually applying industrial action. Furthermore, the political ties of the two major unions frequently gave rise to charges of victimization of workers because of their union/party affiliation and to militant action, including the use of violence, to rectify this situation. Prominent examples of militant industrial action related to victimization and union competition in 1967 and 1968 were, for instance, the strikes and violence at the Alpart site at Nain, at Reynolds in St Ann, at Port Kaiser, on the Kingston docks, and among workers in the water and electricity services (Lacey, 1977:51–2).

Another crucial reason for high worker-militancy was the traditional, highly antagonistic relationship between workers and employers, which was prevalent in many enterprises. Many employers regarded their workers as lazy, cheating, stupid, etc., and believed that only a 'strong hand' could enforce discipline and ensure adequate work performance. Consequently, they maintained an authoritarian relationship to their workers, often bordering on arrogance and outright disdain. This tense and antagonistic relationship was frequently aggravated by racial overtones, as employers and managers were predominantly white or light-skinned and the workers black. In such a climate, misunderstandings as well as real conflicts were difficult if not impossible to solve through direct communication and negotiation, and instead tended to provoke rash actions on both parts, such as suspensions or firings of workers and work stoppages or even physical assaults on employers. Many of these work stoppages were 'wildcat', that is, they were spontaneous reactions of angry workers, not planned collective action cleared with and approved by the union leadership.

There were exceptions to this pattern of antagonism in labor relations and high militancy. Some enterprises enjoyed a reputation for having an excellent industrial climate. The key reason for this lay in their effort to keep communication between workers and management open and to deal with problems and conflicts on a face-to-face basis.[57] In bigger enterprises, this was achieved through an industrial relations department, and in smaller enterprises frequently through the employer personally who assumed a basically paternalistic role. Thus, the former managed to routinize interaction between hierarchical levels in the context of a highly class- and race-conscious society, and the latter managed to overshadow the authoritarianism in the interaction with the benevolent side of paternalism. As stated, however, both cases were exceptions to the general pattern of antagonism, strife and militancy resulting from the combination of structurally and historically rooted class and race conflict with competitive unionism.

Forms of social integration and domination
Given the history of slavery and colonialism, the extremely high degree of inequality, and the strong correlation of race and class, the Jamaican situation begs the question of how the society cohered. This question could, of course, be asked about any society, with the usual competing answers being consensus or coercion, the former being associated with the assumption of lack of fundamental clash of interests in society and the latter with the opposite assumption. Gramsci, as well as the Frankfurt school Marxists, departs from these traditional assumptions in that he argues that the rule of capital can be combined with consensus, albeit a manipulated consensus. Gramsci argues that, in advanced capitalist society, capital rules through ideological hegemony. The control of property and all that it entails in terms of domination of the media, attractiveness as a social ally to other social forces such as the church, cultural elites and so on, as well as the sheer weight of tradition are the basis of this ideological hegemony. As a result, in a process which is not the least bit conspiratorial in Gramsci's formulations, values and 'facts', or rather beliefs about facts, favorable to the status quo are naturally taught in schools, propagated in the media, supported in the church, and reinforced in daily interactions in a variety of social settings (family, voluntary associations, etc.). Gramsci's concept of civil society is the totality of these social institutions and associations which are not strictly economic or governmental (that is, the state) in character. He argues that the strategy of the socialist movement in such a society is to conquer civil society by building a socialist counterhegemony. Using his military analogy, he terms this the 'war of position'.

Gramsci contrasts this with the situation 'in the East', that is, in more backward societies such as turn-of-the-century Russia, where elite rule was achieved through coercion, the application of force or the threat of it. In such societies, civil society is very weak (or it is not 'dense', as he would say). There, he argues, the 'war of maneuver' or movement – that is, armed revolution – is the appropriate strategy. This picture of Russian society and European feudal societies certainly has an element of caricature in it, but, if we take the case of slave society in Jamaica, it comes very close to this polar type of rule purely through coercion.

To characterize the mode of domination and cohesion in Jamaica today, it is useful to take slavery as a point of departure and trace the development of the system very briefly. Here we must elaborate on Gramsci and go beyond his polar concepts of rule and social cohesion through the state via coercion or civil society via consensus. It is important to recognize that rule in pre-capitalist societies such as feudalism was not achieved entirely through coercion. Feudalism and other pre-capitalist forms of social organization were organized around a chain of vassal—lord relationships, a system of personal loyalties built on clientelistic ties and patronage. In the case of feudalism, this system of ties formed the basis of the economic and political system which were one and the same. As Marx points out, with the development of capitalism this fusion of the economic and the political is overcome, and political relationships become distinguishable from economic relationships. Using the Hegelian terminology, he writes that civil society becomes distinct from the state; but this does not mean that civil society in Gramsci's sense is created. At any rate, we cannot say that civil society is 'dense'. In fact, the personalistic system of clientelistic ties and patronage relationships continues in a new form. Or in societies like Jamaica, in which coercion was the sole form of rule, these clientelistic relationships begin to develop. This, of course, is not an either/or thing. Societies can have various combinations of integration via clientelism and via civil society. And substantial sectors of society can remain completely unintegrated and, as long as they do not actively disrupt the social order, can also not be the active subject of coercion. The mode through which a group is socially integrated is clearly related to the class system and productive relations, with the urban bourgeoisie and middle classes most likely to be integrated via the system of ideological hegemony in civil society and those marginal to the capitalist system, the lumpenproletariat and subsistence farmers, most likely to be completely unintegrated.

The two forms of integration are different not only in that one involves a personalistic loyalty to an individual or institution (that is, a political party) while the other involves an ideological commitment to a system, but they also differ in that clientelistic integration is developed and maintained through a system of single channels or ties. Hegemonic integration, on the other hand, is developed through a multiplicity of diffuse channels and ties. The individual receives reinforcing ideological messages in the initial socialization process and throughout adult life from a multiplicity of individuals and institutions which have the appearance of having no link to one another. That is, it does not appear to the individual that they are going through a process of ideological indoctrination. Consensus, belief in the system, appears to be spontaneous (which is one factor accounting for the stability of advanced capitalist societies).

Forms of party organization are obviously related to these forms of integration. Parties of notables are generally clientelistic parties; if they attempt to gain working-class and peasant support, they do so through developing systems of patronage. To the extent that they receive this support, they become important channels of integration of these classes into the capitalist system. Mass parties attempt to gain support through the development of ideological commitment and the promise of class-wide economic benefits (rather than individual gain). The development of a working-class mass party as part of a larger socialist movement as both an instrument in the struggle for ideological hegemony and a vehicle for the acquisition and exercise of power is a key element in Gramsci's strategic prescriptions.

With this framework as a background, we can now return to the Jamaican case. In the hundred years after the abolition of slavery, as M. G. Smith (1967) correctly argues, Jamaica developed not as an integrated society, but as a group of semi-autonomous race–class communities, each with its own set of norms, customs and behavior patterns. In the urban areas, civil society did become denser and increasingly a white upper-class hegemonic rule over the brown middle class developed. The *Daily Gleaner*, the anglophile secondary schools and the European-based churches were important institutions propagating values which portrayed all that was white and colonial as valuable. There were limits to this ideological domination of the brown middle class, as the few nationalist and democratic organizations mentioned earlier showed, but they were few.

For the most part, the peasantry and the working class remained unintegrated. The primary schools and the established churches were points of contact with the dominant value system, though the influence of the latter was limited by the growth of Afrochristian sects. There were also some individualized clientelistic relationships between members of the upper and lower classes. However, this lack of integration should not be taken to mean that they developed oppositional interpretations of society, or radical value systems as Parkin (1971) calls them. Rather, they were accommodative, or subordinate in his terms. There were some clearly oppositional movements in the period, such as Bedwardism and Garvey's movement and, at the end of the period, Rastafari, but they attracted the support of only small minorities of the population. So the lower classes were kept in line by a combination of coercion and lack of organized opposition.

With the development of the two party–union complexes, clientelism became the dominant form of integration of the lower classes. The pervasive nature of clientelism is clearly demonstrated in Stone's (1973:81) analysis of political behavior and attitudes in the Corporate Area (Kingston and St Andrew), which shows that 36 per cent of the working class and 70 per cent of the lower class (marginals) had sought patronage. It is important to recognize here that this system resulted in their integration into the party–union complexes and thus only indirectly into society. That is, this type of clientelistic integration developed loyalty to the party, not the system as a whole. The Jamaican political parties were a hybrid of parties of notables and mass parties. They were elite-dominated, non-ideological, and clientelistic but had a mass membership. This combination made them ideal instruments for the clientelistic dependent integration of the masses.

The electronic media, particularly radio, did reach a large proportion of the population, as 88 per cent of homes had radios and 76 per cent of the adult population listened daily (Brown, 1976:46). But by the late 1960s, the electronic media was not very effective in promoting either the ideological hegemony of national capital or any sort of national integration and nationalism. The radio station ZQY and its successor, RJR, were British-owned and aired popular music from the USA and UK. In 1959, Norman Manley's government set up the JBC radio (television was later added) with the explicit intention that it serve national purposes and promote national development in a non-partisan way. It operated this way until 1964, at which point the JLP government's attempts to manipulate it led to an unsuccessful strike organized by the NWU. Moreover, its influence was limited by the fact that its audience was only half that of RJR. In its early days JBC did promote local music such as ska, rock steady and later reggae, and local artists such as Bob Marley and Jimmy Cliff for the first time. Reggae, an authentic and completely Jamaican cultural expression, did later become the dominant music form on the air and Marley became a national cultural hero revered by Jamaicans of all parties and classes,[58] but by 1970 this breakthrough had not occurred and indeed was impeded by the policies of the Shearer government.[59]

In analyzing the media situation in Jamaica, it is important to emphasize the pre-eminence of the *Gleaner* in forming political opinions on specific issues in the country (as opposed to general societal values, though the *Gleaner* was and is influential there also). In the first Jamaican media surveys (carried out in 1976) only RJR exceeded the *Gleaner* in its reach and its perceived trustworthiness (Stone, 1981c), but compared with the *Gleaner*, RJR devoted little space to newscoverage and analysis. Indeed, the surveys show that radio use is focused on programs other than news and public affairs (Stone, 1981c:320). Moreover, as media specialists point out, the *Gleaner's* influence was magnified by its influence on more educated local opinion leaders (for example, pastors, teachers, etc.). To many Jamaicans, 'it was in the *Gleaner*' meant 'it was true'. Thus the paper, which was owned by a conservative segment of the capitalist class and, by and large, represented their views, was an extremely potent political instrument as well as an important element in the apparatus of capitalist ideological domination of the middle and upper-middle classes.

Even clientelistic integration did not extend to all sectors of the society; large sections of the marginal population, particularly in the urban areas were not integrated in any way. Moreover, a significant proportion of this social group had developed an oppositional interpretation of social reality. By the late 1960s, Rastafari had become a significant social movement. The oppositional nature of Rastafarian doctrine is obvious.[60] They interpret the Old Testament as the story of the black man's enslavement, considering themselves the true Israelites. While the initial emphasis on repatriation to Africa has been moderated in practice, the strong identification with Africa and the black pride remains. So does the identification of white society, particularly police power, the established churches and the colonial power, as 'Babylon', the oppressors of black people. Support for the movement is clearly class-related: Stone's (1973:156) 1971 poll of the Corporate Area shows that less than 10 per cent of the business and professional classes expressed support of Rastafari compared with over 30 per cent of the lower class (marginals). While the proportion of the marginal population which practises Rastafari in its orthodox form (the dietary restriction, deification of Haile Selassie, etc.) is certainly smaller, acceptance of the general interpretation of history and social reality offered by the Rastafarians, that is, acceptance of the 'culture of dread', as Beckford and Witter (1980) call it, is even greater. Indeed, Chevannes (1981:398) contends that this interpretation was so widespread in the Kingston ghetto that it came almost 'naturally' to ghetto youth.

Against the background of the economic situation, the nature of the parties and the weakness of shared national values and national loyalty, the roots of the inter-party violence, which began in the 1950s and then moved to a qualitatively new level in the mid-1960s with the introduction of gun-play and then escalated to unprecedented levels during the Manley government, are easy to understand. The weakness of hegemonic (or counter-hegemonic) integration of the lower classes and the strength of clientelistic integration resulted in a situation where party loyalty is great and appeals to supra-party values are not effective. The high level of unemployment and provision of jobs through party patronage means that which party is in power can make a great difference in the life situation of many people.[61] The highly competitive party system and single-member districts cause relatively small changes in party support to make a great difference in how much patronage can be dispensed by each party. Finally, the strength of party loyalty and weakness of supra-party loyalty means that the party stalwarts are not restrained by overarching value commitments in the lengths they are willing to go to ensure that their party wins.

The coming crisis
By the late 1960s, there were unmistakable signs of a challenge to the economic and political order in Jamaica. The development model of industrialization by invitation had produced growing unemployment and poverty next to growing affluence, which was aggravating the class and race conflicts in the society. These conflicts manifested themselves not only in labor militancy, political violence and the emergence of new radical groups, but even more threateningly in spontaneous riots and in increasing violent crime. In the early 1970s, the exhaustion of the growth phase of the economic development model added to Jamaica's problems and raised the specter of an impending crisis, calling for a serious change in direction in economic and social policy.

The first outbreak of large-scale violence after independence were the riots in Kingston in August–September 1965, which came to be called the Chinese riots because much of the violence was directed against Chinese property. The Chinese were predominantly medium and small business-men, some expanding into large businesses, with a reputation for hard work as well as hard bargains. Because of their economic success, they were envied by many, and they constituted an easy target as a highly visible minority. The disturbances broke out because of a dispute between an employee of a Chinese store and the owner, and because of a shooting incident caused by a Chinese (Lacey, 1977:86). The riots lasted for about a week, leaving several people shot, one of them fatally, and many Chinese businesses destroyed by looting and arson. They involved hundreds of people participating in mob action, and they were concentrated in down-town Kingston, close to the poor areas of West Kingston where about half a year later the politically motivated 'West Kingston War' was to flare up.

The second series of disturbances that shook Jamaica were the demon-strations and violence with political overtones sparked by the banning of Walter Rodney in October 1968. Rodney, a radical Guyanese intellectual who held a post at the University of the West Indies, was not allowed to re-enter the country on his return from Canada.[62] Student demonstrations escalated rapidly into mob action, predominantly by unemployed youths, which lasted for two days and could only be stopped by heavy deployment of security forces. Youth gangs and other participants attacked, burnt and smashed all kinds of property, including foreign-owned enterprises as well as white- or minority-owned Jamaican businesses, cars, buses, etc. Chant-ing of slogans like 'black power' accompanied these acts of violence and caused much fear, speculation and accusations concerning plans and plots of revolutionary violence. However, these riots, which again were concen-trated in downtown Kingston, were nothing but an explosion of pent-up frustration and anger among the urban poor. They lacked any political purpose or coordination with organized radical groups. Nevertheless, they had the effect of profoundly threatening the Jamaican propertied classes and large sectors of the middle class, by revealing the explosive potential underlying the apparently smooth and consolidated surface of the Jamai-can political system.

A further cause for concern among the middle and upper classes was the rising level of violent crime. Lacey's figures (1977:69), based on newspaper sources, show that the number of casualties of violent incidents increased from 111 in 1964 to 152 in 1965, to 302 in 1966 and to 457 in 1967; for 1968 he found 246 reported casualties and for 1969, 399. As he points out, the government discontinued publication of the JCF Annual Report in March 1966 (Lacey, 1977:64), but even though there were no official figures to create alarm in the society, the newspaper reports and the rumor mill made up for this lack. Certainly, the West Kingston War was an important contributing factor to the increase in violent crime, insofar as the guns given out for political purposes remained in the hands of the youth gangs and were easily put to use for criminal purposes.

At the level of organized political life, radical forces emerged in the form of independent unions, political groups with a black power ideology, and the Rastafarian movement.[63] Though none of these organizations managed to mount a serious challenge to the two big union–party blocs, some of them became quite influential ideologically, particularly those identifying with the black-power movement. The most important among them was the weekly *Abeng*, which represented a mixture of Marxist, liberal, African, and Rastafarian points of view and was close to the New World Group at the University of the West Indies.

Economic trends in the early 1970s threatened to push social and political conflict to new levels of intensity. The end of the investment cycle in bauxite/alumina and tourism and the lack of plans for new investment in these industries meant that economic growth was going to decline, and that the labor-intensive construction industry particularly was going to suffer. This would drive unemployment levels even higher. Furthermore, the end of capital inflows from abroad for investment in bauxite and tourism would confront the country with a serious balance-of-payments problem and require import restrictions or devaluation. Given the high import-dependence of the domestic manufacturing sector, such restrictions or devaluation were likely to hamper economic growth further and to aggravate the unemployment problem. In sum, then, the economic and social policies of the previous two decades had brought Jamaica to a situation where economic problems increasingly turned already explosive social conflicts into a zero-sum game, and from which there would be no escape without deep-going attempts to effect structural and behavioral changes.

Unfavorable pre-conditions for democratic socialism
Any process of socialist transformation in democratic societies faces inherent obstacles, which makes the path difficult under the best of circumstances. To win elections, governments need to deliver the material goods to their marginal supporters, and in the medium and long term this necessitates the generation of economic growth, not an easy task when a significant portion, often a majority, of the means of production are in the hands of private owners whose material interests are not being served by the government in question. Moreover, defending the status quo by sabotaging the change process is a lot easier than successfully carrying through a process of transformation.[64] Democratic socialist movements in dependent capitalist societies face further obstacles that their sister movements in advanced capitalist societies do not face: As we will argue in more detail in Chapter 9 the tasks facing movements in dependent capitalist societies are more difficult since the state must lead the growth process and redistribute from present resources, though it has fewer resources, in human and material terms, at its disposal. Furthermore, the transformation of its external relations involves the country in international econ-

omic struggles and often, as a consequence, geopolitical struggles, a factor not faced by socialist movements in advanced capitalist countries to nearly the same degree.[65]

In addition to these problems which Jamaica shared with other dependent capitalist countries, it found itself in a particular economic, historical and geographic situation which was very unfavorable for the successful initiation of democratic socialist development. As we pointed out in this chapter, the Jamaican economy was dependent to an extreme degree on foreign trade, investment and technology. It imported energy, raw materials, roughly half the food consumed, consumer goods, capital goods and semi-finished goods for manufacturing. Export earnings from bauxite and alumina, sugar, bananas, and tourism were not sufficient to cover the cost of imports, and the current accounts deficit on the balance of payments had worsened in the 1960s. Furthermore, the key sectors of the Jamaican economy were under foreign ownership, and the low degree of internal integration of the economy meant that growth in these sectors had virtually no multiplier effects on the rest of the economy. Finally, the state's role in the economy was extremely limited, and the state machinery was uninnovative and inefficient. All this made the introduction of an economic model characterized by state-sector-led growth, trade diversification, increased self-reliance, equalization and employment creation very difficult.

The political pre-conditions were equally unfavorable. The balance of class forces heavily favored capital. Though the domestic bourgeoisie did not enjoy a truly hegemonic position outside the upper and middle classes, it could rely on the lack of organization and of ideological education of the rest of the population, as well as its sheer economic clout to maintain its domination. The split in the labor movement, the purely economistic orientation of the trade unions, and the non-ideological nature of the parties meant that there had not been any efforts at establishing a counter-hegemonic presence and that the base from which to launch such efforts was weak. Thus, the task of channeling protest and the propensity to violent action of politically alienated groups in the society into an organized political movement, in coordination with popular sectors already organized in unions and the party, was a formidable one.

Thus, the problems encountered by the Manley government could stem from various analytically-distinct sources; general difficulties of socialist transformation, difficulties caused by general features of dependent capitalism, factors associated with Jamaica's position in the world economy and geopolitical space, specific features of Jamaica's historical legacy and political and economic situation in the early 1970s, and finally, mistakes made by the leadership of the democratic socialist movement during its tenure in office. An important part of the task of this book will be to analyze the relative weight of these factors in accounting for the shortcomings of the Manley government.

3

The PNP's First Term: Tasks at the Outset and Populist Politics in the First Years 1972–74

To begin the history of the Manley government, it is useful to start with an overall periodization of its period in office. Michael Manley was elected President of the People's National Party in February 1969 and in the period up to the February 1972 election his and the party's energies were focused on winning that election. The period from the election until the declaration of democratic socialism in the fall of 1974 witnessed the announcement of most of the domestic and foreign policies which have come to be associated with the Manley government, but the rhetoric of the government remained populist. These first two phases are covered in this chapter.

Chapter 4 covers the period from the declaration of democratic socialism to the 1976 election. The ideological debate intensified in this period and rifts within the PNP began to surface. The country's economic difficulties became increasingly severe but the PNP managed to increase its parliamentary majority in an election campaign characterized by ideological polarization, class realignment and increasing levels of political and criminal violence. The following chapter covers the watershed year of 1977. In the first four months of the year, the PNP left attempted to use the election victory to mobilize the people and to push for an alternative to the IMF. The party moderates reasserted control, the IMF agreement was signed in the summer of 1977, and the party General Secretary D. K. Duncan, one of the left's leaders was driven from that office in the fall. The remaining periods are covered in Chapter 6. The period from the beginning of 1978 to Fall 1979 was characterized by the political ascendancy of the moderate wing of the party and a catastrophic decline in the party's popularity in the face of the severe austerity policy demanded by the IMF. The left and Duncan were returned to a position of influence in the last period which saw the failure of the IMF test of December 1979, the party's decision to break with the IMF, an election campaign of unprecedented violence and the decisive defeat of the party in the elections of October 1980.

The tasks facing the party
In the Jamaican situation as of 1972, the extension of state ownership (or a controlling interest) into key areas such as the utilities, banking and bauxite, was necessary just to make the state capable of carrying out any plan for economic development and social transformation. Further, essential steps were the reduction of foreign ownership in crucial areas such as bauxite and land, and control of foreign capital in the rest of the economy, diversifying trade relations by reducing partner and product concentration, and increasing self-reliance by developing food self-sufficiency, greater use of domestic raw materials in manufacturing and backward and forward linkages in industry. In order to meet the food self-sufficiency target (as well as for distributive reasons) land reform was necessary. Idle lands needed to be brought into production and currently utilized lands re-oriented to different uses. In addition to moving toward long-term economic transformation there was an immediate pressing need to reduce poverty and social inequality through redistributive policies such as employment programs and provision of free or subsidized goods and services to lower income groups. To pull all this together, there was a need for an economic plan which would specify the overall accumulation target and the role and level of investment expected of the public and private sectors as well as alternatives that could be pursued if the most important economic actors, for any reason, failed to reach their targets.

Such an economic program also called for new foreign-policy initiatives. Trade diversification requires the widening of political and diplomatic ties, particularly with the Soviet Union and Eastern Europe, to expand trade relations. Strengthening of ties to Western European countries, especially those where the left was powerful, and with oil-rich Third World countries, was important not only for trade but also for alternative sources of foreign exchange to core capitalist financial institutions. Given the authoritarian nature of work relations and the elitist character of political institutions and culture in Jamaica, there were also urgent needs for policies aimed at social inclusion and deepening political democracy.

To carry out this program the PNP needed to alter radically the political strategy it had utilized until the late 1960s and move to build an ideological hegemony in society. It needed to develop an ideological consensus and to build the social and organizational apparatus capable of propagating that ideology. Building a mass party with auxiliary organizations (such as women's and youth groups) was the first step. Obviously a long-run goal had to be unification, expansion and conversion (to socialism) of the unions, but given the deep-rooted nature of the split in the labor movement, efforts in this area were unlikely to yield anything much in the short run. The Party also needed to develop a media policy which would serve the movement not only when it was in government but also in opposition and in pursuit of power.

Both the strategy and the goals involve a move away from clientelistic politics to mass party/hegemonic politics and indirectly from clientelistic integration to ideological hegemonic integration of society. To achieve this and, more specifically, to get at a source of political violence and low labor productivity in public sector jobs, the government needed to begin to reduce political patronage in the granting of jobs, housing and contracts.

Preparation for power 1969–71
As we pointed out in the last chapter, the PNP actually presented a more radical platform in the 1967 election than any time since the split in 1952, but this did not result in a general effort to radicalize the party and, in fact, the right wing of the party was far from enthusiastic about the program, which could have contributed to the loss.[1] Far more significant from the point of view of the PNP's future evolution was the election of Michael Manley, NWU leader and son of the founder of the party, to represent Central Kingston in Parliament. Soon thereafter, Norman Manley began to remove himself from the political scene. In the fall of 1968 he announced his intention not to run for re-election as PNP president the next year and he gave up his seat in mid-1969.[2]

That there would be a new direction under Michael Manley was not clear at the outset, at least not to the general public. Manley was urged by younger elements of the party to run for the party presidency and privately he made it clear to his supporters that he was willing to do so only on the grounds that it would involve a clear ideological differentiation from the opposition. While it is obvious now that Manley was much more radical than Vivian Blake, the other candidate for the PNP presidency, Manley's decisive victory (376:155) in the 1969 party presidential election was primarily due to his trade union support, his superior political skills and the Manley name.

The PNP's strategy under Manley's leadership as the opposition in 1969–71 must be seen against the background of the deteriorating social economy discussed in the last chapter and the corruption, repression and ineptness of the JLP government. In 1967, Hugh Shearer took over the post of Prime Minister and effective leadership of the party, though formally Bustamante was still the party leader. There were widespread rumors of corruption at the highest level of government, which seemed only to be confirmed by the acquisition of expensive residential property and luxurious housing by some top government officials. One minister was known as 'Mr Ten Per Cent' because of his alleged practice of taking kick-backs on contracts awarded by his ministry. The government also engaged in questionable manipulation of the electoral system. Electoral boundaries were gerrymandered to the extent that in the parish elections of 1969, the PNP received 51.3 per cent of the popular votes yet won fewer seats than the JLP, failing to gain a seat majority in two parishes where it gained an electoral majority. The government also refused to update the 1969 electoral lists so that in the 1972 election, no-one who had reached voting age (21) after 21 October 1969 was allowed to vote. Furthermore, many potential voters were not registered in that enumeration, by design or accident, thus over 200 000 Jamaicans of voting age were not allowed to vote in 1972.

The Shearer government was probably the most repressive Jamaican government since the advent of universal suffrage. It banned marches not only of smaller radical groups but also of the PNP. In response to the Black Power agitation, it banned literature on the subject, refused re-entry to Commonwealth citizens such as Rodney and C. Y. Thomas, and seized the passports of people suspected of radical activity. The JLP government also manipulated the JBC by covering the government in a favorable light and banning songs protesting social and economic conditions in Jamaica as well as those deemed to be directly supportive of the PNP.

The themes aired by PNP spokesmen in 1969–71 were designed to make the most of the social and economic situation and the failures and abuses of the JLP government. They did not flow from a coherent ideological point of view and issues of controversy were avoided. The main theme of virtually all major PNP speeches or policy statements of this period was the growth of unemployment and inequality as well as the resultant growth of crime, but the party offered few real solutions and certainly none that would indicate a tilt leftward.

The second theme of the PNP attacks on the JLP government was the issue of corruption and abuse of power. Political corruption, such as gerrymandering, the dispensation of jobs and housing to party supporters (called victimization in the Jamaican debate) and the disenfranchisement of voters, and the corrupt use of office for personal financial gains were skillfully interwoven by the PNP with the repressive measures of the Shearer government to present a picture of a government in moral decay.

Manley himself, particularly in the early part of his tenure as leader of the opposition, made speeches which indicated that he had something more than a few populist policies in mind, that he in fact envisioned an alternative path of development emphasizing the need for greater 'economic independence' (*Public Opinion*, 6 June 1969 and 13 October 1969), but he came under some fire for his statements and had to clarify the PNP policy on 'economic nationalism', emphasizing local private ownership and a very limited role for government ownership (*Public Opinion*, 7 November 1969). In his 1970 budget speech, however, he did clearly foreshadow the PNP's bauxite initiative as he strongly argued that massive increases in revenue could be achieved (*Public Opinion*, 19 July 1970).

Thus, the public posture of the PNP and to a lesser extent Michael Manley was almost completely non-ideological and its policies were undefined. But what of the private position of the leaders and their common agreement on what they would in fact do? In Manley's case, the situation is clear. In his book covering the events of the period, Manley (1982:39–57) claims that the overall objectives were clear to him at the outset and then goes on to outline a program similar to that presented in Chapter 1 of this book. Moreover, if one carefully examines the *Politics of Change* (1975) which was completed in the spring of 1973, one finds almost all the policies essential to democratic socialist development: nationalization of the commanding heights of the economy, increased economic self-reliance, a non-aligned foreign policy, popular mobilization, etc. as well as a rationale for these policies.[3]

Manley's ideology, or any ideology for that matter, was not shared by the party leadership, which is not very surprising given the party's non-ideological posture. Furthermore there was not even an agreement as to the concrete policies which the party would pursue in power. One close Manley advisor told us:

> There wasn't really a consensus on policies. The party at that stage wasn't strong on policy, they wanted to win the elections, they were strong on that . . . There were no hard, clear cut positions on anything. What was clear was a general 'people orientation'. The PNP wanted to win on the basis of concern for the people and for unemployment.

This lack of ideological coherence was to prove one of the PNP's worst weaknesses. Retrospectively one can say that it was a serious mistake for Manley and those around him not to attempt to introduce ideology into the party sooner nor to run the 1972 election on a more ideological platform.

In contrast to the lack of effort at ideology formation and ideological education, party organization-building did receive attention from the party after Michael Manley's election to the presidency. At the time, the party organization was at a low point with only fifty recognized groups. In July 1969, the party announced both a major membership drive and the formation of a youth arm, the PNP Youth Organization (PNPYO) (*Public Opinion* , 4 July 1969, 11 July 1969). The new efforts at organization building appear to have met with considerable success in the following two and a half years.

Before moving on to the 1972 election campaign itself, it is necessary to mention one last development in the JLP's second term in order to understand the forces behind the 1972 PNP election victory as well as the dynamics of the PNP government itself. While the Jamaican oligarchy had traditionally backed the JLP since 1949, a significant section of this class in later years of the Shearer government swung to join the PNP's traditional capitalist supporters in support of the party. In part, this change was stimulated by the abuses of power by the JLP government mentioned earlier.[4] Another factor also stimulated this shift: many businessmen felt threatened by some JLP measures, particularly Seaga's efforts at reducing tax evasion, but also Wilton Hill's moves to increase the government's ownership share in the utilities. In his efforts as Minister of Finance to increase revenue without increasing taxes, Seaga introduced measures to reduce tax evasion which were viewed as Draconian by many businessmen. Once he went so far as to suggest that legislation be introduced to imprison people for suspicion of tax evasion, and the combination of this with the measures he did introduce and his early speeches on 'the gap between haves and have-nots' led many businessmen to think that he was a danger-ous radical. One prominent capitalist told us 'He was pretty tough on everybody with taxes . . . he was regarded as very socialist-oriented, maybe even a communist [so he] was feared and hated by the business community'. These actions added to the resentment caused by the more general abuse of power to produce a backlash in the conservative segment of the capitalist class. One representative of that segment told us:

> I and many other private sector capitalists in 1972 felt that the JLP was behaving very badly. They were riding high and not speaking to or listening to anybody. We don't like this sort of thing here. We felt that a new government would be good . . . When Michael Manley got in, many of us felt that this should teach a lesson to the JLP.

Thus the scene was clearly set for a clear PNP victory in almost all social classes: the party could expect to maintain its traditional strong support among the middle strata. Growing inequality and unemployment could only serve to strengthen its lower class support, and an important segment of the capitalist class had been alienated by the JLP government and was swinging to the PNP to join its traditional business supporters.

The 1972 election
The election strategy of the PNP in 1971 and 1972 can be said to have had two primary goals. The first was not to rock the class coalition that had assembled behind it. Thus Manley not only did not put forward new social and economic programs but he also toned down even the more moderate statements he had already made on economic nationalism and economic independence in order to avoid alienating capitalist and upper middle-class supporters. At the March 1971 PNP conference, Manley avoided these issues and focused his attack on the JLP for victimization, incomplete and corrupt voter lists, manipulation of the JBC, crime, corruption and (signifi-cantly) Seaga's attempt to have people arrested on suspicion of tax evasion. Moreover, no real policies were proposed (*Public Opinion*, 5 March 1971).

The second goal was to gain the support of the two most important socio-cultural forces in Jamaica, the traditional Christian community and the Rastafarian community (or rather the broader culture of Dread) by identifying the party with issues and symbols associated with both movements. The fact that the two groups shared symbols and themes derived from the Old Testament made symbolic identification easier, the primary problem being to avoid blasphemy in the case of the traditional Churches. Given the JLP's record of corruption and repression and Manley's charisma, particularly his tremendous gift as a public speaker, it must have seemed natural and obvious that he should be cast in the role of the society's moral redeemer. Manley sounded this theme to an overflow crowd at the party conference in the fall, 1971. He began by saying that the nation was in a state of crisis explaining 'I believe that at the heart of our problem is creeping moral decline'. He went on to condemn gambling and the national lottery (an issue raised by the established churches), victimization, abuse of power, disenfranchisement, and corruption. He then said he had been talking to churchmen as a source of inspiration and moral purpose. He continued:

> I want it to be known that if it is God's will that I should face this awesome responsibility I would want to consult the Church for guidance, to involve the small farmers in the creation of decisions that guide their fate, to get the help of teachers in the planning of a genuine educational revolution; the help and advice of doctors in any plan for social justice so far as medicine is concerned; I would want the Jamaica Manufacturers Association, the Chamber of Commerce, the trade unions, the genius of the University and all of the people actively involved in the decision-making processes. Without them, the future cannot be built nor can it be built without the youth groups and organizations . . . we will face the election, when it comes in the faith that the New Jerusalem is ours to build and we will say with St John in the Revelations: 'And I saw a new heaven and a new earth; for the first heaven and the first earth were passed away . . .' Comrades, let us now put our hands to that holy task. (*Public Opinion* , 15 October 1971).

It was in this period and for this type of appeal that Manley acquired the title of 'Joshua' casting him in the role of a prophetic figure analyzing society's injustices and leading the people to correct them.

The campaign
The strong symbolic appeal to Rastafarianism, and thus indirectly to African and Black cultural identity developed fully during the campaign itself. In the open air mass rallies characteristic of Jamaican election campaigns, the PNP attempted to appeal to the new racial and cultural identity of the younger generation and the Rastafarian movement, playing reggae sometimes with live appearances by such well-known performers as

Max Romeo and Bob Marley. After crowd chants for 'Joshua', Manley would appear on the podium displaying his 'Rod of Correction', a cane given him by Haile Selassie. The same themes were repeated by Manley and other party spokespeople at these rallies and in PNP media advertisements throughout the campaign.[5] Some of them were contained in five election pledges Manley made:

1. legislation requiring parliamentarians to declare their assets publicly annually in order to counter corruption;
2. a fixed formula for the distribution of government jobs to end victimization;
3. permanent voter registration centers and voting rights for 18–20 year olds;
4. Parliament to be restored as the center of government activity;
5. no electioneering and government by promises. The PNP would tell the truth (*G*, 2 February 1972).

PNP slogans also showed little in the way of ideological content: 'Better Must Come', 'A change is coming with the PNP' and 'Power for the People'. The JLP campaign emphasized the party's record of achievement (roads, schools, hospitals built, etc.) in office, and its slogans were equally nondescript 'Keep ahead with the JLP', 'One good term deserves another' and 'Jamaicans agree with the JLP'.

Aside from charges from both sides that the other was responsible for the election violence, these themes dominated the campaign until the final week. At this point the JLP abruptly shifted tactics in newspaper advertisement accusing the PNP of anti-Christian blasphemy and dictatorial intentions.[6] Undoubtedly, the JLP sensed that the popular mood was strongly behind the PNP and this new tactic represented a desperate attempt to turn the tide. But perhaps more significant than the fact that the JLP used such appeals in its desperate attempt to reverse the tide is that, for the only time in its history, it did not use the Communist scare tactic in an election.

The PNP program
It would be unfair to say that the PNP said nothing about the concrete policies it would implement when in office or that its entire appeal was as devoid of ideological content as the themes sounded in the media and in public rallies. The parties were invited by the *Gleaner* to submit policy statements on three dates (12, 19 and 26 February) and the PNP did utilize the second and third occasions to criticize too much dependence on foreign capital for development. The last article was a statement by Manley in which he went into an extensive critique of the Puerto Rican model linking it to the rise of unemployment and crime in Jamaica. He criticized the dominance of foreign ownership in key sectors of the economy and called for a program which would couple industrialization with the development

of agro-industry and agriculture, but, significantly he did not mention what role the state and state ownership would play in this process.

The PNP also published its party program in a series of three full page advertisement in the *Gleaner* (24, 25 and 28 February). A number of the policies pursued by the PNP are included in this document: employment programs, programs aimed at increasing domestic food production, development of agro-industry, industrial development aimed at more use of local raw materials and increasing employment, most elements of the bauxite policy, development of Negril as a tourist area, most of the education programs, youth employment programs, the national youth service, more progressive taxation and subsidies on essential consumption goods. If we compare this program with the one laid out in Manley's 1975 book and with the policies pursued by the PNP in the first couple of years in office, a number of policies are notably absent from the 1972 program; public ownership of the 'commanding heights' of the economy, specifically the nationalization of the utilities and acquisition of 51 per cent ownership of the bauxite companies; land reform, workers' participation, development of cooperatives and the adult literacy program. In short, while being more specific than the rest of the campaign appeals on some policies, the manifesto avoided mentioning many policies key to economic transformation and focused on populist policies aimed a redistribution and employment.

The pattern of the vote
The PNP won the 1972 election by the largest majority ever gained by either party in Jamaican history up to that date. It gained 56 per cent of the popular vote and thirty-seven of the fifty-three seats in the House (Table A.1). The turnout was somewhat lower than in 1967, however, which was probably attributable to alienation of lower-class voters in the corporate area. The swing to the PNP by parish was not uniform. In fact, previously strong PNP parishes swung to the JLP, continuing the long-term process of national homogenization of voting patterns. This, along with the fact that two-thirds of voters voted solely on the basis of party with no consideration of the candidate (Stone, 1974:23), indicates the trend toward the increasingly national character of political life and an underlying social trend toward national communications networks and increasing density of civil society.

For the 1972 Jamaican election one can, for the first time, go beyond these aggregate statistics and examine behavior at the individual level, as a nationwide survey was carried out immediately after the elections by Carl Stone (1974). Stone's study confirms the cross-class nature of PNP support (Table A.21). The capitalist elite is too small to appear in such a sample but our interviews in 1982 reveal that PNP support among businessmen was very significant. Though we did not directly ask how they voted in 1972, nine of the thirteen businessmen we interviewed volunteered the information, and of these nine, six voted PNP. These numbers are small but given that they were considered to be the most influential businessmen in the country they are nonetheless indicative of the opinions of an important segment of the capitalist elite.

In his analysis of new PNP voters and swing voters, Stone (1974:29–30) found that Manley's charisma, JLP corruption, and the symbolic appeal of the 'Rod of Correction' did influence their behavior, but he correctly goes on to argue that Manley's leadership, the opening to black consciousness and Rastafari, and even corruption were unlikely to have had much effect were it not for the underlying social discontent in the country. Most new PNP voters reported that they felt their living conditions had become worse in the previous ten years. Significantly, a majority of all unskilled workers expressed this feeling and it is this traditionally JLP stratum that shifted most dramatically to the PNP (up 15 per cent from 1967 based on retrospective questions on past voting behaviors, Stone, 1974:37).

It appears that the PNP's party-building efforts did pay off in 1972 as three times as many PNP supporters as JLP supporters were actually involved in the campaign. The PNP was particularly effective in mobilizing youth to support its cause actively (Stone, 1974: 47–8).

The traditional non-ideological nature of the parties was reflected not only in the class heterogeneity of their support but also in the reasons given for the voting decision in the 1972 election . Stone (1974: 56–7) points out that 'only 44 per cent of the sample were able or willing to articulate an image of the party they supported which yielded some basis on which to describe the value frames of reference that inform and influence partisan sentiments'. Only 4 per cent gave clearly ideological responses. This does not indicate, however, that if the PNP had run a more ideological campaign it would have been doomed to failure. Stone shows that a plurality of the sample favored the nationalization of the bauxite companies (46 per cent for; 37 per cent against) and about three-fifths favored government appropriation of land belonging to big land-owners for distribution to small farmers.

It should be noted that the 1972 campaign was (and is) the only one since Independence in which violence decreased. The *Gleaner*'s political reporter noted two days before the election that 'up to now violence during the current election has been subdued as opposed to violence in previous elections'. The campaign witnessed frequent rock- and bottle-throwing at rallies and between political youth gangs and there were a number of shootings, but there were very few deaths.

The populist years: political developments
The two and a half years from the 1972 election to the declaration of democratic socialism in the fall of 1974 can be characterized as 'the populist years' as the rhetoric and appeal of the government was primarily populist.

However, as we noted at the outset of this chapter, virtually all the reform programs initiated during the PNP government were either implemented or announced during this period. This is important to recognize as it is the source of the contention in some quarters in Jamaica that Manley's biggest mistake was to introduce ideology into the debate as it was that factor and not the concrete policies of his government which stimulated the reaction of the private sector which led to migration, declining investment, strident political opposition and ultimately to economic sabotage. We contend (and hope to convince the reader) that this view is much too simplistic. However, the attempt to segregate reactions to policy from reaction to rhetoric is, at least in part, made possible by the fact that most of the policies did precede the ideological declaration. Table 3.1, (adapted from Girván *et al.*, 1980:117) lays out the major policy initiatives of the Manley government. Missing from the table are many of the taxation policies introduced to pay for the programs and details of the foreign policy. It is obviously not possible to cover all of the major policy initiatives in this work. In this and

TABLE 3.1   *Principal policies and initiatives of the PNP government*

Year announced	
1972	Promotion of NIEO
	Special employment program
	Skill training program
	Workers' Bank
	Literacy program (JAMAL)
	Lowering the voting age to 18
	Community health aides
	Operation GROW
	Land Lease
	Civil service reclassification
	Youth training increased
	Public housing program
1973	Cultural training centre
	Food subsidies (flour, condensed milk)
	Uniforms for primary school children
	Free secondary education
	Free university education
	National youth service
	Rent restriction act revised
	Equal pay for women and women's affairs bureau established
	Jamaica nutrition holdings
	Property taxes increased
	Initiated founding of IBA
	Home guard
	Promotion of non-aligned movement

1974	Self-supporting farmers development program (loans)
	Family court
	National minimum wage
	Gun court
	Suppression of crime act
	NIS pensions increased
	Poor relief increased
	AMC outlets in low income areas
	New mental health law and free education for handicapped
	Construction of small industries complexes
	Sugar cooperatives
	Bauxite production levy
	Nationalization of bauxite multinational companies
	Development venture capital financing company (loans)
	Jamaica public service company (electricity)
	Jamaica merchant marine
	Jamaica omnibus service company
1975	Capital gains and inheritance taxes increased
	Compulsory recognition of trade unions
	Worker participation
1976	National housing trust
1977	Small enterprise development company
	State trading corporation
	National commercial bank
1979	Maternity leave with pay

SOURCE   Adapted from Girvan *et al.* (1980:117).

the following chapters, we will touch on those policies which were most significant in terms of sheer size (for example, the Special Employment Program) or their transformative potential (for example, bauxite policy and the State Trading Corporation).

Domestic policies
Given the newness of the government, it is not surprising that the 1972 Throne Speech, in which new government initiatives are generally announced, contained few new policies and that the budget announced in the speech was largely a JLP budget. One exception was the adult literacy campaign which had been announced the week before and was to begin as soon as possible. The intention was to eliminate illiteracy within four years calling for 20 000 volunteers to teach the 500 000 illiterate Jamaicans to read and write, (*G*, 1 June 1972). A National Literacy Board was set up to carry out this task. The program was too ambitious in the Jamaican context and a number of criticisms emerged the next summer. The problems continued until the whole program was reorganized in the spring of 1974. The Literacy Board was replaced by a Statutory Board for Adult

Education (JAMAL) and instead of attempting to wipe out illiteracy by 1976, the target was now to involve 100 000 people per year in adult education programs. The JAMAL program subsequently proved to be fairly successful. This is one of the few instances where poor implementation was recognized, corrective action was taken and the new program that emerged was successful.

The PNP election manifesto called for the development of a national youth service program and in October 1972 the government declared its intention to begin a voluntary program in 1973 which would be made compulsory later (*G*, 19 October 1972). The voluntary program would focus on teaching in primary schools, vocational training and the literacy program, with work in health, youth camps and civil service as an alternative (*G*, 3 May 1973). The introduction of a compulsory service was announced in the Throne Speech in 1974. Because of financial constraints, compulsory service would be required only of those 18-year-olds who had completed fifth or sixth forms though plans were that it would apply to all 18-year-olds in the future. The two years of compulsory service could be done at once at 18 years or after post-secondary school or one year before, and one year after. The pay was clothing, room, board, transportation allowance and $10 per week for 18-year-olds or normal government rates of pay for post-secondary students. The penalty for refusing service was to be denial of entry into either government-supported educational institutions, employment in government jobs or contractual service with the government.

Upon taking office, the Manley government began to attack the problem of employment. In March, it announced the Special Employment Program (SEP) or Impact or Crash program as it is more commonly called. At the outset, Manley announced that this was a temporary program of job creation which would give employment primarily to PNP supporters many of whom, because of victimization, had not had a job in ten years. The work would be such tasks as street cleaning, painting of schools and other public buildings and sidewalk improvement in the urban areas, and road work and afforestation in the rural areas. Initially, the program was not too controversial except with the JLP leadership. Even the *Gleaner* (30 May 1972) agreed that it was fair for the government to give jobs to those who had been victimized during the JLP government. By the end of 1972, it became clear that there were a lot of idlers in the program and the nation was not getting much in return for the money spent in the program. This was a point of criticism by the opposition and the *Gleaner*, but it was not until the program was made permanent in August 1974 that criticism of the program became severe. Though jobs in the program were then allocated through local councillors and thus no longer aimed entirely at PNP supporters, the program was beset by the perennial problem of patronage, lack of work effort, as the workers had already 'earned' their rewards through party loyalty. Though the government admitted that productivity was a big problem in the crash program, it also argued that something had to be done to alleviate the social pressures resulting from high unemployment and that this program was better than straight welfare.

In terms of the sheer number of dwellings built, the PNP public housing program has to be considered one of its most successful programs. The primary negative aspect of this program was that, with the exception of those units built under the National Housing Trust, the dwellings were distributed on a patronage basis continuing the practice established by previous governments.

In this context, one 'non-policy' of the PNP should be mentioned. The PNP promised to do something about the system of distribution of jobs, housing and other scarce benefits and Manley (1982) listed detribalization as one of their goals at the outset. In 1972, the government appeared to move in that direction. When Manley announced that jobs in the SEP would go to PNP supporters he made it clear that this was a special case and that the government would be entering into talks with the opposition to work out a mutually acceptable formula for job distribution. Later, Manley proposed to Shearer that government work be distributed by the following formula: 60 per cent of the people should be recommended by the MP for the constituency; 30 per cent by the caretaker (that is, the other party's local representative) and 10 per cent by neutral persons. The JLP rejected the PNP suggestion on the grounds that it violated an ILO Convention on non-discrimination and would endanger secrecy of the ballot (*Gleaner*, 4 December 1972). The Churches then intervened suggesting all work be distributed on a first-come, first-served basis via a public labor exchange. The suggestion was formally accepted by Manley (*Gleaner*, 7 December 1972). This policy was never implemented. With the exception of the National Housing Trust and, for the most part, Land Lease, PNP programs continued the practice of distributing benefits on a patronage basis.

The 1972 PNP manifesto called for working toward the goal of food self-sufficiency. Given the constitutional provision concerning compensation for nationalized property, a comprehensive land-reform program would have been prohibitively expensive. The government itself was already the largest land-holder in the country in 1972, but much of this land was unsuitable for agriculture. The Manley government approached the problem in several ways. It did acquire some land itself, the largest source being the bauxite lands which the government acquired as part of its overall agreement with the bauxite companies. The government also attempted to force larger landholders to bring idle lands into production by serving them (or threatening to do so) with idle-land orders under which the owners had either to bring the land under production themselves or lease to someone who would. The sugar lands which the foreign corporations had unloaded on the JLP government, formed the basis for the PNP experiment with agricultural cooperatives which will be discussed in the next chapter and in Chapter 8. The idle lands owned, acquired or leased by the government formed the basis for a number of programs (Food Farms, Project Land Lease, Pioneer Farms) which were aimed at bringing land to the land-hungry and at increasing domestic food production. Of these, Project Land Lease was by far the largest and the only one which met with any success. Under Land Lease privately-held lands were leased by the government and then leased for a period of five years to small farmers in the area as a supplement to their own holdings. Under this phase (later dubbed Phase I) 2700 farmers were placed on 4300 acres in 1973, the first year of the operation of the program. According to estimates, 3500 acres had already been brought under production by January 1974 and the expected yield was 10 104 tons of crops worth $1.2m. This phase of the program was substantially expanded in 1974 and two more Phases of the program were announced with the goal of placing 10 000 farmers on 6000 acres of land. Under Phase II, idle lands owned or acquired by the government were to be leased for forty-nine years to the farmers who already had some land in the area as supplement to their own holding with the goal of bringing their net yearly income up to $1500–2000. The farmers would have hereditary rights to the land and would be compensated for any improvements to it if terminated through non-performance. Under Phase III, full farms would be leased under the same conditions as Phase II. By the end of 1980, 37 661 farmers had been placed on 74 568 acres of land in the program.

In 1973, Manley announced in his budget speech that both secondary and university education were to be made free of charge (*G*, 3 May 1973). By this point, the government had already moved to expand opportunities for secondary education and plans for further expansion were such that by the end of the term of office everyone would have the opportunity to attend secondary school, either the traditional high schools or the new secondary schools. These policies generated opposition in several ways. First, there was middle-and upper-class resentment based on elitist attitudes and opposition to class mixing. Second, there were some concerns about the expense of the programs. Finally, it quickly became known in elite circles that Manley had announced free education in a parliamentary speech without consulting David Coore, the Finance Minister. Reportedly, the Ministries of Education and Finance had rejected the plan as too costly, but immediately before the budget debate there had been an inflow of back taxes because of the granting of a grace period within which no tax penalties would be charged. So Manley decided that this would go to pay for the cost of free education for the next year and then reportedly told Coore, who was taken aback by the announcement, that they would worry about where the funds for future years would come from later. This was not the only time that Manley announced policies in public speeches without consulting the relevant ministers or civil servants about feasibility of the program. The frequency with which he did this has been exaggerated by some, and experts on public administration in Jamaica, while admitting that this did cause problems, argue that it was of minor importance in terms of the totality of the problem of program development and implementation. However, Manley did this often enough to provide substance for the criticisms both of generally irresponsible management and of Manley's tendency to do and say things – particularly when speaking to a live audience – which were popular, without fully considering the consequences.

In 1973, the Manley government established Jamaica Nutrition Holdings (JNH), a government company which was to handle the business aspects of the government's nutrition program, such as the school lunch program. In terms of long-term social transformation, an important aspect of JNH was that it took over the task of bulk import of basic foods, such as wheat, soy, corn, rice and salt fish. This aspect of its activity was a forerunner to the State Trading Corporation (STC) which was introduced in 1977 (see Chapter 5).

As we pointed out in the last chapter, crime and violence increased significantly in the 1960s. In response to the problem, the PNP government more than doubled the size of the fleet of police cars and increased the salaries and size of the police force. They also increased the frequency of joint police–military anti-crime operations, and introduced a system of voluntary help for the police, the Home Guards. Under this program, citizens could volunteer to help the police to patrol their own neighborhoods. Several Home Guard Volunteers, one of whom was issued a gun at the beginning of the patrol by the police, would accompany a policeman on his patrol duties. However, crime continued to increase in 1972 and 1973 and began to escalate particularly sharply in the later part of 1973 and early 1974 (see Table A.7). After a wave of gun killings in early 1973 in which seven prominent citizens were killed, the government came under intense pressure to act quickly and decisively. In response, the government established the Gun Court.[7] The Gun Court was a special court established to deal with any crime involving a firearm including illegal (unlicensed) possession of a firearm or ammunition, and was to try anyone charged with a firearms offense within seven days of arrest. The penalty for conviction was a mandatory sentence of indefinite detention.[8] A number of other measures accompanied the Gun Court Act. All films that depended on violence for their main theme were banned and scenes with gun-play were edited out of other films. The Prevention of Crime Act was passed increasing the power of the police to search, carry out raids and cordon-off areas. The Ministries of Defense and Home Affairs were combined into the Ministry of National Security in order to facilitate joint police–military operations.

From the speed with which the government moved on the utilities question, it seems probable that the party leaders had decided before the election that the telephone company (JTC), the electrical power company (Jamaica Public Service, JPS) and the Kingston public transportation service (Jamaica Omnibus Service, JOS) should be publicly owned. In August of 1972, Coore announced that the government was considering acquisition of complete control of the public utilities; it was a matter of timing, of finding the funds and ensuring smooth operation with the necessary expertise. In May 1974, the government took control of the JOS buying all shares in the company, the first total nationalization ever carried out by the Jamaican government. (The Water Commission and the Jamaica Railway Company had always been government-owned.) By March 1975, state ownership of shares in the JPS was increased to 93 per cent. In September 1975, the government bought the 68 per cent of the shares of the JTC owned by the US-based Continental Telephone Company, bringing the total state share to 78 per cent. It is clear from the timing as well as from statements by Bell, the Minister of Public Utilities, that the bauxite levy provided the resources for these acquisitions as well as for rehabilitation programs in the JOS and JPS.[9]

Obviously not all these programs could be implemented without increasing taxation. We will cover the taxation increases in our discussions of economic performance and the various budgets and policy packages. Suffice it to say here that increased taxation is always controversial and, in fact, Manley (1982:89) contends that the property tax introduced in 1973 was the most controversial thing the PNP did in its first term.

The bauxite strategy[10]

One of the greatest achievements of the Manley government was the totality of its bauxite policy. Careful planning and analysis was the key to the success in this area. The 1972 PNP election manifesto contained the promise to establish a National Bauxite Commission to investigate what the country ought to do about increasing its revenue from and control over bauxite production and the idle bauxite land, and this was done within two months of assuming office. The terms given to the Commission, which was chaired by businessman Mayer Matalon, were clearly broader than the revenue question, though that became the *cause célèbre* after the imposition of the levy. And it went beyond the question of the bauxite lands and a share in ownership: the commission was to study the whole role of bauxite in Jamaican development.

According to Manley (1982) the full strategy emerged some eighteen months later, somewhat before the Arab oil embargo. The effect of the oil-price increase was to create considerable pressure to deal with the revenue aspect before the other matters had been settled. In his book, Manley (1982:46, 98) lists six goals that had been worked out by the Commission by late 1973:

1.   Repatriation of the lands owned by the bauxite companies;
2.   acquisition of 51 per cent ownership of the bauxite mining operations;
3.   the establishment of the Jamaica Bauxite Institute (JBI);
4.   the formation of a cartel of bauxite-producing countries;
5.   increased revenues through a tax based on the price of aluminum ingot;
6.   the development of a smelter complex in cooperation with Venezuela and Mexico.

More important than the goals was the motivation that lay under them. It was much more than a question of revenue. The whole strategy aimed at taking more control of this natural resource and directing it to development ends decided by Jamaica and not by the multinationals. In the Jamaican situation, expropriation followed by development of bauxite and aluminum completely independently of the aluminum multinationals was not feasible. The constitutional clause on compensation would have made this extremely expensive. Moreover, even without the constitutional clause, it would have been practically impossible to do anything which would have involved a total break with the multinationals for an indefinite period of time given the vertically-integrated oligopolistic nature of the world aluminum industry. Given that Jamaica was the largest bauxite producer in the world at that time and hoped to increase its rate of extraction to increase revenues, there is no way that the country could have found outlets for so much bauxite outside the western aluminum oligopolies.

The Manley government's policy was to begin a process of renegotiation of relationships to the economic system of the core capitalist countries and to begin to exercise local control over the development of the industry. Two key areas were diversification of outlets for its bauxite and alumina and increasing forward linkages in the processing of its bauxite. The two policies were linked since, as an energy-poor country, Jamaica could only hope to develop a fully integrated industry in cooperation with other countries. The smelting of aluminum had to be done in a country with natural energy resources. Jamaica could hope to enter into a joint venture in which it would be able to supply the alumina thus developing new alumina plants and increasing its bauxite extraction and alumina exports and, possibly, the right to market some of the aluminum smelted by its partners. The Jamaica–Venezuela–Mexico (Javemex) agreement was just the first of a series of such joint venture agreements with energy-rich Third World countries (Trinidad, Algeria, Iraq) all of which fell through, though not because of Jamaica's actions.

The specific policies pursued have to be seen in the light of the overall strategy of diversification, independent local development of the industry and increased revenues. The repatriation of the lands, for instance, was not just aimed at bringing the land back into local ownership and bringing idle land into food production. The land ownership question was tied to the control of reserves: some companies had 150 years of reserves under their control at their then rate of extraction. Together the companies controlled 1.5 billion tons of bauxite but were mining only 12 million tons annually. Thus, the land ownership was related to control of reserves and, in turn, to the rate of extraction and therefore revenue. The 51 per cent ownership target was obviously related to revenue in the long run, but it was originally also thought to be related to diversification. It was assumed that the companies would be reluctant to enter into long-term contracts, particularly with Communist countries. The development of such contracts is very important to countries with product-concentrated exports like Jamaica since these guaranteed sales can help to insulate them from slumps in the capitalist world economy. However, as it turned out, under the management contracts granted to the companies, the companies continued to exercise ultimate control over the marketing of bauxite. Nevertheless, given the over-capacity in the world bauxite industry after the early 1970s, the companies were quite ready to accept long-term sales contracts, including those negotiated by the Jamaican government with communist countries.

The goals of the JBI (development of local expertise to help guide the overall bauxite policy) and the bauxite levy (revenue) are obvious. In the case of the formation of the International Bauxite Association (IBA) increased revenue was obviously the primary goal but technical cooperation aimed at reducing the multinationals' monopoly of expertise was also a goal.

To return to our chronology, at Jamaica's initiation most of the world's large bauxite producers met in Yugoslavia in November 1973 and the decision was made to form the IBA, which then took place in Conakry, Guinea, the next February. The original members were Australia, Guinea, Guyana, Jamaica, Sierra Leone, Surinam and Yugoslavia. The headquarters were to be located in Jamaica.

In March, talks with the aluminum companies on the revenue question were opened (*G*, 19 March 1974). The companies initially approached the whole question in terms of Jamaica's balance-of-payments problems created by the oil price increases, but the Jamaican approach was much wider, as we have seen. The Jamaicans approached the question from the point of view of a fair value for their resource and the cost to the companies rather than a narrow balance-of-payments question. The companies were surprised at the level of preparation of the Jamaican team.[11] As the talks progressed it became increasingly clear that it would be impossible to reach an agreement. By this time, Manley had already acted to test what the reaction of the North American governments would be. Trudeau, with whom Manley had a friendly relationship, assured Manley that his government would not object as long as fair compensation was paid in case of nationalization and provided the Canadian company (Alcan) was not treated differently from the other companies (Manley, 1982:99–100). Manley also talked to Kissinger emphasizing two points: (i) the action was purely economic and implied no political hostility to the USA, and (ii) Jamaica recognized the strategic importance of bauxite to the USA and would never block US access to Jamaican bauxite. He asked Kissinger to pass this information on to the National Security Council. Manley (1982:100) believes this resulted in a 'wait and see' attitude on the part of the US government which was important as two of the American companies approached the State Department and asked that Jamaica be black-listed, her aid cut off and so forth. In any case, Matalon had been in touch with Lawrence Eagleburger at the State Department and he had information that the US government would not retaliate.[12]

Jamaica was also keeping other members of the IBA informed about the progress of the negotiations, and the government was also consulting with key interest groups at home: the unions, the media, church leaders and the leadership of various private sector organizations so that by the time it had to take a decision the government was fairly sure it would get broad cross-class support. In the end, when the negotiators told Manley that there was no way that the companies would accept the government's compromise offer (6 per cent of the price of a ton of aluminum ingot for the amount of bauxite required to produce a ton of aluminum (about 4.3 tons), Manley could move with some confidence. On 15 May 1974, he announced that no agreement could be reached and that the government had decided to unilaterally impose a production levy at the rate of 7.5 per cent. This would not only increase revenue sevenfold but would also tie revenues into metropolitan inflation (thus addressing an oft-expressed complaint of Third World leaders about the falling prices of their exports relative to those of developed countries). The levy would be retroactive to January 1974 and would yield $170–$200m in the period January 1974–March 1975. The companies immediately referred the dispute to the International Center for the Settlement of Investment Disputes (ICSID), whereupon Coore announced that the government had already given notice to the ICSID of its withdrawal from the provision of the treaty covering natural resources. Manley then called a meeting of national leaders to Jamaica House to sell the levy to them, explaining why it had to be imposed and saying that it would be used for capital development not for consumption. His speech was met with overwhelming support. Only a part of the most conservative segment of the capitalist class opposed it (on the grounds that it violated the sanctity of contracts).[13] Even the *Gleaner* supported the imposition of the levy (*G*, 16 May 1974).

On 4 June, the House passed the levy bill. The government announced that the bulk of the levy would be placed in the newly created Capital Development Fund (CDF) and would be reinvested in other capital assets. The companies clearly felt the government had the upper hand; they protested that Jamaica had priced itself out of the market and continued to pursue their claim with the ICSID, but they paid the quarterly installment of the levy at the end of June and agreed to continue negotiations on the land question and Jamaican participation in the industry.

After the imposition of the levy, members of the Jamaican bauxite team went on a lecture tour to other IBA countries to explain how the levy was accomplished and persuaded a number of them such as Surinam, Sierra Leone and Guinea to follow suit, but as Manley (1982:102) points out (not without a note of disappointment given his strong feelings about Third World solidarity) they all contrived to fix their level of taxation somewhat below that of Jamaica thus securing a competitive advantage. Whether this was because of the pressures of a contracting market, because they were outbargained or because of an attempt to increase their market share, is still an open question to the Jamaicans.

The negotiations for partial ownership and for return of the land were completed in the next two years, with the Kaiser agreement as the first, a tentative version of which was announced in November 1974. The agreements provided for the purchase of all lands by the government. The government in turn reassigned portions to the companies to mine bauxite at the level desired by the companies guaranteeing them access to reserves for forty years. Thus, the government gained use of the lands for agricultural purposes and gained control of the bauxite reserves. The government purchased 51 per cent of the Jamaican operations of the companies involved in bauxite mining only (Kaiser and Reynolds) and 6 or 7 per cent of the companies involved in both bauxite mining and alumina processing (Alcan and Alcoa). The purchase terms were very favorable as book value and low interest rates were paid; but the government, which had increased the levy to 8 per cent in July 1975 had to reduce it to the original 7.5 per cent. The companies also received management contracts of varying lengths (usually about seven years). The companies agreed to withdraw their ICSID suits. In the case of Alcoa, Jamaica also was entitled to purchase 33 000 tons of alumina yearly which it was free to sell on the world market. In general, these agreements between the government and the companies were amicably achieved. The companies continued to press for a reduction in the levy and expressed hostility toward Jamaica's projected joint ventures such as Javemex and the Trinidad–Guyana–Jamaica proposal, but they were in no position to block these as Jamaica had gained control of its bauxite reserves.

In the Jamaican political debate and in the academic discussion on the bauxite policy, there is still considerable controversy about the costs Jamaica incurred because of the magnitude of the levy and the move to impose it unilaterally. It is often argued that the country suffered substantial cutbacks in bauxite and alumina exports and significant losses in foreign investment in all sectors. These issues are exceedingly complex.

We have conducted an extended analysis of them elsewhere and refer the interested reader to this analysis (Stephens and Stephens, 1985). Suffice it to make two points here based on this analysis. First, very little of the reduction in bauxite and alumina purchases by the North American companies can be attributed to the level of the levy or the act of imposing it unilaterally. Second, the oft-repeated charge that the OPIC insurance for investments in Jamaica was suspended as a result of the levy is almost totally groundless. OPIC was already very over-extended in Jamaica and thus was refusing to insure further investment as a result. The unilateral imposition of the levy may well have contributed to the foreign image of the Manley government as radical and thus to a poor business investment climate, but the total cost to Jamaica of the levy alone in terms of discouraging foreign investments was certainly very small when measured against the financial benefits.

Foreign policy
Under the JLP, Jamaica had pursued a pro-West but essentially isolationist foreign policy. Under the Manley government, Jamaica emerged as a leading spokesperson for the Third World. The contours of Jamaican foreign policy are well-known to social scientists and political observers outside the Caribbean and good accounts from the key actor (Manley, 1970, 1975b, 1976, and 1982) and academic analysts (V. Lewis, 1981, 1982) are readily available. So here we will limit ourselves to a very brief outline of the main thrust of PNP foreign policy and throughout the book our main interest will be in the way that foreign policy relates to the overall dynamics of the broader political and economic developments in Jamaica during the PNP period in office.

The key goals of the PNP foreign policy throughout the 1970s were:

(1) Non-alignment: strong support for the non-aligned movement, development of relations with communist countries and other Third World countries while maintaining good relations with the West;
(2) strong support for Third World solidarity; political and economic cooperation among Third World countries;
(3) advocacy of the New International Economic Order (NIEO).

Concretely, in its first years in office, Jamaica moved to open full diplomatic relations with Cuba and the People's Republic of China, took on a very active role in the Non-aligned Movement and strongly promoted anti-apartheid in international forums. The country was perhaps the leading proponent of the re-ordering of North–South economic relations, with Manley assuming the role as leading spokesman for the NIEO and P. J. Patterson, the Minister of Industry and Tourism (later of Foreign Affairs) emerging as the leading negotiator of the ACP countries in their talks with the EEC. The PNP also reactivated its membership in the Socialist

International and later played an important part in its opening to the Third World under Brandt's leadership, and, of course, the IBA and the whole bauxite strategy for that matter was closely linked to the push for Third World cooperation and the NIEO.

Throughout the Manley period, the aspects of the government's foreign policy that created the most problems were its relations with socialist and communist countries, especially Cuba. By far the most controversial occurrences of this period (1972–4) were the events surrounding Manley's trip to the meeting of the Non-aligned Movement in Algiers in September 1973. Jamaica, Guyana, and Trinidad had all upgraded relations with Cuba recently, so Castro invited the leaders of those countries to accompany him in his jet to the meetings. Eric Williams declined as he was not intending to attend the meeting, but Forbes Burnham and Manley accepted. The trip with Castro and Manley's offer to help raise volunteers for the struggle against South Africa created a storm of protest in Jamaica.

The PNP: organization and appeal
The PNP began an internal discussion on its ideological self-definition in this period, but this was not made public until later. The Cabinet was the most conservative of the entire period. Four of the Cabinet members; Wills O. Isaacs, Florizel Glasspole, Allan Isaacs and Rose Leon, were sufficiently conservative that it is fair to say that their ideological positions were closer to the central tendency of the JLP in the 1970s than that of the PNP. Glasspole and Wills Isaacs were kicked upstairs to Governor-General and Ambassador to Canada respectively, but their seats were eventually taken by two men only slightly less conservative, Eli Matalon of the business family, and Vivian Blake. There was only one radical in the cabinet: Anthony Spaulding, the Minister of Housing.[14] Senator Dudley Thompson, who was Minister of State in the Foreign Ministry (which was held by Manley) and was, for all intents and purposes, a full minister, did publicly identify himself as a socialist in this period, but his economic ideology was not as left-wing as that of the radicals and he did not always side with them in internal party debates.[15] Only Tony Spaulding was more controversial than Thompson in the early period, as much for his flamboyant style as for his radical statements.

One important change took place in this period. D. K. Duncan was elected to the post of General Secretary of the PNP in June 1974. Duncan was one of a number of younger leftists promoted in the party under Manley's patronage in this period. Duncan had been active in the *Abeng* group which also spawned Arnold Bertram, another leading PNP radical. (Trevor Munroe and a number of other founders of the Workers' Party of Jamaica, were also active in the *Abeng* group). Duncan became involved in PNP politics in St Ann before the 1972 election. He developed a reputation as an excellent political organizer there and Manley personally persuaded him to take on the job as national organizer in 1972 telling him of his plans to build a mass party and to resurrect the party's socialist ideology (*G*, 9 October 1977). This move was not without opposition in the PNP: according to Duncan, Eli Matalon threatened to walk out of the 1972 PNP conference if Duncan was elevated to the post (*G*, 26 September 1977).

The party's appeal in this period was basically populist and was built around Manley's charisma. The image Manley projected was the same as in 1971 and in the 1972 election campaign. Manley's and the party's image as a 'people's' party was promoted by symbolic gestures such as the adoption of the Kareba as an alternative acceptable dress to the European jacket and tie, the initiation of voluntary work projects on Labour Day in which Ministers along with the public would work on projects of social utility and the practice of Manley and other Ministers helping in manual labor at the initiation of new government projects.

The symbolic gestures and the National Youth Service were part of the government's efforts at national mobilization. With the possible exception of a brief period at the beginning of the second term, it cannot be said that the Manley government ever had a cohesive program of mobilizing people to work for the country's development that went beyond exhortation to the people to help in the effort, but these symbolic gestures were important steps towards inclusion of the masses psychologically in the life of the country and to building a stronger national consciousness and identity. Along with the opening to Rastafari, the foreign-policy initiatives strengthening ties with Africa, and other policies such as the Status of Children Act which gave full legal status to children born out of wedlock, they helped to give the black masses of Jamaica the feeling that they were full members of the Jamaican community and first class-citizens for the first time. Obviously, social inclusion and strengthened national identity is a prerequisite to national mobilization efforts, since people are not going to work for the development of a community with which they do not identify.

Aside from the ideological developments going on behind the scene (see next chapter) the most important development in the party in this period was the building of the party organization. Jamaican parties were geared toward winning elections and the party organizations particularly of the party in power tended to atrophy between elections. Manley was aware of this and it added to his conviction that building the party should have a high priority. Duncan was to be responsible for this task. Aside from the establishment of the Regional Councils in February 1975, few changes in the party structure were actually made as the party's structure which had been developed in careful work by Vernon Arnett and others in the 1940s was basically sound. There was an effort to get more grass-roots people on the party executive, which carries on the week-to-week work of the party. This body had previously had an elite character in terms of its class composition. There were a number of by-elections in the first PNP term of office and Duncan and his field staff changed previous practice by living 'in the field' and were thus able to build a better personal relationship with local party activists. Overall, it can be said that the PNP's success at party building was the result of having a secretariat that was committed to the idea of a mass party and mass mobilization, and of efforts to integrate the rank and file into the party, giving the party's formally democratic structure some substance.

Managing the economy

The development of the economy has to be seen in the light of the end of investment in bauxite/alumina and tourism foreshadowed in the last chapter. The decline in investments in bauxite and tourism were clearly not the government's fault. Investment in hotel construction in the late 1960s was excessive so that room occupancy fell from about 70 per cent in the mid-1960s to 50 per cent by the time the PNP took office *despite* increases in visitor arrivals (see Table A.19). The fact is that the previous JLP government irresponsibly encouraged hotel construction by guaranteeing loans. The PNP was saddled with these guarantees and as a result was later forced into major hotel acquisitions. The fall in investment in these two areas was the main cause of a balance-of-payments crisis of major proportions which hit the PNP government in its first year in office. An additional factor was the crisis of the international monetary system occurring at the time. For Jamaica this was particularly important as the British pound, which was being allowed to float, was weak and the Jamaican dollar was then tied to the pound. The international monetary situation in general and the fear of devaluation of the pound (and therefore the Jamaican dollar) contributed to an increase in uncertainty of foreign investors and this along with the end of investment in bauxite and hotels caused a decline in foreign investment from $147m in 1971 to $21m in 1972 (Girvan *et al.*, 1980:136).

The government's first statement was the 1972–3 budget presented in June 1972. It represented a spending increase of 18 per cent (see Table A.2). But it must be remembered that it was largely an inherited budget and few of the planned programs (including some that actually did come onstream in that year) were actually included in it. The increase was primarily due to salary increases and commitments of the previous government. As the foreign exchange situation became apparent several measures were taken. A temporary embargo on car imports, a price freeze, and import licensing for a number of goods, notably consumer durables, were introduced. These were only a foreshadowing of what was to come.

On 10 November 1972, Manley made a speech to the nation outlining the direction of the new government's economic policy. The speech shows that at least some people in the government had not only correctly analyzed Jamaica's problems but also had a good idea of what needed to be done in the long run and what steps could be taken in that direction immediately. Manley explained that the balance-of-payments problem itself was just a 'symptom of the failure to introduce changes in the economic structure which we inherited in 1962 and to put the economy on a basis where it would have been capable of self-sustaining growth', and he outlined the areas of failure: (i) passive domestic policies which did not cope with international economic forces, particularly the deterioration of the terms of trade for Jamaica's main export crops; (ii) failure to modernize and increase productivity in export agriculture to utilize the markets which were available; (iii) failure to meet domestic food requirements; (iv) failure to seek out new export opportunities; (v) failure to develop the industrial base to process Jamaica's raw materials or to produce goods for the domestic market; (vi) failure to stem the orgy of consumption of imported luxury goods, and (vii) failure to increase the rate of savings and thus an excessive reliance on foreign capital. The effects of failure could be seen in the increase of the unemployment rate. The agricultural failure and unemployment were linked as that sector had not provided jobs for youth who then migrated to the city increasing the slum population. Increasing unemployment, increasing inequality and the expanding ghetto were at the root of the problem of crime and violence. Manley continued pointing to the:

> deterioration of attitudes. In many ways it is in this area where we find our greatest failure. For there was total failure in winning the commitment and dedication of all sectors of people to working wholeheartedly for the welfare of our country. We find many among the wealthier classes seeking only to maximize profits as quickly as possible but syphoning this off to build nest eggs abroad. Many of our middle income groups seeking only to ape the rich in their consumption habits but having to borrow to do so and therefore being completely thriftless and many in the low income groups imbued with a freeness mentality (*G*, 11 November 1972).

In the short run, Manley said the target was to reduce the import bill, stating that 'we must never again find ourselves in the position where we finance our consumer imports from capital flows' (*G*, 11 November 1972). The composition of imports would also have to be changed to give priority to raw materials and capital goods needed for economic expansion, and particularly for the development of agriculture with the goal of food self-sufficiency and increased exports. The emphasis in manufacture was on more backward integration, increased local value added, import substitution, export development, and employment creation. There would be hardships for importers, salesmen, and consumers, in the last case, because they would have to do with a more limited range of goods and would have to develop a taste for goods produced locally, but there would be 'tremendous opportunities' to those in the private sector 'who are prepared to display the necessary initiative'. Workers were to benefit from both the expansion of jobs and opportunities for advancement (*G*, 11 November 1972).

Along with the speech, the immediate import restrictions were released; fifty-six items were banned, mainly locally-produceable items and luxury imports, and another four items were added to the previous list of ten goods on which there were curbs (mainly consumer durables). Coore announced a series of measures designed to reduce the outflow of foreign exchange such as a limit of $500 per year spent on travel abroad and a requirement that the proceeds of all commodity exports must be channeled through Jamaican banks.

Thus the economic situation in Jamaica was not rosy at the beginning of 1973 and it went from bad to worse as world inflation hit the country in early 1973. Between February and May of 1973, corn prices went up from $58 to $71 per ton; soy from $144 to $237 and wheat from $67 to $90 per ton (Bartley, 1981). Other grain and animal feeds also increased in price and fertilizer prices continued the upward movement which had begun in 1972 with four price increases in 1973. The inflationary spiral was aggravated by devaluation. The government pegged the Jamaican dollar to the $US in January 1973 and in the process devalued 6.5 per cent. A month later the USA devalued by 10 per cent and Jamaica maintained the relation between the US and Jamaican currencies. The combination of these events and the government's policy of restricting imports and controlling prices created a constant problem of food shortages (especially sugar, cooking oil, milk, rice and flour). In response to inflation the government brought more products under price control and introduced rent control. Retailers responded to shortages and price controls by hoarding goods to wait for a price increase (thus aggravating shortages) and 'marrying' goods (that is forcing customers to buy something in addition in order to get a good in short supply). The difficult food situation sparked the first consumer protest ever in Jamaica when, in April, the National Consumer League organized a boycott to protest meat price increases. The government moved to crack down on hoarding by imposing fines or imprisonment on those found guilty of this practice.

The 1973 budget was the first real budget of the Manley government. In the original budget the departure from the past was modest. Expenditure was increased as a number of the government's new programs were to come onstream, but, the increase was moderate and taxes were increased to pay for the new expenditures. Notably, the controversial property tax was introduced. Thus, like previous budgets the original 1973 estimates provided for a substantial current account surplus, but the first supplementary estimates in November showed net increases of $36m, mainly due to increased salaries for public servants ($12.2m) and the increased educational budget ($11.6m). No new taxes were imposed, so the current accounts surplus fell to only $5m by the final estimates, and it became necessary to cover about three quarters of the capital budget with loans.

The oil price increases in the wake of the Arab–Israeli war hit Jamaica hard. With virtually no domestic energy supplies the country faced a $100m increase in its oil-import bill. At the end of 1973, a number of immediate measures to deal with the oil crisis such as a 25 per cent reduction in production of gasoline for local consumption were announced. In late January, Manley announced a more comprehensive package to deal with the oil crisis and its immediate consequence; the foreign exchange situation was so bad that reserves would cover only four weeks of imports. The measures were stringent: bank rates were increased; gasoline prices doubled; car imports cut from $10m to $5m; taxes on cars increased by 50 per cent; 75 per cent duty on imported spirits was imposed; import licensing was made stricter; a number of consumer goods were added to the banned imports list; and new exchange controls were instituted (*G*, 24 January 1974). The next month, Finance Minister Coore announced that the government had decided to make all companies, families and individuals repatriate all foreign assets over $5000 by 31 July 1974. Import licenses for a number of consumer items were also revoked.

In the initial months of 1974, then, the government added to the restrictive measures it had begun to introduce in 1972, to make what was nothing less than an austerity program. The reaction was predictable: hoarding caused near-riots in food stores in January and the private sector sharply protested against the chaos and confusion caused by the introduction of stricter import licensing in February. Nevertheless, the government was still riding the wave of popularity that brought it in, as is shown by the margin of its victory in the 1974 parish council elections that spring. Moreover, the coming of the bauxite levy allowed the government to ease the situation, making this very restrictive period relatively short.

The first moves toward easing restrictions were announced by Coore in his budget speech. The 25 per cent gasoline cutback would be rescinded. Eighteen items would be removed from import licensing requirements, and the total import bill would be increased significantly. The bauxite levy was expected to bring in $210m in the period from January 1974 to the end of the fiscal year (31 March 1975) easing the foreign exchange situation considerably. Of this, $40m would be used for budget support (*G*, 17 May 1974).

Politics: the Opposition

The JLP

For the period up to fall 1974, Shearer remained the *de facto* leader of the JLP (Bustamante was still *de jure* leader), but the party was still deeply divided and was now demoralized by the crushing electoral defeat. Infighting continued and the party was doing very little organizing. Virtually all party statements were given at formal occasions such as the budget debate, party conferences, or New Year's and Independence messages. Three JLP politicians were jockeying to replace Shearer as leader; Seaga, Lightbourne and Wilton Hill. The decisive defeat in the 1974 parish council elections (54 per cent to 44 per cent) was followed by a stormy meeting of the Standing Committee of the JLP in which Shearer declared his intention to remain as party head and in which Hill and another MP walked out. By April 1974 Seaga clearly had won the internal struggle, as Lightbourne had resigned from the party in 1973 and had since formed a new party. (The attempt fizzled and the party never competed in a general election.)

For the period, the only two JLP leaders who received extensive press coverage were Shearer, the party leader, and Seaga, primarily because of his role as opposition spokesman on finance. Shearer's themes (in the budget debates) were mismanagement and (at party conferences, public messages and other public speeches) alleged government moves towards a one-party state and/or communism. The latter charges were made on incredibly weak grounds and to the foreign observer appear to be completely irresponsible, but they have to be taken in the Jamaican context in which politicians (particularly Labour politicians) always use the strongest possible rhetoric in describing their opponents. For instance, in April 1973, in response to verbal attacks on Seaga and Percy Broderick, Shearer charged that the PNP was trying 'to stifle lawful criticism' and continued:

> Now it appears that it is not only to win power at any cost but to stifle all criticism against Government measures, however harmful to the country such measures might be, and to wipe out the concept of political and parliamentary opposition (a cherished plank of our constitution) by dictator-like measures of whatever nature, Communist or Hitlerite (*G*, 10 April 1973).

The next February he accused Manley of 'conceit and megalomaniac afflictions of a "little Hitler" who believes that when he differs with God, God is wrong'. Despite this, Manley and Shearer were friendly to one another and used to have breakfast together on a regular basis![16]

Shearer did use some of the tried and tested JLP critiques of the PNP. At the 1972 party conference he charged that the 'PNP has led Jamaica into the Red Bloc' (which the *Gleaner* ran as a banner headline) because the government had established full diplomatic relations with the People's Republic of China and Cuba (*G*, 4 December 1972). At the time of the establishment of CARICOM, Shearer maintained that it was a 'reimposition of another portion of rejected Federation' (*G*, 8 June 1973). The anti-socialism theme was also strong in his speech to the 1973 party conference, calling on the government to choose 'between private enter-prise and socialism with total government control' and asking 'are they (the PNP) only paying lip service to democracy and moving instead to a one-party state?' (*G*, 19 November 1973). Shearer and other JLP spokes-men also criticized the government for using government agencies such as the JBC and Jamaica Information Service (JIS) for party political pur-poses.

The political attack on the compulsory National Youth Service was led by Robert Lightbourne. His blistering attack on an (as it turned out entirely erroneous) account of a speech by PNP Senator Paul Miller was given major play by the *Gleaner*:

> I am horrified at two statements [by Miller] . . . that young persons in the society who do not volunteer for the National Youth Service are likely to be treated as criminals and even brought within the ambit of the odious Gun Court . . . Senator Miller is reported as making reference to 'our latest attraction, the Gun Court' in the context of saying that all young persons must serve in the National Youth Service or face the fact of being treated as enemies of the state. He also made the significant comment, reported to me, that young people owe no obligation to their parents but only to the state . . . Are we indeed heading for that most dreadful condition, the Police State, of which some of us are already seeing ominous signs in this country? (*G*, 27 April 1974).

Lightbourne followed this up with a telegram to the Jamaica Council of Churches and other organizations calling on them to 'preserve democracy' by taking a firm stand against the compulsory youth service which 'smacks of dictatorship and victimization'. He repeated his attack on Miller and then charged that if Youth Camps were made compulsory they could be 'used as instruments of indoctrination for the brainwashing of our youth' (*G*, 28 April 1974). Lightbourne's irresponsible actions and the copy given to them by the *Gleaner* are most significant as a measure of the upper- and upper middle-class discontent with, and fears of, the compulsory youth service, which Lightbourne hoped to exploit.

Though the anti-socialism/anti-communism/one-party-state theme was present in the JLP's attacks on the government in this period, it was sounded much less frequently than later, as Table A.3 shows. Our reading of the *Daily News* which began to appear in spring 1973 convinced us that this was not merely an artefact of the *Gleaner's* changing agenda. The JLP focused its criticism on the issue of 'mismanagement'. Sixteen of the twenty-two attacks coded for this period were on this ground.[17] It is worth looking more closely at the content of the JLP's criticism of PNP economic management, as we will argue that the PNP did fail in this area. For the historical record it is important to know whether the PNP's opponents clearly recognized its mistakes at the time. In retrospect, it can be said that the PNP's biggest mistakes in this period were poor implementation of its programs and the failure to develop an overall economic plan. It also began to borrow too much, particularly abroad, though not at a magnitude that makes this a major mistake in economic management in this period. Only four of the sixteen JLP attacks concern these areas. Shearer and Seaga (like everyone else in Jamaica) quickly recognized that the SEP, particularly its KSAC component, was very unproductive and they criticized the government on this ground. Seaga, and occasionally Shearer, criticized the government's increased reliance on loans to finance the capital budget. Seaga also contended (probably correctly) that a lack of business confidence, caused by uncertainty about the government's direction and by the closer relations with communist countries had contributed to the decline in investment. However, any impact these criticisms might have made was completely vitiated by the fact that taken as a whole the JLP critique was inconsistent and contained at least as many incorrect solutions as correct ones. The inconsistency was partly a product of a division of labor with Shearer calling for more programs and more subsidies and Seaga criticizing deficit spending. This, of course, reflects the cross-class nature of the JLP's trade union–business base, but the problem goes further: placing Shearer's statements together reveals gross inconsistency. He alternatively called for more subsidies, and then less taxes; more social programs, but a smaller budget deficit.

Seaga's critique was more precise but particularly weak on alternative solutions. Moreover, since his line was generally fiscally conservative, it was not consistent with the party program. For example, the 1973 JLP conference called for subsidies on basic food items, family allowances for mothers, expansion of youth training programs and funds for Christmas work programs (*G*, 19 November 1973). It is not possible to combine this with Seaga's critique of both increased deficit financing and higher taxes unless one calls for substantial cuts in other programs which, of course, he never did. His suggested solutions for various economic problems often lacked plausibility. For instance, in the debate on economic measures introduced in the wake of the oil crisis, he criticized the restrictions and argued that the solution would be to build up foreign exchange reserves to cover a projected $120m deficit by special assistance from the IMF, a possible reduction in oil prices(!), and additional borrowing by the government, but he then warned about the danger of excessive foreign borrowing (*G*, 13 March 1974).

The JLP's actions often had the character of opposition for opposition's sake. When the government introduced the Kareba as an alternative to the European coat and tie, more suitable to a tropical climate, the JLP stuck to the coat and tie. When the government announced that Labour Day would be devoted to collective volunteer work projects, the JLP and BITU responded by encouraging all their members and supporters to celebrate the holiday with leisure thus undermining the government's symbolic attempt at national mobilization for production.

The BITU also opposed another (not so symbolic) move that had the blessing of the government: a serious attempt to promote trade union unity. In April 1972, a meeting with all the unions including the small ones was called by Manley to discuss wage policy in the SEP and his proposals for work on Labour Day. At the meeting, a proposal emerged from the unions to begin discussions on trade union unity. At a subsequent meeting in May both Manley and Shearer spoke strongly in favor of unity as it would help to organize the unorganized (instead of reorganizing the organized) and give labor a single voice on legislation. Later that month the BITU pulled out of the talks giving 'violent attacks and intimidation of BITU members' at various work-sites (notably at the Pegasus Hotel where the BITU was being challenged by the NWU in a representation rights poll) as the reason for its action (*G*, 21 May 1972). While this 'official reason' cannot be dismissed, one cannot help speculating that there were other motivations for the action. The BITU stood to gain from the normal pattern of swing to the union affiliated with the opposition party and the JLP as the party out of power was much more dependent on its union than was the PNP on its union affiliate.

The Gleaner

As we pointed out in the last chapter, the *Gleaner*, which is politically the most influential of the mass media, is controlled by and represents the opinions of a conservative segment of the capitalist class. In assessing the criticism of the government emanating from the *Gleaner*, one has to look at its presentation of the news as well as the editorials and the columnists' opinions. The news presentation has the greatest mass impact while the editorials and columnists have a much narrower audience, but are still important because of their impact on the upper classes. There was always some attempt to keep a non-partisan veneer on the editorials themselves while sticking to a very conservative political line. This was particularly true of the first few years of the Manley government. However, the presentation of the news often belied the more even-handed approach characterizing the editorials.

Because of time constraints, we were unable to read systematically every column by every columnist for the whole period, but we did read enough columns to get the gist of the main columnists' general political line. We paid particular attention to columnists who received a significant number of nominations in the 1974 and 1982 elite samples (see Appendices 2 and 4). The methodology of choosing the sample obviously gives strong indication that such a columnist was considered influential by the elite. In this early period the only columnist who was considered to have considerable influence was Morris Cargill, who wrote under the pen name of Thomas Wright. Cargill was (and is) a planter and his views, which can accurately be described as reactionary are probably a good representation of the views of that most conservative section of the capitalist class. Furthermore, Cargill had always supported the JLP (Cargill, 1979:151–62).Thus, it is not surprising that his columns were uncompromisingly strident in their attacks on the Manley government from the outset. In Cargill's mind democracy and free enterprise were inseparable as were socialism and dictatorship. Thus, every step toward government intervention in the economy from price controls to ownership of the utilities was seen as a step toward dictatorship.

During the first years of the Manley government, neither the *Gleaner's* editorials nor the news coverage showed overt party partisanship. Its socio-economic analysis followed a general neoclassical conservative line. The private sector was the only viable and efficient economic actor. Inequality was necessary because only the rich save and saving is necessary for investment which is necessary for growth. Their attacks on and criticisms of the government flowed naturally from this posture. As can be seen in Table A.3, the *Gleaner* immediately began to press the PNP government to clarify the limits of the public sector and to reassure the private sector about its role in the PNP's plan for the economy. It also began to express concern about the statements of 'some government ministers' (at times openly referring to Thompson and Spaulding) and the new closer relations with socialist countries (Cuba and China) because of their effects on business confidence and thus the level of investment. The following excerpt from an editorial is fairly typical of the tone and the concerns of the *Gleaner* in the first year or so of the PNP government:

> there is a great deal of local investment which has not been made because of uncertainty as to Government Policy. Government ministers can laugh if they want but many Jamaicans are very worried about the sudden interest in relations with socialist countries. The question of whether communism and socialism are good or bad is academic at this stage. The fact remains that Jamaica has always been very firmly on the side of the West. Any sudden departure from this, whether it be good or bad, has to upset some people. And those who are most easily upset are those who have investment and money to invest.
>
> The Prime Minister, Mr Manley, has made it clear that his Government is in favor of free enterprise. However, Mr Dudley Thompson who has a great deal to say on behalf of the Government, and who seems to have a great deal of influence in Government policy has stated very clearly that he is not a free enterpriser. Now how do we reconcile one with the other? . . . The private sector must be assured of its role in development (*G*, 1 November 1972).

Aside from criticisms of rhetoric and lack of clarity on the private sector's role, these editorials are telling in two other ways. First, it is clear that the *Gleaner* editorial writers shared Cargill's view on the incompatibility of socialism and democracy. This was representative of the conservative segment of the capitalist class: one member of this faction told us that 'after the announcement of democratic socialism, we (the private sector) asked "just how democratic and how socialist?" ' For this group there was little if any difference between communism and socialism. Second, these editorials show that, from the outset, there was an attempt on the part of the *Gleaner* to highlight the ideological differences within the PNP and to isolate the left and brand it as anti-democratic.

The *Gleaner* editorials usually spoke in generalities and rarely leveled strong criticism at specific government policies. In fact, in this period, it expressed support for broad policy directions as represented by the 1973 Throne Speech, the November 1972 economic package, the January 1974 oil crisis package and the bauxite levy, but there were exceptions and they are significant. On several occasions, the *Gleaner* expressed opposition to the property tax. In terms of foreign policy, a notable exception, especially in the light of later events, to the absence of specific critiques was the *Gleaner's* expression of opposition to Manley's trip to Algiers with Castro. The compulsory National Youth Service also met with disapproval. Again, it expressed this by giving major play to an event (the Lightbourne attack) ignored by the *Daily News*.

The *Gleaner* did not raise the mismanagement charge as often as did the JLP in these years or as the paper itself did later (see Table A.3). In several of these attacks, the paper's concern was the government's switch to loan-financing of a great portion of the capital budget. Unlike the JLP, the *Gleaner* was consistent on the issue: it accepted the government's explanation that pay rises were needed for public servants but then suggested that the government should have cut some of its programs to keep spending at the level originally projected. Moreover, this was not an isolated comment, on a number of occasions the *Gleaner* criticized the government for trying to introduce too many programs too fast.

Despite the criticisms emanating from the *Gleaner*, the paper was not nearly as critical then as in future years. In the period up to the declaration of democratic socialism, we coded an average of 13.6 attacks from the *Gleaner* per year compared with 31.8 in the next period from the declaration to the 1976 elections. The paper's strategy at this time seemed to be to contain the government and discredit radical elements in the PNP rather than to bring the government down. Thus, while expressing general support for the government's various policy packages and retaining a veneer of non-partisanship, it actually opposed any element of reform, any departure from social, fiscal and political conservatism contained in them. By implication or direct statement, the paper opposed: the compulsory youth service; the level of overall expenditure and number of programs being introduced; key elements of the government's foreign policy, particularly the move away from total identification with the West; greater government intervention into the economy, particularly in ownership and the property tax.

The private sector[18]
In the case of the JLP and the *Gleaner*, the public criticisms of and attacks on the government, which were aimed at influencing mass and elite opinions in Jamaica and abroad were the most important aspects of these two groups' oppositional activity. In the case of businessmen, the situation is quite different. They are officially private persons and even their public spokespeople generally attempt to keep up a veneer of official non-partisanship. Indeed, the attacks on the government from the private sector were much more infrequent than those from the *Gleaner* and the JLP (see Table A.3), but, unlike the paper and the party these 'attacks' and the milder form of vocal opposition which we shall label 'criticism' were not primarily aimed at influencing public opinion but rather were aimed directly at influencing government policy. There was always a latent threat of non-cooperation in the expressions of opposition. Given that the Manley government's model involved a mixed economy, developing a working relationship with the private sector was a crucial element of its development path. Thus it is essential to analyze this relationship and why it deteriorated. Were capitalists alienated by essential features of the path, that is, the policies of the government, or was it other factors such as excessive rhetoric or the close relationship to Cuba, as some have claimed, which alienated them?

In analyzing private sector behavior (and to some extent that of highly skilled personnel) one must look beyond vocal criticism to various forms of 'exit' behavior; disinvestment and migration. In the case of capitalists, the process of disinvestment can take a number of increasingly severe forms. At the lowest level, they may take a 'wait and see' attitude delaying new investments until the 'business climate' seems better, but keeping their money in the domestic economy either in banks or speculative investment like property. As uncertainty increases, they may then attempt to export some of the surplus. In an open economy like Jamaica's, this is quite easy to do as most businessmen are involved in foreign trade and can arrange with their foreign clients to over-invoice imports and /or under-invoice exports. (In fact, export of capital by wealthy Jamaicans began well before the Manley government. Seaga (*Public Opinion*, 29 October 1971) charged in 1971 that this practice had already reached 'alarming proportions'). At the next level up, businessmen can begin to disinvest, to fail to replace depreciating capital goods and then export the proceeds.

The final step would appear to be migration, to leave the country altogether, depriving the country not only of their wealth but also of their managerial skills, but the process is not so straightforward in the Jamaican instance. In the 1970s the overwhelming majority of Jamaicans who migrated were headed for the USA or Canada (see Tables A.4–5), but many Jamaicans, particularly businessmen, kept economic ties with Jamaica after 'migrating'. That is, they can retain their Jamaican citizenship according to Jamaican law even after they have become permanent residents or citizens of the USA or Canada, and, given that the USA has no requirement that a foreigner with permanent resident status remain in the USA for a certain portion of the year and that Canada had no such requirement until 1978, a person could retain their permanent resident status and, for all intents and purposes, continue to live and do business in Jamaica. This, in fact, was quite common. Thus, while it was the usual practice for businessmen to develop 'nest eggs' abroad in anticipation of possible migration, one cannot interpret the fact of migration as a final break with the island's economy. Nevertheless, the decision to attempt to obtain permanent resident status in North America is an important barometer of a given person's opinion of the social, political and economic direction of the country. Where businessmen are concerned, it is highly correlated with export of at least some of their wealth and managerial skills. For other groups, such as professionals, the acquisition of permanent resident status does seem to be a decision to migrate and thus the figures on migration are an accurate representation of the loss to the island's economy.

We have five sources of data with which we can analyze business reactions to the Manley government. First, the main source for public statements, criticisms and attacks was the daily papers and the codings of attacks in the *Gleaner* (see Appendix 3). Second, for migration, the source was figures on immigration collected by the USA and Canadian governments (Tables A.4–5). Third, the data on capital formation from the Jamaican national accounts provided information on investment (Table A.6). Fourth, in the spring of 1982, we interviewed forty-six members of the Jamaican elite, chosen by the positional–reputational method used by Bell and his associates in 1974 and Moskos in 1962 (see Appendices 2 and 4). Thirteen of the forty-six were capitalists. The interview schedule included the core questions on economic ideology, democracy and foreign policy used by Bell and Moskos, as well as a number of supplementary questions adapted to the specific person's role in the events of the Manley period. In the case of business elites, a special interview schedule was added which covered the relationship between the respondent and the business community at large and the PNP government.

The final source of evidence was the 1974 elite study which Professor Bell made available to us for secondary analysis. Twenty-two of the eighty-three interviewed were business people. We supplemented the information gathered in 1974 with data on emigration of the 1974 respondents. On this matter, we relied on information of one member of the elite sample who was well-connected in both business and political circles. The number of business people in the two elite studies is small, but it must be pointed out that, because of the sample selection methods, the people interviewed were a large segment of the most influential and wealthiest capitalists on the island. They controlled very substantial interests in almost all the major corporate groupings in the country.

To begin with the public statements, they show that the Manley government did experience a honeymoon with the private sector. The first real salvo from the private sector came from Meeks, President of the Chamber of Commerce in August 1972 in response to the government's moves to make bulk purchases of salt-fish. He criticized the government for 'extending its tentacles into the domain of businessmen' (*G*, 15 August 1972) and expressed 'fears for the future of Free Enterprise'. Meeks continued to be the government's biggest private sector critic in the next two years, repeatedly raising questions about the government's intentions about encroaching on the domain of the private sector. These criticisms were stimulated both by the import restrictions and licensing and by the government's first moves to acquire the utilities.

The policies laid out in the November 1972 package affected the manufacturing sector much less. The JMA began to express strong concern when the flour mill shut in response to government price controls in April 1973, warning of more closures to come if the policy would persist. The move to acquire 10 per cent in the Caribbean Cement Company in June provoked sharp criticism from JMA President Henderson-Davis as he termed the move a 'flagrant breach of the democratic principles of the free enterprise system which the government professes to believe in and support' (*G*, 15 June 1972).

Manley (1975b:233) argued that there were four issues which generated upper-class, middle-class and/or business opposition to his government the first two years in office: the National Youth Service, the property tax, foreign policy and the role of the government in the economy. We have seen that by summer 1973 the private sector had shown a strong reaction to the government's encroachment (small though it was) in ownership, importing and import licensing. The Youth Service controversy did not heat up until the next summer, but in the other two areas private sector criticism was muted. However, it must be understood that representatives of private sector organizations have generally felt constrained to limit their criticism to matters that infringe on business affairs. Taxes on individuals and foreign policy have generally fallen outside this area. Therefore, one should attach particular importance to the fact that criticism of both policies did come from the private sector. Soon after the announcement of the property tax, the Chamber of Commerce called for the suspension of its implementation. The tax was clearly not a tax on business: the tax was on the unimproved value of land, with agricultural land in production exempted. Thus, the tax was designed to get idle agricultural land in production and to tax individual wealth in the form of residential property. Businesses were little affected since the tax did not apply to the productive assets (factory or office building, etc.) on the land. The aim was to get the rich to pay their fair share of taxes. The government was aware of the fact that many wealthy people (primarily owners of businesses) were declaring little or no income and paying no taxes. Yet they owned palatial mansions in the hills surrounding Kingston. So the government decided to tax what they could see. The reaction of the Chamber of Commerce, then, reflected a broader class interest rather than a narrow interest group concern:[19]

There were some earlier private sector grumblings about foreign policy initiatives, such as the trade mission to Russia in summer 1972, but the first strong criticism came from Douglas Vaz, who succeeded Henderson-Davis as JMA President, after Manley's speech at the Non-aligned Conference in Algiers. Vaz attacked Manley's offer to send volunteers to fight in Africa in no uncertain terms:

> If that is the way we feel about it, why shouldn't Cuba or China send volunteers to help Jamaican subversive groups establish Communism in Jamaica? Or, why for that matter shouldn't the US send volunteer Marines to overthrow the present Jamaican government and make Jamaica safe for democracy? (*G*, 13 September 1973).

Vaz went on to say that the government had better turn its attention to domestic developments and restore confidence in the government in order to stop the outflow of people and capital. The speech is significant for a number of reasons. First, it was a speech by the JMA president at a meeting of the JMA directors on a foreign policy issue that did not directly affect manufacturers, that is, it was not a situation where Vaz was invited to comment on the general political situation to a broader audience. Second, the reference to migration and capital flight at this early date was important. Third, Vaz was a strong supporter of the PNP in 1972.

The oil crisis policy package initially received a favorable reaction from the private sector, but when the import licensing went into effect there was loud protest, particularly from the Chamber of Commerce. While there were special problems in the beginning, these regulations and the operation of the Trade Administrator's Department were a constant source of irritation to business throughout the Manley government. How much of this was attributable to bureaucratic bungling and corruption and how much to the sheer shortage of foreign exchange is impossible to evaluate.

The JMA was less critical of the government, but its action on a non-business issue, the National Youth Service, is noteworthy. Soon after it was announced that the National Youth Service would be made compulsory, the JMA sent a delegation to talk with Manley about it, expressing agreement with the service in principle 'but not . . . with the compulsory aspect' (*G*, 9 May 1974). The year before in an editorial the *Daily News* (10 July 1973) expressed the opinion that the critiques of the youth service were based on fears of class mixing, something which Manley (1975b:233–4) has also observed. There was certainly an element of this in the motivation behind the JMA's action; one businessman told us:

> This [the compulsory youth service] frightened a lot of people. You just couldn't have rural youths, ghetto kids and criminal elements associate with kids from other families.

The persistent difference in the public statements about government policy of the Chamber of Commerce and the JMA in this period raises the question of whether the commercial bourgeoisie did not shift to a posture of opposition more quickly than the industrial bourgeoisie. It is clear that the import restrictions affected commerce much more than manufacturing in this period. Six of the nine attacks by the private sector came from Meeks or the Chamber itself, but one must be careful about interpreting this as reflecting the overall attitudes of clear class segments. As we pointed out in the last chapter, there are in fact no clearly divided segments in the Jamaican capitalist class. While there is no doubt that the Chamber of Commerce did have more to complain about, the personal political ideology of Winston Meeks, who was an ultra-conservative, certainly played a role in determining the character of his statements as the President of the Chamber. In general, it appears that ideology was much more important than sector in the shift away from the government, though sector probably did have an effect on migration.

The government responded to criticism from the private sector sympathetically. There was an occasional counter-attack saying that private sector spokesmen were being unreasonable, but generally Manley, Patterson, and Vivian Blake (Minister of State in the Ministry of Industry) met often with businessmen and reassured them that the private sector had an important role in their plans and that they considered profits legitimate.

Interpretation of the migration figures shown in Tables A.4–5 must be done with some caution. We want to know what economic, social, and political factors stimulated the decision to migrate. The figures in the table are based on the date of arrival in the USA or Canada, not on the date of initiation of the process to arrange for permission to migrate. For migration to Canada, the average time lapse between these two dates is only about four months, so generally the decision to migrate and the date of arrival are in the same year. For migration to the USA, the average time lapse is about one year, so an adjustment must be made in order to interpret the figures.[20]

The data in Tables A.4–5 show that there was already a very significant increase in the migration of businessmen (managers, administrators, proprietors and officials) in 1973 and another large increase in 1974. The increased migration was entirely to Canada, so we can assume it was stimulated by events occurring no later than mid-1973 and mid-1974 respectively. The timing of this migration wave is very significant since it could not have been stimulated by the declaration of democratic socialism, the rise of the PNP left, nor the heightened ideological debate (the 'rhetoric') that followed. One must be careful, however, in interpreting this migration as a straight rational economic reaction to the PNP's policies. The economic austerity policies, particularly the import restrictions, caused by the shortage of foreign exchange, did have a significant impact on the commercial bourgeoisie, and capitalists from this sector did emigrate in disproportionate numbers (see Chapter 4). Specific fiscal and social policies, such as the property tax and the National Youth Service, were also important but they were important as part of a trajectory of a whole program that was aimed at introducing egalitarian change in a very elitist society. Part of that change was the social and cultural inclusion of the masses of Jamaica into the society. And when those who had been privileged in the elitist society that had existed heretofore began to feel their social position threatened, some of them began to abandon the society. We can see this straight elitist reaction most clearly in the case of the storm over the compulsory youth service, and, as we pointed out, there was a clear element of racism in this response. It cannot be denied that the socio-cultural inclusion process as indicated by the emphasis on the African heritage and black identity which the PNP under Manley promoted was resented and feared by many whites, 'socially white' upper-class browns and other ethnic minorities. In the minds of many of them this was tied to the rising crime rate which they felt was directed at them. 'Is Black man time now' meant it was not their society anymore. It is significant in this respect that it was the Chinese businessmen who migrated in disproportionate numbers in 1973 and 1974. With the recent memory of the Chinese riots of 1965, they felt particularly threatened by the rise in Black consciousness.

Turning to the figures on investment (Table A.6), one can see a fall in investment in the percentage of GDP going to fixed capital formation in the first year of the PNP government as well as in the preceding year. The fall was a result of the end of the investment program of the aluminum multinationals and of the tourist industry to which we alluded earlier and thus had little if anything to do with the actions of the government. Moreover, the levels of capital formation reached in these years, about a quarter of GDP, were adequate. Indeed, this was Seaga's target-level in the early 1980s.

The second fall in investment came in 1974 and 1975. Again the timing is important: the investment fall came before the declaration of democratic socialism. While the party's move to adopt socialism as an ideology was first mentioned by the press in August 1974, it was not given much press play even during the party conference in September. It was only after Manley's November speech in Montego Bay (see Chapter 4) that the PNP's new ideological posture became a topic of heated debate. Moreover, given that the process of translating an investment decision into an actual transaction must take some time, the decline in 1974 at least is not likely to have been influenced by events such as the declaration of democratic socialism in late 1974. Reactions of the *Gleaner* and private sector spokesmen to the events of 1972 to mid-1974 suggest that policies of the government introduced in 1973 and early 1974 (for example, the property tax, the youth service, foreign policy, etc.) and the general difficulties of the economy were the primary factors responsible for this decline. Based on our data, it is a fairly safe assumption to say that two groups were most responsible for the decline in investment. On the one hand, those who were adversely affected by the economic situation such as importers (especially of consumer goods) and other large net users of foreign exchange, were obviously constrained by the import restrictions and lack of foreign exchange. On the other hand, ultra-conservative businessmen reacted to the political direction of the government.

The data from the 1982 business people interviews confirm our contention with regard to the posture of conservative businessmen. Three of the thirteen capitalists were coded as 'ultra-conservatives' with regard to economic ideology.[21] These three people (two of whom voted PNP in 1972) accounted for two of the four capitalists who said their own attitudes changed in the first two years, for all three who said the business community's attitudes changed in the first two years, and for both of those who said they began to invest less in the first two years.

As to the reasons given for the changes in attitudes, investment behavior and migration, few of the capitalists mentioned specific policies, but it is significant that such responses came very disproportionately from the ultra-conservative group, particularly when the question referred to the respondent's own behavior. In addition, in response to the question about failures of the PNP government, only the three ultra-conservatives referred to specific policies. Thus, the 1982 elite data strongly confirm our contention based on the previous three data sources that the ultra-conservative segment of the capitalist class, which we estimate to be about 25–33 per cent of the class, turned against the Manley government in the first two and a half years. The policies aimed at state sector expansion, redistribution, and social inclusion were the primary factor that alienated this group. Their response was not just 'voice' but also 'exit'; they began to invest less, to export capital and even to migrate. These people would have been alienated by *any* program of significant change.

Concluding remarks

To summarize briefly: the first two and a half years of the Manley government saw the introduction of a broad range of programs and policies aimed at greater economic self-reliance, more equal distribution, greater social ownership and greater economic and political independence from the Western capitalist world. Most programs associated with the Manley government were in fact initiated in this period. A process of party-building, popular mobilization, and socio-cultural inclusion was also begun. The PNP was going through an internal ideological redefinition but this was not yet public knowledge. The reform program was being carried out in the face of considerable economic difficulties which the government attempted to address with a series of special economic packages.

The popular reaction to the government was positive. In the absence of any public opinion studies between 1972 and 1976 it is not possible to state with any degree of confidence whether and to what extent different social classes and ethnic groups were reacting differently to the government. We do know that the ultra-conservative segment of the capitalist class had realized that the government was serious about introducing egalitarian change into the society and, as a result, had turned against the government. This, along with the rising crime rate and the foreign exchange problem, had already resulted in significant migration. It is a good guess that this alienation from the government extended to the more privileged sections of the professionals. As far as the working classes, peasants and lumpenproletariat are concerned, one can only say (based on the result of the 1974 parish council elections) that the government had picked up enough political support to offset the losses it had suffered among the upper classes.

A full evaluation will be attempted later in the book, but it might be useful here to touch upon the obvious successes and failures of the PNP up to this time. The movement-building and ideology-formation process was proceeding as well as could be expected given the situation at the outset. The party machinery, now under the direction of D. K. Duncan, had produced impressive results winning the parish council elections and all three by-elections by substantial margins. The ideological-redefinition process was underway and proceeding on schedule. These efforts, together with the socio-cultural inclusion policies, initiated a gradual shift in the balance of class power. One weak area was media policy. The government transformed Jamaica Information Service into the Agency for Public Information (API) as part of an effort to make more active use of the Agency to promote the government's policies, but there was no attempt to develop media organs for the party itself.

The government's policies all appeared to be headed in the correct direction, toward the kind of democratic socialist development path we outlined in Chapter 1. Moreover, contrary to most current evaluations, the government's macroeconomic management was not too bad especially when seen from that time-point. We know now that the world capitalist system entered into a phase of stagnation and price inflation just as the PNP took power. So retrospectively, the budget deficit of $100m in the 1973–4 budget and $150m in the original 1974–5 budget estimates (about 6–7 per cent of GDP) was too high given the debt at high interest rates with which it saddled the country. Even with the benefit of hindsight this was not an error of major proportions. It must be remembered that the PNP government faced special problems in addition to the price inflation of oil and other products faced by all non-oil-producing Third World countries. The fall in bauxite/alumina investments, which had been subsidizing the import bill, caused major economic restrictions *before* the price inflation hit the country. Finally, the government has to be credited with the introduction of the bauxite levy which helped to ease some of the problems caused by the fall in investment and the world economic situation.

There were serious problems in the PNP's economic development program and one of them was already obvious; the government had no coherent medium or long term economic plan. Any coherence the policies appeared to have was because they hung together in the mind of Manley,[22] and Manley's strength was not economic planning. The absence of a plan meant there was no real attempt to target levels of investment and then to develop contingency plans if investment failed to come through (as in the case of sufficient private sector investments). The absence of a plan meant that the costs of programs were not forecast over long periods and weighed against one another. Take the National Youth Service. On a number of occasions, Manley stated that it was the intention of the government eventually to make the service compulsory for all youths whether they completed school or not. A simple calculation will convince anyone that with 32 000 youths in each age-year cohort and a two-year service requirement this meant employing 64 000 people a year in a single program, which would be prohibitively expensive even if the government provided only a subsistence living for them. In fact the program, even in the form it did take, proved too expensive and was teminated. Thus, all the abuse which the government took for the program was for nothing.

The second failure, which should have been apparent by this point, was that many of the programs, though correctly conceptualized, were poorly implemented. The most important reason for this was the sheer incapacity of the Jamaican bureaucracy to handle all the new programs coming onstream, but the government has to share the blame in not recognizing this and adjusting to it. Moreover, the PNP must shoulder the full blame for the patronage characteristic of many of the programs. This factor was the second most important reason for the poor performance of the programs as a whole. It virtually destroyed some of them such as Food Farms (see Chapter 8). Furthermore, these failures of program implementation had a direct impact on macroeconomic management in the long run. For instance, the failure of Food Farms not only meant a waste of government funds but also lost domestic food production and thus more imports and a drain on the foreign exchange budget.

4

The First Term: Ideological Definition and Social Polarization 1974–6

During this period, some major tendencies emerged which subsequently came to dominate the political struggle characterizing the remainder of the PNP's period in office. The increasing importance of the ideological debate in the PNP and between the PNP and the opposition aggravated internal PNP splits and brought them into the open, and the reaction from the opposition became more and more hostile and strident. The *Gleaner* spearheaded the attacks; criticism in editorials increased in 1975, escalating particularly sharply both in frequency and tone in late 1975. In January 1975 Seaga, now leader of the party, launched a JLP 'election campaign' focusing on the issues of economic (mis)management and the Communist–Cuban threat. In 1974, the private sector was more concerned with economic issues, such as the call for repatriation of assets held abroad and the nationalization of utilities than with the new ideological turn represented by the declaration of democratic socialism. However, after the announcement of the economic policy package of August 1975, discontent over these measures generated increased hostility, as did Manley's trip to Cuba and his admiration for Fidel. Opposition to the government intensified as the 1976 elections drew near, culminating in a campaign of violence amid charges of destabilization by domestic and foreign forces.

The government reacted to the growing opposition with endless clarifications of its concept of democratic socialism and also countered with pressures on the JBC to give more sympathetic coverage to the government's policy and political philosophy. In this period the process of mass party building and of popular mobilization was stepped up. In reaction to the escalating violence the government declared a State of Emergency in June of 1976 which remained in effect for almost a year. Meanwhile the economy began to deteriorate sharply. In this climate of increased social polarization and intensified political struggle, the PNP scored a massive election victory on the platform of democratic socialism, despite the high degree of violence and the impending economic crisis.

The PNP political offensive

The move to ideological definition
Though the usual periodization of the PNP government takes Manley's reaffirmation of the party's commitment to democratic socialism in his speech to the 36th Annual Conference as the turning-point, this speech is only one event in the process of ideological self-definition of the party. This process became publicly visible in August, and the official launching of the political education campaign on democratic socialism did not take place until 21 November, at a mass rally in Kingston. Shortly after the 1972 elections Manley had addressed the PNP executive reminding them of the party's socialist heritage and had then emphasized the need for an ideological platform and consensus. From then on, some of his closest collaborators were working on a program for a party political education campaign. In 1974 the materials were presented to the relevant party organs.[1] The move toward a renewal of the PNP's socialist tradition was made public for the first time when the *Daily News* published a story about the proceedings of a large (but closed) PNP meeting at a major Kingston hotel in August. The meeting caused a considerable public storm and pressure for clarification of both the party's long-term vision of a desirable society and its short- and medium-term policies to move the society in the desired direction. This pressure prompted the leadership to accelerate the whole process and publish such a document before it had a chance to be discussed within the party as widely as originally planned. Partly because of the acceleration of the process, no consensus could be reached in the PNP on several critical points and consequently there was considerable vagueness in the document. It was not until the publication of *Principles and Objectives of the People's National Party* in 1979 that most of these points were publicly clarified.

Another prior event indicative of the move toward a democratic socialist ideological position of the PNP was the publication of Manley's book, *The Politics of Change*. It was formally launched in Jamaica at the end of 1973 and serialized in the *Gleaner* in the first half of 1974. The book makes a strong case for a society based on the principles of self-reliance, democracy, participation and equality. As operational framework to build such a society the book favors a mixed economy with public, private, small business and co-operative sectors, but it is not very specific on the relative importance of the different sectors in the mixed economy. It merely stipulates that the 'commanding heights' of the economy clearly belong in public ownership and control. The book does not present a class analysis of society and consequently fails to specify whose class interests should be assigned priority in the competition for scarce resources. These two issues, to which the question of imperialism was soon added, became highly controversial from the moment when the internal and the public discussion about PNP ideology started.

Different PNP leaders gave varying interpretations of the concept of democratic socialism.[2] Moreover, outlining the contours of their ideological path was no easy task, since existing models (such as European social democracy or African socialism) were not really appropriate to the Jamaican context.[3] An official clarification of the future role of the private sector in the mixed economy was given by Manley in a speech to the House on 20 November, but the issues of class and imperialism remained without official clarification. Furthermore, external critics still raised the question whether the mixed economy was to be a transient or a final state, and occasional utterances from various party spokesmen continued to provide grounds for such questioning.

In many speeches during this period the key themes with which party leaders attempted to explain what democratic socialism was all about were 'equality', 'brotherly concern', 'love' and 'Christianity'. Given the JLP's traditional tactic of attacking the PNP as communist and thus atheist and given the importance of religion in Jamaican society, the PNP attempted to link democratic socialism to Christian values (for example, see *DN*, 17 October 1974, and *G*, 21 November 1974.)

The 1974 PNP conference had taken place during the visit by President Nyerere of Tanzania, who was invited to address the participants. His presence was intended to emphasize the PNP's commitment to Third World solidarity and to explain and legitimize the adoption of a democratic socialist model of development. The Agency for Public Information (API) prepared the public for his visit with big advertisements featuring quotes from Nyerere as well as various briefs on Tanzanian political history and current policies. The purpose was to present a positive example of ways to overcome the legacy of colonialism and to present an alternative model of self-reliant socialism. At the end of Nyerere's visit, a joint eleven-point Declaration of Principles was published which did nothing to diffuse tensions and clarify matters. The Declaration stated that the aims of domestic policy should be 'ultimate control by, and in the name of the people, of the major means of production, distribution and exchange', (*DN*, 18 September 1974).

Though the definition of 'major' remained open, this statement certainly projected a different thrust from the Prime Minister's speech to the House on 20 November in which he said that the private sector was to be a full and integral partner in the mixed economy. In this speech, he identified the areas which required public sector involvement as human resource development and basic social services, basic nutrition, infrastructure and public utilities, mineral resources, financial institutions (to come under effective government supervision), salvage operations of important firms in economic difficulties, and research and development in areas of trade and industry which the private sector is hesitant or unwilling to develop (*G*, 21 November 1974). The PNP Supplement to both daily papers published on 9 December contained the very same conception of the mixed economy as the one outlined in this speech. In fact, the whole document in both its content and tone was intended to reassure the private sector. On the other hand, the statements by ideologically inclined members of the PNP frequently reflected a more radical spirit than did this document, though – and this is important to emphasize – they did not contradict it in concrete terms (with the exception of some statements from the PNPYO).

It is worth quoting from the document at some length both to illustrate its moderate tone and non-Marxist analysis, and to enable the reader to appreciate the significance of subsequent ideological struggles and developments within the PNP.

Socialism is first an *attitude of mind* that expects people to care for each other's welfare. Socialism is a form of *social and economic organization* that makes all opportunities as far as possible, equal and open to all.

Socialism is the Christian Way of Life in Action. It is the political philosophy that best gives practical expression to the Christian ideal of the equality of God's children.

Socialism recognizes that democracy is fundamental to the *creation of a society in which each individual* has equal opportunities in, influence over, and responsibilities to the process by which decisions on matters of public interest are made and implemented.

In its pure form capitalism is a system which subordinates people to economic and political exploitation by the wealthy. This exploitation of majorities by minorities generates poverty and class conflict. Therefore the capitalist system generates poverty and class conflict.

Private business is not the same thing as capitalism. It can exist either in a capitalist or in a socialist society. Under a capitalist system private business is encouraged to think only in terms of profit without regard to the National Interest of the people's rights and welfare. Under Socialism private business is required to work within the bounds of the national interest and the people's rights and welfare.

We believe in the right of all those that are employed as workers providing the goods and services that the nation needs to trade union representation; to just wages, terms of employment and conditions of work; to job security; to the enjoyment of the benefits of collective bargaining; to a full share of the wealth that their labor creates; and to participation in the making of decisions within the enterprise to which they are employed [all italics in original].

The document also gives a list of examples of 'nations with democratic socialist governments' which includes Australia, Britain, Sweden, Israel,

Malta, New Zealand, Singapore, Tanzania, Guyana, Germany, Holland, India, Denmark and Sri Lanka. Clearly, then, the PNP's ideological position at the end of 1974 might have been acceptable to a wide spectrum of politicians including centrists sympathetic to the conservative wing of European Social Democracy. In fact, the 1974 elite interviews show that this program was compatible with the economic ideology of nineteen out of the twenty PNP leaders interviewed.

Warming relations with Cuba

The warming of relations with Cuba, which began with Manley's trip to Algiers with Castro in 1973, intensified in 1975. Under the auspices of the newly formed Jamaica–Cuba Joint Commission on Economic, Technical and Cultural Cooperation, a whole variety of projects were started, such as in agriculture, fishing, education, and science and technology (*G*, 9 May 1975). In May 1975 the first group of Jamaican youths went to Cuba for a year-long course in construction methods and technology. This program, the Jamaican Brigade or *Brigadista* program, continued throughout the Manley government, with some 1400 youths participating in it. The Jamaica–Cuba cooperation agreement also brought Cubans to Jamaica to build, at Cuban government expense, several schools, a large number of microdams and residential housing. Cuban doctors also came to Jamaica to work in public hospitals, and half a dozen Jamaican policemen eventually received training in Cuba in methods of security provision for VIPs.

Manley visited Cuba at Castro's invitation in July 1975. He received the warmest possible welcome, and he was awarded the highest Cuban order by the Cuban government. While in Cuba Manley made several speeches about Jamaican–Cuban friendship and solidarity which raised controversy in Jamaica, but none was so controversial as his 'Five Flights a Day to Miami' speech made in Montego Bay upon his return. Manley's trip to Cuba was just the first of a constant stream of visits there by other PNP ministers, party leaders and advisors.

In other foreign policy developments, Jamaica moved into a role of leadership in the Third World in this period, probably partly because of publicity generated by the bauxite levy as well as Manley's effectiveness as orator and the support of an able diplomatic corps. In both the Commonwealth and the UN, Manley emerged as the leading spokesman for the NIEO. In 1974 Patterson was elected to head the ACP negotiating team in the negotiations with the EEC for the Lome convention. In 1976, Jamaica was elected vice president of the Non-aligned Movement. The government continued to expand its diplomatic ties with communist countries, as it opened up relations with Czechoslovakia.

In late 1975 Jamaica's strong anti-apartheid and African solidarity posture led it to take a stance which proved very controversial in Washington. Cuba had sent troops to Angola to help the MPLA government defend the country against the South African invasion. It was Manley's analysis, confirmed by his discussions with African leaders, that the invasion represented a threat not only to Angola but would also permanently consolidate South Africa's hold on Namibia and the Smith government's hold on Rhodesia (Manley, 1982: 110–16). Consequently, the PNP government supported the Cuban move diplomatically.

Mobilization, rhetoric and internal disputes
The process of ideological definition, the closer relations with Cuba, and PNP successes in political mobilization heated up the political climate considerably by the second half of 1975. The successes in political mobilization became clearly publicly visible in this period when the PNP swept two by-elections. The combination of the political mobilization and ideological profile gave the PNP left greater prominence within the party and greater public visibility. Duncan and those around him in the party secretariat joined Spaulding and the PNPYO as the principal target of the *Gleaner* and the JLP. 'Rhetoric' increasingly became an issue.

There was considerable internal tension in the PNP by this time, but not only was this not public, it was also muted within the party itself. Manley indeed was the principal force behind the process of ideological definition and political mobilization and had promoted the PNP left, which was enthusiastically supporting this process. Many PNP moderates, particularly those furthest to the right, were unhappy with the direction of affairs, but Manley's position in the party and in Jamaican society as a whole was unassailable, so they dared not confront him publicly or in party forums. They grumbled behind his back. This situation probably contributed to the absence of any strategy on the part of Manley and the left to deal with discontent within the party. Since opposition to content of the ideology was never brought into the open, there was never a serious effort to come to a compromise. Instead, the opponents resorted to behind the scenes sabotage and footdragging. Above all, this meant that they did not take the ideology seriously, regarding it as a bunch of rhetoric.[4]

For the most part, it cannot be said that public utterances of party spokespeople clearly deviated from the party's stated ideology, especially given the vagueness of some of the formulations. One exception was the PNPYO which took a line closer to Leninism than to democratic socialism. Examples of PNPYO behavior which was clearly out of line with the government's policy in this period were a resolution adopted by the YO Conference in 1975 calling for a 'united front of mass power' and support given to an illegal land invasion in Savanna-la-Mar in April 1975.

In its attempts to deal with internal disunity, the government sought to clarify further the concrete policy implications of democratic socialism and to follow disciplinary procedures to handle 'deviationists' in the party. In October 1975 Manley gave a confidential address to the National Executive

Council, which was important because it addressed certain aspects of relationships to imperialism and the question of class struggle. At the request of the Cabinet it was published as policy statement authorized by the Cabinet (*G*, 5 October 1975). It restated clearly the policy of principled relations with other countries and respect for their choice of economic and political systems, while reaffirming the commitment to the construction of democratic socialism at home, and it emphasized the difference between communism and democratic socialism in respect to class struggle and leadership. It stated that whereas communists saw class warfare as a necessary part of their political strategy, to be pursued even where members of the privileged group might wish to cooperate to facilitate significant progress and change, 'we seek the friendship and the support and the help of all who genuinely accept our objectives' (*DN*, 4 October 1975). It also expressed the belief of democratic socialists in building a mass political movement, wide and open to everyone, in contrast to a tight controlling elite party as under communism.

PNP policy initiatives

In this period the PNP government initiated a number of new policies in the area of labor relations and cooperatives. In March 1975 the Labour Relations and Industrial Disputes Act (LRIDA) was passed. One of its clauses provided for compulsory recognition of trade unions by employers if a majority of workers in an enterprise had voted in favor of union representation. In May 1975 the government set up a committee to study and advise on possibilities for worker participation in decision-making in enterprises, for acquisition of a share in ownership by workers and for disclosure of accounts in collective bargaining, and in October 1975 a national minimum wage was decreed for all categories of workers, including domestic servants and agricultural workers. The government-owned sugar estates were transformed into cooperatives in this period.

As part of its economic package in the fall, 1975, the government announced new policies in the areas of land acquisition and housing. Under the new land policy, the government would establish an alternative to the acquisition of idle land by obtaining from the owners a ten-year renewable lease at a rent of 1 per cent of the value of the land on the valuation roll. The National Housing Trust (NHT), which was passed into law in March 1976, was a compulsory national savings scheme based on a 3 per cent payroll tax and a contribution of 2 per cent of gross earnings by employees designed to provide financing for housing construction. The innovative features of this policy were the freeing of some housing construction from the budget constraints and, more important, distribution of housing under this program by lottery rather than patronage.

The agreements with the bauxite companies discussed in the last chapter were signed in this period, though some aspects such as the management contracts did not go into effect until as late as 1980. The expansion of the state budget made possible by the bauxite levy led to substantial increases in a number of distributionist programs of the earlier period, such as the Special Employment Program (SEP) and to an acceleration in the pace of acquisition of the utilities.

Managing the economy 1974–5

To give a brief and somewhat simplified overview of developments in the period 1974–6, one can say that the difficulties of the previous period gave way to a short-lived expansion and optimism which was soon to be followed by renewed and more severe budgetary and balance of payments pressures and to end up in the foreign exchange crisis of December 1976. The revenue from the bauxite levy enabled the government to expand significantly the total expenditures, from J$443m in 1973–4 to J$751m in 1974–5, or from 25 to 35 per cent of GDP respectively. In the following years, government expenditure in real terms increased only slightly, but the revenue side deteriorated significantly because of declines in earnings from tourism, sugar and bauxite. In this situation, the government relied on transfers from the Capital Development Fund, on domestic and foreign borrowing, and on new taxation. However, the increased tax rates did not produce the desired revenue because of lack of economic growth, and substantial borrowing on unfavorable terms greatly aggravated the debt service burden. Thus, the combination of shortfalls in foreign exchange earnings, high debt service, legal and illegal capital outflows and lack of new foreign investment precipitated a foreign exchange crisis by the end of 1976.

At the time of the imposition of the bauxite levy, the revenue from this source from January 1974 to the end of the fiscal year 1974–5 was estimated at some $200m. Initially, it was announced that $40m of this was to be used for budget support, but successive expansionary measures necessitated an eventual transfer of a total of $85m. At the time of the budget, the government announced it would relax certain import restrictions and that the $40m would be used to build up cash reserves, finance new capital projects, and expand the employment program (*G*, 17 May 1974). Throughout the fiscal year the national budget was progressively increased, beginning with a large increase announced in Manley's (August) Independence message, resulting in an expansion of government spending from $596m to $751m (see Table A.2). At the same time, the foreign exchange brought in by the bauxite levy allowed the government to expand the import budget, initially (and probably somewhat unrealistically) targeted at $600m, to $851m (NPA, 1976:39), and thereby ease import controls. Both the expansion of government expenditure and the import budget, as well as the abolition of credit ceilings on bank loans were designed to stimulate the economy, which had been in a stagnant state since the price shocks of 1973.

By early 1975, the budgetary and inflationary pressures built up, which caused the government to formulate a 1975–6 budget with more restricted expenditure and higher taxation and impose an anti-inflation package in two installments in August and October. Recurrent expenditure was to be increased by only 14 per cent and capital expenditure by 51 per cent over the 1974–5 level, to $582m and $329m respectively. New taxes on liquor, cigarettes, road traffic licenses and travel were to raise an additional $18.3m in revenue. Furthermore, increased tax income was to result from taxes on capital gains and inheritance which had been raised shortly before the presentation of the budget. These tax measures can clearly be seen as an attempt by the government to put the burden of the economic adjustment measures on those most able to carry it. This attempt was made more explicit with the introduction of the new tax measures in February 1976 as well as with certain provisions of the anti-inflation package.

The inflation rate had risen to a high of 27 per cent in 1974, and there was no moderation in sight in early 1975. Thus, in August, the government announced an anti-inflation package whose centerpiece was an incomes policy aimed at reducing wage differentials at the same time as containing wage inflation (*G*, 25 August 1975). Top level salaries were to be frozen and a general incomes policy worked out in consultation with management and labor. The government made it clear that if no consensus could be reached it would impose such a policy as a unilateral act, along with the announcement of the national minimum wage. Also, a rent freeze was imposed as an emergency measure until a new rent control system could be put into place, and stricter price controls were to be enforced. Since no agreement was reached in the consultations about wage guidelines, in November the government imposed such guidelines for an interim period of six months in the second part of the anti-inflation package (*G*, 9 October 1975). For incomes under $7000 per year, purchasing power was to be restored to 1973 levels, incomes over $16 000 per year were to be frozen, and incomes in between were to be adjusted so as not to exceed the increase accruing to the lowest income group. The national minimum wage for all categories of workers was set at $20 per week, and a twelve-month freeze on fees for professional services and a ceiling on dividends were imposed as well. Rents in depressed areas were to be rolled back to 1971 levels, and Community Rent Tribunals were to be set up to determine official levels of rent.

The other important provisions in the anti-inflation packages were plans for a slight reduction in government expenditure, tax incentives for the private sector to increase production and employment, measures to stem the outflow of foreign exchange, and the previously mentioned new land acquisition policy and the National Housing Trust. The outflow of foreign exchange was to be reduced by putting lower limits on remittances to migrants from property or businesses owned in Jamaica.

After 1974 the government began to rely increasingly on loans to finance the budget (see Table A.2), with borrowing from private banks abroad increasing particularly rapidly. The proportion of Jamaica's total external public debt owed to private banks had risen from 10 per cent in 1970 to 44 per cent in 1974 and 51 per cent in 1975.[5] Commercial bank loans obviously carry less favorable terms than loans from multilateral or bilateral sources; in fact, the Permanent Secretary in the Ministry of Finance, Horace Barber, publicly warned in August 1975 of increasingly unfavorable terms attached to foreign loans being sought to cover part of the government's capital expenditure. Interest payments on the external public debt jumped from US $33m in 1974 to US $49m in 1975 and US$53m in 1976; expressed as percentage of exports of goods and services, debt service payments rose from 5.1 to 7.2 per cent to 11.6 per cent in these years.

Political reaction and counter-reaction

JLP

Predictably, the opposition sought to turn the events surrounding the declaration of democratic socialism to their political advantage. Not without some justification, the JLP accused the PNP of using President Nyerere to gain partisan political mileage. A long exchange of letters between government and opposition preceded the visit, in which the offer was made that Nyrere would also address a JLP gathering, but the JLP ended up boycotting the visit. The JLP also accused the PNP of admiration of a one-party state, despite Nyerere's careful explanation of the difference in political history between Tanzania and Jamaica.

The JLP seized upon the declaration itself with calls for immediate elections as the PNP 'had no mandate to impose socialism on the people'. Shearer's resignation as party leader in October opened a jockeying for his position causing several aspirants to assume a high profile using the issue to attack the government as 'tied dogmatically and theoretically to a concept of a state-controlled economy, a totalitarian or communist form of economy'.[6] Seaga announced that he was willing to reverse his decision to withdraw from public life as recent events had been taking an alarming turn and that he would be prepared to assume leadership of the JLP. He warned that 'foundations (were being) laid which could be used to so manipulate the country into one belief, one doctrine and one party, that a group of men could arrange for themselves and their successors to rule and rule and rule and rule till God almighty comes', (*G*, 6 November 1974). However, despite the vitriolic tone of the attacks, the frequency of attacks from the JLP as a whole was not too great in late 1974 and early 1975, Seaga's initial period as party leader (Table A.3).

From the moment of his assumption of opposition leadership Seaga used the threat of communism as his major ideological weapon against the PNP.

In July 1975, soon after Manley's return from Cuba, he claimed that the PNP had been following 'to the letter' the formula for transforming Jamaica into a socialist state and that 'the time has now come to fully understand and recognize that the country is being firmly placed on the road to Socialism/Communism', (*G*, 30 July 1975). Whereas this line of attack had little effect on the mass public in the short run, as we will show, it did give a focus for fears among certain sectors of the Jamaican elite and thus prepared the ground for all kinds of rumors, such as about impending limitations on freedom of movement. In the second term, the JLP, with the *Gleaner's* help did managed to associate the PNP with a Communist threat in the eyes of a significant portion of the electorate.

Given the general popularity of the fall 1974 economic package, JLP criticism was muted. It showed the usual contradiction between Shearer and Seaga, Shearer calling for an extension of food subsidies to imported foodstuffs and terming the government's measures 'feeble steps' (*G*, 7 August 1974) and Seaga criticizing the government for overspending.

In the second half of 1975, JLP attacks on the government escalated sharply, particularly in the area of economic management. The anti-inflation package of fall 1975 contained a lot more 'stick' than 'carrot' for the private sector and upper income groups. Seaga sought to exploit this discontent, charging that 'the government is using the national crisis to embed socialism into the economic framework' (*G*, 30 August 1975). Later in the year he warned of impending financial chaos due to overspending and overborrowing, accusing the government of 'squandermania', a theme which he continued throughout the PNP's tenure in office (*G*, 12 November 1975).

JLP strategy in this period brought a new characteristic to prominence, namely the use of secret documents leaked from top echelons in the bureaucracy, which were used in Seaga's attacks on the government's economic policies. A big controversy erupted around a broadcast in December 1975 in which Seaga cited such a leaked document, and in the aftermath of which the Permanent Secretary in the Ministry of Mining was relieved of his duties and the Minister of Mining, Allan Isaacs, a PNP conservative, was forced out of his post. However, the leaks and Seaga's use of them continued during his whole time as Opposition Leader without creating repercussions of similar magnitude again. Seaga's critique of the government's economic policy focused consistently – and rightly so – on the impending balance-of-payments crisis, and on the gap between government revenue and spending. His suggestions of remedies, however, generally mentioned only areas where more spending was required, particularly for stimulation of the private sector, and failed to specify areas for major budget cuts.

Another element in JLP strategy was the boycott of by-elections on the grounds of electoral manipulation. In mid-October 1975 the JLP lost two by-elections in which it made heavy, and apparently unsuccessful, use of the anti-communism issue. At the end of October Seaga announced that the JLP would boycott the by-election in East Kingston 'to shock the country into understanding that the electoral process is being abused' (*G*, 28 October 1975). These boycotts have to be seen against the background of the regularity that the party in power wins by-elections in Jamaica. In the case of the East Kingston constituency, it was a seat which had been held by the PNP since universal suffrage was introduced. Under these circumstances a boycott was the most promising course of action to score at least some propaganda points.

The charge of electoral fraud was then linked to other themes such as political manipulation of the Security Forces, plans for takeover of mass media to silence press and radio opposition to the government, violence against JLP supporters and abuse of public funds for partisan purposes, all of which were claimed to constitute a clear pattern indicative of the government's plans to lead the country to socialism/communism (to use Seaga's favorite compound expression). To support the allegation that the PNP government was leading the country to socialism/communism, JLP spokesmen pointed to the friendship with Cuba and insinuated that the agreements on economic and technical collaboration between Cuba and Jamaica had ulterior political motives. The JLP campaign received some unexpected support in early 1976, when former PNP minister Allan Isaacs, after being forced to resign as a result of the leaked documents, charged that unelected PNP party officials (that is, the left) had acquired a greater voice in the government than the MPs and that 'they were committed to the eventual goal of establishing the Cuban model of socialism in Jamaica' (*G*, 22 January 1976). These charges were continuously pressed up to the 1976 elections and resumed in the second half of 1977 under the new label of 'violations of human rights'.

Gleaner

The *Gleaner's* reaction to the declaration of democratic socialism was hostile, as was to be expected from a conservative paper, but not yet propagandist as in later years. The editorials called repeatedly for clarification of the government's conception of socialism and the mixed economy and they criticized the 'change of course in midstream', but there were neither big headlines on the declaration at the Party Conference nor prominent displays of JLP criticisms. The paper even had some positive comments on President Nyerere and it published reviews of Manley's *The Politics of Change*, most of which were positive. However, things began to change at the *Gleaner* in 1975 when Hector Wynter, who had been chairman of the JLP in the late 1960s, was made Executive Editor of the paper, and by mid-1975 the *Gleaner* had been transformed from a simply conservative to a blatantly partisan paper. At that point, the political struggle assumed a new level of intensity.

The change could first be seen in the *Gleaner's* coverage of Manley's trip to Cuba, which featured headlines selecting the most provocative quotes from his speeches, generally insinuating subversive (that is, pro-communist) intentions on his part, and the coverage of Manley's speech in Montego Bay upon his return was even more propagandist, and damaging (to the PNP) in nature. Manley addressed a gathering of PNP supporters and told them about his impressions. The *Daily News* reported that he emphasized the need for hard work, for a society in which people wanted to work to build a nation, and that he pointed out that in such a process 'there was no room for people who were seeking palaces and wanting to become millionaires and invited those with this in mind to note that there were twice daily flights out of Jamaica to Miami', (*DN*, 14 July 1975). The *Gleaner* did not pick up the story until two days later when it ran it under the headline 'No one can become a millionaire here – PM', quoting Manley as saying that 'anyone who wants to become a millionaire in Jamaica my advice to them is to remember that planes depart five times daily to Miami', (*G*, 16 July 1975). Two days later, Manley's letter of protest and clarification was published, pointing out that he had been referring to people being 'motivated by the selfish desire to become a millionaire overnight' and 'refused to regard themselves as part of the Jamaican society and owing an obligation of service like the rest of us'. However, no clarification could neutralize the frightening and lasting effect of the presumed threat contained in the reference to the 'five flights to Miami'.

This incident provides an excellent example to illustrate part of the problem of 'excessive rhetoric' on the part of prominent PNP leaders. The charge of excessive rhetoric was one of those most frequently brought against the PNP, and a brief discussion of it is in order here, given that the rhetorical battle began to heat up considerably in this period. The problem had two dimensions, namely the use made by the opposition of these statements and the terminology chosen by the PNP left. First, interpretations given and importance assigned by the *Gleaner* to statements like the above, which, in their proper context, were not very radical at all, made them into salient issues with frightening and ominous overtones. The 'five flights to Miami', for instance, were mentioned by several of the business-men interviewed in 1982 as an incident which influenced them to turn against the PNP and reduce their level of investment in the country.

Second, the PNP left introduced a terminology which was new to the larger Jamaican political debate. Thus, if 'rhetoric' is taken to mean the way in which something is said, the charge has some validity, but if it is taken to refer to the substance of what is said, the case is much weaker. For instance the document of December 1974 only uses the terms 'capitalism' and 'wealthy minority', but not 'capitalist'. Yet, it would be unrealistic to think that someone with a socialist analysis of society would refrain from using the term 'capitalist' in a debate or speech dealing with the economic and political dimensions of capitalism. However, the private sector in Jamaica, where ideological debate was a novelty, took exception just to the language used by the left, and the PNP moderates objected that this was needlessly costing the government political support. For instance, the head of one of the largest business families told us that the PNP engaged in all kinds of personal abuse, such as calling people capitalists. Aside from the use of some neo-Marxist terminology, it was very difficult to find concrete public statements which reflected a different political agenda for Jamaica from the one of the document, such as full socialization of the economy or abridgements of basic political and human rights, as implied by their opponents. Moreover, two important factors in creating alarm about PNP rhetoric were the tendency of the *Gleaner* to misquote PNP spokesmen, particularly those on the left, and for relatively moderate statements to be grossly exaggerated through rumor. Frequently, the *Gleaner* did print clarifications and corrections, but by the time those were printed (with generally less prominence than the original report) the damage in terms of fears and confusion had been done.

On the economic front, the *Gleaner*, along with the private sector, was highly positive to features of the August 1974 economic package, such as the easing of import restrictions and the lifting of credit ceilings. Both groups welcomed the nature of the economic package and the paper editorially commended the government on its 'moderate reflation package' (*G*, 7 August 1974).

The reaction to the anti-inflation package in the fall, 1975, was exactly the opposite. This was partly because the government had painted far too positive a picture of the economic situation in the early part of the year and the realization of the depth of the economic difficulties caused by the announcement of the package came as a rude shock, but, perhaps more important for the *Gleaner* and the business interests whose opinions it reflected, was the class orientation of the way in which the PNP government proposed to solve the crisis. Essentially, the government proposed to maintain its social programs and make those who were better off pay for them. Thus, the *Gleaner*, echoing Seaga's critique, contended that the policies in the package were more about redistribution and socialism than about fighting inflation (for example, see the editorial, *G*, 29 August 1975).

After the 'five flights' story, the verbal battle between the *Gleaner* and the PNP escalated. Several prominent PNP leaders from both the left and the moderate wing made strong speeches attacking the mass media and the *Gleaner* in particular for misleading the people and for being 'one of the greatest forces of oppression operating against the people of Jamaica', as PNP moderate, Ken McNeil, said in July 1975 (*G*, 28 July 1975). The

Gleaner hit back with warnings about threats to press freedom and signs of impending communism, and with columnists' attacks on the PNP left, playing up internal disunity in the PNP and spreading rumours about left-wing plots to replace the party leader with a more radical figure.

A first climax in this battle was reached in the beginning of 1976 with a front page editorial which departed from the *Gleaner's* prior practice of using editorials and articles for attacks on government policies and statements while leaving personal attacks on PNP leaders to the columnists. This editorial was a personal attack on Manley, calling him the 'most Messianic figure in Jamaican political history' and warning of 'magical powers' which could lead to destruction of a will to freedom among people (*G*, 2 January 1976). It stated that the speed with which change was being pushed forward indicated a belief in a real 'mission' and that to gain revolutionary leadership Parliament had to be primed and a party machine created, and that MPs were being bullied openly by party activists (that is, the left) who were making policy without standing for election. On the one hand, the editorial clearly implied that Manley as a leader presented a potential threat to democracy in Jamaica, but on the other hand it ended with an appeal to him to put things right as he alone had the capacity to do so. This illustrates the somewhat ambivalent position the *Gleaner* still had at that time, in other words, extremely critical and hostile to Manley and the government, but not yet completely bent on destroying their legitimacy, as was to be the case from 1978 on. Also, despite such heavy attacks on the government on political grounds, attacks on economic grounds far outnumbered them in 1975–6; themes like communism, Cuban threat, totalitarian tendencies, etc., contributed about a quarter, the rest focused on mismanagement, overspending etc. (see Table A.3).

The private sector: the crucial turning-point
In this period, all but the most liberal segment of the capitalist class moved from a posture of reluctant accommodation to determined opposition to the PNP government. In this section, we will present evidence showing that this was the crucial turning-point and elucidate the reasons for the turn. As in the previous period, the timing of this turn is crucial in establishing its causes.

The data on capital formation show that capital formation declined sharply in 1976 to wholly inadequate levels and it never recovered during the PNP's two terms in office (Table A.6). It is clear that this drop in investment is not a reaction to the declaration of democratic socialism as it comes too late. However, it could be a reaction to the increasing rhetorical battle and fears of communism caused by Manley's trip to Cuba and the 'five flights to Miami' speech in July 1975. On the other hand, it is at this point in time that it became obvious to everyone that the economy was in severe difficulty; thus it could be a reaction to the general deterioration of the economy; or it could be a reaction to the way in which the government chose to deal with the crisis as represented by the policies contained in the August–October economic package.

The migration figures (Table A.4–5) confirm this pattern. Remembering that one must interpret the US figures with a one-year lag (see p. 98), it is clear that 1976 was a crucial turning point, representing a very large increase in the decision to migrate to the USA on the part of businessmen. Again, this confirms both the contention that the crucial turning-point was in the first term and that the declaration of democratic socialism *per se* was not all that critical, but again, one does not know what weight to give to various events which occurred in late 1975 and early 1976.

In order to get some insight into the reasons for migration, we analyzed the 1974 elite data, examining what attitudinal, social and institutional characteristics of the businessmen covered in the 1974 interviews correlate with subsequent migration behavior.[7] What this analysis revealed, not surprisingly, was that there was a very strong correlation between economic ideology and political attitudes and migration behavior, with the more conservative businessmen being more likely to migrate. In addition, commercial capitalists were more likely to migrate than industrial capitalists, independent of economic ideology and political attitudes. This would appear to indicate that lack of economic opportunity caused by the shortage of foreign exchange and the deteriorating economy contributed significantly to migration of the business elite.

This secondary analysis has its limitations. The sample is only one of important businessmen with control over large holdings and some variables of importance were unmeasured. One cannot say whether the conservative businessmen were reacting to concrete policies of the government or rhetoric of the party leaders. Moreover, the whole question of the rising crime rate (see Table A.7) was left untapped in the interview. There is no doubt that the rising crime rate stimulated migration. This contention, which appeared frequently in our elite interviews in 1982 and in newspaper reports, is confirmed by Holzberg's (1977a) study of entrepreneurial elites in Jamaica based on anthropological field work in 1973 and 1974. Her study also confirms that fear of crime was linked to race, with the whites feeling that they were the target of crime (Holzberg, 1977a:39; also see Holzberg, 1977b). Apparently, women were particularly fearful and it was often the wives of businessmen who strongly encouraged them to leave.[8]

Turning to the 1982 elite data, some unambiguous findings emerge from this data.[9] First, it is clear that the decisive souring of the relationship came in the first term. As we mentioned in the last chapter, the ultra-conservative segment of the class defected in the first two years. Most of the moderate conservatives,[10] who form the bulk of the class, turned against the government and began to invest less in the period under discussion in this chapter. This squares with the data on migration and capital formation. Two groups emerge as having remained with the Manley government in some fashion into the second term. First, the three capitalists who gave the most liberal responses to our economic ideology questions and who were closely associated with the Manley government, account for all but one of the responses indicating a turning-point in the second term. Indeed, two of these three liberal capitalists remained with the PNP until the return of D. K. Duncan as General Secretary in September 1979. Second, the two capitalists who contended that they did not invest less gave patriotic reasons for doing so. In ideological terms, these men were moderate conservatives; and politically, they were never pro-PNP. To this group of 'patriotic capitalists' we could add an additional moderate conservative who claimed that he personally made many investments as did most of the enterprises with which he was closely associated (generally as top director), but that some with which he was peripherally associated did invest less. Two of the liberal capitalists also claimed to have made many personal investments but companies with which they were associated 'hedged their bets', as one of them said.

As to the reasons for their change of attitude and investment behavior, the businessmen who became alienated in this period gave a variety of causes, such as mismanagement, deterioration of the economy, the hostile attitude toward the USA, the Cuba relationship and rhetoric and 'fear for the future'. Very few mentioned specific policies. However, a number of respondents linked 'mismanagement' and the 'deterioration of the economy' to the government's overspending on distributive programs. On the other hand, the decline in the economy was also linked by many of the respondents (sometimes the same ones) to PNP rhetoric and the relationship to Cuba, which they claimed undermined business confidence in the government. Thus, on the basis of these interviews it is not possible to give an unambiguous answer to the question of what caused the turn of this group of businessmen against the government. In a sense, the very fact that it was difficult to disentangle the various factors causing the deterioration of the PNP government's relation to the capitalist class is a finding in itself. The policies, the rhetoric, the Cuba relation and the deteriorating economy were tied together in the minds of many of the business people to whom we talked. In the course of time, each factor fed the other, generating a downward spiral in their total perception of the government. To get a clearer picture of this process, it is necessary to look at the exact sequencing of events in this period.

To aid in this task, we can make use of the more detailed coding of attacks appearing in the *Gleaner* as shown in Table 4.1. The private sector's response to the PNP's ideological self-definition was initially very mild. They were more concerned at the time with the government's insistence that all assets held abroad be declared and subject to repatriation on notification by the exchange control authorities,[11] and with the implications of Finance Minister Coore's statement that the government should become directly involved in banking where the traditional banking system did not prove satisfactory. In October, Vivian Blake, one of the PNP leaders who had excellent relations with the private sector, was made Minister of Commerce and Marketing, which was clearly a reassuring gesture and met with official approval of the JMA. Also, one has to keep in mind that the economy was still visibly benefitting from the injection of funds from the bauxite levy. At any rate, it is clear that the declaration of democratic socialism itself was not a turning-point in the government–private sector relationships.

For the 1975 codings in Table 4.1, we have departed from our usual dividing line between the second and third quarter (July 1) and used Manley's trip to Cuba as the cutting-point in order to assess the immediate reaction to that event. There is little doubt that 1975 was a decisive turning-point in the PNP government's relationship with the private sector and the *Gleaner*. But it does not appear to us that the Cuba trip and 'five flights' speech was the critical juncture that many people came to believe. Let us remind ourselves of the events. After the levy and the fall 1974 expansive budget, the government was riding a popular wave which allowed it to present its democratic socialist posture without taking too much criticism. Business grumbled about socialism but did not attack the government frontally. The economy did not respond to the fall 1974 package and signs of deeper economic trouble began to surface. However, the government spokesmen continued to paint a fairly rosy picture of the economic situation, (for example, see Manley's speech to the JMA on 18 May 1975), but as these difficulties became increasingly apparent, the *Gleaner* increased its attacks on 'mismanagement' between April and mid-July. In the days after Manley's return from Cuba there was a brief heated interchange between the *Gleaner* and PNP spokespeople, but no sustained campaign. It was in the fourth quarter that there was a dramatic increase in attacks on the government. Moreover, the increase was overwhelmingly in the category 'mismanagement'. There is no doubt that these attacks were a response to the government's economic policy package, which was initially announced in late August but was not spelled out in detail until early October. The critiques focused on two things: (i) the government's economic policies (excessive spending and borrowing) which were held responsible for the economic crisis and (ii) the government's solution to the crisis, which was to make the more privileged groups bear the brunt of economic austerity instead of cutting back social programs. The new land policy also attracted very strong criticism from the private sector.

Because there are generally so few private sector criticisms which were strong enough to be coded as an 'attack', we reviewed all private sector statements on the government to get a better reading of the turning-point

122

TABLE 4.1   *Attacks on the PNP government, 1974–6*

Year	Quarter	Mismanagement		Rhetoric, socialism ideology, etc. (categories 2–9 on Table A.3)		Total
1974	1	G	2	$G(2)$	3	5
	2	JLP	4	JLP	6	10
		G		$G(3)$		
		JLP(2)		JLP		
		PS		PS		
				O		
	3		0	$G(7)$	9	9
				PS(2)		
	4	G	1	$G(6)$	9	10
				JLP(3)		
1975	1	$G(2)$	2	G	2	4
				PS		
	2 (to July 13)	$G(4)$	5	$G(4)$	6	10
		PS		JLP		
				PS		
	3 (from July 14)	$G(4)$	5	$G(3)$	5	10
		JLP		JLP		
				PS		
	4	$G(10)$	15	$G(3)$	7	22
		JLP(5)		JLP(2)		
				PS		
				O		
1976	1	$G(4)$	6	$G(6)$	13	18
		JLP(2)		JLP(6)		
				PS		
	2	$G(10)$	17	$G(2)$	8	23
		JLP(7)		JLP(4)		
				PS(2)		
	3	$G(2)$	7	$G(3)$	6	12
		JLP(5)		JLP(3)		
	4	$G(4)$	6	$G(2)$	4	8
		JLP(2)		JLP(2)		

KEY G=Attack by *Gleaner*;
JLP=Attack by JLP spokesman;
PS=Attack by private sector spokesman;
O=Attack from other source
If more than one attack occurs, the number of attacks appears in parenthesis after the author of the attack.

in the private-sector–government relationship. As was previously mentioned, the declaration of democratic socialism resulted in an increase in private sector 'grumblings' about the ideological posture of the government, and the Cuba visit was not a turning-point for criticism on ideological and political grounds (such as, rhetoric, manipulation of the media, criticism of party statements, etc.). There were four critical statements before and four after the visit. However, there was an increase in criticism of economic policy and administration (from four to eight). Again, this appears to confirm our contention that the economic situation and the government's egalitarian policies were the *initial* stimulus to the second turning-point in the government–private-sector relationship. However, it is significant that the eight critical statements on ideological and political grounds in 1975 constitute a sharp increase over previous years.

The situation began to change in 1976. In the first quarter, the level of attacks on the government remained at a fairly high level, but the grounds shifted dramatically. This was caused in part by the JLP's exploitation of the Isaacs resignation (Cuba/communism issue) but also by the *Gleaner's* attacks on PNP rhetoric. There was a shift to the question of economic management in the second quarter of 1976 (partly because of the budget debate), but the attacks on 'rhetoric' continued at the same level. Moreover, criticism of rhetoric and PNP ideological statements became a major private sector theme in this period. In addition to the two attacks on the government appearing in the codings (significantly one by a moderate private sector spokesperson – Carlton Alexander), there were seven strong criticisms from private sector spokespeople between mid-March and mid-July. It is clear that by this point a major section of the capitalist class was completely alienated from the PNP government. This shows up in the major decline in investment in 1976 and thereafter and in major increases in decisions to migrate to the USA, which manifest themselves in the landed migrant figures the next year. It also shows up in capital flight, estimated at some \$300m in 1975–6 (*DN*, 1 February 1977), a sum of money which could have made the difference in whether or not to go to the IMF.

In this climate it is not surprising that the formation of the Private Sector Organization of Jamaica (PSOJ) in mid-1976, an umbrella organization for all private business regardless of sector, was viewed with great suspicion by the left. There were in fact forces that attempted to push the new organization into a militant anti-government position, but with the election of Alexander as its President the PSOJ assumed an ostensibly non-partisan, pro-private-sector, pro-growth position. In a statement released after the formal launching of the PSOJ its members expressed their commitment to work in partnership with the public sector for the national interest (*G*, 1 July 1976).

So, in summary, what generated the second and decisive turn of the capitalist class was dissatisfaction with the economic situation and opposition to the PNP government's egalitarian policies. This was then fueled by antagonism to the ideological posture of the government (its commitment to socialism, friendship with Cuba, hostility to the USA, etc.), which the business community saw as further undermining the economic conditions in the country. Exactly what caused the increasing weight of rhetoric–ideology as an important factor in business alienation is not completely clear. Certainly, part of it was a self-generating vicious cycle with the economy and PNP policy factor feeding ideology–rhetoric and vice versa. A second factor was the sharper ideological profile of the PNP caused by the increasing influence of the left and the social and political mobilization process. A third factor was the changing role of the *Gleaner*. It is clear that the paper chose not to give prominence to JLP Cuba–communist threat charges in the by-elections between September and November 1975, but then chose to do so in the case of JLP Cuba–communist attacks in the first quarter of 1976. The question is: did this represent shifts in the view of the conservative segment of the capitalist class that owns the *Gleaner*? Or was it the result of the increasing influence of Hector Wynter over *Gleaner* policy? A fourth factor was the destabilization campaign which apparently began in early 1976 (see pp. 131–7). The adverse propaganda in the USA damaged tourism. The arson, violence, oiling of roads, etc. certainly increased the climate of fear, and, of course, it increased PNP charges of destabilization and attacks on imperialism and the USA. This in turn fed the fears of businessmen.

Reactions from other social forces

Against the background of the deteriorating relationship between the government and the private sector and the barrage of attacks coming from the JLP and the *Gleaner*, it is important to point out that there were two major social actors, the church and the labor movement, whose position remained basically supportive of the government because of its policies, though with some exceptions and without engaging in distinctively partisan activity. The major role played by the established churches and their representative organization, the Jamaica Council of Churches (JCC) was one of conciliator in partisan political disputes and political violence. In this role, the JCC criticized the behavior of both sides and called on PNP and JLP to refrain from certain actions. However, many spokesmen emphasized the church's stand on the side of the oppressed and the need to correct social injustice; and some explicitly supported the pursuit of a democratic socialist society, though sometimes coupled with a warning to ensure that the methods used to implement it be compatible with Christian ideals (*DN*, 1 and 19 February 1975; *G*, 30 May 1975).

The trade unions' official statements have to be understood in the context of constant and intense trade union rivalry and the BITU's partisan position. As long as the BITU took a highly visible critical stand, none of the other unions could afford to be clearly supportive of the government, lest they be seen as weak or sell-outs. Though a number of government policies clearly strengthened the position of labor, there was very little public praise from the unions. On the contrary, the unions objected strongly to a number of government actions, though only the BITU took a really strident position. For instance, the unions had objected to a number of provisions in the draft legislation on industrial relations, with the result that the clauses in the final form of the LRIDA were changed accordingly (*G*, 20 March 1975). Also, the unions firmly opposed the government's wage guidelines, and again the government yielded by way of exempting fringe benefits from the $10 per week ceiling put on wage increases (*G*, 3 and 30 March 1976). Constant communication and consultation between the government and unions was carried on through the Labour Advisory Council,[12] as well as frequent special meetings between unions and various ministers, including the Prime Minister.

The government began to experience some pressure from the left from two quarters in this period. The left Catholic Social Action Centre had been active on the sugar estates for a number of years and, by this time, had organized a substantial group of activist sugar workers to demand that the government-owned estates be transformed into cooperatives. They succeeded in pressing the government into substantially increasing the pace of its plans for the establishment of the cooperatives and this was accomplished by mid-1975.[13]

The other challenge from the left came from the communist Workers' Liberation League, (WLL) which was launched under the leadership of university lecturer Trevor Munroe in December 1974. Initially, the WLL was critical of the PNP, which it believed was basically a representative of the interests of the national bourgeoisie, a line which it maintained until late 1975. At this point, a number of events came together to convince the WLL to change its analysis and to take a stance of critical support for the PNP government: the turn of a significant segment of the capitalist class against the PNP, Manley's trip to Cuba and the PNP's increasingly anti-imperialist line, the JLP's use of anti-communism under Seaga's leadership, the endorsement of the Conference of Communist and Workers Parties in Havana of the non-capitalist path and Cheddi Jagan's support of Manley. Thereafter, the WLL played a key role in the anti-CIA agitation in 1976 and provided support for the PNP in the 1976 election campaign. This support was not nearly as visible as that provided in the second term, in part because the communist movement had less than half the cadre in the earlier period than in the later and, in part, because the *Gleaner* and the Jamaica Broadcasting Corporation (JBC), for opposite reasons, chose to give the supportive role of the communists greater coverage in the later period.

The government's counter-reaction

The escalation of attacks from the *Gleaner*, the private sector, and the JLP stimulated counter-attacks from the PNP leadership. There is little doubt that one cause of the increase in 'rhetoric' from PNP spokespeople was the number of attacks aimed at them from opposition forces. With the *Gleaner* now taking a clearly partisan, and not merely conservative, posture, the government began to feel its lack of media support more acutely.[14] Consequently, it started to put pressure on the JBC to politicize radio and television programming to serve as a counterweight to the *Gleaner*. In June 1975, the government asked the JBC to 'develop a more positive attitude toward democratic socialism' (*DN*, 12 June 1976). JBC general manager Dwight Whylie resisted on the grounds that the JBC statutes stated that it should have impartial news. Tensions increased between Whylie and the government and pro-PNP JBC journalists over the next year. In June 1976, the JBC board, which is appointed by the government, fired Whylie, on the grounds that they lacked confidence in him, particularly in his ability to carry through workers' participation, given the tensions between him and the staff. As a result, the JBC newsroom became progressively more partisan over the next four years.

In the case of the private sector, there were conciliatory aspects to the PNP's counter-reaction. The government appealed for collaboration and increasing production both through words and actions. The 1975 anti-inflation package had offered incentives such as tax breaks for fuller utilization of capacity and training of workers and expansion of export credit facilities, and in July 1976 the Minister of Industry published a Green Paper outlining plans for the manufacturing sector until 1980 and the role to be played by private enterprise in the realization of these plans. Yet despite these efforts, the private sector as a whole was not inclined to take advantage of these incentives to increase production. Rather, they adopted a 'wait-and-see-and-support-the-JLP' attitude in the hope that the PNP would lose the elections.

The USA turns against Jamaica[15]

Before the bauxite levy, Jamaica was a relatively obscure country as far as US foreign-policy-makers were concerned. This evaluation of the country's international importance was reflected in the staffing of the Embassy in Kingston. Ambassador Sumner Gerard, like his predecessor, was a Nixon political appointee with no previous diplomatic service. As one Carter administration official told us, the embassy staff was:

> an assembly of misfits . . . if someone was medically not in shape and needed to be close to home, they would assign them to Jamaica . . . [A top state department official] told me this. He also said reporting from Jamaica was emphasizing the sex life of key people (in the PNP govern-

ment). We were to stop this, unless it was really important for portraying the situation.

So the quality of political reporting from Jamaica left something to be desired. The situation at the Embassy did not change until the advent of the Carter administration, despite Jamaica's (and Manley's) growing importance in the Third World and despite Kissinger's recognition that Manley's stature as a Third World spokesman made him and Jamaica important.

Along with Manley's Third World leadership it was the bauxite levy that put Jamaica on the map for US policy-makers. As we saw in the last chapter, the US government made no strong move to censure Jamaica on this account. One can only speculate why. It was not an expropriation, which the Treasury Department under William Simon's leadership censured very hard. The timing, right at the peak of the Watergate affair, was also certainly important, as was the climate in the USA; in this period the actions of multinationals were coming under scrutiny in congressional hearings and so on. By late 1974 the issue began to blow over as Kaiser signed a tentative agreement on the lands and ownership with the Jamaican government. A final factor which decreased the likelihood of US reaction was that, once it was clear that the State Department would not act, two of the companies, Reynolds and Alcoa, turned to their congressional allies, such as Senator Orrin Hatch, in an attempt to get Jamaica's aid cut in order to put pressure on the government, but Kaiser did not go along. The US government continued to encourage the Jamaicans to come to an agreement with the companies, but no pressure, in the sense of threats of counteraction, was put on. The USA also continued to be concerned that the IBA might become another OPEC, and thus monitored this situation very closely.

The events of late 1974 and 1975 led to a decisive souring of the relationship between the US and Jamaican governments. The increasing anti-imperialist and anti-American tone of the statements of some PNP leaders bothered the Americans. In this climate, the embassy also felt it was not being provided with enough security, as shown by the stoning incident of early 1976 (described later). They were also concerned about the rise of the PNP left. They regarded the PNP left in general, and Duncan in particular, as Leninists. Throughout the rest of the PNP government's tenure in office, State Department and Embassy analysts seriously entertained various scenarios in which the PNP left might come into control of the party, dispense with Manley, and, with Cuban help, move Jamaica toward a one-party state.

It was the close relationship with Cuba that disturbed the USA the most. In the US view the Cuban motives could not be honorable, thus, all the exchange programs, and particularly anything with a security aspect to it, were perceived as being, in all probability, part of a Cuban design to facilitate the type of scenario just mentioned, should it become possible. The US administration was also concerned about the diplomatic support which the Manley government gave to Cuba on various issues in international forums and its support for Cuba's admission as a member in good standing of the hemispheric community.

Manley (1982: 115–17) believes it was Jamaica's position on the question of Cuban troops in Angola which was the decisive turning-point in the Ford–Kissinger administration's attitude toward his government. The State Department officials we interviewed denied that this single event was that crucial, arguing rather that it was the whole Jamaica–Cuba relationship, of which the Angola stance was one piece, which resulted in US hostility toward Jamaica. Whatever the case, as we shall see, the US hostility led to actions to undermine the Manley government and help its opponents in the form of reduced aid, negative reports damaging to tourism, and, in all probability, covert funding of the opposition.

The crisis of 1976

Economic crisis

The crucial economic developments in 1975 and 1976 were a severe deterioration of the balance-of-payments situation and negative growth in real GDP (Tables A.8–10). The main reasons for the growing balance-of-payments deficit were the shortfall in receipts from tourism and the increase in net investment income payments abroad. Also, the value of bauxite exports declined in 1975 and remained below the 1974 level in 1976, and sugar export receipts declined sharply in 1976 because of a fall in world market prices. Tourism showed a moderate decline in 1975 and a dramatic one in 1976 (Table A.19). This had a detrimental effect on both hotel room occupancy rates and tourist expenditure in Jamaica. Many hotels got into financial difficulties, and since they had been built with government-guaranteed loans, the government was virtually forced to acquire them. By mid-1976, the government had thus come to own or control about 3300 hotel rooms, that is about half of the total rooms in the industry (*G*, 1 July 1976). A closer examination of figures on stop-over visitors reveals an interesting pattern. The decline is almost completely due to a lower number of visitors from the USA whereas the number of visitors from Canada and Europe even increased slightly. Since US visitors accounted for roughly 75 per cent of the total, the decline in demand for Jamaica on the US travel market hurt the Jamaican tourist industry badly. The concentration of the decline among US tourists shows clearly the effect of the adverse campaign concerning violence, political instability and presumed Cuban influence in Jamaica which was carried on by the US press (see pp. 135–6).

Returning to the causes for the deterioration of the balance of payments in 1975 and 1976, we have to add the legal (and illegal) private capital movements to the picture. Capital flight, together with the shortfalls in foreign exchange earnings and the increase in foreign investment income repatriated abroad, exerted considerable pressure on the balance of payments (Table A.8). Thus, despite the high level of foreign borrowing, Jamaica's foreign exchange reserves declined to −J$74m in 1975 and −J$238m in 1976 (Girvan *et al.*, 1980:138).

The deterioration in the situation of Jamaica's external transactions was accompanied by a negative trend in GDP growth, mainly because of a decline of activity in mining, construction and the distributive trade (Tables A.9 and A.10). The decline in the mining sector resulted from the decline in world demand for bauxite and alumina in 1975, the development of production in other countries by the multinational companies in the course of the ongoing restructuring of the world aluminum industry, and the problems with labor unrest and equipment damage at alumina plants in Jamaica in 1976 (see Stephens and Stephens 1985). The decline in the construction industry was a result of the very low level of investment in new plants and equipment, which in turn was caused by the lack of business confidence. These same reasons along with difficulties in the importation of raw materials and the disruptions in production resulting from the violence in 1976 accounted for the declining performance of the manufacturing sector. The dramatic decline in distributive trade in 1976 also has to be attributed to the foreign exchange problems on the one hand and the election year disruptions on the other.

Despite the negative trends in the economy as a whole, people's living standards were not really negatively affected up to the summer of 1976, with the exception of say, 8 per cent of the population in the high income group.[16] Real median weekly incomes of income-earners in the labor force kept increasing every year up to and including 1976 (Table 15 in Girvan *et al.*, 1980). Small farmers were benefitting from the increased demand for local foodstuffs caused by import restrictions as well as from various programs in support of agricultural development. The high income group, of course, felt particularly hurt by import restrictions, higher taxes, and the limitations on foreign exchange available for travel. Though there were many ways which people in this group found to get around such restrictions, these problems were experienced as a severe nuisance at best and an act of class warfare at worst. Thus, the economic basis was given for the process of class polarization and realignment which manifested itself in the 1976 elections.

At the turn of the year, prospects for 1976 looked rather gloomy. In early February Manley warned that tough sacrifices were ahead and that the government would have to make some hard decisions but that it would ensure that the poor would not suffer any more hardship. In this situation, all kinds of rumors were circulating which prompted Coore firmly to reject speculation about any impending devaluation or 'freezing' of personal savings (*G*, 24 February 1976). In a broadcast to the nation, Manley predicted a shortfall of $120m in earnings from bauxite and sugar alone, which would force the government to impose further import restrictions and to review both the expenditure and revenue side of the budget, with emphasis on the revenue side. Taxation was to be the key, as the government was determined to generate new revenue to make up for the shortfall in order to 'go ahead with other programs which for the first time since Independence have started to address the problem of inequality' (*G*, 26 February 1976). On the next day, Coore outlined the new tax program with increases on liquor, cigarettes, beer; a 10 per cent increase on incomes above $10 000 per year; a property tax increase of 2.5 per cent; an increase of consumption duty on capital goods of 15 per cent, on consumer goods of 10 per cent, on pleasure boats of 25 per cent and on jewellery of 50 per cent. These taxes were to bring in an additional $81.25m in revenue. Also, new wage guidelines were announced, as was a reduction in business travel allowances (*G*, 27 February 1976). Coore criticized particularly the 'illegal activities of epidemic proportions' which prevented a large proportion of foreign exchange earnings from tourism from reaching the Bank of Jamaica, and the abuse of business travel allowances for pleasure trips, which resulted in Jamaicans spending $43m for foreign travel.

Some savings were effected in the budgets of the Ministries of Education, Youth and Community Development, and Health, by way of restructuring certain programs and rephasing construction plans. Notably the National Youth Service was cut from two years to one and the number of new students accepted was drastically reduced because of financial and administrative difficulties. However, the allocations for the Special Employment Program were maintained, though with the promise that changes in the projects were to be effected.

In July, a new round of measures was announced to deal with the dual problem of balance-of-payments pressures and economic stagnation. Imports for the rest of the year were drastically curtailed, particularly in the consumer goods category. Penalties for the illegal export of currency were stiffened to confiscation of the funds and fines up to three times the value of the funds involved and/or up to six months in prison. Production was to be stimulated by public sector construction of small business complexes, new allocations to agriculture for project Land Lease and a $10m credit for the private manufacturing sector. Finally, stricter controls over the allocation and use of travel funds were imposed to counter the many types of fraudulent schemes in operation.

However, none of these measures made any decisive impact on the negative trends. A *Gleaner* editorial in September described the situation rather well as one in which the private sector was not responding at all to the government's appeals and incentives. Many businessmen had left and taken their money out, whereas others who had decided to stay were doing as little as possible to provide production and employment in order to embarrass the government and to make it lose the next election (*G*, 15 September 1976). As a result of declining economic activity, of course, the tax revenues remained below target. Thus, budgetary restraint would have been of utmost importance. In fact, the budget presented in April showed a very modest nominal increase over the final 1975–6 levels, which meant an actual decrease in real terms. However, as one of its last acts before being dissolved in November, Parliament passed the First Supplementary Estimates which amounted to an increase in $83.6m, largely attributed by Coore to salary increases in the public sector and spending on the SEP (*G*, 10 November 1976).

In order to cover the ever-growing budget deficit, the government intensified its borrowing efforts. Externally, important loans were raised from Caricom countries ($70m) and from Canada ($32m in loans and a $59m line of credit). Also, Jamaica received a $14m IMF loan under the Compensatory Financing Facility. Internally, the government relied on transfers from the Capital Development Fund and – to the largest extent – on 'accommodations' from the Bank of Jamaica (in other words, printing money). Along with the July economic package, the House had passed a bill which raised the ceiling on advances to the government from the Bank of Jamaica from 15 to 30 per cent of the estimated revenues and also on the proportion of the public debt which could be held by the Bank of Jamaica. Ultimately, the Bank of Jamaica was called upon to cover $271.5m of the $558.1m deficit in the 1976 budget (see Table A.2).

By late 1976, the balance-of-payments situation had reached such alarming proportions that Coore had entered into secret negotiations with the IMF during a meeting in Manila. The negotiations were secret insofar as most of his Cabinet colleagues were unaware of these contacts. In contrast to the PNP leadership, Seaga had obviously managed to get some information about these negotiations as he predicted in a radio campaign broadcast in December that a PNP election victory would mean an immediate 40 per cent devaluation. The 40 per cent was indeed the figure which had been suggested by the IMF and became the subject of much controversy in the negotiations of the 1977 agreement.

Rising violence and destabilization
Early in 1976, a new phenomenon assumed prominence on the political scene, namely political violence accompanied by a series of unexplained violent events which could only be interpreted as part of a campaign of destabilization. Obviously, political violence was by no means new to Jamaica, as pointed out in earlier chapters. In fact, all through 1975 gang warfare with political overtones had been plaguing the Kingston ghetto and

the government had initiated joint police–military actions and imposed periodic curfews in an effort to contain them. What was new in early 1976 was a type of violence which was neither of the gang warfare nor partisan terrorization nor ordinary criminal variety, but rather destructive acts without an apparent motive.

In January of 1976 political gang warfare in West Kingston flared up to new intensity; there were several fires in the Rema area, and when fire trucks tried to get to these fires they were attacked with stones and bottles and burning tires on the road. In April, violence among rival political gangs spread to Central Kingston, and by November political violence had spread well beyond the ghetto areas to affect campaign activities all over the island.

The new and strange type of violent incident started in the aftermath of a demonstration against the presence of a South African representative at an IMF meeting taking place in Kingston in early January 1976. In this demonstration, the PNPYO as well as some junior ministers figured prominently, the latter with permission from the government (Manley, 1982:136), though it was the government that had lifted the ban to enable the South African to participate in the meeting. After the demonstration, the US consulate was stoned which resulted in damage being done to the building. Consequently, the decision was taken to put two policemen on duty as guards at the consulate. One day later, the two policemen were shot, one of them fatally. During the same few days, several other police-men were shot, which led to strong protests from their colleagues. In May, armed men set fire to a block of tenement buildings on Orange Street in Kingston, kept the residents from leaving the burning buildings and attacked the police and the fire-fighters who were trying to reach the scene. In this attack, ten people lost their lives and some 500 their shelter and belongings. Partisan gang warfare seems to be an unlikely explanation for this event, since an examination of the 1974 returns to the appropriate polling stations showed that the residents had voted in virtually equal numbers for the two parties (*G*, 22 May 1976), and an inquiry into the reasons and perpetrators of this crime conducted by the Chief Justice could not find any links to either of the political parties (*G*, 17 February 1977). Thus, it did not fit into the known pattern of partisan political violence. A further incident in this vein was the killing of the Peruvian ambassador in early June. Yet another incident which indicated that forces were at work capable of carefully planning coordinated destructive acts was the oiling of dangerous (that is, steep) stretches of roads in three different areas on the day when a PNP rally was to be held in Montego Bay at night (*DN*, 12 November 1976).

In this whole wave of violence, the security forces obviously had a very dangerous and difficult role to play. However, pressures on them were not confined to those inherent in fighting crime and violence in the society, but were being aimed at them directly. Besides policemen being shot on guard duty, several police stations were attacked with high-powered weapons, and there were several incidents where police and military personnel got into physical fights with one another. There were indications that there was more to these incidents than simple corporate rivalry; in May, the Commissioner of Police charged that there was a calculated plot to demoralize the police force (*G*, 28 May 1976) and in November the Minister of National Security, Keble Munn stated that the security forces had information about a plan to divide the police and the military (*G*, 21 November 1976). Taken together, these strange events convinced the PNP government that the 1976 violence was, in Munn's words, 'a deliberate, organized attempt to destabilize, undermine and bring down the government' (*G*, 7 December 1976).

The government tried to get control over the situation by supporting intensified operations by the security forces, by seeking to institute preventive measures, and by urging citizens to collaborate fully with the security forces. In a speech to a constituency meeting in January, Manley called on PNP supporters to form their own unarmed defense groups to protect PNP meetings and offices. However, this call caused a highly publicized storm of protest from various quarters, including the JCC, and there was no official follow-up on the part of the PNP. In February, the government set up an Advisory Council on National Security, chaired by the head of the Bar Association, to advise and collaborate with a cabinet subcommittee and the heads of the security forces in the fight against violence. In May, a joint police–military command was set up to be in charge of all crime- and violence-fighting operations, including a joint intelligence organization. In the same month, a restructuring and recruitment drive of the Home Guard was started. The recruitment and training drive did have some success, as the total Home Guard membership increased to 1984 by December 1976 (NPA, 1977:365) from 1574 in May (*G*, 11 May 1976). The PNP called on political leaders to participate in the Home Guard, with Manley and Munn, the Minister of National Security, setting an example, but Seaga rejected the idea and no member of the opposition signed up. Finally, in June 1976, the government asked the Governor-General to declare a State of Emergency which gave the security forces powers of arrest and detention for all persons whose activities were deemed likely to endanger public safety.

The declaration of the State of Emergency received virtually universal support in the society, with the notable exception of the JLP.[17] Seaga argued that the powers of arrest and detention already existed under the Suppression of Crimes Act and that the State of Emergency entailed a withdrawal of the right to trial and enabled the government to do almost anything it would want; and soon after their arrest he started calling those detainees with a JLP affiliation 'political prisoners'. The Prime Minister explained that the State of Emergency had become a necessity because 'recent wanton and ruthless activities' had had 'the effect of not only creating fear throughout the country' but also had been 'slowly bringing the economy to a halt' (*DN*, 20 June 1976). He said that the security forces had warned of a new wave of violence planned to coincide with Carifesta at the end of June and into July, and that the declaration had been moved up several days because of developments including the 'strange and sinister case' of a man who told the security forces he had been forced to make allegations against a number of people associated with the government (*G*, 23 June 1976).[18]

As we have just mentioned, the government believed that the events of 1976 were part of a plan to destabilize the country. Manley (1982:140) himself believes that the US government unleashed CIA directed covert action of the type that occurred in Chile, an opinion which is shared by much of the PNP leadership. The pattern of circumstantial evidence certainly suggests this. So does the timing of the events. Manley discussed Jamaica's stand on the Angola situation with Kissinger in December 1975, in a meeting in which Kissinger also raised the possibility of a significant aid increase (the apparent carrot in the package). The Jamaicans stood fast on the question. No aid increase was forthcoming, of course. The next month seven new staff members were added to American Embassy personnel and the string of events described earlier began.

Initially, we believed that the allegations of CIA involvement were probably true (for example, see Stephens and Stephens, 1983b:407–8), but we did take pains to investigate it in the course of our interviews with State Department and Foreign Service officials. The results of this investigation raised serious questions as to whether the CIA was conducting a covert action operation in Jamaica in 1976. According to the law, such an operation would have had to have been approved by the National Security Council (NSC). Four different Carter Administration officials, most of whom were hostile to Kissinger's Latin American policy and expected the worst about the Jamaican case, volunteered to us that they had checked the NSC notes which indicated no CIA operation in the country.[19] Furthermore, a leading investigative journalist with contacts inside the intelligence establishment also carried out parallel research on this question and came to the same conclusion: it is unlikely that there was any CIA-directed covert action operation in Jamaica.

However, one note of caution should be inserted here. As Hersh (1983:264) points out, Nixon and Kissinger were known to have by-passed the 40 Committee, which was theoretically responsible for approving all sensitive covert operations by the CIA. It is at least possible that this also occurred in the case of the NSC. Thus, our evidence is not conclusive.

Even if no covert action of the Chilean variety was carried out, this does not mean that the USA bears no responsibility for the developments of

1976. The USA did reduce aid to Jamaica in 1975 and 1976 (Table A.20), a timing which suggests that this was a reaction to more general features of the PNP government's policy, such as the bauxite policy, the socialist orientation, Third World advocacy, and the Cuba relationship, rather than specifically the Angola stance.[20]

Another overt action of the US government in this period was the negative picture of Jamaica which it was disseminating to individuals and the press in North America. The alarmist articles, columns and letters in the *Gleaner* had their counterpart in a series of extremely critical articles in the US and Canadian press. Some of these articles contained outright lies, in particular about Cuban influence in Jamaica. On 17 March, James Reston wrote an article in the *New York Times* claiming that 'according to high officials of the Ford Administration' Jamaican security forces were being trained in Cuba. The Minister of National Security, Munn denied the report, stating that a total of two members of the security forces were being trained in Cuba, as compared with 129 in the UK, seventeen in Canada, and several others elsewhere (*G*, 18 March 1976). In April, the *Christian Science Monitor*, the *New York Times* and *Newsweek* all ran articles raising concern about the Jamaica–Cuba connection and the future of democracy in Jamaica. Similar themes appeared in articles in the *Wall Street Journal*, and the *Washington Post* and several Canadian newspapers. These articles, particularly those highlighting the violence taking place in Jamaica, had a highly detrimental effect on potential foreign visitors and thus on Jamaica's earnings from tourism. The *Gleaner* gave wide exposure to these effects through headlines and articles such as 'tourism hit by reports on violence; Canadian/US visitors cancelling their bookings because of adverse publicity in the foreign press' (*G*, 15 January 1976).

Much of the negative propaganda about Jamaica was coming from right-wing sources in the USA unconnected to the State Department, but many of the very reputable US newspapers and magazines, such as those just mentioned, cited 'high administration' or 'State Department' sources. Many of the falsehoods, such as the Cuban threat and dangers to democracy, were actually believed by significant elements in the State Department, but this did not make them any less damaging to the Jamaican economy in general and the tourist industry in particular. In addition, some information such as the exaggerated accounts of the security forces being trained in Cuba was known by the US government to be untrue, yet these reports continued to appear.

The question of whether State Department reports on violence in Jamaica were fair or unfair is tricky. We asked people in the State Department in this period about this and they responded that, yes, they told potential tourists and travel agents that it was dangerous in Jamaica, because, they contended, it was true. As we know, crime in Jamaica was increasing, but it can easily be shown that the US action was not the apolitical act that these officials pretended (and maybe even have believed) it was. First, it is a fact that the crime rates were lower in 1976 than in 1981 and 1982 (Table A.7) and, in the latter period, the State Department was positively encouraging people to 'come back to Jamaica', as it was now safe for tourists. Second, the crime rate in tourist parishes is only about half that of Jamaica as a whole, or about equal to that in the USA for the calendar year 1975.[21]

Finally, we believe, based on our interviews, that the USA attempted to influence events in Jamaica in 1976 by funding the opposition. We have no hard evidence on this, but it is very telling that not a single State Department/Foreign Service official we interviewed denied that this was done even when directly asked about it. The responses were that they had no knowledge of it or could not remember, with a number adding that 'it could have happened'. Clearly, some of the people we talked to would have known if this had happened. This is admittedly the only evidence we have, but one would certainly have expected a denial as a matter of procedure. In addition, the journalist mentioned earlier who also investigated the covert action allegations, came to the same conclusion as he believed that 'they washed some money in'.[22]

Questioning US responsibility for any direct involvement in the acts of violence and other 'dirty tricks' (such as the oiling of the roads) of 1976 begs the question of who was behind these events. Unfortunately, this will probably remain unknown forever and thus one can only engage in educated speculation. The truth is probably that these events were not part of one single plan and that no one group was behind all of them. Some of them were simply a result of the climate of fear created by the JLP and the *Gleaner* by their incessant communist-smear campaign, but there is evidence which suggests that two groups might well have been involved in planning a campaign aimed at destabilizing the country.

The first candidates are elements of the JLP. It is not our suggestion that the party as a whole was involved, but rather that certain leaders and activists who had a long history of association with gunmen may have escalated the tried and true tactics of earlier years. Evidence for this allegation is provided by the contents of a briefcase confiscated by the police in 1976. It belonged to Peter Whittingham, a JLP candidate for the election and former JDF officer, one of the first people to be detained in the State of Emergency. According to the Prime Minister's statement to the House, the briefcase contained three handwritten documents, positively identified as Whittingham's handwriting, with information about weapons, supplies and trained and ideologically indoctrinated supporters and with anti-communist and anti-government propaganda. These documents very clearly pointed to a plot for armed terrorist activities against the government, as they contained a pledge 'to take up arms against the communist regime and purge them from our shores' (*DN*, 30 June 1976).

The second candidates are the Cuban exile groups based in Miami. It is known that they were active in Jamaica. In March 1974, the Cuban National Liberation Front bombed the Cuban mission in Jamaica (*G*, 27 March 1974) and later that year, a bomb blew up on the lawn of the Cuban Embassy (*G*, 7 August 1974). In July 1976, a bomb exploded in a suitcase being loaded on a plane to Cuba at the Kingston airport and an anti-Castro group in Miami claimed responsibility (*G*, 13 July 1976). In November of that year a Cuban plane on the way to Jamaica was bombed and all seventy-eight passengers on board were killed. Again, an anti-Castro group claimed responsibility for the act (*G*, 7 October 1976). These acts were all directed at Cuban targets, but, given the good relations between Cuban exiles and right wing Jamaicans in Miami, as well as the fanatic anti-communism of the Cubans, action against the PNP government does not seem unlikely.

The 1976 elections

The 1976 campaign
The PNP's term expired at the end of February 1977; but by fall 1976, it was apparent that the PNP would call elections for sometime in late 1976. On 22 November the election date was set for 15 December and Nomination Day, the formal opening of the campaign, for 29 November.

The JLP had been campaigning for almost two years. Seaga had announced the launching of the JLP campaign in January 1975 and in September 1975 he had predicted elections within six months (*G*, 29 September 1975). The selection of fifty-three JLP candidates had already been completed in June 1976 and the JLP was holding mass meetings in different parts of the island to present their candidates. In August, the JLP refused to participate in two parish council by-elections on the grounds that what the country really wanted was general elections.

The PNP, on the other hand, had not really started to set its campaign machinery in motion. In September, the party's attention was focused on the 38th Annual Conference, at which the candidates were to be presented. The final day of this conference saw the largest attendance at any public session in the party's history. The crowd was so large that the conference had to be moved to the National Stadium. There, Manley gave one of the most brilliant and charismatic speeches of his career. Manley explained to the crowd that the 'clique' had embarked on four distinct lines of action to turn back the development of democratic socialism. He defined the 'clique' as the controllers of capital who resisted change, including those who ran away, and contrasted them with the honest businessmen who were willing to produce and whose assistance the government welcomed. The 'clique', he argued, had taken full possession of the JLP and let loose upon Jamaica the most vicious propaganda Jamaica had ever seen; and the strategy of the 'clique' involved the use of guns and violence as well as economic sabotage, to force the government to turn back, to throw impact workers out of work, put an end to a number of social programs and to stop supporting Angola. The key themes that Manley emphasized as reaction to the 'clique' were 'We are not for sale', and 'We know where we are going' (*G*, 20 September 1976).[23] These phrases set the tone for the campaign.

A poll conducted in the last week of October showed that the JLP had managed to pick up some support in its campaign and that consequently the PNP's lead had narrowed from 8 per cent in August to 2 per cent, with 36 per cent PNP to 34 per cent JLP and 30 per cent still undecided (Table A.15). In November the PNP campaign got into full swing and was able to increase the PNP's lead to 11 per cent (48 per cent to 37 per cent) within one month. In this campaign, the PNP benefitted greatly from the mass party building efforts pursued in the preceding years. Party groups and the YO supplied cadres to plan and execute campaign activities all over the island. The PNP relied heavily on public meetings to get its message across, and participation at such meetings was promoted through the party's grass-roots organization network. The rally in Montego Bay where Manley announced the date of the election attracted a crowd estimated at between 100 000 and 150 000 (Stone, 1980:165; Manley, 1982:145). Through such meetings and the party channels, the party's message could be communicated in face-to-face contact, which made it possible for the PNP to counter the JLP's financial superiority and its resulting massive media advertising campaign between Nomination Day and the elections. The number of full page advertisements by the JLP in the *Gleaner* from 29 November to 15 December amounted to fifty-nine, as compared with the PNP's thirty-five.[24] In the *Daily News*, the balance in advertising was reversed with a total of thirty-four full page JLP advertisements, and fifty-four full page PNP advertisements. However, one has to keep in mind the *Gleaner's* special position and its circulation combined with the afternoon *Star* of some 154 000 as compared with the *Daily News* with 30 000 in 1976 (Brown, 1977:203).[25]

On the electronic media, both parties were given equal slots of free TV time to present their programs and candidates, and in addition to this they made frequent paid broadcasts on the radio. By virtue of being the government, the PNP clearly got more exposure on the electronic media than they paid for and got as free time on an equal basis with the JLP. This, then, was a second factor which helped the PNP to compensate for the financial superiority of the JLP campaign.

The JLP campaign focused on two general areas, the Cuban – Communist threat and popular discontent resulting from long-standing social and economic problems which the government had failed to resolve, such as unemployment, the bad state of rural roads, etc. On the Cuba/communism issue Seaga made a broadcast listing ten points as proof of a PNP drift towards Cuba and towards an imposition of Communism on Jamaica (*G*, 27 November 1976) and this theme was emphasized in many JLP speeches. Further charges pressed by the JLP campaign were victimization, mismanagement and waste of money by the government, misuse of public funds for PNP partisan activities, and plans for bogus voting. The JLP attempted to use the issue of violence against JLP followers to mobilize support (for example, see, *G* 11 December 1976).

In terms of an alternative political program, the JLP offered 'nationalism' as its ideology and restoration of business confidence as its first priority.[26] At the JLP Annual Conference in December 1975 Seaga had introduced the JLP's new philosophy of nationalism as basis for a program of national reform which would balance the rights of government with the rights of the people (*G*, 1 December 1975). At that time, he had also proclaimed that the two parties were pursuing the same ends, but that the JLP was pursuing a strategy of equalization by lifting up and the PNP by pulling down (*DN*, 3 December 1975). The 1976 campaign sounded the same general themes of nationalism and restoration of business confidence. Further, the JLP would immediately stimulate new demand for production, motivation, new investment and consequently new employment; in short, it would get the country out of the PNP-inspired slump. The election manifesto also held that a fundamental principle of nationalism was the Jamaicanization of ownership and control of all assets; concretely, a minimum local participation of 51 per cent in all enterprises, which was to be achieved by working out a realistic timetable for the transfer of ownership, carefully tailored to avoid counterproductive disruptions. The manifesto listed several areas where the JLP would bring improvements, but the discussion of these areas consisted mainly of critiques of PNP policies without many concrete alternative policy outlines. One of the concrete changes suggested by the Manifesto concerned Project Land Lease, where the JLP suggested that the land should be sold instead of leased to farmers; and another one called for a reduction of land taxes and for subsidies to small farmers. In the area of foreign policy the manifesto urged that the government should not develop a fanatic friendship with a country that locked Jamaicans into organizing their country along the political lines of this other country, and the manifesto promised the establishment of a Ministry of National Justice to protect human rights and freedoms from any abuses, including abuses by the police. However the JLP chose not to campaign on what it would do but rather ran mainly on 'anti-' themes, that is, on criticizing the PNP for not solving Jamaica's many economic and social problems and for bringing the country closer and closer to Cuba and communism.

The PNP campaign was mainly based on stressing the achievements of the first term, promising to proceed along the path of structural reforms towards greater economic independence and social equality in the framework of parliamentary democracy in the next term. The PNP manifesto listed achievements in education, health, youth programs, housing, minimum wage, labor legislation, status of women, agriculture, bauxite and foreign relations, but it also outlined economic constraints and therefore the necessity to continue import restrictions as well as wages, salaries, fees and profit restraint in all areas of the economy. The manifesto also reaffirmed the commitment to a mixed economy and to the provision of employment through the public sector, accepting the criticism that some of this work was nonproductive and promising that new proposals would be implemented to obtain more value for the money spent. Finally, the manifesto announced that a program of constitutional reform with wide popular discussion and participation would be carried out.

The PNP advertisements in the newspapers also focused mainly on the achievements listed in the manifesto, and they ended with the slogans 'Forward with Democratic Socialism' or 'Forward Together'. In terms of straight campaign attacks, some PNP advertisements warned of JLP intentions to 'free up' (alluding to the JLP slogan) bauxite for foreign exploitation, prices for big profits, land for land barons, and others warned the voters of the 'Big Lie' which the JLP would introduce into the campaign to scare the voters, like they had done in 1962 with the claim that a Russian ship was coming to Jamaica to support the PNP. The PNP answer to the JLP charges of violence against their supporters was an advertisement which asked the question: 'Who stands to gain from violence? The Government or those who seek to bring it down?' and listed a series of unexplained violent incidents, such as fires, oil on the roads, the shooting of Bob Marley on the eve of a free concert, the false rumors abroad, etc.[27] In their speeches, PNP leaders frequently pointed to the economic sabotage and political destabilization efforts by internal and external opposition forces. They held these forces responsible for a large part of Jamaica's economic problems and asked the people for support in the government's stand against these pressures. As part of the PNP's uncompromising stand, they emphasized the continued friendship with Cuba as a matter of principle regarding Jamaica's sovereignty and firmly refuted the allegations that this friendship posed a threat to democracy in Jamaica.

The whole campaign, of course, took place under the State of Emergency. At first there were no restrictions on any campaign activities, but after some violent incidents had occurred the security forces imposed bans on a phased basis. On 9 December all marches and motorcades were banned in Kingston and the next day throughout the island; and on the day before the election all public meetings were banned. During the whole State of Emergency the media had been operating under a regulation which prohibited any reports or statements prejudicial to public safety.[28] However, there were no cases in which the media were either censored or sanctioned for breach of this regulation. Thus, one can say that the State of Emergency did not significantly impede normal political activity before and during the actual election campaign. On the contrary, if the level of violence had been left unrestrained, political activity would certainly have been more hampered, which means that the State of Emergency helped rather than hindered the normal course of the campaign and the election.

The pattern of the vote

The most important aspect of the pattern of the vote was the change in the social base of the two parties between 1972 and 1976. The PNP lost heavily among its traditional middle-class base and gained among manual wage labor, farm labor and unemployed (Table A.21).[29] The PNP losses were most dramatic among the business, professional and managerial strata and somewhat less so among white-collar workers. Such losses had to be expected on the basis of the PNP's commitment and policies of equalization and social inclusion, as those upper middle- and middle-class people saw their traditional privileges threatened. The PNP made the biggest gains among skilled and semi-skilled wage labor, much of which has to be attributed to the government's legislation strengthening the position of labor. The government's general pro-labor position and specific policies such as the minimum wage and the employment programs probably also contributed to the gain among unskilled labor and the unemployed, along with the youth vote, and the growth of PNP support among farm labor, despite the traditional strength of the JLP in many rural areas, must also be attributed to the constant emphasis on the rights of the underprivileged in the society and its concrete manifestation in policies such as the inclusion of agricultural workers under the national minimum wage, which had caused strong protests from employers of farm labor, and the establishment of the sugar cooperatives. Among small peasants, in contrast, the PNP's support declined slightly, despite benefits accruing to this group from restrictions of food imports and from the variety of agricultural support programs such as Land Lease and credit facilities. Three factors can be mentioned to explain the continued minority support for the PNP among this class. First, the traditional allegiance of large sectors of this class to the JLP, the party with the image of champion of the interests of the small black man in contrast to the traditional PNP image as party of the educated brown middle class. Second, the relatively low knowledge about government support programs for agriculture. For instance, 43 per cent of people in rural villages had no knowledge of Project Land Lease (Stone, 1980:173). (Among those who knew, however, 96 per cent were in favor and only 4 per cent against it.) Third, the PNP suffered from the lack of a significant youth vote among small farmers.

The youth vote was important in the 1976 election because the electorate had expanded from 605 000 in 1972 to 872 000 in 1976 because of the lowering of the voting age to 18 and the inclusion of the voters who had been disenfranchised in 1972 because of the outdated voters lists. According to Stone (1980:168) the PNP enjoyed a two-to-one lead over the JLP in the group of voters under 30 years of age. The reasons for this have to be sought in the cultural inclusion process, the elevation of Afro-Jamaican culture and values to first class status, and along with it the psychological elevation of the lower class black Jamaican to first class citizenship (see p. 83). As one would expect from any such change, what was a very important positive contribution for those lower on the social ladder was a considerable threat to those higher up and contributed to their disaffection from the PNP. In particular, critics complained about unkempt appearance, and indiscipline resulting from a legitimation of cultural aspects of Rastafari and about the heightened feeling of self-worth among the lower classes. One of the ways in which opponents of these changes described them to us in 1982 was that they had generated a freeness mentality and aggressiveness among the lower classes, expressed in slogans such as 'is I time now'. Whereas these changes deeply threatened members of the middle and upper classes and probably even some of the older members in the lower classes, the youth, especially from the lower classes, welcomed this social inclusion process and aggressively asserted the new cultural identity and social rights, and for the most part, they associated these changes with the PNP. Since young people are overrepresented among the unemployed and unskilled, this certainly contributed to the increase of PNP support among this group, and since young people are underrepresented among small farmers because of their reluctance to go into small scale agriculture, the youth vote was not able to increase PNP support among this group nor even to hold it steady.

Whereas the distribution of the popular vote changed by less than 1 per cent, the PNP increased its seat majority from one of 36:17 seats to one of 47:13 seats. Stone (1980:168) explains this by a combination of three factors, the single member district/ simple majority system, constituency boundary changes, and a more even spread of the vote for both parties. He attributes the loss of two seats by the JLP to the boundary changes, and he also claims that it 'seems to be the case that illegal voting and registration manipulation by the PNP won at least two or three seats for the PNP that would probably have been won by the JLP candidates in rural parishes'. The more even geographical distribution of party strength was partly caused by the large influx of young voters and the disproportionate PNP support among this group which eroded some of the JLP strength in areas where the party had done well traditionally. Stone (1981b:1) also has pointed to a 'trend (evident since the PNP election victory in 1972) whereby the country has been moving more and more towards greater uniformity in regional and parish vote patterns', which in a single-member district system is bound to enhance the seat majority of the party that wins the popular vote. This is indicative of a growing strength of civil society in Jamaica in this period.

An analysis of the effect of the campaign issues on electoral decisions shows that the PNP did benefit from its emphasis on the variety of government policies promoting the interests of the underprivileged, whereas the JLP managed to attract support on the basis of discontent about 'hard times' (Stone, 1980: 170). Among the PNP voters, 32 per cent said that their liking of the policies was the reason for their party choice, and among the JLP voters 49 per cent gave 'hard times' as their reason. The most important motive for PNP voters was party loyalty; 41 per cent of them voted for the PNP because of this; on the JLP side 38 per cent made their voting decision on the basis of party loyalty. Attraction to leader(s) motivated 15 per cent of the PNP voters and 6 per cent of the JLP voters to vote for their party. The fact that they liked the PNP's ideology was offered by 12 per cent of PNP voters as reason for their choice, whereas none of the JLP voters gave a parallel answer. The ideological issue on the JLP side was anti-communism, which was mentioned by 7 per cent of JLP voters as the reason for their vote.

The communism issue merits some further discussion. Despite the JLP's heavy emphasis on the Cuban/communist threat, only some 3 per cent of the whole electorate voted for the JLP because of it. The answers to some further survey questions show that the JLP was not wrong in assuming a basically anti-Communist attitude among a large sector of the Jamaican public. In response to the question 'What do you think about communism?' 49 per cent of respondents in the Kingston metropolitan area gave anti-communist responses, as did 60 per cent in parish towns and 50 per cent in rural villages, whereas pro-communist responses were given by 23, 11 and 5 per cent in these areas respectively, the rest being either ambivalent or without opinion (Stone, 1980:172). However, 63 per cent of people in the Kingston area, 71 per cent in parish towns and 60 per cent in rural villages were in favor of Cubans coming to Jamaica to help build dams, schools and houses and only 28, 19 and 32 per cent respectively were hostile or suspicious. Thus, the JLP had clearly not (yet) managed to establish a link in the voters' mind between Cuba and a communist threat and between the two and the PNP. Also, in 1976 Seaga's Cuban–communist threat clearly lacked credibility among the lower classes; after all, some people were benefitting directly from Cuban aid and the economic conditions had not yet deteriorated to the point where shortages provided some credibility to threats of impending rationing which could then be linked to the threat of communism and deprivation.

A final comment on the issues in the 1976 election concerns the State of Emergency. The JLP tried to use it to rally partisan support around allegations of abuse by the government for political purposes. However, this did not yield the desired results because popular support for the continuation of the State of Emergency was very strong; over 80 per cent of respondents in urban areas were in favor of it in October–November 1976 (Stone, 1980:172). Given this support, the PNP slogan of putting gunmen under 'heavy manners' must have found some resonance among the electorate.

Concluding remarks

Thus, Jamaican politics went through a decisive realignment in the PNP's first term. The redistributive and social and cultural inclusionary policies attracted a substantial number of former JLP supporters and a large majority of young Jamaicans from the lower classes to the PNP. These same policies and the deterioration of the economy as well as the government's ideological posture and the Cuba relationship led to the defection of the upper middle and upper classes.

Had this social polarization process been limited to a class realignment of voting patterns, it would appear to be a natural and even desirable result of the PNP's new political trajectory, as the PNP did not lose aggregate electoral support as a result of the process. Unfortunately, the privileged classes withdrew more than their votes. Capitalists froze investment, disinvested, exported capital and even migrated. The turning-point, late 1975, indicates that the deterioration of the economy and the class-orientation of the government's measures to deal with it were decisive factors, but subsequent events show that rhetoric, Cuba and the alleged communist threat accelerated the defection. In the case of the upper middle-class (administrative and professional personnel) our information on the causes of their alienation is more sketchy. But the timing of their migration to the USA (Table A.4) and Maingot's (1983:26) study suggest that the deterioration of the economy and thus of economic opportunity was decisive for their decision to withdraw their talents and skills from the national economy. In all probability, this group began to withdraw positive political support from the government earlier, in response to social inclusionary policies, taxation, and perhaps the PNP's new ideological posture.

Given the importance of the deterioration of the economy for the alienation of these classes, it is important to examine the causes of the deterioration of the economy. The primary cause was clearly the decline of the world economy and Jamaica's dependent position in it, as Girvan, Bernal and Hughes (1980) argue in their analysis of Jamaica's deteriorating foreign exchange situation in the years leading up to the 1977 IMF agreement. They effectively demolish the IMF's argument that Jamaica's problems were the result of factors such as excessive wage rates and overvalued exchange rates. They argue that the pre-conditions for the foreign exchange crisis were created by a number of structural factors such as the end of the bauxite/alumina investments, import-price inflation and declining export production and that the immediate causes were largely political: capital flight, sabotage of tourism by bad press in the USA and declines in bauxite exports.[30] Both the structural and political factors are clearly directly related to Jamaica's peripheral and dependent position in the world capitalist economy.

Though there is little doubt that Girvan, Bernal and Hughes' argument is largely correct, it is too deterministic and leaves one with the impression that the government had no options. There were other options, and the government's failure to perceive and pursue them increased its vulnerability to external factors. First of all, in terms of economic growth and the foreign exchange situation, the government's macroeconomic strategy was wrong. The critical juncture was the economic package of fall 1974.[31] The following economic rationale could be provided for the program: after two years of slow growth in 1972 and 1973 and a further turndown in early 1974 caused by the international economic situation and the fall-off in foreign investment, the economic situation called for vigorous government action to stimulate growth. This could be provided by increased government spending which would stimulate aggregate demand while at the same time providing sorely needed social programs. Given the import restrictions, this demand would be channeled toward locally produced goods and thereby stimulate growth of output and investment by the private sector, thus regenerating economic growth.

There were two problems with this strategy. First, it was not implemented correctly, as import restrictions were eased not only on raw materials and capital goods necessary for increased production but also on consumer goods,[32] thus allowing some of the created demand to be channeled outside the domestic economy. Second, and more fundamentally, the national bourgeoisie had never led Jamaican economic growth and could not be expected to begin to do so in 1974. It lacked the capital base and the entrepreneurial talents and will, and by this time, a section of the capitalist class was clearly jittery about the direction of the government.

The option that would have been desirable for the PNP government to take in the fall of 1974 was to introduce a type of development plan along the lines of the non-IMF plan elaborated in early 1977: development led by the state sector, development of Community Enterprise Organizations (CEO) based on the use of local inputs, and so on (see pp. 163-6). Economic conditions would have been much more favorable in the fall of 1974. Since the foreign exchange shortage was not acute then, it would not have been necessary to starve the domestic manufacturing sector of imports, thus removing the most important political barrier to implementation of the program. This alternative would have entailed less reliance on foreign loans in 1975 and 1976 which would have eased the foreign exchange pressure.

A greater proportion of the income from the bauxite levy should have been invested in state sector projects such as the planned alumina plant and light manufacturing based on local inputs which would have promoted accumulation and generated or at least saved foreign exchange. This would have meant resisting pressures from the private sector for an easing of import restrictions as well as distributionist pressures from popular forces. Also, an earlier and more intensive search for new trading partners in the Third World and in the socialist bloc might have been more promising than in 1977, in the situation of an acute foreign exchange crisis.

However, political conditions did not encourage the adoption of such a plan in 1974. There was no threat yet of an IMF program, and the ideological development of the party was not advanced enough to promote such an economic reorientation.[33] Success of all of these economic initiatives hinged on their being part of a comprehensive economic plan oriented towards the goals of self-reliance and state sector guidance. The failure to elaborate such a plan in its first two years in office is probably the single biggest mistake of the PNP government. The absence of a plan was clearly part of the legacy of non-ideological politics of the earlier era. With an economic plan, it might have been immediately obvious that as private sector investment fell short, the state sector would have to take up the slack. But, in the absence of a plan, this was not recognized. Furthermore, poor implementation of several government programs aggravated fiscal and balance-of-payments problems. The implementation of Food Farms and many other programs suffered from bureaucratic incapacity, patronage, political resistance and political in-fighting, in that order of importance. Patronage and political resistance and in-fighting, like the absence of an economic plan, were rooted in the low initial development of the political movement.

The economic and political decisions made in 1974 already considerably narrowed the options available in 1975 and 1976, but, with the benefit of hindsight, it is now clear that in those two years the government did borrow too much, particularly from banks abroad at unfavorable interest rates. Since, as we shall argue, for political rather than economic reasons the non-IMF alternative was probably not possible in 1977, this borrowing was the final factor that closed any other option and locked the government into the IMF agreements that led to its downfall.

Finally, the declaration of democratic socialism and the organizational and campaign successes of the PNP are clear manifestations of a further strengthening of the political movement. The massive attendances at PNP rallies and the large margin of the election victory, despite the growing economic problems and violence, demonstrated how far the political mobilization process had come. However, it is important not to overestimate this progress, in particular the ideological strength of the party at the leadership as well as grass-roots levels. At the leadership level, disputes and tensions about the ideological self-definition were simply temporarily patched over by closing ranks to fight the election campaign, and since the political education program had virtually stalled, it had not managed to make an impact at the grass-roots level. Thus, popular support for the government was based on the effects of its policies, particularly the distributive ones, rather than on an understanding of and commitment to democratic socialism as an alternative development path. Differing interpretations by the left and the moderates of the campaign, the victory, and the role of ideology in all this, were to cause severe conflicts in the following years.

5

The Second Term: The Rise and Fall of the Left Alternative

1977 was a watershed year for the PNP government for what it did not do as well as what it did do. What it did do was enter into an agreement with the IMF. With this agreement, the reform process begun in 1972 essentially came to a halt and it was the IMF-imposed austerity policies (under a subsequent agreement) which ultimately led to the downfall of the government. What the PNP did not do was to adopt a left-wing alternative economic plan under which the country would have foregone the IMF loans and opted for a deepening of the reform process and structural transformation of the economy.

Spring 1977: the rise of the left and the debate over the IMF
The PNP left which previously had been almost entirely dependent on Manley had emerged from the 1976 election with an independent political base for the first time. Duncan, Small and Bertram joined Spaulding in the House of Representatives and, under Duncan's leadership, the left continued to dominate the party secretariat. The left interpreted the election victory as giving the party a mandate for its ideological program of democratic socialism. Most important for events to come, the left felt strongly that the Jamaican masses had responded enthusiastically to the PNP's anti-imperialist posture, expressed in the campaign theme of 'We are not for sale'. Specifically, this meant that any move toward the IMF would be a betrayal of the people.

The depth of the impending economic crisis was not public knowledge at this time and the PNP left was not an exception in this matter. Manley, Coore and the leading civil servants responsible for economic affairs, Horace Barber (Permanent Secretary in the Ministry of Finance), G. Arthur Brown (Governor of the Bank of Jamaica) and Gladstone Bonnick (Director of the National Planning Agency) were aware of the seriousness of the foreign exchange situation, but few other PNP politicians were. Indeed, the cabinet as a whole was not informed of Coore's discussion with the IMF in Manila in early fall of 1976. Though no actual agreement was

148

worked out at this meeting, the discussions with the IMF were at a relatively advanced stage by the time of the elections. The Fund had evaluated the Jamaican economy and communicated to Manley and the key financial advisors that they considered a 40 per cent devaluation and sharp cutbacks in budget expenditures necessary. Manley responded that this was impossible during the election campaign but agreed that 'the subject would be taken up again immediately after the elections (Manley, 1982:151). The devaluation itself would have been a political bombshell. Through his contacts in the international banking community and/or the government bureaucracy, Seaga got wind of the negotiations and, three days before the election, charged that the government would devalue the currency if re-elected, correctly citing the 40 per cent figure demanded by the IMF (*G*, 13 December 1976). This was immediately denied by Coore and the government repeatedly denied any intention to devalue in the next several months, as business and unions expressed their opposition to such a move.

Within the party, however, the very fact of negotiating with the IMF was bound to be extremely controversial, given the perceptions of the left of the Fund and of the promises of the election campaign and the electoral mandate. Thus, there were bound to be recriminations and charges of duplicity when it was revealed that not only had the government been talking to the IMF, but also a timetable for an agreement had apparently been worked out (Henry, 1980:25).[1]

The development of the left alternative
On 18 December, three UWI social scientists, George Beckford, Norman Girvan and Louis Lindsay, attended a victory celebration at Duncan's house and on this occasion warned him of the gravity of the economic situation and of the economic and political consequences of the IMF 'solution', as demonstrated by the effects of such policies elsewhere in the Third World. As a consequence of a discussion among PNP leftists that evening, Small and Duncan met with Manley the next day and attempted to convince him of the disastrous economic and political consequences of entering into an agreement with the IMF.[2] After a subsequent meeting with the UWI social scientists, Manley was persuaded that the government should do its utmost at least to explore any alternative to concluding an agreement with the IMF.

Public utterances by the government in the month after the election were consistent with the pursuit of an alternative to the IMF. On 5 January, Vivian Blake, the Minister of Industry and Commerce, announced that the country would be able to import only $600m in goods in 1977, a reduction from $835m the year before (*DN*, 6 January 1944). Though Blake did not say so, the $600m figure is what the government estimated would be available if Jamaica did not seek assistance from the IMF. On the same day, Manley made a radio broadcast in which he predicted difficult times ahead: the public should expect more taxes, shortages of many goods and disappearance of others, but he added that the government had no plans to devalue (*DN*, 6 January 1977). He went on to say:

> The Government on behalf of the people will not accept anybody anywhere in the world telling us what we are to do in our own house and in our own house there will be no other masters but ourselves. Above all, we are not for sale . . . we reject any foreign imposed solution to the present crisis we face (Quoted in Henry, 1980:40).

The new cabinet, which was announced on 3 January, included three new Ministers: Small, Minister of Youth and Sports; Duncan, Minister of Mobilization; and Ralph Brown (center left in the party), Minister of Local Government. Two members of the previous cabinet, Pagan (center right) and Rose Leon (right) were no longer present because of demotion to Minister of State and loss in the election, respectively. Thus the new cabinet was clearly more left-wing than the previous one. However, the overall profile of the cabinet was still centrist. The ideological composition was left – three, center-left – four, center – six, center-right – six, and right – one.

The creation of the Ministry of National Mobilization was closely related to the leftward move of the PNP and the government during the campaign and in the first months of 1977, in general, and, as it turned out, to the development of the alternative economic plan, in particular. The task of the new ministry was publicly described as coordination of the government's people's programs; supervision of the democratization project in education, the community councils, and worker participation; and maintenance of a dialogue with the people through mobilization of popular opinion in the party and in the nation (*G*, 4 January 1977). Personnel of the ministry considered one of its main tasks to be 'detribalization' of society. At the outset, the line between party partisan and national mobilization (and thus obviously detribalization) was not clear, and Duncan himself stated that 'in recognition of the deficiencies of the (PNP) secretariat much of the load of its work was legitimately transferred to the Ministry of Mobilization' (at its creation) (*G*, 11 October 1977). As it worked in practice, during its effective life, the ministry's main task was to mobilize the people for participation in the development of the alternative economic plan.

In a speech on 19 January, Manley outlined a new economic austerity package with a decided left-wing profile (*G*, 20 January 1977). Declaring 1977 the 'Year of Economic Emergency', he set out drastic measures: (1) severe foreign exchange restrictions including limiting imports to essential consumer goods and raw materials and reducing the personal travel allowance to $50 per person per year; (2) increased taxes, among others a new marginal rate of 80 per cent on income over J$30 000; and (3) a temporary wage and price freeze. In a symbolic move, the salaries of the Prime Minister, other Ministers of Government and Parliamentary Secretaries would be reduced. Manley went on to call for a national production drive with the long-term goal of making the country self-sufficient in food, clothing and housing. The concrete goals and plans for 1977 were in the process of being developed (that is, as part of the alternative plan, though this was not explicitly stated). He also announced that the government would acquire the Caribbean Cement Company and three commercial banks,[3] and that RJR would be acquired initially by the Workers Bank but then sold to a number of 'people-based organizations' (such as unions, cooperatives, etc.). Finally, in order to diversify economic relations, the government would seek greater trade relations with Comecon and other socialist countries. Thus, full diplomatic links with the USSR would be established.

The development of the alternative plan
The group of UWI social scientists became the core of the planning group for the Emergency Production Plan. A task force with ten working groups focusing on different sectors of the economy and society began feverish work soon after Manley's speech. Some of the UWI group were brought into the formal bureaucracy on a permanent basis, most notable being Girvan's appointment as head of the National Planning Agency. The working groups were to evaluate the production potential of their sector, set production targets, estimate required resources to meet the targets, and mobilize resources for implementation. Eventually, each group produced a report of several hundred pages in length which was passed on to the government along with a summary of the entire plan.

The intention was for this to be a 'bottom-up' planning effort and this is where the Ministry of National Mobilization came in. The Ministry launched a public education program including 'People's Forums' on the meaning of self-reliant democratic socialism and meetings with interest groups on their role in the production plan. People and organizations were urged to submit their suggestions on how the productive effort might be furthered. The response was gratifying: some 10 000 suggestions were submitted identifying idle land that might be brought into use, new projects that might be initiated, etc. Many of these suggestions were incorporated by the working groups into their proposals and an additional volume was appended to the production plan summarizing these suggestions (Beckford *et al.*, 1978:v). In order to explore the possibilities of expanding economic relations with the countries of the Council for Mutual Economic Assistance (CMEA – the Socialist Bloc), a delegation consisting of Patterson (now Foreign Minister), Duncan and Richard Fletcher

(Minister of State in the Ministry of Finance) went to Cuba for talks with a team headed by Deputy Prime Minister Carlos Raphael Rodriguez.

From the earliest stage of the development of the alternative plan, the UWI team had met with resistance from the established bureaucracy in financial affairs (Barber, Brown and Bonnick) as well as from the political directorate in this area (Coore and Fletcher). This tension increased through time, especially *vis à vis* the senior bureaucrats. Initially, information was withheld on the grounds that it was subject to the Official Secrets Act. The UWI group then agreed to sign the act. When things still did not improve, Manley was prevailed upon to issue a memorandum instructing that the team be given certain information which they considered essential to their assignment. Members of the team told us that an additional complicating factor was that some of the information was not assembled on written documents at all but rather retained in an organized fashion only in the memory of the senior bureaucrats themselves, Barber in particular. It was, of course, a method of staying in control of the situation.

The reasons for the resistance of the established finance team are complicated. Certainly, differences of opinion on the IMF question and ideology in general were important. Ideologically, the senior bureaucrats were liberal not radical: they favored an active state role in the economy, but the state should be adding to what the private sector did, doing what it was unwilling (because of lack of profitability or excessive risk requirements) to do. Beckford and Girvan, who were key figures in the Caribbean dependency school, and the other UWI social scientists were radicals. They advocated a sharp move toward greater self-reliance and a greatly enlarged state sector.

A second source of tension was the opinion of the UWI group that the bureaucracy itself was a major stumbling block and had to be overhauled, an opinion which they committed to paper and circulated in the early stages of the development of the IMF alternative. Finally, there was a cultural gap between the Western-oriented senior bureaucrats and many members of the UWI group, who identified with the popular and more African elements of the indigenous culture of the Jamaican masses. One of the more conservative members of the PNP cabinet told us:

> The reason why the Emergency Production Plan would not work was because of the attitude of the UWI economists. They were abusive to people like G. Arthur Brown; Michael made one of them apologize to Brown once. They would go up to the Bank of Jamaica wearing sandals and a tam, and demand, not ask, for some statistics or data and naturally people resented it. Their personal appearance, all wearing tams, they were known as the 'tam pack'.

Or Manley (1982:154) observes 'I do not doubt that there was an element who would have looked askance at all these young Turks of the left, often sporting beards, tams and jeans, playing so prominent a part in affairs'. This same cultural factor played a part in PNP intra-party disputes also.

Despite these tensions, it is important to note that large elements of the state bureaucracy were harnessed in developing the alternative plan.[4] Indeed, it would have been impossible to produce a plan so detailed in such a short time as the one produced without this help.

Other signs of a move to the left
The movement toward the left in this period was not limited to the development of the IMF alternative. As we have already pointed out, Manley's speech on 19 January contained a number of measures which involved a leftward movement of government policy such as the nationalizations, the tax package, and the expanded economic relations with the Socialist Bloc. In order to stem capital flight, the government expanded and strengthened the Financial Intelligence Unit (FIU), whose primary task was to stop the illegal flow of currency out of the country (*DN*, 1 February 1977). In another effort to bolster its foreign exchange situation, the government decreed that the Ministry of Finance could order holders of foreign property to sell such property if the Ministry was of the opinion that sale would strengthen Jamaica's financial position (*G*, 12 February 1977).

One event that indicated that the government was considering a major expansion of the public sector into areas that were the domain of ongoing private sector activity was the government's initiation of negotiations with two of the largest businesses in the country, Industrial Commercial Developments and Grace Kennedy. Acquisition proved too expensive and the negotiations were ultimately broken off.

In February, the Civil Service Commission, which is responsible for the promotion of civil servants, resigned *en bloc*, six months before their term ran out as a result of pressure from the government. Manley wanted to replace some of the commission members with people who would weigh factors other than seniority more heavily in handing out promotions. This was widely seen as a move to rate political commitment more strongly, but the matter was considerably more complicated than that (see Chapter 8).

In its election manifesto, the PNP had promised to put the question of constitutional review on the agenda. The manifesto made specific reference to questions of a republic, public financing of political parties, and extending integrity legislation to senior public officials, but there was a clear intention not to limit the review to these matters. In early February, the government appointed Paul Robertson, who was also considered to be on the party left, to head the constitutional review process (*G*, 5 February 1977).[5] What the government planned to do was to try to generate a grass-roots discussion on the general issue of constitutional reform and get some kind of broad public support on at least some of its own agenda, such as institution of a republic and modification of the constitutional property clause as it related to land. Then, with this support along with the promise of electoral reform (in which the JLP was obviously interested, given that it was the opposition party) the PNP would attempt to strike a deal with the JLP. If they failed to get JLP support and thus the two-thirds majority in the Senate needed for changing the constitution (they had over two-thirds of the House), they could go to the people and attempt to overrule the Senate with a two-thirds majority in a referendum.

The mobilization process initiated by the PNP during its first term and intensified during the development of the production plan, began to spill over into uncontrolled and illegal mobilization in the first months of 1977. In January the *Gleaner* reported several cases of 'capture' (that is, illegal seizure or occupation) of housing in May Pen and of land in Saint Thomas (*G*, 12 and 13 January 1977). In both cases, the squatters were reported to have been chanting 'Is socialism time now'. The text of articles, particularly the one on St Thomas, makes it clear that the impression given by the *Gleaner* headlines exaggerated the situation, but land capture was a relatively new development and became more significant later in the year.

The total visibility of the left was enhanced by the activities of the communist Workers' Liberation League (WLL). The WLL continued its policy of critical support for the PNP government' and was very active in the campaign against the IMF. It began to gain more prominence in the print media, but almost entirely in the *Daily News*, not in the *Gleaner*. The UAWU also joined other unions (other than the BITU) in their statements of general support for the government's policy.

Reaction of the PNP 'Moderates'
There was no public reaction from the so-called 'moderate' wing of the PNP to the tide of events in the first months of 1977, but behind the scenes, a conflict was brewing which came to a head at the meeting on 26–7 March of the NEC, precisely when the alternative plan was presented to the government.

In the early days after the election, there was no active move, apart from Coore's offer to resign in the face of the proposals from the UWI economists (Henry, 1980:46), to block the development of the IMF alternative. There was, however, considerable footdragging by some ministers. Given the intensity of the dispute later and numerical superiority of the moderate wing of the party, particularly in the parliamentary group, the lack of active opposition from the moderate wing needs some explanation. Manley was still totally dominant in this period and, as previously emphasized, he was sympathetic to the left. Decision-making was still centralized, with Manley making the important decisions after consulting with various advisors and confidants on an *ad hoc* basis.[6] In this period (1975–7) the right was afraid to challenge Manley and the leftward course of the party openly. They grumbled behind the scenes. They were also reluctant to take on the left in debate, because the left, though much smaller, was more articulate.[7] Finally, Manley (1982:81) indicates that the moderate wing of the party was divided on the question of the alternative path at this time between a group who hoped the alternative would work given what the IMF was proposing and a minority who were sure it would not work. Thus, one reason that the moderates did not challenge the left in this period is that they were not yet fully opposed to the left's alternative as it was not yet known what the risks of that alternative would be.

Where the moderates' first counter-action appeared was in the area of foreign policy. The stimulating factor here was the new direction in foreign policy *vis-à-vis* the Third World in general and Jamaica in particular charted by the Carter Administration as it came into office. The toleration of different ideological stances and economic models in the Third World was central to the new administration's policy and a more positive stance toward democratic and progressive governments like the PNP was an integral part of its approach. With Andrew Young, a longtime friend of Jamaica, at the UN, it is no accident that the country was singled out as a showcase of the new policy. Apparently as a response to US overtures of possible economic assistance, in early February, the party was instructed not to refer to 'imperialism' in the coming local election campaign.[8] In turn, Foreign Minister Patterson departed for Washington at the end of that month for consultations with the US administration.

The question of relations with the USA and the Socialist Bloc and the related issue of the role of imperialism in the PNP's ideology and rhetoric had always been (and continues to be) a point of contention in the intra-party debate. Now this took on much greater significance as the left believed that developing economic relations with the CMEA countries was of paramount importance for the development of the IMF alternative. Not only did they believe (and later charge) that Patterson was dragging his feet on this matter, they also believed that the early contacts with Carter would send the wrong signals to the USSR. The moderates, on the other hand, were suspicious of the USSR in the first place and were sure that the CMEA countries could offer little. They believed that the USA, in contrast, had and would come up with help. By late February, it was clear that their line was prevailing.

The moderates were also suspicious of the UWI team. One minister from this faction of the party told us 'They were all very left-wing. Girvan was a communist'. His view was admittedly extreme, but the view that the alternative plan was part of a hidden agenda for the left's power aspirations, a vehicle they wanted to use to take over the party, began to gain wider and wider currency among the moderates. Matters were not helped by Duncan's conflicts with several cabinet colleagues.

The Ministry of Mobilization's task cut across other ministries and this combined with the ideological differences and Duncan's personality led to conflicts between Duncan and the other ministers. Confrontations between Duncan and Isaacs, the Minister of Labor and party rightist, as well as Bell, Minister of Education and center-rightist, surfaced publicly (*G*, 17 March 1977) and, according to our interviews, at least one other serious run in occurred in this period, between Duncan and Coore. In all cases, some aspects of grass-roots mobilization brought Duncan into conflict with the other cabinet members.

By mid-March, tensions and suspicions inside the political directorate were to develop into a rumor (of unknown origins) that the left, led by Duncan, was plotting to replace Manley as party leader. This rumor leaked to the rank-and-file activists and resulted in physical attacks on Duncan in several cases.

The ideological dispute and, even more so, the debate on the non-IMF path, on the other hand, did not extend deep into the party. The debate was confined to senior members of the political directorate and the key financial advisors. Neither was the party as a whole involved in any way in the decision on the alternative path, in sharp contrast to the situation two-and-a-half years later.

The JLP on the defensive

In the first three months of 1977 the JLP was clearly a defeated party and on the defensive politically. As one can see from Table 5.1, we recorded only three attacks by the JLP on the government in this period. One was Seaga's New Year's message and the other two, also attacks on misman-agement, came in the wake of Manley's broadcast to the nation on 19 January.

However, the JLP did lay the basis for a theme that was to join mismanagement and the communist threat as a tool in its campaign against the PNP – the corrupt use of power. Seaga was to lay out his case in a series of proposals to Manley a few days after the elections. He called for a review of the cases of the detainees under the State of Emergency, a Fair Labour Act to end political discrimination in government employment, a Code of Conduct for distribution of government benefits, an impartial Electoral Commission, an impartial Police Commission, a bipartisan Con-tracts Committee and Parliamentary committees to oversee government expenditure, statutory boards and public corporations (*DN*, 18 December 1976). Underlying each of the proposals were allegations of PNP abuses in these areas. Manley's response was to accept the invitation to discuss the distribution of scarce government benefits (jobs, housing, etc.) but to reject most of the others on the grounds that the voters had rejected them as they were included in the JLP's election manifesto (*G*, 22 December 1976).[9]

A week after the election the JLP announced its intention to file for

TABLE 5.1 *Attacks on the PNP government, January–April 1977*

Ground of attack	Month January	February	March	April	Total attacks
Mismanagement	5	4	3	9	21
	(G,2;	(G)	(G)	(G,2;	(G,11;
	JLP,3)			JLP,5;	JLP,8;
				PS,2)	PS,2)
Communism/Cuba		1			1
		(G)			(G)
One-party state/			1		1
totalitarianism			(G)		(G)
Rhetoric undermines		1	1		2
business confidence		(G)	(G)		(G)
– economic problems					
Socialist policies					
undermine business					
confidence					
Clarify limits of			1		1
public sector/			(G)		(G)
reassure business					
Socialist policies		2	1		3
unfair/bad		(G)	(G)		(G)
Manley out of control/	1	1		2	4
disunity in party	(G)	(G)	(G)	(G)	(G)
Total articles	5	8	7	11	31
	(G,2;	(G)	(G)	(G,4;	(G,21;
	JLP,3)			JLP,5;	JLP,8;
				PS,2)	PS,2)

KEY   *G* = attack by *Gleaner*
          JLP = attack by JLP spokesperson
          PS = attack by private sector

NOTE The column totals refer to the number of articles, while the row totals refer to the number of attacks. Since one article can contain attacks on more than one ground, column totals do not equal the number of attacks in the cells and the row grand total is greater than the column total.

recounts in twenty-five seats (*G*, 23 December 1976). On 10 January, the party filed twelve electoral petitions alleging widespread irregularities in the 1976 elections. It charged that the PNP had employed 'a scientifically and expertly organized system of bogus voting previously unknown in Jamaican politics' (*G*, 11 January 1977). In addition, it made charges of rigged election procedures, use of the State of Emergency to impede the JLP campaign, illegitimate use of government funds, false voters' IDs, inaccurate voter lists and the arrival of Presiding Officers hours after the polls opened. Repeatedly for the next three years the JLP was to charge in Jamaica and abroad that the PNP had stolen the elections.

As we pointed out in the last chapter, there were certainly corrupt practices in the 1976 election, but this was not more frequent (probably less so) than in previous elections and certainly not of the magnitude necessary to change the electoral outcome. There can be little doubt about our assessment of this matter. The JLP filed twelve petitions, not enough to change the outcome of the election, even if every one of its petitions were successful. The party did not even follow up eleven of these with applications for hearings (*G*, 1 February 1980). In the remaining case, the JLP candidate did successfully overturn the election results (*G*, 4 January 1980). Only in one other case was the vote margin small enough to have been influenced by the corruption in the system.[10] Additional evidence that the electoral outcome would have differed little in the absence of corrupt practices is Stone's poll which accurately predicted the popular vote.

One incident in this period, which clearly benefitted the JLP, was the so-called Rema affair. In early February, the Ministry of Housing moved to evict a number of illegal tenants in a government housing project in Rema, a JLP-dominated area in a corner of Minister of Housing Spaulding's Southern St Andrew district directly abutting Seaga's West Kingston district on two sides. Considerable force was used in the evictions and they were accompanied by clashes between rival political gangs in the area, probably the most explosive part of the Kingston ghetto. One man was killed and a number of others were wounded (*G*, 3, 4, 5, 6 February 1977). Seaga immediately charged that the Ministry of Housing and the police were working with gangs of PNP gunmen from 'Concrete Jungle' (Arnett Gardens, a PNP housing project) to replace 1000 residents of Rema with 1000 PNP supporters. Despite the statement of PNP ministers to the contrary, it was widely suspected that the Rema incident was a grab for political territory by the PNP. Demands were made by the Jamaica Council of Churches, the Jamaica Teachers Association and the Jamaica Council on Human Rights for an impartial inquiry into the situation.

The government did agree to a judicial inquiry of the Rema incident with retired Supreme Court Judge Ronald Small as Sole Commissioner (*G*, 15 February 1977). Small submitted his report sixteen months later (*G*, 26 July 1978). The report concluded that the root cause of the eruption of

violence was the intense political bitterness in the area and active engage-
ment of gunmen on both sides. Tensions had been aggravated by the
'overwhelming victory of the PNP at the polls . . . resulting in the devas-
tating defeat of the JLP, thereby giving rise to the unquenchable thirst on
the one side for further fields to conquer and on the other side bitter
resentment and calculated embarrassment' [of the government through the
non-payment of rent, etc.]. Small also confirmed that the 'incidence of
non-payment [of rent] has indeed grown to alarming proportions'.[11]

The Rema incident is typical of violent political clashes both in that it
demonstrates the intensity of party tribalism and in that it is usually
impossible for the outside observer (and the judicial system for that
matter) to get to the bottom of things without knowing either the motivations of the party leaders involved or what went on behind the scenes. This
particular incident was an important event in the course of the Manley
government for several reasons. First, despite the fact that Small's report
indicated that Spaulding's account of the events was more accurate than
the JLP's charge of massive victimization, the incident clearly damaged the
PNP government since it was initially widely perceived as an act of blatant
political territorial expansion. It must be kept in mind here that Small's
report appeared almost a year and a half after the incident. Second, the
rent boycott, by questioning the authority of the government, served to
chip away at the legitimacy of the state. It was the first act in the campaign
of delegitimization conducted by the JLP during the PNP's second term.

At the very end of March, the JLP seemed to come alive, perhaps
stimulated by the increasingly public dissension within the PNP and the
decline in the PNP's post-election momentum. It was at this point that the
JLP launched its 'Human Rights' campaign. (Since this campaign continued throughout the year and was not relevant to the IMF decision, we
will defer discussion of it until later in the chapter).

The JLP's attacks on the government focused on mismanagement of the
economy, blaming the government for the economic crisis. As one can see
from Table 5.1, there was a sharp increase in the number of attacks in
April, again indicating that the JLP sensed that the government was now
vulnerable. In January Shearer and the BITU had parted company with
the rest of the trade unions in issuing very negative reactions to Manley's
two speeches on economic policy. At this point and again in April Shearer
was sharply critical of the wage-freeze, calling on workers to resist at the
latter date. Vaz, now a JLP MP, reacted negatively to the January
announcement of the $600m limit on the import budget, contending it
would create massive unemployment. Continuing this theme in April he
demanded that the government seek foreign loans of $300m to expand the
import budget. The government's move to cover the central government
budget deficit with a $300m Bank of Jamaica 'accommodation' sparked a tor-
rent of criticism from Vaz, Buck and Seaga charging that the government's

'printing of money' was 'fiscal indiscipline and madness of alarming proportions' which could lead to hyperinflation (*G*, 9, 13, 16 April 1977).

Private sector
As in the case of the JLP, public criticism of the government by the private sector was very subdued in the first three months of 1977. In fact, we recorded no attacks in the *Gleaner* in this period (Table 5.1) and found little criticism from private sector spokespeople until late March. The PNP's electoral mandate appeared to have given the party a little breathing room.

Unfortunately for the government, that breathing room was only a public phenomenon. Underneath, there was almost panic in the upper classes in general. One can see from the migration figures in Tables A.4 and 5 that business people and managers migrated in massive numbers in 1977 and even more of them began the process of migration. Reports on migration became more and more frequent in the Jamaican daily papers. Investment as indicated by the figures on gross and net capital formation (see Table A.6) hit an all-time low in this year. It is not surprising that the banks, in response to excess liquidity, lowered the interest rate by 2 per cent despite the high rate of inflation (*G*, 18 March 1977). In March the *Gleaner* reported that there had been a dramatic decline in both volume and price of shares traded on the local stock exchange (*G*, 15 March 1977). People were desperate to get their money out of the country, resorting to such crude and easily detectable methods as sending it out in the mail. Munn, the Minister of National Security, reported in late March that the FIU had discovered large amounts of money in mail destined abroad, dating the escalation from 17 January 1977 (*G*, 30 March 1977). The panic was increased by the announcement that government could now legally force people to sell foreign holdings and repatriate the proceeds to Jamaica (*G*, 12 February 1977).

In this climate it is not surprising that the Jamaican rumor mill, active in normal times, was running at a feverish pace grinding out new rumors about Draconian measures planned by the government. The situation became so bad that in mid-February Manley publicly called for a halt to the rumor-mongering. He cited five specific rumors, among them that the government intended to withdraw passports of almost all adults and to ban overseas travel, which he termed a 'pack of lies' (*G*, 16 February 1977).[12]

Publicly, private-sector spokespeople were conciliatory. The PSOJ and JMA extended an olive branch to the PNP after the election and soon thereafter the leaders of all private-sector organizations met with Manley in camera for consultation on the economic situation. With the exception of the tax package (specifically the 80 per cent marginal tax on high incomes) they were generally supportive of the economic measures announced by Manley in January, which is surprising in view of the $600m imports level.

It was not until the second week in April that the real attacks began and then quickly developed into a veritable barrage. The criticisms contained obvious, if indirect attacks on the PNP left, specifically the level of 'rhetoric' and the line being pushed by the left, notably Duncan, that the crisis was due to the failure of the private sector to reinvest and produce. The JMA came out with the harshest attack, strongly criticizing the government for excessive spending and contending that the ongoing migration was caused by 'a campaign of indiscriminate vilification' against ownership and the role of employers, rather than by the changes in the socio-economic philosophy for the nation's development. The manufacturers went on to say that the import restrictions were severely hurting production and called on the government to seek $150m in foreign loans for the purchase of raw materials to 'maintain the economy at a minimum level of viability' (*G*, 9 April 1977). Chamber of Commerce President Avis Henriques argued that the production plan was being developed in too much secrecy and that its 'parentage is suspect' (*G*, 10 April 1977).[13] The PSOJ generally sounded a more conciliatory note but also termed the attempt to lay all the blame on the private sector 'untruthful and dishonest' and added a call for an end to 'devisive rhetoric' (*G*, 9 April 1977).

As to the reasons for the reactions of business, one of our business respondents contended that the closing of the foreign exchange window after the election was a real shock, a significant turning-point in his mind. Certainly this act did bring home to many people just how bad the economic situation was. As in the previous year, the economic decline continued to be an important factor motivating the lack of investment and the migration.

The factor that came to be of greater importance in this period was 'fear of what's around the corner' as many of the capitalists we interviewed called it. People were not reacting to what the PNP had done but to what they thought the PNP might do. This fear was fed by several things. One factor was the use of rhetoric. Of course, this is the whole point of the critique of radical rhetoric. It is obviously not primarily the rhetoric *per se* that makes people react, however much they may object to being called 'rapacious capitalists' or whatever. Rather, it generates a fear that the radical rhetoric is foreshadowing radical action in the future.

A second factor that fed the fear was the rising influence of the party left. The party left was perceived by the business community to be communists. That is, they believed that the left not only wanted to socialize the Jamaican economy but that it also wanted to abolish parliamentary democracy in Jamaica. In our interviews, we found that even the most pro-PNP capitalists held this view.

The opposition to the PNP, particularly the *Gleaner* in this period, magnified the effect of rhetoric and the rise of the left on businessmen's fear for the future. Policy did leave some impact, of course. The picture the

JLP and the *Gleaner* painted of the PNP's intentions would not have been credible if the party had not embarked on a program of significant change. The past policies could easily make some rumor about intended future actions quite plausible. The $50 limit on foreign-travel expenditure could make someone's contention that the government would soon prohibit foreign travel seem reasonable, or if the government could make you sell your foreign property today it might want to confiscate it tomorrow and so on.

The role of rumor in a small society like Jamaica must not be under-rated. One Manley advisor who also had business connections told us that it was quite frequent for, say, a fairly temperate speech critical of the capitalist system by a PNP minister to be turned into a rabid attack on greedy capitalists. Or a suggestion by a left-winger at a cabinet meeting that professionals be made to pay a fee for free higher education received in Jamaica before migration could easily be turned into a definite government plan to prevent professionals from migrating.

A final factor contributing to capitalist class reactions in this period was the election itself. Many had taken a 'wait and see' attitude in 1976. After the PNP was elected, they left and/or began sending their money out.

One point should be made about the wave of business migration during the PNP's second term. This wave was primarily to the USA, in large part, Miami. A significant portion of people who migrated in this period retained their businesses and often homes in Jamaica. By going through immigration in the USA they acquired a green card, which ensured that they could migrate at a moment's notice in the future. These 'Jamaican Americans' ranged from businessmen who had their primary place of business and residence in Jamaica to fly-by-nighters who just continued to use their Jamaican connection for any quick-profit scheme.

The Gleaner

In the first three months of 1977, the *Gleaner* and its columnists carried the weight of opposition to the government. Of the twenty articles with attacks on the government appearing in the paper in this period, the paper itself accounted for seventeen (Table 5.1). The *Gleaner* also went through a transformation which, though not as dramatic as the shifts in 1975 and 1978-9, was definitely noticeable. In this period, the paper moved beyond its previous practice of reporting the events of the day selectively to outright distortion and wholesale manufacture of the 'news'. The least heavy-handed of these new tactics was exaggeration of a single incident into a much larger phenomenon, such as the case of the land capture incident in St Thomas.[14] Much more heavy-handed was the use of extremely misleading headlines on articles. For example, an article on 20 January reporting that the government was studying the possibility of economic relations with the Socialist Bloc was entitled 'Jamaica May Join Comecon'. In March and April, a number of 'news' articles began to appear on the front page which were simply anti-government statements, most often pessimistic assessments of the economic situation by *Gleaner* reporters.[15] Another development in the first four months of 1977 was the increasing prominence of *Gleaner* columnists, first Wilmot Perkins and later John Hearne, in leading a 'no-holds-barred' attack on the government, the PNP left, and D. K. Duncan personally, attacks which made the *Gleaner* editorials look very moderate by comparison.

Thematically, the *Gleaner* opened the year with attacks on the government's economic management and on the expansion of the state sector saying that the government had already taken over so much of the economy that 'there is very little left which can be called the private sector as such' (*G*, 20 and 22 January 1977), but in February, the focus of criticism shifted. Though these themes were continued, the *Gleaner* began to focus on the PNP left and the government's socialist policies to a much greater extent than before. In the months February to April, the majority of *Gleaner* attacks focused on the PNP's left political posture rather than economic management for the first time (see Table 5.1). Moreover, the total number of attacks was higher in this three-month period than in any previous three-month period during the PNP's tenure in office. The main object of these attacks was the PNP left (again Duncan in particular) and now not just for its rhetoric but also for its intention, according to the *Gleaner*, to destroy the private sector 'as in communist countries' and, by very strong implications, to eliminate democracy (see especially *G*, 25 February 1977 and *G*, 5 April 1977).

The People's Production Plan
On 24 March, the economic plan authored by the UWI team with the help of parts of the staff of the state bureaucracy was presented to the Cabinet. Though the most important features of the plan were not ultimately carried through, it is worth looking at this plan in some detail for several reasons. First, the plan was produced by leading proponents of the Caribbean dependency school and thus represented an attempt to work out an economic strategy applicable in a political democracy which was broadly consistent with their theoretical ideas. Moreover, unlike such works as Thomas' *Dependence and Transformation* (1974), the strategy had to be concrete and incredibly detailed, with sub-plans for each section which could be implemented with human, material and organizational resources which already existed or which could be mobilized in a relatively short time.

Second, since rejection of the plan led to the IMF agreement and thus to the downfall of the Manley government, it is important to evaluate the plan in order to answer the question of whether the PNP had any other viable option at this date. The left wing of the party believed, and most still believe, that the plan was viable and a lot of the bitterness they felt (and still feel) was due to the fact that they were sure that the IMF agreement would destroy the government and that there was an alternative that would have furthered the social transformation process.

The main feature of the plan was that it would begin a process of reorientation of the Jamaican economy toward greater self-reliance, greater internal integration and more democratic and egalitarian production relations, while maintaining or increasing the level of production. The constraints were that the plan must work within the economic resources already existing or easily mobilized, limitations on the state budget and, above all, an extremely tight foreign exchange budget.

In reorienting the economy, agriculture was key: the planners stated that 'the production plan implicitly indicates that the development of a self-reliant national economy must be based on rural development' (Beckford *et al.*, 1978:67). The agricultural plan set overall goals for employment, nutrition and production, and set specific targets for production of various crops for 1977. The plan for this sector called for an additional $42m in state budget expenditures but no additional foreign exchange. The planners identified 129 000 acres of idle land, 66 000 of which should be brought into production during the plan period. The 36 000 acres of government owned lands would provide the largest chunk of the land needed. It was estimated that bringing these new lands into production would provide 37 000 jobs. Most of these would go to the rural unemployed but some would be reserved for the urban unemployed who would have to be redeployed for the purpose.

The new lands, as well as some land already under production, in so far as possible would be the object of land reform aimed at achieving a more equitable distribution of land. The land reform would take three forms: an extension of Project Land Lease (in other words individual small farms), cooperatives and Community Enterprise Organizations (CEOs). The CEO, a novel concept developed by economist George Beckford,[16] is a community-owned, cooperatively-operated enterprise. The emphasis in the 1977 plan was to have CEOs in agriculture and livestock, but later they were to be expanded into manufacturing, to promote (forward) integrated manufacturing sectors by using raw materials available in the region, in such areas as agro-industry and furniture manufacture.

The second area of emphasis in the plan was construction, with the main thrust being housing. This sector was to provide 7500 new jobs at the cost of an additional $120m to the government budget and $49m to the foreign exchange budget (above the $600m limit).

Manufacturing, on the other hand, was projected to suffer a loss of almost 700 jobs even with an additional $100m for the foreign exchange budget. The reason for this, argued the planners, was clear: because of the way in which the large manufacturing firm was developed in Jamaica, it demanded very high levels of imported raw materials (not to mention the capital goods necessary). The planners estimated that in seven leading manufacturing subsectors imported raw materials accounted for 39 per cent of the gross value of the product and that it required an average of $3956 per annum in imported raw materials to keep one worker employed! (Beckford *et al.*, 1978:80–1). On the other hand, in small manufacturing and crafts which used local raw materials, it would be possible to create approximately 5000 new jobs.

In terms of structural transformation of sectors other than agriculture, the plan called for the nationalization of all banks and insurance companies, the flour mill, the cement factory and the oil refinery. CEOs were to be developed in new smaller-scale enterprises using local raw materials.

The plan as a whole called for $268m in state expenditure over and above the $1245m to $1412m projected at that time. In the original budget, it was estimated that recurrent revenue and bauxite revenues would amount to $680m, with another $134m coming from internal loans from banks, insurance companies and state insurance funds and from external loans. The planners believed that another $144m could be raised from *quasi*-public agencies and $171m from private financial institutions. This still left a gap of $383m to $550m. They suggested four possible sources for the funds: (1) Bank of Jamaica support; (2) increased fiscal revenues; (3) foreign credit; and (4) reduction in expenditures; adding quickly that (3) did not seem feasible (Beckford *et al.*, 1978:107). The first would be very inflationary and the second would necessitate significant improvement in the tax-collection machinery.

As must be clear by now, the planners found it impossible to accommodate what they wanted within the $600m foreign exchange budget announced by the government in early January. They proposed to close the gap in the following way (Beckford *et al.*, 1978:109):

	$m
Alumina exports to socialist countries	35.0
Suppliers credits from socialist countries	50.0
Line of credit from Hungary	8.0
Moratorium on private debts and investment income payments	52.3
TOTAL	145.3

There is no doubt that even the planners considered these sources uncertain. For example, in the case of the moratorium, they admitted that 'care must be exercised in selecting private debts so as to minimize adverse repercussion on capital inflows' (Beckford *et al.*, 1978:108), and the amount of trade and aid that could have been obtained from socialist countries (primarily the CMEA countries) in the fiscal year immediately ahead was clearly not secure. For this reason, the planners presented three different foreign exchange budgets. The full budget would allow all targets to be met, resulting in a net increase of 48 000 jobs (with a loss of fewer than 1000 jobs in manufacturing). With an import budget of $600m, the agriculture and crafts target could be met (an increase of 36 000 and 5000 jobs respectively) but only 60 per cent of the construction and manufacturing targets, resulting in a loss of 12 000 and 21 000 jobs respectively, in those sectors for a net gain of 8000 jobs.[17] A $650m budget would result in the construction and agricultural targets being met but still with a loss of 21 000 manufacturing jobs for a net gain of 15 000 jobs.

The authors of the plan emphasized that it would require a vigorous effort at national mobilization to implement the plan. Thus, Duncan's ministry was to be assigned a major role. It was to mobilize the people to get behind the plan and the productive effort. The redeployment of thousands from manufacturing and urban unemployment to the agricultural employment would require a major change in attitudes. The tastes for imported foods and metropolitan consumer goods would also have to undergo a similar transformation, given the strict budgeting of foreign exchange and the emphasis on agriculture. The new forms of production relations such as cooperatives and CEOs would also require political education.

Manley decides
The timing and process of decision-making on the production plan are both of considerable importance because they tell something about whether an alternative was possible and why the decision was so divisive in the party. The People's Production Plan was the topic of Cabinet discussions on 24 March and of the NEC meeting on the weekend of 26–7 March and Cabinet discussions the next week. Though the decision was not made at the NEC meeting, the writing was on the wall, as the left took a beating at that meeting. One of Duncan's lieutenants, Maxine Henry, describes the scene:

> At the meeting of the Party's National Executive Council . . . the Left was virtually berated for their failure to appreciate tactics and for creating false expectations among the people, for destroying the class alliance by intemperate speech. Manley castigated them for confusing ideology and pace and noted that 'Socialism alone cannot produce' (Henry, 1980:62).

Manley (1982:155) states that the decision was made at a Cabinet meeting, which probably dates it before the first weekend in April. At any rate, given the time constraints (a revised plan was written, typed, printed and presented by 22 April) it seems fairly certain that it was made no later than a week after that. The timing here is important because it appears that the decision to reject the plan and to go to the IMF for additional foreign exchange was made before the private sector had mobilized (at least publicly) to pressure the government to significantly increase the foreign exchange budget and generally to stem the leftist tide.

Though Manley's contention that the decision was formally made by the Cabinet is most probably correct, the usual characteristics of decision-making in the Manley government and a number of specifics we discovered about this decision (in particular the lack of knowledge of Cabinet members about the contours of the plan) indicate that Manley made the decision himself and then 'sold' it to the Cabinet and Party. Henry (1980:64–6) using the IMF decision as a case-study of decision-making in the government contends that he simply consulted various advisors and groups of advisors in an *ad hoc* fashion, made a decision on the course of action to pursue, and then attempted to convince his colleagues (and opponents) of the wisdom of the course of action. There is complete agreement between this view from the party left and one from the moderate wing:

> Michael's trade union background gives an interesting insight. He was a supreme performer. He had no equal in his facility with figures or debate. He was also tough. Now, the system requires that negotiations be ratified by the workers. Michael's ratification would be obtained by explaining – or selling – his negotiation. Consensus was not by debate but rather by salesmanship. He took this system to the political arena . . . he was the quintessential advocate.

As to the reasons for the decision, Manley (1982:154–5) contends that the alternative plan had weaknesses; namely, that some production targets were unrealistic, foreign exchange requirements were underestimated and there was 'a general miscalculation about the amount of foreign exchange that would be needed and could be forthcoming.' A number of sources confirmed that the foreign exchange budget was the main source of concern. Reportedly, Manley did, in fact, raise the subject with Moscow and OPEC countries and found that no immediate and substantial support was possible.[18] Thus, it appeared likely that the country would have to count on the $600m foreign exchange budget if it did not go to the IMF. This would result in the layoff of 50 000 according to Manley's public statements.[19] Manley feared not only the drastic drop in employment in urban areas, much of which could have been picked up in agriculture only with great difficulty. He also feared the political reaction from the private sector, which when faced with massive cutbacks and/or shutdowns, would 'lock down the country' (as one PNP leader said to us) in order to force a change in policy. The economic chaos resulting from such a private-sector strike would be politically devastating.[20]

On the other hand, there is little doubt that Manley (unlike many of his moderate Cabinet colleagues) understood what the consequences of an IMF imposed austerity plan could be, but there was now a possible countervailing factor: the new Carter government. It seems very likely that the strong possibility of significant aid from the new US government made the IMF pill a little easier to swallow. Thus we would argue that in the end several factors played a key-role in shaping Manley's decision. One was his perception of the likelihood of significant aid from the Soviet Bloc and OPEC countries. Once this was answered in the negative, the decision hinged on his assessment of the balance of class forces within Jamaica. He felt the government could not survive a total confrontation with capital, and finally, the promise of US aid facilitated the decision.

The unifying factor here, of course, was that it was Manley's personal perception or evaluation that counted. This is not to say that Manley could force a decision down the party's or government's throat against its will. Manley was (and is) a man of extraordinarily persuasive powers and could convince key forces to support him. The point here is not that the majority of the party or government disagreed with him but rather that the decision-making was so structured or perhaps better said, unstructured, that other elements in the party and government did not really participate in making the decisions. This opened up the possibility for much greater alienation on the part of those whom the decision went against, which is precisely what occurred in the case of the PNP left in this decision.

Another point to note about this key turning-point in the development of the PNP government is the importance of foreign policy and foreign actions in the decision. Jamaica had always been of strategic importance for the United States, but it had played a passive role until 1972. With the new foreign policy of the PNP – non-alignment, trade diversification, the friendship with Cuba – and with Jamaica's rise to prominence in Third World affairs because of Manley's leadership and the example of the bauxite levy, this small island country assumed a role of importance in world affairs out of proportion to its size. Beginning with the bauxite policy, through the dispute over the Cuban troops in Angola, down to Seaga's special relationship with Reagan, Jamaican domestic political developments cannot be understood without the foreign policy backdrop.

Was the plan feasible?
Whether the People's Production Plan was a viable alternative option to seeking IMF assistance is still a hotly debated topic on the Jamaican left. One comes up with somewhat different answers to this question depending on how one approaches the problem. One way is simply to compare what did happen under the IMF plan with a careful assessment of what the economic effects of the People's Plan might have been. It is probable that the People's Plan would have been preferable on the basis of this type of

comparison. Even if we make a number of negative assumptions about the plan with regard to its inflationary impact and the limited foreign exchange budget, it is unlikely that the People's Plan would have resulted in the degree of suffering which the IMF produced, though there is no doubt that the People's Plan would have imposed hardship and demanded sacrifice of many people. This is true not only in the short run, but also in the medium run. The degree of economic reorientation demanded by the Plan was bound to create at least some hiatus in production, but unlike the IMF plan, its long-term effects would have been positive. It would have made the Jamaican economy more self-reliant, more viable and more egalitarian.

However, the viability of the plan cannot be evaluated in this way for the simple reason that it assumes that the mass of people *know* what the alternative would be like and are thus prepared to make the sacrifice. But this was something they could not know until they experienced it. Even with a massive public education and propaganda campaign, the many people who suffered a loss of employment or a decline in their level of living were bound to be ripe for countermobilization, given the level of ideological consciousness of the mass of the people. It is the political effects of the plan that made it exceedingly risky in the situation faced by the PNP government in early 1977.

Economically, the plan had three potential weak points. First, the production targets may have been too high. What the plan was attempting was simultaneously to raise the production level and structurally transform the economy. Case after case, Chile under Allende, comprehensive land reforms in numerous Third World countries, France under Blum and later Mitterrand, the Portuguese revolution, show that this is very difficult to do. Jamaica did have one advantage in this respect: the most important aspect of the structural transformation involved redistribution (to small farmers, CEOs, etc.) of land that was at that time idle, rather than redistribution (or socialization) of currently utilized productive capacity. The key difficulty, as we see it, was the redeployment of urban labor and unemployed to agricultural work, a problem to which we will return later. Still, given the level of unemployment in the countryside, it seems likely that labor would not be a major problem. So we are willing to give the plan the benefit of the doubt and assume that production targets would not have been grossly undershot.

The second area of weakness was the additional government budget expenditures needed. The subsequent history of the PNP government shows that it would have been difficult to cover much of the deficit through taxation and improved revenue collection. Some trimming of expenditure was also possible, but only in the distributive programs. In the end a large 'accommodation' from the Bank of Jamaica of $250–350m would have been inevitable which would have been highly inflationary. It would have been impossible to compensate people fully in the form of wage adjustments and so on without unleashing another round of inflation. In a sense, this is the way that the mass of people would have been made to pay for the plan, to sacrifice for the social transformation.[21]

The third and most serious weakness of the plan was the foreign exchange budget. The truth is that very little of the extra $145m would have been forthcoming. The Hungarian line of credit was eventually doubled to $16m but it was doubtful that much more in the form of aid from the Socialist countries could have been procured, as the experience of the Allende government clearly indicates (Bitar, 1979:192–5).

The time-frame for the alumina sales to the Socialist Bloc was too short. Full diplomatic relations with the USSR, including a resident ambassador in Jamaica, were not even established until May 1977. The development of trade relations with centrally-planned economies takes time in any case and the Jamaicans had had little experience in this regard.[22]

Finally, the moratorium on payments of private debts and investment income of the magnitude suggested would have stimulated illegal capital flight and inhibited inflows of loans and investment to such a degree that it would probably have been counterproductive. Attempting to control capital movements in such an open economy as the Jamaican is very difficult.[23]

Thus we would argue that with the Hungarian line of credit and the most generous assumptions about aid from OPEC countries, Jamaica would have had no more than $650m, probably less, for its import budget without the IMF loan and seal of approval. This would have meant, at the very least, the loss of 25 000 jobs mostly in manufacturing, because of the shortage of raw materials, about one third of the total jobs in that sector. This would have been concentrated in the larger enterprises, some of which would have had to close, others of which would have had to cut back their workforce. Thus, some 50–66 per cent of large manufacturers would have been seriously adversely affected by the plan. The foreign commerce sector in anything but basic necessities would have been decimated. Only domestic commerce and tourism would have gone untouched. Thus it can be said that the plan would have had a major negative impact on a large segment of the national bourgeoisie, and given the interlocking nature of Jamaican business and families within the Jamaican capitalist class (Reid, 1977), it is likely that an even larger section of the class could have been mobilized for any counteraction against the government which carried some promise of success. Moreover, independent of its direct economic effects, the political character of the plan in envisioning such a radical economic reorientation and popular mobilization would have frightened many capitalists.

The counteraction of the capitalist class, say a sector-wide lock-out, would ultimately have depended on arousing some popular support to be successful. We think that this would have been forthcoming from the economistically-oriented Jamaican working class. Even if the workers who were laid off in manufacturing were redeployed to some of the newly-created jobs in agriculture, they could expect to earn no more than 50 per cent what they earned previously. Obviously, the BITU could be counted on to spearhead the countermobilization effort. Given their record it is probable that the other unions would not have been able to resist the economistic push of their members. True, they had been supportive of the PNP government, but when it came to the bread-and-butter demands of the workers they could not be counted on to go along, as was shown in the case of the six-month wage-freeze and the freeze on retroactive pay. Again, the legacy of non-ideological politics proved to be a barrier to deepening the process of social transformation (or, at least, would have, had this option been tried).

To follow this theme a little further, it also seems that this legacy would have made the national mobilization process deemed essential by the planners and the PNP left much more difficult than they envisioned. They interpreted the election victory as a mandate for the deepening of the social transformation process, creating a more self-reliant and socialistic economy, but, in fact, only seven of the forty-seven PNP MPs elected were on the left. Much more important, it is virtually certain that most PNP voters and clearly the 14 per cent of the voters who formed the margin of victory between the PNP and JLP were expressing support for the redistributive programs and social-inclusion process initiated by the PNP in the first term. As one prominent PNP leftist told us in 1982:

in 1976 we campaigned on the basis of democratic socialism . . . and we got the support of the people, but the people's perception of socialism was more related to what had been done in concrete terms – land lease and the other people's programs – and not really to a theoretical understanding of socialism.

Indeed, the material gains of the people under Democratic Socialism had infused the PNP loyalists with enthusiasm for the campaign and the party, and they had provided the party with the margin of support that ensured victory. The victory was not, unfortunately, a mandate for sacrifice to build a self-reliant socialist economy.

In closing, we would like to emphasize that what made a successful adoption of the plan so difficult was, first, the shortage of foreign exchange and its impact on the capitalist class, and, in turn, on the industrial working class. Second, despite the real progress made in popular mobilization and political education, it is questionable that the level of ideological consciousness was sufficient so that, even with a coordinated national mobilization campaign, the people would be prepared to sacrifice for the alternative without knowing personally what the IMF plan would bring. In short, the development of the political movement (and thus the balance of class power) limited the possibilities at this point. Finally, the economic difficulties in implementing the plan, and thus the sacrifices necessary, would have been aggravated by the limitations on the state's capacity to administer such an ambitious program of economic transformation.

However, it is equally important to emphasize that the plan itself was basically sound, if not in all its details, then in its general direction. If it had been introduced in a situation where the budgetary and foreign exchange constraints were considerably less, such as in the fall of 1974 after the imposition of the bauxite levy, it might have been successful. In this context also, it could have been introduced on a more gradual basis taking into account the limitation of the administrative capacity of the state. The plan would have been the next logical step on the path toward building a more self-reliant, more democratic, more socialist society.

April–December 1977: under the first IMF agreement

Economic and domestic policy
On 22 April, Manley, announcing an Emergency Production Plan, began by saying that the government could not hold down imports to the $600m level without sacrificing the manufacturing sector, and, consequently it would seek an additional $200m in foreign exchange (Manley, 1977). Though unstated, this implied that the government was actively pursuing negotiations with the IMF for a loan.

In the plan presented by Manley the production targets for 1977 remained the same in most sectors as in the one written by the UWI team but the revised plan called for much less in the way of structural transformation of the economy, and the extra budget expenditure was drastically reduced to $23m. Unlike the original plan, which involved no devaluation, the revised plan called for the establishment of a dual exchange rate. The old rate of J$.90=US$1.00 would continue to apply to government transactions, all basic food imports, petroleum, feeds, fertilizers, medical and pharmaceutical products and the bauxite–alumina sector. A new, devalued rate of J$1.25=US$1.00 would apply to all other transactions.

In the agricultural sector the amount of new land to be brought into production was reduced to 36 000 acres, which seems to be the amount deemed necessary to meet the targets.[24] The construction target remained at 13 000 houses with 10 000 of them government-built, though with no extra budget allocation (compared with $120m in the original plan) this appears to have been unrealistic. This plan called for maintenance of 1976 production levels in manufacturing. In terms of structural transformation of the economy, the only new, definite element announced was the 36 000 acres of idle land which was to go to 10 000 farmers under the Land Lease program. The development of CEOs was announced as a future project and no new nationalizations were added to the list of 19 January. It was announced that Jamaica would attempt to further diversify its foreign economic relations, particularly with the Soviet Union, the Comecon Bloc and the People's Republic of China (Manley, 1977:10).

This speech along with the throne speech, the private-sector White Paper, and budgets announced in April and May give the contours of PNP policy in 1977. In the speech on the plan, Manley announced that the government intended to

(1) introduce an incomes policy;
(2) deal with the problem of scarce benefits by introducing the first come first serve principle after consultation and agreement with the JLP;
(3) move toward the establishment of an independent electoral commission but in the context of an overall review of the Constitution;
(4) end the State of Emergency.

Manley concluded by stating that he had invited Amnesty International and the International Commission of Jurists to visit Jamaica to examine the government's human rights record. (This was in response to Seaga's new campaign of which we write more later.) The only new significant area for reform aside from those already mentioned would be workers' participation. In real terms, the budget was actually smaller than that for the previous year (NPA, 1978:28).

In an apparent effort finally to 'clarify the role of the private sector' as the *Gleaner* and the bourgeoisie had so often demanded, the government published a White Paper on the topic along with the Emergency Production Plan. The paper was published in its entirety by the *Gleaner* on 25 and 26 April. The White Paper began with the statement that the public sector would play the leading role in economic development, planning and shaping the direction of the economy. The government would also actively encourage the development of cooperatives. The paper then proceeded to demarcate the public–private sector line, though adding that the line could not be hard and fast, but where and when changes were to be made they should be obvious to all. Moreover, fair compensation would be paid in the case of any government takeover. Finally, the paper went into a very detailed sector-by-sector outline, stating the present relative weight of various ownership forms (state, large private, small private, foreign, joint venture, cooperative) and the proposed weights under the government's long-term plans. This section of the paper is aptly summarized by Bernal (1981:18) in Table 5.2.

At this point the government was involved in intense negotiation with the IMF. In May, Manley announced that the government had rejected the primary conditions demanded by the IMF. These conditions include:

(1) a full devaluation, of 40 per cent (that is, a unification of the exchange rate and a small additional devaluation);

TABLE 5.2   *State participation in the economy: actual and proposed, as of April, 1977*

Sector	Foreign capital		Big national capital		Small capital and simple commodity producers		Cooperatives		State enterprise	
	*A	P	A	P	A	P	A	P	A	P
Domestic food production	0	0	0	–	X	X	–	X	0	X
Export agriculture	X	0	X	X	X	X	0	X	0	X
Livestock	X	0	X	X	X	X	0	0	0	X
Fishing	0	0	0	0	X	X	–	X	–	X
Forestry	0	0	0	0	0	0	0	0	X	X
Mining	X	–	0	0	0	0	0	0	0	X
Manufacturing	X	–	X	X	–	X	0	X	0	X
Construction	0	0	X	X	X	X	0	X	X	X
Tourism	X	0	X	X	–	–	0	–	–	X
Banking	X	–	–	X	0	0	0	0	0	X
Transport	0	0	–	0	–	–	0	0	0	X
Distribution	–	0	X	–	–	X	0	–	0	X
Printing	–	0	X	X	X	X	0	–	X	X
Media and communications	X	0	X	–	–	–	0	0	–	X
Services	X	–	X	X	X	X	0	–	0	0

*A = actual, P = proposed

Notation: X = significant role
            – = small role
            0 = insignificant or none

SOURCE   Bernal (1981:18). Reprinted by permission.

(2) a cutback of expenditures to balance the budget (that is, eliminating the $250m deficit proposed for 1977–8);
(3) an end to foreign exchange controls and to quantitative restrictions and regulations of foreign trade (*G*, 10 May 1977).

Girvan, Bernal, and Hughes (1980:123) report that the IMF was also of the opinion that the government's position on wage restraint was too lax, as, in the face of union criticism, the government was permitting wages to increase above the $10 limit (which became effective after the end of the moratorium) in cases where real wages had fallen below the June, 1973 level. The negotiation became deadlocked.

At this point, Manley began to mobilize international support for Jamaica's position. According to his own account, Manley managed to get Canada and Britain, both of whom had directors on the Board of the IMF, to put pressure on the fund for a favorable agreement (Manley, 1982:156). In the case of Canada, Manley utilized his long-standing friendship with Trudeau. The British situation was influenced not only by the presence of a Labour (Callaghan) government, but also because Callaghan 'had been through his own torment with the IMF' (Manley, 1982:156). In both cases, Manley's now established international prestige certainly aided Jamaica's position. Girvan, Bernal and Hughes (1980:123) point out that the international context was favorable as the IMF had recently come under attack from a number of quarters, including the establishment financial press, and finally, they believe – and our own interviews confirm – that the Carter administration exerted pressure on the IMF to reach a favorable agreement. Though the official State Department position was 'hands off', Andrew Young went directly to Carter on this and let the IMF know informally that the USA wanted a favorable agreement for Jamaica. At other levels the USA argued that the potential social and political effects should be taken into consideration in prescribing the economic medicine.

The agreement, which was concluded in July, was indeed favorable, by IMF standards. The IMF would loan the country US$74.6m over two years with $44.4m coming in the first year in installments of $22.4m in August 1977, $11m in December 1977, and $11m in March 1978. As usual, Jamaica would have to manage its fiscal and monetary policy and balance of payments in a fashion that would make it possible to pass IMF performance tests relating to net foreign reserves, net domestic assets of the central bank, net banking system credit to the public sector, and outstanding arrears and limits on new external medium- and long-term borrowing. Otherwise the terms were relatively good: Jamaica was allowed to keep its dual exchange rate, the wage guidelines were not made more stringent, foreign exchange controls and import restrictions were maintained and the government did not have to balance the budget. With respect to the last point, the agreement allowed the government to use $190m (the counterpart to the anticipated foreign loan total) in Bank-of-Jamaica support to finance the budget, and allowed a net credit expansion for budget support by the banking system of $45m. The resulting $235 million was only $15m below the government's original budget estimates (*G*, 13 July 1977).

In his announcement of the agreement, Manley argued that the agreement would allow the government to maintain foreign exchange resources necessary for industry and basic food and so on, while pressing ahead with new initiatives like CEOs and land reform. The government did move forward with a very modest CEO program in subsequent years, but an accelerated land-reform program announced a few months later with great fanfare was never begun. A few policies announced or initiated earlier were followed-up: RJR was sold to a number of 'people's organizations' (unions, cooperatives, church groups, etc.) and RJR employees, and the Home Guard was further strengthened in response to a Corporate Area crime wave in the fall. However, with one exception, the social transformation process initiated by the PNP government was largely spent by this time. The IMF, frustrated by Manley's politicking this time, was to make sure of that in the next round.

The one exception was the establishment of the State Trading Corporation, which was announced in November. The STC was to expand on the concept begun with the establishment of Jamaica Nutrition Holdings (JNH) in 1973. It would be the sole importer of certain items which were imported in sufficiently large quantities that bulk buying could be an advantage. On a general level, the STC would allow the government to diversify foreign trading relations and to exercise greater social control over the economy. Specific advantages were

(1)   lower costs as a result of competitive tendering, lower shipping costs for the large quantities, purchase from primary sources of supply avoiding the payment of commission, and greater use of bilateral arrangements;
(2)   foreign exchange savings resulting from the lower costs;
(3)   particularly lower prices to consumers because of subsidies of a 'basic needs basket' financed from savings on other items (NPA, 1978:48).

The STC was a holding-company wholly-owned by the government, and consisting of a number of subsidiaries. The first operational subsidiary was JNH with six more to be established. Three of these were to be established in 1978: Jamaica Building Materials Ltd, Jamaica Pharmaceuticals and Equipment Supplies Ltd, and Jamaica Textiles Import Ltd. Eventually, the STC was 'to be the major importer of all goods necessary for national development' (NPA, 1978:47). According to Kirton and Figueroa (1981:157), STC executives originally expected the STC to account for 80 per cent of the value of all imports other than oil and those for the bauxite/alumina sector.[25]

Foreign policy
Lewis (1982:7) identifies three strands in Jamaican foreign policy in the

first two years of the PNP's second term: (1) normalization of relations with the USA; (2) diversification of diplomatic and economic relations as part of the policy of non-alignment, in particular exploration of closer relations with the Socialist Bloc countries; and (3) continued pursuit of the NIEO in international forums. All three strands of the policy, Lewis points out, were directly or indirectly connected to the PNP's contradictory relationship, as both a government and a party, with the IMF. As we have already seen, the potential of economic relations with the Socialist Bloc was critical to the alternative plan favored by the PNP left, while the promise of aid from the new US administration influenced the decision to seek IMF aid. Moreover, the favorable terms Jamaica did receive from the IMF were partly a result of US assistance.

The relationship with the USA was progressively cemented during the year. Patterson visited the USA for talks with Vance in March. In May, a US team from the State Department, Treasury and USAID came to Jamaica for talks on economic aid and collaboration. In the same month, Rosalynn Carter arrived for a visit and talks with the government. The Carter administration, disturbed by the sorry state of affairs in the embassy in Kingston (see Chapter 4), appointed Frederick Irving, a professional diplomat and a liberal known for his progressive views on race relations questions, to the post of ambassador. In August, the same month that Irving presented his credentials, Andrew Young visited Jamaica, as part of an effort by the administration to strengthen ties with the Caribbean. His visit was followed by the announcement of a $63m US aid package over several years for Jamaica, by far the largest US aid package to Jamaica to this date (Table A.20). In December Manley himself traveled to Washington for discussions with Carter.

The PNP left viewed these moves with suspicion. These feelings were reinforced by talks between William Luers, Assistant Secretary of State for Latin American Affairs, and Duncan in May, arranged at the US Embassy's request. The Jamaicans present (Duncan and Henry) report that Luers advised ideological moderation and a quick conclusion of an agreement with the IMF, warned against trade diversification, the STC and other economic reforms, and suggested that Duncan's Ministry should attempt to dampen the people's expectations (Henry, 1980:54). US officials knowledgeable about the meeting deny most of these allegations, pointing out that such pressure for changes in internal policies was against Carter administration policy and Luers' own inclinations. Only the reference to the IMF was consistent with the new government's orientation; it did continue to encourage financially-strapped countries to come to an agreement with the Fund. Whatever the truth of the matter, the important thing here is the left's perception of the US posture and US intentions.

Jamaica also experienced a substantial warming of relations with social-democratically-governed Norway. In November, Manley visited the

Scandanavian country concluding an agreement on collaboration in Jamaica's search for oil and future alumina sales. A month later, Norway came through with a $22m line of credit for Jamaica.

Despite the decision to enter into an agreement with the IMF, the PNP government did attempt to develop relations, particularly economic ones, with the USSR and Eastern Europe. In March, Jamaica established diplomatic relations with East Germany and Bulgaria, and two months later, the first ambassador from the USSR presented his credentials at Jamaica House. Also in May, a Jamaican trade delegation visited the USSR and managed to conclude agreements on trade and economic and technical collaboration. By the end of the year, talks with the Soviet Union had led to the signing of agreements on trade, the building of a cement plant and technical education for Jamaicans in the USSR. Manley also visited Yugoslavia in November for discussions about bilateral cooperation and the non-aligned movement.

Jamaica's relations with Cuba continued to be close and the government used its new ties with the USA to promote normalization of relations between the USA and Cuba and continued to defend its position on Cuban troops in Angola. Exchange and trade relations between the two Caribbean countries were actually strengthened. In May, a new recruitment drive for the one-year construction skills training program (the so-called *Brigadista* program) was held and a new agreement on economic and technical cooperation was signed.

In November, Castro arrived in Jamaica for a week-long state visit. In sharp contrast to Samora Machel, whose speech in Jamaica the week before had deeply offended elements of the bourgeoisie, Castro was extremely well-prepared for his visit and handled every situation with impeccable diplomacy. He took the first opportunity to vow non-interference in Jamaican affairs and expressed his appreciation that the previous (JLP) government had not joined the US trade blockade of Cuba. The government rolled out the red carpet awarding Castro, 'a giant in the struggle against imperialist intervention and aggression', the Order of Jamaica, the highest Jamaican honor given to non-Jamaicans (*G*, 14 October 1977).

Internal struggles in the PNP

The decision to go to the IMF was a defeat and bitter disappointment for the PNP left, and the internal party struggle had demoralized the party and left it directionless. It never really recovered. This state of affairs was not lost on the society as a whole and was reflected in slipping popular support for the government: a May poll showed that only 28 per cent of those questioned thought that the government's economic performance since the election was good, while 31 per cent thought it was bad and 26 per cent said the government was trying but it could do better. By September, these figures changed to 8, 36 and 52 per cent, respectively (Stone, 1980:175; also see Table A.15).

Manley sought to reconcile the left to the decision to go to the IMF. In his speech announcing the favorable terms gained from the IMF, he contended it would allow the government to press ahead with its initiative stating that in the past there had been conditions tied to the IMF loan which were inconsistent with the PNP's goals, but that the agreement finally achieved was consistent with the country's immediate needs and the goals which the party had set itself. However, not many of the IMF critics were convinced by Manley's appeal. The internal party disputes continued unabated throughout the year peaking in September at the party conference and the resignation of Duncan as party General Secretary and Minister of Mobilization. As the internal party debate heated up, the rhetoric and ideological posturing of the left became more publicly visible.

The worst transgression by far, in this regard, came from the PNPYO. Immediately before the party conference the YO issued a position paper stating that the party's policy was too flexible and should be revised in the light of contributions to socialist thought by Marx and Lenin. The media, it argued, must positively encourage the broad masses to destroy the capitalist system. To accomplish this the government should take over RJR and the *Gleaner*. It also called for politicization of the police force and creation of a people's militia and for restructuring of the judicial system into people's courts and people's magistrates (*G*, 2 September 1977). In an NEC meeting soon thereafter, the party clearly distanced itself from the YO's paper, with Manley personally making a strong statement on the matter. Apparently, a number of NEC members called for much stronger action against the YO.

In November, a number of construction workers trained in Cuba in the *Brigadista* program formed the Jamaica Youth Construction Brigade League, a Marxist–Leninist organization, affiliated to the PNPYO. Unlike the position paper, this move seemed to have the support of the PNP left as Spaulding made a speech at the founding. The pro-Leninist stand was echoed again a few weeks later when the YO saluted Lenin and hailed the 'proletarian international position of the Communist Party of the USSR (*DN*, 7 November 1977).

The YO finally made itself totally impossible when it objected to the police placing Anthony 'Starkey' Tingle on the 'most wanted' list for several counts of murder, rape, shooting with intent and robbery. The statement, signed by YO president Paul Burke, continued: 'We recognize that Starkey is not an angel, but neither do we regard him as a most wanted or dangerous man. . . . He has had to defend his life and certain communities against paid political mercenaries which we see as natural and instinctive' (*G*, 15 November 1977). The government immediately dissociated itself from the YO statement. Burke was subsequently summoned to testify before the parliamentary committee on National Security (after refusing an invitation to testify). He was later suspended from his post by the party, whereupon the entire PNPYO 'politburo', that is, the executive committee) suspended itself, taking collective responsibility for the statement. They would remain in the YO and PNP, they said, because they saw the PNP as the only viable alternative to a fascist takeover of state power in Jamaica (*DN*, 3 March 1978).

YO members were involved in several instances of land capture. Early in the year the government had announced that it would acquire land on a compulsory basis where 'social pressures' existed, that is, where there was excessive rural unemployment, yet land on large estates lying idle. It was believed that this played a role in stimulating the increasing instances of land capture which was important because it created an area of uncertainty for land-owners.

Prominent leaders of the PNP left also came out with some statements which could be termed 'excessive rhetoric'. For example, in June, Spaulding made a speech saying that capitalism was not dead in Jamaica and that 'there was one more river to cross' in the struggle to 'obliterate capitalism' (*G*, 6 June 1977). A week later he made another speech saying 'As socialists, our purpose in Jamaica is that as vanguards of the conscience of society, we must ensure that we preside over the death of capitalism, the naked ruthlessness of the rich' (*G*, 11 June 1944). Another example is Duncan's statement in his speech to his constituents: Duncan, understandably bitter about being hounded from office by the PNP right, said that *Gleaner* managing editor Oliver Clarke was upset about a land invasion of his family's estate 'where the PNPYO helped repatriate [land] to the people of Jamaica' (*DN*, 27 September 1977); and, given the Washington, DC, venue, Small's references to 'economic interests in the US who do not want to see the Jamaican people consolidate their independence' and to the struggle of the Jamaican people 'to achieve complete independence by liberating the economy from imperialist economic interests' (*G*, 6 November 1977) could also be considered impolitic (if, at the same time, accurate).

In September, the party set up a committee to monitor the statements of party spokespeople and organizations (*G*, 1 September 1977). The formation of the committee was a response to the YO position paper, but there is little doubt that many hoped it would act to check the left also.

Publicly, the shifting balance of power in the party could be seen in personnel changes, statements of leaders, and the visibility of certain ministers. Businessman Danny Williams was elevated to the post of Minister of Industry and Commerce, joining ex-businessman William Isaacs (Labor) in heading two of the three most important economics ministries. Williams and Isaacs were very prominent, attending meetings of various private-sector organizations, emphasizing the important role of private enterprise in the government's economic development plans. Likewise,

Agriculture Minister Belinfanti, himself a large farmer, assured large farmers of their role and assured them that the government would not be influenced by artificially created 'social pressure' situations.

In the period leading up to the party conference, the internal struggle reached a level of bitterness behind the scenes that was only revealed publicly after Duncan's resignation at the first NEC meeting after the conference, when Duncan made a speech on the topic to his constituency (*G*, 27 September and 9 October 1977). According to Duncan, the right wing of the PNP had conducted a campaign against him which had as its central feature the allegation that he was the leader of the alleged plot (mentioned previously) by the left wing of the party to displace Manley. Duncan's ministry was termed a 'supra-ministry' and was supposed to be a key instrument in the plot. The rumor contended that Duncan and the PNP left were conspiring with the PNPYO, the Worker's Liberation League and Trevor Munroe to carry out the plot. The right wing had made use not only of informal party channels to spread the rumors but had also leaked them to *Gleaner* journalists. The existence of the plot inside and outside the party became widely believed and had led to physical attacks on Duncan by groups of rank-and-file party supporters. His position became untenable, according to Duncan, when the Security Forces also began to believe the rumors. At this point, he decided to resign. It was later revealed that Duncan's illness in this period and again in October was the result of arsenic poisoning (*G*, 13 November 1977).[26]

The left met with defeat at the 1977 party conference. The election of the four vice-presidents was aborted and put off until January. Reportedly, this was done by Manley in order to protect the left from a rout.[27] The results of the NEC election were reflected in the political composition of officers and the party executive, elected by the NEC a week later.[28] Only two leftists were elected to any of these posts and, notably, Small was defeated in his bid for a seat on the party executive. The most important change, of course, was Duncan's resignation. In the wake of this resignation a number of leftists also resigned from their posts in the party secretariat and the Ministry of National Mobilization. (The Ministry was subsequently placed in Manley's portfolio.)

The Cubans played an interesting and somewhat surprising role in these intra-party disputes. After Manley presented the revised plan and announced the decision to seek IMF loans (by implication), he was accused of 'selling out' by the PNP left and the extra party left. To support his position he called on the Cubans, who sent Carlos Rafael Rodriguez. He met with the left, the WLL and the YO. Henry (1980:58) relates his argument:

Rodriguez attempted to place the April 22 document (the revised plan) in the context of 'taking one step backward to take two forward' – a tactical retreat . . . He tried to assure the group that it was merely a

matter of 'pace' not a 'betrayal'. The Cubans as the 'accepted ideo-
logues' were called in to try and obtain the acquiescense of the 'left' in
the policy shift toward the IMF.

Similarly, when Castro came to visit, he backed Manley's position all the
way in discussions with the PNP left.[29]

Content of the ideological disputes
Aside from the IMF dispute, it is not easy to identify what the internal
debates in the PNP were about and precisely what were the positions of
various wings of the party in the debates. The PNP attempted to carry on
these debates behind closed doors and though there were massive leaks,
the information that came out was often distorted and sometimes completely inaccurate. This was particularly true of the information spread by
Gleaner columnists, which on the basis of further investigation, we found
to be very unreliable. Unfortunately, these columnists were the main
source of information for most Jamaicans on the behind-the-closed-doors
disputes. However, we were able to acquire detailed information on the
content of the internal PNP debates from our interviews.[30]

In Table 5.3, we have attempted to summarize the position of various
wings of the party on the internal party debates. We have divided the

TABLE 5.3   *Issues in PNP internal debates*

'Radicals' Left	'Moderates'	
	Center	Right
Mixed economy: Nationalize more now. In the long run, socialist economy with very limited private sector.	State-sector led, but state should mainly add to economy, not take over existing enterprises. Mixed economy is permanent.	State should limit itself to activities private sector will not or cannot do. Mixed economy is permanent.
Class alliance: Class struggle between workers and capitalists is inevitable. Alliance of workers, small farmers and lumpen proletariat.	Classes exist but class struggle is not inevitable. Alliance includes popular classes and middle classes and some capitalists, *but* avoid talking about classes – divisive.	Classes are not the fundamental feature of society. What you believe is the important thing. Do not talk about class – divisive.
Ideology: 'Rhetoric' Necessary for clarification/political education. Only a few 'excesses'.	Important reason for difficulties of party. Avoid talking about imperialism, capitalist, especially attacking better-off people.	
Expertise vs. commitment Ideological commitment is the most important qualification for administrative positions. Experts with no commitment will sabotage your programs.	Expertise is necessary. Commitment cannot replace expertise.	

Political education Very important component of political strategy for social transformation.	Not important and potentially divisive.	
Long-term vision See *Mixed economy*.	*See mixed economy.*	
'Strategy vs. tactics' Make decisions on long-term considerations of social transformation.	All decisions must be judged on the basis of feasibility; take current reactions to policy into account.	
Views of USSR Supporter of national liberation movements. Not imperialist.	Totalitarian, Imperialist.	
Foreign policy: – *US* US is imperialist.	US is imperialist but do not talk about it. Jamaica needs US aid, friendship.	
Imperialism Imperialism, US imperialism, should be emphasized at home and in international forums.	Imperialism exists but don't antagonize US.	You have to accommodate; US is too powerful.
Cuba Favors close, warm relations, expanded trade programs. Identifies with and admires Cuba.	Don't embrace Cuba. Causes adverse reaction from US and private sector. But principled defense of Cuba as full member of Hemispheric Community.	
Trade, economic relations Vigorous diversification, especially with communists countries.	Diversification.	Diversification is limited by geo-political situation.
Relations with communist countries Develop close relationships.	Strict non-alignment. Relations with USA and Communist countries on same level.	Jamaica is inevitably part of the West.
Relations with foreign communist parties Develop warm relationships, invite to party conferences, etc.	PNP is a member of the Socialist International and should have primary (only?) fraternal party relations with those parties.	
Other: *Relations with WPJ* For an alliance with WPJ and all 'progressive' forces.	Against alliance with WPJ.	
Lifestyle Comrades should have very modest style of life and consumption.	Whole debate is stupid.	
IMF No relations with IMF under any circumstances.	IMF demands are unduly harsh but we have no alternative.	IMF demands are too harsh but understandable.

moderate wing of the party into two factions, the center and the right. We make this distinction on the basis of the ideological differences revealed in our elite interviews and on the basis of a similar distinction made by several PNP leaders in interviews on the internal party debates. The right wing actually did not favor key elements of the development model being promoted by the PNP. In particular, they did not favor development led by the state sector, though they did support the egalitarian social programs introduced by the PNP. These people, most of whom either were businessmen or had strong connections to the private sector, were PNP leaders primarily because of historical attachment to the PNP.

In the first term the representation of this group at cabinet-level was larger than that of the left, but retirements (for example, Glasspole, Wills O. Isaacs) and defection (Allan Isaacs) had reduced its number; at the same time the left in 1977 had increased its representation. By 1977 the left and right were about equal in size in the cabinet. In the parliamentary group, the Party Executive, and the NEC the left was probably larger though admittedly this evaluation depends on both classification decisions and the time point chosen. The center was larger than both of the other factions combined in both the parliamentary group and the Party Executive. In the NEC, and to some extent the Party Executive, there were a number of people who were party loyalists without strong ideological convictions. Manley held sway over this group. On the NEC this group was still very large even in 1977, though it did become smaller through time with the left receiving the most converts as a result of the experience of the IMF program, but even in 1980, this group was a critical swing group in the party. Though it is important to distinguish the right from the center, it must be emphasized that the gap between the center and the left was much wider and the internal party debate was carried on across this gap for the most part.

As would be expected, a key area of internal debate was the nature of the mixed economy. The differences were most clear in terms of what the configuration of the economy might look like in the long run, though this was more an implicit agenda than an openly debated point. The immediate points of contention were *much* narrower, with the left advocating the nationalization of banks, cement and flour and in some cases (especially during 1980) of distribution and with the right contending that already achieved state control was sufficient. These discussions were closely related to those about 'strategy versus tactics' or more generally about the 'pace' of change. The extent of STC operations was a point of controversy, but even on these points the divisions were not hard and fast. For instance, in the 1982 elite study, one leading PNP moderate said that he thought that the party should carefully examine the whole financial sector with a view toward nationalization, depending on the outcome of the study. It was not the specific issues but the implied underlying trajectory that made these debates controversial.

The debates on the class alliance and the question of class struggle were much more heated for several reasons. First, more precision was necessary on this question in the writing of the party manifesto.[31] Second, it went to the core of how the party would present itself in public (as a class party or a people's party). Third, as a consequence, it was closely related to the question of rhetoric, that is, who is the enemy?

The left was quite willing to go for a majority class alliance of poor people, whereas the center and right emphasized the necessity of cooperation of professional, technical personnel and business people. Their alliance was an alliance of all 'working people' which included the middle strata, small businessmen and some capitalists. They wanted to de-emphasize class and emphasize that 'we are all working people'. Talk about class struggle should be avoided as it alienated people whose cooperation the government needed. This same theme of avoiding alienating various social groups can also be seen in the group of issues we have somewhat artificially labeled 'ideology'[32] in Table 5.3, particularly in the question of the importance of political education and the role of rhetoric. Movement-building, as we have defined it, did not have a high priority in the agenda of the moderates.

The position of the moderates on questions of foreign policy and the attitude toward the domestic communist movement was also strongly influenced by the desire not to alienate powerful social forces, this time foreign powers, primarily the US government and US corporations, as well as domestic social classes. It can also be said that the right, and to some extent the center, was deeply anti-communist and very suspicious of the Soviet Union.

Three factors help to explain the left's view of foreign policy and the WPJ question. The first is that their view of the strategically necessary class alliance led them to play down the damage of anti-imperialist statements and of the close relations with Cuba. That is, they were less afraid of alienating the Jamaican middle and upper classes than the moderates. Second, their analysis of the nature of the world capitalist economy and what was necessary for the pursuit of the non-IMF or more generally non-capitalist path led them to look to certain sets of countries and not others. One prominent radical explained this to us when questioned about the desirable foreign policy for Jamaica:

You have to look at it in relation to your economic strategy, in our case, the non-capitalist path, this will shape your foreign relations. Look at the present trade arrangements: those which work to the mutual benefit of the countries, leave them in place. Don't change for changes' sake. But

if you want to have more central planning and state-sector-led development, you can look to three sets of countries for trade and foreign
exchange: Scandinavia, Arab countries and the Communist countries,
Eastern Europe. They are willing to help a country on a non-capitalist
path. You have to count on a US reaction.

Finally, the whole picture, especially the tone of foreign policy statements
by the radicals, cannot be understood without taking into consideration the
deep identification of many of them with African national liberation
movements. These men and women, many of whom had political roots in
the black power movements of the late 1960s, were heavily influenced in
their views of Cuba, the USSR and the USA by the respective roles of
these countries in Africa. Moreover, they adopted some of the style of
these movements. As one leftist, who had had second thoughts about it,
told us 'We were identifying with and using the rhetoric of the most radical
element of the third world, the national liberation movements. It was not
appropriate to our situation'.

To the students of the Western European left, many of these differences
seem fairly typical of mass-based socialist parties and, consequently, not
unbridgeable. The problem was that the perception of the ideological
differences was much greater than the actual differences. The right and
significant portions of the center perceived the left to be Communists or,
more politely, 'scientific socialists'. That is, they believed that total state
control of the economy was part of the left's long-term agenda and
suspected that the introduction of a one-party state was, too. They held
this opinion while admitting that the immediate differences on policy,
particularly domestic policy, were not very great. In an interview one PNP
rightist said 'What was wrong with the radicals was all the personal abuse,
anti-Americanism, and the rhetoric. Basically there were not very important policy differences. But they wanted to destroy the private sector'. Of
course, the IMF controversy was a *very* important exception to the general
rule that the concrete, short-term policy differences were not so great as to
make constructive collaboration in the same party impossible.

In fact, the long-term vision of the left did not involve total state control
of the economy. Certainly, like left socialists in any movement, they
harbor Utopian long-term visions of a socialist economy totally dominated
by state enterprises, cooperatives and worker-owned firms, with only a
residual role for private enterprise, but this vision had little practical
impact. To the extent that they had any clear-cut theoretical orientation on
the long-term role of the private sector in national development, it was the
theory of the non-capitalist path, which envisions a significant though
subordinate role for national capital until an undefined point in the distant
future when the productive apparatus and the working class is fully
developed.[33]

As for the direction of democratic institutions, there is no doubt that the left favored thorough-going constitutional reforms to eliminate the constitutional barriers to rapid change. Moreover, they did feel that the highly competitive two-party system was a barrier to national mobilization and they clearly hoped to make the PNP into the dominant, hegemonic party in Jamaican society, but there was no serious suggestion (outside some elements in the YO) that periodic elections should be suspended or that the opposition should be forcefully suppressed. The one-party dominance was to be achieved through popular mobilization in a democratic context.

The left view of the moderates, on the other hand, was that the moderates' desire to hold back the pace of change and above all to enter into the IMF agreement was motivated by the class interests they represented rather than by an evaluation of what was politically possible at the time. It is true, as we have pointed out, that many right-wingers did have roots in the private sector, but the left applied the class background criteria very crudely, lumping a number of centrists with *haute bourgeoise* backgrounds with the right and unfairly abusing them personally. Many of the other centrists were reviled as *petit bourgeois* whose only interest in politics was sinecure. Given the historical class profile of the PNP and the pervasiveness of clientelism in Jamaican politics, there was some truth to these charges. But many of the centrists of varying class origins were sincerely committed to the PNP's social programs, its economic development path and foreign policy, but simply had a different analysis of what was politically possible.

The JLP takes the offensive

In late March, the JLP, sensing the weakening of the PNP, began to recover from the election defeat as can be seen from the large increase in criticisms of the government by the JLP shown in Table 5.1. One can see from this table and Table 5.4 the shifts in JLP attacks during the year. After a spate of attacks in April on economic mismanagement, stimulated by the large Bank of Jamaica accommodation to finance the 1976–7 budget and by the uncertainty of foreign exchange sources, the party toned down its attacks after the announcement of the Emergency Production Plan and the accompanying decision to seek an IMF loan. It picked up the pace again in August when it became obvious that the PNP was clearly publicly on the defensive.

In the fall, the JLP attacks increased and shifted in emphasis to the Cuba/communist threat, movements to a one-party state, attacks on socialist policies, and attacks on the PNP left (disunity). The main events that stimulated these attacks were the RJR takeover, PNP internal disputes and left rhetoric, Castro's visit, the affiliation of the Marxist–Leninist brigade with the YO, the introduction of the STC, and the subpoenaing of the *Gleaner* journalists.

TABLE 5.4 Attacks on the PNP Government, May–December 1977

Grounds of attack	Month								Total attacks (May–Dec.)
	May	June	July	August	September	October	November	December	
Mismanagement	1 (JLP)	1 (G)	1 (G)	6 (G,1; JLP,4; PS,1)	3 (JLP)	2 (JLP)	5 (G,3; JLP,2)	1 (JLP)	20 (G,6; JLP,13, PS,1)
Communism/Cuba						3 (JLP)	1 (JLP)		4 (JLP)
One-party state/ totalitarianism	1 (JLP)			2 (G,1 JLP,1)	6 (G,3; JLP,3)	1 (G)	6 (G,3 JLP,3)	8* (G,4; JLP,2; PS,1;0,1)	24 (G,12; JLP,10, PS,1;0,1)
Rhetoric undermines business confidence→ economic problems	2 (G,1; JLP,1)	1 (G)	1 (PS)	3 (G,2; PS,1)	3 (G,1; JLP,1; PS,1)	1 (JLP)			11 (G,5;JLP,3 PS,3)
Socialist policies undermine business confidence	1 (JLP)								1 (JLP)
Clarify limits of public sector/ reassure business		1 (PS)							1 (PS)
Socialist policies unfair/bad				1 (JLP)	1 (G)	2 (G,1; PS,1)	6** (G,3; JLP,1; PS,2)	1 (JLP)	11 (G,5;JLP,3; PS,3)
Manley out of control/disunity in party					1 (JLP)		1 (JLP)		2 (JLP)
Total Articles	3 (G,1; JLP,2)	3 (G,2; PS,1)	2 (G,1; PS,1)	10 (G,3; JLP,5; PS,2)	14 (G,5; JLP,8; PS,1)	9 (G,2; JLP,6; PS,1)	15 (G,8; JLP,5; PS,2)	9 (G,4; JLP,3; PS,1;0,1)	65 (G,26; JLP,29; PS,9; 0,1)

*Attacks on the threat to press freedom stimulated by subpoenaing of *Gleaner* journalists.
**Including attacks on the State Trading Corporation.

KEY   G = attack by *Gleaner*
JLP = attack by JLP spokesperson
PS = attack by private sector
O = attack from other source

By far the most important development in JLP strategy in 1977 was an internationalization of its political strategy. Lewis (1982:16) argues that Seaga perceived how effectively the PNP had used international contacts to bolster both government and party policies and tactics and that he seemed to have decided that the JLP should abandon its isolationist traditions and seek to use external relations to affect the process of domestic relations. The first indication of this strategy was Seaga's late March call for the release of Senator Pearnel Charles and all other 'political prisoners' held under the State of Emergency, contending that they were being deprived of their 'human rights', a phrase obviously selected for its appeal with the Carter Administration (*G*, 30 March 1977).

In the following weeks the JLP launched a Human Rights Campaign calling on its supporters to mount a campaign of peaceful and lawful resistance against the government. The JLP would boycott the opening of Parliament in protest and Seaga would take the party's case before Amnesty International and the International Committee of Jurists. The JLP's charges concerned the State of Emergency; fraud in the 1976 elections; victimization in job allocation; political manipulation of the security forces, government funds and public information media; and threats to the free media.[34] Throughout the year, JLP spokesmen repeated these charges, but particularly those related to electoral fraud and manipulation of the security forces.

Seaga immediately increased the stakes by taking his campaign abroad. In April, first in Belize and then in Miami, Seaga repeated the human rights charges, characterizing as 'naive' a US government report stating that Jamaica had a 'clean or moderately unblemished' human rights record (*G*, 14 April 1977; Lewis, 1982:15). Later in the year, the JLP leader's campaign shifted to the Cuban threat. In August, he told Andrew Young that Cuba was presented as the 'sample and example' of the type of republic on which Jamaica should be modeled (*G*, 7 August 1977). In October in London he charged that Manley had brought Castro to Jamaica to build up the PNP left wing against the moderates (*G*, 19 October 1977).[35]

Seaga escalated the international strategy to a qualitatively higher level in an October speech (followed by questions and answers) in Washington, attended by some US Congressmen, an event that was so controversial that it resulted in Seaga's censure by the Jamaican Parliament for 'reprehensible conduct and acts inimical to Jamaica' (*G*, 2 November 1977).[36] The gist of Seaga's speech follows (*G*, 7 November 1977). Because of their number Caribbean states were now a considerable bloc in international forums. In this group of states, the Cuban model was gaining influence at the expense of the Puerto Rican model, as could be seen in the governments of Jamaica and Guyana and the oppositions in Grenada and Trinidad. The effect of this would be the replacement of multi-party democracy with single-party systems, as had happened in Guyana. Seaga then asserted 'we are about to lose [multi-party democracy] in Jamaica'. People would reject the government but they could not do so under the present electoral system which was under the total control of the government and therefore open to abuse through manipulation. If this succeeded in Jamaica, it would mean that 'following in the footsteps of Jamaica and Guyana, the Marxist system can be introduced in other countries despite the will of the people'. The only impediment to the spread of the model was the 'utter economic chaos' which the economies of Jamaica and Guyana were experiencing.

In the question-and-answer period, Seaga repeated the charge that the violation of democratic rights under the State of Emergency during the 1976 elections was very serious. On the question of economic aid, he contended that Jamaica should receive increased aid and that the design of the program would determine how much it benefited the people. He continued by saying that he 'could never advocate the reduction of aid for a country that I represent', adding that 'it cannot be said that an increased aid program will in fact benefit the Manley regime' in its present economic difficulties. Thus, as Lewis (1982) concludes after reviewing the events of the period, by late 1977 Seaga had devised a strategy to influence the US administration away from its pro-Manley position to a view of the government as part of a developing Cuba–Jamaica–Guyana axis in the Caribbean.

To the extent that his allegations about human rights violations, electoral fraud and communist subversion were believed in Washington, it is obvious that they would have an effect on economic assistance offered (or denied) to the Manley Government. Seaga denied publicly that this was his intent. But our State Department and Foreign Service interviews supported our own conclusions that the only sense one can make of Seaga's actions is that he indeed did try to reduce US aid to Jamaica. A reduction of economic assistance to Jamaica would increase the economic difficulties for the country which, in turn, would aid his campaign to dislodge the government from power.

The theme of a Cuban/communist threat was also promoted by the JLP in the domestic political arena. There were constant attempts, usually by Seaga but also by other JLP leaders, to link PNP policies to an alleged communist master plan: the Home Guard was patterned after the Cuban People's Militia; the RJR takeover was part of 'a four-part master plan . . . to assassinate free expression in Jamaica . . . [the] plan is the standard communist strategy'; the PNP's constitutional revision, if successful, would introduce 'the Cuban Model of a Constitution' (*G* 17 and 23 October and 29 November 1977).[37] The JLP boycotted Castro's visit to Jamaica on the grounds that the 'communist dictator' abused human rights and that the people of Jamaica distrust communism (*G*, 16 October 1977). They followed this up with a statement that the party would oppose closer relations with Cuba as long as Cuba was involved in Jamaican domestic politics and in espionage in Jamaica, adding allegations about the Cuba–Jamaica–Guyana axis similar to those made by Seaga in Washington (*G*, 17 October 1977). Finally, the JLP had a field-day with the announcement of the affiliation of the Marxist–Leninist brigade with the PNPYO. Clearly, the *Brigadista* program was resulting in Jamaican youth' being indoctrinated into communism and as communist agents' (*DN*, 31 October 1977).[38]

The divisions in the PNP and the visibility of the PNP left also offered opportunities for the JLP charges that the PNP was infiltrated by subversive elements. Seaga called for the removal of the 'gang of four' (Spaulding, Small, Duncan and Bertram) to save the country, as the radicals were bent on wrecking the country and destroying the economy (*G*, 17 September and 28 November 1977).

The JLP sustained its criticism of the PNP's mismanagement of the economy, blaming the PNP for the country's severe economic difficulties. Again citing secret government documents (in this case a letter from the government to the IMF) Seaga claimed that the government had notified its creditors that it could not repay its debts, which was immediately denied by Coore.[39] One specific policy that was attacked was the State Trading Corporation, which JLP spokesman on Industry and Commerce Douglas Vaz called the beginning of 'economic enslavement' by the government and part of an 'attempt to achieve (the) egalitarian goal of a one-party Socialist State' (*G*, 22 November and 12 December 1977).

The JLP rejected the PNP's proposal for 'first-come, first serve' as a basis for distribution of jobs and housing on the grounds that a Labor Exchange (or similar institution for housing) would be subject to government manipulation. The JLP's response was a suggestion that scarce benefits be distributed on the basis of votes in general elections (with abstentions being the basis for distributions to non-party people) rather than seats in the House and parish councils, which, because of the single-member district system, favored the majority party. A parliamentary committee, set up to investigate the question, came to nothing as the JLP members resigned after four months, complaining that the government was not taking it seriously.

The election defeat had made it clear to the JLP leadership that the political game had changed during the PNP's first term in office and now no Jamaican party could win office without an effective political mobilization capacity. In the fall of 1977, the JLP began to lay the organizational ground-work for developing this capacity, founding auxiliaries for women (the Women's Freedom Movement), farmers (Progressive Farmers' Association) and higglers (Jamaican Association of Higglers); revitalizing the youth organization, Young Jamaica, and instituting area councils to strengthen the party machinery.

However, at this point the JLP's mobilization capacity was still not great, as can be seen from the small size of the few demonstrations it did mount.

It is true that the PNP's lead over the JLP in the opinion polls narrowed to 3 per cent, a big change from 11 per cent the year before, but this was due to the defection of PNP supporters to the uncommitted ranks (see Table A.15) rather than gains by the JLP, so it would appear to be a product of the demoralization of the PNP rather than the development of the JLP's mobilization capacity.

In sum, in the second half of 1977 we see an intensification of the JLP's campaign to delegitimize the government. We think it is quite clear that the allegations about human rights violations (electoral fraud, etc.), government-sponsored and/or tolerated communist subversion, and authoritarian intentions of the PNP left were all designed to convince the Jamaican people and the international community that the People's National Party and the government were operating outside the rules of the democratic game and, indeed, were trying to subvert it. The goal of the campaign was to undermine the government's support and build that of the JLP, and to legitimize increasingly radical forms of protest to dislodge the government. A second goal was to demonstrate the government's inability to produce adequate economic results by undermining any will to invest on the part of domestic and foreign investors by bringing into question the intention of the government to maintain a mixed economy. Finally, the goal of the international campaign was to reduce potential sources of foreign assistance for the government, which, in turn, would reduce the chances of economic recovery.

New tactics from the Gleaner

Generally, the pattern of attacks of the *Gleaner* is similar to that of the JLP, with relatively low levels of attacks from April to fall and then an escalation focusing both on economic mismanagement and political extremism. Two differences are worth noticing. First the *Gleaner* showed more concern for the rhetoric of the PNP left, singling out Duncan, Spaulding and the YO for particularly severe criticism. Second, the paper still did not identify itself actively with the JLP's anti-communist smear, though it did promote it more subtly.

Until the STC controversy, the editorials, even the critical ones, were decidedly more moderate in tone, at least when the subject was the government rather than the PNP left. The RJR takeover did provoke a page-one editorial insinuating that the takeover was a response to pressure by the local communist movement and charging that freedom of expression was threatened by the move (*G*, 6 September 1977). In the context of the production drive (which the paper supported) it continued to lay the blame on the government for the crisis as it had been destroying the private sector.

However, a more anti-government political thrust was sustained by the paper through columnists Hearne and Perkins and the gossip and rumor column 'Listening Post'. Joining the numerous front page 'news' articles, based on relatively little real news begun in early 1977, were front-page columns by 'Patricia Smallman', also critical of the government's economic management.[40] The *Gleaner* also played up the crime problem (which admittedly was worsening) in a sensationalist way.[41]

The new *Gleaner* tactic which became frequent in this year was the publication of 'news' articles well after the event in question had occurred. For instance, several months after Duncan made a speech at the opening of an auto repair school built with German aid, *Gleaner* columnists Perkins and Hearne wrote a series of columns strongly attacking the speech. The *Gleaner* then managed to make front-page news of the speech. During Castro's visit, while the *Gleaner* editorials were very gracious, the paper was giving major play to JLP attacks on Cuba and communism, including digging up a ten-day-old speech by Allan Isaacs (alleging that the PNP had charted a 'communist course' for Jamaica) and running the article as front page 'news' (*G*, 19 October 1977).

Like the JLP, the *Gleaner* strongly criticized the introduction of the STC, which it termed 'yet another signpost on the road to complete dominance by the state of all (economic) activities' (*G*, 23 November 1977). At the end of the year, the *Gleaner's* afternoon tabloid, the *Star*, ran a story alleging gross incompetence (resulting in some cases in death) of the Cuban doctors working as part of the aid program in the Savanna-La-Mar hospital. The allegations proved to be completely unfounded, but this fact was obscured by the heavy-handed efforts of a Parliamentary Committee which subpoenaed *Gleaner* editors and *Star* journalists and attempted to coerce them into revealing who was responsible for the article. This action brought a wave of protests not only from the *Gleaner* itself, the Caribbean press, the JLP, and the private sector, but also from groups heretofore sympathetic to the PNP, such as the Jamaica Council of Churches.

Reactions from the private sector
The announcement of the decision to seek an IMF loan was apparently met with considerable relief, as we saw earlier in this chapter. The private-sector reaction to the Emergency Production Plan was basically positive also, but, as the prolonged negotiations with the IMF began to cause foreign exchange shortages, private-sector organizations began to express considerable impatience with the delay. The agreement seemed to come just as the complaints were about to escalate substantially. Moreover, the agreement did not end complaints about the shortages of foreign exchange which, along with those about price controls, continued throughout the year.

In July the JMA president, the ultra-conservative Winston Mahfood, made a very strong attack on a speech by Manley, in which Manley had said the government would not bribe Jamaicans to stay by rescinding tax measures. Mahfood characterized the speech as 'vile and lying rhetoric' and angrily stated that 'Jamaica is not a private laboratory for the experiments of a handful of bitter, gullible, inexperienced theoreticians driven mainly by personal ambitions for political power' (*G*, 21 July 1977). Mahfood's speech led to an escalation of interchanges between him, backed by the Chamber of Commerce and the *Gleaner*, and the PNP Ministers and the party executive. The later summer and early fall were peppered with business criticisms of the YO and the PNP left. Thus, the IMF agreement appeared to have provided only a little breathing-space in the government's relations with the private sector.

The Castro visit did not spark any official reaction from the business leaders, but, based on our interviews, we have little doubt that the Jamaican capitalist class was harboring strong reservations about the development of an even closer relationship with Cuba. Obviously, the JLP campaign was feeding these fears. From the business point of view, the most that could be said about Castro's diplomatic presentation was that it did not make a bad situation worse. One of the leading tourist magnates told us 'Castro did one hell of a job in public relations . . . he is one hell of a politician – but he is still a communist'.

Only two specific policy initiatives sparked any reaction from the private sector. Both the JMA and the Chamber of Commerce expressed criticism of the RJR takeover, contending that it could become another government mouthpiece. The STC unleashed a veritable storm of attacks, most charging that the government was moving toward total state control of the economy. Even the JEA, the most moderate of the private sector organizations, expressed strong opposition to the introduction of the STC (*DN*, 30 November 1977).

One might think that the White Paper on the mixed economy, the IMF agreement and the defeat of the left would have assured the private sector and that relations between capital and the government would have improved. In fact, only the JEA issued a positive response to the White Paper (the rest said nothing at all) and 1978 was a record year for business migration to the USA, indicating a record number of decisions in 1977 to migrate (see Tables A.4–5), and investment hit rock bottom (Table A.6). Several factors probably explain this lack of private-sector turnaround. First, by this point most Jamaican capitalists did not trust the government. Commenting on the mixed economy, Royal Bank of Jamaica chairman Ron Sasso, probably reflecting the opinion of a number of his colleagues asked 'Who among us can say with confidence that this is the official objective?' (*G*, 10 September 1977). JLP propaganda along with symbolic events like Castro's visit, actual policies like the STC, and rhetoric from the YO and the PNP left were enough to nurture these doubts even in the face of the overall moderation of the government's course. Second, the economic situation itself had become an important cause of the migration and lack of new investment.

Reactions from other social forces

The dismal economic situation was also being felt by the middle classes. The lack of economic opportunity was the primary factor contributing to the steep rise in migration of professional and technical personnel in this period, but the crime wave of the fall of 1977, especially a number of well-publicized rapes in St Andrew, was also a contributing factor (see Tables A.4–5 and A.7). The effects of the JLP–*Gleaner* attacks on the government and the rumor mill cannot be discounted. For example, the rumors about the impending withdrawal of passports certainly stimulated some people to leave while they could.

In this period, one can also detect shifts in the posture of other social forces toward the Manley government. The established churches, as represented by the JCC, which had been generally supportive of the government's policies and very rarely critical of the government's action, spoke out against the PNP on several occasions in this year, notably concerning the Rema incident, the YO position-paper and the subpoena of the *Gleaner* journalists, and, significantly, several leading churchmen began to refer to the threat of communism in Jamaica. The JTA, which was also basically sympathetic to the government, publicly took a critical stand on the Rema incident and the YO paper.

Another significant development in this period was that, by 1977, the Governor-General, Florizel Glasspole, a founding member of the PNP, former PNP Minister and Manley appointee to the Governor-General post, was publicly perceived as being anti-PNP, consistently making more or less indirect criticisms of the party, particularly the left. Indicative of the extent of Glasspole's dissatisfaction was his decision not to accept Manley's nominees for the Privy Council, instead substituting his own list of a clearly different political color. For instance, Glasspole appointed ultra-conservative businessman and *Gleaner*-owner Leslie Ashenheim and did not appoint Vernon Arnett, one of Manley's suggestions, who was, like Glasspole, a founding member of the PNP, and had also been General Secretary of the party for years and Minister of Finance under Norman Manley.[42] The shift of Glasspole is significant not only because it shows how former PNP loyalists had abandoned their party as it moved left, but also, and more important, because Glasspole did have a great deal of influence on public opinion.

We will deal extensively with the reaction of organized labor to the IMF plan in the next chapter. Suffice it to say here that the unions, other than the BITU, maintained a positive attitude toward the government, but this was being tested by the wage guidelines. The guidelines along with the difficult economic situation and inter-union competition led to a substantial increase in industrial disputes in 1977 (see Table A.16 and 17).

Economic performance in 1977
The economy declined by 2 per cent in 1977, largely because of the very low levels of capital formation (see Tables A.6 and A.10). Per capita consumption also declined, by 3 per cent, as the inflation rate increased to 11 per cent, but employment was stable when compared with October 1976 (Table A.11). This combination of events was possible because of the differential growth of sectors, with increases in agriculture, services and self-employment (often under-employment) covering declines in other sectors, primarily in construction and large manufacture. Naturally, this shift was accompanied by lower levels of income given the relative wages in these sectors.

Obviously, performance fell substantially short of the targets set by the Emergency Production Plan. This occurred for a variety of reasons: inadequate budgets; overestimation of resources available or mobilizable; overestimation of private investment and factors beyond the control of the government. In the housing sector, the government managed to build 4540 houses (NPA, 1978:158), compared with the target of 10 238, which was primarily because of the budget allocation in this area.[43] Bauxite and alumina did experience a substantial increase but the 12.5m ton target was missed by 1.5m tons because of the slower than expected upturn in the world market and secondarily to the slower than expected pace of diversification (Ministry of Mobilization, 1977:14–19).

The emphasis of the Emergency Production Plan was on agriculture, and here the plan met with some success, though again it fell short of most of its targets. The targets were to bring an additional 36 500 acres of land into production, primarily through Project Land Lease and secondarily through a new Crop Lien programme, and to settle an additional 10 000 farmers under Project Land Lease. The achievements of Land Lease were 7700 farmers settled, an increase of 30 200 acres planted; and an increase of gross output from 58 000 to 86 000 short tons, (NPA, 1977:99; 1978:115). As Table A.18 shows, domestic food production increased substantially. Elsewhere, the results were not so impressive. The total employment in the sector, including Project Land Lease, increased by only 10 000 (Department of Statistics, 1979), far below the goal set in the plan.[44] Production targets in other areas such as milk were also far below expectations.

In the area of balance-of-payments, the overall program was very successful, as the deficit was reduced from $238m to $14.6m. Import restrictions, the partial devaluation, and increased domestic food production were responsible for this positive movement.

In terms of its impact on the PNP government, the economic failures and successes in all the previously-mentioned areas paled beside the economic failure in one area: on 15 December, Jamaica failed one of the IMF performance tests, the net domestic assets test. On that day, the net domestic assets of the Bank of Jamaica were $9m (2.6 per cent) above the ceiling of $355m, because of the failure of certain foreign loans to materialize on time.[45] As a result, Jamaica would not receive the second or third tranches of the IMF loan, and a $30m World Bank loan and a $32m loan from US commercial banks would be held up (Girvan *et al.*, 1980:124). More important, the IMF was now in a position to demand new concessions from the government which had dared to pressure it into concessions which were not consistent with its usual prescriptions. The Manley government had come to the end of its rope.

Concluding remarks
In the last chapter, we concluded that the downturn in the international economy and Jamaica's dependent situation in it, along with mistakes of the PNP government had locked the country into a path that was to lead to the PNP government's downfall. In this chapter, we saw why: it was not because there were no options that were better than the IMF agreement in pure economic terms. Rather, the pursuit of that option, the People's Production Plan, was made exceedingly difficult by the unfavorable balance of class forces in Jamaican civil society and the limited capacity of the state to carry out such a profound departure from the past. The PNP as a political movement had made great progress but the legacies of the past, the non-ideological clientelistic nature of the party at the outset and the divided, economistic labor movement, continued to limit the transformation process. The PNP was in an unenviable position where there was no middle ground between the two options which was economically feasible yet within its political capacity. Either it went to the IMF and accepted all that ultimately meant in terms of dictation of its economic policy, or it went without and all that meant in terms of the dramatic loss of employment in manufacturing and its political consequences as well as the general privation that the difficulties involved in managing a rapid economic transformation would bring in the short to medium term. Both options appeared to lead to political defeat.

The decision on the IMF left the party divided and the left embittered. Though it may be true that no other decision could have been made, it could have been made in a better way. This is the one point of agreement in the otherwise very different accounts of the 1977 IMF decision given by Manley (1982: Chapter 9) and Henry (1980): had the decision-making process been more participatory as, for example, in the case of the 1980 IMF decision, it is likely that it would have been considerably less divisive and the resulting path would have generated more support, whatever the outcome. Still it is probably fair to say that the ultimate outcome in terms of the PNP's downfall in the wake of the second IMF agreement would have been no different.

After the struggle over the IMF had demoralized and divided the PNP, the JLP with the help of the *Gleaner* had the opportunity to take the offensive. It launched a campaign alleging government corruption, communist subversion, and massive economic mismanagement designed to delegitimize the government and impair its ability to produce adequate economic results and, thus, to bring it down.

6

The Second Term: The Struggle with the IMF

The IMF in the driver's seat 1978–9

In the period from the failure of the December 1977 IMF test to the failure of the December 1979 test economics was clearly in command, that is, political dynamics were fundamentally shaped by the constraints of the economy. The government lost virtually all room for maneuver by early 1978. A combination of three factors put the government entirely on the defensive. First, the harsh austerity measures imposed by the IMF caused a dramatic decline of living standards without producing any signs of arresting the economic decline and laying a basis for recovery. They also deprived the government of the means to carry on with its reform policies by way of their budgetary as well as political implications. Second, the severe internal tensions in the PNP and the demoralization of the activists and parts of the leadership made the government appear even weaker. Third, the opposition very skillfully exploited the political vulnerability of the government, waged a relentless delegitimization campaign and attempted to take advantage of the slipping political base of the government to promote popular countermobilization.

The failing fortunes of the government, the demoralization of PNP activists, and the intense pressures from the domestic opposition as well as growing pressure from abroad created the conditions for a successful campaign of the PNP left to revive the spirit of struggle against the IMF and to bring D. K. Duncan back as General Secretary. The 1979 party conference put the secretariat in charge of revitalizing the party and its political education program, and of 'giving priority attention to the very burning question of the economy' (PNP, 1980:2). The subsequent discussion brought rank-and-file complaints about the economy to the center of the debate and prepared the ground for the decision in March 1980 to break with the IMF, to pursue an alternative economic path and to hold elections at the earliest possible date.

Between March and October, the bipartisan electoral commission worked at maximum speed, putting into place the machinery which was to guarantee fair elections. The plan for the alternative economic path did not show the expected results and consequently the economy suffered even

more serious disruptions which manifested themselves particularly in shortages of basic necessities. The political campaign was waged with unprecedented bitterness and violence, resulting in more than 500 deaths. In the
end, the years of economic hardship, the JLP's delegitimization campaign
and the *Gleaner's* anti-communist hysteria, the violence and the government's loss of control over the security forces took their predictable toll;
the PNP was defeated in a landslide, getting only 41 per cent of the vote.

The economy under the second IMF program

After the failure of the December test, the IMF insisted that a new
three-year Extended Fund Facility arrangement had to be worked out.
However, as a pre-condition to new negotiations, Jamaica was forced to
devalue by 10 per cent (Girvan *et al.*, 1980:124); in January the third
devaluation in ten months set the basic exchange rate at J$1.05 and the
special rate at J$1.35 (*G*, 14 January 1978). The negotiations were long and
difficult; the entire Jamaican team, including strong advocates of choosing
the IMF route in 1977, were shocked by the harshness of the new measures
proposed by the IMF. The feeling was widespread among participants and
observers that there was an element of revenge in the IMF team's approach
for Manley's audacity to mobilize political pressure for the first agreement,
yet, the consequences of defiance were too costly. It was made clear to
Jamaica that the lack of an IMF agreement would not only affect the
disbursement of program loans from the World Bank and its willingness to
set up a sub-group for Jamaica, but also loans from bilateral sources, and
significantly so. Thus, the government had no choice but to announce the
new economic measures to the nation in early May.

The new agreement entitled Jamaica to US$220m over the next three
years, provided the following measures were adopted:

(1)   An immediate devaluation and establishment of a unified exchange
      rate at US$1.00 = J$1.55, which implied an effective weighted
      average devaluation of 25 per cent, to be followed by small monthly
      devaluations over the next twelve months amounting to 15 per cent;[1]
(2)   a strict incomes policy, limiting total increases of wages, fringe
      benefits, overtime, etc. to 15 per cent per year despite a projected
      inflation rate of 40 per cent;
(3)   a reduction of the fiscal deficit of the public sector through expendi-
      ture cuts, primarily in public sector wages and subsidies, and through
      a new tax package designed to raise $180m;
(4)   a policy of encouraging private sector investment by guaranteeing a
      20 per cent return on capital, based on price liberalization and a tight
      lid on wages;
(5)   an export promotion policy, involving tax incentives, priority access
      of exporters to foreign exchange, as well as the devaluations;

(6)   an adherence to monetary targets, with special emphasis on ceilings on credits to the public sector and on the orderly management of arrears.

The three-year public sector investment program with projected expenditures of 15 per cent of GNP per year, was to be financed predominantly (53 per cent) by public savings, the remainder coming from domestic (25 per cent) and foreign borrowing (22 per cent), in a sharp reversal from the two previous years when domestic borrowing had covered 85 per cent and more of public sector capital expenditure. The current surplus needed to finance these expenditures was expected to result from wage restraint in the public sector, from reduction and elimination of many of the current subsidies, and from the new tax package and improvements in tax administration. The net amount of foreign loans needed for the investment program was an average of J\$190m per year; together with amortization payments of J\$235m annually this meant that Jamaica would have to be able to raise an average of J\$425m per year in foreign medium- and long-term loans.

The public-sector investment program was important in the context of the overall IMF package because it was to stimulate production despite the induced decline in demand. Thus, it was approved by the IMF despite the general stipulation in the package that public ownership in the economy be restrained. An important element in the IMF-imposed restraint of state intervention in the economy was a ban on any further expansion of the role of the STC.

It is important to understand the IMF program not as a purely technical matter but as an inherently political one. The key to the success of the program was an increase in domestic as well as foreign private investment and lending, and this in turn required a revival of private sector confidence, no matter what the political – and even economic – cost. The STC is a case in point. Since new investors would hesitate to invest in a system where control of the sources of raw material would be taken out of their hands, the functions of the STC had to be restricted. This stipulation restricted not only the government's freedom of choice in promoting structural change but also, ironically, its ability to save foreign exchange by bulk buying. Thus, the hypothetical, or hoped-for, new investment took precedence over the assured foreign exchange saving. Another case in point is the IMF's demand for a higher return on investment. This restricted the government's ability to continue the egalitarian thrust in its economic policies and pitted the government against the unions.

From the point of view of the IMF, of course, and of those sympathetic to its policies, the whole program, including its political components, was practically motivated. In their view the IMF team was very reasonable and business-like, insisting only on the obviously necessary conditions to stimulate investment.[2] From the opposite point of view, the IMF conditions constituted an act of blatant interference designed to weaken critically a government bent on internal and external modifications of dependence and on curbing the power of capital.

The two key concrete tasks to make the program work were the enforcement of austerity provisions domestically, particularly *vis-à-vis* the unions, and the raising of substantial amounts of external loans. Enforcement of the program domestically was not going to be easy. The announcement of the conditions of the new agreement encountered a storm of protests from all social groups. The private sector, though clearly relieved that an agreement was in place, complained about the harshness of the terms and Seaga went as far as to urge the government to 'renegotiate or resign' (*G*, 18 May 1978). The unions, whose members were going to be affected harshly by the austerity, uniformly condemned the IMF terms, in particular the wage guidelines and the greater power given to the Ministry of Labor in wage negotiations in the public and private sector (*G*, 11 May 1978).

Success in dealing with the international financial community was clearly only partially under the government's control. The IMF was apparently committed to helping Jamaica in this endeavor.[3] As part of the IMF's effort to facilitate the achievement of the external loan targets, a World Bank Consultative Group was set up for Jamaica. Yet, despite this assistance and despite the internal sacrifices resulting from adherence to the IMF package, the hoped-for effects in terms of economic recovery failed to materialize. The reasons for this failure were partly straight economic and partly political, just as was the logic of the whole package.

Based on the 1978 IMF agreement, the World Bank projected a growth rate in real GDP of 1.5 per cent in 1978, of 3 per cent in 1979 and of 4 per cent in 1980 (IBRD, 1978). In reality, however, GDP declined by 1.7 per cent in 1978, accompanied by an increase in the unemployment rate from 23 per cent in April to 26 per cent in October (NPA, 1979:15.2). The combination of wage restraint and 49 per cent inflation led to a drastic cut in consumption; average weekly real incomes of wage earners declined by 30–35 per cent (NPA, 1979:ii). Also, the continued very tight foreign exchange situation caused disruptions in production through shortages of raw materials, etc. The recession in turn obstructed the government's fiscal program as tax receipts remained below target. Investment was lagging behind schedule and negotiations for new commercial bank loans were very difficult. Foreign banks did agree to roll over 87.5 per cent of the debt as it became due, but they were very reluctant to extend new loans.

In view of these difficulties for which the government could not be held responsible, the IMF agreed to make certain changes for the second year of the new agreement, starting in May 1979. It agreed to increase its own lending commitments to a total of US$419m over three years. The government was required to reduce further the real size of the budget and make more credit available to the private sector, and the unilateral policy of wage restraint in the face of rapidly-rising prices was to give way to a coordinated wage-price policy, keeping both wage and price increases at 10 per cent. In order to achieve this, the IMF urged the government to call for a social contract, that is, for a coordinated effort of all social and political forces, including unions, the private sector, professionals, farmers, and the political opposition, to work together, exercise self-restraint and devote maximum effort to an increase in production.

Still, availability of foreign exchange remained the key issue and the key impediment to economic recovery. Net foreign borrowing remained behind schedule and negotiations for refinancing US$450m in commercial bank debt due in 1980 failed. Despite reinstatement of OPIC insurance coverage for Jamaica in June 1979, no substantial new foreign investment materialized.

Economic growth remained elusive; real GDP declined by 0.4 per cent in 1979. Inflation, on the other hand, remained at 20 per cent. The lack of growth partly caused by the severe depression of domestic consumption resulted in a severe shortfall in government revenue, and unemployment continued to increase; because of public sector austerity, production cutbacks in the private sector, and flood rains in June, it reached a record level of 31 per cent by October. These economic problems aggravated social strife and political tension, resulting in further disruptions of production.

In December of 1979, Jamaica failed the net international reserves test; the IMF had set the limit at −US$380m, and Jamaica's real position was −US$475–500m. The government asked for a waiver of this test, on the grounds that factors outside the government's control were largely responsible for the failure. The factors mentioned were an unexpected increase in the oil bill, in foreign debt payments, in raw material import prices, and a shortfall in agricultural exports because of flood rains (*G*, 20 December 1979). Girvan, Bernal and Hughes (1980:129) confirm the importance of these factors and add shortfalls in foreign loans, in domestic non-bank financing and in tax revenue to the reasons. Since the original targets and estimates had been worked out in collaboration with the IMF, Jamaica expected an understanding attitude on the part of the Fund in considering the waiver. However, the conditions that the IMF attached to the waiver were extremely stringent, requiring a public expenditure cut of $150m before the waiver would be granted and a further cut of the same magnitude in 1980. These cuts entailed a streamlining of public agencies and enterprises, and a lay-off of an estimated 11 000 public employees in early 1980 (Girvan *et al.* 1980:129–30). The issue of these cuts and the resulting lay-offs led to a deadlock in the negotiations which ultimately resulted in the government's decision to break with the IMF.

As pointed out, one of the crucial reasons for the disastrous outcome of the IMF package was the shortfall in the expected inflow of foreign loans. Clearly, the attitude of foreign bankers toward Jamaica was strongly influenced not only by the IMF's approval of the government's economic management but equally, if not more so, by political factors. Key among these political factors were the attitude of the US government toward Jamaica and the signals sent to the international banking community by the Jamaican opposition via local affiliates of foreign banks and by Opposition Leader Seaga directly in trips to the USA. For instance, the anti-PNP information related through these channels highlighted rhetorical statements of the PNP left, particularly those on imperialism; and it emphasized the divisions within the PNP and the presumed threat posed by the left wing. Three former top-level figures in the PNP government told us independently that negative reactions to left-wing rhetoric and to the return of Duncan as general secretary had been crucial obstacles in their negotiations with foreign investors and bankers. Accordingly, one has to see the shortfalls in foreign loans, and perhaps the hardening line of the IMF in late 1979, in the context not only of domestic Jamaican politics but also of the deteriorating relationship between the Jamaican and the US government and Jamaica's general foreign policy.

The importance of Jamaica's foreign policy
Jamaica's non-aligned stand in foreign policy was, as pointed out previously, intimately connected to the PNP's policy goals of reduction of dependence and of consequent vulnerability to market fluctuations and political reactions in core capitalist nations.[4] The problem was that the development of alternative markets and sources of loans in the Eastern Bloc, in Arab countries, among Jamaica's neighbors and in the Northern European countries was not possible at a rate and speed sufficient to compensate for a reduction of funds from core capitalist nations and ease Jamaica's foreign exchange crisis, while that very policy of non-alignment and of support for Third World solidarity had an adverse impact on the flow of such funds.

In 1978 and 1979, Jamaica pursued cooperation with all four sets of countries.[5] Manley visited Hungary in February 1978 and Moscow in March–April 1979. These trips resulted in an agreement with Hungary on engineering work for Javemex, the joint venture alumina refinery to be built in Jamaica, and on a $22m line of credit, and in an agreement with the USSR on shipping and sales of 50 000 tons of alumina per year until 1983 and 250 000 tons from 1984 on, in exchange for Russian goods and on Russian assistance for the construction of a cement plant. Other bilateral agreements included trade with Nigeria, alumina sales to Iraq, and Venezuelan equity investment of $24m in new business ventures in Jamaica. The most important agreement with a Northern European country involved technical cooperation in alumina and shipping with Norway, along with a Norwegian line of credit. Important as all these agreements were, they did not significantly reduce Jamaica's dependence on loans from Western nations, multilateral lending institutions and commercial banks. In particular, Eastern-Bloc offers of assistance and trade did not fulfill the hopes of those who had regarded them as potential major substitutes for Western partners.

Relations with the USA, which had greatly improved with the advent of the Carter Administration, remained friendly until the summer of 1979. In June of 1978, Andrew Young visited again, followed the next month by a US Economic Mission studying investment possibilities; and Jamaica received various loans from the USA. However, by mid-1979 a growing concern in the Carter Administration and in Congress about developments in the region (that is, Nicaragua, El Salvador, Grenada), along with the ascendancy of the Brzezinski wing and its 'get tough on Communism' line, also affected the relations with Jamaica.[6]

In this context, Manley's speech at the Conference of the Non-Aligned in Havana, 3–9 September 1979, was oil on the fire. His general praise of Cuba and Fidel, the host of the Conference, and of Lenin's contribution to world history, as well as his call for a US withdrawal from Guantanamo Bay and for an end to the trade embargo against Cuba were perceived in Washington as dangerously anti-USA. This perception was reinforced by his call for self-determination for Puerto Rico and the expression of a preference for an independent Puerto Rico.[7] Besides resulting in diplomatic pressures, these tensions with the USA had immediate economic repercussions. It would certainly not be difficult to see a relationship between them and the simultaneous failure of the Minister of Finance to obtain an agreement from US banks on re-financing $450m of Jamaica's foreign debt and to obtain an additional $200m in loans. Furthermore, in the same month an attempt was made in the US Senate to freeze already approved loans of $32m to Jamaica. Under these circumstances one would not expect the US representatives on the IMF board to show particular lenience toward Jamaican requests for a waiver either. Thus, political concerns among US bankers and policy-makers undermined one crucial component of the IMF program and consequently doomed it to failure in its entirety despite the economic sacrifices of the Jamaicans.

The JLP and the Gleaner on the offensive
After the implementation of the second IMF agreement, popular support for the PNP slipped rapidly. The JLP seized upon the opportunity to launch an aggressive campaign to delegitimize the government at home and abroad. The campaign strategy had four dimensions: (1) verbal confrontation strategy, consisting of attacks in public speeches, in official statements, and in the media; (2) organizational strategy, consisting of

mobilization for direct action in demonstrations, strikes and civil disobedience; (3) electoral and parliamentary strategy, consisting of boycotts of
by-elections, calls for early general elections, and obstruction of parliamentary proceedings; and (4) international strategy, consisting of attempts to bring diplomatic and economic pressure to bear on the government by denouncing it abroad for communist leanings.

The verbal attacks centered on four major themes, all continuations
from the previous year: abuse of human rights, mismanagement, Cuban
infiltration, and disarray in the PNP and an impending left-wing takeover
of the party. The campaign which had been started in 1977 under the label
of 'human rights', with a view to the Carter Administration's foreign policy
concerns, was intensified. The main charges continued to be corrupt use of
the state machinery by the PNP, victimization, election fraud, and political
manipulation of the security forces. In particular, the JLP charged that
politically-directed members of the security forces were engaged in a
campaign of terror against the JLP (for example, see *G*, 27 November
1978). Official inquiries and results of court proceedings did not support
the charges, but many of them were not completed until long after the
charges had damaged the government's legitimacy.[8]

The state of the economy provided an obvious target for attack. However, the JLP did not attack the IMF but rather blamed the government for
all the economic hardship, having brought about the foreign exchange
crisis which required IMF assistance, through a squandering of resources.
Seaga called Manley a 'beggar leader' because of Jamaica's search for
foreign loans (*G*, 1 October 1978), and he called the government 'tax mad'
because of its attempts to meet the IMF revenue targets (*G*, 15 January
1979).[9] 'Mismanagement' became the key word in the attacks, subsuming
everything from the waste of money on the crash program and other social
services to the deficits of state enterprises which provided subsidized
services, and to the failure of the IMF tests. A particularly effective
weapon in this campaign was Seaga's repeated use of secret Cabinet
documents on the economy. Thus, he would highlight problems and
predict new economic austerity measures before they were announced,
which lent credibility to his statements on the economy.[10] This credibility
then rendered his predictions of impending economic doom resulting from
the government's mismanagement all the more effective.

Charges of Cuban subversion and of communist infiltration in the
government took many forms. The build-up of the Home Guard was
castigated because of its alleged resemblance to the people's militia in
Cuba and its alleged arming with Cuban guns (*G*, 3 July 1979); the
Brigadista program was accused of training Jamaican youths not in con-
struction methods but in guerrilla tactics (*G*, 1 July 1979); the Cuban
Embassy in Kingston was labeled a center for subversion in the Caribbean
(*G*, 22 October 1979). A major controversy was started about the new

Cuban ambassador, Ulisses Estrada, which ended up in a demonstration against the *Gleaner* and in support of Estrada, with the participation of several PNP leaders, including Manley.[11]

The severe internal tensions in the PNP gave welcome ammunition to the opposition for warnings of an immediate takeover by the 'totalitarian left', calls on the moderate wing to oust the left, claims that Manley had lost all control over the party, etc. After the return of Duncan in September 1979, the JLP charged that the left was now firmly in control of the party and was planning a 'military solution' in the form of a State of Emergency, a terror campaign against JLP supporters, and bogus elections before the new electoral system could be in place (*G*, 23 October 1979).[12]

By late 1978, the *Gleaner's* political agenda had converged fully with the JLP's anti-PNP campaign. It gave extensive coverage to Seaga's speeches and the JLP statements. In 1978, the main theme was mismanagement, and in 1979, the communist–Cuban threat and the danger of totalitarian tendencies assumed great salience, marking for the first time full *Gleaner* attention to this theme (Table A.3). The whole campaign showed the *Gleaner* editors to be masters of propaganda. The use of misleading headlines, misquotations of PNP spokespersons, suggestive and misleading combinations of headlines and pictures,[13] elaborate scandal stories, etc., turned the paper into a very effective tool to create confusion, uncertainty and concern in the population about what was really going on in the country. Thus, this campaign persistently, little by little, eroded confidence in the government as well as the government's general credibility and legitimacy.[14]

In addition to anti-PNP articles and editorials, the *Gleaner* published columns which launched constant attacks on the government and in particular on Manley himself. What the columnists were engaged in we would describe as a campaign of character assassination. As one of them told us in response to the question whether the columnists had exerted any influence on the fall of the Manley government, their primary merit was to 'deflate Michael's magical qualities':

> Michael Manley had such charisma that it is not inconceivable that the economy could have disintegrated and he would still have maintained the loyalty of the people. By cutting him down to size, by ridiculing him, we did reduce his charisma . . . We were able to, in a way, pin it (the deteriorating economy) on Michael . . . It was important for people to be able to laugh at Michael Manley, to take him down from his pedestal.

While the columnists ridiculed the PNP and its leader and portrayed them as villains, they built up the image of Seaga and the JLP as a superior alternative, capable of restoring economic well-being to the country and deserving of strong popular support:

We were also helpful in making Seaga and the JLP more palatable to the people . . . Before, the JLP's image was too 'labourite', . . . too backward . . . the party of ignorants. Seaga was JLP; there was something sinister about it; someone with his education in the JLP was suspicious. We helped to correct this, to open up a support base for him.

The JLP's organizational strategy was designed to strengthen its own mobilization capacity to counter the PNP's by promoting affiliated organizations and drawing them into coordinated activities. In 1978, the WFM and Young Jamaica (YJ) achieved some visibility in statements and protest demonstrations, but neither the Higglers Association nor the Farmers organization, both founded in 1977, did so.[15] The JLP also pursued other approaches to mobilization: It continued to strengthen the party organization itself, attempted to get the BITU involved in political action, and provoked outbursts of popular protests over immediate issues close to the people's hearts. To strengthen its organization at the grassroots, the 1978 JLP Conference called for a party branch with a local leader to be established in every polling division (*G*, 27 November 1978). Though, as in the case of the affiliated organizations, the party's accomplishments fell short of its aspirations, the JLP did succeed in strengthening its organization and enhancing its capacity for political mobilization.

In November 1978, a joint JLP–BITU committee was formed to coordinate a campaign of civil disobedience and a conference was held on the topic (*G*, 7 November 1978). Action soon followed, as the JLP, backed by the BITU, called for a national strike for 19 February 1979, in all sectors except essential services and tourism (*DN*, 16 February 1979). However, the strike call had only very partial results and most unions, as well as the PSOJ and JMA, did not support it (*DN*, 17 February 1979). The PSOJ's reason was that the economy should not be subject to any further strains, 'though we are in agreement with many of the stated issues' (*DN*, 17 February 1979). The trade unions rejected the strike as a partisan political action, contrary to the tradition of the Jamaican labor movement which was oriented toward economic and workplace issues. Seaga continued his attempt to politicize the BITU, telling the BITU general assembly that they should reject the social contract sought by the government, look beyond traditional trade union concerns to the question of which government should be in power, and force the government to hold elections within six months (*DN*, 27 May 1979). Yet, despite verbal support for the rejection of the social contract by Shearer, the President of the BITU and the one top JLP leader closely identified with the labor movement, the BITU did not mobilize its members for the type of political strikes that the JLP leadership hoped would force the PNP to hold early elections. The competitive nature of the Jamaican labor movement and the economic costs of such strikes to the workers would have rendered such action very risky for the BITU in terms of a potential loss of membership. Ironically, the same economistic trade-union orientation which deprived the PNP of a reliable, ideologically-committed support-base among labor, also deprived the opposition of an effective tool to aggravate economic disruptions and social strife in a systematic manner.

Whereas organized labor could not be manipulated by the JLP into planned and systematic disruptive action, outbreaks of popular discontent and general labor militancy could be provoked or exploited and escalated into large-scale protests against economic hardship. The most successful such action was the initiation of the demonstrations against the gas-price increases in January 1979, which brought Kingston to a standstill and also affected other towns. Before the magnitude of the increases was announced, the JLP created alarm by predicting a huge increase through higher taxes on gas and called for resistance against the new prices (*G*, 6 January 1979). The JLP-affiliated National Patriotic Movement (NPM) organized the blockade of certain key roads which paralyzed the flow of traffic in and out of Kingston. Spontaneous demonstrations originating at these road blocks escalated into protests lasting several days (*G*, 9–11 January 1979). On the third day of the demonstrations, the JLP leadership led a march in Kingston and issued a statement to the effect that the refusal to pay the new price for gas was the only way 'to protect the public against still further taxes by government gone mad with greed to pay for waste and corruption' (*G*, 12 January 1979). Thus, the JLP skillfully linked the issue of gas-price increases, which obviously and understandably caused great popular concern, to a wholesale attack on the government, insinuating that governmental waste and corruption were responsible for the increases and that the protests were really directed at getting the government out of office. Another version of this strategy of linking bread-and-butter issues to the issue of legitimacy of the government involved the use of anti-communism by systematically associating price increases and scarcities with the threat of rationing and the close relationship to Cuba.

The JLP's parliamentary and electoral strategy included the boycott of by-elections, boycotts of sessions of Parliament, the resignation of all JLP Senators, and insistent calls for early elections. All these actions were highly publicized and presented as last resorts for a party being victimized by the government through manipulation of the administrative and coercive machinery of the state. In July 1978, the JLP announced that it would continue to boycott all by-elections until a new electoral system was in place, because of the 'need to alert the nation to the problem of abuses and manipulation of the electoral process' (*G*, 17 July 1978).

Given the JLP's minority position in parliament, it could not advance or obstruct legislation.[16] Thus, the party resorted to protest action with a dramatic component here as well. In July 1978, all JLP Senators resigned over the issue of a Commission of Inquiry into the Military Intelligence

Unit accused by the JLP of partisan behavior, only to be reappointed by Seaga some three months later (*G*, 28 October 1978). The only constitutional way for the JLP to speed up a change in its power position was through early elections. Starting in April 1979, Seaga pushed hard for such elections. For instance, the commitment to hold elections within six months was one of the prerequisites presented by Seaga to the government for the JLP's acceptance of the proposed social contract (*G*, 12 May 1979).

Finally, the JLP's international strategy begun in 1977 was pursued to continue to put the government under greater economic and diplomatic pressure. On the diplomatic front, an attempt was made to isolate Jamaica politically by way of spreading propaganda concerning Cuban subversion and a communist threat to Jamaica. In speeches in Miami and Washington, Seaga charged that 'Kingston is the subversion capital of the Caribbean', that the PNP was receiving Russian money through the Communist Party of the USSR (*G*, 22 October 1979), and that the PNP was discussing the possible need for a military solution in collaboration with the Cubans and that the PNP might call in 'friendly' forces in an attempt to hold on to power (*DN*, 20 October 1979; *G*, 23 October 1979). On one of his trips to Washington, Seaga gave a document to US officials accusing fifty-eight top PNP members and officials of links to the KGB. Whereas this particular document was apparently regarded with serious doubts by the US intelligence community (*LAWR*, 23 November 1979), the campaign as a whole strengthened the position of those US policy-makers prone to seeing the whole Jamaican process in an East–West framework.[17]

The campaign directed at foreign bankers and investors accused the government of incompetence and mismanagement, and painted it as a caretaker government with a short lifespan. Furthermore, the JLP announced publicly that it would not consider itself bound by agreements concluded by the PNP government which it might consider 'to be selling out the patrimony of the country' (*G*, 10 December 1979). Naturally, all these criticisms fueled an adverse press campaign abroad, mainly in the USA, which had a detrimental effect on tourism. Thus, the opposition campaign abroad contributed to the failure of the IMF program by exerting a restrictive influence on the inflow of foreign exchange needed to bring about economic recovery.

Private sector reactions
As pointed out in the two previous chapters, most of the capitalist class was strongly opposed to the PNP government by the 1976 election. With extremely few exceptions – namely capitalists with strong political ties to the PNP, such as direct involvement in party politics or in governmental functions – there were no supporters left in this class. The only variation in the relationship between the government and the domestic bourgeoisie from then on lay in the severity of the tensions. Great fear in early 1977

was followed by short relaxation and sharp criticism after the failure of the IMF test. Then, the conclusion of the second IMF agreement and the ascendancy of the moderates within the PNP led to a temporary easing of tensions. However, by 1979 the continued deterioration of the economy, the intense campaign waged by the JLP and the *Gleaner*, and the disappointment over the unfulfilled hope that the left would be ousted from the PNP replaced any remnants of a conciliatory posture with renewed militancy of the bourgeoisie.

The clear defeat of the left inside the PNP in 1977 and the presence of strong pro-private sector members in the Cabinet, such as Minister of Industry Danny Williams and Minister of Labour William Isaacs, helped to smooth government–private-sector relations in 1978. Williams strongly identified as a businessman with a political job to do; to serve as a liaison and foster collaboration between the government and the private sector.[18] The government's attempt to obtain private-sector collaboration took many forms, both formal and informal. The government formed a National Planning Committee with representatives from the private sector, labor and government. Individual Cabinet members as well as Manley himself engaged in frequent institutionalized and spontaneous consultations with businessmen. In August 1978, the government awarded Carlton Alexander, the head of the PSOJ, the Order of Jamaica. In addition to these conciliatory gestures, the conclusion of the second IMF agreement itself reassured the private sector. It cemented Jamaica's continuing relationship to the IMF, and it took care of one of the most contentious issues in the eyes of the private sector in so far as it required a stop to any possible expansion of the STC. Similarly, the wage guidelines and the guaranteed 20 per cent return on investment stipulated by the new agreement could not fail to please the private sector.

Official private sector reaction in 1978 was generally conciliatory but very critical on specifics and highly aggressive against the PNP left, urging that the left be expelled from the Cabinet and the party. Attacks continued to be aimed at the tax package imposed under the new IMF agreement, though conveniently ignoring its parentage, at the shortage of raw materials and capital goods resulting from import restrictions, and at the operation of the Trade Administrator's Department because of 'red tape'. The 'red tape' issue was raised by the private sector in other connections as well; in particular, the government's efforts to collect the data necessary for informed economic planning were regarded as an intrusion into business affairs and as a nuisance causing businesses to waste a lot of time.

Several factors worked together to end the conciliatory phase and aggravate tensions again in early 1979, a trend which took a dramatic turn for the worse in August. The continued deterioration of the economy and shortage of foreign exchange, the decline of popular support for the government manifesting itself in opinion polls and in the behavior of the labor movement, the stepped-up opposition attacks from the JLP and the *Gleaner*, all affected the private sector's attitude toward the government adversely. Some businesses successfully attempted to mobilize their workers to stage demonstrations for import licenses and against general sacrifices. Further, Manley's speech in Havana and its fall-out in terms of US hostility, the problems with foreign loans, the PNP's counter-attacks on the JLP and the *Gleaner*, particularly the demonstration in support of Estrada, were all highly objectionable from the point of view of the bourgeoisie because they were perceived as anti-Western and anti-capitalist and thus anti-business. The return of Duncan as PNP general secretary and the simultaneous resignation of Williams as Minister of Industry seemed to the private sector to have decisively turned the tide against them and thus to have left no option but full confrontation with the government.

The transition to increasing confrontation manifested itself in the broadening of critiques of the government from issues of economic policy to issues of left-wing rhetoric, of communist influence, and finally of the government's incumbency itself. The charges of increasing influence by domestic communists as well as by the Cubans on the PNP and the state apparatus were directed against left-wing officials (Duncan, Small, Spaulding), government programs (the exchange programs with Cuba) and the JBC (particularly the TV newsroom). These attacks clearly developed in interaction with the *Gleaner*. The JLP's and the *Gleaner's* campaign managed to convince many private sector members of the existence of a communist/Cuban threat. This is borne out by our interviews in which 38 per cent of the businessmen mentioned the Cuban/communist threat as a reason why they themselves turned against the government and the same percentage thought that the business community in general had been so influenced.

All the private sector organizations made critical statements on these economic and political issues in 1979, though with different degrees of stridency; the JMA, the C. of C. and the JEF continued to be more militant than the PSOJ and the JEA. For instance, the JMA demanded sweeping concessions from the government in exchange for accepting the social contract, such as more foreign exchange, tax reductions, control over union militancy, and elimination of anti-capitalist rhetoric (*G*, 19 April 1979). By the end of 1979, the private sector had decided that the government should go. The final confrontation was shaping up and manifesting itself in the full-scale attack on the level of spending projected in the Supplementary Estimates (*G*, 14 December 1979), in calls on businessmen to get involved in politics, and in the clear expression of expectations that the JLP would form the next government.

Growing disaffection among the middle class
Middle-class disaffection, which had started in the PNP's first term and

continued in 1977, further increased in the two years under the second IMF program. It became visible in various statements from associations of professionals, in growing emigration of skilled and professional workers,[19] and in conflicts and foot-dragging in the bureaucracy. The reasons for this growing disaffection are to be found in the combination of economic problems, crime, threats to certain privileges and ultimately also in fears of Cuban influence in Jamaica. In the case of government employees, governmental attempts to turn the bureaucracy into an effective instrument to manage change created resentment.

The economic problems affected the middle class through the decline in its buying power, shortages of consumer goods, and threats to job security through lay-offs in both the private and the public sector. The high level of crime, particularly the burglaries and robberies with gun violence and also the rapes created a climate of fear in middle-class neighborhoods. A poll in November 1978 showed that one third of respondents in the Corporate Area had been victims of robbery or theft since the beginning of the year (Stone, 1982:68). Rumors about such crimes and extensive coverage in the *Gleaner* and the *Star*, the *Gleaner* Company's more sensationalist afternoon paper, gave rise to something approaching a bunker mentality in some middle-class quarters.

Threats to middle-class privileges resulted primarily from government policies in the areas of education and foreign exchange controls. In part, these threats were perceived as more dramatic than they actually were. The introduction of universal free secondary education did mean that middle-class offspring had to compete with lower-class children in admission examinations, but their performance in these examinations was, of course, still helped by the cultural advantage of a middle-class upbringing. Another issue causing friction was the requirement to get approval of plans for study abroad in order to obtain the foreign exchange needed. Some of the better-off sectors of the Jamaican upper middle-class have had a preference for sending their children to US universities, even to second- and third-rate ones, rather than to the University of the West Indies, partly for reasons of prestige and partly for fear of 'indoctrination' by radical professors and fellow-students. The need to justify this decision to members of the bureaucracy and just the possibility that approval might be denied greatly upset many of the applicants' families. From there it was a psychologically short step to fears of restrictions on freedom of movement and to a general belief in the charges made by the anti-Cuban/anti-communist propaganda campaign.

Disaffection among the members of the middle class employed in the public sector was aggravated by various attempts of the government to turn the bureaucracy into an effective agent of change. From the very beginning of its tenure in office, the government had shown concern with improving the planning and managerial capacities of the civil service, and it made various attempts to upgrade the structure of the state bureaucracy and its personnel, such as the introduction of emphasis on meritocratic criteria rather than straight seniority for promotion and the establishment of new specialized agencies outside the civil service structure, offering more attractive salaries in order to get qualified people.[20] Both of these attempts caused resentment among the more traditional bureaucrats because they introduced some element of uncertainty and of relative deprivation into the situation. Yet the most explosive issue in the government's relations to the bureaucracy was the discussion concerning the need to politicize the bureaucracy in the sense of ensuring a commitment to new policies among incumbents in high-level positions, in contrast to the traditional doctrine of 'administrative neutrality'.

The intent was to ensure that only people with an understanding of development policy issues and with the willingness and capacity for effective management would be put in charge of overseeing the implementation of social and economic programs. Thus, the interviews by the Civil Service Commission came to cover conceptualizations of the government's policy thrust in the areas of concern to the potential appointee. This procedure, however, was perceived as a highly partisan political one, that is, as an attempt to keep non-PNP supporters out of all high level positions in the civil service. Though there were extremely few controversial cases of civil service appointments in reality, the interview procedure and the issue of 'political qualifications' became a convenient scapegoat for people disappointed about their record of promotion.

Matters were not helped by the appointment of an 'Accreditation Committee' after the 1976 election victory, a committee of high-level PNP leaders in charge of screening potential appointees to boards of public institutions and to various committees. Though such positions have nothing to do with the civil service and have traditionally been discretionary on the part of the government, the perception that the PNP committee was using ideological criteria lent itself to the drawing of parallels to the Civil Service Commission's functions. The charge leveled against both screening procedures by the opposition was, as one might expect, that the PNP was trying to pack the whole state apparatus with their supporters and that any non-supporter was going to be victimized. As in other cases, internal PNP discussion caused by a serious concern about the difficult problem of how to manage social change through an administrative apparatus characterized by traditionalism and lack of initiative, as well as public statements of left-wing PNP leaders on the subject were used to bolster these charges. These controversies contributed not only to a loss of votes for the PNP and of skilled personnel for the bureaucracy, but also to resistance in the form of foot-dragging within the bureaucracy. Such foot-dragging aggravated the problems with the implementation of various programs, problems which were caused by shortages of funds, skills and experience.

Growing tensions in the relationship to the unions
Under the IMF imposed wage restraint policies industrial disputes increased (Table A.16). The first significant increase came in 1977, in all categories of reasons, but particularly noticeable in disputes over bargaining rights. This together with the greater involvement of the BITU in disputes (Table A.17) suggests that the IMF policies and the rapid decline of popular support for the government were perceived by the BITU as favorable conditions for challenging representation rights held by the NWU.[21] The NWU attempted to resist the BITU's challenge to its numerical membership position by formally distancing itself from the government and the PNP. It invariably criticized the government's austerity policies and changed its status from being an 'affiliate' of the PNP to being an 'associate' at the end of 1977. Nevertheless, there is general agreement among Jamaican participants and observers that the BITU managed to outstrip the NWU in the second half of the 1970s, both by way of raiding and by way of organizing new sectors of workers particularly white-collar workers.[22] It is a traditional trend in Jamaica for the union linked to the party in power to experience some losses in membership relative to the union linked to the opposition party. In 1977 and thereafter, of course, this traditional trend was greatly aggravated by the economic austerity measures and the resulting decline in living standards, and by the visible weakening of the government.

With the hardening of the IMF's wage policy under the 1978 agreement, wage issues became the most important cause for disputes. In early 1978, during the negotiations for the second IMF agreement, the unions issued pre-emptive warnings that they would under no circumstances accept a wage freeze. As a result of IMF pressure, the government strengthened its enforcement capacity by passing legislation enabling the Minister of Labor to refer all wage disputes to the Industrial Disputes Tribunal (IDT) for compulsory arbitration and to ask the IDT to take the 'national interest' into account in making awards.[23] The legislation also required that all collective agreements reached between union and employers be sent to the Ministry of Labor (*G*, 25 May 1978). The guidelines and the government's will to enforce them were heavily tested in 1978, as more and more disputes failed to be solved in direct negotiations or through conciliation and had to be referred to the IDT. Union rivalry was the key reason behind this intransigent and militant attitude, as no union could afford to accept voluntarily a wage settlement within the 15 per cent limit lest it be accused of cowardice and suffer losses in membership. Yet, increasing strike pressure and several instances where workers defied IDT 'back-to-work' orders, did not manage to deter the Ministry of Labor, with the support of the IDT, from enforcing the guidelines.[24]

In 1979, the continued economic deterioration brought the spread of unemployment to the forefront of labor's concerns and made dismissals and suspensions the leading cause of disputes. The steep decline in wage disputes in 1979 can be attributed to the enforcement of a two-year bargaining cycle under the IMF agreement and to a certain moderation of the impact of the guidelines, as well as to a certain learning effect among unions concerning the insistence of the Ministry of Labor on the wage guidelines. The impact of the guidelines was moderated somewhat by the elimination of the crawling peg devaluations and their resulting inflationary effects, and by the exemption of contributions to NIS, NHT and pension funds from the calculation of the wage fund. Though the unions as well as the private sector rejected the social contract, the Minister of Labor insisted that the guidelines would continue to be enforced by the IDT and through tax policy in that any increase above the limit could not be deducted as costs.

In comparative perspective, labor militancy in Jamaica has generally been high. One might wonder why strike rates did not soar even higher under the IMF austerity program and why no general nationwide strikes paralyzed the economy, as has happened in other countries in protest against IMF policies. Certainly, the political divisions in the labor movement were a key obstacle to large scale coordinated protest strike action. Furthermore, Manley's trade union background and his good relationship with Shearer were instrumental in keeping channels for communication with the unions open and in mediating many difficult negotiations, particularly in the public sector. Despite Shearer's public attacks on the government and despite official rejections by the unions of all appeals for collaboration, participation of the top union leadership in institutionalized consultations with the government as well as informal communications with Manley personally were very frequent.[25]

Despite such consultation and despite a certain flexibility on the part of the union leaders, however, their ability to exert a moderating influence on union militancy was subject to limits set by the competitive tradition and the nature of the relationship between workers and leaders. This relationship has been characterized by a certain lack of mutual trust, as a result of the rather authoritarian structure and operation of most unions.[26] Thus, the union leaders were engaged in a difficult balancing act, trying to appear tough and militant in the eyes of the workers without needlessly adding to the problems of a government which was clearly more pro-labor than any government in Jamaica's history and which was equally clearly unable to make any significant concessions in violation of the IMF agreement.

A final important development in the area of the government's relationship with the unions in the period under consideration here was the significant scaling-down of the workers' participation program. In the face of strong employer resistance, considerable union indifference and partly outright union opposition, conflict among leading members of the commission, and heavy constraints on administrative expenditures, the government abandoned all plans for legislation on the subject and cut back the personnel in charge of organizing participation schemes.[27] The program was to become an experimental one only, confined to pilot projects and set up on a voluntary basis, and the importance of the new guidelines tabled in the House in June 1978 was played down with the accompanying comments that they were not to be considered as stringent rules. In practice, only two schemes of any significance were ever set up, one at JBC and the other at JAMINTEL, that is, both in the public sector and with predominantly white-collar employees with above average education.

Thus, in this area as in many others, the government had lost the initiative by 1978. On the one hand, one might argue that scaling-down this program was a mistake on the part of the government, as it would have been a useful instrument for a reform strategy seeking to substitute redistribution of power or psychological rewards for redistribution of material goods which had been made impossible by the IMF program. On the other hand, given the lack of support for the program from any significant organized force in the society, and the IMF insistence on an improvement in the 'business climate', the government could ill afford to stir up additional opposition. Again, its room for maneuver had narrowed considerably in political as well as economic terms by that point.

The PNP on the defensive
The negotiations for the second IMF agreement and the implementation of the agreement itself put the PNP entirely on the defensive. Politically, the first fatality of the failure of the December 1977 test was Finance Minister David Coore. Manley decided that, given the circumstances, Coore would have to go. As Finance Minister, he had political responsibility for the failure.[28]

The dramatic decline in living standards caused an equally drastic erosion of the government's popular support, which demoralized the party activists and added to the internal tensions in the leadership. The government planned a large-scale communication campaign to explain the 1978 IMF agreement to the population. Also, Manley and key Cabinet ministers briefed all the interest groups in the society. However, there were problems at the top in terms of generating enthusiasm for the campaign (which is not very surprising) and there were problems at the bottom in terms of comprehension by activists of what was happening in the economy. Clearly, the lack of previous political education among party cadres aggravated the difficulty they had in absorbing and passing on such information. Finally, of course, the best information campaigns would not be able to convince most people whose real wages were being reduced by a third within one year that the government presiding over this decline deserved their continuing support; at best, the campaign would be able to moderate the magnitude of the defections and the intensity of resistance to the program. The poll results of June 1978 which showed that the government's support base had slipped to 28 per cent, must have been expected but nonetheless were a blow to the government's and the party's morale (see Table A.15).

Party morale in 1978 was low to begin with, because the internal struggle continued in the aftermath of the defeat of the left. As pointed out, the moderates were in control of the major ministries (Industry, Finance, Foreign Affairs); from their positions of strength, they attempted to restrict the areas of responsibility and influence of the left. However, the left offered resistance to such pressures and continued their efforts to regain positions of influence. At the 1978 Party Conference Francis Tullock, supported by the left, defeated the moderate William Isaacs in the election of Vice President, and Arnold Bertram, clearly identified with the left, was appointed Minister of State for Mobilization, Information and Culture in May. Duncan remained vocal, making several controversial attacks on PNP MP's and on Glasspole.[29] Also he pushed forward with preparations for a political education campaign, which was formally launched in December 1978.

The one very significant achievement of the PNP in this period was the final revision and adoption of its ideological document *Principles and Objectives*.[30] The issues discussed in the last chapter were intensely debated at all levels of the party, in groups, constituency organizations, Regional Councils and the NEC, and the draft document was further revised and amended by the 1978 Party Conference and finally returned to the party leadership with the mandate to complete the editorial work on it and publish it as the party's official statement of purpose and policy. The sticky points regarding the role of the class alliance as opposed to class struggle, and the composition of the class alliance were resolved as follows:

> The existence of class divisions is a reality of capitalist society. Essentially, each class tends to protect what it perceives to be its own interest. This results in conflicts between classes. This conflict is known as the class struggle (*Principles and Objectives*, p. 13).
>
> The struggle between social classes can only be resolved through the building of socialism . . . In the building of socialism in Jamaica, and as the process unfolds, the natural alliance will comprise the working class, the small farmers, middle strata and reclaimed elements from the lumpen proletariat. In addition, there are capitalists who are willing and able to contribute to the building of the just society, which is the objective of socialism. All these must be united around clear objectives in a politics of purpose (p. 14).
>
> The dynamic nature of the process allows for one's class outlook to differ from one's class origin (p. 14).
>
> The basis of the alliance must be the struggle for national liberation

and democratisation of our economy moving towards the building of socialism. Therefore, all those who are a part of this alliance must, through action, promote these objectives. At all times, every decision which is taken and every programme implemented, must ensure that the interests of the working people predominate (*Principles and Objectives*, p. 15).

Thus, on the one hand the existence of class struggle under capitalism was not denied, but on the other hand the class alliance as political base for the construction of democratic socialism was given an inclusive character. The middle strata were included without qualification, in contrast to earlier drafts which had only included 'middle-class elements who identify with the goals of democratic socialism' and which had made critical reference to vacillation and inconsistency among the middle strata. Furthermore, allowance was made for capitalists to contribute to the implementation of the party's program.

Other controversial issues, such as the shape of the mixed economy and its status as stage of transition versus permanent feature of democratic socialism, and the difference between 'democratic socialism' and 'scientific socialism' were also clarified.

Democratic Socialism is a political and economic theory under which:

the means of production, distribution, and exchange are owned and/or controlled by the people (pp. 65–6) . . . The Jamaican economy is a mixed one. It includes the following types of enterprises: state, cooperative, and private . . . In the transition to a Democratic Socialist economy, the state sector leads the way in planning, directing and transforming the economic structure . . . Our economic policy seeks to maximize the degree of social control over the economy while, at the same time, recognizing that private enterprise will continue to play an important part . . . Social ownership though fundamental, is not the only basis for the exercise of social control. Control can be exercised directly by the people through Cooperative and other participatory institutions and indirectly by the State acting on behalf of the working people or by Worker Participation in private enterprise (p. 14–15) . . . Every socialist economy (even the most advanced) retains areas of private enterprise (p. 29).

This is a very clear statement and obviously it was hoped that it would lay to rest the fears in the private sector concerning 'what's around the corner'. Similarly, the statements on the political process under democratic socialism should have answered opposition attacks concerning the threat of totalitarianism from the PNP:

The Democratic Socialist process will provide for: 1. The right of every Jamaican to form or join any political party of his/her choice, and to compete for state power in democratically contested elections (p. 10) . . . As distinct from scientific socialism, its [Democratic Socialism's] method is based on the alliance of classes around clear objectives (p. 66) . . . Scientific socialism . . . believes in the accentuation of that (class) struggle to the end that the working class will overthrow and destroy the capitalist state leading to the setting up of the dictatorship of the working class (pp. 62–63).

There were sectors inside the PNP whose acceptance of the principles was all but enthusiastic, but, contrary to opposition claims, the more influential one among them was the sector on the right. A large sector of the moderates did accept and support the document, but some of the people on the right considered it a waste of time and objected in particular to the class analysis laid out in it. Also, the reference to imperialism was unsatisfactory to many. In the section on international policy, the document lists anti-imperialism first among the fundamental elements of party policy, explaining it in the following way:

The PNP supports passionately the right of all people to self-determination and to the exercise of their national sovereignty. Hence, our participation in, and our support of, the struggle against imperialism, which is by its very nature actively opposed to the principle of self-determination (Principles and Objectives, p. 53).

On the one hand, this statement did not satisfy the YO because it contained no reference to active intervention, particularly on the part of the USA. On the other hand, it did not satisfy the right either because they saw any reference to imperialism as unnecessarily offending potential foreign lenders and investors. The issue of imperialism remained contentious and the debate later broadened to the question whether there are 'two imperialisms' (Western and Eastern, or American and Russian) or whether there is a fundamental difference between them because of the difference in economic relations. Despite such remaining instances of dissent and controversy, however, the adoption of *Principles and Objectives* was a significant milestone for the PNP.

In contrast, the government achieved little in its program of social transformation in this period. The combination of budgetary austerity, loss of popular support, and the opposition campaign absorbed most of the government's time and energy in attempts at self-defense and left little resources for old and new programs. Land-lease virtually stalled, the establishment of CEOs proceeded extremely slowly, and workers' participation was scaled down, as was the constitutional reform effort. In particular the programs with a transformative thrust aimed at changing the structures of power, such as workers' participation and CEOs, were hampered by the IMF's insistence on maximum efforts to create a favorable business climate. With a premium on private-sector confidence, it was clearly impossible to encroach on their control rights.

If 1978 was an extremely difficult year, 1979 was to bring the real low points in the government's position. The economy continued to deteriorate, and the great escalation of the gas-price demonstrations in January, the massive opposition campaign on the theme of a Cuban/communist threat, the Estrada affair, increasing US hostility and growing political violence projected an image at home and abroad of a government beleaguered. The government and the party fought back with statement after statement refuting the charges, as well as with counter-attacks on the opposition. Even Patterson, a leading moderate and generally a very diplomatic politician, responded to Seaga's allegations of Cuban influence with the counter-attack that the purpose of these allegations was none other than to 'create panic and hysteria' in society and thereby prevent economic recovery from taking place; he characterized Seaga's strategy as repeating the lie so often that people would believe it (*G*, 6 July 1979).

The Workers' Party of Jamaica (WPJ, formerly Workers' Liberation League) complicated the picture when it made a public announcement that it would enter an alliance with the PNP (*G*, 22 May 1979), which took the government by surprise and, of course, provided more ammunition to the opposition for its communist campaign. Manley, in a carefully worded response, established a clear distance between the two parties, clarifying that this was a unilateral act on the part of the WPJ, that any organization was free to support the PNP, but that the PNP would not at any time in the future enter into any political alliance with any other political organization with respect to any election in Jamaica (*G*, 22 May 1979).

The split inside the party came to a head over the return of Duncan as general secretary. The PNP Annual Conference was scheduled for September and Duncan's announcement that he was going to campaign actively for the position alarmed the center as well as the right. Privately, some of them claimed to have concrete evidence that foreign lenders and investors involved in crucial current negotiations with the government would react strongly to Duncan's return. These strong concerns contributed to a move by the right to caucus and organize a coordinated attempt to prevent Duncan's return to the position. Reportedly, they got thirty-three out of forty-seven MPs who opposed Duncan to attend a meeting to discuss the signing of a document stating that they would resign if he was to return.[31] Though all thirty-three opposed Duncan's return, the right was unable to get them to act in concert and the move failed, probably because it was perceived that Manley favored Duncan's re-election. The Women's Movement also strongly supported Duncan, as did the YO. Furthermore, the demoralization of the party and the dire need for an infusion of a new resolve to deal with the economy weighed heavily in Duncan's favor. The central themes of delegates' complaints at the conference were the state of the economy, their strong feeling that the IMF program was not working despite the privation visited on the population, and their own incapacity to deal with grass-roots discontent. Duncan's capacity to inspire a 'spirit of struggle' and his organizing talents seemed to provide the only hope to revive the party's failing fortunes. Finally the Party Executive, MPs and Cabinet members were swayed to support Duncan's reappointment or to at least accept it without resigning in protest.[32]

The conference gave rise to the process which ultimately resulted in the break with the IMF. It established three priorities for party work, namely, political organization, political education and economic policy (PNP, 1980). Work in all three of these areas was carried on, but the economy rapidly became the focal point of all party work. The secretariat solicited proposals for economic policy initiatives from all the regional councils. Also, questionnaires were circulated among all party groups soliciting information on economic and social projects to be initiated or completed in their communities. An NEC meeting in November was devoted primarily to a discussion of these proposals and suggestions and the general question of how to deal with the continuing economic crisis. The party's newly-constituted Economic Affairs Commission was given the task of integrating these party suggestions into the planning of the 1980–1 budget, in collaboration with the Ministry of Finance. However, the failure of the December IMF test put all the budget projections in limbo and moved the question of the relationship to the IMF to the center of the discussion about the economy.

From the break with the IMF to the elections

The decision to break with the IMF
The failure of the IMF test in December 1979 and the IMF's hard line on conditions for a waiver and a new agreement served as catalysts in the PNP's deliberations. While negotiations with the IMF were going on and austerity measures already being implemented, the economic commission started to work on a non-IMF economic plan. The most visible of the new austerity measures was the partial reorganization of the government itself. The number of ministries was reduced from twenty to thirteen and studies were carried out to improve the efficiency of public sector enterprises. These measures fell far short of saving the amount of resources demanded by the IMF, and they were explained as part of the continuing attempt to confront the acute budget problems, the implication being that more public sector austerity measures lay ahead (*G*, 20 December 1979). In fact, the IMF demanded a budget cutback of $150m before a waiver could be

granted, and further cutbacks under a modified program.[33] The government agreed to cutbacks in subsidies, wages and areas such as travel
expenses, but it refused to accept cutbacks involving laying-off more than
10 000 workers in the public sector.

In January, a special conference with some 2000 PNP delegates was held
to discuss the economic situation further. This conference gave the economic commission the job of continuing to elaborate a more detailed plan
for a non-IMF path. The groundswell of opposition against any new IMF
measures was clearly gaining momentum, and it was reinforced by numerous discussions of party groups and activists on formal and informal levels
with the technocrats in the economic commission.

Resistance to any new austerity policies was not confined to party
forums. At the end of January and in the first days of February, a number
of street demonstrations took place. Media workers, workers in charge of
preparing and delivering school lunches, workers at the Ministries of
Construction and of Agriculture, many other groups of workers, as well as
teachers, students, junior doctors and journalists took part in protest
demonstrations, urging the government not to make any new concessions
to the IMF (*DN*, 1 and 2 February 1980). The NWU also made a public
appeal to the government to the same effect. In the midst of such protests,
Manley announced that elections would be held as soon as the new
electoral machinery was in place, and that these elections would be a
fundamental choice between different economic strategies (*DN*, 5 February 1980). There was little doubt in anybody's mind that the PNP's
trajectory pointed to a break with the IMF. What remained in doubt was
the timing of the break.

While anti-IMF pressures were building up, Minister of Finance Bell
continued to negotiate with the IMF. Besides the budget cutbacks, there
were two other issues of contention, the amount of foreign exchange to be
made available by the IMF and the performance targets to be reached by
Jamaica over the next year. Specifically, the possibility of failing an IMF
test scheduled for September, in the middle of an election campaign,
loomed as a great danger under the conditions proposed by the IMF. Thus,
a special NEC meeting in early March expressed not only overwhelming
support for a break in the long run but also a strong inclination to an
immediate break. However, Manley and others were not satisfied with the
alternative plan as presented by the economic commission. When a revised
plan was presented to another NEC meeting two weeks later, the NEC
voted virtually unanimously, with the sole exception of Bell, in favor of a
long-term break with the IMF. The vote on the short-term break was 103 in
favor, forty-five against, and four abstentions (Manley, 1982:189). Despite
some concessions on the part of the IMF concerning the magnitude of the
budget cuts and of the foreign exchange to be made available, the September test remained the stumbling-block. The only way to ensure that the net

foreign reserves test would be met at that point, would have been to revoke millions of dollars worth of import-licenses already issued. This would have had obvious political repercussions. Consequently, the concern about the certain negative political implications of the new IMF agreement, one way or the other, sealed the fate of Jamaica's relationship with the IMF. Significantly, all but two cabinet members (Small and Spaulding) voted against the immediate break, but the government accepted the party's decision and carried it out nevertheless.

As a result of this decision, Bell resigned as Minister of Finance and Hugh Small was appointed his successor.[34] The appointment of a left-winger to this important ministry sent shock-waves through a private sector which was already paralyzed by the break with the IMF. These shock-waves were further reinforced by the NEC recommendation to establish an Economic Intelligence Unit in charge of monitoring production, distribution and lay-offs (*G*, 26 March 1980). Thus, the battle lines were drawn. On one side was a government attempting to pursue an entirely untried economic path and a party attempting to mobilize people to support this alternative. On the other side were a private sector bent on proving the foolishness of such an attempt and an opposition bent on ousting the government at any cost. In the following months, the country became engulfed in the most bitter and violent election campaign in its history.

The non-IMF path
The key problem in the short term economic program, of course, was financing the foreign exchange gap. The deficit in the current account of the balance-of-payments was projected to reach US$393m.[35] On the capital side, the inflow of US$10m in Special Drawing Rights and of US$139m in already committed loans to the public sector, and an outflow of US$64m would result in a new inflow of US$85m, leaving a gap of US$308m. The strategy to bridge this gap had two essential components, namely the build-up of arrears of US$105m and the raising of special balance-of-payments assistance loans from friendly countries. An estimate based on commitments received from friendly countries put this special foreign financing at US$128m. This still left a gap of US$75m, which would force even tighter management of foreign exchange allocations for imports. As it was, the plan was built on the assumption that the commercial banks would continue to roll over the 87.5 per cent of the principal on the debt as in 1979, and that already committed and expected loans would not be affected by the break with the IMF and the build-up of arrears. The first of these assumptions turned out to be correct, but not the second. The government also made attempts to reschedule US$186m in commercial foreign debt as well as principal payments due to the World Bank and the Inter-American Development Bank, both of which were unsuccessful.

Given the foreign exchange gap of some US$300m, the final IMF offer of

US$135m in drawings for 1980 would have been less than half what was needed. Acceptance of this offer would have entailed the requirement to reduce arrears rather than to build them up. Thus, the 'seal of approval' of the IMF would have been its main contribution to the short-term foreign-exchange situation of the government. Furthermore, the disbursement of the full US$135m was highly unlikely because of the foreign reserves tests.

Other important short-term economic policies involved a cutback in real government expenditures of some 17 per cent in the fiscal year 1980–1, leaving the projected budget deficit at 11.7 per cent of GDP. Should the foreign financing target not be achieved, either domestic bank credit would have to be expanded or credit to the private sector curtailed. Both these options would have undesirable consequences, the former a higher infla-tion rate than the projected 22 per cent, the latter an even greater decline in GDP than the projected 2.6 per cent. Other measures to keep inflation at the projected levels were the expansion both of the list of goods under price controls and of the training of voluntary price inspectors. Finally, the 10 per cent wage guidelines adopted in 1979 were to remain in force.

The central components of the non-IMF path in the medium and long run were the following:

(a) increasing domestic food production in order to save foreign ex-change allocated to food imports;
(b) increasing exports of manufactured goods as well as agricultural products, which required that foreign exchange be allocated to ex-port industries on a preferential basis and, again, that agricultural production be raised;
(c) increasing bauxite and alumina exports by bringing the existing facilities into full production, expanding these facilities further, and building a new state-owned alumina plant in cooperation with other countries;
(d) further developing tourism and making even stronger efforts to stop the leakage of foreign exchange;
(e) reducing energy imports through an energy conservation and devel-opment program.

In order to achieve all this, the planning mechanisms of the state were to be strengthened and management in the public sector to be made more efficient.

It is difficult to assess the relative success of the short-term economic program in exact figures because the projections were either for the whole calendar year or even for the whole fiscal year, and the October election, of course, changed the whole situation. However, the available figures, Manley's account (1982:190–1) and our interviews all point to the same conclusions, namely that the foreign financing targets were not achieved. In the half year from 31 March to 30 September 1980, total loans received amounted to J$119.6m, outflows on account of the national external debt amounted to J$4.2m, resulting in an increase in the national external debt of J$115m (Bank of Jamaica, 1981:32.1). If we compare this with the total anticipated foreign financing for the fiscal year 1980–1 of J$530m, or J$265m for the half-year, we arrive at a shortfall of J$150m or US$84m in this half-year.

There were several reasons for this shortfall. For instance, Jamaica asked OPEC for a loan of US$100m (*G*, 3 May 1980) but received only about a quarter of this amount. Loans from Venezuela remained below expectations as well; of the promised $50m oil credit only $20m were granted before the elections. The Jamaicans felt strongly that some governments were hedging their political bets in anticipation of a change in government in October. Also, the assumption that loans and customary credits would not be affected by the break with the IMF and the build-up of arrears was mistaken. The Thatcher government in Britain cancelled its export insurance for Jamaica (*G*, 29 April 1980) and expected loans of some $60m from the USA and Britain did not materialize (*G*, 27 July 1980).

The unwillingness on the part of official and commercial banks to reschedule substantial amounts of the Jamaican debt was heavily influenced by the anticipated change in government. Seaga's public threat that the JLP would not necessarily honor agreements concluded by the PNP government (*G*, 10 December 1979) could not but reinforce hesitation on the part of foreign lenders. Furthermore, according to one person closely involved in the debt renegotiation attempts, Seaga used his good contacts with the international financial community in a very systematic and deliberate way to undermine the government's efforts. Yet, despite all these adversities, the government managed to avoid any default on debt payments, which was important to the government because of the value in terms of credibility of governmental commitments in the long run.

The shortfall in foreign financing showed the expected effect in terms of a higher inflation rate (27 per cent) and a lower growth rate (−5.4 per cent) than projected. The most visible and politically-damaging effects of the foreign-exchange gap were the shortages of imported raw materials and the resulting lay-offs in the manufacturing sector, as well as the acute shortages of basic foodstuffs and articles of daily use. The disruptions in production and the shortages were further aggravated by the rising political violence, by politically-motivated actions of economic sabotage, and by damages done by Hurricane Allan, estimated at $167m (*G*, 4 September 1980).

Implications for a non-IMF path in the long run
What does the experience with the non-IMF path in 1980 tell us about the viability of this path in the longer run? Setting aside the lack of political support as demonstrated by the election outcome and focusing narrowly on

the economic problems, it can be said that the path would have been extremely rocky, but also one where Jamaica would not have been without some support nor completely without options. Conjunctural factors, such as the recession in the developed world in 1981–2 which depressed the world demand for bauxite would have dealt severe blows to Jamaica's plans on the one hand. On the other hand, one can speculate that the precedents set by Nicaragua and then the major debtor-nations Mexico, Brazil and Argentina in rescheduling their debts might have made it somewhat easier for Jamaica to do the same.

Certainly, in 1980 the debt negotiations as well as contracting new loans were made more difficult by the impending election and the probability of an imminent change in government, yet problems in the area of foreign loans and investment would have persisted. The break with the IMF was perceived by many bankers as a step toward a total break with the capitalist system and an inexorable move toward the Eastern Bloc. Seaga's disappointing experience with attracting foreign investment suggests that no impetus to export promotion would have come from there either. Friendly countries, in particular in Northern Europe, the Arab world and, to some extent, in Latin America, could have been relied on to continue offering some loans and to be willing to expand trade relations, technical assistance, and possibly enter into joint ventures with the Jamaican government, but their actual capacity to do all this would have depended on the state of their own economies. In particular, the world recession, the drop in oil prices, and the debt crisis would have affected existing joint venture plans for alumina refining and would have made the search for new partners in the Third World more difficult.

Promotion of tourism was an important and promising strategy; despite the state of the world economy, Jamaican tourism has done well since the elections. However, one important factor changed with the election victory of the JLP, namely, the adverse press campaign in the USA, fueled by opposition propaganda, came to a halt. This probably would not have happened in the case of a PNP victory, and potential American tourists would have continued to receive negative messages concerning Jamaica from the media as well as from their travel agents. Though less susceptible to negative propaganda, the European market does not have the same numerical potential for Jamaica as the North American market.

Promoting agricultural production for domestic consumption as well as for export certainly had to be a corner-stone of any path directed toward greater self-reliance. The progress made by the government in the area of domestic food crops in the previous years suggests that there was further potential for growth. Significant increases in production, however, would have required substantial improvements in transport and storage facilities. Still, it seems reasonable to assume that agriculture would have made an important contribution to the non-IMF path in the medium run.

In conclusion, then, the early 1980s would have been an extremely difficult period for a Jamaican non-IMF path. Continued economic hardship would have been imposed on the population. By the mid-1980s an increase in agricultural production, a diversification of bauxite–alumina markets, and a renegotiation of the foreign debt might have improved the situation. In the end, some sort of coordinated action on the part of Third World debtor-countries might well have been essential. Furthermore the economic hardship imposed by the IMF under Seaga hit the Jamaican people so hard in 1983 and 1984 that the living standards of the masses would probably not have been significantly different under the new path. However, there is one factor which would most likely have made things a lot harder for a PNP government on a non-IMF path than warranted by straight economic conditions. The Reagan administration's Cold-War policy towards the region would certainly have brought such heavy overt and covert pressures to bear on Jamaica that the country would have been brought to a state of ungovernability.

Work of the electoral committee
After it had become clear that the IMF-imposed austerity measures forced a retrenchment of the constitutional reform project, the government agreed to deal with the issue of electoral reform separately. In November 1978, the government and the opposition reached a preliminary agreement to establish an Electoral Advisory Committee (*G*, 22 November 1978). After protracted discussion, a final agreement was reached in August 1979 to set up an Electoral Advisory Committee as an interim body, later to be replaced by an electoral commission under new constitutional provisions. The interim committee was composed of seven members, two appointed by the Prime Minister, two by the Leader of the Opposition, and three including the chair by the Governor-General on the recommendation of those four members. The committee was to recommend a Director of Elections to the Governor-General for appointment, and to serve as advisory body to the director, with the understanding that its advice would be accepted. This whole process was completed, the director appointed and the committee ready to appoint lower-level election officials and to review registration and voting procedures by December 1979.

The central concerns of the committee were to eliminate flaws in the registration and voting systems which allowed for multiple voting and impersonation. As part of the establishment of a national registration system, each voter was to be issued an identification card with a photograph. On election day, every polling station was to use 'integrity equipment' in the form of indelible ink which could be detected by ultra-violet light. However, the announcement of early elections by Manley, the insistence of the JLP on the earliest possible date and the intense election campaign put the committee under time pressure and caused it to postpone the plan to issue identification cards with photographs to a later date. Instead, great care was taken in a fresh enumeration of voters, whereby the certificate of enumeration served as identification on election day. New election officials were selected, trained, and supervised by the committee, and new checks were built into the procedures at polling stations.[36]

Despite the great difficulty in carrying out these preparations, caused by high levels of political tension and violence, there was a general agreement that the new measures were successful in ensuring an election with less abuse of the electoral system than any previous one.[37] Isolated incidents of multiple voting, failure of the integrity equipment, and tampering with ballot boxes were still reported, but none were remotely of a magnitude to have an impact on the election outcome.

The JLP campaign and the Gleaner
A poll taken by Stone in December 1979 showed the JLP holding a considerable lead, with 47 per cent over the PNP's 37 per cent (see Table A.15). Seaga began exuding confidence in victory while at the same time disseminating warnings of the PNP's intention to steal the election. The JLP suggested three possible scenarios how the PNP would deprive the JLP of an election victory, namely by postponing elections and redrawing electoral districts (*G*, 28 February 1980), or by calling elections before the new system was in place (*G*, 1 March 1980) or by calling a State of Emergency and intimidating JLP supporters (*G*, 12 March 1980). The latter scenario was deemed the 'military solution' planned by the PNP, which became one of the dominant themes of the campaign, linked to the theme of communist subversion and the Cuban threat (*G*, 7 July 1980). Another major theme, of course, remained mismanagement, sometimes also linked to the 'military solution' by the allegation that the government was deliberately pushing the country over the brink of economic disaster in order to impose a communist system.

The Security Forces were a key target in the JLP campaign. If the Security Forces could be brought to passive resistance or – even more dramatic – active opposition to the government, then the population would perceive the government as completely out of control and unable to maintain public order, and strong sympathies for the government's immediate removal would emerge. Furthermore, this would mean that the PNP campaign would be severely hampered by lack of protection of its activists from political violence. Thus an interesting shift was made in the JLP's approach to the Security Forces. Whereas the attacks on 'politically-directed' abuses by the Security Forces, which had been repeated over and over in the previous years, were continued, the JLP started taking greater pains to emphasize that this involved only a very small group (*G*, 8 December 1979). In a new twist, the Security Forces as a whole were praised for doing their best to protect the public despite their very precarious position in terms of equipment, which in turn was blamed on the government's deliberate attempt to weaken the Security Forces (*G*, 30 April 1980). In fact, the JLP became the champion of the interests of the Security Forces, deploring their vulnerability which was caused by a scarcity of vehicles in running order and emphasizing the need for stronger governmental support for the forces (*G*, 18 April 1980). Furthermore, the JLP promised full support for the Security Forces in the fight against the PNP's alleged plans to replace the regular forces with the Home Guard and/or a People's Militia. By the same token, the JLP and the Security Forces would stand united against the threat of a communist takeover in which the Home Guard and a militia trained with Cuban assistance would figure prominently. To underline the immediacy of the threat, the JLP alleged that there were 1500 Cuban-trained *Brigadistas* at large in armed guerrilla-type cadres (*G*, 7 July 1980). Seaga insinuated that 'regular members of the police force must be asking themselves the question daily, what is in store for them when they are required to face trained squads of terrorists, armed with machine guns, against which their own weapons are as ineffective as sling shots?' (*G*, 30 April 1980). Thus, the campaign attempted to use the Cuba–communist threat to frighten the Security Forces and consequently turn them against a government that was conspiring with the subversive elements. As we will see, this campaign was remarkably successful.

In addition to the Security Forces, the anti-communism campaign was directed at another institutional target, namely the churches. If church leaders could be convinced that Jamaica was threatened by communist forces as long as the PNP was in office, then the anti-PNP campaign would be infused with moral fervor and the churches' considerable influence would work in favor of the JLP. Thus, a strong element in the attacks was the immorality of communists, for whom the end would justify any means. This element lent itself to all kinds of allegations and defenses; for instance it could be used to blame violence committed against PNP supporters on the PNP itself, suggesting a 'hurt-your-friend-to-blame-the-enemy' plot, which of course could only be the product of sick, immoral communist minds:

> It is this characteristically evil Communist technique which has caused Communism to be abhorred by outstanding leaders . . . There are no fixed immutable principles, consequently almost anything, force, violence, murder, lying is a justifiable means to the millenial end (*G*, 12 February 1980).

Apparently, this campaign was very effective among the evangelical churches; several of our respondents and other observers emphasized the frequency and intensity with which preachers in these churches had picked up the communist threat theme in 1980. Among the leaders of the established churches as well, there was concern about the issue leading to a generally more critical attitude toward the PNP.

In this campaign, the JLP not only repeated general allegations like the ones just discussed but it seized upon any occurrences of significance and wove them into the communist-threat scene. The break with the IMF was explained as a result of a Marxist takeover of the PNP (*G*, 25 March 1980). In May, the Moonex affair broke, involving allegations that the manager of the Moonex company, a Cuban national, had tried to smuggle cartridges into Jamaica.[38] This, the JLP interpreted as evidence that the Moonex company was being used as a front for espionage and subversive activities, and it made the further accusation that there was a close relationship between the Moonex ring of companies and the Jamaican government (*G*, 20 June 1980). When Thompson, the Minister of National Security, was found a few days later on the same plane as the Moonex manager, bound for Cuba, the JLP claimed that the 'military solution' planned by the government to regain power in the next election had taken on an international involvement (*G*, 20 June 1980).

In June, a plot, involving members of the JDF, to overthrow the government was swiftly put down by the command of the JDF. Seaga, on a visit to Washington, commented that he was 'deeply suspicious about the abortive coup attempt', as the Prime Minister was trying to use it as a political weapon (*G*, 24 June 1980). At home, the accusations were much more blunt; the JLP was publicly 'taking note' of the fact that conspiracies of this kind, designed to camouflage electoral defeat, were tools promoted by Communist nations, and that there was an inextricable alliance bordering on subversion between the PNP and the Cuban government (*G*, 24 June 1980).

In essence, the strategy in terms of criticism regarding the economy remained the same, that is, forecasts of impending disaster based on confidential as well as public information, charges of overspending, and allegations that no economic recovery would take place until the JLP with its superior management capacities would get a chance to replace the inefficient, corrupt, and communist-infiltrated PNP government. In February, while negotiations with the IMF were going on, Seaga claimed that the $50m which separated the government and the IMF in the negotiations could easily be cut, without requiring any lay-offs, by eliminating the 'political fat and gravy' in the budget. In contrast, a break with the IMF could lead to a 91 per cent closure of the industrial sector, the disappearance of 80 000 jobs, and a total breakdown in the services sector. Furthermore, the commercial banks would no longer roll over their loans as they had done before but rather see them as subject to immediate collection; thus, all further credit would stop and 'life would become totally impossible' (*G*, 7 February 1980).[39]

In April, Seaga claimed that he had identified half of the $300m in additional foreign-exchange needed (*G*, 21 April 1980). In September, it became public that Seaga had held discussions with the IMF in Washington in June, which boosted his image in Jamaica as an expert financial manager enjoying (already) greater legitimacy in crucial international financial circles than the incumbent government. He also held discussions with a wide variety of political and private sector figures in the USA, using his contacts with the American Enterprise Institute and the American Conservative Union, whose Washington headquarters reportedly provided him with office space and services (*Boston Herald*, 9 December 1980). In addition to such private talks, he worked through the public relations firm Anne Sabo Associates in New York, and he made many public appearances sounding warnings like the foregoing on the economy as well as on the dangers of Cuban expansionism and communist subversion in Jamaica.

The JLP received considerable financial and material support for its campaign, which gave it a great advantage over the PNP in terms of availability of vehicles, radios, public address systems and the like. Part of this support came from the JLP-affiliated Jamaica Freedom League (JFL), an organization of Jamaicans living abroad.[40]

The *Gleaner* remained the most valuable asset in the JLP's campaign. It continued to give wide coverage to Seaga's and the JLP's statements, as well as to wage its own propaganda campaign in the editorials and through tendentious headlines, pictures and articles. The frequency of full-scale attacks on the government had risen strongly in the second half of 1979 already and rose even more in 1980 (Table A.3). In contrast to the JLP's 1976 campaign, the *Gleaner* now gave full exposure to the communist smear. Not only did it give great prominence to Seaga's allegations, such as placing his press conference of 30 June 1979, on the front page for three days (*G*, 1, 3 and 4 July 1979), but it contributed many suggestive articles, such as the series on the accidental drowning of a Jamaican, a National Gallery employee, in Cuba.[41]

In terms of positive campaign themes, the JLP's main promises were 'money jingling in your pockets' and 'deliverance from economic hardship and communism'. It promised all kinds of measures for rural development, for industrial recovery and job creation, for better health care, and so on. The JLP claimed that it would be able to do all that by bringing about economic recovery, which in turn could be done simply by restoring business confidence at home and abroad and by introducing efficient economic management.

The private sector's move to total opposition
The failure of the IMF test in December 1979 and the PNP discussion of a possible break with the IMF led to the final official move of the private sector to irreconcilable opposition. In the very beginning of January, the

PSOJ criticized the government in sharpest terms, blaming the acute crisis of the economy on bad management of the country's affairs. To deal with this crisis, the PSOJ called for a Government of National Unity, made up of the best brains, whether PNP, JLP, or non-partisan (*G*, 6 January 1980). The JMA was even more militant, calling on the government to resign, and discussing the possibility of a mass close-down of operations (*G*, 12 January 1980). Despite some internal opposition in the PSOJ, the militant JMA forces led by Winston Mahfood successfully pushed the adoption of a similar resolution by the PSOJ, accompanied by a call for June elections (*G*, 15 January 1980; *DN*, 18 January 1980). The demand for elections at the earliest possible date remained foremost among private sector demands in the following months.

There were two key issues causing severe tensions between the government and the private sector: the lack of foreign exchange for imports of industrial inputs, and a highly political issue, concerning the charges of hoarding levelled by forces close to the government, and the attempts to control prices and oversee distribution of basic necessities. When the PNP suggested the establishment of an economic intelligence unit to monitor imports, production, and distribution, the whole private sector sounded extreme alarm. Even the PSOJ – together with the JEA the generally most moderate private sector organization – claimed that this would be part of the apparatus of a totalitarian state and that it would threaten fundamental rights and freedom (*G*, 27 March 1980). Other suggestions urging the government to ensure adequate minimum supplies and equitable distribution of basic necessities met with equally strident opposition. For instance, a ten-point proposal from the PNP's Women's Movement which was approved by the PNP NEC and included the establishment of a Food Monitoring Council as well as sharpened legislation on hoarding (*DN*, 28 April 1980) caused a storm of protest. Also, the commercial sector complained bitterly about being victimized and harrassed by aggressive price inspectors.

The private sector became particularly irate over the JBC's treatment of the issue of hoarding. The JBC, both on radio and television, picked up the issue, giving coverage to consumer complaints about shortages and allegations of hoarding. At times, such as in phone-in programs, these allegations were very specific, causing the Chamber of Commerce to complain about a calculated move to incite shoppers against supermarkets, resulting in runs on supermarkets and mob behavior (*G*, 16 April 1980). Reaction against the JBC went beyond complaints; there were open calls to put pressure on the JBC through withdrawal of advertising (*G*, 1 August 1980), calls which clearly were heeded.[42]

The charges leveled against the private sector in 1980 are not easy to evaluate. On the one hand, there were clearly instances of favoritism in the sale of scarce goods, of overpricing, of withholding goods in expectation of a price increase, etc. On the other hand, the shortages were real; there was simply not enough foreign exchange available to maintain a consistent and adequate supply of imported and domestically produced goods.[43] Still, the question remains whether the private sector, or significant segments thereof, played politics with the real shortages. Circumstantial evidence in the form of private sector attitudes and threats at the time, as well as a concrete example, seem to indicate that this was the case. In our formal interviews and many informal conversations it became clear that a large number of businessmen were prepared to emigrate if the PNP were to win the 1980 elections, and that they were also prepared to incur costs in attempting to prevent this. An overt example of what could legitimately be called sabotage, or a not-so-subtle attempt to influence the election outcome, was the decision by Jamaica Detergents, a member of the Seprod Group and the larger of Jamaica's two major detergent manufacturers, to stop manufacturing detergents at the beginning of October on the grounds that the government had refused to grant certain price increases (*DN*, 2 October 1980).

Increasing USA hostility

During 1979, Jamaica's relationship to the USA deteriorated markedly, because of developments in the region as well as internally in the Carter administration.[44] In March 1979 the New Jewel Movement took power in Grenada and some four months later the Sandinistas celebrated victory over the forces of Somoza; and opposition forces grew stronger in El Salvador and Guatemala as well. In August, Senator Frank Church sounded the alarm over an alleged Soviet combat brigade in Cuba, and Carter came under increasing pressure to adopt a firm line against all regimes with left-wing tendencies in the region. These hemispheric events, together with the Iran hostage crisis, shifted the internal balance of power in the Carter foreign-policy establishment from the moderate faction around Secretary of State Vance to the more hard-line faction around National Security Advisor Brzezinski. The Brzezinski faction, of course, was operating entirely in a framework of East–West conflict and accordingly was focusing explicitly on the Jamaica–Cuba connection.

Among the career people in the State Department, there had always been a strong sector who believed the PNP left to be Leninists and who regarded the government's relations with Cuba with great suspicion. They were also concerned about Manley's leanings towards a Third World development model 'closer to the Cuban model than we would feel comfortable with', as one State Department official expressed it. However, in the first two years of the Carter administration, their views had been overshadowed by the positive approach of Jamaica's friends in the administration, and by the general principle of uncoupling North–South from East–West issues and exercising greater tolerance toward different development models. With the exit of Young and the shift of power to the Brzezinski faction, they came to shape US policy decisively toward Central America and the Caribbean and toward Jamaica.

In concrete terms, this shift resulted in a strengthening of US military presence in the region through the establishment of the Caribbean Task Force in Key West and a general increase of naval activity in the region.[45] Also, attempts were intensified to influence the outcome of the struggle in Nicaragua, and after the revolution to channel aid such as to strengthen the private sector. In the Jamaican case, the disbursement of aid was reduced, although not cut altogether as demanded by some sectors led by Senator Schweiker, and the high-level visits back and forth decreased significantly. Also, the signals from the State Department to the US press, businessmen, bankers and potential tourists became decidedly negative.[46]

In the context of this general policy-orientation, Manley's speech in Havana with its praise of Fidel and Lenin was oil on the fire. It was followed by expressions of indignation from the State Department,[47] as well as a spate of articles from the US press decrying Cuban subversion, economic disaster and violence in Jamaica. The adverse press campaign, which continued through the election was partly a result of deliberate action on the part of some foreign policy personnel. There were instances where members of the National Security Council leaked documents with allegations about Cuban subversion to the press. For instance, Jack Anderson's column of 25 October 1979, which appeared in newspapers across the USA reported that according to State Department sources the Manley government had been making use of Soviet and Cuban intelligence agents. The press campaign involved exaggerations of real problems in Jamaica as well as outright distortions. For instance, the *Wall Street Journal* (7 April 1980) reported a Jamaican default on its foreign debt, which had not in fact occurred.

Some sectors in the State Department were seriously entertaining a scenario at that point which involved a left-wing takeover of the PNP and then, possibly with Cuban help, of the entire island, installing a left authoritarian regime. At least the view that the PNP left was Leninist was almost universally accepted in the foreign policy establishment. The hawkish sectors backed up their position with confidential intelligence reports. However, closer examination sheds considerable doubt on the accuracy of these reports.

The intelligence apparatus was collecting information through phone-tapping and observations of contacts between key Jamaican actors and Cubans. These fragmentary pieces of information were then construed to fit into an elaborate picture derived from preconceived notions of the intelligence community and the political staff about what was happening in the country.[48] These preconceived notions had their roots in the East–West mental attitude of the analysts themselves, the pervasiveness of the

Gleaner opposition line, and feedback from some right-wing quarters in the PNP itself. Also, the change of ambassadors had an impact on US perceptions of what was going on in Jamaica. Under the new ambassador, Loren Lawrence, who started his tour of duty in March 1979, Embassy reporting became markedly critical of Manley's Third World posture, his sympathies for the Cubans, and his management of the economy. The Embassy also saw the return of Duncan and the break with the IMF as a sign that Manley had lost control over the PNP. By mid-1980, the Ambassador was generally perceived as being openly pro-JLP.

The increasingly obvious US hostility generated renewed charges of US covert operations in Jamaica. All our research points to the conclusion that no covert destabilization campaign *à la* Chile was orchestrated by the CIA in Jamaica, but that it is quite likely that the CIA 'washed in' some money to support opposition groups. For instance, it is known that the German Christian Democrats greatly increased their financial support for the JLP, and that this channel served as a conduit for CIA money in other cases, such as in El Salvador in 1984 (*New York Times*), but it is not at all clear that CIA involvement was needed for destabilization to be successful; the *Gleaner* had become master in propaganda, and political violence and terrorism were not alien to Jamaica.

Violence

The level of violence in society assumed unprecedented proportions in 1980. The same forms of violence which had terrorized the country in 1976 recurred. Acts of violence directed at innocent people, such as shooting and arson, created fear and panic. In addition, a new violent phenomenon occurred, the operation of well-organized para-military-like groups, equipped with semi-automatic weapons. This escalation was particularly tragic (though not surprising, given the degree of political polarization) because only two years before it had seemed that peace might come to the Kingston ghetto.

After gang warfare with political overtones had continued in the West Kingston ghetto throughout 1977, rival gang-leaders there surprised the society by meeting in public in January 1978, calling a truce and pledging allegiance to a peace treaty (*G*, 11 January 1978).[49] The key issue on their agenda *vis-à-vis* society were an improvement of the relationship with the security forces,[50] and assistance for community development in roads, rehabilitation of buildings, youth training programs, and jobs. Wide approval of the peace move was forthcoming immediately; both political parties, the churches, the security forces, the private sector and other groups expressed their support and promised help in bringing about the desired improvements.[51]

Almost immediately, however, two areas of tension emerged: the continued illegal possession of guns, and the control over the various economic and social initiatives. Manley called for all guns to be turned in under an amnesty for their illegal possession (*G*, 13 January 1978). However, this call did not fare any better than a similar amnesty initiative after the 1972 election. Seaga did not throw his weight behind this call, nor were the gangs prepared to give up their guns. Part of their reason was certainly the suspicion that the truce might be of limited duration, the other was their fear of the security forces. An agreement was reached between the Minister of National Security Thompson, the heads of the security forces, and the peace leaders that the latter should carry special identification and accompany members of the security forces in their areas, and that special Citizen–Security Forces Community Councils were to be established in the ghetto areas (*G*, 27 January 1978). However, relations remained tense. For instance, in March, the peace leaders criticized Thompson for a speech in which they perceived an anti-slum, anti-popular and pro-security forces hard-line bias (*G*, 10 and 13 March 1978). The issue of control over support projects caused tensions between the government, the peace leaders, and an advisory committee made up of representatives from both political parties, the churches and the private sector. The peace leaders insisted on leaving all initiative and control in the hands of their Central Peace Council, but they were not able to provide the necessary leadership in organizing projects in coordination with other groups and institutions in the society. Also, progress in these projects was hampered by the budgetary austerity imposed on the government by the IMF, and by the rather slow speed with which private donations, as opposed to lip-service support, were forthcoming.[52]

Bob Marley, the international reggae star who enjoyed universal popular admiration in Jamaica, gave a special Peace Concert, the proceeds of which were handed over to the Central Peace Council. The concert at the National Stadium was attended by some 25 000 people, and at the end Marley got Seaga and Manley on the stage together to shake hands in a symbolic show of reconciliation and a promise of peace (*G*, 24 April 1978). Yet, despite the aura of conciliation and the euphoria surrounding the concert, the truce was already wearing thin. Attendance at meetings of the Central Peace Council dropped off, some members were expelled and others resigned, meetings virtually ceased to be held, irregularities in the handling of funds – particularly, the proceeds from the Peace Concert – emerged, and disappointment about the pace of improvements in the area mounted (*DN*, 30 July 1978; *G*, 1 November 1978). By October, gun play had returned to West Kingston, and the police reported a slow re-emergence of gang warfare (*DN*, 26 October 1978).[53]

By early 1979, any remnants of a peace effort had disappeared. Claudius Massop, one of the key peace-leaders on the JLP side and several companions were killed by the police (*G*, 5 and 6 February 1979).[54] In the following weeks, several incidents of attacks on policemen, believed to be in reprisal for Massop's killing occurred (for example, see *DN*, 20 march 1979). Also, partisan political violence increased, such as in the form of a gun attack on Minister of Housing Spaulding and his party while on a tour of a housing scheme (*G*, 3 August 1979), several clashes between PNP and JLP gangs, and a shooting incident at a ceremony on National Heroes Day.[55]

The announcement of early elections in February 1980, then, signalled the beginning of a veritable campaign of violence and terror. People in the ghetto were terrorized by gunmen and arson, the Eventide home for the aged burned down, costing 153 lives (*G*, 21 May 1980),[56] dances of both political parties were invaded and people killed (*G*, 21 April and 11 May 1980),[57] party activists killed in their sleep (*G*, 14 July 1980), and more. Violence started to affect all areas of life; public utilities and services, particularly in Kingston, suffered from disruptions and staff anxiety over surrounding violence. Buses had to be re-routed to avoid areas of frequent shootings, etc. The high level of violence meant that not only party supporters but practically anyone could be hurt by it. The feeling of terror in the population at large was further reinforced by the sound of the guns used which included high-powered weapons like the M16 and others.

The 1980 campaign was peculiar in a further respect. The violence affected more top political leaders directly than ever before. Manley and a touring party were fired on (*G*, 9 October 1980), Shearer was hurt on his way to a rally (*G*, 28 July 1980), a PNP MP was shot at and his chauffeur was beaten to death (*G*, 14 October 1980), and two-and-a-half weeks before the election, the Minister of State for National Security, Roy McGann, was shot to death in an incident where the police were on the scene. Despite joint statements issued by Manley and Seaga calling for a halt to violence and warning that any prospective candidate involved in violence would be removed from the election campaign (*G*, 18 July 1980), despite repeated calls for an end to violence from the churches and various other organized groups in society, and despite the use of curfews, road-blocks and the like by the security forces, the violence did not stop. The total number of murders reported in 1980 was 889, that is, 538 more than in 1979, a number which has to be attributed primarily to politically-motivated violence.

The security forces, of course, were caught in the crossfire in their attempts to control violence. On top of that, they frequently suffered direct attacks by gunmen, on policemen on patrol as well as on police stations.

The turn of the security forces against the PNP
The 1980 election campaign saw a shift of the security forces from a neutral stance to an overtly anti-PNP one, though the JDF as a whole formally continued to respect its constitutional role. This shift was caused by a variety of factors. First, in 1980, the security forces were not only affected by the violence in their professional roles, but also by the violence and the

economic hardship as individuals and family members. In 1976, they had also been caught in the crossfire of the election campaign, but this had not led them to turn against the government at that point. The level of violence was higher in 1980, of course, and the equipment situation more precarious, particularly with cars,[58] but this should not be considered the key reason. Rather, the key reason lay in the social and political dynamics leading up to the 1980 election, which affected the security forces as members of the middle classes and as members of the coercive arm of the state.

If we assume that the political sympathies of the security forces in 1980 reflected those of their social classes, then we would have to assume that a great majority of the officers as well as a smaller majority of rank-and-file members wanted a change in government. If we further assume an 'environmental effect' on political attitudes, that is, a tendency for wavering people to gravitate toward the majority opinion in situations with a high degree of in-group interaction, which is typical for members of military institutions and, to a certain extent, also for members of a police corps, then we would predict an even stronger anti-PNP sentiment among the security forces. Yet, besides the general economic malaise and the social polarization affecting them as members of the middle classes, and besides the reinforcement effect of their corporate environment, there were further political factors which had an impact on the security forces.

Most importantly, the Cuban/communist threat campaign managed to raise considerable concern. The JDF officers' predominantly British training – for the top at Sandhurst – had made them strongly anti-communist. For them, communist was equivalent to enemy, a term carrying heavy connotations and evoking strong reactions. Thus, when they, along with large sectors of the population, came to believe that there was some truth in the incessant allegations that communists had infiltrated the PNP, they naturally started regarding the PNP itself as a threat. Among the rank-and-file, ideological predispositions were much weaker, but the specter of a physical threat posed by the Cubans and by Cuban-trained forces inside Jamaica, alleged by the opposition, took its toll in the form of hostility to a government with obviously friendly relations to Cuba.[59] In the police force, neither officers nor rank-and-file have generally had any ideological leanings.[60] However, the frequently repeated threat that they might be replaced by the Home Guard and/or a similar militia-type organization, modelled after the popular militias in communist countries, also made them highly suspicious of the government's intentions. Finally, for the security forces as a whole, the damage done to the government's legitimacy reduced their respect for its legitimately constituted authority and weakened the constitutionalist norms inculcated in their training.

The government again arranged for joint police–military operations to keep the lid on the violence, and it extended the Suppression of Crime Act throughout the 1980 campaign. However, as discussed above, none of these measures had the desired effects. This situation, the security forces being faced with an unachievable task, under orders from a government whose authority was increasingly disregarded by the society at large, could not but create anger and resentment against this government and the forces supporting it. The fact that, on top of this, the security forces were exposed to direct physical attacks of unprecedented proportions, such as the machine-gun attacks on police stations, induced at least parts of the security forces to challenge the authority of the government openly.

There were two instances of obvious and direct challenges to the government, the coup attempt in June and the call of the Police Federation for Thompson's removal from his post as Minister of National Security in May. The plot for the coup was detected by the command of the security forces in its early stages. According to the chief of the JDF, information about contacts between civilians and some members of the JDF led to regular surveillance of the suspects and to the discovery that the coup was planned for 23 June (*G*, 24 June 1980). Thus, the coup could easily be prevented and the suspects, three JDF officers, twenty-three JDF members, and three civilians, detained for questioning.

The Police Federation, an association representing interests of the policemen in labor relations, became increasingly vocal and critical of alleged political interference in police work in the early months of 1980 (see for example, *G*, 27 March 1980 and 7 April 1980). At the Federation's annual conference, its chairman McBeth launched a frontal attack on Thompson, charging him with neglect in the area of security of police stations, of mobility of the force, of retaliative action (*sic*) for the killing of policemen, as well as with negligence toward political interference and with other actions inimical to the interests of the police. As a result, the Federation expressed a collective 'no confidence' in Thompson and urged Manley to remove him (*G*, 28 May 1980).

The open challenge from the Police Federation, which constituted a clear breach of discipline, cannot be understood without reference to the actions of the civilian opposition. Since late 1979, the JLP with the support of the *Gleaner* had unrelentingly pressed the charge of political interference in and deliberate weakening of the security forces by the government (for example, see *G*, 28 March 1980). At the conference where McBeth launched this attack, Seaga had been the invited guest speaker, also pressing charges of blatant political manipulation, particularly interference in transfers and promotions for political reasons (*G*, 29 May 1980). Moreover, the JLP used graphically suggestive full-page political advertisements in the *Gleaner* to incite the security forces against the government.[61] Such incitement and support from the party which had a 14 per cent lead in the opinion polls at the time could not help but encourage breaches of discipline like McBeth's speech and strong hostility to the party in power.

The effects of the shift of the security forces against the PNP were several. Most importantly, they impaired the PNP's capacity for political campaigning. PNP activists were harrassed, detained for longer periods than legal, and worse; details of such harrassment were exposed in a debate in the House by many MPs (*G*, 21 August 1980). Also, headquarters of the PNP candidates were searched and damaged (*DN*, 1 August 1980), and PNP candidates were hassled at road blocks. In general, the high command officially condemned any abuses of authority by the security forces, insisting that only a very small minority was involved in such abuses, but it was obviously unwilling or unable to take the disciplinary measures which would have put a halt to the abuses.

Besides impairing the PNP's door-to-door campaigning capacity, which had contributed so much to its large victory in 1976, the hostility of the security forces had a further, indirect, effect on the PNP's support base. It caused fear among rank-and-file supporters, decreasing the attendance at political rallies, and it convinced wavering voters that the PNP offered little promise of a return to safety and stability.

The PNP campaign
The May poll showed the PNP lagging behind the JLP with 36% and 49% respectively (Table A.15). Up to that point, virtually all the party's energies had been absorbed in the discussion of the break with the IMF. After the campaign had been launched, the gap slowly started to narrow, down to 10 per cent by September. However, the campaign was beset by a number of problems: First of all, the government, and thus the PNP leadership, continued to have preoccupations other than campaign plans and speeches, most prominently the management of the economy, and in particular, the provision of basic foodstuffs and services. Second, the high level of violence and the hostility of the security forces made campaigning difficult or even hazardous for PNP activists as well as leaders. Third, the aura of scandal and suspicion resulting from the controversy about the legality of nomination procedures for a by-election won by Thompson in 1978, and from the Moonex affair, put the government on the defensive.[62] Fourth, the high profile of the WPJ in the PNP campaign played right into the opposition's communist smear tactics. Fifth, the strong influence exercised by some members of the WPJ on the JBC newsroom gave an explicitly radical slant to news coverage which hurt the credibility of the government.

In the face of all these problems, the PNP campaign became more a defensive one rather than one projecting an image of strength and promising new initiatives. PNP spokespersons and official statements devoted much attention to refuting the JLP's charges and to launching counter-attacks on the opposition. Two instances of Seaga's conduct were particularly sharply criticized; his speeches in the USA alleging communist subversion in Jamaica and links of key government-personnel with Cuban and Russian intelligence circles, and his attempt to paint Manley as wavering and out of control over the course of governmental policy by using a doctored tape-recording of Manley's speech at the NEC meeting which decided on the immediate break with the IMF.[63] In counter-attack, Manley claimed that the JLP was using fascist tactics (*G*, 13 June 1980). He further charged that foreign reactionary agencies and people were working with the JLP, and that the JLP was receiving money from the John Birch Society.

In the issue-oriented parts of the campaign, the PNP pointed to its achievements in the areas of workers' rights, land reform, and bauxite, whose effects had clearly survived the years of IMF austerity. For the future, it promised continued austerity and an uphill struggle in the pursuit of economic independence and maximum development of human and material resources.[64] The election manifesto emphasized that after an immediate renegotiation of the foreign debt, priority would be assigned to agriculture in order to achieve greater self-reliance, that state sector management and planning capabilities would be strengthened, that great efforts would be made to prevent sabotage in all areas of economy and society, and that greater production and discipline would be needed. The PNP also stressed the need to bring violence under control by way of defeating political tribalism. On the whole, the manifesto had a rather somber tone, honestly and – in the case of an election victory – wisely so, which, however, made it a weak competitor for the JLP's promises of 'jingling in your pockets' in the appeal to voters who had just suffered more than two years of declining consumption.

In terms of concrete promises and proposals, the PNP campaign was quite moderate, fully reaffirming the party's commitment to the goals laid out in *Principles and Objectives*. That the campaign nevertheless projected a radical image was due to instances of militant rhetoric from PNP spokespeople, the role of the WPJ, the campaign coverage by the JBC newsroom, and the distortion of the PNP positions by the opposition. Particularly remarkable rhetorical statements were Spaulding's proclamation at a PNP rally that he had 'appointed myself as the General of the Streets from now until then', as he was going to 'unite the roots to fight the fascists' (*DN*, 11 February 1980). Also, Small's statements that in its third term the PNP would need to take state power and that the little resources that the poor country had would need to come under people's power had a distinctly radical ring to them and lent themselves easily to ominous *Gleaner* headlines and insinuations (*G*, 6 October 1980). What made opposition distortions particularly harmful was the fact that the PNP had virtually no organ of mass communication remotely equal to the *Gleaner* in reach and credibility with which to counter.[65] The *Daily News* never achieved more than a fraction of the *Gleaner's* circulation, and the JBC was progressively losing credibility among large sectors of the population. The reasons for this loss of credibility merit some more detailed discussion.

The Role of the WPJ and the JBC Newsroom

In August 1978, the Workers' Liberation League was transformed into the Workers' Party of Jamaica, a Marxist–Leninist party. The new party continued the policy of 'critical support' for the PNP and the government, that is, support for the government's anti-imperialist and pro-people policies, and attempts at collaboration with the left wing in the PNP. From the start, it maintained a stance of strong opposition to the IMF and it engaged in attempts at popular mobilization against the IMF. The PNP repeatedly rejected any formal collaboration, but it publicly welcomed the support for its struggle expressed by the WJP, and on an informal level collaboration took place on several issues.

Mobilization against the IMF's demands was a key area where the WPJ and the PNP left pursued the same objectives. Enforcement of price controls and other action for the protection of consumer interests was an area where the PNP Women's Movement and the WPJ-affiliated Committee of Women for Progress (CWP) worked together. Political rallies and demonstrations against the JLP's communist-smear campaign and against the *Gleaner's* propaganda also invited common action.

As we noted, such collaboration was controversial within the PNP, but whereas the moderates prevailed in enforcing a clear official distance, the left prevailed in implementing its strategy of 'collaboration of all progressive forces' on an informal level.[66] The issue came to a head in 1980, when the WPJ first launched an all-out anti-IMF offensive and then announced that it would not put up any candidates of its own for the election but would instead actively campaign for the PNP. Again, the moderates were strongly opposed to this, fearing an anti-communist backlash against the PNP, whereas the left insisted that the PNP must join forces with all progressive people in order to be able to win the election.[67] In fact, according to several reliable sources, the secretariat did make contact with the WPJ to coordinate their help in campaign activities. This whole question was never formally discussed and decided on by the party leadership, which became the subject of strong criticism in a post-election analysis by a leading PNP moderate. During the campaign, the moderates continued to clarify publicly the differences between the PNP's and the WPJ's positions and voicing their displeasures over the WPJ's activities on behalf of the PNP. Still, the WPJ did visibly participate in PNP rallies as well as door-to-door campaigning, which certainly resulted in an identification of the two parties in many a voter's mind.

Much of the WPJ's public visibility was due to the coverage given to its activities by the JBC newsroom. The JBC, as public broadcasting station, had traditionally been strongly influenced by the government in power, with more or less direct interference in its programming depending on the particular government in office. As we discussed in Chapter 4, the Manley government was no exception in the sense that it expected a generally favorable exposure of the government's plans and policies. However, during its second term, a new element entered into the picture – the workers' participation scheme introduced with the government's encouragement. Though the scheme did not achieve a high degree of formalization, it meant, among other things, that employees had a greater influence on the hiring and firing of colleagues.[68] This influence, together with some degree of self-selection, made it possible for a small group of dynamic journalists with WPJ ties to make their mark on the perspective from which news was reported, as well as on the selection of topics to be covered by the newsroom. In general, this meant that news was reported from a left-wing perspective and that topics like popular struggle, anti-imperialism, reactionary politics, etc., and events like demonstrations and statements by left-wing groups received much attention. In particular, this meant that the WPJ, a party with an extremely small social base (between 1 and 4 per cent in opinion polls) compared with the two others, tended to receive a widely disproportionate amount of coverage for its actions and statements. Its leader Munroe figured almost as prominently as Seaga and Manley.[69]

In addition to selection and interpretation of news from a left-wing perspective by the newsroom journalists, there were controversies over attempts by the head of the current affairs division, John Maxwell, to stifle criticism of governmental conduct by censuring the statements of commentators (*G*, 4 and 22 October 1979; 5 November 1979). These controversies and the obvious ideological slant of the newsroom did further damage to the traditionally low credibility of the JBC among the general public, and the JBC's history of manipulation by the government in power suggested to the public the conclusion that the government had to approve of these operations. Thus, the lack of credibility of the JBC reflected negatively on the credibility of the government. Also, the wide coverage given to events in which the PNP as well as the WPJ were involved played into the hand of the oppositions's attempt to create fear of a communist takeover of the PNP and the country. In sum, the JBC was damaging rather than helping the government's image among marginal voters.

The election outcome
The October 1980 election brought a record voter turnout of 77 per cent of eligible voters (Table A.1), which reflected the high degree of politicization and polarization caused by the change process initiated by the PNP. The election was a massive swing to the JLP, with 59 per cent of the vote, giving them fifty-one of the sixty seats in Parliament. The pro-JLP swing affected all social classes, to the extent that the JLP carried a majority in all of them, though the class re-alignment of 1976 was not reversed (see Table

A.21).[70] The JLP also managed to obtain a majority of the vote in all parishes, including the traditional PNP strongholds of Kingston, St Andrew, St Ann, Westmoreland and Manchester. The similarities of the swings showed a continuation of the trend toward greater national uniformity in voting patterns, which had already manifested itself in clear fashion in the 1976 election. This trend to uniformity was reinforced by the intensity of the national political debate over the issues on which the election was fought, namely the state of the economy, the role of democratic socialism, the Cuban/communist threat, and the high level of violence.

The largest swing toward the JLP occurred in the category of skilled and semi-skilled manual wage labor, though the PNP still retained 48 per cent of the vote, the strongest support it achieved in any class grouping. On the one hand, the strong decline of support reflected the deterioration in the relationship between the government and organized labor caused by the wage guidelines and by the decline in real wages over the three preceding years. On the other hand, the continued comparatively strong support for the PNP among blue-collar workers can be explained by the perception of a marked difference between the two parties in their commitment to the protection and promotion of workers' rights and interests.

Large swings against the PNP also occurred among the unemployed and unskilled labor, and among white-collar workers (Table A.21). The white-collar PNP vote followed the downward trajectory established in 1976. Whereas the strong traditional PNP attachments among middle- and lower middle-class employees had still kept a majority of voters in this category in the PNP camp in 1976, the spread of disaffection from the upper and upper middle- to the middle- and lower middle-class had grown stronger than tradition for many white-collar employees during the following years, shrinking the PNP base to a low of 37 per cent in 1980. Unskilled workers and the unemployed had given 60 per cent of the vote to the PNP in 1976, partly because of the youth vote which comprised a particularly large group in 1976 (see Chapter 4). However, partisan attachments after one or two (in local elections) votes were still weak among young voters, with the exception of party activists, of course. Thus, they defected relatively easily when the economic hardships and the violence turned the tide against the PNP.

The smallest swing of any category occurred among businessmen and higher-income professionals, mainly because the 40 per cent swing against the PNP in 1976 had left only one fifth of these classes in the PNP camp. Most of them, one has to assume, were from families with close PNP ties, remaining loyal party voters in 1976 and again in 1980.[71]

Among agricultural workers, the PNP vote declined to 42 per cent. The shortages, the threat of growing unemployment, and the decline in real wages all contributed to an erosion of PNP support in this category. Still, agricultural workers remained more loyal to the PNP than did the unskilled and the unemployed and white-collar workers, becoming the second strongest support base of the PNP in 1980, in clear contrast to 1972.

Small farmers, in contrast, remained the second lowest category of PNP support, slightly lower even than white-collar workers. Despite its policies promoting domestic agriculture, the PNP had not managed to make any inroads into the traditional JLP hold over the majority of this class by 1976, partly because of a lack of visibility of programs like Land Lease. During the IMF years, of course, this visibility was doubly impaired, as little money was available for the programs proper as well as for education and mobilization purposes. On the other hand, the experience of shortages of farm inputs and credits took their toll in terms of growing opposition to the party in power.

By far the most important reason for the PNP's dramatic loss of political support was the state of the economy, followed by violence and the communism issue. In a September 1980 poll, voters were asked which was the most important issue in the election. Economic issues, predominantly unemployment, economic recovery, and shortages, were mentioned by 51 per cent of respondents in the Metropolitan Area, 66 per cent in other towns and 61 per cent in rural areas (Stone, 1981b:11). Unemployment topped the list in all three areas, with 21 to 26 per cent of voters considering it to be the most important issue. Whatever the particular economic concerns, the general perception was one of an economy – and a people – in deep trouble, and of a government incapable of solving this fundamental problem. In March 1980, 77 per cent of voters in the Kingston area and 75 per cent in the rest of the island said that their living standards had deteriorated over the previous year (Stone, 1982:70), and in response to the question as to which among a list of five factors contributed to the economic hardships being experienced in the island, 60 per cent of voters mentioned the government, 51 per cent the world economy, 27 per cent the IMF, 14 per cent private business, and 14 per cent enemies of the government (Stone, 1982:74). Thus, regardless of the granting of some extenuating circumstances, primarily the world economy, the government had to shoulder the bulk of the blame, with obvious electoral consequences.

Violence was clearly more important to voters in the Kingston area than elsewhere, as 23 per cent saw it as an important election issue there compared with 10 per cent of respondents in towns and 7 per cent in rural areas; party tribalism, intimately connected to political violence, was mentioned by 5 per cent of respondents in Kingston and only 1 per cent elsewhere. Again, in the all important question of who was to blame for the increased level of political violence, more respondents in a June 1980 poll blamed the PNP only (34 per cent) than blamed the JLP only (10 per cent), or both political parties (20 per cent), or unspecified politicians (14 per cent), criminals (9 per cent), communists (2 per cent), or the CIA (1 per cent) (Stone, 1982:25). Given that there is no evidence that the PNP initiated more political violence than the JLP, one can point to two reasons to explain this. First, just as in the case of the economy, the government was held responsible for providing security for the citizens and consequently the party in power was punished for its inability to do so. Second, the relentless opposition campaign highlighting the JLP victims of violence and blaming the PNP for instigating violence and weakening the security forces was bearing fruit. The role of the *Gleaner* in reporting and playing up PNP attacks and not JLP attacks was particularly important in this respect. The extensive coverage given to the Gold Street Massacre as compared with a similar attack on a PNP dance (which, significantly, remained nameless) is just one example of this.

Communism figured as the most important election issue in a comparatively low percentage of voters' minds; 2 per cent mentioned it in the Kingston area, 3 per cent in other towns, and 7 per cent in rural areas; socialism was mentioned by 8, 6 and 4 per cent respectively (Stone, 1981b:11). This may come as somewhat of a surprise, given the length and intensity of the opposition's communist-smear campaign. However, one has to keep in mind that voters were asked for *the* most important issue in the election. If second and third choices had been tabulated, it is quite likely that the issue of communism would have figured more prominently. There are indications that the issue was in fact more important than it had been in 1976 and that a stronger link had been established in the voters' perception between the PNP and the Cuban and communist threat. According to Stone (1982:25), 43 per cent of respondents in a poll in June 1980 agreed that the PNP was heading toward communism. He also reports that 45 per cent of respondents in the same poll felt that they had something to fear from the Cuban presence, whereas in November 1976 only 25 per cent of the respondents had been opposed to the Cuban presence (Stone:1981b:13).[72] These pieces of evidence taken together suggest that a credible link between the PNP and the alleged communist threat had been established in many voters' minds, and that the threat was perceived as real by more voters than in 1976.

The opposition campaign, particularly the *Gleaner's* masterful use of propaganda tools, was certainly of key importance in bringing about this change,[73] but there are at least three more factors which played a role. First, the economic hardships and the violence created fear, confusion and uncertainty, and thus rendered people more susceptible to the anti-communist propaganda. Second, the perception of an association between the PNP and communists was reinforced by the WPJ's campaign and by the JBC newsroom's coverage of events. Third, by 1980 the Evangelical churches had picked up the communism issue and were warning and threatening the faithful and attacking the PNP for godlessness from the pulpits. They exhorted people to pray for 'Deliverance'.

The importance of the *Gleaner's* role in making the charge of communist

leanings and support for Cuban subversion stick on the PNP becomes clear
if its reach and credibility compared to other media are taken into account.
In addition to its wide reach, the *Gleaner* enjoyed a considerable advantage in credibility. A poll in October 1980 showed that 25 per cent of
respondents in the Kingston area and 33 per cent in other areas regarded
the *Gleaner* as the most reliable news source (Stone, 1982:42). Only RJR,
the radio station sold to various popular organizations, which had a clearly
non-partisan position, surpassed the *Gleaner's* credibility, with 41 per cent
of respondents in the Kingston area and 37 per cent elsewhere regarding it
as most reliable. However, one has to keep in mind the relatively small
proportion of air-time devoted to news coverage by RJR, as well as the
influence of the *Gleaner* on local opinion leaders. As discussed above, JBC
radio and television did not enjoy strong credibility outside PNP partisan
circles; in the poll, 14 per cent selected it as most reliable in the Kingston
area and only 5 per cent in the rest of the island. The *Daily News*, which
had a moderately pro-PNP position, was regarded as most reliable by 9 per
cent in the Kingston area and 6 per cent elsewhere. Thus, the blatantly
pro-JLP *Gleaner* continued to benefit from the credibility it had acquired
on the basis of its long-term monopolistic position as the key source of
printed news. This meant that it was able to put across extremely strong
partisan propaganda with much greater credibility than the JBC, and even
with greater credibility than the *Daily News* could put across its own much
more moderate partisan line.

In summary, then, one certainly has to assess the state of the economy as
the key reason for the 1980 election outcome. It is hard to imagine how any
government could survive the test at the polls after implementing an IMF
austerity program with the harshness of the one forced on the Manley
government.[74] Second, the high level of violence and the turn of the
security forces against the PNP further eroded its popular support, and
third, the relationship to Cuba and to the domestic communists also hurt
the PNP in that it provided material for the long-lasting opposition propaganda. These three factors mutually reinforced one another in that the
disastrous economic situation had exhausted many Jamaicans and rendered them highly susceptible to propaganda raising the specter of even
further austerity, the imposition of rationing, and a communist take-over
aided by Cuba. Thus, fear for the future and fear for personal safety from
violence in the present made a majority of Jamaicans long for the election
and a change in government.

Besides having a direct effect on the election outcome via voters'
perception of a communist threat, the combination of the PNP's actions
vis-à-vis Cuba and the opposition's propaganda campaign had an indirect
effect on the election via the economy. The fear of communist subversion,
or simply 'what's around the corner' affected the business community both
earlier and more sharply than the mass public. This fear contributed to the

flight of capital and of entrepreneurial and managerial skills, and consequently to the deterioration of the economy. Also, Jamaica's close relations with Cuba had a negative effect on the willingness of foreign bankers to extend new loans and on the disbursement of US aid. Again, fact and fiction, or the reality of these fears and their impact on business behavior, and the exaggerated opposition claims that the key reason for the deterioration of the economy was the destruction of business confidence by PNP rhetoric, worked together to create a perception among voters at large that the PNP's pro-communist leanings were, at least in part, responsible for the economic difficulties. On the basis of these indirect effects then, the issue of the Cuban or communist threat has to be assessed as more important than on the basis of the foregoing analysis of public opinion alone.

Concluding remarks
The economic and political developments in the years from 1978 to 1980 again demonstrate Jamaica's vulnerability resulting from dependency. Economic policy was dictated by the IMF and primarily oriented toward restoring confidence among foreign and domestic investors and foreign lenders. This orientation, together with the imposition of the austerity measures, closed not only economic but also political options for progress on the democratic socialist path. Ultimately, compliance with the IMF policies and the resulting sacrifices failed to create economic recovery, as foreign exchange inflows remained way below expectations. Negative feedback from the Jamaican opposition and from an increasingly hostile Carter administration influenced foreign lenders, investors and tourists not to commit themselves to Jamaica. Finally, the experience of 1980 demonstrates how extremely difficult it is for a small country deeply in debt to break out of the IMF dictates.

In emphasizing Jamaica's dependence and vulnerability, however, it is important to keep in mind that the pressures on Jamaica in this period were by no means exclusively due to international economic interests. Rather, the dominant motivation for US behavior was the perception of threats to US security interests. In fact, threats to economic interests, except for the hypothetical case of a default on the foreign debt, were reduced in this period, as the IBA proved to be much weaker than expected and as the Jamaicans renegotiated and reduced the bauxite levy. It was the close relationship with Cuba, in particular the presence of Cubans in Jamaica, which greatly concerned the ascendant faction among the Carter administration's foreign-policy personnel, because of their own view of the world through an East–West conflict lens.

The development of the political movement in this period demonstrated both its continued limitations and the progress achieved. On the one hand, grass-roots support crumbled and activists were demoralized rapidly under the onslaught of the economic hardships. On the other hand, the PNP finally arrived at an official formulation of its program and ideological orientation which could serve as a basis for internal political education as well as for explaining the party's plans to the larger public. Also, the process leading up to the break with the IMF involved strong inputs from rank-and-file activists and illustrates the progress in deepening internal democracy in the party. And the PNP's increased organizational strength forced the JLP to strengthen its own organization and mobilization capacity in order to be able to compete with the PNP for political support.

The important role played by the opposition, particularly the JLP and the *Gleaner*, in this period in delegitimizing the government highlights a crucial difficulty for any political movement and government pursuing a democratic-socialist development path. First, it is always easier for the opposition to criticize, create fears, and sabotage policies than it is for the proponents of change to project a clear, concrete, and understandable picture of their path and to implement new policies successfully. Second, the propertied classes as key opponents of democratic socialism are in a position to take advantage of their resources and the democratic principle of freedom of the press to undermine the very process of open and truthful political debate and opinion formation.

The administrative and coercive machinery of the state also presented problems for the government in this period. Foot-dragging in the bureaucracy and the turn of the security forces against the PNP hampered the government's ability to manage the difficult economic situation, maintain public order and run its election campaign. It is important to note, however, that the behavior of the state apparatus changed in step with the middle classes. Thus, it is more appropriate to see it as an effect rather than a cause of declining popular support. This is not to say that particularly the defection of the security forces did not aggravate the government's political weakness, but it is to say that it was not some inherent quality of the 'capitalist state' which proved to be the stumbling-block. We would argue that the state apparatus would not have been a bigger problem in 1980 than in 1976, if the government had been able to avoid recourse to the IMF (and thus the resulting economic hardships), and to construct a class alliance with the middle- and lower middle-classes included, and thus maintain enough popular support to win the elections.

7

Seaga's Return to Dependent Capitalism

With the election of the JLP in 1980, Jamaica returned to a new variant of the model of dependent capitalist 'development' that had been pursued in the 1950s and 1960s. By 1983, it was already clear that the attempt to resurrect dependent development had failed even when measured by its own narrow criteria. In this chapter, we will briefly examine the reasons for this failure, both because it helps to put the successes and failures of Manley's years in perspective and because developments during the JLP government are a necessary background for assessing the chances for the successful implementation of a democratic socialist development model in the future.

Seaga's economic model

The economic development strategy of the JLP government is properly called 'Seaga's model' because he not only designed the policy but also exercised very tight control over its implementation, holding the minister-ial posts of Prime Minister, finance, mines (to January 1984) and culture, as well as heading special projects such as 'Agro 21' which ordinarily would fall under another portfolio. To understand Seaga's model, it is essential to put it in the context of both his past actions as Finance Minister under the Shearer government and his political strategy as opposition leader in relation to domestic capital and to the US government. As Finance Minister, Seaga was a proponent of state intervention in the economy in the forms of ownership and control, taxation, and public welfare expendi-ture, but, during the Manley period, this position was progressively modi-fied, at least rhetorically, as Seaga attempted to capitalize on the PNP's deteriorating relation with the private sector and to play the 'American card'. As we saw in Chapters 5 and 6, 'playing the American card' under the Carter administration consisted of a campaign alleging human rights violations on the part of the PNP government, but after the 1980 US and Jamaican elections, 'playing the American card' meant emphasizing the role of private enterprise and market forces in the JLP's development model. Seaga played this for all it was worth with the Reagan administra-tion and, as it turned out, it was worth quite a bit.

Because of the public-relations nature of the private-sector orientation of Seaga's model, there was a certain disjunction between rhetoric of the government and its image, especially abroad, and the reality of its policies. Nonetheless, two agreements entered into by the government, the Extended Fund Facility (EFF) agreement with the IMF and the Structural Adjustment Loan with the World Bank, did bind it to a definite set of policies. These policies were similar to those pursued in the 1950s and 1960s in that private capital – domestic and foreign – was to be the primary engine of growth. Of course, state intervention in the economy would not actually be reduced back to the pre-1972 level, but there was an explicit commitment to the IMF and World Bank to investigate divestment of all state enterprises other than the utilities. Under the IMF and World Bank agreements, state sector capital expenditure was to be concentrated on infrastructure. The IMF agreement also committed the government to reducing state-sector employment by attrition. The Seaga government also intended to introduce market-pricing for all goods produced by all state-sector enterprises. A final similarity with the 1950s and 1960s was that the government moved toward an open licensing system for imports.[1] Of course, the implications of this were quite different in the context of a shortage of foreign exchange since such a more inherently created pressures for devaluation.

Despite these similarities, Seaga's model was by no means a straight recapitulation of the earlier dependent development path. Both the EFF agreement and the Structural Adjustment Loan, but particularly the latter, involved a commitment to shift the economy from import substitution to export orientation. In the short run, this would involve promotion of both traditional (bauxite, alumina, sugar and bananas) and non-traditional exports. In the long run, progress towards an export-oriented economy would depend on the growth of non-traditional exports. Promotion of exports would be achieved in part through incentives offered to present exporters and new investors, domestic and foreign. However, the government also wanted to eliminate the 'anti-export bias' of the economy, that is, the protection of import substituters which allowed them to make large profits because of insulation from competition. Under the terms of the IMF loan, the government agreed to introduce no new quantitative restrictions on imports and, under the World Bank loan, further committed itself to eliminate all existing quantitative restrictions over a five-year period. It was assumed that this would make producers for the domestic market more competitive and encourage investment in exports. Finally, the Seaga model, more by circumstance than intention, differed from the earlier dependent-capitalist model in that it relied on foreign loans rather than investment inflows to cover the trade deficit.

Of course, the IMF package did demand austerity policies, which have no parallel in the pre-Manley dependent capitalist model. The EFF agreement called for reduced budget deficits, wage restraint, a real reduction in government expenditure, reduction in government employment, rationalization of public enterprises, limitation of monetary expansion and maintenance of a 'realistic' exchange rate. It is worth pointing out here that the March 1981 package was not as severe as the one demanded of the Manley government the previous year though one must keep in mind the fact that Seaga was able to borrow large amounts abroad in the first few months of his administration. For instance, the state was allowed to reduce the workforce through attrition and no figures for wage restraint were publicly specified.

Whereas policies such as rationalization and increased efficiency of tax collection were as characteristic of the 1960s Seaga as of the 1980s Seaga, the reduction in the role of the state was not. However, it is important to recognize that, even at the outset, there were ways in which the old Seaga showed through here also. Social services were not subject to a wholesale Reagan–Thatcher type of attack, which in the face of the heightened level of political mobilization and the patronage expectations of JLP supporters would have been politically very costly. Even the Special Employment Program was maintained for a time, albeit under another name, Relief Employment Program. The State Trading Corporation was renamed the Jamaica Commodity Trading Company Limited and actually expanded to include motor vehicle imports. Even the Managing Director, a PNP appointee and former campaign manager for Manley, O. K. Melhado, was retained in his post, and, though the World Bank loan agreement mentions exploring the possibility of selling government-owned hotels, government actions suggest that it never had any intention to go beyond leasing them, a policy initiated by the PNP government.

Seaga's cultivation of Reagan could hardly have been more skillful or more successful. His approach to the American President had two aspects. On the one hand, he pushed the private enterprise–free-market line very hard, which naturally had great appeal in Washington. On the other hand, Seaga's anti-communist/anti-Cuba line fitted perfectly with the Reagan administration's foreign-policy posture. One cannot help but presume that one motivation behind the break of diplomatic relations with Cuba in October 1981 was currying favor with the US administration at precisely the time it was mounting a major ideological offensive against Castro's government.[2]

Seaga was the first head of state to visit the USA and meet the new President after his inauguration. Seaga's visit not only established very warm relations between the two countries but also had several concrete results. First, Reagan set up the US Economic Committee on Jamaica, a group of US businessmen, whose task it was to promote US investment in the island. At Reagan's personal request, Chase Manhattan Chairman, David Rockefeller, headed the committee. Second, Seaga took the opportunity to suggest to the

President that the USA develop a Marshall-plan-type program for the Caribbean Region. This suggestion eventually evolved into the Caribbean Basin
Initiative (CBI). Finally, the USA increased aid to Jamaica massively (Table
A.20), so much so, that by 1983, the country ranked third only to Israel and
El Salvador in per capita US aid. Moreover, these figures do not include
income from the agreement with the USA for the sale of 1.6m tons of bauxite
for its strategic stockpile in 1982 and again in 1983; nor does it include any
potential benefits from the CBI.

Reagan announced the CBI in February 1982. The centerpiece of the
program was duty-free entry into the USA for twelve years of all goods
produced in the Caribbean Basin except textiles and apparels. The CBI
also included tax incentives for investment in the area; a $350m aid
package, with Jamaica and El Salvador being the largest beneficiaries; and
technical assistance to the private sector in the region. The CBI was passed
in a modified form by Congress in fall 1983.

A final important aspect about the Reagan aid package to Jamaica
should be noted. As one can see from Table A.20, US aid to Jamaica in
this period included a small but significant military component.

Economic performance
The performance of the economy in 1981 appeared at least in part to justify
the official optimism. In 1982, the weaknesses of the heralded recovery
became rather visible and caused the government to adopt a somewhat
more cautious outlook and public posture. By early 1983, the problems
grew so grave that the government was forced to admit certain shortcomings and to take drastic corrective measures. By the end of 1983, the
government had failed the quarterly IMF tests twice and was forced to
negotiate a new agreement with the Fund, which involved a massive
devaluation.

Balance of payments
The central problem for the government has clearly been the availability of
foreign exchange. The Extended Fund Facility Agreement with the IMF,
reached in March 1981, was to be the key to the solution. It involved IMF
loans to Jamaica of US$650m over three years, US$260m of which were to
be disbursed in 1981–2. In addition, Jamaica received US$48m from the
IMF's Compensatory Financing Facility in 1981 and another US$24m in
1982, to make up for the shortfalls in traditional export earnings.

The two most important short-term purposes of the agreement were to
stimulate exports and revive economic growth. They were to be achieved
by fuller utilization of capacity in the bauxite/alumina industry; taking
steps toward a rehabilitation of the tourism, sugar and banana industries,
and by making much more foreign exchange available for imports of
industrial inputs, primarily to stimulate new manufacturing production for

export and second, to utilize more fully the capacity of industries producing for the domestic market. Of course, the resources provided by the IMF proper would not have been sufficient to achieve these objectives, but with the IMF seal of approval the Seaga government managed to achieve massive borrowing and refinancing targets in its first two years in office. Jamaica's foreign debt increased from an estimated US$1.2bn at the end of 1980 to US$3.1bn (including outstanding debt servicing) at the end of 1983 (*JWG*, 4 June 1984), or from J$1492m to J$5334.8m in November 1983 (Bank of Jamaica, 1984). Nevertheless, these policies did not produce the desired results in terms of increased production and generation of new export revenue. The trade deficit grew from US$75m in 1980 to US$323m in 1981 and US$476m in 1982. The total current amount deficit showed a similarly negative trajectory, from US$148m in 1980 to US$426m in 1982 (NPA, 1983a:3.6).

The major reasons for the growing deficits were the significant increase in imports, the poor performance of traditional exports, and the poor response of non-traditional exports. The worst setback was certainly suffered in the bauxite/alumina industry, a setback which could not have been averted by any government policies because it was a direct result of the recession in the world economy and of the diversification strategy of the aluminum corporations. Total bauxite shipments declined from 12m tons in 1980 to 7.3m tons in 1983; accordingly, total government revenue from the industry declined from US$206m in 1980 to US$137m in 1982 (NPA, 1983a:9.3–5). Production did not improve in 1983, and the closure of Reynolds' operations in early 1984 was a further setback. The other traditional exports, sugar and bananas, also performed poorly as sugar production declined from 242 000 tons in 1980 to 192 000 tons in 1982; and banana production declined from 33 000 tons in 1980 to 22 000 tons in 1982 (NPA, 1983a:8.1).

The reasons for the disappointing performances of non-traditional exports, which grew from J$197m in 1980 to only J$235m in 1982 (NPA, 1983a:4.10), were the traditional response of Jamaican businessmen and the slow response of foreign investors. Jamaican businessmen persisted in their traditional preference for quick and easy profits over entrepreneurial risk-taking, new investments and a search for new markets. The opportunities to reap quick and easy profits were provided by the government's policies of deregulation of the economy, liberalization of imports, and first quasi- and then full legalization of the black market or, as it came to be called, the parallel market in foreign currency. With the hope of drawing black market dollars into specified types of imports, the government issued so-called 'no-funds licenses', that is, import licenses which did not entitle the importer to draw the required foreign exchange from the central bank. The problem was, however, that regular as well as no-funds licenses were abused for imports of illicit but highly profitable finished goods, rather than for the explicit purpose of importing raw materials, intermediate and capital goods to stimulate manufacturing for the domestic market and for export.

To satisfy pent-up consumer demand, the government allowed an increase in consumer goods imports, including food, durables and non-durables, from 11 per cent of total imports in 1980 to 17 per cent in 1982 (NPA, 1983a:4.3). Total imports increased from US$1038m to US$1203m between 1980 and 1982 (NPA, 1982; 1983a:3.2). Clearly, in the face of the sluggish export performance, these policies of import liberalization exerted an intense pressure on the balance of payments. The foreign-exchange problem was further aggravated for the government by the considerable leakage of foreign-exchange earnings from the tourist industry. In 1982 total visitor arrivals had increased by 21 per cent over 1981 and estimated total visitor expenditures by 19 per cent but total cash receipts by the Bank of Jamaica from the tourist sector by only 9 per cent (NPA, 1983a:14.3).

By early 1983, the foreign exchange situation had become so difficult that some corrective action imposed itself. Seaga opted for the establishment of a two-tier exchange rate in January 1983, which effectively devalued the Jamaican dollar. The issue of devaluation had been a very sticky one for the Seaga government, as he had previously attacked the devaluations under Manley as a result of 'PNP mismanagement'. In line with its initially flexible attitude toward Seaga, the IMF had not insisted on a devaluation as part of the EFF agreement. This clearly helped Seaga to lower inflation in his first two years in office and to impose the wage restraint desired by the IMF. By introducing the dual exchange rate, Seaga could attempt to insist publicly that this was not a devaluation but rather only a formalization of the parallel market which was already in effect. The effect of the *de facto* devaluation was, of course, a significant increase in the price of imported goods and, given the high import component of all sectors of the Jamaican economy, a ripple effect on prices of all other goods. Accordingly, the inflation rate for 1983 was projected to reach 18.5 per cent (NPA, 1983b:i).

At the end of March, Jamaica failed the IMF's performance test, the IMF suspended further disbursements under the EFF agreement, and Seaga, blaming unexpected delays in the inflow of foreign loans, asked for a waiver. In anticipation of IMF deliberations, Seaga introduced a series of austerity measures such as a 10 per cent cutback in foreign exchange allocations for imports, new taxes, and a shift of many new items, such as gas, air fares, drugs, educational books, and edible oils and soap to the parallel market rate. The IMF was flexible again and granted the waiver in June, thus allowing Jamaica to receive disbursement of the US$40m held up at the end of March.[3] With the passage of the June performance tests, Jamaica could receive disbursement of another $40m, and at the same time two World Bank loans totalling US$80m were disbursed (LARRC, 23 July 1983). However, neither these belated import cutbacks, nor the IMF's flexibility, the World Bank loans, and official US approval of Seaga's policies changed the minds of international commercial bankers, who had become concerned about the Jamaican situation and repeatedly refused the US$200m in loans which Seaga continued to seek.

In October 1983, the IMF again suspended the EFF agreement, disputing the figures on the basis of which the government claimed to have passed the September performance tests. As a result, negotiations for a new agreement were initiated for a fifteen-month stand-by credit of US$180m, supposed to start 1 January 1984. The IMF's key demands were for a unification and devaluation of the exchange rate and a reduction of the fiscal deficit. At the end of November the exchange rate was set at J$3.15, and by May 1984 it had reached J$4; the supplementary estimates of February 1984 cut US$25m from the capital budget for public sector projects in the fiscal year 1983–4 and the new budget presented in May 1984 proposed to reduce the budget deficit by half, from 15.4 to 8.3 per cent of GDP (*JWG*, 4 June 1984). As part of the measures to achieve this reduction, new taxes on motor vehicles, drivers' licenses, beer and spirits were imposed, estimated to bring in J$45.1m in extra revenue (*JWG*, 4 June 1984). Also, the government asked its creditor countries to reschedule 100 per cent of arrears of principal and interest outstanding, as well as the principal and interest falling due in 1984 and 1985, and it asked private commercial banks for re-scheduling (*JWG*, 4 June 1984). After protracted negotiations, an agreement for a US$143.5m credit from the IMF came into effect on 2 June (LARRC, 20 July 1984), and the next month the Paris Club agreed to re-schedule US$135m of Jamaica's external debt payments due up to March 1985 (*JWG*, 20 July 1984).

The question imposes itself, why did Seaga, who had carefully cultivated a public image of himself as a financial wizard allow this import boom to continue for so long and thus lead to such a disastrous balance-of-payments situation? The answer lies in the combination of his strategy of economic reorientation toward export and his getting caught in his own rhetoric and by his own supporters. Seaga apparently really believed that the manufacturing sector had to be exposed to competition with foreign imports and thus forced to produce more efficiently for the domestic market as well as to reorient toward export markets. Furthermore, the World Bank loan agreement imposed a progressive liberalization of import restrictions, particularly the dismantling of any quantitative restrictions. The Reagan administration's strong economic support for Jamaica also demanded action in accordance with the free market rhetoric. Finally, Seaga had to pay off political debts to the middle class in the form of satisfying a certain extent of consumer demand.[4]

Investment

Besides creating greater space for the free play of market forces, the second major ingredient of Seaga's ideological platform was reliance on the private sector as the engine of growth. Before the election, he had proclaimed that all it would take to stimulate private domestic and foreign investment was a restoration of business confidence. After the election, he worked hard to cultivate this confidence with promises and reassurances, and with the help of the US–Jamaican business committee. Clearly, new investment in production of non-traditional exports was an indispensable part of the solution of the balance-of-payments problem.

Despite the great fanfare around the US–Jamaican business committee, the press conferences and the optimistic announcements of 'hundreds of investment inquiries',[5] actual commitments of investment resources and initiation of projects materialized very slowly. Seaga's proclaimed goal was to bring the ratio of gross fixed capital formation to GDP up to a level of 25 per cent, but the performance of 18.2 per cent in 1981 was only marginally better than the 1979 level of 17.4 per cent; in 1982, the ratio increased slightly to 20.3 per cent (NPA, 1983a:2.1). Obviously, the response of both domestic and foreign capital lagged far behind expectations. In particular, the hoped-for return of Jamaican capital and skilled personnel from abroad failed to occur. In his 1984 budget speech, Seaga stated that, as of April 1984, some 251 new investment projects had been established, with a total capital outlay of $360m, employing 7363 workers (*JWG*, 4 June 1984). Over the three-and-a-half year period, this amounts to roughly $100m per year of investment in new projects and 2100 new jobs, hardly a dent in the pool of unemployed. Of these new projects, 150 were locally owned, seventy-one foreign and thirty joint ventures. However, even where foreign capital was involved, alone or in joint ventures, businessmen apparently preferred to borrow on the local market rather than bringing in foreign funds. The NPA's figures on sources of foreign exchange show no inflow in the category 'foreign investments' in 1981, and a total of only US$2.4m in 1982 (NPA, 1983:3.8). Furthermore, as we will discuss below, many of the joint ventures were initiated and partly financed by the government.

Several reasons for the poor response can be mentioned. First, the international economic climate in 1981 and 1982 was certainly not favorable for the commitment of significant new investment. High interest rates, particularly in the USA, and depressed demand everywhere rendered new investment projects rather unattractive. Second, there were some specific factors which reduced the attractiveness of Jamaica as an investment site. In the beginning, US investors still shied away from Jamaica because of its reputation as a place with high degrees of violence and leftist infiltration, though Reagan's and Rockefeller's manifestations of confidence in and support for Seaga slow managed to assuage these concerns. Among Jamaican businessmen, the opportunities mentioned already for quick profits in imports remained most attractive, and furthermore the memory of Seaga's policies as Minister of Finance in the Shearer government created some doubts about the genuineness of his pro-business rhetoric. Also, the unreliable supplies of power all over the island and of water in the Kingston area weighed in as factors unfavorable to efficient production. Finally, the complexity and inefficiency of the Jamaican bureaucracy served as a deterrent to potential investors. Though the Seaga government created a new state agency, the Jamaica National Industrial Promotion, Ltd. (JNIP), to deal with investors in all matters from the planning stages to the actual start of production, there were still complaints about delays, customs and inefficiency in the port facilities. According to several people closely involved in the attempt to encourage foreign investors to go into Jamaica, the problem of the bureaucracy has been perceived as the most serious one in considerations of Jamaica as an investment site.

Both Reagan and Seaga have put much emphasis on the CBI as a cure for Jamaica's investment and export problems. However, the long delay in implementation and the exclusion of textiles, apparel and other categories of goods, greatly reduced its impact on Jamaica in the short and medium run. By late 1983, Jamaican hopes focused on alcoholic beverages, electronics and electrical equipment, and non-traditional agricultural exports as potentially the most important sectors.[6] However, it is highly unlikely that foreign capital will flow into Jamaica in significant amounts without very special concessions, which then would reduce the benefits from this investment to the Jamaican economy. In the bargaining about such concessions, foreign capital will clearly be in a position of greater strength, given the crucial dependence of Seaga's development model on such investment in order to be able to handle the balance-of-payments problem.

Reduction of the state's role in the economy
The disappointing response of the private sector, both domestic and foreign, to its assigned role as the principal engine of growth was clearly perceived, although not officially admitted, by the government by the second quarter of 1982.[7] Thus, without changing his free market/private enterprise rhetoric, Seaga started to change his mode of action toward greater involvement of the state sector. In July 1982, the government announced the purchase of Caymanas Estates as part of its efforts to upgrade the sugar industry, and of the Montego Freeport complex whose foreign owners threatened to close the facilities. Around the same time, the government announced the initiation of a rice-growing project on government-owned land. In September 1982 the government purchased the Esso Refinery, in response to what it considered excessive demands in the renegotiation of the expired agreement with Esso.

The divestment process advanced exceedingly slowly. The only enterprises of any significance that were sold to the private sector were Versair, a service company for airlines, and Southern Processors, a canning factory. The JOS was greatly pared down but not sold, and route assignments to minibuses were formalized. Hotels were leased (but not sold either) to as many takers as could be found. The utilities, in accordance with the IMF and World Bank agreements, were slowly upgraded through a public investment program, and at the same time the prices for their services were raised so as to reduce their deficits substantially, with the ultimate goal of making them financially viable.

Overall growth and sectoral performance

The government's projections of GDP growth envisaged rates of 4–5 per cent during a three-year recovery period. The growth performance of 3.3 per cent in 1981 lent some temporary credibility to the renewed optimistic projection of a 4 per cent growth rate for 1982 despite the rising concern among the business community over intensifying pressures from the balance-of-payments problem. However, in 1982 the economy remained virtually stagnant, with a growth rate of only 0.17 per cent, and in 1983 it grew by a modest 1.8 per cent.

Clearly the key sector depressing the overall growth rate in 1982 and 1983 was mining. Jamaican bauxite production suffered greatly from the world recession and the diversification policy of the North American corporations and it would have suffered even more if Reagan had not come to the rescue with his purchase for the US strategic stockpile.[8] It is worth noting here that the Seaga government successfully pursued an agreement for bauxite sales to the USSR, for 200 000 tons in 1983 and from 1984 on for 1m tons for seven years (LARRC, 13 May 1983) despite the criticism that Seaga had heaped on the PNP for its agreements with the USSR.

The performance of the manufacturing sector also lagged behind expectations. Though the allocation of foreign exchange to the sector increased by 28.5 per cent in 1981, the value of production increased by only 1.3 per cent (NPA, 1982:11.1; and Table A.10). The production level in 1982 was still 4.2 per cent below the 1979 level. The reasons for this disappointing performance were the large-scale abuse of import licenses, facilitated by corruption in the Trade Administrator's department, the damage done by the liberalization of imports, the legalization of the parallel market, the scarcity and unpredictability of foreign exchange allocation and the scarcity of credit for small businesses.[9] The abrupt exposure to foreign competition was particularly detrimental in the face of the foreign-exchange shortage, which forced manufacturers partly to buy dollars at the higher parallel market rate and partly to buy from countries which offered lines of credit, regardless of the competitiveness of the goods from these countries. Also, a reorientation toward export required obviously a transition period for the identification of suitable markets and products and possible retooling, a period which was not granted to manufacturers because of the rather abrupt exposure to competition from imported goods. The sectors hardest hit were shoes, leather, textiles, and parts of food processing.

Agriculture was also performing poorly, (Table A.10), not only in export crops but also in production for the domestic market, which was hit hard by the competition from imported foods. Agricultural production in 1982 was 9 per cent below the level of 1979. In sugar, which declined in both 1981 and 1982, Seaga was forced to admit the existence of deep structural problems, although during his time in opposition he had maintained that the decline of the industry was due to 'PNP mismanagement'. Bananas also performed poorly; pimento, ginger, cocoa, coffee and rum were the only exceptions to the generally poor agricultural performance between 1980 and 1982.

Clearly, the balance-of-payments problem makes an increase in agricultural production indispensable. Traditional and non-traditional agricultural exports have to be increased and produced efficiently to earn, and domestic crops to save, foreign exchange. Since private initiative was obviously not forthcoming to satisfy this requirement, Seaga stepped in again and launched the program Agro 21 in August 1983 (*JWG* 24 August 1983). This was to bring some 200 000 acres of unutilized or under-utilized land into production and provide employment for some 142 000 persons over a period of four years. The program was to be carried out in large part by private developers, producing on a commercial scale and with advanced technology. In the hope of attracting suitable developers, Seaga hired a well-known agribusiness executive as coordinator. The program had several components which clearly addressed long-standing obstacles to improvements in agricultural production in Jamaica, such as crop zoning, erosion control, irrigation systems, and upgrading of transport, packaging and storage facilities. The big question marks behind the program, of course, concern the willingness of private developers to invest in it and the spill-over effects on small farmers in terms of benefits from crop zoning, erosion control, etc.

Tourism was clearly a bright spot in 1982. Visitor arrivals increased by 21.4 per cent from 1981 to 1982; with a total of some 670 000 visitor arrivals, 1982 surpassed the 1979 number of some 594 000. Accordingly, hotel occupancy rates were up to 53.3 per cent (NPA, 1983a:14.1–4). Partly, this positive result has to be attributed to the intensive advertising and promotional efforts of the Jamaica Tourist Board in North America, but certainly the supportive attitude of the Reagan administration and the resulting positive publicity in the USA contributed considerably to it. The benefits from this increase in tourism to the economy as a whole, particularly to the balance of payments, are reduced by three factors, the high import content (35–40 per cent) of the sector, the cost of the promotion campaign abroad, and the diversion of tourist dollars to foreign bank accounts or to the black market.[10]

Employment
From a social and political point of view, of course, the most crucial failure of Seaga's development model lies in the area of (un)employment. In his 1981 budget speech, Seaga proclaimed his goal of creating 100 000 jobs over a period of three years, which would quite significantly reduce unemployment. However, after a decline from an annual average level of 27.3 per cent in 1980 to 25.9 per cent in 1981, unemployment increased again to an annual average of 27.4 per cent in 1982. In October 1982, unemployment stood at 27.9 per cent of the labor force, the second highest level ever recorded in Jamaica (Table A.11). In addition, under-employment grew, as the percentage of employed people who worked less than 33 hours a week increased from 14.9 per cent in October 1980 to 19.4 per cent in October 1981 and 21.4 per cent in October 1982 (NPA, 1983a: 17.17).[11]

Job losses between October 1981 and 1982 occurred in agriculture, mining, transport, communication, public utilities and public administration whereas manufacturing, construction, commerce and other services remained stable or had slight increases in employment (NPA, 1983a:17.8). According to Seaga's own target, 30 000 new jobs are needed annually, just to reduce unemployment marginally (*G*, 12 May 1982). Given his commitment to the IMF to reduce the workforce in the public sector, the private sector would need to create an even higher number of jobs than that. Clearly, the response of the private sector up to 1984 did not leave much room for optimism that this target would ever be approximated.

Admitting the obvious, Seaga in November 1982 explained that the government would step in to help to solve the unemployment problem in so far as it could not be solved by economic development alone. For this purpose, he launched the Human Employment and Resources Training (HEART) Trust, which was to provide young people with relevant job-training. An employment program for the young would be particularly important, because unemployment among the 14–29 age group was the highest to begin with and increased above average from 1981 to 1982. However, HEART will be unlikely to make more than a marginal impact on youth unemployment, because it is a training program only, and presupposes that the private sector will create jobs to absorb the newly-trained workers. The Seaga government's inability to avert a rise in unemployment and to deliver on its election campaign promises of 'jingling in the pockets' of the masses, was bound to erode its political support base.

Political dynamics
Whereas it was not surprising that the JLP government's popular support

declined, given the economic difficulties it encountered, it was surprising how fast it declined. In May 1981 the JLP held a 48 to 20 per cent lead over the PNP in the opinion polls; by November this lead had declined to 41% to 34%, where it remained until May 1982. Then, in October 1982, the PNP pulled ahead of the JLP with 43% to 38% and maintained that lead into 1983 (Table A.15).

The primary explanation for the rapid loss of popular support lies not simply with the economic developments, but rather the interaction of the economic developments with the political appeal of the JLP in the 1980 elections and the increased political consciousness and mobilization of the Jamaican people which had occurred during the PNP years. As we saw in Chapter 6, in the 1980 campaign, the JLP appealed heavily to people's immediate economic interest promising rapid economic recovery, 'deliverance' from mismanagement and 'jingling' in people's pockets, proclaiming that 'the poor can't take no more'.

From the outset, the JLP was viewed as a government which favored the 'big man' and the PNP as the party more interested in the concerns of the poor. Stone's July 1981 poll showed 54 per cent of the people saying that the PNP was 'most interested in interests of the poor' compared with 36 per cent for the JLP (*G*, 30 August 1981). In his poll in May 1982, 71 per cent of the people responded that 'the businessmen' had obtained 'benefits since the JLP has been in power' far more than mentioned 'consumers' (45 per cent), 'farmers' (25 per cent), 'higglers' (23 per cent), 'workers' (17 per cent) and 'unemployed (15 per cent) (*Star*, 9 June 1982). However, up to mid-1982 Stone's polls also consistently showed that the JLP was perceived as the party that could manage the economy best, that things would be worse under the PNP, and that things were better under the JLP than they had been under the PNP. As the economy stagnated, unemployment rose and inflation accelerated in 1982, however, the picture changed. By early 1983, polls showed that 44 per cent of the people believed things had become worse under the JLP, while 32 per cent thought they had become better (LARRC, 13 May 1983).

The JLP's difficulties were not limited to the economic problems, though these were by far the most important. Within the government, several factors were contributing to demoralization. Seaga's concentration of so much power in his own hands led other JLP leaders to feel left out of the decision-making process. Corruption, involving the issuance of import licenses among other things, was widely believed to have reached the ministerial level.[12] Finally, the JLP let the party machinery built up in its drive for power atrophy while in office.

Not only did the government lose support among the population, it also lost among the group that was perceived to have benefitted most from its policies: business people. This process was already far advanced by the time we interviewed Jamaican elites in the Spring of 1982. The business people we interviewed contended that Seaga's projections for investment were unrealistic at the outset, and they privately, as well as the business associations publicly, expressed their dissatisfaction with the availability of foreign exchange and the operation of the parallel market. They complained that Seaga was not accessible to the business community; it was a lot easier to see Manley during his period in office than Seaga. Their severest criticism, at least that of the domestic manufacturers, was reserved for the structural adjustment policy:

> By and large, the policy is worthy of consideration, but it is being implemented too rapidly and it has been prepared entirely without consultation with the private sector . . . you can't do that [i.e., reorient the economy to export] if you don't supply foreign exchange to manufacturers for retooling to be competitive in export markets and there hasn't been any retooling here for years . . . It's hard to be competitive when you have to buy raw materials where you have lines of credit. For instance, I have to buy steel from the UK where a line of credit is available, but it's 20 per cent more expensive than the same thing from Japan.

This dissatisfaction with Seaga had not resulted in any significant shift to actual support of the PNP, at least by spring 1982, but, it had led to a certain restiveness which increasingly became public, on the pages and later even in the editorials of the *Gleaner*.

Battered from the 1980 campaign, the PNP was even further demoralized by its crushing defeat in the parish council elections of March 1981. In February, Manley had offered his resignation, but the NEC rejected his move by a vote of 109 to zero, with 3 abstentions, which firmly re-established Manley's leadership of the party. Manley's first decisive move was to denounce the covert alliance with the WPJ, contending that the party's association with the small communist party had contributed to the margin of the PNP's defeat in the 1980 election. At the same time, Manley reasserted that the general parameters of the development model that the PNP had pursued in the 1970s were correct and would not be changed under his leadership.

The election defeat and the party's failures in office regenerated the internal party debate with a focus on how to interpret these events. The lines of debate followed those described in Chapter 5, though now the right wing had, by and large, left the party and the left was stronger than in 1977. Aside from the general issues discussed in the earlier chapters, the debate centered on the causes of the election defeat. The moderates emphasized that the WPJ alliance, the left's rhetoric and the close relations with Cuba fed the JLP/*Gleaner* communist-smear campaign. The left played down these elements, emphasizing the defection of the security forces and destabilization from the domestic opposition and the USA. Both sides agreed that the economic situation was the main reason for the defeat and the IMF austerity policies had contributed heavily to it. The moderates added that left rhetoric and ambiguity about the permanence of the mixed economy had contributed to the economic difficulties by frightening the private sector. The debates, though still better, now contained an element of soul-searching and, in the absence of the need to make policy could be carried out at a more reasonable pace. Manley continued to attempt to hold the two wings together.

The first year of opposition was a quiet one for the PNP and the country. This was purposeful policy on the part of the PNP leadership, as it wanted to allow time for internal debate and to give the country a breather from the conflicts of the late 1970s. Indeed, Manley vowed to avoid the type of confrontationist and destabilizing style of politics in which the JLP had engaged during that period.

The theme of the party conference in fall 1981 which marked the beginning of the PNP's active opposition, was 'Rebuilding for the Future'. A number of aspects of the PNP's opposition period became clear at this conference. First, the education program would be pursued, as Manley, with the left behind him, fully supported it. The program, which was financed in part by the Friedrich Ebert Stiftung, aimed at providing a thorough education in party principles, ideology, development policy and political strategy to 1000 constituency level leaders who in turn were to be responsible for education of rank-and-file party members. The conference also passed a resolution requiring all PNP officers and candidates for office to attend a specified number of the political education sessions.

The political education programs did move forward the next two years with the establishment of party schools in Kingston and Montego Bay and the implementation of the program outlined at the 1981 party conference.[13] Manley took a very active interest in the education program; he himself gave each political education lesson to the NEC before it went out to the constituencies, thus legitimating its content. The NWU agreed to participate in the political education program and to co-publish a monthly paper, the *Rising Sun*, with the party. In addition, the NWU started an internal educational program, assisted and funded in part by the Norwegian LO, which focused both on concrete trade union education (union structure, collective bargaining, etc.) and on the position of the worker in the wider society.

By the time of the 1983 party conference the emphasis in the PNP's political education program had shifted to the constituency and group levels. Every PNP group was required to institute education programs, and prospective candidates were required to attend 80 per cent of the meetings of the national level education program (PNP, 1983:102). However, one should be careful not to overestimate the progress of the movement's ideological strength. Resistance from some quarters of the party's moderate wing continued, as they still regarded the political education program as a tool of the left, but, instead of attempting to modify or change the content of the program, they chose to try to undermine it by not participating and by telling their constituency leaders to do likewise. Moreover, and very importantly, the education program made little headway in the Parliamentary Group (PNP, 1983:104–5). It was clear that these people still did not realize that the PNP's failures in the 1970s were, in part, connected to the lack of ideological and programmatic understanding of many people in the party, not least among them many of the MPs. The critical factor for future progress wil be how strictly the political education requirements for candidates are enforced.

Second, Manley set the tone for the policy of an eventual new PNP government at the 1981 conference, declaring at the same time that the direction of the 1970s democratic socialist path was a correct one but that this time economic not social policy would take the first place. This was, in part, a tacit admission of some of the mistakes of the previous government, but it was also a recognition that under the changed conditions, among other things the tremendous debt incurred by Seaga, there would be little room for social policy innovation. Manley repeatedly declared in his public speeches over the next two years that the PNP would not try to fool people that things would be easy; sacrifices would be necessary, and those who were not willing to work hard and sacrifice for Jamaica's development should not support the PNP. This emphasis on economic strategy and the need for sacrifice was reflected in the party's social and economic commission's documents in these years. Given the disastrous experience under Seaga, the potential for a favorable popular response to this change in appeal was greater than ever before.

The PNP also repeatedly stated its intention to develop a coherent economic plan for its next term in office, to be presented to the electorate before the next general elections. In point of fact, although the Economic Commission continued to exist, there was little work done on the plan until 1983. The PNP's capture of the lead in the opinion polls in October 1982 caught the party by surprise and it was only then that the party realized not only that it might be back in power at the next elections but that, if a crisis intervened, those elections could take place as early as spring 1984, once the agreed electoral reforms were entrenched in the Constitution and the new enumeration of voters and issuance of photograph voter-IDs would be completed. The PNP conference in September 1983 reconstituted the Economic Commission and gave it the task of developing a comprehensive economic plan by the time the electoral reform process was completed.

The third aspect of the PNP's opposition period which became obvious at the 1981 conference was the dismal state of party finances. The problem faced by the PNP had obvious causes. Before 1972 it could rely on business financing along with help in kind from the NWU at election time. After its turn to the left, it was in office, so it could draw on state resources, particularly the time of party cadre employed by the state, but now, having failed to address the problem of party financing while in office (see pp. 304–5), it was in desperate straits. It only had the NWU support which was not very great in financial terms (PNP, 1983:30).

As it turned out, the victim of this situation was D. K. Duncan, who was forced out of his position as General Secretary in January 1983. Liberal capitalists made it clear that they would not renew their financial support for the PNP until Duncan went. For them it was not really a matter of the economic policy direction of the PNP.[14] Rather, he was a symbol of the radical left, which they saw as anti-democratic and essentially Leninist in orientation, harboring intentions of introducing Cuban-style communism in Jamaica. Unfortunately for the PNP, Duncan's exit hardly ended their financial problems. The report to the 1983 party conference emphasized the dismal state of party finances which, in turn, was hampering virtually every area of party work from political education to organizing to media exposure (PNP, 1983).

At the time of writing, it is unclear how much the PNP has shifted to the right. Manley's own speeches show no indication whatsoever of any such move. P. J. Patterson, the most prominent moderate leader, did return to active party politics in 1983, taking the post of party chairman.[15] On the other hand, Duncan's replacement was Paul Robertson, who was programmatically aligned with Manley in the party. Moreover, the report to the 1983 conference gave no indication whatsoever that the party as a whole was backing down on its commitment to movement building, both in terms of organization and political education, or to the democratic socialist model of development (PNP, 1983).

Seaga's snap election

By the early fall of 1983, it seemed that a PNP victory in the next election was in the cards. With the JLP trailing in the polls and the economy in bad shape and with little hope for rapid recovery, the PNP appeared to be headed toward a victory in 1985 if not sooner. Parish council elections were expected in 1984, as soon as the electoral reforms and an enumeration were complete, and this would present the opportunity to show the JLP's lack of popular support, perhaps a prelude to early elections. With Reagan in the White House, the debt-burden skyrocketing, and the economy in great difficulties, it was unclear how much the PNP would be able to do, but it seemed that they would get a chance to try.

But then the events in Grenada in October 1983 intervened to change the situation completely. After the coup and the murder of Maurice Bishop and his comrades, the JLP recognized an opportunity to recoup their losses of popular support by reviving the communist smear-tactics of the 1970s.[16]

The JLP immediately issued a statement saying that such events could happen in Jamaica, and proceeded to revive the propaganda it spread in its drive for power, such as the allegations about the State of Emergency, the stealing of the 1976 elections, PNP intentions to replace the army and police with a people's militia, Cuban subversion in Jamaica, etc.

The JLP government took an active part in the invasion of Grenada, which the PNP opposed. The Jamaican people were horrified at the killing of the Bishop group and thus Seaga's move did have popular support. The government used its access to Grenadian government documents captured in the invasion to show that the PNP had taken part in an allegedly secret and subversive meeting in Nicaragua with other Socialist International parties of the region. Seaga then kept the red scare going by expelling four Soviet diplomats and a Cuban journalist for allegedly plotting to kill a senior officer of the Protocol Division of the Ministry of Foreign Affairs (*JWG*, 7 and 14 November 1983).[17]

Events came to a head in late November. On 23 November Seaga announced that Jamaica had failed the September IMF performance test and had agreed to a 77 per cent devaluation in order to secure a new standby agreement. The PNP condemned the devaluation and demanded the resignation of the Finance Minister (Seaga) from his post on the grounds that he had mismanaged the country's affairs. Seaga used the call for his resignation as a pretext to call snap elections on 25 November, with Nomination Day scheduled for 29 November and elections for 15 December. The PNP then announced that they would boycott the elections on the grounds that the agreed electoral reforms had not been carried out and that holding elections using the 1980 voter lists would disenfranchise anyone who came of voting age since the last elections. No PNP candidate filed on Nomination Day. The JLP had won the election before a vote was cast.

Seaga was of course aware of what a devaluation of this magnitude would do to the government's popularity. It would make it impossible for them to win, or even come close, in an election, since the devaluation was bound to cut the real-income levels of the people by at least one-third, probably more. The events in Grenada were a godsend for Seaga and, in retrospect, it seems likely that all the JLP's subsequent actions in whipping up anti-communist sentiment and implicating the PNP were done with an eye on eventual elections. Only the inter-party agreement on electoral reform stood in the way, but Seaga apparently found it so easy to sweep this agreement aside, despite his own statements as to its necessity in the period 1976–80.[18]

There were two key reasons for the PNP to boycott the elections. First, it was the principled thing to do, as participation in the elections would have legitimized the abrogation of the inter-party agreement. Second, though the PNP would clearly have won more seats than they had in 1980, its chances to win a majority were hampered by a number of factors *directly related to the abrogation of the electoral reform agreement.* The development of the economic plan and candidate selection were timed according to the expectation that elections would not be held before electoral reform would be completed, and thus an election at this early point, particularly a snap election, found the party ill prepared. More important, polls showed that the PNP had a comfortable lead among 18–20-year-olds, precisely the group which would be disenfranchised by using the 1980 voter lists. In fact, a poll taken the night before and published five days after the election showed that the PNP would most probably have lost narrowly on the old voter lists but would have won on new lists (Table A.15).

In 1984, signs of strong support in the society for new elections after a speedy completion of the new voter-registration system mounted. The JCC officially urged the government to go ahead with this, and opinion polls showed that 70 per cent of the people wanted new elections (LARRC, 11 May 1984). Discontent over their rapidly-deteriorating buying–power grew strong among large sectors of the population. Tensions among JLP factions in the West Kingston ghetto, caused by disappointed patronage expectations, led to violent confrontations (Stone: *JWG*, 4 June 1984). Despite these signs of a mounting challenge to his government, however, Seaga in May 1984 indicated no willingness whatsoever to hold general elections before 1988.

Concluding remarks

Jamaica's experience during Seaga's first three-and-a-half years in office demonstrated clearly the pitfalls of the free-market/private-sector-oriented development model in the context of the world economy in the 1980s. The model failed not only in socio-economic terms (employment, support for the poorest sectors), but also in terms of its own narrow growth-criteria. The failure of foreign investment to come into Jamaica in any significant proportion, and the failure of foreign and domestic entrepreneurs to develop production of non-traditional exports is particularly impressive in the face of the enormous material and symbolic support from the Reagan administration and prominent capitalists in the USA. If the presumed model case Jamaica failed to produce even the minimum expected of the free market/private sector path, namely sustained growth and an alleviation of the balance-of-payments problem, does not this suggest considerable skepticism as to the ability of other countries in the region with a small, dependent capitalist economy to do better on this path?

8

Jamaica's Democratic Socialist Path: An Evaluation

Because of the seven consecutive years of economic decline, most observers, left and right, consider the PNP experiment with democratic socialism in Jamaica to have been a failure, and, indeed, we have argued that it was in the area of economic strategy that the Manley government made its most serious mistakes. However, this should not obscure the significant, and permanent, achievements of the PNP government, such as the bauxite policy, land reform, the State Trading Corporation, labor legislation and social inclusion policies. Moreover, since some of the PNP's failures were correctable and others were due to the very unfavorable conditions for pursuing a democratic socialist path faced by the PNP at the outset, the economic decline experienced by Jamaica in the 1970s does not demonstrate that the democratic socialist path is not a viable one. To evaluate that question, one needs to assess whether idiosyncratic and country-specific features of the Jamaican experience in the 1970s were primarily responsible for the decline or whether it was caused by the very characteristics of the path itself. We will address this question both in this chapter and, in a comparative perspective, in the final chapter.

In the process of evaluating the successes and failures of the Manley government, we will identify four chronically difficult problems encountered in such attempts at gradual socialist transformation in politically relatively open societies, of which the first two problems concern the relationship of the socialist movement to the capitalist class and other privileged groups:

(1) The model requires the successful operation of a mixed economy. What is the role of private capital in the economy and what are the capitalists expected to contribute in the way of investment and so on? Is it reasonable to think that they will do this?

(2) What are the roles of the capitalist class (or segments thereof) and the middle strata in the class alliance underpinning the movement? Are they in it, outside it but somehow neutral, or are they the enemy? If they are in it or neutral, can this be reconciled with the

need for political mobilization of the lower classes required by the political strategy?

(3) The third problem area lies in the difficulties of a young political movement in finding the proper balance between the need for political education and the danger of alarming people with unnecessarily provocative ideological sloganeering. The Jamaican movement was doubly 'young' in that it not only confronted privileged groups as a government based on an ideological movement for the first time, but in that it was also in the initial stages of forming its ideological posture.

(4) The fourth problem area has to do with geopolitics, in Jamaica's case with the proximity to the USA. Do the degree of foreign economic penetration and the security concerns of the USA make a democratic socialist model impossible?

The goals and policies of the PNP's democratic socialism

Reducing dependence

The PNP government's efforts to reduce Jamaica's economic dependence on and vulnerability to external forces met with mixed success. The most successful of these efforts were the ones designed to reduce the control exercised by foreign capital, in the form of direct investment, over the domestic economy. Further success was achieved in reducing two aspects of trade dependence, partner concentration and food imports. Other aspects of trade dependence, however, such as the overall importance of the external sector, product concentration in exports, and the debt burden remained the same or became even stronger.

The takeover of the utilities, urban transport, RJR, three banks, the sugar estates and sugar factories, half the hotel capacity, the bauxite lands and 51 per cent of the bauxite mining operations, all of which had been under foreign ownership, significantly reduced the extent of direct control exercised by foreign capital in the Jamaican economy. With the exception of the banks and the bauxite operations, these takeovers constituted a burden rather than an asset for the government in financial terms. The utilities needed major investments to upgrade their capacities to provide service to larger sectors of the population, and they required substantial subsidies for their operations because the government kept prices for basic services to consumers low. The sugar estates and many sugar factories had been heavily decapitalized before being sold to the government. The hotels were not economically sound either; they came under government ownership because of defaults on loans guaranteed by the previous JLP government. By putting a financial burden on the government, then, these takeovers added to the inducements for foreign borrowing which resulted from the distributionist pressures and thus, paradoxically, they aggravated

Jamaica's foreign dependence in financial terms, while at the same time constituting a potential asset for national development by eliminating foreign control over crucial sectors.

The advantages were that the utilities could be upgraded according to the criterion of need for the service, and the leakage of foreign-exchange earnings from the sugar and the tourist industry could be reduced. The takeover of RJR from its British owners and the sale of shares to various organizations eliminated foreign control over one important instrument of opinion formation and turned it over to a plurality of groups independent of the government as well as of any other special interest.

The banks and the bauxite operations were economically sound, and thus promising assets in financial terms in the medium and long run after amortization of the purchase price, as well as in control terms. Control over a larger share of bank credit gave the government the opportunity to channel it to areas important for national development, such as agriculture and small business, which would enjoy low priority for lending on purely profit considerations. Acquisition of the bauxite lands gave the government control over reserves and thus the opportunity to search for new investors and partners for forward integration of the industry. Acquisition of 51 per cent of the existing bauxite operations increased the government's insight into the companies' operations in the country.

Other aspects of the bauxite policy also worked to reduce Jamaica's dependence on the TNCs. The establishment of the Jamaica Bauxite Institute significantly strengthened national technical, managerial and research capacity. The 'apprenticeship' period for national directors, managers and technicians under the management contract with the TNCs has worked in the same direction, and the formation of the International Bauxite Association has led to information-sharing among the producer-nations, thus strengthening their bargaining positions *vis-à-vis* the TNCs and their capacity to develop an alternative network of production and marketing outside the TNC network.[1]

The PNP government's strong efforts to diversify its foreign trade partners for bauxite/alumina and other exports, as well as for imports, were successful in reducing Jamaica's dependence on the North American and British markets. Whereas the USA, the UK and Canada accounted for 71.2 per cent of Jamaican exports and 63.6 per cent of imports in 1972, their share had declined to 60.3 per cent of exports and 44.1 per cent of imports by 1980 (Tables A.13 and A.14). In terms of a reduction of dependence on the developed capitalist countries, the increase in the combined share of Caricom, the Latin American Common Market, Japan and other countries outside North America, the ECM, and EFTA, from 10 per cent of total trade in 1972 to 40 per cent in 1980 shows considerable progress indeed. In contrast to the successful reduction of partner concentration, the government's efforts to promote non-traditional exports in order to reduce product concentration did not achieve the desired results. Bauxite and alumina, sugar and bananas accounted for 79 per cent of the total value of exports in 1972 and for 82.5 per cent in 1980 (Table A.12). Ironically, this increased dependence was in part a direct result of the success of the government's bauxite policy.

If financial transactions are taken into account, Jamaica's situation of dependence on the international capitalist system has clearly increased. The ratio between the combined value of imports and exports of goods and services (including financial services) and the GDP increased from 72 per cent in 1970 to 107 per cent in 1980 (IDB, 1982a:24). The total external public debt outstanding increased from US$370m in 1972 to US$1697m in 1980; and debt service as percentage of exports of goods and services increased from 4.7 per cent in 1972 to 16.5 per cent in 1979 and 13.1 per cent in 1980 (IDB, 1982a:393). Furthermore, the structure of the debt shifted as loans from foreign commercial banks became more prevalent than loans from bilateral and multilateral institutions. The greater proportion of loans contracted on commercial rather than concessionary terms brought not only higher interest rates but also shorter maturities, implying greater difficulty in meeting debt-service obligations without substantial refinancing and new loans. The percentage of the total outstanding debt having maturity periods of 0–5 years increased from 40 per cent in 1970 to 51 per cent in 1980, whereas the percentage with maturities of more than ten years declined from 33 to 29 per cent in the same period.[2]

This greater indebtedness and more intense debt-service pressure are clearly the most serious obstacles to the pursuit of policies designed to reduce dependence. Bankers have been unwilling to renegotiate the debt or extend new loans without the IMF's seal of approval, and the IMF's policy prescriptions obstruct efforts to increase self-reliance by imposing policies of deregulation and insisting on concessions to attract foreign investment. The pursuit of an alternative path to the IMF, in turn, becomes more difficult, the more acute the foreign exchange shortage is. Severe disruptions in production and the resulting shortages and lay-offs are certain to produce strong political reaction against an alternative path. The fear of such political reaction was decisive in the rejection of the People's Production Plan in 1977, and the experience with the alternative path in 1980 confirmed the extreme difficulty in maintaining minimally adequate supplies of imports for domestic production and consumption, even if one makes allowances for the extra problem presented by the short prospective life-span of the government. The only way through which severe disruptions could be avoided is renegotiation of the debt and a change in IMF policies towards structural adjustment programs allowing for and even promoting the development of greater self-reliance. Certainly, a country like Jamaica cannot bring about such change alone. Rather, only collective action among developing countries and some sympathetic allies among the Western European countries could wring concessions from the IMF and bring bankers to renegotiate. For this purpose, as well as for the development of a new international network of production and trade, not under the control of the developed capitalist countries, the pursuit of greater South–South cooperation is crucial.

A (if not *the*) key role in reducing dependence certainly has to be played by agriculture, both in reducing dependence on food imports and, in the case of export agriculture, reducing dependence on loans as a source of foreign exchange. Greater self-sufficiency in food production can cushion consumers of basic foodstuffs against the impact of foreign-exchange shortages. The PNP government had some important successes in this area. Domestic food production increased, as shown in Table A.18 and the proportion of food declined from 14 per cent of total non-fuel imports in 1973 to 10 per cent in 1980.[3] Though the increase in domestic food production did constitute a success, the overall results of the government's considerable efforts in the promotion of agriculture fell short of expectations. During the PNP's two terms in office, a variety of policies and programs were pursued, some of which were more successful than others. Restrictions on agricultural imports effectively raised demand for local crops, and the development and marketing of new products, such as a type of bread made out of cassava, were designed to further increase this demand. Among the various agricultural programs, Land Lease was the most successful; various credit schemes, such as Crop Lien and support programs for medium farmers were partly successful. Food Farms and the sugar cooperatives, in contrast, were beset by so many problems that they have to be considered failures.[4]

The most important barriers to success of any agricultural policy or program were the steep slopes, the lack of adequate water supplies and the inaccessibility of much of the land owned by small farmers or the government. In order to increase productivity significantly on these lands, heavy infrastructure outlays for terracing, irrigation and roads were required (IICA, 1981), or productivity could be increased by implementing a land reform designed to bring better (that is, flat, accessible, with adequate water supplies) but idle land forming part of large estates into production. Some of the land owned by large farmers was acquired or leased by the government under the provisions for idle land. However, acquisition again was costly, and pressure on unwilling landowners to sell or lease to the government had unfavorable political repercussions, thus making a large-scale land reform very difficult. Under some pressure many landowners did agree to sell or lease but the provisions for compulsory acquisition or lease were virtually never invoked.

Other problems which hampered agricultural production regardless of the government's programs were the shortage of farm inputs caused by the foreign exchange crisis, the problem of praedial larceny, and the secular decline of the Jamaican sugar and banana industries. Praedial larceny has been and still is a problem plaguing farmers of all sizes. The important role of higglers in the food distribution system provides ample opportunity for stolen farm products to be sold and thus for agrarian larceny to be a worthwhile undertaking. Various farm security programs have been under study by different governments, but none of them have had any significant impact on the problem.

The obvious reason for the secular decline of the sugar and banana industries is their non-competitiveness with other producers. For bananas, the underlying problem is quality. A large proportion of bananas are produced by small farmers, and the transport over the bumpy roads tends to bruise the bananas which renders them unacceptable for the – mainly British – customers. Also, small farmers have problems in correctly applying pesticides and fertilizers. However, large plantations have quality problems as well, because of difficulties in spraying in windswept areas, for instance, and unreliable water supplies. Furthermore, the plantations in the north-eastern part of the island are exposed to very strong winds and vulnerable to hurricanes.

The problems in the sugar industry have their roots in the period of rapid growth of output and of high profits between the 1940s and the 1960s.[5] The foreign companies, prominent among them Tate and Lyle (UK) and United Fruit (USA), derived their profits primarily from processing, shipping and refining sugar, not from the cultivation of sugar cane. Thus, they increased cane production on their estates by including marginal sugar lands rather than by increasing efficiency. Cane yields per acre increased only marginally between 1940 and 1960, and cane quality actually deteriorated between 1950 and 1960. At the same time, production costs increased rapidly in the cane fields as well as in the sugar factories. By the early 1960s, the sugar factories had become technologically outdated and inefficient. The state of the industry deteriorated even further during the 1960s, as the companies decreased replanting in the fields and neglected maintenance and replacement of equipment in factories. One of the reasons why the foreign companies did not invest sufficiently to keep the productivity of cane-fields and factories in an internationally competitive position was that they did not need to do so for the sake of their profits. Commonwealth sugar arrangements protected them from outside competition and thus allowed for inefficient but profitable production. From the mid-1960s on, the Jamaican sugar industry was clearly on the decline, and the major estates lost money every year. This decline continued throughout the 1970s, despite the government's efforts to arrest it.

In addition to the problems with the availability of land and farm inputs, and the secular decline of the banana and sugar industries, the government's efforts to increase agricultural production through various programs were beset by problems in the implementation of these programs. For instance, insufficient screening of candidates for participation in programs, interference of politicians in the selection of participants, inadequate supervision of the use of credits, inadequate provision of advice on different crops and technology, and little or no action against non-performers, all hampered the production drive and made it expensive for the government. The key underlying reasons for these problems were the limited managerial capacity of the state (which we shall discuss later) and the clientelistic nature of Jamaican politics.

The Ministry of Agriculture was a particularly traditional and inefficient branch of a generally inadequate state bureaucracy. Its structure was over-centralized, its personnel policies dominated by favoritism and much of its personnel characterized by a lack of commitment to agricultural improvement programs and their peasant clientele. A reorganization of the ministry in 1977, on the basis of recommendations from the UNDP,[6] decentralized its operations by creating three regions under the control of regional directors to which a fourth region was added in 1978. The parishes within each region were further subdivided into a total of 65 divisions and 401 extension areas. Under this organization, new extension officers were to be placed to achieve a ratio of one officer to each 500 farmers. However, finding sufficient suitably qualified personnel was a problem (NPA, 1978:115).[7]

The clientelistic character of Jamaican politics and the importance of agricultural programs as a patronage base because of their wide numerical reach meant that MPs and local politicians frequently put pressure on the officials in charge of these programs to have their supporters included, even if they did not meet eligibility criteria, or, where programs could not accommodate enough people, for instance because of a shortage of available land, pressures sometimes caused them to be expanded to include marginal lands. Both these situations, of course, had a negative impact on productivity in the government-sponsored agricultural programs.

Finally, the agricultural marketing network was inadequate to deal with the increase in production. Higglers accounted for the marketing of 70–80 per cent of the domestic food crops, but they clearly could not provide outlets at guaranteed prices for sudden or massive increases in certain crops. In order to provide such an outlet and to ensure adequate supplies of basic foods at controlled prices for poor areas, the government expanded the functions of the Agricultural Marketing Corporation (AMC). However, the AMC was also beset by a multitude of problems, such as the lack of adequate information and planning of transport and storage facilities, over-centralization and overstaffing. Furthermore, beneficiaries of agricultural programs who were supposed to sell their crops to the AMC at fixed prices and thus repay their loans found it frequently more attractive to sell to higglers, hide their income and delay repayment on loans.

These various problems affected all the government's programs to some degree, but in some cases – for example, Land Lease – they only made the program less cost-efficient, whereas in other cases – for example, Food Farms – they destroyed the program. By the end of 1980, Project Land Lease had placed 37 661 farmers on 74 568 acres of land. Thus, 26 per cent of the 144 605 farms (and presumably farmers) listed in the 1968 agricultural census as having less than five acres benefitted, and the total acreage covered by these small farms was increased by 32 per cent. By far the largest proportion of beneficiaries (71 per cent) had received land under the provisions of Phase I, and only 3 per cent had been settled under the provisions of Phase III, mainly because Phase III was by far the most expensive because it included provision of a house.[8] The success of the program was twofold; on the one hand, it contributed to the increase in domestic food production, and on the other it improved the living standards of the beneficiaries both in kind and in cash. The problem with the program was that it was relatively expensive; the accumulated cost by 1980 was $39.1m, of which $13.7m were recoverable loans. These loans were extended for soil improvements and agricultural inputs. The farmers were supposed to sell their products to the AMC at fixed prices and then repay the loans out of their earnings. However, by the end of 1980, only $2.8m had been recovered. Thus, the average cost per beneficiary to the government amounted to roughly $960. Given the budgetary austerity imposed by the IMF, it is not surprising that very little progress was made in the program between March 1978 and December 1980. In this period, only 3459 farmers were given land under Phases I and II, and not a single one under Phase III. One specific problem which hampered productivity of land leased under Phase I provisions, which accounted for 64 per cent of the total acreage leased, was fragmentation; farmers frequently leased land at a considerable distance from their own, which involved additional costs in time for commuting and in transport.

The Crop Lien program was initiated under the Emergency Production Plan in 1977, designed to provide credit to small farmers quickly and on terms easier than commercial terms, to encourage the production of selected crops. Land Lease as well as the Crop Lien program were important because they were both aimed at small farmers who produce almost entirely for the domestic market and who are the primary domestic supplier for that market. In the first year of the program, $20.7m were to be made available for special credit to Land Lease participants and other small farmers (NPA, 1978:115); by January 1978, $7.9m in loans had been disbursed, and by December 1980, a total of $37.5m had been approved and $24.8m disbursed. The loans carried an interest of 6 per cent and their duration was for the life of the crop, which amounted to a significant negative real interest rate under the prevailing high inflation. Nevertheless, the repayment record was poor; a total of $3.2m, or 13 per cent of the disbursed amount, had been collected by December 1980 (Ministry of

Agriculture, 1981). Crop failure resulting from inexperience with the designated crops as well as adverse weather conditions contributed to this low collection rate, as did poor investigation of loan applications and the general deterioration of living standards in the country which caused many small farmers to cover the basic needs of their families before repaying the loans.

Loan-repayment problems were not confined to programs for small farmers. They also affected support programs for medium farmers financed by the Agricultural Credit Board and by the Agricultural Development Program of the Jamaica Development Bank. Farmers who owned between five and twenty-five acres were provided with loans and technical services, and farmers with up to 100 acres could obtain assistance for constructing or upgrading buildings and irrigation facilities and for land preparation. Besides such general support programs, there were industry-specific ones, such as the replanting and increased production loans granted by the government and administered by the Banana Board, which did not fare much better in terms of collection of repayments (for example, see *DN*, 27 February 1977). However, whereas the various farm-support programs were a financial burden on the government and were clearly in great need of more efficient implementation, they did contribute to the increase in production of domestic food crops and thus to the decrease in dependence on food imports.

The least successful of the agricultural programs was Project Food Farms. Its purpose was twofold, that is, the farms were supposed to train farmers to become efficient cooperative farmers and to contribute to domestic food production. They started out as state farms on which people were to be trained in farming techniques. Eventually, the best participants were to be selected and permanently settled on this land, and the farms were to be transformed into cooperatives. The farms were supposed to become self-supporting through the sale of their products, but this never happened. By January 1976, accumulated expenditures for the ten Food Farms amounted to $3.9m, of which only $0.4m had been recovered (Ministry of Agriculture, 1976). During 1976, the program was discontinued and the land was allocated under project Land Lease. The key reason for the failure of project Food Farms was patronage. Local MPs put pressure on the farm managers to admit their supporters to the program, even if these supporters had no interest in farming whatsoever and even if the farms had sufficient personnel already. As a result, the farms became a source of relief employment rather than centers for training and efficient production. Furthermore, the farms suffered from considerable predial larceny. The idea behind the Food Farms cannot be faulted; the lack of understanding of the importance of the concept and of its successful implementation for the PNP's development path among PNP MPs themselves obstructed its realization.

A similar concept, but on a smaller scale and with concentration on rural unemployed youth, formed the basis for the Pioneer Farms program which was initiated in 1978. Young people were employed on farms on land owned by the government. These farms were under the supervision of farm managers, assigned by the Ministry of Agriculture, and they were organized as pre-cooperatives. In the first year, nine Pioneer Farms were set up with a total of 193 members, and by December 1980 eleven farms were in existence but total membership had decreased to 120 farmers. The acreage planted went up from 370 acres by the end of 1978 to 706 acres two years later (NPA, 1979:7.4; Ministry of Agriculture, 1981). The accumulated costs over the three years of the program were $2m, of which $1.2m was recoverable; but again, only $0.08m had been repaid. In its first two years, the program suffered to a certain extent from political pressure like Food Farms, and in 1980 political violence added to their problems. The farms were correctly perceived as PNP creations and their members were easily identified as PNP supporters, thus making them easy targets of anti-PNP violence. Despite these problems, however, production on the farms increased from 193 276 lbs in 1978 to 545 713 lbs in 1980 (NPA, 1979:7.4; NPA, 1981:6.3).[9]

A further program designed to deal with the problems of rural youth unemployment and agricultural production was the special youth employment program in soil conservation. Young people were employed in projects such as terracing and irrigation on government land. Whereas this program was reasonably successful in providing some relief employment and rendering some land potentially more productive, it suffered somewhat from the problem of deficient work efforts typical of all relief employment programs in Jamaica.

The problems encountered in the agricultural sector should not be allowed to obscure the fact that this sector did comparatively well during the PNP's tenure in office (Table A.10). Two of the three bad years for agricultural production were caused by bad weather – in 1979 the floods in western Jamaica and in 1980 Hurricane Allen. Moreover, as Davies (1984) points out, domestic agriculture was performing much better than export agriculture. For instance, in 1977 and 1978, domestic production grew at an annual average rate of 15 per cent compared with 6 per cent for the whole sector. Indeed, during the whole period sugar experienced a secular decline. Given this, there is a strong argument that the more marginal lands on the sugar estates should have been transferred to domestic agriculture.

A further effort to promote self-reliance and provide employment was the establishment of Community Enterprise Organizations (CEOs). The CEOs had been conceptualized as part of the People's Production Plan in 1977 (see Chapter 5) as socially-owned, worker self-managed enterprises. They were to be linked to agricultural activities through their use of locally produced raw materials in manufacturing, construction, and marketing activities. Thus, they were to provide employment in rural as well as depressed urban areas. The initiative for such projects was to come from community organizations which were then to be assisted with financing and advice, originally by an inter-ministerial committee, later by the Ministry of Parliamentary and Regional Affairs, and still later by the Ministry of Youth and Community Development. However, the development of the CEOs lagged far behind expectations. During 1977 and 1978, while the administrative support machinery was being put into place, few CEOs were set up. From the beginning of 1979 to December 1980, eighty-six CEOs were financed, with a total expenditure of $6.6m (NPA, 1981:9.4). Fifty were in agriculture; the rest in small manufacturing (mainly furniture), food processing and handicrafts.

The problems which hampered the development of the CEOs were the lack of an appropriate legal status and of financial and administrative support, and the scarcity of organizationally skilled local leadership. The creation of an appropriate legal framework for the CEOs was originally linked to the process of constitutional reform. One of the aims of the constitutional reform was decentralization, involving a strengthening of local government and of direct citizen involvement. For this purpose, Community Councils had been created, and these councils were to be given legal status and to become the legal carriers of the CEOs. As the constitutional reform effort got bogged down, the creation of Community Councils was promoted by simple legislation, yet the Act giving legal status to the councils did not get to the stage of a first reading in parliament until October 1980, a few short weeks before the election (*DN*, 7 October 1980).

In the interim, CEOs could be set up under a provisional legal status, but the lack of adequate financial arrangements constituted another obstacle. Scarcity of funds under the budgetary austerity, combined with problems of evaluation of CEO proposals meant that existing lending institutions were not likely sources of financing. Thus, a new public sector institution, the Community Economic Organization Project Development Company, was created, which finally came into operation on 1 April 1979. It was in charge of providing technical assistance as well as financing for the development, implementation and operation of CEO projects.

The slow development of this new company itself and thus of the CEOs can in part be attributed to problems of higher-level administrative responsibility. Shifts from an inter-ministerial committee to one ministry and then to another created problems in terms of delays and in terms of continuity of support personnel. Davies (1984) indicates that there was also a lack of real belief in the project on the part of the central authorities. The availability of support personnel to provide assistance in managerial and technical aspects was crucial for the development of CEOs because of a scarcity of local leadership with the necessary experience to initiate, organize and manage entrepreneurial projects. Like so many other programs, some of the CEOs suffered from the fact that some members viewed the operation as part of the usual state bureaucracy and thus saw profitability as of negligible importance (Davies, 1984).

Finally, many CEOs were hampered by political violence which increased dramatically in 1980, during or soon after the establishment of most of the CEOs. Like the Pioneer Farms, CEOs were perceived as PNP creations and became targets for attacks, such as vandalism. Certainly, most people employed in CEOs were either PNP supporters or at least non-partisan, as the concept of the CEO had a clearly socialist character, and the degree of political polarization prevented JLP supporters from becoming associated with such a concept. On the whole, then, the concept of the CEOs was imaginative and an essential ingredient in a self-reliant, democratic socialist development path, but the implementation of the program suffered from financial and administrative weaknesses of the state, as well as from the economic disruptions and political repercussions in the society.

In his review of internal obstacles and policy mistakes of the PNP government in its efforts at creating a more self-reliant economy, Davies (1984) argues that the government missed an opportunity to promote self-reliance and production by failing to promote the small-business sector. Drawing on detailed information from a study which included a survey of small businesses (that is, with fewer than twenty-five workers) conducted by him and several associates in 1979, he points out that this sector accounted for 80 000 jobs including 30 000 in manufacturing which amounted to 40 per cent of all employment in manufacturing. Moreover, the sector, in sharp contrast to large manufacturers (see Chapter 5), is not very dependent on imported raw materials. Only 22 per cent of the small businessmen mentioned raw material supplies (domestic or imported) as a problem and only 8 per cent as their most important problem, which is impressive given the severe shortages of imported raw materials experienced by the economy as a whole at that time. Inadequate demand and finance were much more important. Davies argues that state aid in financial record-keeping (as inadequate record-keeping is a barrier to acquiring loans) and in consumer identification could increase the output of the small-business sector. With regard to demand it could also be observed that the IMF-imposed austerity in this period quite certainly had adverse affects on this sector.

This brings us back to the question of alternatives to IMF stabilization policies. We have shown that the government on the one hand managed to reduce dependence in terms of control exercised by foreign capital over the domestic economy and in terms of partner concentration and food imports, but that on the other hand it let dependence on foreign loans increase and with it the control of foreign lenders over the domestic economy via the IMF. The factors impinging on the 1977 IMF decision as well as the problems experienced in attempting to do without IMF loans in 1980 demonstrate just how difficult it is for a country which is *already* deeply in debt *and* still very economically dependent on the developed capitalist countries (especially the USA) to develop rapidly new sources of loans and trade outside Western commercial banks, multilateral lending institutions and corporations. Indeed, for a country very deeply in debt it may be almost impossible, on its own, to find financial assistance outside the IMF–Western commercial banking system at anywhere near the level available within the system.

This is a very strong argument for extreme caution in contracting large amounts of loans, particularly from commercial banks, in the first place. At the same time, developing more economic insulation through diversification of trade and cultivation of alternative foreign exchange sources, such as loans from oil-exporting countries, lines of credit from the Eastern bloc, and assistance from social-democratic-governed Western European countries may allow a country to forego IMF 'assistance' when faced with a debt problem of moderate proportions. Another important factor in this regard is internal. As we argued in Chapter 5, it was political factors that made the non-IMF option exceedingly risky in 1977. The strength of the political movement, and thus, the internal balance of class power, is a strong factor conditioning a country's ability to alter external economic relations rapidly.

Establishing and operating the mixed economy
In addition to the nationalization of foreign holdings discussed in the last section, the flour mill, the cement company and a textile mill were taken over by the PNP government. Also, another public bank was established, RJR transferred from foreign to 'popular' ownership,[10] cooperatives introduced on the sugar estates, CEOs established primarily in agriculture and agro-industry, and a substantial portion of imports transferred to the State Trading Corporation (STC). State and cooperative ownership increased from 2 per cent of the total to 20 per cent.

It is true that, in the case of state sector expansion, much of this would have been done by any government in power at the time. As Phillips (1982) points out, expansion of the state sector in the 1970s is a Caribbean-wide phenomenon occurring in a variety of countries with different ideological orientations. In Jamaica, the JLP government of the 1960s had already begun the process by buying into the utilities and acquiring some sugar lands. Acquisition of the hotels and sugar estates was forced on the government, and it seems likely that the utilities would also have been forced on the government eventually. Only in the cases of the flour mill and the cement company, which were Jamaican-owned and profitable, did the government encounter opposition to its bid for ownership, and, of course, the establishment of the STC caused a big furore from the private sector, *Gleaner* and the JLP.

Regardless of what a JLP government in the same period might have done (and it most certainly would have done less), the expansion of the state sector was a necessary feature of the democratic socialist developmental model. The question is whether the transformation of ownership relations was successful both in terms of its extent and the efficiency of operation of the new state sector enterprises. The question of the proper extent of state sector expansion is a complex one, since it involves two separate questions which can work in opposite directions. The first is whether the size of the state sector was sufficiently large for the government to be able to plan and direct development. The second is whether the state could effectively manage the enterprises it had acquired.

The first question could again be subdivided into (1) whether the threshold for effective state-sector-led development had been reached and (2) whether further expansion might have made the process more effective. We would give an affirmative answer to both questions. Given the level of public ownership achieved by the middle of the second term, the government did have sole ownership, joint venture shares, or a substantial portion of capacity in all sectors making up the commanding heights of the economy. On the other hand, the benefits derived from the STC could only have been increased by its expansion and it seems probable that investment planning could have been made more effective by greater ownership and control in the financial sector,[11] but by and large we would argue that the government's mistake was not in the area of insufficient nationalization, but rather in not expanding the state sector through new investment in existing enterprises and new ventures.

Whereas from the point of view of the ability of the state to plan and direct the economy one can generally say the more state ownership the better, efficient state management of public-sector enterprises may act to limit the desirable level of state expansion, particularly when the former middle- and upper-level management personnel are unwilling to continue to work for the enterprise in question once it is transferred to the state sector. This, along with any financial outlays involved, would be the key considerations in the case of further bank nationalizations. As for the nationalizations which the Manley government did carry out, we get a mixed picture of the effectiveness of management.

The most negative result in this regard was the transformation of the nationalized sugar estates into cooperatives. This experiment was important both because of its ambitiousness, as the estates accounted for one-third of the country's second largest export and because the failure of the cooperatives became a symbol of the government's 'mismanagement' and its utopian and unpractical schemes to its opponents. We have dealt with the problems of the sugar cooperatives extensively elsewhere (E. Stephens, 1984; also see Feuer (1984) and Schecher 1981a, 1981b); suffice it to highlight the most important here.

The cooperatives were very hastily established as the government was under pressure from activist sugar workers and the left Catholic Social Action Centre (SAC) to move in this area. Moreover, there was deficient follow-up in correcting the initial problems experienced. There was no education program to teach the workers about cooperative management, and no system of effective cost-accounting. The problems which had made the estates inefficient in the first place: under-capitalization, over-staffing and cultivation of marginal lands, were never rectified. Moreover, the cooperatives were structured in such a way that there was no connection whatsoever between wages, on the one hand, and workers' efforts and cooperative productivity on the other. As a consequence of all these problems, the cooperatives were plagued by constant cost-overruns and accumulated a large debt over the years.

The reasons why none of these problems were adequately addressed are complex. The lack of sufficient follow-up was partly because of the failure of the top political directorate (including Manley, who was the main promoter of the process at the top) to exercise adequate supervision of the project. At the middle level, the cooperatives suffered from (i) bureaucratic hostility as the main officials in the relevant bureaucracies (the Sugar Industry Authority, Frome Monymusk Land Company, the Ministry of Agriculture) had no faith in the cooperative concept; (ii) overlapping bureaucratic responsibility for the cooperatives; and (iii) the transfer of responsibility for the cooperatives from one ministry to another. Finally, the cooperatives suffered from political competition as the government pushed the SAC, which did have an effective education and cost-accounting program, off the cooperatives partly out of fear of autonomous mobilization of the sugar workers by the independent left SAC.

Despite the problems, a government committee (the Lindsay Committee) appointed to suggest corrective action produced a report in October 1979 which would have gone a long way toward making the cooperatives viable enterprises. Its proposals included bringing the SAC activists back to introduce and supervise the educational program and a management and budget-control program, and cutting overstaffing through attrition and the offer of severance pay. However, because of IMF-imposed financial constraints and time constraints from the coming election, the committee report was never fully implemented (E. Stephens, 1984). Seaga did not follow-up on this effort, but rather terminated the cooperatives in 1981.

Not surprisingly, in the case of other 'forced' nationalizations – and here we include the utilities as well as the hotels – there were also serious difficulties. In the state sector in general, but particularly in these forced nationalizations, one is faced with a difficulty in evaluating the performance of the enterprises because profitability is not the only criterion to be taken into consideration. As Brown and McBain (1983) document in their survey of public-sector enterprises in Jamaica, these enterprises had such goals as maintenance or creation of employment (as in the case of the hotels), price subsidization, delivering essential services at affordable prices (the utilities), etc. Thus, one cannot look at the bottom line in the ledger to evaluate their efficiency.

In the case of the hotels, the government simply did not have the capacity to run the hotels itself. Recognizing this, the government began a policy of leasing the hotels, selling management contracts while retaining ownership of the hotels, a policy which was continued by the JLP government.

The effectiveness of management in the utilities varied. The telephone company appears to have been effectively run. The service by the JPS definitely deteriorated after improving immediately after the take-over, but this was primarily because of the shortage of foreign exchange.[12] The JOS definitely deteriorated under government management but this was primarily because the theft of parts crippled the bus fleet. The government was considered fair game for theft; and it was much too lax about this.

In the case of other public-sector enterprises, the picture is somewhat better but still mixed. In an interview, one leading public-sector manager contended that, generally, the newly-developed state enterprises and statutory bodies fared better than those which were simply nationalized previously (usually inefficient) private ones, citing the STC, JBI and its subsidiary Jamaica Bauxite Mining as examples of efficient operations. On the other hand, the banking sector does not fit the pattern: the Workers' Bank consistently suffered major losses, while the National Commercial Bank was a successful business despite the fact that the year before nationalization (as Barclays) it had lost money. (*G*, 2 March 1977).

So, how do we make sense of this admittedly complicated picture? There is no doubt that there were managerial problems in public-sector enterprises, some of which were correctable and deserve attention in the future, as Brown and McBain (1983) argue, but it is unlikely that many of these would have fared better in the private sector, and thus the government's take-overs were appropriate even on efficiency grounds. The fact that Seaga announced his willingness to divest these enterprises and got very few takers (except in the case of the hotel management contracts) strongly supports this contention. Thus, with the reservations expressed above we would term the PNP's state-sector expansion policy moderately successful. Moreover, as in the case of the sugar cooperatives, the proper course of action would have been to attempt to correct the managerial difficulties, not to reverse the policy, in this case, divest the properties.

The attempted economic transformation was not limited to the expansion of the state and cooperative sectors. There was also an effort to transform relationships in the private sector. The government attempted to strengthen labor's position through labor legislation and its schemes of workers' participation. Though the extensive labor legislation fell short of what the unions wanted, the labor legislation clearly strengthened the hand of organized labor and individual workers against employers. Replacing the century-old (and appropriately named) Master and Servants Law, the Labor Relations and Industrial Disputes Act provided for compulsory recognition of the union (or unions) democratically elected by the workers, for recourse to a tribunal in the case of dismissal, for the right to compensation and reinstatement in the case of wrongful dismissal, and for arbitration on the demand of either party to an industrial dispute. Another law passed by the PNP provided for severance pay giving workers in bankrupt enterprises priority treatment among creditors.

The workers' participation plans, on the other hand, never went very far. Given the fanfare with which the plans were announced, their crucial importance for the process of structural transformation, and Manley's own strong commitment to the project, it is worth examining why.[13] Essentially, the whole project fell victim to the combination of lack of strong support from the labor movement, opposition from the private sector, and the economic crisis.

Given the non-ideological character and the authoritarian structure of the labor movement, it is not surprising that the unions were less than enthusiastic about the project. All but one of the unions paid lip-service to the goal of workers' participation. Unofficially, however, they were concerned about a possible erosion of their power. The private sector, of course, was virtually unanimously opposed to the introduction of workers' participation, particularly to any legislation on the issue. Reactions ranged from mild and pragmatically argued to quite rabid and intransigent opposition.

Despite this strong entrepreneurial opposition against anything more than management-controlled consultation schemes, and the lukewarm reaction of the unions, Manley pushed the project announcing in his budget speech in May 1977 outlines for the establishment of workers' participation schemes involving joint consultation on economic and technical matters and possibly co-determination on personnel affairs, as well as worker representation on the board of directors (*G*, 25 May 1977). However, in the following years, the impetus behind the project largely dissipated. In February 1978, eight of fifteen field-organizers trained to promote the organization of participation schemes within enterprises were laid off, and in June 1978 new guidelines concerning participation in the public sector were issued, along with the universal restriction that only experimental schemes were to be set up, and on a purely voluntary basis. The lay-off of the field organizers was a result of strong union objections to the personalities and political inclinations of the particular people chosen and trained. The scaledown of the project as a whole was largely a result of the economic crisis. The aftermath of the failure of the IMF test of December 1977 absorbed the energies of the top-level political directorate, which means that the only force which could have overcome union opposition as well as bureaucratic inertia in the Worker Participation Unit of the Ministry of Labor was otherwise occupied. Even if there had been more support for it, the second IMF agreement, with its premium on the cultivation of private-sector confidence, would have made a compulsory introduction of workers' participation against the strong employer opposition altogether impossible.

For future progress on the path towards social transformation, a reactivation of the workers' participation project is clearly crucial. The first task for the PNP will be to swing the unions behind the project. An education program directed at union leaders, emphasizing how unions in other countries have been able to strengthen their position along with the position of workers as a whole by becoming actively involved in participation schemes, will be a necessary first step.

The private sector, needless to say, did not produce as the PNP hoped it would. We have extensively discussed the reasons for this in the preceding chapters and will return to this topic in the context of our subsequent discussion of the class alliance. Suffice it to emphasize here that the PNP could have handled the relationship to the capitalist class better and thus could have obtained better performance from the private sector to produce the levels of economic growth it hoped to achieve.

This leads us directly to the key mistake that the PNP government made in the area of economic management: its failure to increase the level of state sector investment to make up for the fall of private sector investment. As we argued in Chapter 4 and again in our discussion of the People's Production Plan, the critical turning-point for the PNP was fall of 1974, after the imposition of the bauxite levy, when it had the resources to do this (see Chapters 4 and 5). Instead, the budget increase of over $100m went primarily to consumption. At the same time, import restrictions were relaxed, wasting valuable foreign exchange on non-essential consumer imports. In this same period, the government shifted to a much greater reliance on foreign commercial loans at high market interest rates to finance the government budget (see Table A.2). Again, this proved to be a mistake.

Davies (1984) points out that the key problem with the foreign borrowing was not so much the level of borrowing but rather the type of project that was supported with these funds. While they were targeted for the capital budget, most of the loans went to projects such as schools, housing, and health centers that were only indirectly productive and only very remotely, if at all, connected to a saving or earning of foreign exchange that would equal the outlay. He suggests, correctly we believe, that foreign funding be contracted primarily for directly productive projects which are net foreign-exchange earners either through import substitution or export, and secondarily for physical or social infrastructure directly required by such projects.

Obviously what we are arguing for, in a sense, would be a more 'conservative' approach in this period. Though expanding state-sector investment, increasing taxes, and restricting middle-class consumer imports can hardly be termed conservative, that label could be applied to the greater restraint in redistributive spending, lower levels of foreign borrowing, and smaller budget deficits that this formula implies. While stepping up land reform and the development of CEOs would have been redistributive as well as productive, and the suggested tax program and import restrictions also could have had a redistributive impact, it seems likely that this formula would not have had as great an effect on income distribution, at least in the short run, as the one pursued by the government. At any rate, the urban unemployed would have been worse off and this would have had social costs for the society and political costs for the PNP, but this economic formula just might have put the country on a viable economic development path and would have had a very good chance of allowing the government to avoid the agony of the IMF.

In addition, there were problems with the management of some state-sector enterprises, as was just mentioned, and serious problems with the implementation of a number of the programs introduced. In some cases, such as the National Youth Service, which should have been recognized at the outset as being prohibitively costly, this was a matter of poor planning and faulty conceptualization of the program.[14] These programs should have never been started. In other cases, such as Food Farms, the program was properly conceived but implementation was abysmal for the reasons cited already (and again later) in this chapter. In these cases, corrective action should have been taken, or where that was not possible, they should have been terminated.[15] These steps would have saved the government money and/or resulted in greater production, both of which would have had a favorable macro-economic impact.

It should not be surprising that, in the 1982 elite study, we found that there was remarkable agreement in the whole elite that the central failure of the PNP government was its failure properly to manage the economy (see Table 8.1). The criticism fell into four areas: (1) mismanagement, overspending; (2) rhetoric, policies, and/or Cuba relationship leading to loss of confidence of business and skilled personnel and thus flight and economic deterioration; (3) poor implementation of programs, and (4) lack of a coherent economic plan. 92 per cent of businesspeople, 86 per cent of JLP politicians, 63 per cent of PNP politicians and 72 per cent of other elites listed at least one of the four of these as one of the main failures of the PNP government. As one can see, there were differences in the

TABLE 8.1 *Elite perceptions of failures of the PNP government (% of respondents)*

	PNP	JLP	Capitalists	Other	All
Economy: mismanagement, overspending, no growth, foreign exchange shortage	0	43	46	22	28
Economy: destroying confidence of capital and skilled personnel	25	57	54	28	39
Poor implementation of programs	13	29	31	56	37
Lack of an economic plan	38	0	0	6	9
Too close to Cuba and domestic communists	0	0	23	22	15
Anti-Americanism	0	0	23	6	9
Lack of appropriate policies to deal with opposition, sabotage, security forces, constitutional limitations, media	50	0	0	11	13
Lack of strategy to maintain support among key interest groups (labor and professionals)	25	0	0	11	9
Indecisiveness; disunity; lack of leadership	0	0	15	17	11
Self-criticism: lack of ideological preparation and confidence in capacity for transformation	50	0	0	0	9
Pace of change too rapid	13	0	0	17	9
Divided country; too much conflict	0	43	15	0	11
Abuse of party and state machinery for repression of opposition	0	0	8	11	7

TABLE 8.1   *continued*

	PNP	JLP	Capitalists	Other	All
Corruption	0	0	15	0	4
Anti-elitism; anti-successful people	0	14	8	0	4
Encouragement of indiscipline; resulting in lack of personal security	0	14	15	6	9
Other	0	0	8	33	15
Total number of respondents	8	7	13	18	46

categories emphasized by the various groups: Business and JLP elites emphasized the first two, PNP elites the fourth and other elites the third.

That the political mobilization process frightened the capitalist class is to be expected and counted as a cost of the whole transformation process. The negative effects of political mobilization should have been partially offset by efforts at national mobilization for production and nation-building. A Ministry of National Mobilization and Human Resource Development was created in the second term. The ministry almost totally atrophied after Duncan's resignation, but even under his leadership it did not perform its task. In Duncan's defense, he did not head the ministry very long. Moreover, the first few months were taken up with developing the economic plan (in which the ministry did perform an important function) and after that, at least from his point of view, he was mobilizing people for the 'IMF plan', something he was not very enthusiastic about for obvious reasons. Nevertheless, there were serious deficiencies in the operation of the ministry that make it unlikely that it would have been able to perform its function without major reorganization.[16]

It should be made clear at the outset that national mobilization in the context of a highly competitive two-party system is a very difficult task. From the very beginning of the Manley government almost every attempt it made to mobilize people to make its development program work or simply to get people to identify with collectively building the country was obstructed by the JLP, who saw all these efforts in party partisan terms. So, when Manley in 1972 called on the nation to put in a day of voluntary work on some community project on Labor Day, the JLP and BITU announced that they would continue to celebrate the day in the traditional fashion. In April 1977, when all other social forces, including PNP opponents like the

Gleaner and the private sector organizations, were lining up behind the government's production efforts, Seaga issued a blistering critique of the production plan. Numerous other examples could be cited.

In this context, it is probably safe to say that Duncan, who remained as PNP General Secretary, was a bad choice for Mobilization Minister, despite his considerable talents as a political organizer. Not only was he strongly identified with the party apparatus, which made him suspect from the point of view of the JLP and its supporters and allies, but he was also strongly identified with one wing of the party, which made his actions controversial within the PNP. This situation was aggravated by the cross-cutting nature of the ministry. As Jones (1981a: 20–1) points out 'one of the ministry's major functions was to coordinate and monitor aspects of the fieldwork of other ministries', a function usually carried out by Finance or the Prime Minister in the Westminster model, and thus 'the role of the New Ministry overtly contradicted administrative tradition of autonomous departmentalism'. This led to the conflicts between Duncan and other Ministers which are described in Chapter 5.

In fact, the whole ministry was staffed by party cadre and these were drawn mainly from the left, who were the only ones interested in the Ministry and its task in the first place. The production side of the task was not emphasized and thus the cadre were primarily involved in conscious-ness raising, which, without the productive effort, left what was perceived as rhetoric by the public, and which, taken alone, tended to alienate people, Moreover, some of Duncan's lieutenants and the field cadre took the attitude that 'if you are not for socialism you are against it' which further alienated people. The situation was aggregated by the cultural style of many of the field cadre. As one PNP advisor who was sympathetic to the left related:

the symbols of mobilization, the tam and the unprofessional presenta-tion and unkempt appearance, became associated with socialism espe-cially in the rural areas . . . thus, socialism became associated with anarchy and disorder. The discipline necessary in a genuine mobilization process was not there.

In addition, the structure of the ministry made its smooth operation yet more difficult since there were no intermediaries between the center and the field cadre. This made it very difficult to monitor the cadre's work and, at the same time, made it possible for the cadre to give the center feedback which the cadre felt they wanted to hear but which did not really reflect the situation in the field. Thus, no corrective action was taken when it was actually necessary.

The standard leftist remedy to counter anticipated adverse reactions to efforts at social transformation is to stop or control capital flight. The assumption is that by eliminating or reducing possibilities for capital export, the government can stop disinvestment and possibly even induce domestic capitalists to invest some of their money given that this is their only alternative. The experience of the Manley government argues that controlling capital flight in any significant way is very difficult if not impossible to do, at least in an economy as open as the Jamaican economy. Some of the currency controls and restrictions on foreign exchange for travel may have had a positive effect, but the more dramatic moves, such as the legislation on declaration and possible repatriation of foreign assets were almost certainly counterproductive because they frightened people and thus stimulated further capital flight. In Jamaica, almost all large businesses are involved in foreign trade, at least in a small way, either in exporting products or importing inputs. This gives them an easy opportunity to export capital which is almost impossible to stop: by over-invoicing imports and under-invoicing exports in agreement with their foreign customers or suppliers.

Increasing social equality

The PNP government attempted to increase social equality through many domestic programs, most of which were initiated in its first three years in office (see Chapter 3). These programs were aimed at economic redistribution, cultural inclusion, increased political participation, and equal opportunity, or some combination of these. The employment programs; the housing program, which resulted in the construction of 40 000 new units; rent control; basic needs subsidies; the minimum wage; health care; property taxation; and land reform all contributed to economic redistribution. It is certain that together these programs effected significant redistribution, but just how significant it was, and whether it was significant enough to offset the effects of the rising unemployment caused by the faltering economy, is unclear, given the lack of adequate statistics on the matter.[17] However, it seems certain that the redistribution between 1972 and April 1976, when unemployment began to rise after declining in the early years of the government (see Table A.11), was very significant, and it is very likely that the poorer segments of the population were better-off in both relative and absolute terms up to the time of the second IMF agreement. Moreover, the dramatic decline of the infant mortality rate from 30.9 per 1000 live births in 1972 to 12.4 in 1979 indicates that an improvement at least of health conditions took place throughout the period (NPA, 1981:17.2).[18]

In the case of social and cultural inclusion, on the other hand, there is no doubt that the country went through a very significant and permanent change. It is not possible for the most part to put one's finger on a specific policy here, but rather the whole thrust of the government to include the mass of people in the life of the society, the political mobilization process, and the PNP's openness to and encouragement of the African cultural heritage contributed to the change. One of the few specific policies one can point to was the Status of Children Act, which abolished bastardy. In doing so, the government made the norm of race–class subcultures which form the great majority of the Jamaican society, the legal norm in society. The inclusion of domestic servants in the minimum wage law, quite apart from its effect on their financial situation, made these people, in an often socially degrading occupation, feel more like full members of society. The education and literacy programs, in a quite different way, aided the process by giving many people (over 200 000 in the case of the literacy program) the skill to participate in society. But these policies were just smaller pieces to the general process set off by the direction the government was moving in. As one PNP leader said:

I think our biggest success was the extent to which, as a government and as a party, we were able to raise the level of consciousness of the people. People were saying for the first time 'is black man time now'. For example, domestic servants, for the first time, felt entitled to walk through the front door.

This cultural and social inclusion process was closely linked to the political inclusion process and the increased political participation which occurred during the Manley years. This manifested itself in the rising levels of electoral participation (see Table A.1) and in the massive attendances at political gatherings held by the PNP throughout the period and by the JLP in the last two years. For instance, 40 000 people came to the public session of the PNP's 1976 conference and 120 000 to the election campaign rallies in Montego Bay in 1976 and 1980. (For comparative purposes, the latter figure is equivalent to 3.4 million in the UK or 12 million in the USA.)

However, the process resulted in more than sheer mobilization of vast numbers of people. The people's level of political awareness was raised and the average Jamaican felt like a full citizen in the country for the first time. As one can see from Table 8.2, when questioned about the successes of the Manley government, this was by far the most frequent answer. People became aware of the political issues of the day. For instance, Stone (1982:72) found that, in an opinion poll, 72 per cent of the respondents were aware of what the IMF was. Moreover, the people became aware of the potential power they had. As to the successes of the PNP government, a JLP leader said:

The Manley regime advanced and developed the political consciousness of the Jamaican people in a very fundamental way. People became aware of their political potential and of the use to which political organization and influence could be put.

In short, the Manley government changed the balance of class power in Jamaica. Two factors contributed to this raised political consciousness and increased political awareness of the people: (1) the general progressive thrust of the government, especially the social and cultural inclusionary aspects and distributive policies; and (2) the efforts at organization building and political mobilization, detailed in previous chapters, carried out first by the PNP and then, as a response, by the JLP.

The processes of cultural, social and political inclusion and of increased

TABLE 8.2   *Elite perceptions of successes of PNP government (% of respondents)*

	PNP	JLP	Capitalists	Other	All
Raising the political consciousness of the people	63	57	23	61	50
Introduction of ideology; party organization and mobilization	13	0	8	17	11
Awareness of needs of the poor	0	0	8	11	7
Redistribution of power in society; broader participation at all levels	13	0	8	17	11
Labor legislation	25	0	0	11	9
Minimum wage	13	0	8	22	13
Social legislation: Status of Children Act	38	14	0	17	15
Equal status of women; equal pay	25	29	15	0	13
Social programs: education, housing	38	14	0	6	11
Promotion of agriculture, land reform, sugar cooperatives	63	0	0	6	13
Expansion of state's role in economy	13	0	8	6	7
Bauxite policy	38	0	31	11	20
Foreign policy of non-alignment; Third World leadership role	50	0	0	11	13
Other	25	0	15	17	15
None	0	29	31	11	17
Total Number of respondents	8	7	13	18	46

political mobilization and consciousness were not without costs. As was pointed out in earlier discussions of the reactions of the capitalist class, businessmen and other elites resented and were frightened by the developments. Much of the reaction to these phenomena was inevitable and had to be counted as part of the change process.

The education and literacy policies were also aimed at expanding and equalizing access to more privileged positions in society, as were the cultural inclusion policies. The government furthermore made a number of specific appointments to various statutory boards and governmental agencies which expanded the representation of black people in these organizations.

The educational policies, primarily free secondary and tertiary education, are difficult to evaluate in the absence of hard data on the number and class composition of students graduating, the average level of competence of graduates, and the jobs in which they ended up. However, based on research on the effects of educational expansion on mobility and growth (Collins, 1971; Walters, 1981) it seems likely that the reforms may have had some effect, and that it is a good guess that it was limited. Expansion of secondary and tertiary education does not appear to increase social mobility, particularly if it is unaccompanied by expanding job opportunity due to economic expansion. Moreover, expansion of education at this level, as opposed to the primary level, does not appear to contribute strongly to national economic development. Finally, there were not enough funds allocated to these reforms to provide high-quality education to all those who were now able to attend. Given all this, it might have been a better use of the funds available to devote them to upgrading primary education.

The PNP also instituted a number of reforms which promoted equality between the sexes. Prominent among these were the minimum wage, which helped women most because they were in the lowest paying jobs, equal pay for equal work, and maternity leave with pay.

In enumerating the achievements of the PNP government in increasing social equality through these various programs, we do not want to give the impression that all these programs were effective or, even if effective, should necessarily have been instituted. Like some of the other policies which we have examined, a number of these programs were poorly implemented. Given the space constraints here it is impossible (and unnecessary) for us to evaluate each individual program thoroughly. Suffice it to remind the reader here of our contention that state-sector investment should have been expanded and that this would have necessitated a corresponding restraint on the expansion of some of these social programs. Obviously, those which performed poorly should have been the first victims. The importance of financial constraints also argues that legislative changes that could be achieved without financial outlay, as in the cases of the labor relations legislation and the Status of Children Act, might have been further explored.

Deepening political democracy

There can be no doubt that the PNP not only adhered to the rules of the democratic game,[19] but that it also deepened political democracy in the narrow sense of making the electoral process fairer and in the wider sense of bringing more people into active participation in the process. The latter was discussed in the previous section on the processes of political inclusion and popular mobilization. As to the former, the PNP made some moves in the first term such as extending the vote to 18-year-olds, updating the electoral lists to include many people unfairly excluded from voting in the 1972 election, and re-drawing electoral districts so the outcome in seat distribution would more closely reflect the outcome of the popular vote. Though they were never given legal status as originally intended, the community councils, of which over 400 were established, did provide a non-partisan forum for grass-roots political participation. After years of discussion, the government appointed an Ombudsman, whose duty it was to receive, evaluate, and propose redress to citizens' complaints about actions of the governmental bureaucracy. Most important, the PNP in cooperation with the JLP enacted the electoral reform which made the 1980 election the fairest in Jamaican history.

Forging an independent foreign policy

The PNP's foreign policy of non-alignment, promotion of the NIEO and Third World economic cooperation, support for national liberation movements and political independence, and broadening of foreign economic and political ties has to be viewed against the background of its economic strategy, particularly the goal of reducing economic dependence. The foreign-policy achievements of the PNP government were impressive: under Manley's leadership backed by Foreign Ministers Patterson and Thompson and an able corps of diplomats such as UN representative Donald Mills, this small country moved from virtual isolation, obscurity and total subservience to the West to a position of leadership of the Third World, particularly on the issues of the NIEO and anti-apartheid. Manley became the leading spokesman for the NIEO and Vice President of, and the leading Third World advocate in, the Socialist International; Patterson was elected head of the ACP group of countries in the negotiations for the Lome Convention; Thompson spearheaded the drive for the passage of the Law of the Seabed; and Jamaica was elected to the Security Council of the UN.

Critics of Jamaican foreign policy have argued that there were costs to this policy and that Jamaica got nothing in return. JLP leaders argue that the pursuit of the NIEO was 'pie in the sky' and that antagonizing the USA damaged Jamaica economically. It is true that the short-term benefits from the pursuit of the NIEO and Third World economic cooperation were limited, but a movement must start somewhere, and if the Third World is to get anywhere economically, greater economic cooperation and greater solidarity in negotiatiohs with the developed world will be a necessary feature of that progress. Moreover, the Lome Convention did materially benefit the sugar industry. The country was rewarded for its efforts at Third World economic solidarity and the pursuit of the NIEO with the siting in Jamaica of the IBA headquarters and the Law of the Seabed Authority, which will bring not only diplomatic contacts and prestige to the country but also badly needed foreign exchange. Third World leadership brought the country loans from OPEC, Libya and Algeria and concessionary oil prices from Mexico and Venezuela. Manley's role in the Socialist International was responsible for the Norwegian and Dutch aid and trade packages. New ties with the socialist bloc brought a line of credit from Hungary and, more important, trade diversification (see above). Caricom, though not living up to expectations, did increase Caribbean trade. Finally, it seems reasonable to assume that Manley's international stature also increased Jamaica's bargaining powers *vis-à-vis* other Third World countries as well as core capitalist institutions.

The precise costs of the foreign-policy posture are much more difficult to calculate, particularly if one wants to specify the costs which were necessary features of the development path pursued by the PNP and those which were, so to speak, unnecessary elaborations. We will deal with this question extensively in the section on 'managing geopolitics' below. Suffice it to make several points here. First, the costs were primarily attributable to the political aspects of the policy, such as the extensive exchange programs with Cuba and verbal attacks on imperialism, and only secondarily to the economic aspects such as the bauxite levy or trade diversification. Second, we are prepared to argue that, with adjustments for the 'unnecessary elaborations', the policy promises to bring benefits that outweigh the costs in the long run, but that the political slant of the incumbent US administrations can substantially change the cost–benefit calculations in the short run.

Democratic socialist political strategy

Constructing a class alliance
The two key elements of the political strategy for placing the country on a democratic socialist development path were the construction of an alliance of social classes behind the program and the building of a political movement to create and sustain support for it. As we saw in earlier chapters, the nature of the class alliance, in particular the role of the capitalist class and the middle strata, was a point of contention in the PNP intra-party debates. We have presented extensive information on the reactions of the capitalist class to the PNP government and it is worth reviewing the results of our analysis briefly here, in order to evaluate what can be expected of the

capitalist class under the sort of development path pursued by the Manley government.

Our analysis of capitalist class reactions runs contrary to popular opinion in two ways. The first is the emphasis that we have put on the policies of the government in generating the reactions of the capitalist class. For the first wave (1973–4) the record is totally clear and cannot be read in any other way: the socialist (nationalizations), egalitarian and social inclusionary policies were the most important factors stimulating increased criticism and decreased investment and they were the second most important factor (to crime) stimulating migration.

Our contention that the government's policies continued to play a major role in the second wave (1975–6) will be more controversial, but the historical sequence of events makes it relatively clear that the government's ideological posture *per se* (that is, 'rhetoric', 'Cuba', etc.) did not become a major issue until early 1976. One flaw in previous discussions of private sector reactions is the one-sided focus on opposition to specific policies rather than the level of expenditure which the policies as a whole generated and how the government proposed to pay for these policies, particularly when the crunch came in the second half of 1975. Whereas strong opposition to specific policies was confined to the ultra-conservative segment of the capitalist class, opposition to the overall level of government expenditure, taxation and borrowing was widespread. Jamaican businessmen attributed the difficulties of the Jamaican economy, which became obvious to everyone in late 1975, to these government policies. Thus, we would argue that it is false to separate the issue of economic management from the government's policies. Many of the critiques of management were indirectly or even directly attacks on the Manley government's reform program. It was argued that the government needed to reduce the level of spending, borrowing and taxation so that the private sector would and could invest. The measures in the government's anti-inflation package in fall 1975 were entirely counter-productive from dominant business points of view. Indeed, the *Gleaner* and Seaga argued that the package had nothing to do with inflation and government was using the crisis as an excuse to introduce its socialist policies.

Nevertheless, it cannot be over-emphasized that the bottom line for the capitalists was the state of the economy. Had the Manley government followed a somewhat different set of policies with the *same* class-orientation but with a *better* economic outcome (which we argue would probably have been possible), the capitalist class would have grumbled about the policies but would not in its entirety have turned against the PNP government. The accommodation between the government (which at that time was at the peak of its political strength) and the capitalist class could have been maintained.

Though the deteriorating economy and the government's responsibility for it (in the eyes of the capitalist class) initiated the second phase of alienation of the capitalist class from the PNP government, there can be little doubt that social and political mobilization, the increase in rhetoric, the rise of the PNP left and the Cuba relationship *combined with* skillful exploitation of these issues by the *Gleaner* and the JLP generated a tremendous amount of fear in the Jamaican upper classes which cannot be accounted for by the policies alone. Indeed, it is worthwhile reflecting on why there was not at least some recovery in domestic investment once the IMF imposed its policy prescriptions – that is, austerity, real wage decreases and profit guarantees – on the government. In addition to the continuing foreign-exchange shortage, rhetoric from the left and psychological warfare from the right certainly go a long way to explaining why that never happened.

The second surprising result in our analysis is the decisive clarity with which the first term of office appears as crucial in the PNP–capitalist class relationship. The impressive electoral victory of December 1976 tends to obscure this. We argued in Chapter 5 that, given the balance of class power and the low level of ideological development of the PNP, it was politically very difficult for the PNP to deepen the reform process in 1977 by adopting the People's Production Plan and foregoing the IMF loan. If this is correct, then the book on the Manley government was basically closed by the time of the 1976 election, because by that time there were no progressive options open to the government, given its political resources.

What does our analysis of capitalist class reactions say about the role of the capitalist class in the class alliance and about the viability of the model of development pursued by the Manley government? Let us be clear at the outset that we must address here not only the basic policies necessary to the model (social programs, state-sector-led development, etc.) but also the political means necessary to carry out the policy. It is simply not possible to carry through such a reform process without building a political movement in organizational and ideological terms (that is, if such a movement does not already exist). Social and political mobilization and ideological definition and education are essential elements of the model. Thus, some of the so-called rhetoric of the PNP was essential to the process and not excessive verbiage. For example, one of our respondents, in answer to a question about rhetoric, said: 'I didn't know I was a capitalist until I was told (by the PNP) I was one'. Any kind of process of ideological definition would have to let this person in on this secret. On the other hand, there definitely were instances of excessive rhetoric (for examples, see Chapter 6).

The same sort of thing could be said about the relationship with Cuba. Third World solidarity and cooperation were necessary elements of the development model pursued by the Manley government. Thus, cordial relations with Cuba, defense of its territorial integrity and cooperation on issues such as anti-apartheid were necessary, but the extensive exchange relationships (the *Brigadista* program, etc.) and the effusive praise of Cuba were not. These things were not politically advisable, because of their potential for exploitation by the *Gleaner* and the JLP, a potential used to the hilt by them. Despite the fact that Cubans had only the best intentions in giving Jamaica the aid and that (ironically, given the counter-propaganda) the Cubans generally cautioned the PNP toward a moderate course when asked for their opinions, it is certain that the net effect of the close ties to Cuba was negative, because of their impact on the capitalist class (and thus investment) and the USA.

Given the fact that not only most of the policies of the government but also social and political mobilization and ideological definition were essential to its model, it is clear that the model, as pursued, was not a viable one because it depended on the private sector to produce more investment than it would even if adjustments in toning down rhetoric and in foreign relations were made. Again, as we have repeatedly emphasized, greater levels of state-sector investment were necessary.

As to the role of the capitalist class in the class alliance, we would contend that neither the radicals' not the moderates' position was entirely correct. The moderates, especially the right wing, were wrong in arguing for an inclusion of the capitalist class in the class alliance, because the PNP's policies were not in the interests of capitalists, particularly when we consider their broader interests as wealthy individuals concerned about taxes and upper-class family men concerned about their wives' security or their offspring's career chances and marital partners (and thus social mixing) in addition to their interests as capitalist *qua* capitalist. When one speaks of a class being part of a class alliance, one generally expects that most members of the class will actively support the program and not just tolerate it. It is probably fair to say that once the general contours of the Manley government's program became clear, most capitalists did not *support* it though they did *tolerate* it until late 1975.

On the other hand, the position of the PNP left cannot be accepted either because it did not sufficiently recognize that it was necessary to ensure toleration of the program by the capitalist class to make the mixed economy work. In correctly rejecting an *alliance* with the capitalist class which was impossible given the opposition of interests, the left did not realize the necessity of pursuing a *compromise* with the capitalist class.

A related error, in our view, in the analysis of the PNP left, as well as the extra party left, was its one-sided focus on the class forces within the party as a barrier to change. The capitalists within the party were seen as the main obstacle, and it was sometimes added that the petty bourgeois backgrounds of other party leaders predisposed them to 'reformism'.[20] Without denying that some PNP leaders with business backgrounds did have a conservative influence on the party, (see Chapter 5), there is little doubt in our minds that the main obstacle to further progress in the process of social transformation was the balance of class power in civil society not in the party itself. The 1977 People's Production Plan is a case in point. The implication of this is that deepening the process required extensive, painstaking work in building the movement. It was not just a matter of kicking the capitalists out of the party.

The centrists, on the other hand, generally recognized that the barriers were in society, though they would not use the language of class power as we have but rather the language of public opinion. That is, the people (or the workers, or the middle classes, or the unions, etc.) would not support such a policy, would not cooperate, were not ready to sacrifice, etc. The error of the centrists was that they reified the present state of 'public opinion' or the present level of social consciousness, which is determined by the underlying balance of class power, by the present state of development of the political movement. Thus, they downgraded the political education program, seeing it primarily as a vehicle for the left's power aspirations. Mobilization was reduced, in their minds, primarily to a method of influencing electoral outcomes.

To return to the question of the construction of an accommodation with the capitalist class, based on the literature on Latin America, we expected, given the structure of the Jamaican economy, to find two distinct segments of the Jamaican bourgeoisie, a *comprador* (or commercial) segment, and a national (basically manufacturing) segment. Moreover, it should be obvious that the policies of the Manley government were much more damaging to commercial interests than to manufacturing interests. Under these conditions, it would be natural to assume that the Manley government should have been able to construct a satisfactory compromise with the manufacturing bourgeoisie.

Unfortunately, the only segment of Jamaican capital with a distinctively more tolerant attitude toward the government was the JEA representing the exporters (which makes sense given the PNP government's incentives for exporters). The JMA was, if anything, more militantly anti-Manley than the C. of C. One might argue, with some justice, that this was because of the ultra-conservative politics of its president, Winston Mahfood, but the members of the JMA did constantly re-elect Mahfood, so there must have been some level of approval of his strident posture.

The reason for this, as we pointed out in Chapter 2, is that the Jamaican capitalist elite is heavily interlocked both in economic and kinship terms. The larger concerns often include holdings in commerce, manufacturing, tourism and sometimes agriculture, and even if their own concerns are not diversified, the heads of these concerns are virtually always closely related to people in the other sectors. This is not to say that there are no ideological differences within the Jamaican capitalist class. As shown in Chapters 2, 3, and 4, there were significant differences. However, these were not consistently related to structural fissures in capital, and thus may not be as stable as in other cases where the two are strongly related. In any case, the PNP would have to relate to the ideological (rather than structural) division within the capitalist class in constructing its compromise with capital.

Had the PNP government followed the policies with regard to state-sector investment, rhetoric and foreign policy suggested here, it could have strengthened its relationship with the liberal bourgeoisie, who favored state-sector-led development anyway. (In our interviews one of them criticized the PNP for not having a greater focus on state-sector investment.) Also there is a good possibility that it could have come to an understanding with the 'patriotic bourgeoisie' (see Chapter 4) to insure its continued investment and to minimize the disinvestment of all but the ultra-conservative segments of the rest of the capitalist class. The latter, which we estimate as comprising 25–33 per cent of the whole class, was irredeemable; it was bound to migrate and/or disinvest, and the government would have had to make up for the fall-off. To this group we also have to add those who migrated because of the violence, particularly the Chinese medium and small businessmen. The level of state-sector investment necessary would have had to be at least as large as these segments' previous share in order to have improved the economic situation in 1975. Let us remind the reader once more of how critical the economic situation that year, and the PNP government's response to it, were in initiating the decisive turn of the capitalist class against the government.

Second only to the capitalist class in controlling economic resources crucial to any path of development is the professional and managerial class. It must be admitted that the material interests of this class were adversely affected by the Manley government's policies, even if one ignores the negative effects of the economic decline. The taxes, the luxury import restrictions, minimum wage for domestics, and so on were not in this class' interest. Though a significant minority of this class is black, the social inclusionary policies represented a threat to hereditary privilege, and the mobilization process threatened them almost as much as it did capital. Thus, the professional and managerial class as a whole cannot be counted as part of the class alliance. However, given their skills, the democratic socialist movement needs to come to some sort of compromise with them in order, at the very least, to induce them to stay in the country and contribute to its development. From the timing of migration (see Chapter 5) as well as from Maingot's (1983:26) study of Jamaican migrants to the Miami area, it appears that these highly-skilled people left primarily because of the deterioration of the economy. Thus, economic performance would seem to be the key to keeping this class in place.

In the case of one segment of this class, state-sector managers and technocrats one can go further. Given their leading role in planning and executing the development process, they experience an increase in power, and presumably prestige, under democratic socialist development as compared with private-capital-led development. Moreover, in the Jamaican case, the traditional nationalist ideology of this class segment gives the party an ideological entry-point into the group with appeals to economic nationalism and self-reliance. This, combined with a set of policies to recruit, train and develop state managers and technocrats as suggested by Davies (1984) forms the basis for inclusion of the class segment in the class alliance.

With regard to material interests, the salaried middle class and the petty bourgeoisie are in an ambiguous situation. As was pointed out earlier, the petty bourgeoisie benefits from the emphasis on self-reliance since these small concerns are much less dependent on imported goods than larger concerns, but they are adversely affected by price controls and, in the case of medium-sized enterprises, labor legislation. The salariat is positively affected by labor legislation, employment policies and price controls, but negatively by income taxes. Many members of both groups are home-owners and thus negatively affected by property taxes. On the balance though, the material interests of both these two middle strata predispose them toward support of democratic socialism, and thus they should be targeted as potential members of the class alliance. In the case of small business, the type of support policies advocated by Davies (1984) might further cement them into the alliance, and indeed, the PNP, though losing ground between 1972 and 1976, still retained the support of a substantial majority of these classes in the 1976 election (see Table A.21).

The whole situation was greatly complicated for the PNP government by the cultural permeability affecting not only the capitalist class but particularly also the professional and managerial and the middle classes. The Dutch and Spanish countries in the Caribbean (with the possible exception of Puerto Rico) do not suffer from the same degree of US cultural penetration. The cultural permeability made exit an easier option especially for professionals. It made it much more difficult than elsewhere in the Caribbean and Latin America to find a receptive audience for criticism of the USA in the domestic population. The universal adoption of American consumer tastes made import restrictions more unpopular and promotion of domestic agriculture (and manufacture) more difficult. In short, US cultural penetration made the introduction of a development model which involved the weakening of ties to the USA in economic, political or cultural terms all the more difficult. This, in turn, made an accommodation with the capitalist and professional and managerial classes more difficult and at the same time more important.

The remaining classes – small farmers, farm labor, the lumpenproletariat and the urban working class – which make up some three-quarters of Jamaican society are clearly favored by the policies of democratic socialism and it is these classes that must form the core support base for the movement. Of course, even with regard to the interests of these groups, adequate economic performance is necessary or their material situation cannot be improved. Bernal (1982) has shown how the IMF imposed austerity policies shattered the class alliance constructed by the PNP in its first term, undermining the positions of virtually all classes in the alliance, but even a progressive economic plan cannot demand sacrifices without hope of an eventual economic turnaround. Thus, economic performance is a key element in constructing the class alliance of popular classes as well as striking a compromise with capital and the professional and administrative class.

Building the political movement
If the objective interests of the people, as structured by class relationships, were the only or even the main factor determining the outcome of political competition, democratic socialism would be an incomparably more successful movement than it is today. The class structure is only the terrain on which movements competing for ideological and social hegemony and political power fight out their battle. Though the terrain favors socialism, the capitalist forces have a natural advantage in owning the instruments of economic and ideological warfare and are favored by the deep trenches that the status quo makes on the outlook of all classes in society, particularly the middle classes. Building the organizational and ideological weapons to overcome this advantage is a long, painstaking, difficult process, a process which, though begun by the PNP in the late 1930s, was at a very low level of development when the party took office in 1972.

We have documented the successes of the PNP in the area of party-building and political mobilization earlier in this chapter and in previous chapters. Certainly, there were missed opportunities in this area, particularly during Duncan's absence in 1977–9, but only one is very glaring: the PNP never passed legislation regulating the financing of political activity. Legislation forbidding corporate and foreign funding of parties, other political organizations and political campaigns, limiting personal contributions and campaign expenditure, and providing for support of parties in relation to their electoral support from public coffers was (and is) essential to the long-run development of the PNP as a socialist party. This type of legislation is particularly important in the Jamaican situation because, given the competition of the unions for members, the unions have generally not been willing to contribute heavily financially to the parties, making their main contribution in manpower and material at election time. The effect of this absence of party-financing legislation can clearly be seen not only in the JLP's tremendous financial edge in the 1980 election campaign, but also in the PNP's totally desperate financial situation in 1981 and 1982. In the end, the refusal of liberal capitalists to contribute to the party as long as Duncan remained as General Secretary forced his resignation in early 1983.[21]

The PNP's progress in forming a coherent ideology and propagating it within the party and the larger society was substantial but still far short of what was (and will be) necessary. Given the internal party divisions and the economic crisis, it is easy to explain why the party did not make more progress, but with a little more understanding of the importance of ideology formation and ideological education from party moderates, the advances in this area could have been much more significant. As it was, it was not until 1978 that the party could agree on an ideological document, and as we saw in Chapter 6, the 1978–9 education effort did not make much headway.

The problem was (and is) that many moderates understandably see the party ideology and more so the political education program as opportunities for the left to engage in sloganeering and rhetorical excess. Unfortunately, as was pointed out in the previous chapter, instead of trying to influence the tone of the program, they have tried to kill it. The moderates failed to understand that ideology, as opposed to dogma or rhetoric, is an essential element of any attempt at social transformation. Using the definition of ideology given in the initial chapter of this book, in the PNP's case, an appropriate ideology would include an analysis of the nature of capitalist society in Jamaica, a coherent critique of the development model pursued in the 1950s and 1960s and an understanding of the PNP's alternative model of self-reliance and democratic socialism and of the political strategy and, when needed, the economic sacrifices necessary to implement the model.

The lack of ideological understanding at every level of the PNP was debilitating. Earlier in this chapter, we saw how the tradition of clientelism and the lack of understanding of the PNP's program on the part of PNP MPs undermined the Food Farms program. This is no isolated instance; a large number of programs suffered the same fate.

At the rank-and-file level in the party, there was relatively little understanding of what the democratic socialist path entailed. It was associated with the distributive programs of the government. This was also the view they propagated in society. One negative consequence of this was that it tended to legitimate and promote a get-something-for-nothing mentality which had detrimental effects on work motivation, which, for the structural and historical reasons outlined in Chapter 2 was already low among employees (though not among the self-employed). The PNP activists did not understand that sacrifice might be necessary at some point despite speeches by Manley and other PNP leaders emphasizing this. One PNP Minister, referring to what he would have the party do differently if he could go back in time, put it succinctly:

I would precede the programs of change with the development of dedicated political cadre who had an understanding of the programs and ideology and the sacrifices necessary. They [the PNP activists] were not prepared for struggle or adversity. They were lost once the material benefits from the programs, which sustained their enthusiasm stopped coming. This is how you can explain that there was a massive enthusiasm for the process in 1976 despite [the communist smear, destabilization, etc.] But when the strains and difficulties began in 1977 and 1978, they didn't know what to do, they were not prepared.

In addition, a better understanding of the ideology and the purpose of various programs among the cadre might have helped to moderate pressures for patronage benefits from programs whose primary intention was production not redistribution (Food Farms).

Manley himself was cognizant of the defects in, and the importance of, internal party ideological education, and the PNP has made an effort to rectify this deficiency in its first years in opposition. Though the political education program of 1978–80 got off to a slow start and then the effort was deflected into the election campaign, the materials produced for the program (for example, see PNP, 1980) did contain a comprehensive and popularly accessible explanation of the PNP's democratic socialist ideology (using the word in the sense defined in the paragraph above). This material was used in the PNP's election campaign in 1980 and further developed for the education campaign during its period in opposition.

One of the mixed successes in movement building was the YO. On the one hand, the PNP absolutely needed a youth organization to be able to reach out to the thousands of unemployed youths who were to benefit from various training and employment programs and to youths in general as they were to be the backbone of a new self-confident and self-reliant Jamaican people, and the YO was also a potentially great asset in running election campaigns. On the other hand, the YO's mobilization activities and ideological statements created considerable difficulties for the PNP. One of the key problems was that the parameters of their relationship and of ideological discourse were not yet defined, because of the low stage of ideological development of the party itself.

Another missed opportunity in the area of movement building was media policy. It is probably fair to say that the PNP had no plan for the media; their policy was primarily reactive. The development of the JBC as a whole and the newsroom in particular in the late 1970s, and the handling of the *Daily News* are indicative of this lack of coherent policy. However, the flaws in the PNP policy could most clearly be seen *after* they left office. With the demise of the *Daily News* and the return of the JBC to its late-1960s style after the replacement of the board and the firing of the newsroom, the PNP is now almost without access to the mass media. RJR is the only exception, thanks to the insightful policy of the government in this one case. Since any attempt to convert any of the existing major organs (*Gleaner, Daily News*, RJR, JBC) into a PNP organ would have been either politically impossible in the short run or easily reversible by a subsequent government in the long run, the best course of action would have been for the PNP to create what we would term a democratic (rather than socialist) media structure. The RJR solution was one way to do this. In the case of JBC, the institution of a board selected by popular organiz- ations, such as those eligible to buy shares in RJR, and access to a certain amount of air-time based on organizational membership, polls – or some other means of ascertaining popular support — would be another way of democratizing the structure of the media. In addition to the time allocated to the parties, the present system whereby the government through the API (or JIS) is allocated time for programs explaining its policies and promoting national mobilization might be retained. Either the RJR solution or this JBC fomula could have been applied to the *Daily News*. As for a PNP-controlled media organ, this could have been provided for either directly or indirectly through the party financing provisions discussed earlier.

Another area that needs further investigation is whether the perform- ance of the API, whose task it was to inform the people about the government's programs and mobilize support for them could not have been improved. We have no specific deficiencies or remedies to point to in this regard, but it is clear that many Jamaicans, who were or could have been, direct beneficiaries of the PNP's programs or, at any rate, would have supported them, were unaware of what the government was doing. As we mentioned in Chapter 4, this was the case with Project Land Lease, which is most probably one explanation why the PNP government never achieved an electoral majority, even in 1976, among small farmers despite the emphasis on domestic agriculture and land redistribution in its program.

What we have tried to outline is a media policy which would have been politically workable in Jamaica in the current era. A fully democratic media establishment, by which we mean an establishment which gives representation to views according to popular support and not economic (or political) power, would include democratization of the *Gleaner*, whose abuses of its near-monopoly position in the print media to defend the interests of privileged groups in society have been thoroughly documented in earlier chapters. Private ownership and control of such an important mass media organ by a tiny privileged economic group even more clearly violates principles of democratic opinion formation than does government ownership and control of such an institution because the government (in Jamaica) is, at least, democratically elected. (We hasten to add here that we are not suggesting government control of the press but rather demo- cratic control, as in the solutions mentioned above). However, the traditional conception of freedom of the press is so deeply entrenched in both the Jamaican upper and middle classes and in US political elites and foreign-policy-makers that the democratization of ownership and control of the *Gleaner* would be politically impossible, without any doubt.

In the struggle for ideological and social hegemony, the socialist movement's main instruments of warfare to conquer, bit by bit, a few yards of terrain across a broad front reaching all target classes, are the party and media. In advanced capitalist societies, one would add, no, one would begin with the trade union, an instrument which is the prerequisite for even beginning an offensive, and whose weakness would mean sure defeat in any serious battle. In dependent capitalist countries, the party takes this pre-eminent role, because unlike in advanced capitalist countries where the huge majority of the population has been converted to wage-earners and thus potential union members, the wage-earning classes (the urban working-class, agricultural labor, and the salariat) are a minority of the population in the class structure of these countries. Thus, the party rather than the unions must structure the class alliance. Nonetheless, the strength, unity and ideological posture of the union movement is extremely important to any social transformation attempt in a Third World country.

On numerous occasions, we have stressed the tremendous handicap which the divided and non-ideological union movement was for the socialist movement in Jamaica. Unfortunately, it cannot be said that matters improved much during the Manley government. The BITU gained substantial ground *vis-à-vis* the NWU especially in the last years of the PNP's period in office. As we pointed out earlier, the union affiliated with the party in power always tends to lose membership to the union affiliated to the opposition. This trend was much more exaggerated than usual in the latter half of the PNP's second term because of the austerity policies, particularly the wage restraint. The BITU gains were especially large among white-collar employees, who were organizing in large numbers for the first time. The combination of the economic situation and the swing of the social class as a whole to the JLP attracted this group of employees to the BITU. Fortunately for the PNP and NWU, the tendency for the union affiliated with the opposition to gain membership had already set in within a year of the JLP's 1980 election victory.

During the Manley government, the NWU's main contribution to the PNP continued to be manpower and in-kind resources for election campaigns. The union continued to neglect political education. Though some steps were made, promotion of leadership from the rank-and-file still was the exception rather than the rule. This also meant that the PNP leadership remained overwhelmingly from middle-strata origins, as the union was one of the few potential channels for developing working-class leadership. From the point of view of the class composition of a party leading a mass movement, the significant under-representation of cadre from the lower classes at all leadership levels of the PNP was a real weakness.

One small step toward trade-union unity was made with the establishment of the Joint Trade Union Research and Development Center which includes JALGO, TUC, as well as the NWU and BITU. The main barrier to greater unity is, of course, the political affiliation of the two large unions. The problem here is that the two goals, greater union unity and promotion of political education within the NWU, are partly contradictory. It might be possible to promote the kind of ideological, but non-partisan, education program that the NWU itself has been pushing (see Chapter 7), while at the same time pursuing union unity, but realistically the near future is unlikely to witness much progress toward unity. As a consequence, the divided labor movement will probably remain a key obstacle to the pursuit of a democratic socialist development path in Jamaica.

Whereas the union can provide an additional link to the employed classes, the party is the only organizational link the movement has to the lumpenproletariat and small farmers. As we just pointed out, the PNP failed to effectively penetrate the peasant population. The party continues to have strong links to the urban lumpenproletariat, though competition with the JLP is very stiff.

These links might well have been weakened had the PNP been more successful in overcoming clientelism. Clearly, there was simply a lack of will in this area. Though there were difficulties in coming to an agreement with the JLP, in the last analysis, the PNP was the government and could have made unilateral steps to reduce the extent of patronage in the system. While it is obviously utopian to believe that such a pervasive characteristic of the system could be eliminated overnight, the party could and should have taken steps to cut the extent of it in productive programs. Ironically, the one step that they did make, the establishment of the National Housing Trust, was in the distributive side of the public housing program. Naturally, we are not arguing that this was a bad move. Rather, we are strongly arguing that the success of the PNP's development path depends on effective implementation of programs initiated by the state and on efficient operation of state enterprises, and that this is incompatible with patronage. The disastrous state of the Guyanese economy should make this point abundantly clear.

Despite the possibility that the reduction of patronage might weaken the PNP's ability to mobilize the lumpenproletariat politically, it would clearly benefit the PNP in purely party partisan terms. The blow to the JLP would be much more serious because patronage is the major mechanism through which a clearly pro-capitalist party like the JLP under Seaga can retain a strong lower class base in Jamaican society.

As we saw in the last chapter, the PNP unofficially accepted the support of the WPJ. The PNP Women's Movement entered into an open alliance with the communist Committee of Women for Progress, and the PNP secretariat – without a decision on the matter from the party as a whole – asked for and received active WPJ support in districts where the PNP organization was weak in the 1980 election campaign. This unofficial alliance came under attack after the election, with the PNP moderates arguing that the relationship with the WPJ had contributed to the election defeat. Manley came down strongly on their side; after the party refused to accept his resignation as PNP president, he laid down the distancing of the PNP from the WPJ as one of the conditions for his continuing in the post. For its part, the WPJ in its analysis of the election outcome argued that the PNP had done better in districts where it had been active than in those where it had not been active (WPJ, 1981:42–3). The PNP moderates, in contrast, attacked the WPJ in the very stongest terms, accusing the party of opportunism, of 'riding on the PNP's back'.

There is no doubt that the tacit alliance, particularly in that it involved toleration of WPJ influence in the JBC newsroom, did benefit the communists, but the decision to support the PNP was not made for purely opportunistic reasons; it grew out of a variety of factors including the communists' analysis of the meaning of the capitalist class' opposition to the PNP and the general move of Latin American and Caribbean Communist and Workers Parties to an adoption of the non-capitalist path theory (see Chapter 4).

Nevertheless, the balance of the evidence does support the contention that the WPJ–PNP alliance did more harm than good to the PNP. Even if one accepts the WPJ's claim that the PNP did better in districts where it helped them than where it did not *and* that this was the reason for the differential performance,[22] it is probable that the resulting general public perception that the PNP was cozy with the domestic communists hurt the PNP across the board in all districts to a greater degree, because it fed *Gleaner*–JLP propaganda about the danger of a communist takeover in Jamaica. The very logic of coalition formation and the numbers involved argue against the PNP making such an alliance. To make up for the alienation of centrist voters, a party at the end of the political spectrum must be able to offer a more centrist party large numbers of its own activists and voters to make the move worthwhile electorally. The WPJ, commanding no more than 3 or 4 per cent of the electorate, simply could not offer this. From a comparative perspective, the Communists do not become an attractive coalition partner for the Socialists until they gain the support of at least 10 per cent of the electorate and then only in the context of a proportional representation system.

Using the state as an instrument of transformation
The very logic of the development model pursued by the PNP was built on

the use of the state to initiate and carry through a process of social transformation. The key question for any such model, of course, becomes how good an instrument the particular state is, how well it can be controlled and made to perform efficiently the tasks assigned to it. In the Jamaican case, there were both structural and behavioral problems in terms of the quality of the instrument, as well as control problems in terms of ensuring a consistent effort behind the transformation process or, at least, preventing any obstruction.[23] Furthermore, certain rules of the game constrained the latitude of action of the state, which made the issue of constitutional reform important.

The structural problems hampering the effectiveness of the state in carrying out policies of social transformation were its small size at the outset, institutional fragmentation leading to overlapping responsibilities, over-centralization, and a scarcity of skilled personnel. The development model of the 1950s and 1960s left the state sector very small. As we saw earlier in this chapter, this had an adverse effect on the expansion of the state-enterprise sector, though on the balance performance here was not too bad. This also meant that there were very few public sector institutions and members of the civil service available for and capable of performing the tasks posed by the expansion of the state's role in managing the economy and the introduction of new social programs. Besides being small, the public sector was characterized by duplication and fragmentation of functions and authority. After the achievement of independence, new tasks of public administration were frequently handled by the creation of new semi-autonomous institutions outside the structure of the civil service.[24] This made coordination and implementation of policies through the ministries formally in charge of a given area often exceedingly difficult. For instance, a former top-level civil servant whom we asked why the 'accelerated land reform' announced in September 1977 had not materialized, told us:

> There were too many individuals, from too many different disciplines involved. The accelerated land reform program was not under the authority of the Ministry of Agriculture, but rather under the Ministry of Mobilization. Every meeting I ever attended ended in utter confusion; no clear-cut policy was ever set and decisions were given many different interpretations afterwards.

Likewise, the sugar cooperatives suffered from the fact that responsibility for them fell under a number of different boards, agencies, and ministries (E. Stephens, 1984).

Internally, authority in the various agencies and ministries was highly centralized. The lack of significant delegation of authority meant that decision-making and implementation processes were slowed by the many hierarchical levels through which they had to go. Furthermore, the scarcity of skilled personnel impaired the managerial capacity of the state. From the start, the state was competing with the private sector for people with managerial and technical skills and their competition got keener as the deteriorating economic situation stimulated increasing migration among this group. At the same time, the state's position in this competition was weakened because of fiscal austerity which made it impossible to match the remunerations offered by the private sector.

From the outset, the government made efforts to improve the quality of the state apparatus. Immediately after winning the 1972 election, Manley set up a task force for the reorganization of the civil service (*G*, 21 April 1972) and built up new organizational structures for economic and social planning (*G*, 11 May 1972). In 1973, a new Ministry of Public Service was created to select and train profesionally-competent personnel and to improve organizational structures and procedures. Merit criteria were assuming gradually more weight than seniority for promotions, and in 1975 the rules were changed to base promotions on merit only. This created considerable difficulty in that it required that supervisors had to write annual evaluative reports which could serve as a basis for the Public Service Commission's assessment of merit for appointments and pro-motions. Frequently, the quality of these reports left something to be desired, and the interview part for appointments of officials to important positions by the Public Service Commission became crucial.

In February 1977, a new Public Service Commission was appointed, which was controversial in two respects.[25] First, the head of the new commission was the general secretary of JALGO, which raised the issue of a possible conflict of interest between his union position and his 'public employer' position. Second, and more important, the new commission was perceived as too PNP partisan to make impartial appointments on the basis of merit. This perception was reinforced by the importance of the interview procedure. As we explained in Chapter 6, the commission attempted to assess the candidates' understanding of development policy issues, but its function and procedures were interpreted and attacked as highly political. Though even the strongest critics of the new commission could point to only two cases where partisan loyalty had been put above expertise for an appointment, the perception of political bias created by the attacks on the commission caused some demoralization and loss of personnel, and con-siderable resentment.

Given the magnitude of the task and the considerable difficulties encountered in improving the quality of the state as an instrument to manage change, the government made a mistake in overloading the instrument. It started too many programs, at too fast a pace, for the available state machinery to be able to handle them efficiently. As a result, many of these programs were poorly implemented and constituted a greater drain on the government's resources than they were supposed to do and than the government could afford. If fewer programs had been initiated, they could have been better planned and their implementation could have been more closely supervised.

The attitudinal and behavioral obstacles to managerial effectiveness of the state apparatus, which pre-dated the controversy over political criteria for appointments, deserve some further discussion.[26] These obstacles had two dimensions, namely, intellectual inertia and politically-motivated hostility. A study of top-level civil servants carried out in the early 1970s found that only a very small percentage emphasized scope for creativity as a central value in a civil service career (Mills and Robertson, 1974). Rather, they valued their jobs because of job security, pensions and advancements. Furthermore, almost two thirds of them were found to be marginal readers, that is, reading at most one item besides newspapers or popular magazines. In part, one can certainly interpret this inertia as a legacy of the colonial bureaucracy where the goals of occupational socialization were reliability in the execution of decisions handed down from above, with strict adherence to formal rules. The resulting 'pass-the-buck' mentality and reliance on bureaucratic procedure often prevented effective follow-up and corrective action in the implementation of the PNP's social and economic policies.

The PNP's problems in ensuring a commitment and a consistent effort of the bureaucracy in carrying out its policies of social transformation were largely caused by the class position and class bias of civil servants. Partisan political hostility was of much less importance. If anything, partisan loyalties in the career civil service should have favored the PNP, since middle-class employees and professionals were a traditional PNP support base. In appointments to positions on statutory boards, the PNP had followed Jamaican practice and asked all the incumbents to resign after the 1972 and 1976 elections, in order to replace the JLP appointees with its own and to weed out uncooperative appointees after the first term. However, like large sectors of the middle class, many upper-level civil servants resented the PNP's social inclusionary policies, and they continued to prefer to interact with people of their own social standing rather than with the lower class clientele that was the target public for programs such as land lease, the youth service, rent control, etc. Accordingly, responsiveness to this new clientele and initiative in promoting the programs often left much to be desired.

Commitment of civil servants to the PNP's programs declined even further with the government's general loss of support. Not only did the disaffection of large sectors of the middle class affect civil servants as members of this class, but the obvious political weakness of the government and the consequent prospect of a JLP election victory affected them also as members of a bureaucratic apparatus likely to undergo significant changes which might threaten careers under a new government in the not-too-distant future. Thus, in 1980 many bureaucrats avoided being identified with PNP programs and policies by dragging their feet on implementation.

For the future, then, some structural and behavioral problems (scarcity of skilled personnel, class bias of civil servants) are likely to persist, whereas others (size, structural fragmentation, loyalty to the incumbent government) might be alleviated through the expansion already in place, a serious continuation and improvement of the reform efforts directed at the state apparatus itself, and greater political strength of the PNP when returning to office. Even in the case of scarcity of personnel, Davies (1984) suggests measures that might help alleviate the problem. Furthermore, the effects of the persistent problems could be moderated by the adoption of a slower pace and stricter supervision of program implementation.

The argument about the effect of the PNP's loss of political support on the civil servants also applies to the security forces. As we have argued, their turn against the PNP in 1980 made an important contribution to its election defeat, but it was primarily a turn against a politically weak government, not against democratic socialism *per se*. In 1976, when all the major programs had been initiated and the ideological battle was waged openly as well, the security forces had remained neutral. By 1980, they were turning with the majority in the society, under the impact of the economic hardship, the rising political violence, and the opposition's intense delegitimization campaign, and despite this turn, the top command of the JDF remained loyal to its constitutional role and foiled the coup attempt. Thus, it is reasonable to assume that a politically stronger PNP government in the future could maintain the security forces in their constitutional role and could count on their neutrality.

The constitutional rules of the game which constrained the latitude of action of the state most noticeably were the clause on compensation for expropriation, the structure of the top of the civil service, and the role of the Senate in blocking constitutional changes. As discussed in Chapter 5, the PNP had a clear plan for generating a process which could lead to a change of these and other rules through a revision of the constitution. The public education and discussion component of this plan fell victim to the economic crisis and the IMF. The crisis and the negotiations assumed absolute priority on the agenda of the government, at the expense of virtually all other projects. The budgetary austerity affected the constitutional reform program to an even greater extent than other programs because it was clearly an 'unproductive' expenditure in the eyes of the IMF and its supporters. The bargaining component of the PNP's plan worked slowly towards the desired end, despite the intense struggle with the opposition. The government was able to use the electoral reform as a bargaining chip and to achieve an agreement with the JLP in August of

1979, which included changes in the electoral system, the replacement of the Monarchy with a Republic, and a change of the property clause. However, the whole process of putting this agreement into legal practice would have taken some eighteen months, and thus the call of early elections obstructed its realization. For the future, a resumption of the constitutional reform effort is clearly essential. By pushing for it while in opposition and starting work on it soon after returning to power, the PNP could benefit from this reform in terms of enjoying greater room for action and having a more effective instrument available to promote its process of social transformation.

Managing geopolitics

The foreign policy of the PNP government did have its costs. As we argued above (see 'Constructing a class alliance') the close relations with Cuba along with rhetoric and the WPJ relationship fed the fears of the capitalist class and the middle classes of a communist threat by playing into JLP – *Gleaner* propaganda. Moreover, as the discussion in previous chapters (based primarily on our State Department and Foreign Service interviews) showed, the close exchange relationships with Cuba constituted the single most important factor in causing the deterioration of Jamaica–US relations in 1975–6 and again in 1979–80. The other policies of the government – its internal economic policies (state sector expansion, redistribution, etc.), the STC, the bauxite initiative, trade diversification and non-alignment – had only a secondary impact on relations with the USA during the Ford–Kissinger period and almost none at all during the Carter administration. Thus, the Jamaican case indicates that during the period in question, East–West relations and the USA's perception of its self-defined security interests were far more important than the government's development model or even direct challenges to US economic interests in determining the posture of the USA toward Third World countries.

For the greater part, the Cuba relationship, the cooperation with the WPJ and at least some of the so-called rhetoric were not, in our view, essential to the development path and therefore adjustments could be made without compromising the key elements of the democratic socialist model of development. In the view of the PNP left, close relations with communist countries, including party-to-party relations, support for their posture in international forums and so on, was necessary in order to encourage trade diversification and other forms of economic cooperation with these countries. Blasier's (1983) work on USSR–Latin American relations shows that this is not the case. In the case of the large Latin American countries, Brazil and Argentina, which were by far the largest Soviet trading partners in the 1970s in the region outside Cuba (Blasier, 1983:51), the USSR was willing to develop its economic ties with these right-wing military dictatorships despite their internal repression of the left and anti-communist foreign policy. In the case of smaller countries, there is some connection of economic relations to other policies, but a posture of non-alignment and the existence of full diplomatic relations with the USSR are generally sufficient.

Let us be clear about what will be forthcoming from these countries in any case. Most of the economic relations will involve lines of credit at concessionary terms (in comparison with prevailing bank rates) and purchases of Latin American and Caribbean countries' exports. Actual aid will be limited to such emergencies as disaster relief. The lines of credit, though concessionary, are designed to promote Soviet exports to this region (in which the Soviets incur a huge trade deficit) and thus are similar to US Export–Import Bank credits (Blasier, 1983:66). These economic relations are in the Soviet Union's economic interest. So, for example, in the face not only of Seaga's pro-USA, anti-communist foreign policy but also his ejection of four Soviet diplomats from the country on incredibly flimsy grounds in November 1983,[27] the economic relations in bauxite trade were continued. It is arguable, then, that with a return to non-alignment and a less hostile posture to the USSR, but without the close relations advocated by the PNP left, Jamaica's economic relations with the USSR and other communist countries could be further developed. Thus, there are no real dilemmas between choosing to adjust foreign policy in the ways suggested earlier in this chapter and diversification of external economic relations which is an essential feature of the democratic socialist development path.

However, there were aspects of the foreign policy which did present the PNP with genuine dilemmas. Small Third World countries cannot hope to defend their political independence militarily. Within the context of a non-aligned policy, their only hope *vis-à-vis* the superpowers is to hold together in a solidaristic front supporting each other, at least diplomatically, if not with materials and men, when their independence is threatened. Thus, Jamaica felt compelled to support the Cuban aid to Angola as it was the PNP government's analysis, reinforced by consultation with African leaders, that the South African troops would have entered Angola in the absence of the Cuban reinforcements. Jamaica's position on this issue contributed to the sharp deterioration of relations with the USA in the PNP's first term. As we documented in Chapter 4, the US administration reduced aid, contributed to negative press reports which damaged tourism, and probably funded the opposition as a result.

The ideological stance of the government domestically and in international forums presents a similar dilemma. In particular, the liberal use of the term 'imperialism' did have costs. The negative impact of its use in the domestic arena could be seen in that it influenced local affiliates of international banks to feed reports hostile to the government to their head office, and in that it led to negative attitudes towards tourists in the Jamaican population and thus damaged tourism. In international forums, speeches such as Manley's at the Non-aligned Conference in Havana contributed to the negative attitudes and actions of the US government toward Jamaica.

Some PNP moderates contend that, given the negative consequences, the PNP should drop the term since the idea is implicit in the NIEO anyway. However, it must be admitted that advocating the NIEO does not have the same impact in making clear that current international economic relationships are exploitative that the use of imperialism does, and it seems likely that any term that did make the exploitative nature of the system clear would also evoke a similar negative reaction. There may be some gain in avoiding the use of US imperialism and using instead corporate or economic imperialism, but the dilemma and the need to weigh the costs and benefits is still there.

Some of these dilemmas appear only because of Jamaica's geographical situation and thus its importance to the USA's self-defined security interests. Jamaica's break with the IMF confronted the government with this problem. From our interviews with US policy-makers, it was clear that the main motivation of the USA in wanting Jamaica to continue to deal with the IMF was related to national security.[28] The fear was not of economic ties with the Eastern Bloc *per se* but rather that these would lead to closer political and perhaps military ties. Again, the costs and benefits have to be balanced against one another.

The difficulty in making such an assessment of costs and benefits is that both sides of the equation, but particularly the costs of incurring the displeasure of the USA, are often difficult to assess before the fact. Not only is bluffing, exaggerating your intended sanctions, a standard part of the game, any covert action is denied even after the fact. Moreover, for various reasons, domestic or international, the US response to a given measure can change through time even in the absence of a change in administration. The shift of US policy in the Caribbean in the second half of 1979 is a case in point. Anticipating such moves is obviously extremely difficult.

The advent of the Reagan administration injects a note of extreme caution in generalizing from the experience of the Manley years. Aspects of the development model do now matter. Even if they avoid the type of policies like the Cuba exchange that led to much of the PNP's trouble, Third World regimes following a non-aligned foreign policy and progressive domestic policies, at the very least can expect little or no aid, unless they are very important strategically. In the worst case, well, one does not really know what the Reagan administration is doing in the area of covert action. A further problem in generalizing is that we do not know whether the post-Vietnam, post-Watergate years of Ford and Carter were exceptional interludes or whether the Reagan years represent an exceptional temporary return to cold war Third World policies.

Concluding remarks

In summing up our evaluation of the Jamaican process, we can come back to the questions posed at the beginning of this chapter. On the basis of our analysis, we suggest that the demise of the PNP government was the result not only of structural constraints resulting from dependent capitalism, but also of country-specific structural and historical constraints and mistaken policy choices, and thus not primarily the result of the inherent difficulties of the democratic socialist path itself. Accordingly, chances for a successful pursuit of this path elsewhere and in Jamaica in the future have to be assessed against the background of the specific structural and historical conditions there and then.

Structural characteristics of dependent capitalism, such as high import dependence, export concentration, a chronic balance-of-payments problem lay at the root of the foreign-exchange crisis and thus the IMF agreement, and others, such as the small size of the working class and cultural penetration by core-capitalism constituted important obstacles to the formation of a strong socialist movement. In several respects, Jamaica suffered from an extreme degree of dependence. The importance of the external sector was the fourth highest in the region in 1970 (IDB, 1982a:24); the secular decline of sugar and bananas and the energy-related restructuring of the world bauxite/aluminum industry caused declining export production. The importance of tourism and the North American tourist market made Jamaica particularly vulnerable to US perceptions of and reactions to developments in the island, and the geographical proximity to and linguistic compatibility with the USA resulted in particularly strong cultural penetration. Finally, the geopolitical situation put Jamaica squarely in the US sphere of interest.

Both with respect to movement-building and the use of the state as an instrument of transformation, country-specific features aggravated the obstacles presented by structural characteristics of dependent capitalism. The historically conditioned divisions in the working class, the unions' strong partisan political alignments and economistic orientation, and the weakness of an ideological tradition in Jamaican politics aggravated the difficulties of building a strong socialist movement in a society with the class structure typical of dependent capitalism, such as a comparatively small wage- and salary-earning proportion of the population and great internal stratification of the working class. The small size of the state at the outset, the tradition of patronage, and the scarcity of managerial and technical personnel further limited the capacity of the state to serve as an instrument of social transformation beyond the limits posed by institutional fragmentation which is a frequent characteristic of the state in dependent capitalist societies and by the attitudinal deficiencies of civil servants which can be regarded as legacies of colonialism.

Within the context of these constraints, we can point to some policy-choices which, if made differently, could have alleviated rather than contributed to the economic deterioration and loss of political support for the government. Most crucially, if the post-bauxite-levy economic package had focused more on productive state-sector investment rather than distributive programs, if more care had been exercised in foreign borrowing regarding the foreign-exchange earning or saving capacity of the respective projects, and if program implementation had been more carefully monitored, the severity of the foreign exchange crisis in 1976 might have been reduced. Better economic performance, in turn, would have facilitated attempts at accommodation with the liberal and patriotic sections of the bourgeoisie and thus moderated the decline of investment levels, and it would have reduced the incentive for migration of professional and managerial personnel.

In addition to moderating the economic deterioration, different policy choices could have directly affected the government's relationship to the capitalist and professional and managerial classes. Greater care in making rhetorical statements and less intensity in the relationship to Cuba would have removed important points of irritation in this relationship. More distance from Cuba and less rhetorical anti-Americanism would have had further favorable effects on the government's relationship to these classes, besides sparing Jamaica some of the effects of US suspicion and hostility.

Finally, we have pointed out some missed opportunities in policies for movement-building. The failure to develop a media strategy and legislation on party financing reduced the PNP's ability to construct and maintain a strong social support base. Thus, even given the unfavorable pre-conditions for democratic socialism, if the PNP government had chosen the policy alternatives mentioned here, it might have been able to avoid the IMF dictates and it would have lost less of its political support. This would have enabled it to continue with the process of transformation in the second term and perhaps to win the 1980 election or at least lose it by a smaller margin. Of course, this is not to say that the PNP could have completed the process of democratic socialist development in two or even three terms, but it is to say that it could have implemented more permanent structural changes towards this goal and thus improved conditions for the lower classes on the one hand and facilitated a resumption of the process after a period in opposition on the other hand.

9

Lessons of the Manley Government: Democratic Socialism as an Alternative Development Path

In this final chapter, we will make use of our analysis of the Manley government to reflect upon and clarify several theoretical and strategic issues. First, we will draw out the theoretical implications of our case study for the theory of the peripheral state and for class formation, particularly the interests and action of the capitalist class. Second, we will re-examine the nature of the political project of the PNP and differentiate it from related but distinct political phenomena; state capitalism, populism, non-capitalist development and social democracy. In this context, the conditions for the emergence of the democratic socialist project in Jamaica will be examined. Then we will draw lessons from the successes and failures of the Manley government for democratic socialist projects elsewhere. Finally, we will briefly analyze the conditions for the emergence and success of democratic socialist development models elsewhere.

Theories of state and class

State and society in democratic polities in the periphery: class power, autonomy and dependence

In the initial chapter of this book, an extremely brief sketch of an alternative view of the state in dependent capitalist societies was presented, and throughout the following chapters numerous observations were made on the relationship of state action and its limitation to economic dependence, class organization and power, the strength of civil society, state capacity and so on, based on the experience of the Manley government and comparisons of that experience to socialist governments elsewhere. It is incumbent on us here to bring together these diverse observations to piece together a theory of the state for democratic polities in dependent capitalist countries.

320

Precisely because we are interested in the limited range of countries implied in the last sentence, our discussion does not directly address many of the questions posed in various debates on the state in the periphery, as the main concern of these discussions has generally been authoritarian regimes or party plural regimes with limited suffrage and limited popular mobilization (for example, see Alavi, 1972; Goulbourne, 1979; Canak, 1984; Thomas, 1984; Young and Turner, 1985), which is understandable since most Third World states fall into one of these categories. Given the nature of these societies, it is not surprising that the debates have focused on the relationship of the state to foreign capital, various segments of national capital and the landholding classes, and on the degree of autonomy the state does or does not enjoy from these elite economic factions. This is not to say that the popular classes play no role in regime outcomes in this literature. On the contrary, popular mobilization is an essential element of Stepan's (1978) analysis of various types of corporatism and O'Donnell's (1973) of the origins of the bureaucratic authoritarian regimes. Rather, the point here is that a sustained theoretical discussion of the state in dependent capitalist societies with democratic polities and relatively mobilized populations is conspicuously absent. Our goal here is to make a modest attempt at this. Though we will not discuss other theories at length, our criticism of others purporting to present general theories of the Third World state should be obvious.

We contend that our analysis of the Manley government demonstrates the utility of analyzing political developments in dependent capitalist societies with democratic polities within the political class struggle frame of reference. The changes made in Jamaican society by the PNP government against the resistance of the upper classes clearly show not only the potential of popular organizations at the outset but the significant shift in the balance of class power during the Manley period. The real proof of the latter lies, somewhat ironically, in the developments leading to and occurring during Seaga's first years. The fact that the JLP felt compelled to make such a heavy appeal to the material interests of the masses to win the 1980 election, its reluctance to weaken labor legislation or eliminate the PNP's peoples programs, including the much criticized 'make work' program, its resistance despite its conservative rhetoric, to the introduction of the austerity programs demanded by the IMF, and finally its rapid loss of popular support once the loan-subsidized consumer-orgy subsided and the ugly hand of reality began to push through; all these are indicative of the change in the relative power of classes in Jamaica. The days when the upper classes and a few political brokers ruled over subservient masses are gone forever.

So we will begin our discussion of the state with an overview of the basic insights of the political class struggle approach and then suggest modifications that need to be made for the theory to fit dependent capitalist societies, based on our study of Jamaica and comparative observations. Common to all adherents of this school of thought is the view that the most fundamental factor determining state policy is the balance of power between class forces in civil society and that organization as well as property is a source of power in capitalist societies, particularly democratic (that is, democratic in the narrow, formal sense) capitalist societies. The balance of power between capital and labor is determined primarily by the level of labor organization in economic (unions) and political terms (parties) and secondarily by the degree of centralization of capital. This balance of power is reflected in the hegemonic balance in society (and thus in the distribution of 'public opinion') and the struggle for hegemony – in the Gramscian sense – is the central arena of the class struggle in democratic capitalist societies. Bourgeois hegemony is based on the control of property and all it entails in terms of domination of the media, attractiveness as a social ally to other forces such as the church, cultural elites and so on. Organization – primarily unions and parties, but also youth organizations, cultural and educational associations and so on – is the basis of a socialist movement's attempt to build a counter-hegemony. The socialist counter-hegemony influences people not only through the party and union media but, more crucially, through the network on inter-personal contacts developed through organization. To put it crudely, the growth of socialist counter-hegemony results in expansion of support for the movement's program and support at the polls. Electoral support is obviously critical to achieving a governmental position. Furthermore, holding the achievement of governmental position constant, the extent of support, the publicly perceived 'mandate', can expand (or limit) a socialist government's ability to pursue its policies.

We have just alluded to the most important confirmation of the class-power hypothesis: the JLP's actions in its drive to displace the PNP government, its action while in power and its rapid loss of support. This change in the balance of class power was caused by the increased political mobilization and increased political consciousness of the masses of the Jamaican people which, in turn, were created both intentionally by the party as part of its political strategy and as a by-product of its policies (see pp. 292–4).

The effects of the balance of class power on the ability of a government to implement its program are not limited to the effect of hegemonic balance and its expression in public opinion and electoral outcomes. Class power also finds an expression in naked economic terms, principally through slow-downs, disruptions, or stoppages of production. Depending on its degree of opposition to a government's policy and its evaluation of the effectiveness of its potential counter-action, capital can slow investment, stop investment domestically and invest abroad, disrupt production or even stop production of goods and services altogether, which in fact is precisely the sequence of escalating acts of resistance which we saw in the Jamaican case. The milder forms of capital counter-action may be aimed, consciously or unconsciously, at reducing political support for the government and effecting a turnover the next time the electorate goes to the polls. The most radical counter-action, such as employers' strikes or lockouts, may be aimed at provoking an armed overthrow of the government. The socialist movement also has the capacity to exercise naked economic power, primarily through the strike weapon, to force changes in government policy, but at any given level of popular organization, capital enjoys a greater edge over labor in this arena than in the struggle for hegemony.

The two modes of exercising class power are not independent. Economic power is often aimed at reducing the opponent's hegemonic potential by reducing its source, organization or property. Conversely a strong hegemonic presence can weaken the effectiveness of the exercise of naked economic power. Put in other words, a government with very broad support is less vulnerable to such action. In such a situation, radical action by the opposition may be viewed as disloyal by a large majority of the population thus justifying strong countermeasures by the government. Such was the case in early 1977 when, in the wake of the PNP's massive electoral victory of December 1976, the capitalist class' attacks on the government were very muted despite the fact that the government was considering a more radical path with major implications for capitalist interests.

The balance of class power in civil society is not the only determinant of state policy. Were that so, incumbency would not matter. Not only does control over the executive and legislative bodies matter, but the class orientation, cohesion and political attitudes of the occupants of posts in the military, bureaucracy, and judiciary and the division of powers between these elements of the state are also important. In short, the balance of class and political forces within the state itself must be examined. The historical legacy in terms of such factors as the constitutional and factual division of powers, experience with past socialist administrations, patterns of recruitment and so on contribute to or limit the ability of a socialist movement to use state power once it is achieved in order to implement its policies. The bureaucracy and the judiciary, particularly if it has the power of judicial review, can obstruct efforts at social transformation. As is obvious from the Chilean case, the course of action of the military is absolutely crucial to the very survival of any government.

In the Jamaican case, the allegiance of the security forces and the bureaucracy shifted with shifts in the middle strata as a whole. In 1978 and 1979, as it became increasingly apparent that the government could not stem the deterioration of the economy, the middle classes moved from a posture of accommodation to open opposition to the government. Inside the state, this manifested itself in bureaucratic foot-dragging, information leaks to the opposition, outright sabotage, and finally in late 1979 defection of the security forces, particularly the officers corps.

Early formulations of the political class-struggle view allowed too little room for state autonomy from civil society, for the autonomy of politics more generally and for the variability in the capacity (or incapacity) of the state to act in the direction desired by the holders of state power, but in her analysis of the New Deal, Skocpol (1980) convincingly argues that state capacity, state autonomy and party formations can have an important impact on state policy in advanced capitalist democracies. These factors are even of much greater importance in dependent less-developed capitalist democracies.

State autonomy can be broken down into two elements: (1) the independence of the state from international and domestic class forces in setting goals and deciding on policy and (2) the capacity of the state to carry out any given set of goals or policies.[1] State capacity depends on the degree of centralization of the state, its size and strength in terms of the extent of state ownership and tax extractive capacity, and the availability of skilled personnel. Tax extractive capacity and the availability of skilled personnel are clearly lower for peripheral states because of the weaker resource base and brain-drain phenomenon. Lower state capacity in peripheral states would seem to reduce state autonomy from civil society compared with core capitalist states, but the independence of goal setting factor works strongly in the opposite direction.

One important factor influencing the independence of goal setting is the density of civil society (see pp. 52–3). In advanced capitalist countries, this factor constrains political debate to a narrow range of options and in turn constrains governments (with the exception of times of crisis) to act roughly within the broad limits set by the balance of class power in civil society. The lower density of civil society in less-developed capitalist societies allows the government more leeway in policy formation. This was certainly one factor explaining how it was possible for the PNP government to depart so radically from the past in its policy as well as ideological orientation. In this regard we would pose as a tentative hypothesis that lower density of civil society also gives greater room for charisma to work. This, we think, helps to explain why Manley's charisma had such a profound effect in reorienting the political and social system.

One might also argue that the dominance of clientelistic parties increases the autonomy of office-holders in setting goals and policy. Certainly, it is clear that parties which depend on clientelistic loyalties rather than ideological commitments allow the party leadership a much greater flexibility to change its ideological stance without alienating (or educating!) its supporters. This was the case in the PNP's declaration of Democratic Socialism in 1974. On the other hand, dependence on clientelistic loyalties does make the party in question more dependent on its ability to deliver the patronage benefits, which makes it even more difficult for such a party in government to weather bad economic times. Moreover, reliance on clientelistic loyalties and, thus, on the dispensation of patronage may reduce the capacity of the state to implement its programs. As we saw, this was a serious problem during the PNP's tenure of office.

As far as the relationship between the state and capital is concerned, economic dependency is certainly a factor reducing state autonomy, that is, limiting the latitude of action of state incumbents in less-developed countries (Rueschemeyer and Evans, 1985). However, there are often factors which work in the opposite direction, putting the state in a relatively stronger position in dependent than in advanced capitalist societies (Evans, 1985). The private sector depends on state protection and support in the competition with imports and foreign capital, and only the state can generate sufficient resources for major investments in infrastructure and basic industries. Moreover, the very existence of external capital makes it possible, on occasion, to construct *alliances* directed against foreign capital which include national capital. The bauxite levy of the Manley government was one such occasion. Along similar lines, Klapp (1982) argues that stronger domestic political coalitions opposing state expansion in advanced capitalist countries may constrain a government's ability to act against foreign capital to a greater extent than in developing countries.

Nevertheless, the net effect of economic and political dependency undeniably works strongly in the direction of reducing state autonomy, that is, limiting the latitude of action of state incumbents in less-developed countries. Penetration by foreign capital, trade dependence, and foreign indebtedness can so limit a government's latitude of action that foreign economic actors are in a position to dictate government economic policy, as the IMF has so often been able to do. Moreover, countries in subordinate positions in the world system of states are subject to powerful pressures, through both overt and covert means, from dominant states to adapt their policies to the political, military and economic interests of the powerful states.

The whole experience of the Manley (and Seaga!) governments is yet another confirmation of the degree to which external dependence can limit a Third World government's options. This is particularly true in a period of downturn in the whole capitalist economy. Indeed, while the PNP's prospects of returning to office in the event of a new election look rosy, if the world recession continues, Jamaica's economic prospects look very gloomy. Saddled, in addition, with a huge debt inherited from Seaga, a new PNP government's room for maneuver will be extremely small.

The extremely narrow latitude for action in Jamaica currently as compared with, say, the period immediately after the imposition of the bauxite levy cautions one to keep in mind the *variability* of all of these factors which serve to increase or reduce state autonomy. While we have generalized about the relative degree of state autonomy in dependent and advanced capitalist countries, it is clear that there are great differences across countries and through time in both groups, but particularly among dependent capitalist countries. Indeed, one can hardly imagine less autonomy of politically independent states than that experienced by those deeply in debt and operating under IMF conditionality.

Still, it is important to emphasize again, in closing, that while our study of the Manley government and our comparative observations do confirm the importance of dependence in accounting for the demise of the Manley government, they also point out the importance of the balance of class forces, particularly the weakness of the political movement and the divided labor movement, as well as of the managerial capacity of the state. Moreover, the balance of class forces and the deficiencies in the managerial capacity of the state can only in part be explained as consequences of Jamaica's peripheral position. The small size of the industrial working class, a characteristic of dependent capitalist societies, does constitute an important obstacle to building a strong socialist movement, but the divisions in the working class, the unions' partisan political alignments and the weakness of the ideological tradition in Jamaican politics are due to particular historical factors. The institutional fragmentation of the state and attitudinal deficiencies of civil servants can be explained as legacies of colonialism,[2] but the institutional weakness of the state in terms of initially minimal penetration of the economy can be attributed to the particular development model followed in the period immediately after the Second World War.

Our examination of the Jamaican experience also shows certain successes in the attempt to modify structures of dependence. Project Land Lease and support policies for small farmers did show results in greater food production for the domestic market. The bauxite strategy gave the government greater control over the country's bauxite reserves, greater revenues and the beginning of diversification of export markets, and it set examples for joint ventures between the state and foreign capital in areas where foreign capital is essential. The State Trading Corporation helped to save foreign exchange by bulk buying and competitive bidding and it also furthered the diversification of trade relations. These successes question the views of analysts such as Wallerstein and Gunder Frank who see the world system as essentially closed and allow for virtually no latitude of action for third world states, particularly small peripheral nations. This is fortunate, because despite the important contribution of these viewpoints to our understanding of underdevelopment, the adoption of the more orthodox versions of these theories can lead to extreme pessimism and political paralysis. Fortunately, the system is not completely determined and there are options open to socialist movements in the Third World. The task is to find and exploit the alternatives that are available within the constraints set by the domestic and international system.

The capitalist class: class interests and class action

Some authors (for example, see Lewin, 1982; Ambursle, 1981) have argued that the Manley government's policies were a product of the interests of the national bourgeoisie and that the nationalization programs represented efforts to rationalize capital. Given that, by late 1975, the large majority of capitalists were strongly opposed to the PNP government, this contention cannot be supported within what Gold, Lo and Wright (1975) call an 'instrumentalist' frame of reference. This school of Marxist thought on class and state views the state as invariably consciously controlled by the capitalist class, with the class using the state to further its own interest; this was clearly not the case in Jamaica in the mid- and late 1970s.

Structural Marxists, on the other hand, begin with the assumption that capitalists often do not see their own interests. Rather, there is a structural relationship between the interest of the dominant class and outcomes of state action. This type of Marxist functionalism has been criticized because, like structural–functionalism, it generally fails to specify the mechanism which insures that the institution (the state) carries out its function for the maintenance of the (capitalist) system (Skocpol, 1980; Gold *et al.*, 1975). But one can go beyond this: capitalists' perceptions of their interests do in fact strongly condition their actions, and thus if they perceive a policy or an entire government to be working against them they will move to oppose it politically, then perhaps to reduce investment, to export capital, and even to migrate. Thus, their actions can undermine a government that is 'really' acting in their interest. In sharp contrast to the arguments of the structuralists, it **does** matter what the capitalists perceive to be their interests.

Moreover, it is questionable, to say the least, that the Manley government's policies were 'really' in the interest of national capital. Again, this can only be defended from a structural Marxist conception, in this case, of class (rather than the state). This conception of class sees classes as 'empty places' and class relations as relations between positions in the class structure. Thus, class interests are perceived to be only those aspects which affect the capitalist *qua* capitalist or worker *qua* worker, and not, say, the capitalist as upper-class property-holder or upper-class husband concerned with his wife's feelings about security or his offspring's chances also to move into a privileged position in society. With regard to the capitalist *qua* capitalist, it could be argued that the Manley government benefitted them; the PNP nationalizations were, with only a few exceptions, focused on foreign capital and/or enterprises in danger of ceasing operations. Then, the structuralists might argue, the PNP's social programs were necessary to legitimate the system in the eyes of the people and thus to demobilize them.

First this point of view can be questioned on its own terms. It would be hard to argue that things like the PNP's labor legislation were in the interest of capitalists *qua* capitalist. Also, there can be little doubt that the social and political mobilization process which the PNP intentionally ignited was a threat to capitalists, and moreover, it is probable that the social programs of the PNP fueled, not dampened, the social mobilization process. Second, and more important, it is a misleading abstraction to analyze the capitalist as only 'a location in the class structure' if one wants to analyze class interests and class actions. Capitalists are also upper-class people with homes, spouses, offspring, etc. set in historical situations with memories of the past and expectations for the future for themselves and their families. As one top PNP politician, who was with the government from the beginning to end, put it:

> The first factor causing a fall-off in investment was that the things we did fundamentally challenged the privileges of the private sector (or were perceived as such) much more than the labor movement ever did; because the union is in the factory, but our policies touched their homes and families. A number of our policies caused a great reaction; though they were not really that great a threat: Educational changes which forced middle-class kids to compete with poor kids for places in secondary schools . . . the National Youth Service which caused a tremendous concern among mothers and forced us to hold numerous meetings trying to assure them that we were not 'taking little Johnny away'; the wealth and property taxes which caused a first wave of migration . . . and an angry and frightened reaction.

He went on to name a number of other policies, as well as rhetoric, foreign relations and so on, but the point is sufficiently clear: we have to analyze capitalists in the totality of their social (and historical) situation to understand their political actions and reactions. To do this we have to reject a structuralist conception of class in favor of one which considers kinship and family as central aspects of the analysis (for example, see Zeitlin *et al.*, 1976) and places class relations in historical perspective (for example, see Thompson, 1963). One can still begin with production relations as the primary determinant of the structure of class relations, but then, in examining class formation, one must examine the inter-generational reproduction of classes and the degree of class closure of social intercourse. With this pattern of social interaction analyzed, one can then proceed to examine the historical development of the consciousness of the class. Only then is past action of the class understandable and future action predictable.[3]

The nature of the political project of the PNP

Democratic socialist development
Before attempting to analyze the conditions for the emergence of the democratic socialist experiment in Jamaica, and its applicability elsewhere, it is necessary to reiterate our definition of the political project and differentiate it from other, related social and political phenomena. In Chapters 1 and 8 we have defined the democratic socialist development path as characterized by the following goals or policies:

(1)   reduction of economic dependence through increased self-reliance, trade diversification, and increased national ownership and control of the economy;
(2)   state-sector-led development in the context of a mixed economy with state ownership of the commanding heights of the economy, vigorous state investment, promotion of cooperatives, but still a significant private sector;
(3)   increased social equality – economic redistribution through land reform, employment creation, wage and price policies, workers' participation, cooperative development, etc. – cultural equality through cultural inclusion policies – political equality through strengthening people's organizations such as unions, neighborhood associations, etc.;
(4)   deepening political democracy through enforcement of basic political and civil rights and encouraging political mobilization;
(5)   a foreign policy of non-alignment, Third World solidarity and cooperation, and struggle for international economic reorganization.

Strategically, this democratic socialist development path requires:

(1)   construction of an alliance of the working, peasant, marginal and lower middle classes and the liberal and nationalist sections of the upper middle class;
(2)   coming to a working accommodation with the other elements of the upper middle class and with the liberal and nationalist sections of the bourgeoisie;
(3)   building a political movement centered on an ideological (but not dogmatic), programmatic, mass-based party, buttressed by unions and other popular organizations.

The process of transformation initiated by this democratic socialist development project is best conceptualized as a 'development path' rather than a relatively brief 'transitional stage' to socialism. This conception gives the proper balance between the accumulation processes and the socialization of the economy. It is not the brief, revolutionary but 'peaceful road to socialism' conceived of by large sections of the Popular Unity Government in Chile.[4] This is not to say that the end state will not be socialist in the sense that the means of production will eventually be democratically owned and controlled, but the method by which this is achieved is not primarily by takeover of existing enterprises by the state. Rather, once the commanding heights of the economy are brought under state control, a process which will involve socialization of existing private enterprises, the socialization of the economy proceeds primarily through the expansion of the state and cooperative sectors in relative terms, though the private sector may grow in absolute terms. This change in the relative weight of the sectors is achieved by the fact that public-sector investment outweighs private-sector investment in the accumulation process.

Thus, democratic socialist development is transformative but gradual. Indeed it must be so. Otherwise, no accommodation with any section of the capitalist class can be worked out. Without any compliance, however reluctant, from a significant section of the capitalist class, the model cannot be economically successful and if it is not economically successful it cannot be politically successful, as the events covered in this book make abundantly clear. No rapid takeover of an entire economy is possible without severe economic dislocation and decline as the privileged withdraw their skills and, where possible, capital, from the system, and as external economic sanctions aggravate disruptions. No democratic government can survive this. It will be replaced, democratically or undemocratically.

A process of rapid socialization of an entire economy is certain to generate an extremely intense political struggle which affects the security forces. The government's response to the danger of intervention by the security forces can be, on the one hand, an attempt to win them over to its side or neutralize them by splitting the officer corps, retiring hostile officers, and propagandizing among the soldiers, and on the other hand, an attempt to arm its supporters and thus create a deterrent to intervention. However, either attempt is highly likely to provoke greater hostility against the government on the part of the security forces, in the form of self-defense against governmental interference violating corporate autonomy and against the loss of the monopoly of organized armed force. This hostility, in turn, increases the likelihood of a coup attempt, or, if attempts to split the officer corps are successful, there is a potential for civil war.

The intensity of the political struggle in a process of rapid socialization results not only from the severity and militancy of the opposition, but also from the large-scale popular mobilization required to support the process. Mobilization efforts by the socialist movement entail the potential for uncontrollable militancy and consequent disruptions in enterprises even after their transformation, and efforts at counter-mobilization by the opposition entail the potential for violent clashes between various organized popular forces. In this situation, a government has three options:

(1)   it can enforce order in a legal and impartial way, which forces it to act against its own supporters as well as against opposition forces and thus weakens its own support base;

(2)   it can tolerate such violent confrontations, which increases the likelihood of intervention by the security forces;

(3)   it can act partially towards opposition forces, prosecuting them for violent acts and imposing preventive measures in the form of restrictions on civil liberties, which constitutes a step towards the abandonment of the commitment to democracy and, even more importantly, is highly likely to provoke intervention by the security forces, as the violation of constitutional norms lifts the barrier to intervention in the eyes of those officers committed to their constitutional role.

History makes it totally clear that intervention of the security forces to overthrow a democratically elected government and re-establish order in the context of intense popular mobilization will end up in an authoritarianism of the right not the left. The only case of an eclipse of democracy from the left was Czechoslovakia in 1948 which was occupied by the Red Army at the time.

Analysts of the Manley government, often in a critical vein, have variously argued that the government's project was populist, state capitalist, 'non-capitalist' or social democratic. Each of these alternatives is inferior to its interpretation as democratic socialist development. Some of the aspects of the PNP as much before as during the Manley period, such as the multi-class nature of the movement, the recruitment of labor leaders from the middle and upper classes, the elite origins of many of the leaders, and emphasis on nationalism, have led Ambursle (1981, 1983) and others to suggest that the PNP's political project was simply a Caribbean variant of Latin American populism. However, the movement-building and the popular participation aspects of the PNP's project in the 1970s do not fit the mold. Latin American populism generally involves control of workers by labor leaders, and broad popular mobilization occurs only as an unintended by-product of efforts of populist leaders to increase their own political clout, not by intentional design. Certainly the internal democratization of the party, and the efforts at ideological education and the very content of the ideology (the emphasis on participation, democracy, socialism, etc.) are entirely contrary to what populist leaders generally promote. Thus, populism is not an appropriate interpretation of the PNP's path.

Similarly, the state capitalism thesis as an explanation for changes in the Jamaican political economy under Manley is inadequate. The PNP government would appear to be a perfect example of this type of development as the expansion of the Jamaican state was preceded by many of the conditions which Canak (1984) identifies as typical of the arguments of the proponents of the thesis:

(1)   a weak national bourgeoisie;
(2)   an accumulation crisis linked to the exhaustion of import substitution;
(3)   penetration of the international economy.

But the PNP's emphasis on popular mobilization and changes in production relations through the introduction of workers' participation in privately and state-owned enterprises, through cooperatives and through CEOs does not fit the model outlined by the state capitalism thesis and, indeed, gives the whole process a different class character than implied by the thesis.

In Jamaica itself, the dominant frame of reference which left academics and politicians used to analyze the PNP's development path has been the theory of the 'non-capitalist path'. This theory was developed by Soviet social scientists to analyze national liberation movements in the Third World, primarily in Africa and Asia.[5] The theory gained influence among Latin American and Caribbean communists, and its basic propositions were adopted unanimously at the 1975 Conference of Communist and Workers' Parties of Latin America and the Caribbean. The WLL and then the WPJ actively promoted the theory and it became quite influential because of the active presence of Trevor Munroe and a number of other WPJ members at the Mona campus of the University of the West Indies.

Doubtless, the non-capitalist path is a better frame of reference within which to analyze Jamaican developments than populism or state capitalism. It emphasizes that, in contrast to the social movement in developed capitalist countries, the movement in less-developed countries must develop the forces of production and that, given the weakness of the bourgeoisie and the working class, the state must lead development and the progressive movement must be an alliance of classes. Moreover, the immediate goals, such as reduction of foreign economic domination and agrarian reform, are similar to those pursued by the PNP.

However, there are weaknesses in the theory. As Thomas (1978:19–26) points out in his incisive (though basically sympathetic) critique of the theory, in practice far too broad a range of countries has been described as pursuing a non-capitalist path, such that in the end little more than an anti-imperialist posture (hostile to Western economic domination and a political tilt toward the East) is necessary. Thomas argues that the class character of the government and presence of political democracy must be essential characteristics of the path. As it is, analysts often include countries which repress the working class, unions, strikes, etc., in the category of those pursuing a non-capitalist path.

We would argue that Thomas' critique does not go far enough and, in the end, the concept is of very limited utility. The primary problem is that it attempts to present a development path for countries (or movements in countries) which differ far too much in their current economic and political situation, from extremely under-developed African and Asian states to medium-developed countries in Latin America and the Caribbean, and from repressive dictatorships to political democracies. A set of political and economic prescriptions to fit left strategy in all these countries would have to be so general that it would be useless.

A first step toward developing a theory or rather a set of theories of socialist transformation is to distinguish sharply the situations and tasks of social transformation faced by movements in countries at different levels of capitalist development, with a second dimension being the political form of the countries. Not only do the tasks differ but, perhaps more importantly, the class structures differ and thus the whole process – the class alliance, class confrontation and class compromise differ (see Table 9.1). At the lowest levels of development, such as the peasant societies of Africa, the domestic bourgeoisie is minuscule and thus the problem of class compromise entirely different from the more-developed countries. The urban proletariat is a secondary class and thus the class alliance has a different configuration. In these societies, which are, after all, those for which the theory of the non-capitalist path was developed, the theory does seem most appropriate.[6] In these countries, one central task is to carry out a process of capital accumulation in the state and cooperative sector. Without a significant private sector, the term 'non-capitalist path' does fit the situation. These countries confront capitalism primarily as an international force in their dealings in world commodity and financial markets and only secondarily (if at all) as a domestic force. In most cases, their primary domestic opponent is the large landed class.

In countries at higher levels of capitalist development, a socialist movement will inevitably face a more entrenched bourgeoisie and thus one task for the movement once in power will be that of reaching some kind of accommodation with the domestic bourgeoisie. This is true of pluralistic revolutionary governments, such as the Sandinista government, whose economic model includes a mixed economy with a subordinate private sector as well as of attempts at democratic socialist development, such as the Manley government's. These differ from the advanced capitalist countries in that they must deal with the problem of dependence in the world capitalist economic and political system.

There are so many similarities between the PNP's democratic socialism and European Social Democracy that the PNP's project has often been viewed as a variety of social democracy. Both involve some variety of reformist socialism operating in the context of competitive electoral politics. The PNP's active membership in the Socialist International strengthens the association of the party with its European sister parties.

However, there are several reasons why it seems inadvisable to view the PNP's project as 'social democratic'. The first is that social democracy as an

TABLE 9.1 Schematic comparative analysis of democratic socialist movements: sociological nature of the movement and tasks faced

Level of development/ mode of production	Sociological nature		Tasks facing movement		
	Organizational and social base *Party*	Main opponent	Colonial or authoritarian regime		Democracy
			Pre-transition	Post-transition	
Low/peasant or semi-feudal	Peasants, emerging working class, state bureaucrats, intelligentsia	International capital Landlords	National liberation or Revolutionary seizure		Non-capitalist path (TANU Tanzania)
Medium/ dependent capitalism	*Party with union* working class, peasants, lumpenproletariat, middle strata	International capital National capital Landlords	Revolutionary seizure (Sandinistas in Nicaragua) Negotiated opening (left in Peru, Argentina, Brazil, Chile)	Pluralist socialist development	Democratic socialist development (PNP in Jamaica)
High/advanced capitalism	*Party and union* manual and non-manual employees	National capital International capital	Not applicable		Socialist transition from welfare statism to economic democracy (SAP in Sweden) (PSF in France)

analytical category applied to movements in Latin America and the Caribbean generally covers such widely divergent phenomena as the Allende government in Chile and APRA party in Peru. Many center-right politicians from the region (including one Edward Seaga!) have identified themselves with social democracy which they equate with social reform, democracy and capitalism, a position closer to that of European liberals.

Still, with some specification, one might argue that the analytical category 'social democracy' could be usefully applied to some movements in Latin America and the Caribbean as well as the usual European labor and socialist parties. However, we contend that there are systematic differences in the goals, policies and strategies of these movements because of the positions of the countries in the world system and in historical time and of the level of capitalist development that make it seem wise to reserve the term social democracy for the left-wing movements in the core capitalist nations of the contemporary world.

The essential difference lies in the nature of dependent capitalism, in how the class structure affects the movement-building process and the problem of generating economic development in such societies. Because of their inability to develop support for their more radical, socialistic policies, European social democratic parties pushed these goals into the background and concentrated on a welfare statist program of redistribution through expansion of taxation and public expenditure, a phase of development which lasted until the mid-1970s.[7] The parties and labor movements depended on working out a compromise with the bourgeoisie to produce growth. In dependent capitalism, this purely redistributive phase is not possible, for several reasons.[8] As Cardoso's (1964) early work on the national bourgeoisie in dependent capitalist countries argued, the domestic capitalist class does not have the dynamism to lead development. Thus, the state must step in. The drive to create self-generating domestic growth also calls for an encroachment of the state on the previous preserve of private capital (for example, as in the PNP's nationalization policies, see Chapter 8). Finally, as the cross-national studies of dependence show, growth generated by the private sector in alliance with foreign capital often leads to perverse distributive consequences (Bornschier *et al.*, 1978). Thus, attempting to graft a social democratic style distributive policy onto private-sector-led growth would be a self-negating policy. State-sector-led development and related policies to bring the national economy under national control (thus reducing dependence) are necessary features of the model. So, for example, the PNP's nationalizations, which brought some 20 per cent of the economy under state control were essential to its project whereas Swedish Social Democratic policy generated a pattern of rapid economic growth and substantial equalization in the 1950s and 1960s while the government's role in total ownership did not exceed 5 per cent.

The necessary task of directing substantial resources toward public-sector investment is hardly made easier by the existence of much greater inequality and unemployment in dependent capitalist than advanced capitalist countries. Thus, a redistribution of current resources rather than a redistribution of future growth (the primary social democratic strategy) is necessary in dependent capitalist countries. In short, the scarcity of resources makes these tasks much more difficult in the Third World context. Economic dependence also demands policies such as trade diversification and aspects of foreign policy (Third World solidarity and economic cooperation and promotion of the NIEO), of countries pursuing a democratic socialist development path, which has no parallel in the case of social democracy.

The differing class structures of dependent capitalist and core capitalist countries impose differences on the political strategy of the movements in these countries. This is not only a matter of differences in the alliance of classes underpinning the movement (manual and non-manual workers versus workers, peasants and marginals) but also of the structure of the movements themselves. As we pointed out in Chapter 8 since marginals and, to a large extent, peasants, cannot be reached by unions, the party must play the central role in structuring, unifying and leading the movement in dependent capitalist countries. Because these groups are not united by a common position in the productive process and, in the case of the peasants, are dispersed in physical space this is a much more difficult task.

There are also differences in the role of the state in dependent capitalism and advanced capitalism, because of the configuration of the class structure, position in the world system, and the weakness of civil society in dependent capitalism, which leads to a simultaneous constriction of some options and a greater autonomy in other areas. Again, this entails important differences between European social democracy and the PNP in terms of the political project involved and the sociological nature of the movement. As a result of the differences outlined here, we would be prepared to argue that the category 'social democracy' be reserved for the labor and mass socialist party movement of the core capitalist countries. A logical consequence of this argument would be that social democracy is (was) a phenomenon associated with a specific group of countries in a particular phase of the historical development of the world capitalist economy and that the social democratic strategy for change is probably not appropriate elsewhere in historical time and social space.

As one can readily see, both in terms of the policies and goals to be promoted and in terms of the strategic tasks to be accomplished, the democratic-socialist development project is much more difficult than that facing social-democratic movements in advanced capitalist countries. Moreover, the resources, material and human resources in society, organizational resources and state capacity, are much more limited.

Social origins of Jamaican democratic socialism
To account for the social origins of Jamaica's experiment with democratic socialism, one must first address the question, what social conditions led to the development of democracy in Jamaica? To anyone familiar with Moore's (1966) work on the subject, the plantation origins of modern Jamaica would seem to predict quite another outcome. The brutal suppression of a peasant rebellion in 1865 (the Morant Bay Rebellion) by the plantocracy shows that there was potential for development in an authoritarian direction, but from an examination of Jamaican history, it becomes apparent that more than one factor prevented the coalition of landlords, a politically dependent bourgeoisie, and a strong state,[9] which Moore shows is fatal to the development of democracy, from forming.

At two points in modern Jamaican history, challenges from the lower classes have occurred which, in other countries, might have led to a modern form of authoritarianism. The first was the labor rebellion of the 1930s. By this point in time, several social and economic developments had occurred which reduced the chances of development of an authoritarian coalition. First, after emancipation, an independent smallholding peasant class began to develop, mainly populating the hilly interior. This development was considerably accelerated by the decline of sugar and the rise of bananas as Jamaica's main export, since bananas could be efficiently grown on small plots. The number of large estates fell drastically in this period to one third of their previous number, though this occurred in part through consolidation, increasing the size of the remaining estates. Second, some of the largest estates passed into the ownership of foreign corporations (Tate and Lyle, and United Fruit). These developments served to weaken the economic power and potential political clout of the domestic planter class.

Third, the growing commercial bourgeoisie developed independently of the plantocracy. Its ranks were filled by the new ethnic minority immigrants: Lebanese, Syrians and Jews. Thus, the kinship linkage between the landed class and nascent bourgeoisie was weaker than in, say, Chile (Zeitlin *et al.*, 1976).

Fourth, and most critical, the state and coercive forces were controlled by the British colonial masters in this period. The advisory Legislative Council was dominated by the plantocracy and the Governor generally ruled in their interests, but if anything, the colonial power served as a break on the exploitative objectives of the landholders. It is doubtful if the local oligarchs would have ever abolished slavery without being forced to do so by outside edict (or by internal rebellion), and given their chronic difficulties in recruiting labor in the post-slavery period, it seems very likely that the plantocrats would have resorted to more coercive methods of labor control. However, even if they had maintained their economic dominance up to the time of the 1938 labor rebellion, they could not have chosen the path of repression at that point, simply because the choice was not theirs to make. The class and political alignments in Britain were more important for the path chosen than the domestic alignments in Jamaica. The former pointed to constitutional decolonization, the introduction of universal suffrage and the institutionalization of the labor movement.[10].

By the time the Manley government came to power, the growth of tourism, bauxite-mining and alumina-processing and manufacturing had led to a further differentiation of the class structure, strengthening the bourgeoisie and expanding the working class and the lumpenproletariat. Moreover, and perhaps most important, the labor movement had laid deep roots in the society. These class structural and organizational aspects of Jamaican society and West Indian society in general go far in explaining why democracy endured in most of these societies whereas it did not in Britain's former African colonies. In the Jamaican case, the decline of sugar after 1965 and the exit of the foreign corporations leaving the old sugar estates in the hands of the government meant that by 1972, the old plantocracy was a minor political force. Thus, the dominant class configuration in Jamaica was quite different from Chile, and different in ways important for the survival of democracy.

Finally, one has to question whether the security forces in Jamaica had the firepower and manpower to carry out a coup had they so desired. With a total force of less than 1500 and a ground force of around 1000, the JDF alone is certainly too small for such a task, and the police force, though perhaps large enough at 6000, is too indisciplined. As for mentality, the officers' outlook is certainly influenced by the Sandhurst training of the top officers and thus is conservative and anti-communist, but there would be no parallel coherent school of thought to the Latin American 'new professionalism'.[11] The general middle-class outlooks of the security forces did lead them to turn against the government, and the actions of the forces definitely aided the JLP and hurt the PNP in the 1980 election campaign. Still, an authoritarian take-over planned and carried out by the security forces at the present level of strength and discipline is quite unlikely.

The importance of having a security establishment of limited size is certainly one factor in explaining the survival of political democracy in most of the English-speaking Caribbean and in Costa Rica. In this regard, it is significant that in the two regimes in the English-speaking Caribbean in which the democratic process did break down, Burnham's Guyana and Gairy's Grenada, electoral corruption, not military take-over, was the *modus operandi* of the 'seizure' of power.

On the question of what accounts for the emergence of the democratic-socialist project in the context of Jamaican democracy, the answer we can give must be much more tentative because of the limited number of relevant cases for comparative analysis. First, there are certain Caribbean-wide pre-existing forces and new trends that facilitated the development of democratic socialism in Jamaica. The changes in the international economy in the 1970s stimulated state-sector expansion all across the region as governments of varying political color tried to adjust to the down-turn of the world economy and the oil price shocks. In the British West Indies, the strong labor movements created a populist current in national political consciousness which, combined with the Fabian tradition picked up in British education by sections of the intelligentsia, formed points of departure for democratic socialism.

Viewing the British West Indies comparatively, it is clear that size is an important factor in explaining democratic socialism's emergence in Jamaica and not elsewhere. In the microstates (those smaller than Barbados), the economic constraints of the very small monocrop or tourism economies as well as the class-structural features created by these economic relations clearly militate against such a development. Among the larger democracies, the ethnic divide in Trinidad is probably one factor impeding the emergence of democratic socialism. In the remaining cases (Jamaica and Barbados), the economic situation; the bauxite resources and the lower level of dependence on tourism of Jamaica in comparison with Barbados, were facilitating factors favoring the emergence of the project in Jamaica. Indeed, a lot of the flexibility Jamaica had in the 1970s was created by the bauxite levy; furthermore, a crucial factor was certainly an idiosyncratic one, namely, leadership. Place Michael Manley at the helm of the Democratic Labour Party (Barbados) or the People's National Movement (Trinidad) instead of the People's National Party and it is arguable that the outcomes would have been very different.

Jamaican lessons for other democratic socialist movements

Pre-conditions, strategies and problems in Jamaica
At the outset of this summary of the lessons of the PNP's successes and failures for attempts at implementing this development path elsewhere, it is worth re-emphasizing how unfavorable conditions were for this type of political project in Jamaica in the early 1970s. The small size of the country meant that the economy was very open and the possibilities for self-reliance, greater economic integration, and diversification of trade were much less than in the case of one of the larger South American countries. The cultural permeability made it easier for the upper classes to make the decision to migrate once their privileges were challenged. The country was very dependent on the USA in economic terms and, given its physical proximity to the USA (and to Cuba) is critically located in geopolitical terms from the US point of view. The resources available to initiate the new path were also limited: the state sector was extremely small and the political movement was underdeveloped, that is, the PNP was a non-ideological, clientelistic party and the labor movement was divided and economistic.

Despite this, the Manley government did have its successes. Its bauxite offensive resulted in very greatly increased revenues from the resource, the repatriation of substantial tracts of land, control over its bauxite reserves, and diversification of outlets for its bauxite and alumina. Jamaica's leadership in Third World affairs and advocacy of the NIEO led to successes such as the formation of the IBA and spread of the bauxite levy, the conclusion of the Lome Convention and the location of the Seabed Authority in Kingston. The establishment of the State Trading Corporation resulted in substantial savings on imports, subsidization of basic necessities and diversification of trade. There were also some successes in the area of land reform. Project Land Lease did bring land to the land hungry and resulted in higher domestic food production. Finally, the movement-building and social-mobilization process did deepen political democracy in Jamaica; it did increase the political consciousness of the mass of the people and include them in the social, political and cultural life of the country for the first time. In short, it permanently changed power relations in Jamaican society.

If these successes point to potential opportunities for other Third World countries, some of the failures of the PNP government point to pitfalls that may be avoided elsewhere. The mistakes in economic strategy are some of the most important of these. The Manely government's policy, particularly in 1974–5 after the bauxite levy substantially increased the state's resources, was too distributionist, much like that of the new socialist governments of Chile in 1970 and France in 1936. These parallels remind us that there were reasons for this policy: both the crying needs of the underprivileged and the movement's desire to deliver to its constituency pushed these governments in that direction. Nonetheless, with the decrease in private-sector investment – which was partly the result of the opposition to the government from an ultra-conservative section of the capitalist class – the government had to pick up the slack with state-sector investment in order to maintain growth in the economy. With hindsight, one can also say that the government resorted to too much foreign borrowing at unfavorable commercial interest rates in 1975–6. As we pointed out repeatedly in earlier chapters, the failures in economic planning and management were largely a result of the absence of an overall plan for economic and social transformation on the PNP's part, and this in turn was related to the non-ideological, clientelistic nature of the party at the outset.

The second area of failure that contains clear lessons for other movements was the inability of the PNP to construct a viable accommodation with substantial sections of the capitalist class and the managerial and professional class. The ultra-conservative segment of the capitalist class was a lost cause, as we argued in earlier chapters, but the rest of the class, though clearly not enthusiastic about the government as many of its policies cut into their traditional privileges, were willing to accommodate to the situation as late as early 1975. Let us be clear about the situation of these people: while the PNP's policies were not in their interests, they could still make money (and many did). Moreover, exit is not without its costs. One simply cannot dig up sunken investment and move to another country. Top Jamaican businessmen, well connected in their own country and operating in a known (and in some cases protected) economic environment, do not have these advantages in the USA or Canada. Thus, there was room for the PNP government to push and to coax the moderate-conservative and liberal capitalists into an accommodation.

To come back to our conclusions developed in the last chapter, we suggest that two adjustments of its policies might have achieved this. First, taking into account how crucial the deterioration of the economy was to the alienation of this group of capitalists, the alterations of the PNP's economic policy just suggested, might well have resulted in better economic performance in 1975–6, and thus might have helped to cement the accommodation. Second, a toning-down of the excessive rhetoric of some PNP spokesmen and of the Cuba relationship, though less important than the state of the economy, would also have helped. It should be re-emphasized here that these adjustments would not have entailed a conservatizing of the PNP's policies, that is, a big concession to the capitalists' interests. Indeed, these alterations of the economic policy would have accelerated the process of economic transformation.[12]

The mention of Cuba brings our attention to the last area where, in retrospect, it seems clear that the Manley government made avoidable mistakes: geopolitics. The warm relations with Cuba, in particular the extensive exchange programs and shuttling of top PNP leaders back and forth to Cuba, was definitely the most important factor leading to US hostility to the PNP government in 1975–6 and 1979–80. The direct attack on US economic interests entailed in the bauxite offensive generated nothing like the reaction that the Cuba connection did. That the charges of Cuban subversion of Jamaica – believed by a substantial section of the US foreign-policy establishment – were almost totally groundless is beside the point. Jamaica still lost more than she gained by the relationship. Moreover, it was possible to pursue a policy which would have combined a principled defense for Cuba's right to full membership in the hemispheric community with a toning-down of the exchange programs which were the basis of US fears (and JLP propaganda!) of Cuban subversion.

One area where the PNP failed to achieve what it might have done – though not through any mistake that Jamaica made – that contains a lesson for other Third World countries was in the area of Third World cooperation and solidarity. The limitations of the IBA and the failure of any of the Manley government's cooperative aluminum smelter projects to materialize are only the most obvious cases where the failure of other Third World countries to follow-through led to less than total success of the PNP's policy. Both in the 1970s and now in the 1980s one can see numerous opportunities for Third World advancement through cooperation (such as various economic joint ventures) and solidarity (such as debt cartelization) which have not been realized often simply because the path of least resistance in the short run was to go it alone and gain some temporary advantage and avoid some risk.

Relevance of the model for other third world countries
This book has given anyone who was initially skeptical of the possibilities for democratic socialism in the Third World many reasons for continuing to be pessimistic. Though we hope to have convinced the reader that the demise of the PNP government was not inevitable, that it did have its successes and that other countries might have even greater potential, it is nonetheless true that the People's National Party government in Jamaica failed to put the country on a viable development path. Moreover, in comparing the strategic and political problems faced by democratic social-ist movements in the Third World with social democratic movements in the First, we stressed the greater obstacles facing the former. Nonetheless, we are prepared to argue (1) that democratic socialist development is the best alternative open to the left in democracies in the Caribbean and Latin America; (2) that there is a good possibility that more left-wing move-ments, at least in South America, will find themselves in democratic contexts where this model is relevant; and (3) that given the economic alternatives that the right and center-right are likely to offer, the chances for generating and sustaining support for democratic socialism are not as bleak as one might assume.

First, one can ask what alternatives the left has in political democracies in the region. We have alluded to the tremendous obstacles facing a more radical path than democratic socialism and have analyzed this at length elsewhere (Stephens and Stephens, 1980). Suffice it to re-emphasize the basic points here. History clearly shows that left revolutionary movements cannot succeed in the context of political democracies and that maximalist attempts at rapid socialist transition through electoral means will fail at the polls or be crushed by military coups. We would not absolutely rule out such developments, but chances of victory are so slim and the costs of failure in terms of repression and loss of life so enormous that such attempts are foolhardy.

If one accepts this argument then democratic socialist development is the most radical political project feasible and the only political project with any structural transformative potential that can be implemented in the context of political democracy. Moreover, in the present conjuncture, despite its difficulties, it is not an unattractive electoral alternative precisely because the alternative offered by the other side of the political spectrum (and supported by the IMF and international financial circles) is so bad both from the point of view of the privations it visits on the people and from the point of view of its chances for success. The disastrous results of this free market, monetarist, export-oriented, private-sector-led model in Jamaica are the rule rather than the exception.[13] (Try to count how many IMF-imposed stabilization plans have actually stimulated export-led, private-sector-led growth). The Seaga débâcle allowed the PNP to surge ahead of the JLP in the polls *at the same time* that Manley preached that the return of the PNP would mean sacrifice and not a distributive bonanza.

The very relevance of the democratic-socialist development model depends on the existence or development of political democracy in a given country.[14] It is for this reason that we have limited our discussion to Latin America and the Caribbean, the region in the Third World where democracy is most likely to take root for a variety of structural and historical conditions, the most important of which are the existence of a large working class (by Third World standards)[15] and a recent experience with highly repressive authoritarian regimes.

The parallel between Europe in the first half of this century and South America since the Second World War is instructive. In large part because of working-class pressure, all European countries made some halting moves toward democracy before the First World War. The war itself and its outcome which discredited the countries ruled by the type of authoritarian coalitions mentioned earlier in the chapter created a rush to democratic institutions (J. Stephens, 1979:112–17). In the early 1920s, 75 per cent of the countries of Europe were fully democratic politically. By a decade and a half later only 50 per cent were: all those countries which had modernized under the rule of the authoritarian coaltion (virtually the whole of Europe from Germany east and the Iberic peninsula) and, for different reasons, Italy, were ruled by authoritarian or fascist governments. The most aggressive of these regimes crashed on imperialist expansion schemes which led to a war killing tens of millions, and the regimes were further discredited by the massive internal repression they employed. Thus, where the Red Army occupation did not rule otherwise, the countries eventually became democratic. This is a tribute to the importance of two factors. On the one hand, industrial capitalism creates the conditions for mass mobilization and organization, thus creating a pressure for democracy (Rueschemeyer, 1980: 219–20). This pressure can only be resisted by highly repressive measures; yet, experience with these measures tends to delegitimize these regimes among their erstwhile supporters and, at least as important, they make the regimes' leftist opponents realize the value of political (that is, 'bourgeois') democracy. Thus, Austria, Italy, Germany and Spain emerged from the authoritarian period with a strong negative memory of the recent past which created a much stronger base for democracy. On the economic front, this often led to the development of covert or overt 'social pacts' between capital and labor (J. Stephens, 1979:127–8).[16]

Like Europe in the 1910s and 1920s, South America went through a period of popular (though not always democratic) mobilization from the mid-1930s to the mid-1950s. For a variety of reasons, now well analyzed in the debate between O'Donnell and his critics (O'Donnell, 1973; Linz and Stepan, 1978; Valenzuela, 1978; Collier, 1979) the economic elites, perceiving a developmental or social crisis, conspired with the military to end popular organization and democracy. However, again as in Europe, the cost of doing so – given the growth of the working class and other changes in the social structure since the traditional authoritarian period of the past – were much higher. Particularly in the Chilean and Argentinian case the level of repression was massive. We would argue, and we think there are signs showing this is so, that this repressive period is likely to strengthen support for democracy as democracy returns to these countries.[17] In this situation, the left is likely to find the democratic-socialist model an attractive alternative and a large enough section of the capitalist class may now find accommodation to it palatable.

If developments do move in this direction, a number of features point to much more favorable pre-conditions for democratic socialism in countries like Argentina and Brazil than in Jamaica. The large domestic market creates greater possibilities for increased self-reliance and for forward and backward integration from existing resources and industries. The economic size also increases the possibilities for diversification of trade, and the higher level of aggregate wealth of these societies opens more opportunities for direct redistribution.[18] Furthermore, these countries are less economically dependent on the USA: as Bitar (1983) shows, economic dependence on the USA in this hemisphere in all its aspects decreases strongly and directly with geographic distance from the USA. The state plays a much greater role in the economies of these countries now than it did in Jamaica in 1972, and their cultures are more distinctive from that of the USA.

In the area of movement-building the advantages of the South American countries over Jamaica are less than in the area of economic policy. Here the critical variables are labor's ideological legacy, the unity of the labor movement and the strength and ideological orientation of the parties of the left. Together these factors suggest advantages for Chile on the one end and disadvantages for Argentina (labor's ideological legacy) and Peru (division on the left) on the other end, with Brazil somewhere in between.

For one of these larger countries to take a democratic-socialist path would be very important for democratic socialism elsewhere, given the importance of the current debt situation for any government's options in the debtor countries operating under IMF agreements. The international financial community could easily let Jamaica default and then use the country as an example of the negative consequences of such an action. Brazil or Argentina would be quite another matter. This leverage, combined with a determination to bring Third World debtor-countries together for collective action, could give a government in one of the countries a chance to initiate a 'debt offensive' which would brighten the prospects for democratic socialism elsewhere. Indeed, it may be an essential pre-requisite to progress anywhere.

Notes

1 Democratic Socialism: An Alternative Path of Development?

1. In this book, the name 'Manley' used alone refers to Michael Manley. Norman Manley and other members of the Manley family will be referred to by their full name or initials and last name.

2. Obviously, not all governments profess adherence to democracy defined as a method by which rulers are chosen in periodic competitive elections (Schumpter, 1962: 269). However, those who do not do so still profess to be promoting a more meaningful type of democracy in the sense of mass participation and rule in the interest of the mass of the population.

3. This literature is too voluminous to cite in more than a highly eclectic way. Frank (1967) is representative of the original, more extreme formulations. For surveys of the literature and evaluations of different positions, see Caporaso and Zare (1981) and Munoz (1981). For crossnational data analysis testing various propositions derived from the dependency school see Bornschier *et al.* (1978) and Evans and Timberlake (1980). One of the most useful formulations and analyses of dependent development in Latin America is Cardoso and Faletto (1979). For dependency perspectives on the Caribbean, see Beckford (1972), Girvan (1976) and Payne and Sutton (1984).

4. Among the many cases of breakdowns of democracies, there is only a single example (Czechoslovakia in 1948) of a democratic regime being overthrown from the left and replaced with a revolutionary socialist regime. For a related point in reference to maximalist strategies for transition to socialism, see Chapter 9, pp 330–1.

5. Ul Haq made an early convincing case for this (1973). For a more recent discussion of strategies to meet basic human needs in Latin America, see Brudenius and Lundahl (1982).

6. To postulate greater self-reliance as a goal of development runs counter to the neo-classical economic view of the world. Certainly, we do not suggest *total* self-reliance, that is, autarchy, as a goal. Rather, we suggest that the foreign exchange constraint may make the substitution of local for imported goods worthwhile even where local production costs are somewhat higher, particularly if the goods in question are essential. Such self-reliance can protect developing countries from the effects of drastic fluctuations in exchange earnings (as mentioned in the text) as well as from politically motivated economic pressures. Even developed countries often opt for protecting higher-cost domestic production of essential goods, particularly in agriculture. Given the distortions in international markets resulting from power differentials between economic actors, the incentive for developing countries to increase self-reliance is even greater. Thus, the choice of areas for increasing self-reliance requires careful weighing of straight economic as well as political considerations.

346

7. The 'political culture' school is in general agreement that attitudinal factors, particularly feelings of political efficacy, increase political participation, see for example, Almond and Verba (1968). Nie *et al.* (1969) have shown that organization has a direct independent effect on political participation.
8. Of course, it can be argued that clearly aligned states are better able to extract concessions and expand economic co-operation with 'friendly' states. However, this argument overlooks the factor of independence. The key to gaining greater room for maneuver is diversification. Close economic relations with 'friendly' countries do not ensure stability and predictability of foreign exchange earnings; furthermore, such countries may change their minds (or rather, their governments), withdraw their concessions, and thus push the dependent country into great economic difficulties.
9. Brenner (1976, 1977) and others have effectively attacked this point of view, which is most closely associated with the names of André Gunder Frank (1967) and Immanuel·Wallerstein (1974, 1980). While agreeing with the empirical evidence presented by Brenner and other critics, we feel that the theoretical critique goes too far. The theoretical point in question is their assertion that surplus value can only be created *and* realized in the process of production not in circulation, thus exchange in commodities (international trade) cannot be a process of transfer of surplus value. The clear implication of this for Third World strategy is that one simply has to nationalize or rather just localize ownership and then one can no longer be exploited in the international economic order. (For obvious reasons, none of these authors, at least to our knowledge, has drawn out this implication.) We would argue that while surplus value can only be created in production, it can be realized in exchange. Thus, on the general point that a country can be exploited in the process of exchange, we would side with Frank and Wallerstein. All issues considered, our point of view is closest to that of Cardoso and Faletto (1979).
10. This school of analysis of the state in capitalist societies has also been called the 'new political economy' (Hollingsworth and Hanneman, 1982) the 'social democratic model' (Shalev, 1982), the 'power resources' approach (Korpi, 1983), and the 'working-class power approach' (Weir and Skocpol, 1985).

2 State, Party and Society in a Post-Colonial Plantation–Mineral Enclave Economy

1. The other distinctive feature is, understandably, the emphasis on smallness. For important contributions to this approach, see Beckford (1972), Patterson (1967), Best (1966), Girvan (1976) and the contributions to the volume edited by Girvan and Jefferson (1971).
2. See Patterson (1967) for the social structure of this period.
3. See Beckford and Witter (1980) on the development of the Jamaican race–class structure through time.
4. Garvey had launched the United Negro Improvement Association in Jamaica in 1914. However, his activities and appeals to black pride made a greater impact in the USA, from where he was deported back to Jamaica in 1927.
5. However, this legislation did not legalize peaceful picketing nor did it remove the liability for damages in case of strikes.
6. For a biography of Bustamante and an interpretation of his role in Jamaican politics and society, see Eaton (1975). Post (1978) offers an interesting discussion of Bustamante's role in his extremely well-documented work on the 1938 labor rebellion and its aftermath.

7. *Public Opinion* was launched by three young men, O. T. Fairclough, Frank Hill and H. P. Jacobs, early in 1937. See Post (1978:215ff) for a discussion of the origins and orientation of the weekly paper.

8. The National Reform Association was also founded by a group of young men, two of whom, Ken Hill (Frank Hill's brother) and Noel N. Nethersole, were later to play important roles in the PNP. See Post (1978:218ff) on the formation of the NRA.

9. Fragments of an unfinished autobiography give some insight into Manley's early years (N. W. Manley, 1971:xcv–cxii). His thinking in later years is evident in the selected speeches and writings published in the same book. Nettleford's introduction to the book (pp. xi–xciv), as well as his introductions to the various sections, provide an excellent discussion of the social and political context in which Manley's work developed.

10. N. W. Manley and Bustamante were distant cousins (a family tree is provided by Eaton, 1975:xii), and Bustamante (then Alexander Clarke) spent a year as junior overseer with the Manley family at their Belmont property (N. W. Manley, 1971:xcvii).

11. There is much speculation about the reasons for this break. The interpretations range from personality rivalry, the less-educated Bustamante wanting to outdo his brilliant cousin (Post, 1978:253), to suspicion sown by an editorial in the *Jamaica Standard*, making Bustamante fear that the PNP leadership was trying to push him to the sidelines (N. W. Manely, 1971:6), to a deal between the Governor and Bustamante that he would be released from prison on the promise that he would break the union alliance with the PNP (Munroe, 1972:23); Eaton (1975:79–84) also discusses the break.

12. All tables numbered A.1–21 are in Appendix 1.

13. Post (1981:84ff) gives a very detailed discussion of the controversy over the publication of the report.

14. See Munroe (1972:26–8) and Post (1981:113ff) for discussions of the US and the global influences on the process of constitutional decolonization in the Caribbean.

15. Under heavy pressure from the PNP right wing, the TUC finally withdrew from the World Federation of Trade Unions (WFTU) before the 1949 elections. A prominent figure among the right wing was Glasspole (who was appointed Governor-General in the 1970s) who resigned from the TUC executive in protest against its hesitation to follow the PNP executive's request for withdrawal from the WFTU. The impetus for the PNP executive's demand came from the British TUC which withdrew from the WFTU because of increasing communist influence in that organization, and which strongly urged the Jamaican TUC to follow suit. See Eaton (1975:135–50) and Munroe (1972:79–80) for a discussion of the break and the internal conflicts in the PNP.

16. A full discussion of the reasons for this change is beyond the scope of this chapter. It can certainly be regarded as pragmatic adaptation to the prevailing political currents and economic trends in the region at the time. Though socialism more or less disappeared from the public political debate, N. W. Manley himself continued to profess a socialist commitment, defined as a commitment to equality, and he argued that he did 'not find it difficult or contradictory to invite capital to Jamaica and to help and to pledge the utmost good faith in our dealings with its enterprise (N. W. Manley, 1971:90).

17. The CLC's primary purpose was to integrate the unions in the region and to form international connections, but it also got involved in wider political issues. The PNP strongly supported the development of the CLC and its

political activities. In a meeting in 1945, the CLC affirmed its support for the creation of a democratic, self-governing federation, and in 1947 a CLC conference drafted a detailed constitutional proposal.

18. Munroe (1972:88–91) provides figures for the educational and occupational background of the members of the House of Representatives and the Executive Council, which show the convergence between the two parties.

19. Manley (1975a) gives a vivid account of these organizing experiences.

20. Munroe (1972:116ff) discusses the imperial origins and the progress of the plans for a federation.

21. N. W. Manley, who was considered a highly likely candidate for this office, had decided to remain in Jamaica and continue his political work there to stop a growing anti-federation trend. See Munroe (1972:127) and Eaton (1975:170).

22. Munroe (1972:156–62) offers a very enlightening discussion of the wrangling over the entrenchment of property rights.

23. See Lewis (1950) for the classic statement of his position. Also see Lewis (1954) and (1955).

24. This section on economic development leans heavily on Jefferson (1972). Also see Palmer (1968) and Girvan (1971).

25. See the next section for a fuller analysis of the employment trends.

26. On the development of the Jamaican bauxite industry and the world context, see Girvan (1967, 1976). Also see Banks (1979), Chambers (1980), Davis (1980, 1981), Jefferson (1972), and Stephens and Stephens (1985).

27. Of course, this figure is an average; therefore, it would be lower early in the period and higher later.

28. This is the reason given by Jefferson. In fact, migration was not substantially greater in the 1950s than in the 1960s nor was population growth. It is possible that migration was more concentrated among those in the labor force in the 1950s and shifted to dependents later, but the data for the 1950s do not allow us to make this breakdown.

30. As Orlando Patterson pointed out in oral comments on a paper we presented at the Wilson Center, Jamaican society is not coterminous with the Jamaican nation.

31. The abbreviation *DN* refers to the newspaper *Jamaica Daily News*, and the date to the issue in which the referenced article appeared. To refer to *Gleaner* sources, both the *Daily Gleaner* and the *Sunday Gleaner*, we will use the abbreviation *G* and the date; *JWG* stands for *Jamaica Weekly Gleaner*, North American Edition.

32. See the section below on unions.

33. For the analytical approach to class used here, see J. Stephens (1979a, 1979b:15–38).

34. See Beckford and Witter (1980), Smith (1967) and Stone (1980:11–71) for the class structure in general. On the capitalist class, see Holzberg (1977a, 1977b), Phillips (1977), Reid (1977) and Stephens and Stephens (1983a). On the urban marginals, see Chevannes (1981), Harrison (1982) and Phillips (1981). On rural workers, see Mintz (1974).

35. Stone's (1980:51–71) discussion of the profiles of the classes makes it clear that these groups also suffer from considerable amounts of material privation.

36. The one bit of evidence indicating such a distinction came from the elite interviews carried out in 1974 and 1982 (see Appendices 2 and 4). Twenty-two and thirteen capitalists were interviewed at those dates respectively. We classified each respondent by the sector (manufacturing, tourism, finance, construction and real estate, and commerce and agriculture) in which the largest portion of his or her holdings lay. The correlation between ideology

and party preference and class segment ranged from 0.34 to 0.44. The correlations were entirely due to the contrasting positions of manufacturers (more pro-PNP, more liberal) and commerce and agriculture (more pro-JLP, more conservative). However, these sub-sample numbers are small. For example, in the case of party and sector in 1982 (the highest correlation, 0.44) the two independents and one pro-PNP capitalist among our respondents were manufacturers; thus the whole correlation was due to the position of these three people. Given the social cohesion of the class and heterogeneity of the large empires mentioned in the text, as well as the fact that we found no systematic difference between the political stance of the manufacturing association (JMA) and Chamber of Commerce during the PNP's period in office taken as a whole, we are reluctant to say more than that there may be a tendency for capitalists from various economic segments of the class to adopt segment-specific political and ideological postures. Given how much more negatively the Manley government's policies affected the commercial bourgeoisie, it is amazing that this tendency was not much more evident.

37. See, for example, Munroe (1972) and Kaplan *et al.* (1976:200–9) for basic information on constitutional provisions.

38. Mills (1974:229–34) discusses the problems of state regulation and control of private enterprises in the area of public utilities. See also Swaby (1981) for a discussion of relations between the government and the omnibus, electricity, and telephone companies.

39. In the monopoly license given to the Jamaica Telephone Company in 1967 for twenty-five years, the government insisted that no company, firm or individual could hold more than 20 per cent of the shares (Mills, 1974:231).

40. Jones (1970) and Jones and Mills (1976) discuss the continuities from colonial to post-colonial administrative structures and practices, and their negative impact on national development and popular participation.

41. Mills and Robertson (1974) offer a detailed discussion of behavioral obstacles to efficiency and innovation in the civil service.

42. Nunes (1974) explains the reasons for the decline in the status of the civil service. Besides the reasons discussed here in the text, he also mentions the increased authority of local politicians which came to overshadow that of top-level civil servants, and the expansion of the middle class which meant that a high-level civil service position no longer guaranteed an upper middle-class status.

43. Both Mills (1974) and Jones (1981a) discuss the linkages between the political parties and the private sector and the resulting constraints on the operation of the public sector.

44. For a detailed discussion of the structure and functions of the Jamaican security forces in the 1960s, see Lacey (1977:102ff).

45. The Rodney riots will be discussed later in this chapter: see pp. 56–7.

46. Stone (1980:133) presents data on the occupational background of parliamentary candidates for the JLP and the PNP in 1944 and 1976, which show that in both parties the proportion from élite professions increased from about 20 per cent to about 50 per cent, with the JLP having a higher percentage in this category than the PNP by 1976 (56 per cent versus 45 per cent). The proportion of capitalists also declined slightly, with the JLP having 15 per cent of its candidates belonging to this category compared with the PNP's 10 per cent in 1976.

47. Stone's figures (1980:135) for 1976 show that roughly 33 per cent of the activists in each party were unemployed, small farmers or working class.

Certainly, we can assume a roughly similar composition for the late 1960s.

48. Both Robertson (1972:42) and Stone (1980:124) classify the parishes by party strength.

49. Parris (1976:212–15) discusses the YSL and the resulting conflicts in the PNP, as does Lacey (1977:58).

50. Lacey (1977:87–94) offers a carefully researched analysis of the West Kingston War.

51. These figures are taken from Gonsalves (1977:93), whose main sources were reports of the Ministry of Labour. Though these figures cannot be regarded as entirely accurate, because they are ultimately based on the reports from the unions which tend to inflate their membership figures, most observers agree that 20 per cent of the labor force is a reasonable estimate of unionization.

52. Henry (1972:57) concurs with the assessment that the NWU had reached parity with the BITU by the late 1950s. The rapid growth of the NWU has to be attributed in part to the internationalism of its leaders which caused them to seek support from experienced unions abroad. The United Steel Workers of America, a union with members in the USA as well as Canada, assisted in the establishment of the NWU in the bauxite industry with advisors, organizers, finances, and research and education (Harrod, 1972:26ff).

53. This opinion was expressed to us by union leaders as well as social scientists in interviews in 1981–2. Gonsalves (1977:98) disputes the existence of such a pattern, arguing that except for the spectacular growth of the NWU in the period 1962–4, membership figures indicate a general tendency for workers to choose the union whose political ally has won the elections. However, he looks at trends from 1944 on, which of course were heavily influenced by the rise and decline of the TUC and then the setup of the NWU; thus, a 'normal' pattern could only be established in the 1960s, where he finds more support for the thesis. Furthermore, observers speak of a trend, not of massive swings, which would be more visible in the results of representational rights polls, for instance, than in marked fluctuations of membership figures.

54. For a discussion of Peruvian practice and references to the practice in Mexico and Brazil, see E. Stephens (1980:183–6); for a discussion of the political aspects of labor relations typical for developing countries, see Millen (1963).

55. In trying to put a data series on work stoppages together, we found considerable discrepancies between the *Statistical Yearbooks*, the *Economic and Social Surveys*, and Parris (1976:198). When we questioned experts in Jamaica about these discrepancies and the general reliability of the data, they told us that the data collection is deficient in that essentially only reported work stoppages are recorded and many stoppages never get reported.

56. Ross and Hartman (1960:65) found in their comparative fifteen-nation study that rival unionism was conducive to high militancy. To emphasize the importance of union rivalry for the high militancy of Jamaican workers is not to claim that most strikes were caused by raiding and representational rights disputes. The figures on causes of work stoppages (see, for example, Gonsalves, 1977:97) for what they are worth, indicate that wage disputes were by far the most important cause, followed by dismissals and suspensions. According to many businessmen, union leaders, and observers, the immediate cause of strikes was mostly employer-arrogance. However, union rivalry created the climate for militant reaction of workers to employer-arrogance and for the frequent use of the strike weapon by unions in wage disputes.

57. These 'secrets of good industrial relations' were emphasized to us by several businessmen, union leaders, and observers. Their general consensus was that

it was quite possible for employers to have good labor relations, if only they exercised the necessary care and did not indulge in arrogant behavior towards workers.

58. The National Dance Theater Company was also important in promoting Jamaican culture, though its reach was much more limited than reggae. For a valuable discussion of culture, development and the race question, see Nettleford (1970, 1978).

59. It should be noted that Edward Seaga was an exception in the JLP government in that as Minister-in-charge of Development, Welfare and Culture (before he switched to Finance) he aggressively promoted Jamaican national culture with an emphasis on its African roots.

60. See Owens (1976) for a presentation of Rastafarian beliefs. Also see Nettleford (1970:39–113) for a discussion of Rastafari in Jamaica and the reaction of the middle and upper classes to it.

61. One member of the PNP secretariat cautioned us that one should not exaggerate how many people actually get patronage on housing or jobs, even including temporary work. If one's own party wins it might be only a 1-in-5 or even a 1-in-10 chance. However, if the other party wins there is no chance. Moreover, if one includes the indirect benefits via friends, relatives, and neighbors, which is quite important given the Jamaican lower class tradition of 'share pot' (that is, sharing one's dinner with the neighbors in the tenement), which party wins does affect a significant number of people.

62. See Lacey (1977:94–9) for a description of events around the Rodney riots.

63. Lacey (1977:56–60) discusses these various groups and political currents; see also Parris (1976).

64. This is hardly an exhaustive list of even the most important obstacles to socialist transformation in democratic capitalist societies. See J. Stephens (1979b) and Stephens and Stephens (1980) for our view on this question.

65. We compare strategic problems faced by movements in advanced and dependent capitalist societies at length in Stephens and Stephens (1980). A first draft of the final chapter of this book attempted a sustained comparison but it proved too ambitious. This is the topic of work now in progress.

3 The PNP's First Term: Tasks at the Outset and Populist Politics in the First Years 1972–4

1. However, even if the party had won the popular vote, the gerrymandering of districts by the JLP government made it unlikely that the PNP would have attained a majority of seats.

2. Norman Manley died a few months later. Though there is little doubt that the transition from the elder to the younger Manley profoundly affected the PNP, it is important to note that the themes that Michael Manley emphasized and developed as PNP leader were a continuation of the concerns his father began to express in his last years. The failure of the Puerto Rican model, especially the growing inequality, became his central concern. For example, see his farewell speech to the PNP (N. W. Manley, 1971:368–84).

3. Socialism as an ideology was not emphasized in this book because the party was not yet prepared to unveil its new ideological definition.

4. For example, see the speech by Leslie Ashenheim reported in *Public Opinion* (10 December 1981).

5. We are relying on the reading of the *Gleaner* in its entirety (not just the front page as for the rest of the period) day by day for January and February 1972.

In the 1972 campaign, both parties spent tremendous amounts of money on newspaper advertising. In 1976, there was a marked shift to the use of electronic media to carry out the campaign.

6. The blasphemy issues stemmed from (unwelcome) support for the PNP by a Rastafari-influenced preacher and convicted traitor, Claudius Henry. Through a complicated set of events involving misunderstandings on all sides, the Jamaica Council of Churches ran advertisements (paid for by the PNP) condemning the JLP's action on the issue. This led to a public perception that the churches were 'clearly pro-PNP partisan' (Stone, 1974:19), and it probably increased the strength of the popular wave which the PNP rode its first two years in office.

7. See Manley (1975b:247–52) on the crime problem and the development of the Gun Court and related legislation.

8. The mandatory indefinite detention sentence was later declared unconstitutional. It should be noted that it was up to the discretion of a board as to how long the detention period would last. In some cases, such as illegal possession of a firearm (or in one case two bullets) the detention period was in fact very short, often only a few months.

9. These were not the only nationalizations accomplished by the Manley government. For example, sugar factories, half the hotels, the cement company, the flour mill and shares in the bauxite companies came into public ownership.

10. The Manley government's bauxite policy is dealt with at length in Stephens and Stephens (1985).

11. This was reported in the *Gleaner* (20 April 1974) and confirmed in our interviews with aluminum company executives.

12. This information and that on the treatment of Alcan mentioned above in the paragraph stems from one of our confidential interviews conducted in the spring of 1982 in Jamaica. Subsequently, we will refer to this material, described in Appendix 2, as 'confidential interview', or 'interview with actor from category X'.

13. In the 1974 elite study, fourteen of the twenty-two capitalists mentioned the bauxite policy as 'one of the three most important pieces of legislation' passed since Jamaican independence, adding that they favored it. Only two opposed it and another two were equivocal. The remaining four did not mention it. The bauxite policy was the most popular piece of legislation with the elite at the time of the study; 54 per cent favored it, while only 7 per cent opposed it or were equivocal about it.

14. The ratings of the ideology of cabinet members is based on interviews with eighteen of the thirty cabinet ministers done in 1974 and 1982, public statements of the ministers appearing in the paper and ratings done for us by two members of the PNP executive for most of the Manley government.

15. Confidential interviews with PNP leaders.

16. Confidential interview.

17. See Appendix 3 for the methodology used in these codings.

18. For a sustained treatment of the relationship between the PNP government and the Jamaican capitalist class, see Stephens and Stephens (1983a).

19. Another action concerning a 'not strictly business' issue, which was an indication of the depth of fear felt by the upper classes (capitalists and the managerial–professional class), especially the white segments, at the rising crime rate, was a telegram protesting the wave of gun terrorism, which Meeks sent to Manley in early 1974.

20. The information here on the migration process was acquired through an interview with Michael Carpenter, US Consul General in Jamaica and a

specialist in US immigration, and a consular officer in the Canadian High Commission.

21.   A respondent was coded as ultra-conservative if, in response to our questions about the role of the state in the economy, he/she responded that he/she favored development led by the private sector, minimal public ownership, divestiture of virtually all state enterprises including public utilities and very limited social programs, usually only education and others, and 'only if we can afford them'.

22.   We are not denying the importance of the social and political analyses promoted by academics and younger PNP members; we are simply arguing that among the top-level political directorate only Manley saw the policies in a wider context.

4   The First Term: Ideological Definition and Social Polarization 1974

1.   There is an alternative interpretation of the PNP's adoption of democratic socialism to the one offered here. Some influential observers have argued that the PNP's ideological self-definition was nothing but an attempt to rationalize and popularize the policies they were forced to implement by the economic problems which they encountered. The argument holds that the deteriorating balance-of-payments situation forced import restrictions and a greater role of the public sector on the government, and that the government then felt a need to introduce an ideology based on self-reliance, egalitarianism, and popular mobilization for nation-building. The obvious weakness in this argument is that Manley's push for ideological definition began right after the election, well before the economic difficulties in question were encountered.

2.   Manley (1982:128) relates the following anecdote: During a meeting in a rural parish an important local PNP politician explained to the audience that there was nothing to fear as socialism meant that 'you will pay a little more to the maid in your home'.

3.   See Chapter 9 for our argument on this point. One university-based PNP advisor argued to us, correctly we think, that, given this difficulty, the PNP lacked the intellectual equipment effectively to elaborate such an ideology at this time.

4.   See Chapter 5 for a sustained discussion of PNP internal disputes.

5.   Sources for the data in this paragraph are IBRD (1976), OECD (1975), IDB (1977, 1978). See also Bernal (1980) for an analysis of government borrowing from international commercial banks.

6.   Senator Ian Ramsay in State-of-the-Nation debate (*G*, 2 November 1974).

7.   See Stephens and Stephens (1983a) for a detailed version of this analysis of the 1974 data.

8.   Given that crime was a motivating factor in much of this migration behavior, it is ironic that the destiny of many of these Jamaicans was the Miami area. The *Uniform Crime Reports for the United States* shows the murder rate increasing from 18.3 per 100 000 in 1975 to 32.7 per 100 000 in 1980 in the Miami *SMSA*. A comparison of the figures with those in Table A.7 shows that the murder rate in Miami was higher than in Jamaica in all years except the election year of 1980. The perception of the crime problem was quite different and in this regard the *Gleaner* played a key role in frightening people. The paper's behavior in 1981 and 1982 is instructive. It played down the issue and thus the perception was of less crime despite the fact that there was as much crime as in the Manley years (except 1980).

9.   See Stephens and Stephens (1983a) for an explanation of the strengths and

weaknesses of the 1982 data and for the analysis on which the following remarks are based.

10. Respondents were coded as 'moderate conservatives' if they favored development led by the private sector but approved of public ownership of the utilities and believed that services provided by government should include education, health care and old age insurance (NIS).

11. Actually, a law concerning declaration of foreign assets had been on the books for many years but had never been enforced. By November, a total of $70m in foreign assets had been declared (*G*, 6 November 1974), but this was clearly only a fraction, as the Federal Reserve Bank of New York reported that $39m were held by Jamaicans in about 4000 US commercial banks alone (*DN*, 26 September 1974). If one adds to this the other 10 000 banks in the USA and holdings in real estate, etc., the total assets certainly have to be estimated at more than $70m.

12. The Labour Advisory Council had been enlarged in November 1973 to include representatives from JALGO, the Jamaica Civil Service Association, the Master Builders' Association of Jamaica and the Associated Chambers of Commerce, in addition to the previous members NWU, BITU, TUC and JEF (*G*, 11 November 1973).

13. For a discussion of the sugar cooperatives, see Chapter 8, E. Stephens (1984), and Feuer (1983; 1984).

14. How biased the media as a whole were against the government's policies was pointed out by Manley in a speech to the Press Association of Jamaica in December 1975. He noted that there were twenty-nine regular contributors to opinion formation in the *Gleaner*, the *Daily News*, JBC and RJR, of whom nineteen were clearly conservative, two non-ideological, seven progressive and one defying classification, which meant that the score was 3:1 against progress, in the context of a society in search of progress (*G*, 13 December 1975).

15. Our observations in this and subsequent discussions of US policy are based primarily on interviews with ten State Department and foreign service officials who worked closely on US relations with Jamaica.

16. Stone (1980:52–4) classifies 0.5 per cent of the population as capitalists and 7.5 per cent as upper-middle-class professionals and property owners, a majority of whom had incomes above $150 per week in late 1977, whereas only 6 per cent of the lower-middle- and working-class had incomes above this level.

17. That the State of Emergency had wide popular support can be seen in a poll conducted in October/November 1976 in which over 80 per cent of respondents in the Corporate area and parish towns supported its extension (Stone, 1980:174).

18. In 1978, the JLP and the *Gleaner* were to revive the bizarre story of this man, Albert 'Spy' Robinson, and to start a massive campaign charging corrupt political use of the State of Emergency. What speaks against this charge is that the security forces detained people who were involved in violent activities regardless of party affiliation; in the first week, ten PNP and fourteen JLP supporters were detained, according to the Minister of National Security (*G* 26 June 1976). And in his book about his experience in detention, Pearnel Charles (1977), a JLP Senator, describes how adherents of the two parties had to be physically separated into different tents at the camp where they were detained, in order to prevent violence between them (Charles, 1977:50–1). And an inquiry conducted by the Chief Justice whose report was

published in 1981 came to the conclusion that there was no corrupt use of the State of Emergency for political purposes (*G*, 24–28 August 1981).

19. We expected people associated with the administration at the time to deny the existence of any CIA operation, even if one had existed. What we found convincing about the statements of the four people in question was: (1) they were Carter Administration appointees; (2) they were hostile to covert action; (3) three of the four expressed a general dislike for Kissinger's policies; (4) three of the four are no longer in the public service and thus are not motivated by protecting their State Department careers, and (5) they volunteered this information; (since they were Carter administration officials we did not probe as deeply into the previous period). The increase in US intelligence personnel in the embassy does not contradict this as it is unlikely that covert-action agents would be provided with diplomatic cover.

20. O'Flaherty (1978), a former aide to the Senate Committee on Select Intelligence, suggests that this is the case.

21. This statement is based on breakdowns of crime rates by parish for 1979 and 1982, when the national crime rates were about the same as 1976. Unfortunately, this data is not publicly available and we were only able to get the 1979–82 data and then only indirectly through a third party.

22. In addition to allegations about US government action there were some directed against the bauxite companies, alleging that they reduced production in Jamaica for political reasons, that is, to punish the government for the levy (for example, see Girvan *et al.*, 1980:145). This is an exceedingly complex question, but the bulk of the evidence does not support this allegation (see Stephens and Stephens, 1985). Due to the specialization of alumina refineries on bauxite from a given location (and thus of a certain grade and with specific chemical qualities) such rapid shifts in production were not possible.

23. C. L. R. James said of this speech: 'I would like to say that in fifty years of political activity and interest in all sorts of politics, I have never heard or read a speech more defiant of oppression and in every way more suitable to its purpose' (Beckford and Witter 1980:92).

24. We counted the advertising space in the *Gleaner* and the *Daily News* used by the two parties in the election campaign, as part of our detailed analysis of election themes and strategies.

25. In October 1981, the *Gleaner* alone had a readership of some 321 000, as opposed to the *Daily News* with 81 000 (Market Research Services, Ltd:1982).

26. Both the JLP and the PNP 1976 election manifestoes are reprinted in Stone and Brown (1981:275–98).

27. In the whole advertising campaign in the *Gleaner* and the *Daily News*, the PNP focused predominantly on the themes of achievement and further progress, whereas the campaign attack themes received less emphasis; the former were the subject of fifty-two of the full page advertisements, the latter of twenty-four while thirteen of these advertisements had other themes.

28. Regulation 15 of the State of Emergency Regulations stated:

No person shall publish either orally or in writing any report or statement (whether true or false) which is intended or is of such a nature as to be likely to be prejudicial to the public safety, or to incite or provoke any person to commit a breach of the peace or contravene any provision these Regulations or any order made or any notice given thereunder.

29. Stone (1980: 153) also performed an ecological analysis which confirmed the class polarization that occurred in the 1976 voting patterns.

30. See note 22 above.
31. Retrospectively, all the PNP government's conservative critics point to this economic package as the beginning of massive overspending and wasting of public resources. As we have documented (see pp. 114; 117 and 121), they were basically supportive of the government's economic policy at the time, and, in fact, attacks on the government for 'mismanagement' in this period were the lowest of any other period in the PNP government's two terms in office except during the honeymoon in the first few months of the first term (Table A.3).
32. Some Jamaicans on the left have argued, retrospectively, that this was a concession to the commercial bourgeoisie and the middle classes. This may be true, but it was probably not clear to the political directorate of the PNP that a choice between different options was being made. At the time, the PNP left was not pushing for the option emphasizing state-sector investment for which we argue here. Moreover, from the point of view of our argument, it is critical that the PNP could have put a viable class coalition together behind the policies suggested. The consumer-goods import restrictions were in the interests of small farmers and manufacturers, and a small liberal segment of the bourgeoisie actually favored a much greater emphasis on state-sector investment. One capitalist from this segment told us that he warned Manley about the error of opting for more consumer-imports and distributive policies rather than restrictions and state-sector investment at this time.
33. However, it must be emphasized here that this does not mean that the options were closed for political reasons in 1974 in the same way that they were in 1977. In 1974, clear perception of the situation on the part of Manley, Coore and a few others could have resulted in a different set of decisions. The total package of the 1977 non-IMF plan would not have been possible (it was too radical for 1974 conditions), but significant features of it (including, above all, more state sector investment and less emphasis on distributive programs, as well as CEO development, use of local raw materials, and emphasis on domestic agriculture) would have been possible.

5   The Second Term: The Rise and Fall of the Left Alternative, 1977

1. It is unclear how committed the government was at this point. Henry, a PNP organizer (later Senator and Deputy General Secretary) and confidant of Duncan, indicates that the government was fairly committed. She cites a letter dated 11 December from Brown (who had just come from a meeting with IMF officials) to Coore laying out a time-table leading to an agreement which included the closing of foreign exchange transactions on 20 December. This was in fact done on that date (Henry, 1980:20). Manley (1982:152) contends that the talks were being resumed and that no commitment had been made.
2. The information in this paragraph is based on interviews with actors involved and on Henry (1980).
3. The three banks which were later nationalized were Barclay's, Citizens, and Montreal. Together they accounted for 29 per cent of the total assets of all Jamaican banks.
4. In his preface to the plan, Girvan specifically mentions the staffs of ten ministries, government agencies and statutory boards as having been deeply involved in developing and writing the plan.
5. The information in this paragraph is based on an interview with a PNP advisor. Our informant told us that the establishment of a republic and

modification of the property clause, particularly with regard to the compensation paid for compulsory acquisition of land, were the main items on the PNP internal agenda. In addition, they favored the institution of 'offices of confidence' at the top of the bureaucracy. That is, they wanted to be able to appoint political appointees to the top bureaucratic post in each ministry, a sharp departure from the traditional Whitehall model. They also favored a popularly-elected executive presidency with broad powers, abolition of the Senate, a change in the representational system to a combination of geographical and proportional representation, and entrenching the right to an education in the constitution. The PNP leadership (with a few notable exceptions), also favored electoral reform. It was originally thought that the whole matter of constitutional reform could be disposed of within two years. The reason the PNP leadership did not reveal its own agenda was that it felt that the JLP was behaving so opportunistically that they would jump on any PNP proposal, distort it and then use it for all the political mileage they could get.

6.   See Henry (1980) for a discussion of decision-making in the PNP.

7.   These observations are based on an interview with a PNP Minister.

8.   Henry (1980:51–3) indicates that these overtures were directly related to US concerns that, in not taking the IMF route as it then appeared, the government might become more deeply entangled in the Socialist Bloc as an alternative. We brought up her contention in several of our state-department interviews. The direct link was doubted but our respondents made no mistake that encouraging IMF agreements was US policy. There would also be a concern about a turn to the Soviet Bloc, but seeking assistance from other Third World countries was not problematic.

9.   As previously mentioned, the PNP intended to use the electoral reform issue as a bargaining chip in the discussion about constitutional change. The party was opposed to placing the police out of the control of elected officials.

10.   This squares with Stone's (1980:168) argument that the PNP may have gained two or three seats because of illegal practices. It seems unlikely that the JLP leadership believed their own charge that the election was stolen. The fact that they filed only twelve petitions, that they followed up only on one, the poll results, and the fact that the *Gleaner* (9 April 1977; 24 August 1977) did not think so, all point in this direction. It is probably fair to say that in Jamaica, only the JLP faithful put any credence in the party's charge that the election had been stolen. Unfortunately, it might not have been so difficult to convince people abroad.

11.   Housing Minister Spaulding had argued that the rent strikes and the housing occupations were orchestrated by Seaga and his cronies to undermine his ministry and the government as a whole. Interestingly, Seaga refused to testify. Other JLP spokesmen argued that the reason why the tenants were in arrears was that the rental office was in a PNP zone and the JLP tenants were often harrassed when they went to pay rent. For this reason, the JLP spokesmen contended, the tenants were advised by the JLP to stop paying rent.

12.   It was in this period that a rumor was widely circulated – and believed – in the Jamaican community in Miami that Manley would announce the introduction of communism in Jamaica.

13.   It was well-known both that the UWI team was working on the plan and that their political orientation was left-wing.

14.   Later in 1977, land capture did become a significant movement.

15. For instance, on 22 April, an article by the *Gleaner* Business Reporter entitled 'How the Economic Crunch Hits Workers', appeared. It began with a theoretical exposition on how import restrictions hurt production but without referring to any concrete case. Then, a letter to the editor from a group of workers but signed by only one worker was cited. The article ended with an admission by the author that they were unable to contact the company in question to verify the contentions made in the letter! The *Gleaner's* overtly propagandistic use of the paper, particularly the 'news' columns became so bad that the Council of Ministers (the Cabinet and Ministers of State) issued an official criticism of a page 1 article by 'Economic Analyst', complaining of inaccuracies and illogical conclusions. The Council also noted that this was at least the seventh time since January that the Prime Minister or other ministers felt forced to complain about *Gleaner* reports.

16. The idea of the CEO is typical of the grass-roots participatory socialism which runs through Beckford's thought. For example see Chapter 10 in Beckford and Witter (1980).

17. There is a discrepancy in the estimates of job-loss at two different points in the summary of the plan made available to us. One indicates a gain of only 20 000 jobs in agriculture under the $600m budget (p. 72) resulting in a net loss of 8000 jobs. The other figure (cited in the text) indicates a gain of 36 000 jobs (p. 118). Unfortunately, we could not locate (in 1982) a copy of the full text of the employment task-force. In fact, the only full task-force report we were able to locate was agriculture. The summary report made available to us by one of the planners and cited here as Beckford *et al.* (1978) is a typeset version of the report. It was never printed and contains many typographical errors which is probably the source of the discrepancy. The figures we have used in the text are those which seem the most consistent with the rest of the plan and actual employment figures.

18. Our source on this is an insider who would definitely be in a position to know that such contacts were made and the content of the discussions themselves. The person is very pro-Manley in his point of view and so might tend to justify Manley's actions, but on balance we believe we were given correct information.

19. This figure is given in Henry (1980:62) referring to manufacturing only. Manley gave the same figure without referring to a specific sector (*DN*, 28 April 1977). The figure of 40 000 jobs in manufacturing is certainly too high since only 75 000 people were employed in this sector. Another 36 000 people were employed in construction so it is possible that the foreign exchange constraints could have resulted in a loss of 50 000 jobs overall but the planners' figure of 33 000 seems more reasonable. See note 17.

20. Henry (1980:61) contends that the decision was influenced by the mobilization of private sector pressure, but as we have pointed out, the timing of the decision makes this seem unlikely. Moreover, though the 'parentage' may have been considered suspect (see the text), it is very unlikely that more than a few, if any, capitalists were aware of the actual content of the plan. Indeed, upon discussing the plan with a private-sector-point man in the cabinet, it became clear to us that he had no idea what was proposed. On the other hand, Henry's contention that Manley consulted Mayer Matalon with the logic that if Matalon, as a representative of the most liberal section of capital, could not be convinced, then the plan would not work, is probably correct as Manley did keep in close contact with Matalon on such matters. But again, it is unlikely that Matalon read the plan, so the bottom line, we would argue, is

what Manley's assessment of the economic impact of the two alternatives
would be *and* what the political reactions of various social forces to the
economic repercussion would be.

21. It might be worth pointing out that, in our estimation, based on the experience of the $300m Bank of Jamaica accommodation for the 1976–77 budget,
inflation-induced cuts in living standards would not have been anything like
the cuts caused by the devaluation of the Jamaican dollar from US$1.10 in
March 1977 to US$0.56 in June 1979.

22. The left has charged that the slow development of trade with the Eastern Bloc
was a product of purposeful foot-dragging on the part of Patterson, citing for
instance one incident in the Spring of 1977 when he kept a Cuban Sovietolo-
gist, who was brought in to advise Jamaica on trade development with the
USSR, waiting for two weeks before seeing him. It may be true that, in
general, trade with the Socialist Bloc was not pursued as vigorously as it
should have been, but very reliable sources told us that this was not so in the
case of alumina, Jamaica's most marketable commodity. The alumina deal
with the USSR was consistently pursued but did not materialize for several
years.

23. The little that the Manley government did in this respect was counterproductive; see Chapter 8.

24. The original agricultural task force report estimated necessary acreage as
being 44 000.

25. The first announcement of the STC indicated that *all* importing would be
taken over by the government. This was quickly changed to the position
indicated in the text. Because of IMF demands, the STC was eventually
limited to JNH, building materials, and pharmaceuticals and medical supplies. See Chapter 6.

26. It is unknown whether the poisoning was related to internal party politics,
politics in general, or whether it was unrelated to policits. There is little doubt
that it was widely believed that there was a plot by the left against Manley,
and it can be verified that the *Gleaner* columnists propagated the view that
such a plot existed. It seems extremely unlikely to us that such a plot, in fact,
did exist, for the simple reason that the left was acutely aware of its own
numerical inferiority to the moderates and of its dependence on Manley's
support to achieve anything. Whether Duncan's allegation that the right
purposely generated the rumor to attack him is correct or whether the rumor
had some other origin (in the opposition, spontaneous generation through
the rumor mill because of the left's high profile in early 1977) is unclear.

27. There is some ambiguity as to how this event should be interpreted. We have
given the standard interpretation here. One rightist cabinet minister confirmed this: 'we (the moderates) were about to regain control of the party and
Michael intervened to protect the left'. However, one leading leftist told us:
'The YO had a candidate, Desmond Leakey, who wasn't really a left-winger
and the Women's Movement also had a candidate who was also a moderate,
and only one of them could win . . . [Beverly Manley's] speech was perceived
by the YO as an election speech and [she] was booed. The Women's
Movement was determined not to give up their candidate and this led to a
clash . . . tempers were high . . . so the election was postponed. The left
gave support to the YO candidate though he wasn't left-wing and not even
young'. The *Gleaner* reports (11, 18 September, 1977) for what they are
worth, support the standard view, since according to these reports the
withdrawal of Spaulding and Leakey, both supported by the left, was the

event that led to the postponing of the elections. The defeat of Spaulding, who was an incumbent, would have been a blow to the left.

28. The NEC, the president and the vice-presidents are elected by the conference. The party executive and the other officers (chairman, deputy chairman, general secretary, and deputy general secretary) are elected by the NEC.

29. The advice for moderation is similar to that given by the Cubans to the Sandinista government in Nicaragua.

30. Initially some PNP leaders were reluctant to talk to us about this topic as they attempted to keep up a veneer of greater party unity than, in fact, existed, but we did eventually get reliable information which we were able to cross-check from several sources. Our sources for the content of the debates were six interviews with top PNP leaders, all of them members of the party executive for extended periods of time, and one lengthy post-election analysis laying out the centrist position by a leading PNP moderate. Our eight interviews with PNP 'elites' in 1982 also yielded considerable information relevant both to the debates and to the respondents' personal stance on key questions of economic ideology and foreign policy.

31. The question of the role of the state could be and was fudged by referring to 'ownership and/or control'. See Chapter 6.

32. All these points of division could be called ideology in some sense of the word.

33. See Thomas (1978) for a succinct summary of the non-capitalist path. We will argue that the non-capitalist path model is not applicable to Jamaica. See Chapter 9.

34. Charles was released on 2 April 1977.

35. Obviously, this charge was not without its irony, given the role which the Cubans did play in PNP internal politics.

36. See Lewis (1982) for an extended discussion of the contents and implications of this speech.

37. The allegation about the constitutional revision was that the voter would only vote for the Community Council which, in turn, would elect the parish council which, in turn, would elect the House. This allegation was widely circulated and believed. For example, see a speech by a PSOJ spokesman (*G*, 3 December 1977). In fact, the PNP had no such plan.

38. It is quite obvious that the youths came back from Cuba with a very positive view of the country and its ideology, but a reliable source close to the program told us that this was largely a result of osmosis facilitated by the availability of literature. Thus it did not go beyond what any host country (including the USA) would do to give exchange students a positive view of the country. In this case the ideology was more controversial. Moreover, even an examination of the public evidence indicates that it is unlikely that the construction workers were forced to take formalized courses on Marxism–Leninism and so on, as implied by the JLP. In that case it would seem certain that the JLP would be able to get at least one of the 1400 Jamaican youths who went to Cuba in the programs to level such a charge. They were unable to do this. This argument also applies to the JLP's subsequent charge that the Brigadistas were trained in guerrilla warfare. One observation that might be made on this topic of the ideological influence of the visit to Cuba is that its effect was certainly magnified by the lack of ideological education received by the youths from the PNP itself before they went.

39. The quotation from the letter, once in context, did not support Seaga's allegations.

40. Reportedly, a pen name for *Gleaner* editor Hector Wynter.

41.   For instance, on 3 June, it ran a headline on the bottom part of the front page spanning six columns: 'Gunman on Rampage in St Andrew'. The article was about three robberies in a two-week period.
42.   Arnett was so closely identified with the PNP that he was known as 'Mr PNP'. Arnett was a man of very high scruples and declined to take advantage of his position, even honestly, to enrich himself. The appointment was reportedly an attempt on Manley's part to make Arnett's modest retirement a little more comfortable. So Glasspole's passing over Arnett was a real slap in the face to an old colleague.
43.   See p. 172.
44.   It is not completely clear what the goal, in fact, was. The People's Plan set the figure at 36 000. Manley (1977) did not mention a specific goal for the whole sector. The EPP Progress Report, while repeating the People's Plan figure, estimated that putting 36 000 acres into production as envisaged by the EPP would result in the employment of 20 000 people. This seems like a more reasonable figure given the cutbacks of acreage to be put into production from the People's Plan to the EPP.
45.   This is the version of events given by Girvan *et al.* (1980). Sharpley (1983:246) claims that the country also failed the outstanding foreign arrears and net foreign assets tests.

6   The Second Term: The Struggle with the IMF

1.   Unless otherwise noted, all the figures in this discussion of the IMF agreement are drawn from IBRD (1978).
2.   This opinion, for instance, was communicated to us in an interview by a former PNP Minister.
3.   A telegram from the head of the IMF team to the Bank of Jamaica, which was published by the government and reprinted in Girvan *et al.* (1980:126–7) stated that the executive directors of the IMF fully realized Jamaica's 'need for additional external financial assistance beyond amounts being provided by the IMF and World Bank . . . [and the] importance of quick disbursing assistance from friendly countries'.
4.   For an excellent discussion of Jamaica's foreign policy in the PNP's second term, see Lewis (1982).
5.   Bernal (1981) gives an overview of the development of Jamaica's relations with countries in the Eastern bloc.
6.   See pp. 234–6 below for a discussion of US policy toward Jamaica in this period and up to the 1980 election.
7.   For Manley's own account of his speech and its subsequent repercussions, see Manley (1982:175–178).
8.   The most important of these inquiries dealt with the JLP charges that the State of Emergency had been used corruptly. The Chief Justice issued a long report in July 1981, finding no evidence to substantiate the charges. The report was published in the *Gleaner* between 24 and 28 August 1981.
9.   The 'beggar leader' attack appears rather ironic in retrospect, given that Seaga borrowed more money abroad in his first two years in office than the PNP had borrowed in eight years.
10.   For instance, in a debate in the House in March 1978, while the government was negotiating with the IMF, Seaga correctly predicted the outline of the IMF agreement which was officially announced in May, and severely criti-

cized the government for its insistence on a political direction which was destroying the economy (*G*, 16 March 1978).

11. This demonstration, of course, was further used to bolster allegations that the government was 'under their (the Cubans) thumb', that Estrada was Manley's tutor and boss, and that Fidel was 'Michael's master and Michael Fidel's Uncle Tom', and so on (G, 28 September 1979; 2 October 1979).

12. It is interesting to note that the JLP included bogus elections in their scenario of a 'military solution', rather than predicting a seizure of power through a coup. This suggests that the JLP was quite convinced that the PNP would not deviate from the electoral path.

13. A good example of this is the layout of the paper on the day after Easter Sunday in 1979 (*G*, 16 April 1979). At the top of the front page, near the center, was a large picture of an Easter service at a major Kingston church. The headline under the picture read 'Churchmen urged to form alliance against Communism'. The article, however, was about a Senate debate the previous week in which Pearnel Charles, a JLP Senator, urged such an action.

14. This propaganda was so strong and skillful that Fred Landis, a North American political scientist who had served as a consultant to the US Senate Sub-committee holding hearings on the CIA's involvement in Chile, built a case for CIA involvement in the campaign against the PNP, based on an analogy to the kinds of propaganda techniques used by *El Mercurio* during the Allende years in Chile. He testified to the Press Association of Jamaica, claiming that the kinds of techniques used by the *Gleaner* amounted to psychological warfare and indicated to him that the CIA was financing the *Gleaner*, having basically 'opted for a military solution'. His documented comparisons with *El Mercurio*, which were published by the Press Association of Jamaica, were indeed impressive, but how he could establish CIA involvement with the *Gleaner* by the similarity of its propaganda techniques to *El Mercurio*, much less that the techniques involved showed that the CIA had 'opted for a military solution' is beyond us. These allegations in his testimony were so poorly supported by evidence that they have to be considered irresponsible.

15. Seaga continued to urge the WFM to play a crucial role in the process of getting rid of the government (*G*, 9 October 1978). Certainly, the example of Chile, where women had proved to be a very visible and active component of the opposition movement, was enticing. The 'march of the empty pots' and the demonstrations of officers' wives in front of the house of General Prats, urging him to resign, were important factors in the political dynamics of the Up period. However, the JLP's mobilization efforts fell far short of such results. The same was true for the Higglers Association. Higglers are the street vendors who perform a crucial function in the food distribution system in Jamaica. Thus, it would have been a great political asset for the JLP if it had been able effectively to mobilize and influence the higglers. However, the association never really came to function effectively.

16. This, of course, stands in stark contrast to the situation in the presidential system in Chile, where the opposition had a parliamentary majority and its constitutional powers enabled it to block important legislation.

17. It is interesting to note in this regard that *none* of the JLP leaders we interviewed in 1982 mentioned close ties with Cuba or communist leanings as a major failure of the PNP. See Table 8.1 p. 289.

18. Interview with a PNP Minister.

19. Actually, emigration of professional and technical personnel in 1978 was still

below the level of the late 1960s, with 1400 professional and technical people emigrating to the USA and Canada, but it showed a clear increase over the mid-1970s and in 1979 it reached the level of 1968 and 1969, with 2000 people in this category emigrating (Tables A. 4–5).

20.   For an excellent discussion of the reasons underlying the attempt to reform the administrative machinery, of the fall-out of this attempt, and of the whole issue of 'politicization versus neutrality' of the state bureaucracy, see Jones (1981a, b). We will discuss the Civil Service Commission and its procedures in some detail in Chapter 8.

21.   In 1975, a similarly steep increase in representational rights disputes occurred; we can interpret this also as a response to economic austerity measures, namely the package introduced in August and October of that year. This package did not really affect workers much, but it dramatized the problems in the economy and provoked harsh attacks from the opposition, which projected the image of a government under pressure.

22.   Unfortunately, reliable data on union membership are not available since all the blanket unions inflate their membership figures. However, most participants and observers agree that the NWU represented more workers than the BITU in the first half of the 1970s and that their relative strength was reversed by the end of the 1970s.

23.   Before that, the Minister of Labor could only refer a dispute to the IDT if both parties agreed to it, except for disputes in essential services. The list of services regarded as essential was subject to parliamentary approval. Under the new legislation, the Minister could refer disputes to the IDT on his own initiative. The IMF originally wanted the legislation to force the IDT to make their awards within the guidelines. Minister of Labor Isaacs told them that this would unite the unions for the first time since 1938 and might result in a general strike, and that he personally would resign. The IMF then relented, which resulted in the compromise outlined in the text. (Information based on interview with a PNP Minister.)

24.   The IDT sometimes made awards above the guidelines, particularly in some much publicized cases, which created a public perception of the government's inability to enforce wage restraint. However, these awards were not much above the guidelines at all; on the whole, wage increases exceeded the 15 per cent limit set by the 1978 IMF agreement by a 1–2 per cent margin only. (Interviews with a PNP Minister and with an expert in areas of labor relations.) It is worth noting here that the competitive nature of the Jamaican labor movement made it extremely difficult to enforce a policy of wage restraint and that it was only the external (IMF) pressure which forced the government to incur the political costs of and the unions to comply with the enforcement of the policy. Failure to follow the guidelines would have resulted in further IMF imposed devaluations and thus erosion of any wage increases.

25.   Institutionalized consultation took the form, for instance, of an advisory council to the Ministry of Labor with representation of all major and even some minor unions, of a tripartite National Planning Committee set up in 1978 and of a special tripartite committee appointed in the same year to deal with all lay-offs.

26.   This authoritarianism and lack of trust among workers in the union leadership is the second of the two major reasons for the high number of wildcat strikes in Jamaica. The most important reason which, according to a highly placed person in the Ministry of Labor, accounts for 60–70 per cent of wildcat

strikes, is management attitudes and behavior, such as resistance to dealing with grievances, rash and unexplained actions, etc.

27. The whole development of the workers' participation project and the reasons for its abandonment are analyzed in E. Stephens (forthcoming).

28. Coore was offered another Cabinet post, but he declined and also resigned his posts as PNP Chairman and Member of Parliament, and he later left the country to accept a position with the IDB.

29. In a speech to his constituency (*G*, 20 June 1978) he accused some elements in the PNP parliamentary group of not being fully behind Manley, and he drew parallels to internal party disputes in the 1950s. He attacked Glasspole and Wills O. Isaacs, which provoked a particularly strong reaction among party moderates. Duncan was asked to apologize formally to the PNP MPs and did so (*G*, 25 June 1978). This incident is characteristic of the depth of interpersonal hostility with political overtones plaguing the party.

30. The foreword to *Principles and Objectives* is dated February 1979. Since then, it has been distributed widely for educational purposes inside the party, as well as for clarification purposes in the larger society. The document is 67 pages long and covers general ideological points as well as concrete programmatic ones.

31. Interview with a PNP Minister.

32. In a related shift, Howard Cooke, an opponent of Duncan, was defeated in the election for party chairman by Dudley Thompson, a person who was not really identified with any wing but sympathetic to the left. See *G*, 15–17 September 1979 for an account of the conference.

33. The figures given on IMF demands and the government's positions are not entirely consistent, which is a result of the fact that both shifted somewhat during the negotiations. However, according to most sources, the government agreed to a $100m budget cut and the negotiations deadlocked over the remaining $50m gap, which would have involved lay-offs of some 11 000–15 000 workers in the public sector. (See *Gleaner*, 9 and 26 February 1980;), Girvan *et al.* (1980:129–30), and Manley (1982:184).

34. Soon thereafter Bell accepted a position with the IMF.

35. The figures presented here are from the World Bank (IBRD, 1980). The discussion of intent and success of the program also relies on the published document, 'PNP Step the Way Forward', and on our interviews. For discussions of the alternative path and announcements of various measures, see also *G*, 26 March 1980 and *DN*, 26 March 1980 and *DN* 31 March 1980.

36. For a very informative account of the origins and the work of this committee by its chairman, see Mills (1981).

37. This was a remarkable achievement for the committee, given the circumstances under which it had to operate. The achievement was largely due to the dedication of the members of the committee, who perceived the high stakes of their work for the legitimacy of Jamaica's democratic institutions, and also to the reputation for high integrity of the members of the committee and particularly of its chair.

38. The case gave rise to a long court battle in Jamaica; one court acquitted the defendant and another court convicted him. We will not attempt to pass any judgement on the complex legal matters. In political terms, what is important is that the cartridges were shells for shotguns, whereas most gun violence in Jamaica has been conducted with pistols and rifles.

39. At a press conference in Miami, Seaga warned that the alternative plan was largely based on cancellation of loan repayments of some $200m, which could

have dramatic effects on credits and induce some banks to try to seize Jamaican assets abroad, such as Air Jamaica planes. He went on to warn that all agreements to be concluded with the Jamaican government should be checked with the JLP because 'desperate men might enter in agreements which would require renegotiation after a JLP victory' (*G*, 5 April 1980).

40. The JFL was said to have 2000 members in Miami alone (*G*, 26 April 1980). For instance, in a well-publicized action about a month before the election, in the midst of a severe shortage of basic foodstuffs, the JFL sent tons of rice to Jamaica for distribution by the JLP. For other sources of funds, see our discussion of US policy in this chapter.

41. This series of front-page articles suggested foul play in the drowning, reaching the bottom level of taste with the report that the body was shipped back without entrails; it was only stopped after the man's widow pleaded that a halt be put to the playing of political football with her husband's death (*G*, 6 July 1979).

42. Several sources confirmed that there was an inordinate drop in advertising on JBC. We will return to the role of the JBC, particularly its newsroom, later.

43. A former PNP Minister closely involved in this issue told us 'I took a good look at the food shortage; the whole pipeline, the whole system was dry. Everything went straight from production to the shelves. Whenever there was a disruption in production, there was a food shortage'.

44. The following discussion of US–Jamaican relations is based on our interviews in Jamaica and in the USA with seven present and former officials directly involved in US policy-making towards Jamaica.

45. The *Latin America Weekly Report* (16 November 1979) discusses the US 'two-track' approach to the region at this point, that is, the combination of military measures and economic and diplomatic pressure.

46. These negative signals were effective, both directly and via the mass media. They inclined bankers to respond negatively to Jamaican requests and they induced travel agents to advise their clients against a Jamaican vacation 'as long as things were so unstable down there'. Talking to tourists in Jamaica in 1981 and 1982, we several times heard comments like 'I used to come here regularly, but this is the first time since 1978, because my travel agent then told me it would be dangerous here'. In fact, crime rates in 1981 and 1982 differed little from those in 1979.

47. Manley (1982:175–9) relates how Philip Habib confronted him and criticized his speech on the occasion of a conference in Miami in December 1979.

48. This information is based on interviews with people who had access to these intelligence reports.

49. Harrison (1982) offers a fascinating account of ghetto organization, gang warfare, and the truce. She argues that the truce was a reaction to the 'Green Bay killings', an incident where the security forces killed five JLP gunmen under suspicious circumstances. The *Gleaner* 11 January 1978 ran a report claiming that the initiative was spurred by the encounter in prison of members of rival gangs who found out that they were being held under accusations of shooting people which the other side knew not to be true.

50. The gang-members had reason to fear the security forces. Police brutality is serious in Jamaica, affecting not only known gunmen but also those suspected of minor crimes and sometimes innocent bystanders; of course, ghetto-dwellers are particularly subject to such violence. Lacey (1977:117–21) discusses this phenomenon and its reasons in the 1960s; the rising crime levels and political violence in the 1970s, of course, aggravated the problem.

51. For instance, Seaga started a collection of funds to finance community service and production schemes, Small made the truce area the first priority for the Social Development Commission (*G*, 12 January 1978), the Cabinet decided on a special unemployment relief program in the area, the JEA launched a fund, and firms were donating equipment (*G*, 17 January 1978), the PSOJ agreed to support projects (*G*, 23 January 1978), and the *Gleaner* supported fund collection efforts.

52. In the beginning of November, a good ten months after the start of the peace effort, the *Gleaner* handed over funds which it had collected in a public campaign, to the former chairman of the advisory committee (*G*, 2 November 1978). And after the divisions and violence were already on the scene with renewed strength, Seaga opened a community center and a small factory built with business donations in his West Kingston district, claiming this to be proof that the peace program was working (*G*, 16 November 1978). It is interesting to note that no attendance of representatives from the General Peace Council, nor of figures with a PNP affiliation was reported; the whole affair was an apparently partisan one.

53. The reasons for the failure of the peace effort are as important to understand as they are difficult to pin down with certainty. Obviously, the legacy of years of hostility, lack of trust not only in former rivals but also in the government, in the security forces, in the political parties, as well as organizational inexperience of the leadership all played a role, as did material self-interest among parts of the leadership. However, one may also suppose that there were groups in the society who did not exactly welcome and support the truce, either because ghetto violence was believed to direct gunmen's attention from other targets, or because of the political implications of a unification of ghetto dwellers on the basis of their common economic and social interests. One might even speculate that there were individuals in the political parties who did not like losing their customary strong-arm support base.

54. The policemen involved in the shooting were accused of murder. The coroner's report stated that Massop had been murdered; that he had been shot while holding his arms over his head. However, the policemen were acquitted in court.

55. The reports of this incident in the *Gleaner* and *The Daily News* were predictably different, the *Gleaner* blaming the PNP and the *Daily News* giving both the JLP and the PNP versions (16 October 1979). A big controversy followed, in which *Gleaner* columnist Wilmot Perkins even accused Archbishop Samuel Carter of hiding the truth because, according to Perkins, the Archbishop, who was present at the ceremony, had been in a position to see where the shooting was coming from. In fact, the Archbishop was not on the podium at the time, but Perkins never contacted the Archbishop to check his facts before the column went to press.

56. The Eventide fire was widely suspected to be the result of arson, as an element in the ongoing terror. A controversy immediately arose as to whether the home's inhabitants were predominantly supporters of one or the other party.

57. The shooting at the JLP dance received wide coverage by the *Gleaner*, which termed it the 'Gold Street Massacre', whereas the shooting at the PNP dance was treated as just one incident among many. Similarly, the funeral of the JLP victims was attended by representatives from the private sector and other associations, in contrast to the funeral of the PNP victims.

58. Stone (1981b:6) gives figures based on *Gleaner* reports which show that the

number of members of the Security Forces killed in 1980 was forty-two, more than double the numbers in 1978 and 1979, when there were eighteen and nineteen respectively. Also, the foreign exchange shortage caused disruptions in the import of car parts, which affected the security forces. However, JDF chief Neish assured Seaga that the JDF was prepared to cope with the situation (*G*, 30 May 1980); this implied that the shortages were not as disastrous as Seaga claimed.

59.   For instance, there were rumors that some 1000 Cubans were about to be parachuted into Jamaica, and, as already discussed, the JLP alleged that there were Cuban-trained guerrilla groups inside Jamaica.

60.   It is widely believed that sectors of the police are corrupt. The flourishing ganja trade (and analogies from other countries with a heavy drug traffic) certainly does nothing to convince one of the contrary. Also, occasional instances of corruption coming out into the open reinforce this impression. A rather ironic case was the one of the former Secretary of the Police Federation who absconded to the USA with $60 000 of federation funds (*G*, 28 May 1977).

61.   For instance, such advertisements, built on the occurrence of physical attacks on the security forces showed a picture of a policeman and a soldier from behind, with a target between them, and asked 'What are the PNP and the Communists, and the JBC setting the Security Forces up for? . . . They want a break-down in law and order so that peaceful and fair elections cannot be held to put them out of office . . . Why are they desperately trying to turn the people against the police and soldiers? Keep the Security Forces free!' (*G*, 14 October 1980).

62.   The opposition had disrupted the nomination procedures by getting several people named Thompson to register (*G*, 14 July 1978). Thus, the procedures were repeated. However, there were no legal guidelines for such cases. When the Supreme Court ruled that the nomination procedures were unlawful and unconstitutional, Patterson (in Manley's absence from the island, Acting Prime Minister) relieved Thompson of his portfolio until the legal situation regarding Thompson's seat would be clarified. After getting legal advice (*G*, 1 June 1980) on the implications of the written judgement, Manley reappointed Thompson (*G*, 12 June 1980). However, after Thompson was found on the same plane bound for Cuba with the suspect in the Moonex affair, he was given sick leave and Justice Minister Rattray was appointed Acting Minister of National Security for the duration of Thompson's leave.

63.   For the controversy over the doctored tape, see Perkins' column (*G*, 1 June 1980), articles by Bowen (*DN*, 8 and 22 June 1980), and the PNP's response to Seaga (*DN*, 24 and 31 May 1980).

64.   For the key points, see the reports on Manley's presentation of the manifesto to the public (*G*, 19 September 1980).

65.   A media survey carried out in 1981 showed a total readership of 321 000 for the *Daily Gleaner*, 476 000 for the *Sunday Gleaner*, and 314 000 for the *Star*, the Gleaner Company's sensationalist afternoon paper. In contrast, the *Daily News* had a readership of 81 000 only and the *Sunday Sun* 114 000. If one considers in addition the importance of word-of-mouth transmission of news from the paper by prominent people in rural communities, such as the teacher or minister of religion, the difference widens even more, under the assumption that teachers or ministers were just as likely as the general readership to read one or the other paper. For instance, if we assume that one in five readers of the *Daily Gleaner* and the *Daily News* communicated some of its

contents to two further people, we arrive at a total of 449 400 people reached by the *Daily Gleaner* compared with 113 400 people reached by the *Daily News*. The field-work for this media survey was carried out in October 1981 by Market Research Services Ltd, Kingston, on behalf of RJR, the *Gleaner* Company, and JBC. We gratefully acknowledge the access to this information granted to us by the research firms.

This difference in reach between the *Gleaner* and the *Daily News* presented a dilemma for the PNP's campaign insofar as the party obviously did not want to support the paper with its advertising funds, but by boycotting the *Gleaner* and shifting all its printed advertising to the *Daily News*, which is what the PNP did in 1980, the campaign suffered a loss in its ability to reach people. Furthermore, this decision left the field too much to the JLP, as no PNP advertisements countering those of the JLP containing the communist smear would reach the same reading public with the same regularity.

66. We will attempt to evaluate these positions in Chapter 8.

67. See, for example, Small's statements in the *Daily News* (26 August 1980).

68. This information is based on various interviews, such as with the former General Manager of JBC, a professor of mass communication and several journalists. Again, an evaluation of the government's media policy will follow in Chapter 8.

69. This did not remain unnoticed by the PNP and caused explicit complaints. However, there were two obstacles to action to put an end to this lopsided coverage: the left's defense of the alliance of all progressive forces, and the government's commitment to workers' participation. The minister in charge of the JBC, Arnold Bertram, was a left-winger and not willing to risk a fight with the newsroom staff.

70. Analyses of the election outcome, the pattern of the vote, and public opinion are offered by Stone (1981a and b). Our discussion here will draw heavily on the data in these articles and in Stone (1982).

71. How hard it was for many to break their traditional party loyalties is illustrated by remarks such as 'my wife and her sister cried, but they voted JLP in 1980', which we heard repeatedly in different versions from members of upper- or upper-middle-class PNP families.

72. Given the difference in the wording of the question at the two points in time, it is difficult to interpret this evidence with accuracy. Stone presents additional evidence on the Cuba–communism question in Stone (1982:24, 26, 47, 49, 51). Unfortunately, some of these questions are leading, perhaps because of Stone's increasingly hostile posture toward the PNP left and the WPJ, and thus the results have to be treated with some care. Nonetheless, in our opinion, there is ample unbiased evidence from these polls to support the point of view that marginal voters were influenced to some extent by the Cuban–communism issue to the PNP's disadvantage.

73. It is important to keep in mind here that the JLP had widely used the Cuban and communist threat in the 1976 campaign, but that the *Gleaner* had not fully picked up the issue then. Since 1979, however, the *Gleaner* had devoted its full mastery of propaganda to attempts to establish a strong link between the PNP and a communist threat to Jamaican democracy, with the Cubans looming in the background.

74. Were it not for the re-election of the Thatcher government in Britain in 1983, we would have said it was impossible. Though the opposition was divided, which under the British system greatly helped Thatcher's Conservatives, and though she lost popular support compared with the previous election, her

election victory demonstrates that other factors, such as voters' perceptions of available alternatives and foreign policy issues, can constitute a counterweight to economic hardship conditions in influencing voters. As for the relevance of this example to Jamaica, one has to keep in mind that Thatcher's measures did not have as dramatic an effect on the British economy as the IMF measures had on Jamaica.

7   Seaga's Return to Dependent Capitalism

1. Actually, some quantitative restrictions on imports already existed in the 1950s and 1960s. However, in the 1950s they were used only for political reasons, namely against South Africa and some communist countries, with the exception of the footwear industry which was granted protection from foreign competition. In the mid-1960s the government deliberately began imposing quantitative import restrictions to protect the development of the domestic manufacturing industry. However, it was not until the 1970s that the restrictions became motivated by balance-of-payments concerns and thus came to include an ever larger list of items (Ayub, 1981: 32–3).

2. See U.S. Department of State (1981) for the US allegations of Cuban subversion in Latin America.

3. This uncharacteristically flexible attitude on the part of the IMF should certainly be interpreted in the context of the Reagan administration's commitment to turning Jamaica into a model case of prosperity under dependent capitalism.

4. It is even harder to understand why Seaga consistently and dramatically exaggerated projections for bauxite production, when the JBI told him that much less would have to be expected. In 1981, he projected an increase of 6m tons per year in bauxite exports over the following three years (*G*, 1 June 1981).

5. At the beginning of March 1982, a figure of 500 projects before the JNIP was mentioned (*G*, 25 March 1982), and by the end of the same month the figure was 600 (*DN*, 31 March 1982).

6. The most visible investment projects were a joint venture between the government and an Israeli consortium for the production of vegetables, horticulture and fruits for export to the USA and Western Europe, and an expansion of Blue Mountain coffee production with involvement of Japanese interests.

7. We conducted our interviews between January and July 1982. In this period, we could observe a clear trend towards greater skepticism and disillusion on the part of government ministers concerning the response of the private sector.

8. These dramatic cutbacks in production occurred *despite* the 1979 revision of the bauxite levy, which the companies had pressed for so hard on the grounds that it was the only way to make Jamaican bauxite competitive again.

9. From the middle of 1981 on, there were frequent complaints from government representatives about the abuse of import licenses, as well as complaints from private sector representatives about the liberalization of import restrictions, the parallel market, and the shortages or high price of credits and of foreign exchange for raw materials. See, for example, *G*, 18 September 1981; *DN*, 12 February 1982; *G*, 6 February 1982; *G*, 16 May 1982; *G*, 22 April 1982. See also Stone's columns on the subject in *G*, 20 May 1982 and *G*, 2 June 1982.

10. How important the growth in tourism is, and how crucial it would be to stop the leakage from the tourist industry becomes clear if we consider that in 1982 tourism was Jamaica's second most important foreign-exchange earner, bringing in US \$184m, behind the bauxite–alumina industry with US \$284m (NPA, 1983:3.8). The experience of both the Manley and Seaga governments shows how exceedingly difficult it is to solve the leakage problem.
11. In 1983, the basis for the calculation of the size of the labor force was changed; thus, the figures from April 1983 on are not comparable with the earlier ones (NPA, 1983b: 15.1).
12. These rumors were affirmatively commented on in a confidential interview.
13. We attended the first graduation of the Kingston Vernon Arnett School in 1982. The student who gave the graduation speech was a woman from an obviously lower-class background. Her mastery of the material covered in the course was so impressive that it gave one a very positive impression of the quality of teaching provided and the amount of discipline demanded in the school.
14. These statements are made on the basis of interviews with businessmen in the spring of 1982.
15. In 1982, Tony Spaulding resigned his post as PNP vice-president, but this was apparently connected with a personal dispute with Manley rather than a political change.
16. In a sense, the tactics never went away, as they were periodically revived for various purposes, such as breaking relations with Cuba. Events of October 1983 were different in that they led to a sustained campaign.
17. Just on the surface of it, these allegations were extremely difficult to believe, to say the least, and in Jamaica they were widely believed to have been trumped up.
18. Seaga's breaking of the agreement is a sad comment on this man's commitment to the democratic rules of the game. One wonders if this is how one 'makes freedom work in the Caribbean' (to use Reagan's own words)!

8 Jamaica's Democratic Socialist Path: An Evaluation

1. A detailed discussion of the PNP government's bauxite policy and its effects is given in Stephens and Stephens (1985). See also Maule and Litvak (1980) on the International Bauxite Association.
2. A detailed analysis of Jamaica's foreign borrowing and its economic effects is given by Richard Bernal (1980).
3. Calculation by the authors on the basis of figures from NPA (1976) and (1981).
4. The following discussion of the various agricultural programs owes much to Derrik Stone, former Permanent Secretary in the Ministry of Agriculture. He offered us much information and many interesting insights. Of course, the assessments we made on the basis of our interview with him and the responsibility for the opinions expressed here are entirely our own.
5. This discussion of the problems in the sugar industry relies heavily on Carl Feuer (1983). He provides figures which document the changes in productivity, in costs, etc., and he also offers an insightful discussion of social dynamics in the industry.
6. The United Nations Development Program report, prepared by the Food and Agriculture Organization (FAO, 1975) provides an excellent introduction to the problems of Jamaican agriculture and the development of the government's reform programs in their early phases.

7. For instance, in 1977, the Ministry of Agriculture issued a warning to extension officers concerning complaints about the reluctance of certain extension officers to leave their car to inspect fields, and about rum-drinking and skittles-playing in working hours, etc. (*DN*, 14 May 1977).

8. For a description of the provisions of various phases, see Chapter 3. The figures cited in this paragraph are from Ministry of Agriculture (1981).

9. Knowledgeable observers expressed some skepticism about these figures, citing examples where the same truck loaded with produce would repeatedly drive through the gate and be counted, thus artificially inflating the production figures.

10. See p. 176.

11. Because of the experience with shortages in 1980, many PNP leftists favor substantially greater ownership in the distributive sector. This would not appear to be a wise move, because (1) the degree of decentralization in the sector makes it very difficult to manage it efficiently, (2) it would have generated a reaction not only from large businesses but also smaller ones, (3) it would not have affected the availability of goods to a sufficiently great degree since hoarding was the secondary cause of the shortages, and (4) the move would only be of much use in an economic crisis which caused severe shortages. Such a crisis would be sufficient to defeat the government. Eliminating hoarding would not save it.

12. Knowledgeable people to whom we talked were divided on the efficiency of JPS. Two liberal capitalists felt that Manley's appointee was not appropriate and that he was partly responsible for the decline in service. A public sector manager contended that he did an effective job.

13. See E. Stephens (forthcoming) for a more extended analysis of the demise of workers' participation in Jamaica.

14. The cost of the National Youth Service could have easily been calculated as the approximate number of school-leavers and the level of wages to be paid must have been known (see Chapter 3). It is quite amazing that it was not immediately recognized that this program would be excessively expensive.

15. In all fairness to the PNP government, these steps were taken in some cases. Food farms were eventually terminated, if a little late. Problems in the literacy campaign were recognized and it was successfully transformed into a continuing adult literacy program.

16. For a more extensive analysis of the problems of the ministry, see Jones (1981a, 1981b). The following discussion relies heavily on these two articles as well as interviews with experts in the area.

17. Income distribution data for Jamaica are only available for a few random years in the whole post-Second World War period. The type of redistribution effected by governmental programs is very imperfectly reflected in the income distribution statistics usually available for industrial countries anyway (see J. Stephens, 1979b: 96–7).

18. Much of this decline is due to demographic and economic factors not affected by the government in power, but there does seem to be some effect of policy; the infant mortality rate declined by 37 per cent in ten years of the JLP rule (62–72) compared with 60 per cent in seven years of PNP rule.

19. This is not to say there were not cases of corrupt electoral practices under the PNP government.

20. In the debate in Jamaica, 'petty bourgeois' is not used in the strict Marxist sense but rather is a catch-all term used to denote anyone who is not a worker, peasant, lumpenproletarian, or capitalist. In this sense, the PNP

leadership is definitely petty bourgeois both in terms of present position and social background, but this is as true of the left as the center of the party. This is not to say that the lack of representation of cadre from working-class and peasant backgrounds in the leadership of the PNP and NWU was not a weakness.

21. We believe that this event supports our contention that power relations in civil society were and are a larger obstacle to deepening social transformation in Jamaica than is the class composition of PNP leadership. Duncan's resignation was forced by the character of the Jamaican labor movement and the consequent dependence of the party on financing from liberal capitalists, not by pressure from capitalists in leading roles within the party.

22. The analysis presented in the Central Committee report (WPJ,1981:42–3) is not systematic; it mentions various districts in which the WPJ worked, observing then that either the PNP won the district or that the swing against the PNP was smaller than the national average (that is, 15 per cent). (In one case, the swing was not in fact smaller than average.) Even assuming that the list given was a comprehensive list of where the WPJ worked, it still remains to be shown that there were not other explanations for the difference. For instance, one district was Portia Simpson's South West St Andrew district (that is, part of the West Kingston ghetto) where the PNP actually improved on their 1976 results. Surely, patronage is largely responsible for this outcome. Nevertheless, it seems probable that in districts like this which are dominated by marginals (among whom the communism issue was not very salient) the WPJ's targeted support may have helped.

23. The following discussion owes much to conversations we had with Professors G. E. Mills and Edwin Jones. We are grateful to them for sharing their knowledge and experience with us, and we hasten to add that the responsibility for the opinions expressed here is ours.

24. Jones and Mills (1976) discuss the practice of creating non-departmental (that is, non-civil service) agencies such as public corporations and other statutory boards and advisory committees.

25. See the article by G. E. Mills, the head of the former Public Service Commission, in the *Daily Gleaner*, for some of the issues involved (*G*, 6 March 1977).

26. Jones (1981b) offers an excellent discussion of these and other factors accounting for bureaucratic incapacity.

27. See p. 268.

28. In this sense, it can be charged that even the Carter administration put indirect pressure on debtor countries to adopt a certain set of internal policies since it did encourage them to come to an agreement with the IMF.

9 Lessons of the Manley Government: Democratic Socialism as an Alternative Development Plan

1. Dietrich Rueschemeyer pointed out this useful distinction to us.

2. For an insightful discussion of the effect of the legacies of colonialism on the African state see Young and Turner (1985).

3. See J. Stephens (1979a). Our view has changed somewhat since this article was written but it contains the broad outlines for what we consider to be a viable approach to the study of class formation and class consciousness.

4. Originally, we conceptualized this research as a study of transition to socialism in the context of Third World democracies with Chile and Jamaica as our

two main cases. It was only after study convinced us of the difficulty, and danger, of attempting a rapid transition that we recast the question. The following, necessarily extremely compressed discussion of the maximalist strategy in the transition to socialism is based on Stephens and Stephens (1980). For another view of the Manley government as 'democratic socialist' and an analysis somewhat similar to ours, see Payne (1984).

5. See Ulyanovsky (1974) for the most influential statement of the theory of the non-capitalist path. Though using a different terminology, Brutents (1977) represents a similar analysis, which has gained great currency on the intellectual left in Jamaica because of WPJ General Secretary Munroe's promotion of the work. See Thomas (1978) for a summary of the non-capitalist path.

6. This is not to indicate that the pursuit of this development path is any easier than the pursuit of a democratic socialist development path. The limited capacity of the state is an even greater constraint in these societies. Moreover, the positive feature of the absence of the capitalist class as a domestic opponent is more than offset by the danger of the development of an entirely self-interested 'state bourgeoisie', which in many cases does not even carry out its task of accumulation and thus becomes a complete parasite on the rest of the society.

7. For a more complete explication of our view of social democracy, see J. Stephens (1979b) and Stephens and Stephens (1982). The logic of our analysis leads us to include the Eurocommunist parties under the category of social democracy. For instance, sociologically, the Italian Communist Party is more 'social democratic' in our sense than either of the two Italian Socialist Parties.

8. We say 'phase' here, because it now appears that, with the changes that occurred in the international economy in the 1970s and with the growth of public expenditure nearing its limits in the advanced welfare states, the welfare-statist phase of European social democracy's development is no longer a viable option. These movements must go beyond this phase or abandon their progressive stance altogether. For an elaboration of this argument see J. Stephens (1981).

9. The importance of the state's capacity for repression for the political outcome, a hidden variable in Moore's argument, is highlighted in Skocpol (1973).

10. This same process occurred everywhere in the British West Indies. Domestic forces primarily influenced the speed at which it happened.

11. For a discussion of the concept of the new professionalism and an analysis of it as a factor in Latin American politics, see Stepan (1973).

12. This is not to argue that this would always be the case. In the situation faced by the UP government in Chile, moderation in policy would have been necessary had the government opted for democratic socialist development (gradualism) rather than rapid transition to socialism. See Stephens and Stephens (1980) for our analysis of the options before the Allende government.

13. We would consider the two alternatives here to be the ones that would arise in most cases. Two other possibilities suggest themselves. On the center left, a form of social democracy is sometimes possible when the path of dependent development, for a variety of fortuitous circumstances, does not generate rapidly-growing inequality. An example is Barbados. From the center right, a form of state capitalism might at least produce growth. This path may be an alternative where the debt problem has not forced the country to turn to the IMF. The IMF, of course, will block state expansion and offer 'incentives' for reduction of the state's role.

14. Actually, Thomas' (1984) work gives this model broader relevance than is implied here. He argues for strategies to oppose and dislodge the authoritarian state and to initiate changes in social and economic relations, which are similar to the ones outlined here. These strategies include the formation of an alliance of all major classes, strata and social groups committed to democratic political practice, maximum efforts to promote the organization of oppressed groups, and simultaneous struggle for political and economic democratization.

15. A large working class is not a necessary condition for the development of political democracy, but in the majority of cases in Latin America, the Caribbean and the developed capitalist world it was a major if not the major force behind the drive for universal suffrage and responsible government. Most of the exceptions to this rule are countries in which smallholdings dominated agriculture and small farmers along with the urban petty bourgeoisie were the primary force behind democracy (for example Canada, Switzerland, the north and west of the United States, Costa Rica).

16. Austria would be the most extreme case here, moving from a civil war in the 1930s to a coalition of the political opponents in the war and corporatist compromise between their economic counterparts, capital and labor, a decade and a half later. This corporatist bargaining arrangement between capital, labor and the state is the most fully institutionalized form of the social pact referred to in the text. Most of the corporatist countries in Europe, generally the smaller democracies, did not go through the authoritarian phase Austria experienced. Thus, we are not suggesting that the phase is a prerequisite for the development of a social pact.

17. We are dealing here with factors that might serve to strengthen democracy in the post-authoritarian period, not with factors leading to the transition. Among the factors leading to the transition, the economic difficulties and the ensuing defection of the bourgeoisie from the authoritarian regimes are crucial. On the transition from authoritarian to democratic regimes, see O'Donnell and Schmitter (forthcoming).

18. It has to be emphasized that increased self-reliance, particularly in food production and in the use of local raw materials for manufacturing, is important but does not eliminate the need to foster export-competitiveness. Argentina, for instance, has a great advantage compared with Jamaica in food self-sufficiency, but the country is nevertheless constrained by the need to develop competitive manufactured exports. Our comments here on strategies and conditions in different countries are of necessity cursory. A more detailed and systematic comparative analysis of conditions and strategies for democratic socialist transformation in European, Latin American and Caribbean countries is the subject of a study in progress by the authors.

Appendix 1: Tables

TABLE A.1 *Comparison of general elections: 1944, 1949, 1955, 1959, 1962, 1967, 1972, 1976, 1980*

Year	No of seats	Seats won						% Accepted Ballots			% Voted*	
		JLP		PNP		IND		JLP	PNP	IND	Of[1] electors	Of[2] eligible voters
		No	%	No	%	No	%					
1944	32	22	69	5	16	5	16	41	24	35	59	X
1949	32	17	63	13	41	2	5	43	43	14	65	X
1955	32	14	44	18	56	-	-	39	51	10	64	X
1959	45	16	36	29	64	-	-	44	55	1	65	X
1962	45	26	58	19	42	-	-	51	49	1	73	X
1967	53	33	62	20	38	-	-	51	49	-	82	60
1972	53	16	30	37	70	-	-	44	56	-	79	58
1976	60	13	22	47	78	-	-	43	57	-	85	71
1980	60	51	85	9	15	-	-	59	41	-	87	77

NOTES *In 1976 the legal voting age was changed to 18 years. X – No reliable data available.
[1] % of registered voters
[2] % of population of voting age

SOURCE Chief Electoral Officer (various years) and Director of Elections (1980).

TABLE A.2 *Government expenditure and revenue 1971–83*

	1971–2	1972–3	1973–4	1974–5	1975–6	1976–7	1977–8	1978–9	1979–80	1980–1	1981–2	1982–3
GDP	1280.1	1438.8	1735.1	2169.6	2614.3	2715.0	2988.6	3753.6	4289.0	4730.9	5309.8	5672.3
ORIGINAL												
Recurrent expenditure	NA	250.8	321.3	419.8	582.2	718.0	837.1	1113.0	1180.4	1683.4	1683.4	1869.2
Capital expenditure		103.8	128.7	176.3	328.9	408.5	436.7	711.0	585.1	948.4	948.4	875.2
Total		354.6	449.0	596.1	911.9	1126.0	1273.8	1834.8	1765.4	2631.8	2631.8	2744.4
% of GDP		24.6	25.0	27.5	34.8	41.2	42.6	48.6	41.2	55.6	49.6	48.4
REVISED												
Recurrent revenue	NA	276.5	331.4	445.1	546.1		645.8	851.1	877.1	920.6	1080.5	1386.3
Capital revenue								6.0	5.6	8.3	12.2	8.4
Transfers from CDF	–	–	–		54.4		126.6	261.0	300.0	312.0	324.0	342.0
Total								1112.1	1182.7	1240.9	1416.7	1736.7
ACTUAL												
Recurrent expenditure	218.3	268.1	342.7	509.5	614.1	782.0	839.7	1147.9	1257.8	1552.0	1655.2	1874.0
Capital expenditure	91.6	104.4	128.4	218.5	306.6	524.8	422.3	657.5	602.8	813.3	816.1	872.3
Total	309.9	375.5	471.1	728.0	920.7	1306.8	1262.0	1806.3	1860.6	2365.3	2471.3	2746.3
% of GDP	23.3	25.9	27.2	33.6	35.2	48.1	42.2	48.1	43.4	49.9	46.5	48.4
Recurrent expenditure	213.7	263.2	340.2	493.2	614.1	758.0	838.9	1163.7*	1242.8*	1547.3*	1655.2	
Capital expenditure	85.6	96.5	102.9	257.4	325.9	406.9	403.1	662.6	564.3	844.2	816.1	
Total	299.3	359.7	443.1	750.6	940.0	1164.9	1242.0	1826.3	1807.1	2391.5	2471.3	
% of GDP	23.3	25.0	25.5	34.6	36.0	42.9	42.6	48.7	42.1	50.6	46.5	

continued on page 378

378

TABLE A.2 · *continued*

	1971–2	1972–3	1973–4	1974–5	1975–6	1976–7	1977–8	1978–9	1979–80	1980–1	1981–2
GDP	1280.1	1438.8	1735.1	2169.6	2614.3	2715.0	2988.6	3753.6	4289.0	4730.9	5309.8
Recurrent revenue	244.4	280.7	343.3	421.9	509.0	520.3	529.1	777.1	834.2	964.8	1222.7
Capital revenue	4.6	5.0	4.4	10.6	6.7	6.5	17.3	3.8	1.5	180.4	31.9
Transfers from CDF	–	–	–	85.0	125.0	80.0	110.0	268.0	232.5	230.0	300.0
Total	249.0	285.7	347.7	517.5	640.7	606.8	656.4	1048.9	1068.2	1375.2	1554.6
Loans – domestic	20.3	53.3	64.3	112.4	192.5	555.7	NA	NA	578.2	700.3	393.2
– foreign	23.9	19.1	33.3	70.8	138.3	85.3	NA	NA	232.8	319.9	630.1
Total	44.2	72.4	97.6	183.2	330.8	641.0	579.3	711.5	811.0	1020.2	1023.3
Other	1.7		30.5	27.7			6.3	65.9	9.2		
Total	294.9	358.1	475.8	728.4	971.5	1247.8	1242.0	1826.3	1888.4	2395.4	2577.9

NOTES Capital expenditure does not include capital net amortization.
  *Provisional.
SOURCE NPA (various years).

TABLE A.3a Table attacks on the PNP government appearing in the Gleaner

	1972		1973		1974		1975		1976		1977		1978		1979		1980	
	1	2	1	2	1	2	1	2	1	2	1	2	1	2	1	2	1	2
Mismanagement	–	7	6	6	6	1	6	21	23	13	23	18	49	25	33	36	64	25
Communism–Cuba	–	2	–	1	–	–	–	3	5	1	1	4	4	–	15	17	14	7
One–party state – totalitarianism	1	1	1	–	1	6	2	5	6	1	2	23	1	12	7	24	19	5
Rhetoric undermining business confidence – economic problems	–	5	2	–	2	4	–	3	10	6	5	8	8	5	5	14	5	1
Socialist Policies undermining business confidence	–	–	–	–	–	4	1	–	2	–	1	–	1	6	8	11	4	4
Clarify limits of public sector; reassure business	4	7	2	–	2	3	2	–	–	–	1	–	–	–	–	–	–	–
Socialist policies unfair or bad	1	–	–	–	2	4	2	3	–	1	3	10	2	1	1	1	1	–
Manley out of control – disunity in party	–	–	1	–	2	–	2	1	–	1	3	2	–	1	–	–	5	–
Other	–	–	1	–	–	–	1	–	–	1	–	–	1	–	–	–	19	9
	6	20	13	8	15	19	13	33	41	20	37	59	63	48	61	82	109	45

The numbers in the cells refer to the number of articles on page one of the *Gleaner* or editorials attacking the government on the ground indicated by the row heading. Since an article may contain attacks on more than one ground, the column totals are often less than the total number of entries in the column.
Tables A.3b, A.3c and A.3d are analyses classified by the author of the attack: the JLP, the private sector, or the *Gleaner* itself.

TABLE A.3b *Gleaner attacks on the PNP government*

	1972		1973		1974		1975		1976		1977		1978		1979		1980	
	1	2	1	2	1	2	1	2	1	2	1	2	1	2	1	2	1	2
Mismanagement	–	–	–	3	2	1	5	15	14	6	12	5	24	15	15	22	38	19
Communism–Cuba	–	–	–	1	–	–	–	1	–	–	1	–	–	–	7	8	4	2
One-party state – totalitarianism	1	1	–	–	–	3	–	2	1	–	1	11	1	3	3	8	5	4
Rhetoric undermining business confidence – economic problems	–	3	2	–	1	4	–	2	5	5	4	3	7	4	3	12	5	–
Socialist policies undermining business confidence	–	–	–	–	–	3	1	–	1	–	–	–	1	6	5	11	4	3
Clarify limits of public sector; reassure business	3	5	1	–	2	3	2	–	–	–	–	–	–	–	–	–	–	–
Socialist policies unfair or bad	1	–	–	–	–	3	–	–	–	1	4	5	1	1	–	–	–	–
Manley out of control – disunity in party	–	–	1	1	–	–	2	2	–	–	5	–	–	1	–	1	1	–
Other	–	–	–	–	2	–	–	–	–	–	–	–	–	–	2	2	13	8
	5	9	4	5	7	14	10	21	20	10	23	22	34	27	33	51	64	33

TABLE A.3c *JLP attacks on the PNP government*

	1972		1973		1974		1975		1976		1977		1978		1979		1980	
	1	2	1	2	1	2	1	2	1	2	1	2	1	2	1	2	1	2
Mismanagement	–	6	5	2	3	–	–	6	7	7	9	12	22	10	14	10	11	6
Communism – Cuba	–	2	–	–	–	–	–	2	4	1	–	4	3	–	8	9	10	4
One-party state – totalitarianism	–	–	1	–	–	3	1	2	4	1	1	9	–	9	4	6	9	1
Rhetoric undermining business confidence – economic problems	–	1	–	–	1	–	–	–	2	1	1	2	–	–	1	–	–	1
Socialist policies undermining business confidence	–	–	–	–	–	–	–	–	1	–	1	–	–	–	3	1	–	1
Clarify limits of public sector; reassure business	–	–	–	–	–	–	–	–	–	–	–	–	–	–	–	–	–	–
Socialist policies unfair or bad	–	–	–	–	1	–	–	–	–	–	1	2	–	–	–	–	–	–
Manley out of control – disunity in party	–	–	–	–	–	–	–	–	–	1	–	2	–	–	–	–	–	1
Other	–	8	7	2	5	3	1	9	14	10	10	27	23	17	29	27	30	11

TABLE A.3d *Private sector attacks on the PNP government*

	1972		1973		1974		1975		1976		1977		1978		1979		1980	
	1	2	1	2	1	2	1	2	1	2	1	2	1	2	1	2	1	2
Mismanagement	–	1	1	1	1	–	1	–	1	–	2	1	2	2	4	4	10	–
Communism – Cuba	–	–	–	–	–	–	–	1	–	–	–	–	1	–	–	–	–	–
One-party state – totalitarianism	–	–	–	–	–	–	1	1	–	–	–	1	–	–	–	–	4	–
Rhetoric undermining business confidence – economic problems	–	1	–	–	–	–	–	1	3	–	–	3	1	1	1	2	–	–
Socialist policies undermining business confidence	–	–	–	–	–	1	–	–	–	–	–	–	–	–	–	–	–	–
Clarify limits of public sector; reassure business	1	2	1	–	–	–	–	–	–	–	1	–	–	–	–	–	–	–
Socialist policies unfair or bad	–	–	–	–	1	1	–	–	–	–	–	3	1	–	–	–	1	–
Manley out of control – disunity in party	–	–	–	–	–	–	1	–	–	–	–	–	–	1	–	!	–	–
Other	–	–	–	–	–	–	–	–	–	–	–	–	–	–	–	–	–	–
	1	3	2	1	2	2	2	2	4	–	3	8	4	4	5	6	14	–

TABLE A.4 *Jamaican migration to the USA, 1967–80*

Occupational category	1967	1968	1969	1970	1971	1972	1973	1974	1975	1976	1977	1978	1979	1980
Professional, technical and related	1347	1777	1704	1056	1078	810	562	566	503	493	899	1369	1459	n.a.
Managers, officials and proprietors	110	150	176	222	183	194	158	175	181	222	826	1049	1013	n.a.
Clerical and sales	769	1493	1521	1189	904	902	677	807	689	587	918	1949	2138	n.a.
Other occupations	5423	10104	8407	5568	5089	4405	2808	3372	3097	2504	2532	4748	4643	n.a.
Housewives, children, others	2834	3946	5139	6998	7317	7116	5758	7488	6606	5220	6326	10150	10461	n.a.
Total	10483	17470	16947	15033	14571	13427	9963	12408	11076	9026	11501	19265	19714	18970

n.a. = not available.
SOURCE NPA (various years)

384

TABLE A.5 *Jamaican migration to Canada, 1967–80*

Occupational category	1967	1968	1969	1970	1971	1972	1973	1974	1975	1976	1977	1978	1979	1980
Professional and technical	407	294	351	334	194	154	267	266	119	214	202	171	108	118
Administrative and managerial	37	15	40	52	56	45	223	386	245	177	288	116	66	52
Clerical and sales	604	446	681	773	570	341	1058	607	519	524	610	350	236	197
Other occupation	1349	1029	1387	1838	1524	1079	4588	4837	1765	1224	996	669	643	700
Housewives, children and others with no occupation	1062	1102	1430	1662	1559	1473	3227	5190	5563	5143	4195	2552	2160	2094
Total	3459	2886	3889	4659	3903	3092	9363	11286	8211	7282	6291	3858	3213	3161

SOURCE NPA (various years).

TABLE A.6 *Capital formation 1969–82* (millions of dollars)

Year	Gross fixed capital formation	Gross as % GDP	Consumption of fixed capital	Net fixed capital formation	Net as % of GDP
1969	315.3	32	93.0	222.3	22
1970	367.2	31	117.0	250.2	21
1971	356.0	28	122.0	234.0	18
1972	366.8	25	144.0	222.8	15
1973	448.2	26	172.7	275.5	16
1974	478.2	22	205.0	273.2	13
1975	610.0	23	231.2	378.8	14
1976	450.8	16	248.4	202.4	7
1977	349.4	12	284.1	65.0	2
1978	502.1	13	342.8	159.3	4
1979	724.6	17	393.4	331.2	8
1980	698.9	15	417.9	281.0	6
1981	953.3	18	485.5	467.8	9
1982	1153.6	20	537.3	616.3	11

SOURCE   Department of Statistics (1981, 1983).

TABLE A.7 Crime, 1973–81 (reported cases, absolute)

	Murder	Rape	Manslaughter	Felonious wounding	Robbery	Burglary and other break-ins	Breach of Firearms Act and shooting with intent	Population
1970	152	553	57	364	2241	5403	NA	
1971	145	544	68	609	2595	4722	NA	
1972	170	571	52	450	2605	4782	293	
1973	227	671	81	395	2944	6589	305	
1974	195	460	93	395	2387	5668	332	
1975	226	540	57	411	2964	7828	304	
1976	367	672	42	384	2895	7557	791	
1977	409	829	58	522	3511	8853	1960	
1978	381	709	52	476	3990	9150	855	
1979	351	730	35	538	3654	8484	1749	
1980	889	767	29	652	4731	8292	3882	
1981	490	756	31	588	4617	8437	2557	

TABLE A.7 *(continued) (reported cases, per 100 000)*

	Murder	Rape	Manslaughter	Felonious wounding	Robbery	Burglary and other break-ins	Breach of Firearms Act and shooting with intent	Population
1970	8.2	29.9	3.1	19.7	121.2	292.3	NA	1,848,500
1971	7.6	28.7	3.6	32.1	136.9	249.1	NA	1,896,000
1972	8.7	29.4	2.7	23.2	134.0	246.1	15.1	1,943,500
1973	11.4	33.7	4.1	19.8	147.9	331.0	15.3	1,990,900
1974	9.6	22.7	4.6	19.5	116.4	279.9	16.4	2,025,000
1975	11.0	26.2	2.8	19.9	143.9	379.9	14.8	2,060,300
1976	17.6	32.2	2.0	18.4	138.9	362.6	38.0	2,084,200
1977	19.4	39.3	2.7	24.7	166.4	419.7	92.9	2,109,400
1978	17.8	33.1	2.4	22.2	186.4	427.5	39.9	2,140,500
1979	16.2	33.7	1.6	24.9	168.8	392.0	80.8	2,164,500
1980	40.7	35.1	1.3	29.8	216.4	379.3	177.6	2,186,100
1981	22.0	34.0	1.4	26.4	207.4	379.1	114.9	2,225,700

SOURCE: NPA (various years).

388

TABLE A.8 *Balance-of-payments Summary, 1969–82* (US $m, current)

	1969	1970	1971	1972	1973	1974	1975	1976	1977	1978	1979	1980	1981	1982
Current account balance	−123.6	−152.6	−174.8	−125.3	−180.7	−167.0	−282.7	−302.7	−68.2	−86.7	−142.6	−166.3	−336.8	−426.4
Capital movement (net)	118.2	160.9	195.7	74.6	137.1	243.2	208.9	48.3	101.5	9.8	−10.4	105.1	247.2	508.2
Government external borrowing	12.4	−1.4	4.9	23.2	36.7	90.1	124.2	79.2	38.6	178.9	71.2	226.6	240.2	469.1
Identified private capital	105.8	162.3	190.8	51.4	100.4	153.1	84.7	−30.9	62.9	−169.1	−81.6	−121.5	7.0	39.1
Allocation of SDRs	–	6.3	5.7	5.9	–	–	–	–	–	–	10.0	10.0	10.0	–
Net errors and omissions	−8.2	6.5	17.8	−9.6	13.1	−16.7	−7.2	−7.5	−34.9	−0.6	2.1	1.0	−10.9	n.a.
Overall surplus/deficit (increase = −)	13.6	−21.1	−44.4	54.4	30.5	−59.5	81.0	261.9	14.6	77.5	140.9	50.2	90.5	−81.8

SOURCE Except for 1977 and 1982, all data from Bank of Jamaica. 1969 cited in Girvan *et al.* (1980: Table 7). 1969–76 converted to US$ using IFS conversion rate. 1977 data from IDB (1982: Table 40). 1982 data from NPA (various years).

TABLE A.9 *Gross domestic product by industrial sector in purchasers' values at constant prices ($ million)*

Industrial sector	1970	1971	1972	1973	1974	1975	1976	1977	1978	1979	1980	1981	1982
Agriculture, forestry and fishing	149.8	167.5	170.6	146.9	153.2	156.0	157.6	162.3	178.0	160.6	150.6	156.4	145.9
Mining and quarrying	139.7	149.3	158.9	181.6	197.0	157.2	124.9	146.7	150.4	148.0	162.7	164.8	117.0
Manufacture	348.1	356.1	397.8	401.1	387.2	396.5	377.2	350.6	331.9	318.3	287.5	291.1	303.2
Electricity and water	16.4	18.5	21.0	22.2	22.2	23.1	23.7	23.4	23.7	23.3	23.6	23.9	23.9
Construction and installation	261.7	263.1	255.5	225.7	213.5	210.8	168.6	133.6	138.3	137.4	98.3	99.9	112.7
Distributive trade (wholesale and retail)	423.2	435.2	509.4	481.9	401.7	413.0	337.0	310.5	306.3	293.7	273.1	287.8	304.4
Transport, storage and communication	109.1	115.6	122.6	124.3	137.0	142.6	137.7	130.0	129.4	129.9	124.5	125.6	130.8
Financing and insurance services	78.6	77.7	86.0	91.6	93.4	94.6	92.1	98.0	97.8	90.9	98.7	108.4	99.8
Real estate and business services	194.1	191.1	197.8	208.9	204.6	211.9	212.9	216.7	210.4	216.0	215.4	222.6	233.6
Producers of government services	180.1	181.7	207.2	250.9	251.4	265.1	307.3	328.3	344.1	360.5	358.5	369.5	370.9
Miscellaneous services	106.1	110.9	126.5	125.9	119.6	112.2	108.8	105.0	105.5	98.6	93.5	94.5	102.1
Household and private non-profit institutions	27.9	29.0	33.1	39.9	38.0	29.7	25.7	27.1	21.7	19.0	18.2	18.9	20.5
Less imputed service charges	52.6	53.5	55.1	60.3	65.7	68.9	64.0	70.4	68.0	55.0	67.1	65.8	64.0
Total Gross Domestic Product at Constant Prices	1982.2	2042.2	2231.3	2240.6	2153.1	2143.8	2009.5	1961.8	1968.5	1941.2	1837.5	1897.7	1900.9

SOURCE   Department of Statistics, (1981; 1983).

TABLE A.10 *Rate of growth of gross domestic product by industrial sector at constant prices (%)*

Industrial sector	1970	1971	1972	1973	1974	1975	1976	1977	1978	1979	1980	1981	1982
Agriculture, forestry and fishing	5.9	11.8	1.8	-8.5	4.3	1.8	1.1	3.0	9.7	-9.8	-6.2	3.9	-6.7
Mining and quarrying	29.1	6.9	6.4	14.3	8.5	-20.2	-20.6	17.5	2.5	-1.6	9.9	1.3	-29.0
Manufacture	6.1	2.3	11.7	0.7	-3.5	2.4	-4.9	-11.6	-5.4	-4.1	-9.7	1.3	4.2
Electricity and water	7.9	12.8	13.5	5.6	0.0	4.1	2.7	-1.6	1.3	-1.7	1.4	1.2	0.0
Construction and installation	20.9	0.5	-2.9	-11.7	-5.4	1.3	-20.0	-20.8	3.6	-0.6	-28.5	1.6	12.9
Distributive trade (wholesale and retail)	5.6	2.8	17.0	-3.8	-16.6	2.8	-18.4	-7.9	-1.4	-4.1	-7.0	5.4	5.8
Transport, storage and communication	11.4	6.0	6.1	1.4	10.2	4.1	-3.4	-5.6	-0.5	0.4	-4.2	0.9	4.1
Financing and insurance services	6.4	-1.1	10.9	6.4	2.0	1.3	-2.6	6.4	-0.1	-7.1	8.6	9.9	-8.0
Real estate and business services	12.8	-1.5	3.5	5.7	-2.1	3.6	0.5	1.8	-2.9	2.7	-0.3	3.4	4.9
Producers of government services	19.5	0.9	14.0	21.1	0.2	5.5	15.9	6.8	4.8	4.8	-0.5	3.1	0.4
Miscellaneous services	12.9	4.5	14.1	-0.4	-5.0	-6.2	-3.0	-3.4	-0.4	-5.7	-5.2	1.1	8.0
Household and private non-profit institutions	26.2	3.9	14.1	20.7	-4.8	-21.9	-13.3	5.3	-19.8	-12.6	-4.0	3.6	8.6
Total Gross Domestic Product at constant prices	12.0	3.0	2.3	1.2	-3.9	-0.4	-6.3	-2.4	0.3	-1.4	-5.3	3.3	0.2

SOURCE   Department of Statistics (1981; 1983).

TABLE A.11   *Employment and unemployment 1972–82 (in 1000 and %)*

Date	Total labor force ('000)	Employed labor force ('000)	Unemployed labor force ('000)	Unemployment rate (%)
April 1972	783	598	185	23.6
October 1972	809	624	185	22.8
April 1973	811	637	173	21.4
October 1973	801	621	180	22.4
April 1974	820	642	178	21.8
October 1974	815	648	167	20.4
April 1975	849	677	172	20.3
October 1975	869	685	184	21.2
April 1976	872	693	179	20.5
October 1976	896	679	216	24.2
April 1977	902	680	222	24.6
October 1977	918	699	219	23.8
April 1978	929	715	214	23.0
October 1978	949	702	247	26.0
April 1979	945	715	230	24.4
October 1979	963	663	299	31.1
April 1980	975	703	272	27.9
November 1980	1007	737	270	26.8
April 1981	1007	743	264	26.2
October 1981	1023	761	262	25.6
April 1982	1037	757	281	27.0
October 1982	1049	756	292	27.9

SOURCE   NPA (various years).

TABLE A.12   *Exports of select goods, 1970–80 (current US $m, f.o.b., and %)*

Product	1970	1971	1972	1973	1974	1975	1976	1977	1978	1979	1980
Banana	14.2	15.3	14.8	18.3	12.6	16.1	13.2	13.9	17.3	18.2	10.4
Sugar	35.3	39.1	42.1	39.6	81.8	153.8	61.4	63.4	59.5	56.9	54.4
Bauxite	91.0	98.0	86.2	89.4	104.6	149.6	187.5	205.3	234.0	213.5	197.5
Alumina	127.6	136.9	151.1	165.9	297.8	324.8	237.6	323.2	348.3	368.2	534.7
(A) Sub-total	268.1	289.3	294.2	313.2	496.8	644.3	499.7	605.8	659.1	656.8	797.0
(B) Total exports	342.1	370.9	373.7	399.4	605.1	760.0	630.1	724.0	792.1	814.7	965.5
(A)/(B) %	78.4	78.0	78.7	78.4	82.1	84.8	79.3	83.7	83.2	80.6	82.5

SOURCE   Bank of Jamaica and Department of Statistics, cited in: IBRD (1982: Statistical Appendix, Table 3.2).

TABLE A.13   *Share of exports to major trading partners, 1970–80*

	1970	1971	1972	1973	1974	1975	1976	1977	1978	1979	1980
United States	51.9	45.0	42.4	41.2	47.1	40.3	48.0	47.4	43.2	44.9	37.1
United Kingdom	15.6	19.6	21.7	22.8	16.8	22.3	15.7	18.5	22.2	19.1	19.3
Caricom countries	3.1	4.8	5.8	6.3	5.3	4.5	6.9	6.7	7.3	7.6	5.9
Canada	8.2	8.3	7.1	5.5	5.6	3.3	5.0	8.0	7.7	6.0	3.9
Norway	7.9	8.7	11.5	10.4	11.5	9.5	10.1	9.5	6.4	5.1	10.8
Latin America	1.1	1.1	0.9	1.4	1.8	1.0	3.5	1.9	2.8	2.7	1.6
EEC countries	1.3	0.7	0.9	3.2	1.1	0.6	1.6	1.1	1.2	1.0	0.9
Other	10.9	11.8	9.8	9.2	10.8	18.4	9.2	6.9	9.2	13.7	20.6
Total Jamaica	100.0	100.0	100.0	100.0	100.0	100.0	100.0	100.0	100.0	100.0	100.0

NOTE   Figures may not all add up to 100% because of rounding.
SOURCE   Bank of Jamaica and Department of Statistics. As from: IBRD (1982: Statistical Appendix).

TABLE A.14   *Share of imports from major trading partners, 1970–80*

	1970	1971	1972	1973	1974	1975	1976	1977	1978	1979	1980
United States	43.0	39.6	37.2	37.9	35.2	37.4	37.2	36.0	36.8	31.8	31.4
Latin America	6.0	6.6	7.0	9.4	17.6	16.1	16.4	18.3	18.5	19.3	17.0
United Kingdom	19.1	19.8	19.2	16.4	12.4	13.1	10.9	9.7	10.4	9.8	6.7
EEC countries	8.1	9.1	8.7	9.8	8.3	6.8	6.3	5.9	6.1	6.7	4.6
Caricom countries	1.7	2.4	5.3	5.2	7.6	8.4	7.0	5.7	5.5	5.7	7.2
Canada	9.0	7.5	7.2	6.7	5.4	4.9	5.9	5.6	5.6	4.9	6.0
Other	13.1	15.0	14.6	14.5	13.5	13.3	16.4	18.8	17.1	21.9	27.0
Total Jamaica	100.0	100.0	100.0	100.0	100.0	100.0	100.0	100.0	100.0	100.0	100.0

NOTE   Figures may not all add up to 100% because of rounding.
SOURCE   Bank of Jamaica and Department of Statistics. As from: IBRD (1982: Statistical Appendix).

TABLE A.15   *Opinion polls 1976–83*

	PNP	JLP	WPJ	Uncommitted
August 1976	37%	29%	–	34
October 1976	36	34	–	30
November 1976	48	37	–	15
November 1977	39	36	–	25
March 1978	33	32	–	35
June 1978	28	32	–	40
November 1978	29	33	–	38
March 1979	32	36	2	30
July 1979	34	40	3	23
December 1979	37	47	*	16
March 1980	32	42	a	26
May 1980	36	49	*	15
September 1980	38	48		14
October 1980	37	50	*	13
January 1981	29	46	*	25
May 1981	20	48	2	30
July 1981	30	36	2	31
November 1981	34	41	1	24
October 1982	43	38	a	19
March 1983	41	38	1	20
October 1983	38	43	1	19
December 1983**	39	32	a	29

*WPJ and PNP figures combined by Stone due to WPJ support for PNP

**Among committed voters, the PNP had 55–45 per cent over the JLP when all voters eligible for enumeration on the new list were counted. Among committed voters on the 1980 list the JLP held a 51–49 per cent lead.

a   Less than 0.5 per cent.

SOURCE   Stone (1982: 4, 5, 6, 15, 40) for 1976–82, (1981a:40) for September 1980, and *Daily Gleaner* for 1983.

TABLE A.16 *Industrial disputes by cause, 1972–82*

Year	Wages and conditions of employment	Bargaining rights	Dismissal/ suspension	Other	All	Number involving work stoppages
in absolute numbers						
1972	156	157	58	24	395	117
1973	159	145	47	20	371	109
1974	185	135	81	42	443	137
1975	215	211	73	52	551	205
1976	198	178	83	55	514	142
1977	217	245	148	69	659	163
1978	238	181	142	126	687	NA
1979	128	152	187	141	608	182
1980	160	109	156	132	557	144
1981	172	165	204	165	706	145
1982	173	189	195	102	659	142
as percentages						
1972	39%	40%	15%	6%	100%	30%
1973	43	39	13	5	100	29
1974	42	30	18	9	100	31
1975	39	38	13	9	100	37
1976	39	35	16	11	100	28
1977	33	37	22	10	100	25
1978	35	26	21	18	100	NA
1979	21	25	31	23	100	30
1980	29	20	28	24	100	26
1981	24	23	23	23	100	21
1982	26	29	30	16	100	22

SOURCE   NPA (various years).

TABLE A.17 *Industrial disputes by union, 1972–82*

Year	NWU	BITU	TUC	Other*	Total
in absolute numbers					
1972	235	120	30	46	431**
1973	201	140	50	44	435
1974	232	150	66	45	493
1975	248	174	116	74	612
1976	202	150	88	72	512
1977	263	221	107	98	689
1978	221	227	79	164	691
1979	170	197	73	168	608
1980	149	150	74	183	556
1981	224	184	96	202	706
1982	218	169	76	196	659
as percentages					
1972	54	28	7	11	100
1973	46	32	11	10	100
1974	47	30	13	9	100
1975	41	28	19	12	100
1976	39	29	17	14	100
1977	38	32	16	14	100
1978	32	33	11	24	100
1979	28	32	12	28	100
1980	27	27	13	33	100
1981	32	26	14	29	100
1982	33	26	12	30	100

*Includes situations in which two or more unions held joint bargaining rights.

**Totals differ from Table A.20 since more than one union can be involved in the same dispute.

SOURCE NPA (various years).

TABLE A.18   *Domestic food production 1971–80 (in m pounds)*

Year	Total root and vegetable crops	Crops produced by project land lease (mostly roots and vegetables)
1971	638	
1972	670	
1973	608	
1974	658	17
1975	663	68
1976	631	29
1977	793	56
1978	1010	82
1979	915	139
1980	771	150

SOURCE   NPA (various years).

TABLE A.19   *Tourist arrivals* 1970–82*

	In thousands			Index (1975 = 100)		
Year	Jamaica	Other Caribbean**	Mexico	Jamaica	Other Caribbean	Mexico
1970	309.1	1437.4	2250.2	78	74	70
1971	359.3	1529.5	NA	91	78	NA
1972	407.8	1678.5	2912.2	103	86	91
1973	418.3	1875.2	3238.8	106	96	101
1974	432.0	2055.0	3362.0	109	105	104
1975	395.8	1950.6	3217.9	100	100	100
1976	327.7	1981.5	3107.2	82	102	97
1977	264.9	2167.4	3247.2	66	111	101
1978	381.8	2336.2	3754.3	96	120	117
1979	426.5	2643.6	4141.8	108	136	129
1980	395.3	2690.3	NA	100	137	
1981	406.4		NA	103		
1982	467.8		NA	118		

*Refers to number of persons staying over at least one night.

**Barbados, Trinidad and Tobago, Dominican Republic, Puerto Rico, and Haiti.

NA   Not available

SOURCE   Caribbean Tourism Research Centre, cited in IBRD (1982: 65, 97).

TABLE A.20 US loans and grants to Jamaica, 1956–82 (US fiscal years – US$m – new obligations)

	Annual average 1956–60	Annual average 1961–5	Annual average 1966–70	1971	1972	1973	1974	1975	1976[d]	1977	1978	1979	1980	1981	1982
Economic Assistance – total	1.0	5.3	3.7	23.1	6.1	8.4	13.2	4.3	5.1	32.2	23.3	18.1	14.6	73.5	138.6
AID	0.2	3.1	1.0	20.9	1.2	5.6	9.9	0.6	0.9	17.5	11.6	6.0	2.7	53.9	119.4
(Security Supporting Assist.)[a]	( )	( )	( )	( )	( )	( )	( )	( )	( )	( )	(11.0)	( )	( )	(41.0)	(90.5)
Food for Peace	0.8	1.9	2.1	1.1	3.9	1.4	1.8	1.6	2.6	13.4	10.5	10.2	10.0	17.1	17.5
Other Economic Assistance[b]	–	0.3	0.7	1.1	1.0	1.4	1.5	2.1	1.6	1.2	1.2	1.9	1.9	2.5	1.7
Military Assistance – total	–	0.1	0.1	–	–	–	–	–	–	–	–	–	–	1.7	2.1
Total economic and military	1.0	5.4	3.8	23.1	6.1	8.4	13.2	4.3	5.1	32.2	23.3	18.1	14.6	75.1	140.7
Loans	–	2.3	–	20.0	–	4.4	9.9	1.4	2.4	28.5	19.5	12.7	10.0	69.4	129.4
Grants	1.0	3.1	3.8	3.1	6.1	4.0	3.3	2.9	2.7	3.7	3.8	5.4	4.6	5.8	11.3
Other US Loans[c]	–	0.9	5.6	0.9	17.5	7.3	15.9	16.1	0.2	0.5	–	–	–	7.4	1.5
Ex-Im Loans	–	0.9	5.6	0.9	16.7	7.3	15.9	16.1	0.2	–	–	–	–	6.4	–
All other	–	–	–	–	0.8	–	–	–	–	0.5	–	–	–	1.0	1.5

NOTES (a) Includes Economic Support Fund
(b) Includes $3m grant by the Inter-American Foundation
(c) Represents Private Trade Agreements under Title I, PL 480 and OPIC direct loan.
(d) Includes transitional quarter.

SOURCE AID (1983).

TABLE A.21 *Class realignment 1972–80* (as percentage)

	PNP vote 1972	PNP vote 1976	PNP vote 1980
Unemployed and unskilled	52	60	40
Manual wage labor	61	72	48
White-collar wage labor	75	57	37
Business and management class and high income professionals	60	20	14
Farm labor	52	56	42
Small peasants	47	45	35

SOURCE   Stone (1981:37). Reprinted by permission from *Caribbean Review* 10(2).

Appendix 2: Interview Data

One of the sources of primary data for this study was a series of in-depth personal interviews with eighty-six people carried out in Jamaica in 1981–2 and March 1984 and in the United States in 1983–4. Forty-six of the people interviewed in Jamaica were selected by the elite sampling methods used by Moskos (1967) in his 1961–2 study of West Indian elites (including Jamaica) and by Bell and his associates (Bell, 1977–8; Bell and Gibson, 1978; Robinson and Bell, 1978; Bell and Stevenson, 1979; Bell and Baldrich, 1982) in their 1974 study of the Jamaican elite. For the purposes of this book, the systematic comparisons that these studies make possible have not been extensively exploited, though this will be done in the future. For our purposes here, the advantage of the method was that it drew a systematic sample of powerful people, from different sections of the elite and with different political points of view, whom we could question about various aspects of Jamaican politics in general and the Manley period in particular.

Following the Moskos–Bell method, we began by interviewing five people (each representing a different institutional sector in the society) who had considerable influence in Jamaica by positions alone. The five sectors were the JLP, the PNP, the mass media, the public sector and business. In addition to the standard interview question, we asked these people the following question:

> Considering all aspects of Jamaican life, who would you say are the most important influential individuals on the entire island? That is, who are the people who can influence or control other people's opinions and actions?

Subsequent respondents were chosen from the lists supplied by these first respondents. Each of them in turn was asked this question and handed the combined list and asked to 'check those whose opinions really mattered most' and then 'Is there anyone you would add to the list?' We attempted to interview those who received the most nominations as 'influential individuals'. We interviewed 89 per cent of those who were nominated by at least one-quarter of the other elites.

Of course, this is only one method of selecting elites and it has been shown that other methods, such as a decision-making method will identify somewhat different people as the most influential or powerful. But it was not our purpose here to identify the universe of 'powerful people' in Jamaica and no use we have made of the data depends on this being the case. It was our purpose to identify a group of people who were influential, whose public stature made them opinion leaders, who represented the spectrum of political views in Jamaica, and who represented various sectors of the elite (particularly business, media, the two parties and the unions) in order to gain access to them and interview them. Any educated observer of Jamaican politics and society can verify that this is the case by examining the list of people identified (Appendix 4).

As one can see from Appendix 4, the same methodology resulted in an elite group of quite different sizes at the two dates. We believe the decline in the sample size between 1974 ad 1982 reflects an actual decline in the number of influential people during the period. The ranks of business were diminished: 27 per cent of those interviewed in 1974 had left by 1982. The number of PNP leaders nominated was obviously affected by the fact that they had lost power and by the fact that a number of former PNP leaders left the country to take jobs with various international organizations once they left office. The JLP group did not increase in size between 1974 and 1982, which, at first, may seem surprising given that they were in power at the latter date. The explanation here is that, as we pointed out in Chapter 7, Seaga held a large number of portfolios and took personal responsibility for an ever-larger number of key decisions. It was widely perceived that power in the Seaga government was very concentrated and that relatively few people influenced Seaga's decisions. Furthermore, we have argued that political organization and mobilization made the mass of the Jamaican people more important political actors, and thus political leaders had to be better able to appeal to large numbers of people in order to be very influential. Aside from Manley, Seaga and Shearer, there were not many political leaders who could do this, which prompted some answers from our respondents like 'only Manley, Seaga, Shearer and Bob Marley are really influential'.

The interview schedule included a set of questions taken from the 1974 questionnaire designed to tap the respondents' economic ideology, attitude toward democracy and desired foreign alignments, as well as a set of background and biographical questions. We also asked all respondents what they thought were the biggest successes and failures of the Manley government. Then, in the case of the businessmen, we asked them a number of questions tapping changes in their attitude toward the Manley government and in their investment behavior during the period, and in the attitudes, investment behavior and reasons for migration of the Jamaican business community in general. (See Stephens and Stephens 1983a for the exact wording of these questions.) For the other respondents, we spent the remainder of the interview questioning them on specific aspects of the dynamics of the period into which they, from their vantage point, had particular insight.

The elite sample did not include all the people with knowledge about the PNP's period in office to whom we wanted to talk, so we supplemented the elite interviews with twelve interviews with key informants about the period, primarily PNP politicians and advisors. We also identified eight crucial areas we wanted to explore in depth (management of the economy, sugar co-operatives, workers participation, bauxite, agriculture, media, unions and public administration) and interviewed eight people with special expertise in these areas. Professor Rex Nettleford of the Trade Union Education Institute organized a collective interview for us with delegates (shop stewards) from five unions. In general, these interviews in Jamaica ranged from one to three hours and, in a number of cases, we returned for a second interview.

In the USA, in the fall of 1983, we interviewed eight present or former State Department officials, former ambassadors and former (that is, Ford and Carter period) top foreign policy advisors about US relations with Jamaica during the Manley and Seaga periods, as well as two people professionally involved in promoting US investment in the region. In the fall of 1983 and spring of 1984, we interviewed seven executives from three of the four major North American aluminum corporations about relations to Jamaica since the beginning of the Manley period. Most of these executives were heads of the primary products divisions, heads of the Jamaican operations, and/or negotiators for the companies during the talks over the levy and the subsequent agreements on the lands, equity ownership and so forth.

Appendix 3: Reading and Coding of Newspaper Reports

At the time of our field research, the history of the Manley period could not be pieced together using secondary source materials, so we were forced to resort to primary materials: reading daily newspapers and interviewing the participants in the historical process (see Appendix 2 for the latter). We read the articles appearing on the front page and the editorials of the *Gleaner* from January 1972 to November 1980 and the first three pages and the editorials of the *Daily News* from its inception in May 1973 to November 1980. Given the key role of the *Gleaner* in the opposition to the Manley government, we coded attacks made on the government which appeared on the front page of the paper or in its editorials (see Table A.3). For each attack the following information was coded: the date, the author (or source) of the attack, and its content. Almost all the attacks came from one of three sources: JLP politicians, private sector organizations or spokespersons, and the *Gleaner* itself. The grounds for the attack were coded on the basis of eight categories and a residual category. Most of these categories were developed before we began the newspaper work on the basis of our discussions with Caribbean social scientists and our readings on the period. A few categories were added as we read through the first years and some were collapsed in the final coding (e.g. charges of totalitarian directions and charges of moving toward a one-party state). In retrospect, we made one mistake in the coding process: as attacks began to appear in 1977 and 1978 charging the PNP with election fraud and corruption, we initially decided to exclude these attacks (almost all of them from the JLP) as these are standard charges made by Jamaican opposition parties against the government. By the time we realized our mistake it was too late to rectify it, as the newspaper work was so time-consuming. (The reading and coding took us eleven person–months to complete). We did, however, begin to code attacks on these grounds from March 1979 on (these are *not* included in Table A.3) and we took notes for the whole period on attacks on the government on these grounds, so we do have a check on this. When these factors became significant issues, it was noted in the text.

Not all criticisms of the government were considered attacks. For instance, if the private sector complained that import licenses were not being processed fast enough or if the *Gleaner* said that the government should cut taxes instead of subsidizing foods, this was not coded as an attack. But when, for example, the Jamaica Manufacturers' Association said that the government's price-controls policy caused the closing of a mill and there were more closures coming, the charge was coded as an attack. The most difficult aspect of the coding was deciding in marginal cases whether a given charge was an attack. In these marginal cases, the authors consulted one another in order to arrive at a decision. In reviewing the data we noticed a slight tendency for the threshold to move up in later years, that is, the criticism had to be somewhat stronger to be considered a codeable attack.

Thus, there is probably a slight underestimation of the increase in attacks on the government in the data.

One last point that should be made about this data is that it is quite obvious that it is not an objective reflection of the trends in attitudes, or even in attitudes expressed in public utterances, of the private sector or the JLP leadership. If a spokesperson for the JLP or the private sector made an attack and the *Gleaner* chose not to put it on the front page then it is not coded. Thus, the *Gleaner* in some sense had to pursue a similar agenda, and the trends represent the *Gleaner's* agenda as well as the critic's. This is much less important in the case of the private sector, since throughout its history the *Gleaner* generally has given very prominent coverage to private sector spokespeople, particularly any strong criticism of the government.

But in the case of the JLP this factor was very important, and, as we argued particularly in Chapter 6, part of the story of the Manley government's second term is how the *Gleaner's* agenda increasingly came to coincide with the JLP's in promoting attacks on the government, particularly on the communist threat issue. In this respect our reading of the *Daily News* was important as a method by which we could evaluate the question of whether an increase in the attacks in the *Gleaner* represented a true increase in opposition or a change in the *Gleaner's* agenda.

Appendix 4: Jamaican Elite: 1974 and 1982

Number of nominations	Political/Labor	Economic	Other
		1974	
79	M. N. Manley		
76	E. Seaga		
71			G. A. Brown
			T. E. Sealy
70	H. Shearer		
69	E. Matalon		
68	P. J. Patterson		
64	D. H. Coore		
63			R. Nettleford
62		A. Matalon	
61		L. Ashenheim	
60		C. D. Alexander	
59	E. Bell	Mayer Matalon	
	R. Lightbourne		
	A. Spaulding		
58	V. O. Blake		
	C. Dunkley		
57	T. Munroe	Moses Matalon	
56	F. Saunders		
55			E. Richardson
54			H. Barber
53	K. Munn	K. Hendrickson	
		P. Rousseau	
52	A. Isaacs		
51	P. Charles		
50			A. Smith
48			J. C. Proute
47	O. K. Melhado		W. A. Powell
46	K. McNeill		
45	H. Cooke		S. Carter
43			G. Bonnick
			J. Maxwell
42	D. Thompson		A. Preston
41	W. Hill		
	R. Leon		

403

Number of nominations	Political/Labor	Economic	Other
		1974	
40			F. Glasspole
			A. McIntyre
39			J. Robinson
38		W. Meeks	
37		M. Cargill	J. T. Burrowes
36	R. Fletcher	D. Judah	C. Grant
35		D. Williams	
34		B. Ewart	A. Bailey
33	A. Bustamante	D. Stone	
32		J. Issa	
		J. Lim	
		T. Tatham	
31	I. Ramsay	A. Issa	E. Manley
30	E. Peart	J. Ashenheim	G. Bustamante
29	Leacroft Robinson		J. Hearne
	E. L. Taylor		E. Miller
			W. Wainwright
28	W. Jones	Henderson-Davies	J. Swaby
		T. Donaldson	
27	P. A. Broderick	N. Chin	S. U. Hastings
		M. Facey	D. Whylie
26	E. A. Abrahams		R. Mahfood
	D. K. Duncan		H. Wynter
	M. Tenn		
24	E. Allen	P. Geddes	K. Smith
		D. Tretzel	
23	S. Pagon	R. C. Thompson	B. Manley
			Father Meany
22		W. Mahfood	C. Campbell
		R. Sasso	V. Mendes
			A. A. Rattray
			V. Reid
			P. M. Sherlock
21	E. Nelson		R. Mason
20		H. Sherlock	E. Bailey
19			W. B. C. Hawthorne
			R. M. Murray
			K. Rattray
			S. Reid
18	T. A. Kelly		L. Bennett
	D. Manley		W. Isaacs
17	L. Beckford	O. Jones	E. Clark
	C. Sinclair	S. Mahfood	D. Gascoigne
			C. Henry
			W. Roberts
			Peter Rousseau
			I. Woodstock

Number of nominations	Political/Labor	Economic	Other
		1974	
16		A. Hart	D. Dyer
			B. Glouden
			P. Henzell
			Father HoLung
15		G. Desnoes	G. Beckford ·
		W. W. Isaacs	
		F. Tulloch	
14	R. Brown	O. Daley	A. S. Phillips
		E. George	
		H. Pengelly	
13		D. Banks	R. B. Campbell
12		C. Clark	
		A. Foreman	
		L. Ramson	
11			J. Akar
			I. Carnegie
			L. Mair
			L. R. B. Robinson
			D. Vaz
10	C. Fletcher	C. Charlton	C. Meeks
		T. Kelly	
8			Leila Robinson
7		E. Gordon	V. Arnett
		O. Hudson	N. Dawes
6			R. Nelson
5			M. Henry
4		S. Chen See	G. Ellington
			S. Gerard
2			E. Maxwell
1		D. Myers	L. Bannett

Number of nominations	Political/Labor	Economic	Other
		1982	
42	E. Seaga		
39	M. Manley		
38	H. Shearer		
33		C. Alexander	
32			F. Glasspole
			C. Stone
26	P. Charles		
25			H. Wynter
24	L. Beckford		R. Nettleford
	T. Munroe		
23	D. K. Duncan		

Number of nominations	Political/Labor	Economic	Other
		1982	
22			W. Perkins
20		A. Henriques	O. Clarke
		M. Matalon	
18	B. Golding	L. Ashenheim	S. Carter
	H. Small		J. Hearne
			R. Thwaites
17	P. J. Patterson	W. Mahfood	
16		R. Sasso	P. Abrahams
15			U. Parnell
14	P. Broderick		S. Reid
13	R. Ennis		N. deSouza
12	H. Caven	R. Collister	
	M. Gilmour	A. Matalon	
	R. Irvine		
	A. Spaulding		
11	E. L. Taylor		
10	D. Thompson	A. Issa	J. Robinson
		J. Issa	
		S. Mahfood	
		R. D. Williams	
9	H. O. Thompson	A. Williams	H. Blair
8		D. Lalor	E. Bailey
			C. Wint
7	C. Dunkley		L. Lawrence
			E. Manley
			O. K. Melhado
6			E. Davis
			P. Hart
			H. Sherlock
5	J. A. G. Smith		E. Gordon
4	A. Bertram		H. Barber
	B. Manley		D. Boxer
	D. Vaz		
3	W. Spaulding		
2			S. Clarke
			H. Hart
			K. Jones
			S. Jones
			K. Smith

References

Ahiram, E. (1964) 'Income Distribution in Jamaica, 1958', *Social and Economic Studies*, 13 (September).

AID (Agency for International Development) (1983) *US Overseas Loans and Grants*, vol. II, Latin America and the Caribbean (Washington, D.C.: AID).

Alavi, H. (1972) 'The State in Post-Colonial Societies: Pakistan and Bangladesh', *New Left Review*, 74:59–81.

Almond, G. and Verba, S. (1968) *The Civic Culture* (Boston: Little, Brown).

Ambursle, F. (1981) 'Jamaica: The Demise of "Democratic Socialism"', *New Left Review* 128:76–87.

Ambursle, F. (1983) 'Jamaica: From Michael Manley to Edward Seaga', in Ambursley, F. and Cohen, R. (eds) *Crisis in the Caribbean* (New York: Monthly Review Press).

Ayub, M. A. (1981) *Made in Jamaica: The Development of the Manufacturing Sector*, World Bank Staff Occasional Papers, no. 31 (Baltimore: Johns Hopkins University Press).

Bank of Jamaica, various years, *Annual Reports* (Kingston: Bank of Jamaica).

Bank of Jamaica (1981) *Statistical Digest, October 1981* (Kingston: Bank of Jamaica).

Bank of Jamaica (1984) *Statistical Digest, February 1984* (Kingston: Bank of Jamaica).

Banks, F. E. (1979) *Bauxite and Aluminum: An Introduction to the Economics of Non-Fuel Minerals* (Lexington, Massachusetts: Lexington Books).

Barrett, R. and Whyte, M. K. (1982) 'Dependency Theory and Taiwan: Analysis of a Deviant Case', *American Journal of Sociology* 87(6):1064–89.

Bartley, E. (1981) 'A Conspiracy to Obscure', *Jamaica Sunday Sun*, 8 November 1981.

Beckford, G. (1972) *Persistent Poverty* (New York: Oxford University Press).

Beckford, G., Girvan, N., Lindsay, L. and Witter, M. (1978) 'The People's Plan for Socialist Transformation', (Kingston: unpublished manuscript).

Beckford, G. and Witter, M. (1980) *Small Garden, Bitter Weed* (Morant Bay: Maroon Publishing House).

Bell, W. (1964) *Jamaican Leaders* (Berkeley and Los Angeles: University of California Press).

Bell, W. (1977–8) 'Independent Jamaica Enters World Politics: The Start of Foreign Policy in a New State'. *Political Science Quarterly*, 92:683–703.

Bell, W. and Baldrich, J. (1982) 'Elites, Economic Ideology and Democracy in Jamaica', in Czudnowski, M. M. (ed.) *International Yearbook for Studies of Leaders and Leadership* (Dekalb, Illinois: Northern Illinois University Press).

Bell, W. and Gibson, J. W. (1978) 'Independent Jamaica Faces the Outside World', *International Studies Quarterly*, 22(1):5–47.

Bell, W. and Stevenson, D. L. (1979) 'Attitudes Toward Social Equality in Independent Jamaica', *Comparative Political Studies*, 11(4):499–532.

Bernal, R. (1980) 'Transnational Commercial Banks, The International Monetary

Fund and Capitalist Crisis in Jamaica 1972–1980', paper presented at the Conference on Finance Capital and Dependence in the Transnational Phase: A Latin American Perspective, Mexico City, 4–7 March 1980.

Bernal, R. (1981) 'Jamaica's Economic Relations with Socialist Countries 1972–1980', paper presented at the Second Congress of Third World Economists, Havana, 26–30 April 1981.

Bernal, R. (1982) 'The IMF and Class Struggle in Jamaica', paper presented at the World Congress of Sociology, Mexico City, 16–21 August 1982.

Best, L. (1966) 'Size and Survival', *New World Quarterly*, 2(3).

Best, L. (1967) 'Independent Thought and Caribbean Freedom', *New World Quarterly*, 3(4), reprinted in Girvan, N. and Jefferson, O. (eds.) *Readings in the Political Economy of the Caribbean* (Kingston: New World Group, 1971).

Bitar, S. (1979) *Transición, Socialismo y Democracia: La Experiencia Chilena* (Mexico: *Siglo Veintiuno Editores*).

Bitar, S. (1983) 'Latin America and the United States: Changes in Economic Relations During the 1970s', Working Paper no. 127, Latin American Program, Wilson Center, Washington, D.C.

Blasier, C. (1983) *The Giant's Rival* (Pittsburgh: University of Pittsburgh Press).

Blumberg, P. (1968) *Industrial Democracy: The Sociology of Participation* (New York: Schocken Books).

Bornschier, V., Chase-Dunn, C. and Rubinson, R. (1978) 'Crossnational Evidence of the Effects of Foreign Investment and Aid on Economic Growth and Inequality: A Survey of the Findings and a Reanalysis', *American Journal of Sociology*, 84:1064–89.

Brenner, R. (1976) 'Agrarian Class Structure and Economic Development in Pre-industrial Europe', *Past and Present*, 70:30–75.

Brenner, R. (1977) 'The Origins of Capitalist Development: A Critique of Neo-Smithian Marxism', *New Left Review*, 104.

Brown, A. and McBain, H. (1983) 'The Public Sector in Jamaica', in *Studies in Caribbean Public Enterprise* (Mona, Jamaica: Institute of Social and Economic Research, University of the West Indies).

Brown, A. (1976) 'The Mass Media of Communications and Social Change in the Caribbean: A Case Study of Jamaica', *Caribbean Quarterly*, 22(4):43–49.

Brown, A. (1977) 'The Mass Media of Communications and Socialist Change in Jamaica', in Stone, C. and Brown, A. (eds) *Essays on Power and Change in Jamaica* (Kingston: Jamaica Publishing House).

Brudenius, C. and Lundahl, M. (1982) *Development Strategies and Basic Needs in Latin America* (Boulder, Colorado: Westview Press).

Brutents, K. N. (1977) *National Liberation Revolutions Today* (Moscow: Progress Publishers) (2 vols).

Cameron, D. (1978) 'The Expansion of the Public Economy: A Comparative Analysis', *American Political Science Review*, 72(4):1243–61.

Canak, W. L. (1984) 'The Peripheral State Debate: State Capitalist and Bureaucratic–Authoritarian Regimes in Latin America', *Latin American Research Review*, 19(1):3–36.

Caporaso, J. A. and Zare, B. (1981) 'An Interpretation and Evaluation of Dependency Theory', in Munoz, H. (ed.) *From Dependency to Development* (Boulder, Colorado: Westview Press) pp. 43–58.

Cardoso, F. H. (1964) *Empresario Industrial e Desenvolvimento Economico no Brasil* (Sao Paulo: *Difusao Europeia do Livro*).

Cardoso, F. H. and Faletto, E. (1979) *Dependency and Development in Latin America* (Berkeley: University of California Press).

Cargill, M. (1979) *Jamaica Farewell* (Secaucus, New Jersey: Cinnamon Books).

Chambers, W. G. (1980) 'The Evolution of the Bauxite Mining Laws in Jamaica', *JBI JOURNAL*, 1(1):29–33.

Charles, P. (1977) *Detained* (Kingston: Kingston Publishers Ltd).

Chen-Young, P. (1966) 'An Economic Evaluation of the Tax Incentive Programme in Jamaica', unpublished Ph.D. thesis, University of Pittsburgh.

Chevannes, B. (1981) 'The Rastafari and Urban Youth', in Stone, C. and Brown, A. (eds.) *Perspectives on Jamaica in the Seventies* (Kingston: Jamaica Publishing House).

Chief Electoral Officer, (1955) *General Election 1955, Report* (Kingston: Chief Electoral Officer).

Chief Electoral Officer, (1959) *General Election 1959, Report* (Kingston: Chief Electoral Officer).

Chief Electoral Officer, (1972) *General Election 1972, Report* (Kingston: Chief Electoral Officer).

Chief Electoral Officer, (1976) *General Election 1976, Report* (Kingston: Chief Electoral Officer).

Clarke, C. G. (1975) *Kingston, Jamaica* (Berkeley, California: University of California Press).

Collier, D. (ed.) (1979) *The New Authoritarianism in Latin America* (Princeton: Princeton University Press).

Collins, R. (1971) 'Functional and Conflict Theories of Educational Stratification', *American Sociological Review*, 36(6):1002–19.

Concerned Citizens Committee (1980) 'Report on the Destabilization of Jamaica', unpublished paper.

Davies, O. (1984) 'Economic Transformation in Jamaica: Some Policy Issues', *Journal of International Development Studies*, 19(3).

Davis, C. (1980) 'Jamaica in the World Aluminum Industry: The Discovery and Commercialization of Aluminum', *JBI JOURNAL*, 1(1):3–28.

Davis, C. (1981) 'Jamaica in the World Aluminum Industry II: The Discovery and Commercialization of Jamaican Bauxite (1939–1952)', *JBI Journal*, 1(2):89–135.

Department of Statistics (1966) *Employment, Earnings and Hours in Large Establishments 1965* (Kingston: Department of Statistics).

Department of Statistics (1973) *National Income and Product 1972* (Kingston: Department of Statistics).

Department of Statistics (1979) *Statistical Yearbook of Jamaica 1978* (Kingston: Department of Statistics).

Department of Statistics (1981a) *Employment, Earnings and Hours in Large Establishments 1979* (Kingston: Department of Statistics).

Department of Statistics (1981b) *The Labour Force 1980* (Kingston: Department of Statistics).

Department of Statistics (1981c) *National Income and Product 1980* (Kingston: Department of Statistics).

Department of Statistics (1983a) *The Labour Force 1982* (Kingston: Department of Statistics).

Department of Statistics (1983b) *National Income and Product 1982* (Kingston: Department of Statistics).

Department of Statistics (1983c) *Statistical Yearbook of Jamaica 1981* (Kingston: Department of Statistics).

Director of Elections (1980) *General Election 1980, Report* (Kingston: Director of Elections).

Duncan, N. C. (1970) 'The Political Process, and Attitudes and Opinions in a

Jamaican Parish Council', *Social and Economic Studies*, 19(1):89–113.

Eaton, G. E. (1975) *Alexander Bustamante and Modern Jamaica* (Kingston: Kingston Publishers Ltd).

Esping-Andersen, G. (1985) *Politics Against Markets: The Social Democratic Road to Power* (Princeton: Princeton University Press).

Esping-Andersen, G. and Friedland, R. (1982) 'Class Coalitions in the Making of West European Economics', in Esping-Andersen, G. and Friedland, R. (eds) *Political Power and Social Theory*, (Greenwich: JAI Press) vol. 3.

Evans, P. (1979) *Dependent Development* (Princeton: Princeton University Press).

Evans, P. (1985) 'Transnational Linkages and the Economic Role of the State: An Analysis of Developing and Industrial Nations in the post-World War II Period', in Evans, P. *et al.* (eds.) *Bringing the State Back In* (Cambridge: Cambridge University Press).

Evans, P. and Timberlake, M. (1980) 'Dependence, Inequality and the Growth of the Tertiary: A Comparative Analysis of Less Developed Countries', *American Sociological Review*, 45(3):531–51.

FAO (Food and Agriculture Organization of the United Nations) (1975) 'Agrarian Reform and General Agricultural Development: Jamaica', report prepared for the Government of Jamaica by the FAO (Rome: FAO).

Feuer, C. (1983) 'The Internal Political Economy of Democratic Reform: Sugar Workers' Co-operatives in Jamaica', paper presented at the XXXVII Conference of the New York State Political Science Association, New York City, 9 April 1983.

Feuer, C. (1984) *Jamaica and Sugar Workers' Co-operatives: The Politics of Reform* (Boulder, Colorado: Westview Press).

Foner, N. and Napoli, R. (1978) 'Jamaican and Black American Migrant Farm Workers: A Comparative Analysis', *Social Problems,* 25(5):491–503.

Frank, A. G. (1967) *Capitalism and Underdevelopment in Latin America: Historical Studies of Chile and Brazil* (New York: Monthly Review Press).

Friedland, R. (1983) *Power and Crisis in the City: Corporations, Unions and Urban Policy* (New York: Schocken Books).

Girvan, N. (1967) *The Caribbean Bauxite Industry* (Mona, Jamaica: Institute of Social and Economic Research, University of the West Indies).

Girvan, N. (1971) *Foreign Capital and Economic Underdevelopment in Jamaica* (Mona, Jamaica: Institute of Social and Economic Research, University of the West Indies).

Girvan, N. (1976) *Corporate Imperialism: Conflict and Expropriation* (New York: Monthly Review Press).

Girvan, N., Bernal, R. and Hughes, W. (1980) 'The IMF and the Third World: The Case of Jamaica', *Development Dialogue* (2):113–55.

Girvan, N. and Jefferson, O. (eds) (1971) *Readings in the Political Economy of the Caribbean* (Kingston: New World Group).

Gold, D., Lo, C. and Wright, E. (1975) 'Recent Developments in Marxist Theories of the Capitalist State', *Monthly Review*, October:29–43, November:36–51.

Gonsalves, R. (1977) 'The Trade Union Movement in Jamaica: Its Growth and Some Resultant Problems', in Stone, C. and Brown, A. (eds.) *Essays on Power and Change in Jamaica* (Kingston: Jamaica Publishing House).

Goulbourne, H. (1979) 'Some Problems of Analysis of the Political in Backward Capitalist Formations', in Goulbourne, H. (ed.) *Politics and the State in the Third World* (London: Macmillan).

Harrison, F. (1982) 'Semi-proletaranization and the Structure of Socioeconomic and Political Relations in a Jamaican Slum', unpublished Ph.D. dissertation, Stanford University.

Harrod, J. (1972) *Trade Union Foreign Policy* (Garden City, New York: Doubleday & Co., Inc.).

Henry, M. (1980) 'Getting into the IMF', unpublished paper, Department of Government, University of the West Indies, Mona.

Henry, Z. (1972) *Labour Relations and Industrial Conflict in Commonwealth Caribbean Countries* (Port-of-Spain: Columbus Publishers).

Hersh, S. M. (1983) *The Price of Power: Kissinger in the Nixon White House* (New York: Summit Books).

Hewitt, L. (1974) 'Internal Migration and Urban Growth', in Roberts, G. W. (ed.) *Recent Population Movements in Jamaica* (Kingston: CICRED Series).

Hibbs, D. (1977) 'Political Parties and Macroeconomic Policy', *American Political Science Review*, 81(4):1467–87.

Hicks, A., Friedland, R. and Johnson, E. (1978) 'Class Power and State Policy', *American Sociological Review*, 43(3):302–15.

Himmelstrand, U. (1970) 'Depoliticization and Political Involvement', in Allardt, E. and Rokkan, S. (eds.) *Mass Politics* (New York: Free Press) pp. 64–92.

Hollingsworth, R. and Hanneman, R. (1982) 'Leftist Governments, Working Class Power, and the Political Economy of Advanced Capitalist Societies', in Tomasson, R. (ed.) *Comparative Social Research* (Greenwich: JAI Press) vol. 5.

Holzberg, C. (1977a) 'Race, Ethnicity and the Political Economy of National Entrepreneurial Elites in Jamaica', unpublished Ph.D. dissertation, Boston University.

Holzberg, C. (1977b) 'Social Stratification, Cultural Nationalism and Political Economy in Jamaica: The Myths of Development and the Anti-White Bias', *Canadian Review of Sociology and Anthropology*, 14(4):368–80.

IBRD (International Bank for Reconstruction and Development–World Bank) (1976) *World Debt Tables* (Washington: IBRD) (2 vols).

IBRD (1978) 'Economic Memorandum on Jamaica', report no. 2076–JM, 26 May 1978.

IBRD (1980) 'Jamaica's Short Term Economic Program', report no. 3023–JM, 16 June 1980.

IBRD (1982a) 'Jamaica: Development Issues and Economic Prospects', report no. 3781–JM, 29 January 1982.

IBRD (1982b) 'Jamaica: Structural Adjustment, Export Development and Private Investment', report no. 3955–JM, 3 June 1982.

IDB (Inter-American Development Bank) (1977) *Latin America's External Indebtedness: Current Situation and Prospects* (Washington: IDB).

IDB (1978) *Economic and Social Progress in Latin America* (Washington: IDB).

IDB (1982a) *Economic and Social Progress in Latin America: The External Sector* (Washington: IDB).

IDB (1982b) *External Financing of the Latin American Countries* (Washington: IDB).

IICA (Inter-American Institute for Agricultural Sciences) (1981) 'A Review of Land Reform in Jamaica 1972–1978', report for IICA (Kingston: IICA).

Jackman, R. (1980) 'A Note on the Measurement of Growth Rates in Crossnational Research', *American Journal of Sociology*, 86(3):604–17.

Jefferson, O. (1972) *The Post-War Economic Development of Jamaica* (Mona, Jamaica: Institute of Social and Economic Research, University of the West Indies).

Jones, E. (1970) 'The Role of Statutory Boards in the Political Process in Jamaica', *Social and Economic Studies*, 19(1):114–34.

Jones, E. (1981a) 'Bureaucratic Obstacles to Change in Jamaica: A Preliminary View on the Decade of the Seventies', unpublished paper, Department of Government, University of the West Indies, Mona.

Jones, E. (1981b) 'Issues of Public Management in the Jamaican Election of 1980: An Unorthodox View', Department of Government, University of the West Indies, Mona.

Jones, E. (1981c) 'The Political Economy of Public Administration in Jamaica', in Stone, C. and Brown, A. (eds.) *Perspectives on Jamaica in the Seventies* (Kingston: Jamaica Publishing House).

Jones, E. and Mills, G. E. (1976) 'Institutional Innovation and Change in the Commonwealth Caribbean', *Social and Economic Studies*, 25(4):323–46.

JWG (Jamaica Weekly Gleaner) North American edition, various dates.

Kaplan, I., Blutstein, H. I., Johnson, K. T. and McMorris, D. S. (1976) *Area Handbook for Jamaica* (Washington, D.C.: US Government Printing Office).

Kirton, C. and Figueroa, M. (1981) 'State Trading: A Vital Element in Caribbean Economic Development', in Stone, C. and Brown, A. (eds) *Perspectives on Jamaica in the Seventies* (Kingston: Jamaica Publishing House).

Klapp, M. G. (1982) 'The State – Landlord or Enterpreneur?' *International Organization*, 36:3 (Summer).

Korpi, W. (1978) *The Working Class in Welfare Capitalism* (London: Routledge & Kegan Paul).

Korpi, W. (1983) *The Democratic Class Struggle* (London: Routledge & Kegan Paul).

Korpi, W. and Shalev, M. (1979) 'Industrial Relations and Class Conflict in Capitalist Societies', *British Journal of Sociology*, 30:164–87.

Lacey, T. (1977) *Violence and Politics in Jamaica 1960–1970* (Manchester: Manchester University Press).

LAWR (Latin America Weekly Reports) London, various dates.

LARRC (Latin America Regional Reports, Caribbean) London, various dates.

Lewin, A. (1982) 'The Fall of Michael Manley: A Case Study of the Failure of Reform Socialism', *Monthly Review*, February.

Lewis, W. A. (1950) 'The Industrialization of the British West Indies', *Caribbean Economic Review*, 2:1–61.

Lewis, W. (1954) 'Economic Development with Unlimited Supplies of Labour', *Manchester School of Economic and Social Studies*, 22:139–91.

Lewis, W. (1955) *The Theory of Economic Growth* (London: George Allen & Unwin).

Lewis, V. (1981) 'Issues and Trends in Jamaican Foreign Policy 1972–1977', in Stone, C. and Brown, A. (eds) *Perspectives on Jamaica in the Seventies* (Kingston: Jamaica Publishing House).

Lewis, V. (1982) 'The Small State Alone: Jamaican Foreign Policy 1977–1980', paper presented at the VIII Meeting of the Caribbean Studies Association, Kingston, 25–9 May 1982.

Linz, J. (1978) 'Crisis, Breakdown and Re-Equilibration', in Linz, J. J. and Stepan, A. (eds) *The Breakdown of Democratic Regimes* (Baltimore: Johns Hopkins University Press).

Linz, J. J. and Stepan, A. (eds.) (1978) *The Breakdown of Democratic Regimes* (Baltimore: Johns Hopkins University Press).

Lowenthal, A. F. (1982) 'The Caribbean', *The Wilson Quarterly*, (Spring) 113–141.

Maingot, A. (1983) 'Cuba and the Commonwealth Caribbean: Playing the Cuban Card', in Levine, B. B. (ed.) *The New Cuban Presence in the Caribbean* (Boulder Colorado: Westview Press).

Manley, M. (1970) 'Overcoming Insularity in Jamaica', *Foreign Affairs*, October.

Manley, M. (1975a) *A Voice at the Workplace* (London: André Deutsch).

Manley, M. (1975b) *The Politics of Change* (Washington: Howard University Press).

Manley, M. (1976) John Hearne (ed.) *The Search for Solutions* (Canada: Maple House).

Manley, M. (1977) *A People's Plan* (Kingston: Agency for Public Information).

Manley, M. (1982) *Jamaica: Struggle in the Periphery* (Oxford: Third World Media Ltd).

Manley, N. (1971) *Manley and the New Jamaica* Rex Nettleford (ed.) (London: Longman Caribbean Ltd).

Market Research Services Ltd (1982) 'Media Survey', unpublished results of survey conducted for RJR, *Gleaner* Company, and JBC, Kingston.

Maule, C. and Litvak, I. (1980) 'The International Bauxite Agreement; A Commodity Cartel in Action', *International Affairs*, Spring.

Millen, B. H. (1963) *The Political Role of Labor in Developing Countries* (Washington: Brookings Institution).

Miller, M. (1981) 'A Comparative Content Analysis of the Issue Content of the 1967 and 1976 General Elections in Jamaica', in Stone, C. and Brown, A. (eds.) *Perspectives on Jamaica in the Seventies* (Kingston: Jamaica Publishing House).

Mills, G. E. (1970) 'Public Administration in the Commonwealth Caribbean: Evolution, Conflicts and Challenges', *Social and Economic Studies*, 19(1):5–25.

Mills, G. E. (1974) 'Public Policy and Private Enterprise in the Commonwealth Caribbean', *Social and Economic Studies*, 23(2):217–41.

Mills, G. E. (1979) 'Public Administration in Developing Countries: Public Administration and Change in a Small Developing State: Jamaica', paper presented at the International Conference on the Future of Public Administration, ENAP, Quebec City, 27–31 May 1979.

Mills, G. E. (1981) 'Electoral Reform in Jamaica', *The Parliamentarian*, 62(2):97–104.

Mills, G. E. and Robertson, P. D. (1974) 'The Attitudes and Behavior of the Senior Civil Service in Jamaica', *Social and Economic Studies*, 23(2):311–43.

Ministry of Agriculture (1976) *Annual Report* (Kingston: Ministry of Agriculture).

Ministry of Agriculture (1981) *National Production/Extension Report*. (1980/81 Annual Report) (Kingston: Ministry of Agriculture).

Ministry of Mobilization and Human Resource Development (1977) 'Ministry Paper no. 48, Emergency Production Plan-Progress Report no. 2', mimeo.

Mintz, S. (1974) *Caribbean Transformations* (Chicago: Aldine).

Moore, B. (1966) *The Social Origins of Dictatorship and Democracy* (Boston: Beacon Press).

Moskos, C. (1967) *The Sociology of Political Independence* (Cambridge, Massachusetts: Schenkman Publishers).

Munoz, H. (ed.) (1981) *From Dependency to Development* (Boulder, Colorado: Westview Press).

Munroe, T. (1972) *The Politics of Constitutional Decolonization: Jamaica 1944–1962* (Mona, Jamaica: Institute of Social and Economic Research, University of the West Indies).

Nettleford, R. (1970) *Mirror, Mirror: Identity, Race and Protest in Jamaica* (Kingston: Collins & Sangster).

Nettleford, R. (1978) *Caribbean Cultural Identity: The Case of Jamaica* (Kingston: Institute of Jamaica).

Nie, N. H., Bingham Powell, G. Jr. and Prewitt, K. (1969) 'Social Structure and Political Participation: Developmental Relationships', *AMERICAN POLITICAL SCIENCE REVIEW*, 63(2):361–78, (3):808–32.

NNICC (National Narcotics Intelligence Consumers Committee) (1983) *The Supply of Drugs to the US Illicit Market from Foreign and Domestic Sources in*

1981 (with Projection through 1985) (Washington: US Drug Enforcement Administration).

Nolan, P. D. (1983) 'Status in the World System, Income Inequality and Economic Growth', *American Journal of Sociology*, 89(2):410–9.

Nordlinger, E. (1977) *Soldiers in Politics: Military Coups and Governments* (Englewood Cliffs, New Jersey: Prentice Hall).

NPA (National Planning Agency) (1976) *Economic and Social Survey – Jamaica 1975* (Kingston: National Planning Agency).

NPA (1977) *Economic and Social Survey – Jamaica 1976* (Kingston: National Planning Agency).

NPA (1978) *Economic and Social Survey – Jamaica 1977* (Kingston: National Planning Agency).

NPA (1979) *Economic and Social Survey – Jamaica 1978* (Kingston: National Planning Agency).

NPA (1981) *Economic and Social Survey – Jamaica 1980* (Kingston: National Planning Agency).

NPA (1982) *Economic and Social Survey – Jamaica 1981* (Kingston: National Planning Agency).

NPA (1983a) *Economic and Social Survey – Jamaica 1982* (Kingston: National Planning Agency).

NPA (1983b) *Economic and Social Survey – Jamaica January–June 1983* (Kingston: National Planning Agency).

Nunes, F. E. (1974) 'The Declining Status of the Jamaican Civil Service', *Social and Economic Studies*, 23(2):344–57.

O'Donnell, G. (1973) *Modernization and Bureaucratic Authoritarianism* (Berkeley: Institute of International Studies).

O'Donnell, G. and Schmitter, P. (forthcoming) 'Political Life After Authoritarian Rule: Tentative Conclusions and Uncertain Transitions', introductory essay in a forthcoming volume on the transition from authoritarian rule to democracy.

OECD (Organization for Economic Co-operation and Development) 1975. *Total External Liabilities of Developing Countries* (Paris: OECD).

O'Flaherty, J. D. (1978) 'Finding Jamaica's Way', *Foreign Policy*, 31:137–59.

Owens, J. (1976) *Dread: The Rastafarians of Jamaica* (Kingston: Sangster).

Palmer, R. W. (1968) *The Jamaican Economy* (New York: Praeger).

Parkin, F. (1971) *Class Inequality and Political Order* (New York: Praeger).

Parris, C. N. (1976) 'Political Dissidence in Post-Independence Jamaica and Trinidad: 1962–72', unpublished Ph.D. dissertation, New School for Social Research.

Patterson, O. (1967) *The Sociology of Slavery* (London: MacGibbon & Kee).

Payne, A. (1984) 'Jamaica: the "democratic socialist" experiment of Michael Manley', in Payne, A. and Sutton, P. (eds.) *Dependency under Challenge: The political economy of the Commonwealth Caribbean.* (Manchester University Press).

Payne, A. and Sutton, P. (eds.) (1984) *Dependency under challenge: The political economy of the Commonwealth Caribbean.* (Manchester University Press).

Phillips, P. (1977) 'Jamaican Elites: 1938 to Present', in Stone, C. and Brown, A. (eds) *Essays on Power and Change in Jamaica* (Kingston: Jamaica Publishing House).

Phillips, P. (1981) 'Community Mobilisation in Squatter Communities', in C. Stone and A. Brown (eds) *Perspectives on Jamaica in the Seventies* (Kingston: Jamaica Publishing House).

Phillips, P. (1982) 'Models of State Formation and Transformation in the Caribbean: Jamaica after World War II', unpublished paper, Department of Government, University of the West Indies, Mona, Jamaica.

PNP (Peoples National Party) (1980) 'Political Report to the 42nd Annual Delegates' Conference of the PNP', Montego Bay, 4–5 October 1980.

PNP (1983) 'Report to the 45th Annual General Conference', Kingston, 21–5 September 1983.

Post, K. (1978) *Arise ye Starvelings* (The Hague: Martinus Nijhoff).

Post, K. (1981) *Strike the Iron* (The Hague: Martinus Nijhoff).

Reid, S. (1977) 'An Introductory Approach to the Concentration of Power in the Jamaican Corporate Economy and Notes on its Origin', in Stone, C. and Brown, A. (eds) *Essays on Power and Change in Jamaica* (Kingston: Jamaica Publishing House).

Robertson, P. D. (1972) 'Party "Organization" in Jamaica', *Social and Economic Studies*, 21(1):30–43.

Robinson, R. V. and Bell, W. (1978)' Attitudes Towards Political Independence in Jamaica After Twelve Years of Nationhood', *British Journal of Sociology*, 29(2):208–33.

Ross, A. M. and Hartman, P. T. (1960) *Changing Patterns of Industrial Conflict* (New York: Wiley).

Rueschemeyer, D. (1980) '*Über Sozialökonomische Entwicklung and Demokratie*', in *Weltgesellschaft und Sozialstruktur: Festschrift für Peter Heintz* (Diessenhofen, Switzerland: Verlag Ruegger).

Rueschemeyer, D. and Evans, P. (1985) 'The State and Economic Transformation: Towards an Analysis of the Conditions Underlying Effective Intervention', in Evans, P. *et al.* (eds) *Bringing the State Back in.* (Cambridge University Press).

Schecher, J. J. (1981a) 'Submission to Enquiry by the Co-operative Department into the Sugar Workers' Co-operatives on Behalf of the Bernard Lodge Co-operatives' (Kingston: Social Action Centre).

Schecher, J. J. (1981b) 'A Final Report on Organization Development and Budgetary Cost Control in the Sugar Workers' Co-operatives in Jamaica', (Kingston: Social Action Centre).

Schumpeter, J. A. (1962) *Capitalism, Socialism and Democracy* (New York: Harper Torchbooks).

Shalev, M. (1983) 'The Social Democratic Model and Beyond: Two Generations of Comparative Research on the Welfare State', *Comparative Social Research*, 6.

Sharpley, J. (1983) 'Economic Management and IMF Conditionality in Jamaica', in Williamson, J. (ed.) *IMF Conditionality* (Cambridge: MIT Press).

Skocpol, T. (1973) 'A Critical Review of Barrington Moore's Social Origins of Dictatorship and Democracy', *Politics and Society*, 2(1):1–34.

Skocpol, T. (1980) 'Political Response to Capitalist Crisis: Neo-Marxist Theories of the State and the Case of the New Deal', *Politics and Society* 10(2):155–201.

Smith, M. G. (1967) *Plural Society in the West Indies* (Berkeley: University of California Press).

Stepan, A. C. (1973) 'The New Professionalism of Internal Warfare and Military Role Expansion', in Stepan, A. C. (ed.) *Authoritarian Brazil* (New Haven: Yale University Press).

Stepan, A. C. (1978) *The State and Society: Peru in Comparative Perspective* (Princeton University Press).

Stephens, E. H. (1980) *The Politics of Workers' Participation: The Peruvian Approach in Comparative Perspective* (New York: Academic Press).

Stephens, E. H. (1984) 'Producer Cooperatives, Workers' Participation and Democratic Socialist Development: Jamaica in Comparative Perspective'. Paper

delivered at the Meetings of the Caribbean Studies Association, St Kitts, May-
–June 1984.

Stephens, E. H. (forthcoming) 'Rise and Demise of Workers' Participation in
Jamaica, Chile and Peru', in Sirianni, C. J. (ed.) *Comparative Studies in Worker
Participation* (Philadelphia: Temple University Press).

Stephens, E. H. and Stephens, J. D. (1980) 'The 'Capitalist State' and the
Parliamentary Road to Socialism: Lessons from Chile', paper presented at the
Meetings of the Latin American Studies Association, Bloomington, Indiana.

Stephens, E. H. and Stephens, J. D. (1982) 'The Labor Movement, Political Power
and Workers Participation in Western Europe', in Esping-Andersen, G. and
Friedland, R. (eds.) *Political Power and Social Theory* (Greenwich: JAI Press)
vol. 3.

Stephens, E. H. and Stephens, J. D. (1983a) 'Democratic Socialism and the
Capitalist Class: An Analysis of the Relation between Jamaican Business and the
PNP Government', *Documentos de Trabajo* no. 8 CISCLA, *Universidad Inter-
americana de Puerto Rico*. Also forthcoming in *Social and Economic Studies*.

Stephens, E. H. and Stephens, J. D. (1983b) 'Democratic Socialism in Dependent
Capitalism: An Analysis of the Manley Government in Jamaica', *Politics and
Society*, 12(3):373–411.

Stephens, E. H. and Stephens, J. D. (1985) 'Democratic Socialism and Bauxite in
Jamaica', in Evans, P., Rueschemeyer, D. and Stephens, E. H. (eds.) *States vs.
Markets* (Beverly Hills: Sage Publications).

Stephens, J. D. (1979a) 'Class Formation and Class Consciousness', *British Journal
of Sociology*, 30(4):389–414.

Stephens, J. D. (1979b) *The Transition from Capitalism to Socialism* (London:
Macmillan).

Stephens, J. D. (1981) 'Impasse and Breakthrough in Sweden', *Dissent*,
Summer:308–18.

Stone, C. (1973) *Class, Race and Political Behavior in Urban Jamaica* (Mona,
Jamaica: Institute of Social and Economic Research, University of the West
Indies).

Stone, C. (1974) *Electoral Behavior and Public Opinion in Jamaica* (Mona,
Jamaica: Institute of Social and Economic Research, University of the West
Indies).

Stone, C. (1980) *Democracy and Clientelism in Jamaica* (New Brunswick, New
Jersey: Transaction Books).

Stone, C. (1981a) 'Jamaica's 1980 Elections: What Did Manley Do; What Seaga
Need Do', *Caribbean Review*, 10(2):4–7, 40–3.

Stone, C. (1981b) 'Public Opinion and the 1980 Elections in Jamaica', unpublished
paper, Department of Government, University of the West Indies, Mona,
Jamaica.

Stone, C. (1981c) 'Ideology, Public Opinion and the Media in Jamaica', in Stone,
C. and Brown, A. (eds.) *Perspectives on Jamaica in the Seventies* (Kingston:
Jamaica Publishing House).

Stone, C. (1982) *The Political Opinions of the Jamaican People* (Kingston: Jamaica
Publishing House).

Stone, C. and Brown, A. (eds) (1981) *Perspectives on Jamaica in the Seventies*
(Kingston: Jamaica Publishing House).

Stump, M., Marsh, R. M. and Lake, D. (1978) 'The Effects of International
Economic Dependence on Development: A Critique', *American Sociological
Review*, 43(4):600–4.

Swaby, R. (1981) 'The Rationale for State Ownership of Public Utilities in
Jamaica', *Social and Economic Studies*, 30(1):75–107.

Thomas, C. Y. (1974) *Dependence and Transformation* (New York: Monthly Review Press).

Thomas, C. Y. (1978) 'The Non-Capitalist Path as Theory and Practice of Decolonization and Socialist Transformation', *Latin American Perspectives*, 5(2):10–28.

Thomas, C. Y. (1984) *The Rise of the Authoritarian State* (New York: Monthly Review Press).

Thompson, E. P. (1963) *The Making of the English Working Class* (New York: Vintage Books).

Tingsten, H. (1973) *The Swedish Social Democrats: Their Ideological Development*, trans. Greta Frankel and Patricia Howard-Rosen (Totowa: Bedminster Press).

Ul Haq, M. (1973) 'The Crisis in Development Strategies', in Wilber, C. K. (ed.) *The Political Economy of Development and Underdevelopment* (New York: Random House).

Ulyanovsky, R. (1974) *Socialism and the Newly Independent Nations* (Moscow: Progress Publications).

US Department of State (1981) 'Cuba's Renewed Support for Violence in Latin America', a Special Report (Washington: Department of State).

Valenzuela, A. (1978) 'Chile', in Linz, J. J. and Stepan, A. (eds.) *The Breakdown of Democratic Regimes* (Baltimore, Maryland: The Johns Hopkins University Press).

Wallerstein, I. (1974) *The Modern World System: Capitalist Agriculture and the Origins of the European World Economy in the Sixteenth Century* (New York: Academic Press).

Wallerstein, I. (1980) *The Modern World System II: Mercantilism and the Consolidation of the European World Economy 1600–1750* (New York: Academic Press).

Walters, P. B. (1981) 'Educational Change and National Economic Development', *Harvard Educational Review*, 51(1):94–106.

Weir, M. and Skocpol, T. (1985) 'State Structures and the Possibilities for "Keynesian" Responses to the Great Depression in Sweden, Britain, and the United States', in Evans, P. *et al.* (eds.) *Bringing the State Back in* (Cambridge: Cambridge University Press).

Wilber, C. K. and Weaver, J. H. (1979) 'Patterns of Dependency: Income Distribution and the History of Underdevelopment', in Wilber, C. K. (ed.) *The Political Economy of Development and Underdevelopment* (New York: Random House) 2nd edn.

WPJ (Workers Party of Jamaica) (1981) 'Report of the Central Committee to the Second Congress', Kingston, 17 December 1981.

Young, C. and Turner, T. (1985) *The Rise and Decline of the Zairian State* (Madison: University of Wisconsin Press).

Zeitlin, M., Neuman, W. L. and Ratcliff, R. E. (1976) 'Class Segments: Agrarian Property and Political Leadership in the Capitalist Class of Chile', *American Sociological Review*, 41(6):1006–29.

Index

African socialism 106, 108, 113, 186
agriculture 22–4, 28, 31, 34, 68, 85, 164,
  196, 261, 274–9, 371, 372, 396
  bananas 11, 28, 255, 261, 275, 318, 337
  sugar 11, 13, 16, 28, 31, 128, 255, 261,
    271, 275, 279, 297, 318, 337–8
  see also Land Lease, Food Farms, sugar
  coops
Alcan 26, 78, 80, 353
Alcoa 80, 127
Alexander, C. 123, 211, 403, 405
ambassadors (US to Jamaica) see United
  States embassy
Angola 108–9, 128, 134, 138, 168, 178,
  316
anti–imperialism see imperialism
Army see security forces
Ashenheim, L. 21, 185, 352, 403, 406
austerity measure 87, 150, 168, 169, 200,
  202–3, 215, 249, 252–3, 277, 280, 281,
  321, 364
  see also IMF
authoritarianism 3, 321, 331, 334, 337,
  338, 343–4, 375

balance of payments 25, 26, 58, 59, 78,
  87, 111, 128–31, 196, 224, 254–7, 258,
  269, 318, 370, 388
  crisis 4, 84–5, 111, 114, 144–5
  deterioration 128, 144
Bank of Jamaica 131, 148, 151, 152, 159,
  165, 167, 175, 187, 197, 360, 362
banks, banking 29, 61, 71, 121, 160, 165,
  184, 204, 271–2, 285, 357, 366
Barbados 20, 339
Barber, H. 113, 149, 152, 403, 406
bauxite 19, 22, 25, 26–7, 29, 34, 58, 61,
  69, 84, 128–9, 144, 227, 234, 255, 260,
  318, 351, 370, 400
  development of industry 349
  levy 76, 78–80, 87, 108, 111, 126–7,
    145, 168, 196, 249, 287, 297, 318, 325,
    339
  strategy of the PNP government 63, 68,
    70–1, 73, 76–81, 271–2, 326, 340, 353,
    371
Beckford, G. 56, 149, 151, 152, 164–5,
  346, 347, 349, 356, 359, 405
Bell, E. 76, 156, 223–4, 365, 403
Bell, W. 36, 95, 399
Bernal, R. 144–5, 173–4, 175, 304, 354,
  362, 371
Brown, A. 148, 152, 357, 403

budgets 84, 86–7, 111–12, 130–1, 172–3,
  175, 200, 203, 257, 377–8
bureaucracy see public administration
business, businessmen see classes, private
  sector
Bustamante, A. 13–21, 32, 43, 47, 48, 87,
  347, 404

Canada 27, 29, 30, 33, 78, 95, 98–9, 128,
  131, 135, 175, 272, 363–4, 384
capital flight see investment
capitalism 3, 25–32, 52–3, 58, 62, 116–17,
  180, 252, 305, 343
CARICOM 88, 131, 297
Carter, J./Carter Administration 126, 127,
  155, 168, 175, 177, 189, 205, 206, 234,
  249, 251, 315, 317, 356, 373, 400
Castro, F. 82, 93, 108, 178, 182, 187, 189,
  193, 194, 205
CBI 254, 259
CEO 145, 164–5, 169, 172, 176, 220–1,
  279–81, 282, 288, 357, 358
Chamber of Commerce 66, 96–8, 161,
  194, 212, 233, 301, 350
churches 54, 55, 65–6, 73, 124, 230–1,
  247, 353
CIA 125, 134, 236, 356, 363
civil service see public administration
civil society 52–4, 68, 143, 197, 301, 322–
  4, 336, 373
Clarke, O. 180, 406
classes 14, 16, 19, 35–8, 43–4, 51, 53–4,
  56, 59, 65, 68–9, 74, 89, 105–6, 141–4,
  197, 212, 245, 293, 313, 322, 326, 327–
  8, 333, 334–6, 338, 347, 349, 352, 357,
  372–3
  alliance 6, 35, 166, 182, 185, 218–20,
    250, 270, 297–304, 332, 333, 336
  capitalist 6, 18, 19, 29, 36–8, 43, 49, 55,
    57, 64–5, 68–9, 91, 93, 94–6, 98–100,
    116–24, 130–1, 144, 145, 160–2, 170,
    173, 184, 195, 210–11, 255, 263–4, 267,
    270, 290, 295, 298–302, 319, 322–3,
    327–8, 330, 332, 333, 335, 337, 340,
    344, 349–50, 353, 371, 375 see also
    private sector
  lumpenproletariat 6, 7, 43, 54, 55, 303–
    4, 309
  peasants 6, 7, 11, 28, 35–7, 43, 54, 129,
    303–4, 307, 309, 337
  professionals 6, 36–7, 43, 144, 195, 213,
    302–3, 319, 340, 363, 364
  struggle 110, 182, 185, 218–20

418